RAVES FOR

GENEEN

"Brisk and highly readable biography."
—*New York Times Book Review*

"Splendid . . . Robert J. Schoenberg, a free-lance writer and former advertising executive, has succeeded in bringing Harold S. Geneen nearer to us as a human being. No mean feat since his subject, the social architect of post–World War II Corporate America and the inventor of the multinational conglomerate, was and remains one of the most complex, paradoxical and enigmatic characters ever to occupy the business landscape."
—*Los Angeles Times*

"May well preserve his status in this decade."
—*St. Louis Post-Dispatch*

"Eye-opening insights into the politics of big business with its constant struggle for the very limited room at the top."
—*San Francisco Examiner*

"Revealing . . . shows how Geneen single-mindedly pursued growth and increased earnings . . . abounds with detailed accounts of Geneen's well-known successes, failures and scandals . . . and analyses of the Geneen style and management-by-the-numbers philosophy."
—*Publishers Weekly*

"A fascinating study of one of the most productive lives that I have encountered."
—*J. Peter Grace, Chairman and Chief Executive Officer, W. R. Grace & Co.*

"The four deadly sins of business biography are adulation, antagonism, inadequate research and overwhelming dullness. Mr. Schoenberg's book avoids all four and is certainly the best text so far on the most dynamic business figure of our time."
—*Winston V. Morrow, President and Chief Executive Officer, TICOR*

"A substantial contribution to the literature of business . . . highly recommended."
—*Library Journal*

GENEEN

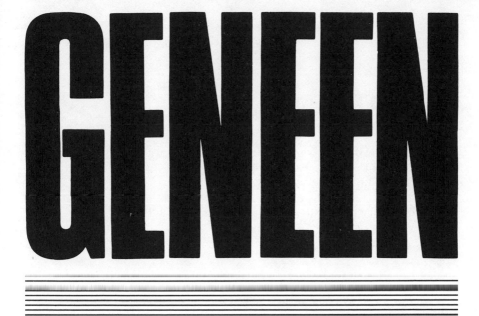

ROBERT J. SCHOENBERG

WARNER BOOKS

A Warner Communications Company

Warner Books Edition
Copyright © 1985 by Robert J. Schoenberg
All rights reserved.

This Warner Books edition is published by arrangement with
W.W. Norton & Company, 500 Fifth Avenue,
New York, NY 10110

Warner Books, Inc., 666 Fifth Avenue, New York, NY 10103

W A Warner Communications Company

Printed in the United States of America
First Warner Books Printing: January 1986
10 9 8 7 6 5 4 3 2 1

Library of Congress Cataloging-in-Publication Data

Schoenberg, Robert J., 1933–
    Geneen.

    Bibliography: p.
    Includes index.
    1. Geneen, Harold. 2. International Telephone
and Telegraph Corporation—Biography. 3. Tele-
communication—United States—Biography. I. Title.
HE8846.I64S36   1986   384.6′092′4 [B]   85-20386
ISBN 0-446-37008-8 (U.S.A.) (pbk.)
     0-446-37009-6 (Canada) (pbk.)

To Nick and Janet Wedge
for everything,
for a long time

CONTENTS

ACKNOWLEDGMENTS

First, my deep thanks to the people who spoke with me. This book would not have been possible without them. Over two hundred people who were part of Harold Geneen's life and career generously took the time and trouble to remember and analyze for me their experiences with him. Many of the interviews lasted for hours, and sometimes there had to be more than one session. Credit for specific quotes, information, analyses, and perceptions is given either in the text or in the Notes. The names of those people I interviewed are listed in Appendix I, with the date (or dates) of interviews, plus a short identification. For the reader's convenience, I also list names that recur in the text without further identification on the second or subsequent mention.

I also want to thank those I cannot name because they prefer to remain anonymous.

If there are errors in the book, the fault of course is mine, not that of the people I interviewed.

Special thanks are due to those who both talked with me and shared certain documents in their possession. Details of their generosity can be found at the beginning of the Notes. But I do want to specify my gratitude to: Meade Alcorn, Tim Dunleavy, Lewis Gilbert, John Kehoe, John Koskinen, Robert Kenmore, Norman Krim, John Lobb, Bud Morrow, Lou Rader, Bob Savage, Dorothy and Eleanor Smith, and Stanley Sporkin. Thanks also to those who gave me documents anonymously.

For the most part, interviews took place on two research trips, both of them literally around the country, during the period from mid-November 1979 to mid-September 1980. For their gracious hospitality during that time, I want to thank: Anita Kane (and the late Sam Kane, sorely missed by all of us) in Chicago; Burt and Shirley Wellenbach in Philadelphia; Nick and Janet Wedge in Ossining, New York, and London, England; Marty and Joan Conroy in Greenwich, Connecticut; John and Joy Pratt in Cambridge, Massachusetts; Lenore Ebling Brown in Springfield, Virginia; Dorace Schwartz in Bal Harbour, Florida; Bill and Lil Cohen in St. Petersberg, Florida (now of Palm Springs, Florida); Barton and Marcie Lee in Tempe, Arizona; Ted and Marj Schoenberg in Los Angeles, both before and after the trips.

Thanks also to some advisors. Charles McIntosh, long my science and technology explainer for advertising matters, as well as general business lore, made contributions of huge value that are credited, passim, in the Notes. Jack Langguth read the manuscript as it was being written and made many valuable suggestions; at every stage he gave me good advice and generous encouragement. Forrest Stichman, at the very beginning of this project, explained business and balance sheets to me. Three people formed a panel that I often consulted: Bud Gobler on business practices and the book trade (and special thanks to him for locating a paperback copy of *The Sovereign State of ITT*, which contains a chapter missing from the hardback edition); Dick Helfend on accounting; and Tom Krebs on statistics and computer matters. Of course, none of these advisors is responsible for my mistakes; but they do have my gratitude for much of whatever is right about the book.

Research help. Thanks to the archives of the following newspapers: the *Hartford Courant* (especially Kathy McKula); the *Memphis Press-Scimitar*; the *Seattle Post-Intelligencer*; the *Miami Herald* (especially James Russell, finance editor); the *Kansas City Times*; and the *Greensboro News-Record*. Thanks to the staffs of the UCLA Law Library and Public Affairs Library; the research desk of the Santa Monica Public Library; the staff of the Maryland annex of the National Archives; the staff at the Federal Court House, New Haven, Connecticut; and the staff of the Suffield Public Library. At NYU, Bayard Sills of the University Archives was most helpful in finding for me both people and documents. Thanks to Sandra Smith, genealogical researcher in Southampton, England; to Miss M. E. Barnaby, Home Office, Croyden, England; to the staff at the Dorset County Library (especially Mrs. R. Popham), Bournemouth, England; to Deborah Lane, Register Office, Bournemouth; to Father David Lowis, Sacred Heart, Bournemouth.

At the Justice Department, I thank E. Jeffrey Ross and William B. Jones, Criminal Division, Washington; Melvin Straughter and Edie Monroe, Immigration and Naturalization Service, Los Angeles.

Various PR people and departments were most helpful. Thanks especially to: Lois Robinson, Bell & Howell; William H. Gibbons, Jr., and Linda Jackson, Jones & Laughlin; Garden Newell and Doris Relf, Raytheon; Rick Battaglia and Daniel A. Conforti, American Brands; Charles H. Thorne, Montgomery Ward; Ned Gerrity, ITT.

The people at Norton could not have been more gracious or helpful. I especially want to thank Roberta Conroy and Winnie Shea Torrano, miracles of efficiency. Ed Barber, who edited the book with a fine eye and firm hand, added immeasurably to tautness and pace. He also added a number of vivid phrases for which I shall take shameless credit. My wholehearted gratitude to him and to his assistant, Amy Boesky. And to Janet Byrne for splendid copy editing.

And thanks as always to Don Congdon, without whom, not.

o   o   o

Permission to reprint photographs from the following sources is gratefully acknowledged: Mrs. Daryl Chapin (p. 25), Bell & Howell (pp. 44 and 46), Jones & Laughlin (pp. 57 and 66), Mr. Ronald G. Nestor (p. 59), Mr. Ralph C. Graham (p. 77), Mr. Francis J. Dunleavy (p. 316), *Time* Magazine (p. 21, top), Ted Polumbaum/*Time* Magazine (p. 234), the U.S. Immigration and Naturalization Service/David A. Schoenberg (p.21, bottom), UPI (p. 83), and AP/WIDE WORLD PHOTOS (pp. 103, 207, 221, 263, 274, 278, 285, 320, 332).

INTRODUCTION

When I started to research my last book, all I knew about Harold Geneen was what any newspaper reader during the early 1970s did: the Kleindienst/Dita Beard/Hartford/San Diego Convention scandals, then a year later the Chile scandal. I knew ITT only as a large company.

The concept of that book was first to ascertain what questions young managers had about being better bosses, then to get answers from people, already at the top, who had demonstrated particular strengths in each area. A surprisingly large number of these top bosses around the country mentioned the influence—either direct or by precept—that Geneen had had on them. Two of the most impressive I spoke with, William B. Roesch and Michel C. Bergerac, credited Geneen as the single most important influence in their business lives. Roesch was then head of Kaiser Industries and later became president of U. S. Steel; Bergerac was chairman of Revlon.

I wanted to find out more about Geneen. The result is this book.

When I started research, Geneen was naturally the first person I wrote to for an interview. I phoned him; and that was the only time we spoke. He said he was not being unfriendly but that he really did not want a book about himself and would not cooperate. He was still in business, he explained, and was sure that every remark about everyone mentioned in the book would be attributed to him if he did cooperate—despite any possible disclaimers. But he wished me well. At the end of our conversation he again stressed that his decision was not to be mistaken for unfriendliness. Then he said, "You didn't really expect me to talk with you, did you?" I still haven't quite figured out why not.

A few months later, someone opened an interview by saying, "I probably shouldn't be talking with you." He showed me a letter—a form letter that had been personalized with the man's name, address, and salutation—from Geneen. It said that there was a fellow going about talking with people from Geneen's past and that Geneen was not sure about the fellow's motives: he seemed all right, but he might be looking for scandalous stuff. In any case, Geneen preferred that his old friends and associates not talk about his private life.

The person being interviewed was of relatively peripheral importance in Geneen's career, so obviously these letters were going out to nearly everyone Geneen could think of. When it became obvious to him that I was determined to talk with everyone I could from every period of his life, his position hardened, and he asked some people not to talk with me at all. Not all of those refused interviews, although a number of them (including the man who showed me the letter) wanted to remain anonymous.

Geneen need not have worried. I did delve into his private life—necessarily, in a biography, to show how he lived and what sort of person he was. But the purpose was not to unearth personal scandal. I am convinced that there was none worth mentioning; there was neither time nor interest in a career riveted on business. What is interesting about Geneen—both the triumphant *and* the the scandalous—is his business career. And that is of consuming interest.

o   o   o

To describe past activities I naturally use a past tense. However, to avoid confusion, I also use it to describe attributes of people who are still alive and quite active. For instance I may write that Harold Geneen *was* brilliant, his memory *was* prodigious, his energy *was* super-human. He still is; they still are. As I write this note he is at age seventy-four alive and well and by all indications as keen and active as ever. May he continue so for many years, and may all the others whose attributes I write of in the past, for clarity's sake, forgive me—and continue to thrive.

Except to describe ongoing events or conditions, or when quoting people, the only present-tense verb I use is "says." I use that when I quote someone whom I interviewed for this book. In contrast, "said" indicates what someone told someone else—generally a reporter or someone who later told me of a conversation. Again for clarity's sake I stick to that practice, even though at least three of the people I interviewed have since died.

GENEEN

PROLOGUE:

The Lion in Winter ... Pounces

On February 9, 1977, Harold Geneen was teary-eyed.

That day it became official: the sixty-seven-year-old chairman of the International Telephone and Telegraph Corporation, eleventh largest company in the United States, would soon have to surrender his post as ITT's chief executive officer. Geneen did not want to step down; he had bitterly fought it. Nevertheless, the ITT directors decreed that on March 1 Lyman Hamilton would become president and chief operating officer of ITT, and that on January 1, 1978, Hamilton would take over as CEO.

The announcement startled everyone, coming as a double surprise. No one had imagined that Geneen would be deposed so soon. And no one expected that Hamilton would be the one to take his place. The new chief operating officer had neither operated any of ITT's 250-odd businesses nor grappled with executive decisions since joining the company. Hamilton was chief financial officer and had always been in finance. He was a staff man. But that might not matter. Harold Geneen would continue as chairman even after January 1, so Hamilton would have plenty of guidance.

Surprise aside, the announcement delighted the people who were expected to assess such matters—bankers, investors, brokers, and analysts. Hamilton had always been outstandingly popular with them. They pronounced his elevation a "favorable development" and a "big plus" for the company. The worrisome problem of succession at ITT had at last been solved, and to them Hamilton seemed the perfect choice.

As it happened, he was not Geneen's choice, though almost no one knew that at the time. Of course, since Geneen did not want to step down, ever, no one was truly his choice as successor. But he specifically did not want Hamilton. And later, when Hamilton was no longer president and Geneen no longer chairman, the central fact emerged that Geneen had built and run ITT in such a way that no one *could* ever be his successor in any usual sense. He was unique. At ITT people used to ask, not entirely jokingly, if the "G" in Geneen was pronounced soft as in Jesus or hard as in God (soft, as in genius). And a favorite prayer went, "Harold be thy name. . . . "

Despite the master's opposition, the new CEO appeared to take hold. While Hamilton chaired the 1978 annual meeting, Geneen sat mute, just another director. Afterward Geneen told reporters, "There can be only one chief executive officer in the company. My sole role will be to give him any help I can. Even if he makes mistakes, it's my job to support him. We aren't going to have two chief executives." Once, when Geneen did try to meddle in line management, Hamilton complained and the board slapped Geneen down. The business press wrote of ITT's "hodgepodge of nearly unmanageable ventures." Hamilton's task, they claimed, was to "fix the machine Geneen made." Geneen appeared to be in decline, and Hamilton appeared to be in charge.

Things were not, however, what they seemed. On July 10, 1979, Hamilton returned to New York from a three-week business trip and was asked to breakfast by several ITT directors the following morning, day of the monthly board meeting. At that breakfast he was fired.

The ITT version is that Geneen had nothing to do with it. "Lyman's been going around town telling everyone that it was Geneen who got him," says the company's director of public relations, "but it was really two other guys, directors, who did it." Others concede that Geneen may have animated the decision but that the board made it. "Geneen was not the one who fired him," says one director. "He did not come to the board and say, Fire this guy. He said what he thought to us, and we discussed it a lot, and then the executive committee fired Hamilton."

That is the triumph of truth over accuracy. Geneen did not have the legal power to fire Hamilton or to compel the board's action; but they would never have moved except for Geneen. His position as chairman had nothing to do with it; in this matter the title was hollow. It was the man himself. Aging, shorn of power, devastated, even humiliated by the ITT board, Geneen could still tower above those rich, powerful men. He prevailed because he was Geneen. He always had.

1

Making the Most of It

Years later, asked why his parents emigrated from England to the United States when he was an infant, Harold Geneen laughed and said, "Well, I don't really remember. But I suppose my parents thought there were some opportunities here."

The opportunities were not immediately evident. In the England of 1910 Samuel Geneen could style himself a master jeweler, living at Wood Grange on St. Mary's Road, Bournemouth; a year later, in New York, he was a secretary, living in a rooming house at 1133 Broadway. Still, at that point the new land promised more for him than the old.

Around the turn of the nineteenth century the Geneen family had left Portugal for Russia, settling in Chedrin, near Minsk. In 1872 Lazar Woolf Geneen, a ferryman, and his wife, Hana, had the first of thirteen children, a son, Maurice. The family was Jewish, and by the late 1880s recurring pogroms impelled young Maurice to flee Russia. He found his way to the Whitechapel section of London. As he prospered he sent for some of his brothers, a sister, and his mother (Lazar Woolf had disappeared; he went for a ride one day and the sled returned without him). Samuel, Harold's father, was one of the brothers Maurice brought over.

In the late 1890s Maurice moved to Southampton, where he married Minnie Cohen and continued to prosper, opening a shop in Southampton and later two in Bournemouth. Like Samuel, Maurice called himself a jeweler. But the shops were really haberdasheries, with a sideline in trinkets favored by the many sailors in the port of Southampton and the seaside town of Bournemouth. Samuel helped in the business, and all went well. Then Samuel married Aida Cruciani, whose family lived in Southampton, and his prospects in England rapidly deteriorated.

Although she was always known as Aida, her birth certificate read Eda Valentina Cruciani. If the registrar erred, Aida's mother, Georgina, would not have caught it, being unable to read or write. Aida's father, Francesco, was a stewart on a P.&O. mail steamer. The Crucianis were of Italian extraction (Georgina had been a Gizzi), and they were Roman Catholics. They deplored the marriage, unmollified by Samuel's strategic conversion to Catholicism. As for the Geneens, in a manner not uncommon to Jewish families of their era they simply wrote Samuel off. He was not just dead to them, he was expunged.

Harold Sydney Geneen was born January 22, 1910, in Bournemouth. Eleven months later his parents gave up the struggle in a now-hostile environment and took their baby son to America.

He was not Jewish according to Jewish law, which requires a Jewish mother. In fact he was baptized a Catholic. He was not Jewish by cultural exposure or association, home atmosphere or parental precept: his father had minimal influence on him and was probably not around long anyway. He would later describe his father as an entrepreneur, claiming on one hand that Samuel was "quite a guy," while admitting on the other that "I never saw much of him" and "I really didn't know him." Within four years the new American entrepreneur had become president of the Spa Lunch Company and had moved his family to a house in Berkeley Heights, New Jersey. Neither the business nor the marriage flourished, and when Harold was five his parents separated. A year later, in 1916, Samuel started the Postal Restaurant Company at 35 Nassau Street in Manhattan. This time he did reasonably well.

After the separation, Aida pursued a career as a singer and actress. Blessed with a good voice, intelligence, and a splendid personality, Aida was able to thrive in the minor reaches of show business, doing musical comedy, along with some concert work. Her voice was not top quality, and neither were her roles. Never a star, she was generally cast as the star's best friend. But it was enough, with Samuel's help, to support Aida, Harold, and daughter Eva, who had been born in the United States.

Perhaps the greatest problem Aida's career raised was what to do with the children. Many of her engagements were road shows, and she refused to expose them to that sort of gypsy life. Her English background made boarding school an obvious solution. So in 1917, at age seven, Harold became the youngest pupil at what is now Suffield Academy in Suffield, Connecticut, about twenty miles north of Hartford.

The school was founded in 1833 by the Connecticut Baptist Education Society to prepare young men for the ministry. Originally called the Connecticut Baptist Literary Institution, the school's Baptist connection is intact today. But soon the school moved beyond theological training, dropped "Baptist" from its name, admitted girls, and became a standard college preparatory boarding and day school. By 1918 the name became Suffield School and then, around 1934, Suffield Academy.

Harold at age 3.

Samuel Geneen's 1942 naturalization certificate, a duplicate issued when he lost the original. His birthplace, Kopatkevich, is about 100 miles southeast of Chedrin, where his brother Maurice was born some sixteen years earlier.

When Harold started about two dozen boys made up the junior school, from eighth grade down. Called the Preps, they all lived together, superintended by William Janes. Pop Janes seemed immensely old; he had been at Suffield when the headmaster was a boy. And he was a stern disciplinarian. Shoes must be lined up just so, every day. No sass was tolerated. "Any backtalk to Pop," says a former student, "and he'd come over and give you a damned good slap." But the boys were his life. He devoted himself to their well-being and amusement, organized games and outings, staged plays and Wild West shows with a part for each boy. "They loved him and hated him, were scared of him and respected him, all in the same breath," the former student adds. Pop brought them up. He was the towering authority, a fountain of bachelor wisdom and advice, such as his favorite adage, "A woman is only a woman but a good cigar is a smoke."

Harold came to Suffield when America was at war. The school had answered the call by requiring all students, girls included, to wear uniforms at all times, ready at a moment to hurl back the Hun from central Connecticut. They were drilled by Captain Harry Johnson, variously described as "a Canadian marinet released from overseas service" and "shell shocked." When a student dropped a tray of dishes in the dining room, poor Captain Johnson hit the ceiling, all nerves. He was unbendingly severe. Defaulters walked off demerits with guard tours of the town common. "You walk your guard and you walk it right," he would bark, interspersing such general orders with his famous regulation for roll calls, "Commencing tomorrow, anyone that is not here is absent."

Harold's career as Suffield's littlest trooper was not glorious. The upper school drilled with real Springfields, but the Preps shouldered wooden rifles. Furthermore, Harold never got the hang of winding his canvas leg coverings. "So there I was," he recalled, "the smallest kid in the school, carrying my little wooden rifle with one hand and trying to keep my puttees up with the other."

School was Harold's home for most of the year, and when school was over, camp took its place. The first summer, he went to Camp Wampanoag at Grey Gables on Cape Cod, the start of his lifelong love for the Cape. Next he attended Morgan's Camp on Lake Maranacook in Redfield, Maine, a place remarkable in his memory because one year he won the running, swimming, and canoe-paddling events. This triumph left him, he later wrote, "agreeably surprised, since I had never won anything much before." But Harold was so tiny and desperately unathletic, imagination fails to conjure a group he could have outrun, outswum or outpaddled. At Suffield that was of consequence, because sports were of paramount importance. Harold sat out organized athletics—and maybe more important, the usual boyish roughhousing. Younger than his classmates (he graduated at sixteen and a half), he remained very short and slightly built, almost frail. Indeed, his small size is the only thing one classmate remembers about him.

All this may seem the recipe for a difficult, lonely childhood. Certainly it hurt Harold that he was so often away from a mother he adored—even over most holidays. A once-close associate speculates that the separation scarred, that the man's notorious mistrust even of intimates derived from the boy's sense of betrayal: a father who decamped; a mother who returned his adoration, yet functionally abandoned him to schoolmasters and camp counselors. But, in fact, Harold did not seem miserable.

"Harold was a very happy boy," says one who knew him well. "He didn't go around brooding." And Captain Johnson's bark or the occasional cuff from Pop Janes notwithstanding, Suffield was no Dotheboys Hall. The headmaster's wife, Alice Truesdell, scrutinized young boarders for homesickness and intervened effectively. The housemother, Agnes Massiglio, was one of those comfortable, childless women who can hug limitless numbers of children to an ample bosom.

Certainly Harold enjoyed the school and later spoke of feeling "how full those years were." The setting was idyllic. Harold loved the town, the smell of burning leaves in fall, the aroma of fresh bread wafting from the town bakery of George Martinson and Sons. In winter he hopped rides to skating ponds on two-horse tobacco sleds that plied the main street. As an older student he could roam to Hartford or Springfield, each about an hour away on the interurban trolley that skirted the common, the only other serious transportation being the "Huckleberry," a one-car passenger and freight spur of the New Haven Railroad.

The Huckleberry's history impressed Harold so much it keynoted an important speech he made almost forty years later. In the early 1800s Suffield rivaled Hartford in size and importance. It was the center of Connecticut's tobacco industry and supplier of ice cut from local ponds to be stored throughout the year. The prosperous burghers, early environmentalists, did not want the noisome train chugging through their town, so the Hartford-Springfield line shunted across the Connecticut River. Without rail transport, Suffield languished. The Huckleberry was a doomed attempt to bring back the railroad and recall the glory traded for mere peace and quiet. Harold would remember it as a cautionary tale for those opposed to change.

Of course, Hartford was the exciting place to visit. From the Travelers Life Insurance Tower one could view the homes of America's most powerful insurance tycoons. Later events suggest that Harold climbed the tower and was impressed.

People at school were impressed with him—mostly as nice little boy who gave gratifying little trouble. Margie Thompson graduated in 1906 and became a Suffield fixture, secretary to each headmaster. "You could depend on him to have his hair combed and make a good appearance," she says, speaking of a day when fashion prescribed sweaters out at the elbow. Harold was an appealing child. "My main recollection is how pretty he was," says Tirzah Walker (now Mrs. Daryl Chapin), who was two grades ahead of Harold. "He was the prettiest little boy I ever saw. Georgeous! He had great big eyes, long lashes, curly hair. My girl friends used to call Harold my baby. I kind of looked out for him." Once, for a Halloween party, he dressed as a girl and was so prettily convincing that no one knew who he was. Not that he was effeminate or a goody-goody. Quite the contrary, says Tee Walker; at times "he was a little devil." For instance, the Reverend Jesse Smith, an English teacher, radiated such dignity that his nickname, "Itch," was never breathed in his presence. But Itch he was, out of earshot, because while lecturing he habitually scratched either his head or (depending who tells it) his crotch. One day his class heard the piping cry, "Itch . . . Itch . . . Itch . . . " through a window. They saw Harold's big eyes pop over the sill as he jumped up, shouting "Itch" at the apogee of each leap. English was never his best subject.

Neither was religion. Compulsory chapel took place in the Baptist church every morning, the headmaster officiating. The services were distinctly Protestant in a specifically Protestant school, not an environment congenial to active Catholic communion. There was no overt pressure on Harold, no prejudice or proselytizing. One of his favorite teachers, Daniel Sweeney, a staunch Catholic, attended mass in West Suffield. But why should Harold waggle in the faces of his peers a difference not quite acceptable? It would be a bother. And for what? Religion never interested him, and steadfastness in this case was plainly not worth the trouble. Or, as he later explained his lapse from Catholicism to a friend, "I had knots on my knees by the time I was ten."

At Suffield Harold built a life for himself that was friendly and secure. The homogeneous Preps provided an extended family, and he always had *a* home nearby. Tee Walker's mother, widely known as Mrs. Tee, was much taken with Harold, thought it a pity he had to stay at school so much, and became, as Tee puts it, his "time-being mother." Harold was often at the Walkers'—for holiday dinners or just to talk with Mrs. Tee and gobble her renowned maple walnut cookies.

Changes came when Harold passed from the Preps to the upper school. Social life under Pop Janes's supervision had been organized; now it was haphazard and voluntary. And Harold was unfortunate in his roommate. Johnny Myers, scion of the Myers thread company, was thought aloof and stuck-up, so hanging around with him isolated Harold. Not that Harold was, himself, unpopular. "He was a real good kid," says a classmate, "very polite. He'd talk to everybody, and he always had a good word for you." His classmates recognized his brightness, counting him one of the best students —and the wittiest. Bright, not arrogant.

Even so, the characteristics that had set Harold apart from the other Preps were magnified in high school, with far-reaching consequences. Most pervasive was his continued lack of athletic skill. Like other Connecticut Valley prep schools, Suffield was a little football factory, complete with scholarships. The school was sports-mad. "All we wanted to know about a guy was, Can you play ball?" says one of the hardier classmates. Harold could not. He was the class baby, considered preternaturally innocent. So even in the shelter of Suffield, Harold was early forced onto his own resources. As a result he had to forego the politics of involvement. (At the peak of his career,

Sophomore class picture in the Suffield Yearbook, 1924. Harold is next to the pillar, left, back row. Roommate John Myers is next to him, leaning against the pillar. Meade Alcorn is third from left, second row.

the man's want of political guile was a marvel to his streetwise associates, though they never doubted the steel of his character.) Once he opted out of the only activities that counted, Harold was let alone, free to follow his own interests.

His characteristic phrase was "I got an idea." But his ideas were never on the order of, Let's all do something that I suggest. They were interior interests (and everything interested him), points that arose in class or his reading. The phrase signaled his disappearance to the library or his room while he tracked down *all* the facts. For Harold, facts were to be a lifelong obsession.

Generosity was to be another. By 1924 Samuel Geneen had gotten into show business, himself, as president of National Concerts, Inc., at 1451 Broadway. He booked acts and managed performers. He also had some connection with the Bluebird Record Company—enough to keep Harold supplied with the latest hits. Harold immediately turned the records over to Tee Walker, because after school students congregated at her house to dance. That was generous enough, since vaudeville and show tunes (songs his mother taught him) would always entrance him, and it was all the more generous since he seldom came to the dances. "Harold," wrote Tee fifty years later, "was usually back at school, researching for one of his 'ideas'." Even when there, it was never to dance; he would sit and talk with Mrs. Tee, munching cookies. But giving up his records was not enough; for him generosity meant overkill. So to mark his gratitude and affection for the Walkers, Harold enlisted Jimmy Austin, a boy two grades down, and between them they sanded and varnished the Walkers' dance-scuffed living-room floor.

Implicit in all this is another lifelong pattern. Tee, Mrs. Tee, Agnes Massiglio, Margie Thompson, the girls in his class—Harold had a gift for charming females. At Suffield romance was not the object; he never had a girlfriend there. Nevertheless, the other girls shared Tee's opinion that he was a winsome, vivacious boy whose brightness was cute, not threatening. He would always feel easy with women, always retain a knack for flattering attentiveness that would win them—though, even later, he seldom won them for romance.

When roommate Myers did not return for the junior year, Harold's closest friend became Meade Alcorn. The Alcorns were a mighty force in the school and town of Suffield, and indeed throughout the state. An Alcorn graduated from the school in the early 1870s, and twenty-three have followed; a Suffield board of trustees without an Alcorn would scarcely be legal. At the time, Meade's father was a trustee, as well as Connecticut State's attorney. Meade very early displayed the political bent that would propel him to the chairmanship of the Republican National Committee under Dwight D. Eisenhower. He tirelessly manipulated even minor school elections. Though considered the best student in the class—and the snappiest dresser—he was also thought something of a "Mexican athlete," the current slang for bull-thrower. He was not universally popular. But as an egregious overachiever —who, as a classmate says, "had to be the best in *everything*"—he did not need to court popularity.

It took someone of Meade's intelligence and disdain for schoolboy notions of acceptability to appreciate Harold. Meade befriended him, and the Alcorns replaced the Walkers when Tee graduated, often entertaining Harold over weekends and holidays.

Harold admired Meade and envied his excellence. Of course, Meade had to work harder for things than Harold did. "Meade was book-smart," says a classmate, "not as naturally smart as Harold." But at school he gathered greater honors than Harold, and in more fields. Harold surely envied Meade's easy superiority, his position. There was no need for Meade to gaze wistfully down from the Travelers Tower; he was an Alcorn. So rivalry between the two keenest minds in the school was as natural as friendship. And Meade retained an indefinable edge. For example, Meade played the banjo as part of a musical quintet. Harold later engaged in a lifelong contest with the banjo, loving it, idolizing banjo stars, playing himself, though never with convincing skill—but never over the years did he let Meade know he was interested in the instrument.

The one subject in which Harold plainly bested Meade was mathematics —algebraic equations and Euclidean demonstrations being no more persuasive when expounded by a Mexican athlete. Unfortunately, the class ignored Harold's mastery of numbers and selected Frank Blenkhorn treasurer.

"Farmer" Blenkhorn, a lumbering, good-natured fellow, had to repeat junior year with Harold's class. In charge of funds for the senior yearbook, he so bungled that no money was left for printing. So Suffield's class of '26 had no yearbook—an episode that perhaps generated what would eventually become writ at ITT: the only unforgivable sin was running out of money.

On Tuesday, June 15, 1926, Harold and his class graduated. As always, the ceremonies were held in the Baptist church. Meade won the best-all-around-student award of $5, the Latin prize ($12), and the prize for highest four-year rank in English ($20). Harold was runner-up in the number of awards received, including a prize for the "Highest attainment in mathematics during four years" ($10) and a medal from the Hartford alumni of Rensselaer Polytech for the best work in math and science.

Harold and his class were ready to go forth and conquer, fortified by the baccalaureate sermon of the Reverend Dr. Gilkey, "Making the Most of an Ordinary Personality." At the time, the clergyman's theme would not have seemed inappropriate for Harold. Some people show early signs of greatness. They proceed from childhood in a commanding posture of achievement that has nothing to do with reality; the world might see them as failures, but they know better and they show it. They seek not a job but a path to vocation. Harold needed a job.

"We had the impression that Harold was from a well-to-do family," says a classmate. Except for inveterately scuffed shoes he always dressed well and had ample spending money. But something happened before his graduation. Perhaps his father failed in business again or stopped financial support; it was such a tender point that neither he nor his mother would ever discuss Samuel. Whatever the reason, the money was gone. "I went to work instead of on to day college as I had originally planned," he wrote years afterward. That disappointment stunted his self-image and view of life's promise. His expectations were modest. He was sure he could get a job if he sent out enough letters and résumés, went on enough interviews; and once in a job, he would strive to be in the top 20% to render himself immune from cyclical firings. These are not the precepts of a Napoleon. Even well into his thirties, his stated ambition was to earn $50,000 a year and, someday, to "run something." It would be a while before he recognized himself.

His first job was as a page for the New York Stock Exchange. Members called it the "Room," and they traded stocks at designated posts on the main floor. Around the sides of the Room clerks manned booths with direct lines to their brokerage firms, writing orders that the pages ran to the trading posts. Not all traders worked for brokerages. Some independents, called "two-dollar-brokers," handled surplus sales whenever regulars were swamped. Each trader had a number and was summoned when that number was lit up on the huge call board dominating one end of the Room. In the usual frenzy, traders had no time to keep tabs on the call board, yet it was essential to respond quickly. So each page would monitor two or three numbers in addition to his regular duties. A page would also run traders' errands off the floor, fetching food and drink, picking up dry cleaning and so on. These extras were important, because a page's salary for a five-and-a-half-day week was only $15. Tips, which were called "graft," made all the difference. Graft averaged about $10 a week, though experienced pages could pull down $100 or so.

When Harold started, the Room was a raucous and colorful place, full of the practical jokes and high spirits born of a long bull market. It was thought rare wit to paste a sign saying "genius at work" on the back of any particularly dim trader, or to give some newcomer an immense (fake) order, then crowd him so he could not get to the post, pushing, shoving, finally ripping his clothes off. On slower days the Room might shift to sentimentality, bursting into song. "Wait 'Til the Sun Shines, Nellie" and "Sidewalks of New York" were the favorites.

Possibilities abounded even for those without money or family backing. A page could become a quotations clerk; then his broker might buy him a seat on the Exchange. Of course, society figures predominated: there were the Fishes and Havemeyers; there was John Bouvier—called "Black Jack" for his indelible tan and constant scowl, a dedicated snob and envied womanizer; there were numberless cadets of the robber-baron families, whose money, once thought vulgar, was now as good as anyone's. But there were also an encouraging number of self-made outsiders: Horace Goldsmith, a Jewish thread dealer; Horsecock Jones from Chicago; Sell 'em Ben Smith, who started as Rockefeller's chauffeur; and many more who, if less notable, were most agreeably fixed. None of this stirred Harold. "I got a hell of a lot of feeling of companies and finance in those years," he later said, "but I decided I didn't want to be on the end of it where I'd be gambling on what other people did." The risk was especially unattractive since it had unacceptable downside consequences. Even before 1929 Harold saw that people who lost Wall Street jobs had no skills to sustain them elsewhere; the situation after the crash, when it appeared that waiting till the sun shone might be a life's work, confirmed his view. He would be better off in business. Success there, he said, would give him "something solid to build on."

On one hand, this decision evinced a lack of the self-confidence so evident in Harold's later career. On the other hand, it showed he was willing to strike out on his own. Though ultimately chancy, the Exchange was highly paternalistic. Leaving was a decision that separated the boy from the man.

In the fall of 1928 Geneen finally started college, enrolling in night classes at New York University's School of Commerce. There was no question of regular, day-time enrollment; he had to work full time, especially since NYU was a private school that charged $9 a point, with 18 to 22 points required each year. Geneen was aiming for a Bachelor of Science degree in accounting. At 128 points, it would be a long haul, taking six years to graduate.

In the 1934 night students' yearbook, the class historian wrote, "With reverence we recall the prosperity wave of 1928, which brought us into our

Freshman Year, innocent of difficulties ahead of us." Their prosperity, like their innocence, was relative. These were people who even before the crash could not afford full-time college. From the start their schedule was brutal. Two class sessions met each weekday night, from six to eight and from eight to ten. The usual load was five classes a week, and scheduling conflicts generally forced students to stay from six to ten at least one night a week— after a full day's work. NYU tried to simulate "college life" for them. The student center offered dances every Wednesday night, but since Thursday morning brought another day's work, attendance was sparse. "Most night students," says Edmund Butler, a classmate of Geneen's, "would come to class, study, then just go home." Butler involved himself more than most. He was one of seven elected to Arch & Square, a senior honor society. He also belonged to a fraternity, living in the house for $6 a week, a blessing since he, too, was a page in the Room, surviving on his $15-a-week salary as the graft dried up.

Geneen was certainly one of those who came, studied, and left, his presence registering on virtually no one. Butler does not remember him. Neither do the class president, Alfred Grossman, the first vice president, Lester Mossberg, the class historian, Hyman Federman, and the student voted most likely to succeed, Bernard Rackmil (who, in fact, *did* do pretty well, becoming vice president of Daylin, a chain of retail stores). Three professors who had Geneen in their classes are still alive; none remembers him. He did not make the senior honor roll of 188 students.

During this period, "ordinary" might have seemed a generous estimate of his personality, and a downright reckless assessment of his prospects.

He roomed in a boardinghouse at 302 Lexington Avenue and spent his days soliciting ads for the *World-Telegram.* It was only barely a living. A very junior salesman, he traveled the less promising advertising pastures of Long Island, then largely a potato patch. One day he wandered into the Rockville Center offices of a firm newly set up in the home-building business. William J. Levitt, three years older than the nineteen-year-old Geneen and sparkplug of Levitt & Sons, Inc., figured it paid to advertise—though in a small way, commensurate with his company's size. "We took an inch or two," Levitt remembers. "Geneen probably made a commission of sixty or seventy cents." Levitt continued to place the occasional ad with Geneen for a year or so before the young solicitor got a different territory and stopped coming around. When they met again, some thirty years later, Geneen had to remind Levitt of their early relationship. Levitt had not remembered him.

By 1932 Geneen had absorbed enough accounting in school to land a job as a bookkeeper for Mayflower Associates, a modest investment firm. It was steady work, a boon in those rocky times. Prices were low: a men's store near NYU proclaimed a going-out-of-business sale with the "same merchandise formerly on sale here at high prices" now going cheap—$32.50 suits were $14.50, and the top of the line, once $47.50, were now only $25.50. Around the corner at Thomas's, where waiters resplendent in floor-length aprons presided over tables snowy with real linen, you could feast for seventy cents, including tip. But seventy cents was a fortune. Later, Geneen told associates that he used to watch people eating in restaurants and desperately wish he could join them. At times his diet consisted of bread and taffy. "They had a one-cent sale on taffy," he explained, "two pounds for nine cents, and bread filled me up."

There was no money to waste on anything. The NYU student newspaper announced that December 10, 1933, was the last day for seniors to have their yearbook pictures taken. The notice warned that "A $1.50 cut cost charge must be paid to the studio before the sitting." That amount could buy a lot of bread and taffy. Geneen's picture is not in the yearbook. Neither is Ed Butler's, nor those of many other night students. "I was broke and discouraged," says Butler, "and a dollar-fifty meant too much then."

Geneen's enthusiasm for the festival rites of graduation would have been negligible anyway, since he did not graduate with the class in June. That was no disgrace; many night students fell a few points shy during the six years. Geneen recouped over the summer and got his degree in October 1934, three months short of twenty-five years old.

Despite an indifferent academic record, his degree gave him an important edge in those days of tight job competition. Following his usual formula for job hunting, Geneen wrote his letters, sent his résumés, and tried to get interviews. Among the few responses was that of Lybrand, Ross Brothers & Montgomery, now Coopers & Lybrand, one of the country's largest accounting firms. At his interview with senior partner Norman J. Lenhart, Geneen asked for twenty dollars a week and was momentarily dismayed when Mr. Lenhart said, "We can't pay that." Geneen needed the job yet knew he could not get by on less. Mercifully, Mr. Lenhart went on, "We'll start you out as an extra—at $30 a week. That's our minimum."

Even today public accounting is not considered a fast track; in the 1930s, when business reckoned accounting mere bean-counting, it promised even less meteoric a career. The eight years Geneen spent at Lybrand, from 1934 to 1942, are instructive only for what they reveal about the development of his mind and interests. In fact the most lasting effect of these years for Geneen was a by-product. The peculiar schedule of public accounting established a work habit that stayed with him to the continuing distress of colleagues. Most clients wanted audits toward the end of the year, so during the fall and winter Lybrand teams went all out. "It was nothing to put in fourteen- to sixteen-hour days," says a contemporary of Geneen's. "You'd be going regularly until ten, eleven o'clock, even twelve or one in the morning." Conversely, it did not matter how early you started; auditors did not punch time clocks. For the rest of his life Geneen would be a slow starter in the morning but would work long into the night.

During his years at Lybrand, he was qualifying as a CPA, learning about accounting and, more important, about business. But much of what he learned was repetitive. Audit groups were formed for each job, led by a manager, the top rank at Lybrand below partner. One or more seniors or "semiseniors" acted as straw bosses over the troop of junior accountants. Since Geneen's prior accounting experience had been with a financial company, he regularly drew audits of brokerages, mortgage companies, finance companies, and the like. There was one important exception. The American Can Company, a big client, needed many bodies for its yearly audit, and Geneen was included.

It was not enough to stimulate him, and narrowness of experience was not all that galled. There had been no new partners at Lybrand since 1929; there would be none until 1940, and even by then Geneen was nowhere near partnership. His prospects were not brilliant. In a profession that cherished time-in-grade, where seniors felt they were running an academy for juniors, Geneen was not only well down the ladder but considered overaggressive as well. "This guy will never get anywhere here," said one of the two who made partner in 1940; "he's too impatient."

Not all of Geneen's superiors agreed. There is division among some now-retired Lybrand executives about how far Geneen might have gone had he stayed with the firm. His work was never an issue: it was always "in apple pie order," as one superior puts it. Geneen was quick, both in number crunching and decision making. And he routinely took responsibility for decisions. Furthermore, he displayed a hard-driving, tireless intensity. Only his motivation was suspect. Those in Lybrand who cared passionately about accounting as a calling were convinced that Geneen saw it simply as a step to something else, not as a sacred rite whose service was its own justification.

Alvin Jennings became a managing partner at Lybrand; Louis H. Rappaport made partner and was author of a standard text on SEC regulations. Both were strong technicians who reveled in accounting as vocation. "A lot of Harold's contemporaries would have gone much further than he would have," says Jennings. Rappaport says, "He was no ball of fire as an accountant," but he adds, "We may have had a lower opinion of him than he deserved."

Walter Staub, who also became a managing partner, felt differently. His joy in accounting was the view it afforded of many varied businesses. "If you're in steel or railroads," says Staub, "you know only that; I'd find that monotonous." Staub thinks Geneen would have made it to the top at Lybrand on his brilliance—though that brilliance was somewhat offset by a tendency toward brusqueness, an important defect in a profession where a gift for ingratiation with clients is useful.

Others in the firm also understood and admired Geneen's broader view of accounting. "I was just senior to Geneen," said Philip Bardes, another who made partner, "and I would always ask for him on any job," and this specifically because of Geneen's wider vision. "He got tremendously enthusiastic," said Bardes. "He was one of the few men on the scene who got a lot of satisfaction creatively from analyzing figures and financial situations. Some men have hobbies or other enthusiasms to give them personal gratification. But not Harold. His job did that for him." It was not the audit but its implications that engaged Geneen's interest. The figures revealed the life of a department or company during the year, the ratios of profitability. Explicating those figures was the auditor's usual job. But Geneen was seized with a personal involvement in the results. If the ratios were off, demonstrating some fault in operation, he took the shortfall as a personal affront and eagerly devised a way to set matters right. This identification with each client's results made Geneen willing from early on to step into management's shoes, which inevitably meant stepping on some toes.

It happened at American Can. In 1936, twenty-one-year-old Norman G. Strobel started there as a bookkeeper in accounts payable. During the 1936 annual audit he heard a crescendo of argument in the corner office of his boss, Julius Cannold. Cannold's was a "showcase office," a low wooden partition surmounted by plate glass. Inside, he and someone from the outside audit team were having it out. Loud voices from the corner office were no rarity; but someone hollering back was unusual. At the battle's height, Cannold beckoned to Strobel. When Strobel went in, Geneen thrust a bookkeeping form under his nose. "Did you make this out?" he snapped.

"Yes."

"Do you know what you're doing?"

"Well, I'm doing what I've been told to—"

"You're overstating the inventory and overstating the payables every time you make this out!"

Geneen was right. As soon as each factory's clerks learned that ordered material was on the way, they approved the bill for payment so as to realize maximum cash discount. The material was entered in a special transit account. On arrival, it went into inventory, and a transfer form supposedly took it out of transit and charged it to payables. But often that did not happen. Geneen tried to explain to Cannold that if material was not immediately taken out of the transit account, it appeared twice on the books. To be sure, the entry would be reversed the next month. But it was a sloppy procedure that distorted inventory and payables at any given moment. "We don't make mistakes in my department," was Julius Cannold's invariable (and inaccurate) response to criticism. Besides, he was not an accountant and could not understand Geneen's explanation or concern. It was only when he realized that Geneen would not drop it that he called in the person who had made the entry.

Strobel got the point at once and was upset for two reasons. He was stunned to see an outsider acting like his boss, shouting, "Don't do it anymore," attacking standard operating instructions. "Our independent auditors were generally very deferential to the client," says Strobel, "but not Harold." He was equally upset for not having realized the significance of the entry. "From then on," he says, "I went into the background of reports I made to see what their end use was. It was a valuable lesson for my career."

The accounting profession has changed enormously since those days, as has the position of accountants and what is expected of them. Much of this change flows directly from Geneen's later career, for he demonstrated what accounting could mean to management. He was lucky he got his start at Lybrand, since they looked more benignly than most on the accountant's involvement with the client's business. It had been a dictum of Colonel Montgomery, one of Lybrand's founders, that "if you don't give at least one good idea for improving the client's operation, you haven't conducted a good audit." Still, Lybrand's zeal for "operating audits" stopped well short of Geneen's. He did not want to give one idea or a dozen; he wanted to tell them how to run the business. If not exactly stifled at Lybrand, he was mightily frustrated.

It did not help that he could see no clear escape. In 1936 he met and married Deeda Tilghman, who was from the South and had been a nurse. It was a short-lived marriage; they were evidently separated by 1942 and divorced in 1946. Geneen never talked about this aspect of his life, neither while it was going on nor afterward. During his separation, some close friends remained unaware that he had ever had a wife. Whatever the exact reasons for eventual disaffection, Deeda certainly had a lot to put up with, married to a man who was married, before anything, to a job that left him unsatisfied. But for the time being, with a wife to support and jobs still scarce, Geneen was trapped.

So the 1930s wore drearily on. Geneen passed much of his free time surf fishing. Deeda often complained about the endless hours spent with him at Jones Beach while he wandered restlessly into the surf, pacing back and forth, solitary and brooding. "I remember," said Philip Bardes, "one whole summer we ribbed him because he never caught a fish. But that didn't bother him. He could walk all day on the beach and cast. He had no interest in the fish."

When the Japanese attacked Pearl Harbor in December 1941, Geneen must have seen release from his stultifying job and marriage in the coming turmoil. Surely, with the ferment, things would change; in dislocation there is always opportunity.

2

For the Duration

If the United States was short of practically everything when it plunged into World War II, at least the pattern for mass production was in place. Heroic effort was needed, but it was mostly a matter of adapting and hugely expanding existing capability for the manufacture of airplanes, guns, ships, tanks, and so on. Torpedoes presented a different problem. Until Pearl Harbor, torpedo manufacture had been almost a cottage industry in Newport, Rhode Island, where craftsmen created the weapons virtually by hand. Blueprints were greasy papers shoved into a back pocket, unheeded, and they often varied anyway from parts that experience had modified. The Newport torpedoes were exquisite. But the system that crafted them could not expand, and now the navy needed a lot of torpedoes in a hurry.

The situation was a natural for American Can. Torpedoes are immensely harder to produce than tin cans, but the core machine-shop disciplines are similar. With wartime restrictions crimping the tin can business, the company had a surplus of highly skilled people. Besides, while war-work profit might be limited, the profit from nonessential manufacture in metals nearly vanished. American Can quickly formed a wartime subsidiary, Amertorp, to make torpedoes.

However, much more was involved than simply turning can plants over to Amertorp. Torpedoes required special machinery, tools, and assembly lines. The navy already had a suitable plant in Forest Park, Illinois, a suburb west of Chicago; Amertorp took that over and built another in St. Louis.

To oversee Amertorp staffing, the company reactivated Arthur Carpenter, a retired auditor. It was easy for Carpenter to find excellent machine shop and factory people, but accounting staff was a problem. At American Can, as in most businesses at the time, accountants were called "clerks," and were thought to possess only the most trivial abilities. Few at American Can had any formal training as accountants. One who enjoyed a distinguished career as controller says he became an accountant "by osmosis." "It wasn't all that hard," he claims; and for the level of accounting at the time that was no doubt true. Instruction manuals detailed every step.

But no manual could cover the conditions at Amertorp. Compensation was cost-plus-fee for each torpedo: substantiated costs were reimbursed and a fixed fee was profit. That might seem to have invited negligence, but in fact it impelled strict control: while American Can's profit was fixed in numbers of dollars, expressed as return on investment, it depended on how diligently expenses were controlled, itemized, and recovered. In the wartime emergency, normal procedures were regularly ignored. For instance, the frantic clip of three-shift production never allowed time for physical inventories. So accounting had to be incredibly tight. Furthermore, recovery of costs was far from automatic. Both the navy and the government's General Accounting Office scrutinized all expenditures, and Amertorp would eat any expense it could not justify. Once, money was spent futilely trying to fix a defective warhead; the navy ruled that it should have been scrapped and would not pay for the repairs.

It was also necessary to separate the cost of building the St. Louis plant from torpedo-making costs, since Amertorp had two distinct contracts: the torpedo fee multiplied with production; the building fee stayed the same, no matter how much money American Can sank into it. And, unlike any other American Can plant, Amertorp had to do all its own accounting, including assignment of overhead, costs, payroll, purchasing, general ledger—the works. All this was plainly beyond the abilities of American Can's regular clerks.

Arthur Carpenter understood the situation. Still, it was unthinkable that the department head be other than an old hand, so he appointed William Cameron as controller. Bill Cameron had started with the company as a boy, his accounting skills acquired in best American Can tradition, osmotically. But he was a good leader, adept at handling people. The real work would be done by a chief accountant and his lieutenants. For those, Carpenter was willing to go outside.

"I went to see the army fellow about a commission," Geneen once said, talking about the days right after Pearl Harbor, "but they turned me down." He had heard that the navy needed CPAs and offered them his services. "They were delighted until I put my glasses on to sign the papers," he said, "then they stopped me. If I was unfit for sea duty, I was unacceptable to the navy." Soon the armed forces would be less finicky about noncombatant commissions, and myopia would be no bar to a draft call. At the same time it was no secret that those engaged in vital war work—which Amertorp certainly was—would be exempt from military service.

Moreover, Geneen saw Amertorp as a god-sent chance to break out of his dead end at Lybrand. As soon as Geneen got word of Amertorp he submitted a plan for production and financing. Impressed, Carpenter appointed Geneen to the number two spot of chief accountant.

Geneen started his new job in the winter of 1942. First came a brief executive training program in New Jersey, then several weeks of planning at American Can's New York City headquarters. Geneen knew enough American Can clerks to realize he would need help from another source, so he recruited two fellow Lybrand employees, Charles W. Plum and Andrew Johnson, to run the general ledgers at the St. Louis and Forest Park plants.

By May, Geneen was hard at work in Amertorp's Forest Park headquarters. "He inherited a zero system, absolutely zero," says Charlie Plum, "and he designed, practically himself, an entire system for the two plants." A comprehensive general ledger was only the beginning. Geneen also had to construct a massive property-record accounting system in an environment so hectic that physical inventories were impossible. But his biggest challenge was building the system to recover costs. "We had to corral *all* the expenses," says Charlie Plum. "Here are the categories we spent in, and this was the authority —because we had to get approval from the naval commanding officer's people for every purchase. And all that was set up by Geneen, the whole system."

In addition, there were hard renegotiations of contract terms to be made in Washington and New York. For instance, there was the question of tools. "Harold had an obsession," says a close Amertorp associate, "that once the contract was over, if we didn't properly account for all the assets in the business, particularly those thousands of tools, we'd be given a great pounding by the navy, coming out of the fee." Some tools, like jigs or holding fixtures that might last forever, had to be accounted for. Others, like drill bits and grinding wheels, were steadily consumed by the thousands. Tracking them would be a monumental task. But what if the navy popped up after the war and said, Okay, we paid for one hundred thousand drill bits and grinding wheels, now where are they? Suppose they charged Amertorp for them? Geneen got the navy to agree that once perishable tools left the stockroom, they were written off. That part was relatively simple. Then came the question of tools that could fit into either category. A saw blade is plainly perishable, a vise plainly not. But what about a hammer? A chisel? The latitude for negotiation was immense.

Geneen had little help with any of these sorts of accounting-management problems. Bill Cameron's affability and personnel talents did not serve here. "It was completely obvious to us from the start," says Charlie Plum, "that Geneen was running things; Cameron became a figurehead." It did not affect relations between them. They quickly formed a firm and workable friendship. Cameron valued Geneen's ability and relied on it. For his part, Geneen liked Cameron, appreciated his nonmeddling, and often found his way eased by Cameron's warm diplomacy. Even one of Geneen's chief admirers admits that the sharpness of his hero's mind was "sometimes to the discomfort of his slower-minded associates." Since that included everyone, Cameron's gift for smoothing ruffled feathers came in handy. The two men grew close, going off together, when they could steal the time, to shoot pheasants in South Dakota.

Had Geneen chosen, there could have been plenty of time. With so much responsibility, it may sound as though he had to be incessantly busy; but he did not. Once his systems were on-line their routines went smoothly. Plum and Johnson were entirely competent, and Geneen could confidently leave the accounting chores to them—which he gladly did. "Often," says Plum, "when he came to Saint Louis I didn't even see him. When I did, the questions would be, Were we able to substantiate all the money we spent? How does the construction contract stand against the operating contract? And when the answers were what he wanted to hear, that was it."

Other matters in St. Louis attracted Geneen. The plant was much more rough-and-ready than the one at Forest Park; the roof was still partly blue sky when production started. Also, all the brass was in Illinois; in St. Louis lines of authority were less distinct. People would more readily accept help and advice from an outsider.

John Devaney was especially willing. He was executive chief clerk of cost accounting. Since his boss, the chief clerk, did not know much about cost accounting, Devaney ran the department. He and Geneen hit it off from the first. Although Devaney was another American Can earn-while-you-learn product, he had been to night school at the University of Cincinnati, after his hours in a machine shop. "He was one of the few," says Charlie Plum, "who even tried to become a real accountant." Geneen liked that spunk. Here was someone who had bothered to learn accounting and did not just follow the company's General Book of Instructions. Furthermore, Geneen could not help liking the way Devaney treated him, with a mixture of deference and devotion. But most of all, Geneen liked the man's utility. Devaney introduced him to a revelation: in St. Louis, Geneen discovered hands-on cost accounting.

It was instant infatuation. The intricate control procedures immediately entranced Geneen, especially since they were linked to the production line. He saw the connection clearly, as well as the potential, and he set out to capitalize on his perception.

To grasp the possibilities Geneen saw one must understand the problems of torpedo manufacture. For its size and weight, a torpedo was the most complex piece of machinery extant in the early 1940s. About 25 assemblies clustered in the warhead, upwards of 100 in the afterbody, each comprised of 150 to 250 parts, machined to tenths of a thousandth of an inch. The gyroscope, guidance system, propulsion unit, and propeller were miracles of accurate delicacy. The tailcone had fin and propeller controls of extraordinary balance. This clockwork fantasy, weighing a couple of tons, had to run true at a set depth even after plummeting from a 100 m.p.h. airplane. Almost every part was custom-made, with an average of six factory steps—lathe work, grinding, and so forth. Some parts took a few hours to machine; the gyroscope wheel took about three months. Yet to send one torpedo out the door, every part had to be ready at the same time. And since there was no room for stockpiling, work had to begin three months ahead on the gyro wheel, less than a week before assembly on some trifling, yet essential, little part. The schedule demanded a peak flow of hundreds of torpedoes a month.

So far, this was pretty standard machine-shop stuff, though the pace was feverish. The novel element that captured Geneen's attention was the intimate and reciprocal relation between production control and accounting procedures. For reimbursement, management had to document the exact cost of every part in every torpedo. Since each part had to be tracked step by step in manufacture, necessity forced a shotgun marriage of cost and production control. A lump of metal sat in a stockroom bin, its cost known. At the prescribed time on the scheduled day, the lump was placed on a hand truck, with blueprints and a job envelope specifying the tools needed for the first operation. These tools would also be delivered to the appropriate machine. When one job was done, the next was waiting. No machine time was lost: that was the crux of production. A ticket was punched to record the time each operation started and ended on every part. Each ticket went to accounting while the job envelope accompanied the part through machining. No more than four days after the part was finished, accounting knew its exact cost: raw material, machining time multiplied by each operator's hourly rate, plus the assigned burden of overhead and direct labor. This was powerful information that could be used a new way. What Geneen saw was that an analysis of costs could instantly pinpoint any slowdown, inefficiency, bottleneck, or other production problem.

Something akin to this, in crude form, was already known. Standard cost systems existed—and were steadfastly ignored by businesses. Only the simplest repetitive operations (making paint, for instance) ran on standard costs. American Can itself did not go on standard costs until 1962, and even at Amertorp the implications of the system eluded management. If a part cost more than standard, so be it; the navy would pay. On the floor, foremen still kept track of hours with hand-postings, by guess and by golly, to locate and puzzle out problems.

Geneen set out to learn as much as he could about the system, however rudimentary and imperfectly used. It did not matter that his interest naturally pushed him into areas beyond his authority or supposed competence. "I think he designed the stockroom at St. Louis," says Charlie Plum. Actually he did not; but he was deeply involved with those who did, as well as those implementing the "mastercard system" of production and accounting control. If his presence was not thought intrusive, it was because he was so clearly able, even in areas new to him, and so adept at solving problems.

"Whenever I try to explain Harold to people," says a later associate, "I tell them I can envision a workman coming into his office and telling him he's having trouble drilling holes in some metal. Geneen would ask him a lot of questions, then he'd say, It's obvious that you'll have to increase the rake angle on the drill. The workman would nod and say, Oh yeah! I see it now—sure, that'll do it, thanks. And as he's on the way out, Geneen would call to him: By the way, what's a drill? *That's* the kind of mind the man has."

Help from such a mind was not resented for another reason. People generally become territorial only when they do not have much to do; at Amertorp almost everyone was fearsomely busy. Even the relatively placid general ledger section worked a forty-eight-hour week. For many others the regular hours were 8:00 A.M. to 6:00 P.M., six days a week, and the average week for managers, at peak, was seventy hours. There were no holidays. One New Year's Eve a man who forgot that the next day would be just another workday celebrated too hard. He made it to the plant, punched in, then keeled over.

With Geneen gravitating to St. Louis, accommodations were a problem. He had an apartment in the Chicago suburb of Oak Park, near the Forest Park plant. But now he was spending a third or more of his time in St. Louis, and he needed something permanent. He had a brainstorm. Like most Amertorp bachelors, John Devaney roomed in the Coronado Hotel, and hated it. At Geneen's urging Devaney found an apartment they could share, a second-floor walkup on Brentwood Boulevard in nearby Clayton. Geneen would pay one-third of the rent. There was only one trouble. Since Geneen's trip expenses were business, the navy would end up paying, and they bridled at subsidizing part of an apartment. That the rent was demonstrably less than Geneen's hotel bills invoked a logic beyond immediate comprehension. "It was off the beaten path," says Devaney, "but once Geneen explained the arrangement, the navy went along."

The apartment was a great success, an edifying domestic interlude for Geneen. His marriage to Deeda was finished, although the divorce was not final until 1946. Deeda did not accompany him to Chicago, and most people who knew him there were not aware that he was married. ("He seemed such an attractive man to be single," one Amertorp wife remembers thinking.) Social life in Forest Park was sporadic: the occasional cocktail party at the Oak Park Arms, a reception when the army/navy "E" was awarded. Generally the executives went their own way.

In St. Louis things were different. John Devaney was courting a local girl (now Madeline Devaney) who came complete with family and social circle. "Harold fit right in," says Devaney. When Geneen came from Chicago, Devaney and Madeline would meet the train around ten at night. After dropping Madeline at her home, the two men went on to the apartment. Geneen was always keyed up, wanting to talk about operations at both plants. "I'd say, Aw c'mon, Harold, lemme go to sleep," says Devaney. "But he'd go on and on, and finally I'd say, Oh the hell with it, and I'd just fall asleep and let him rattle away."

Geneen would stay in St. Louis days at a time, often over weekends. He and Devaney breakfasted in the apartment, lunched at the plant, and dined half the time at home, half at the Candlelight, a Mt. Vernon colonial restaurant that was the pride of Clayton. Madeline usually joined them for dinner out, and sometimes Geneen would squire a friend of Madeline's or her sister, Jane. "Date" is too strong a word; it was more a matter of making a foursome. Jane was in fact engaged to a fellow away in the army.

Sundays in St. Louis were especially homey. While Madeline and Devaney went to mass, Geneen would prepare an enormous brunch, featuring his speciality, green tomatoes, sliced and broiled with cheese. "Damn fried tomatoes," says Devaney, "he used to love those things." Afterward they would sit and talk, or go for walks in Shaw Park across the boulevard. In fine weather Geneen and Devaney played tennis in the park or swam. Geneen's early lack of athletic skill notwithstanding, he came near fanaticism in his lifelong devotion to exercise. He did calisthenics every morning, even in winter, before an open window.

The idyll ended in May 1943, when Devaney and Madeline married. And the intensity of Geneen's involvement with production slackened when Devaney was promoted later that year and transferred to Forest Park. "Harold was not as close to plant operations in Forest Park as in St. Louis," Devaney says. For instance, he joined production meetings only when contracts were discussed. Meanwhile, with his chief disciple gone from St. Louis, Geneen had less ambit there, too. Not that his advice was less welcome; others just did not turn to him quite so automatically.

In any case, his routine at both locations was humdrum, nothing to stretch his abilities. Most of all, his job denied him the complete responsibility he craved. "Knowing Geneen," says Devaney, "there's no way he would have stayed in that job, except it was a wartime thing that had to be done." Besides, as Devaney also points out, the chances of getting another job during the war were not good.

This is not to suggest Geneen was looking for another job, or that if offered one he would have taken it. He always demonstrated a compelling sense of duty and identification with his current company. He was ever the fierce partisan of "his" company's interest, right to the end. Even when conditions turned intolerable (as they later would at Jones & Laughlin), for Geneen, leaving a company was a wrench.

This talent for total commitment, allied with his brilliance, was Geneen's ineluctable strength. His weakness was the direction that his commitment took. There is an essence in any enterprise that merits unflinching dedication. It was Geneen's tragedy never to grasp first causes, never to find the center.

We can observe this flaw in its early stage at Amertorp. When the old-line torpedo crafters in Newport heard Amertorp's plans for mass production they scoffed: the new, unskilled help would produce few torpedoes, they predicted, and surely not ones that would run true. Ten months after the initial conferences at Newport, Amertorp's first torpedo left the factory, on time and on budget. Soon torpedoes by the thousands were delivered. The cost of each started out lower than at Newport and continually declined until prices were halved. But Amertorp's purpose was neither to mass produce torpedoes nor to save the navy money. It was certainly not, despite Geneen's obsession, to recoup costs or to turn a profit. The reason for Amertorp's existence was to help sink enemy ships.

Anyone who remembers those times, or has seen World War II submarine movies, knows that the Newport elite had a point about quality. There were crippling problems with Amertorp torpedoes. Some went around in circles. Others ran too deep, skittering harmlessly under enemy hulls. Still others hit their targets only to bounce off when the cranky firing mechanism failed to detonate.

These were flaws of design and engineering, in no way Geneen's responsibility. Given his later-proven ability to master and coordinate technical subjects, the war effort might have been better served if he had been consulted. As it was, a mere bean-counter dared not invade design and engineering. He would have been snubbed both by the navy and by his own company. It never occurred to him to interfere, and the scandal of failed torpedoes evidently never exercised him. His focus was on increased manufacturing efficiency, reduced cost, and, supremely, the safety of Amertorp's fee. Had he been asked to supervise a solution to the torpedo problem, his dissatisfaction over not having bottom-line responsibility would have been no less acute. Solving a problem central to the company's purpose would have been hollow, because that purpose did not include profit and corporate growth. These issues were the ones that truly spoke to Geneen about any enterprise.

On August 31, 1945, three years after the first torpedo came off the assembly line in St. Louis, the end of Amertorp was announced. Geneen stayed on for the turn-back of plant and tools to the navy and was gratified to see his precautions pay off. There were few disallowed expenses, no major penalties.

What now? At Amertorp, under the lash of war and the navy's eye, American Can's reverence for seniority was set aside. Time-servers were shunted aside to make way for those who could produce. Now it was back to business as usual. American Can could assess Geneen's talent, but not his value. They offered him a spot in New York on the usual schedule: years of service before moving up, working at jobs he would inevitably find trivial.

His first duty was to conduct a manpower survey. Geneen was to chart all elements of the company's personnel so management could weigh present and future needs. "Management didn't think it was an inconsequential job," says an associate in the accounting department, "but Geneen did. We all said if he wasn't made an immediate VP, he wouldn't stay around very long." But his rise would not be immediate, or even swift. American Can did not work like that in those days. Few businesses did—and especially not for accountants. If you wanted people to count beans (or in this case, noses), seniority makes sense just as practice makes perfect. Geneen started looking for another job.

Meanwhile, he continued to show a brusque intolerance of bumbling, which in that environment precluded many friendships. One fellow worker announced that if Geneen ever became boss of the department he would jump out the window. But the old friendships continued. Bill Cameron was in New York now, too; they stayed friends. Geneen would go out to Cameron's Long Island home to fish. Years later he would interrupt a busy schedule to visit his dying friend in the hospital, and he was especially kind to Cameron's widow. He also made a friend of Martin Conway, manager of general accounting. Like Geneen, Conway was a bachelor, and they often dined together. One morning Conway dragged himself into the office, looking haggard. After dinner the previous night, the two men had shared a cab to upper Manhattan, and Conway had asked Geneen in for a nightcap. "That damned fool, Geneen, he kept me up until two in the morning—talking *business!*" The amazement in his voice was echoed by his audience: Marty Conway was a hard man to keep focused on business. But Geneen could do it, and at times that talent was resented. American Can regulars disliked this outsider's unflagging dedication to their company almost as much as his patent scorn of their shortcomings. "You knew he was brilliant," an associate says, "by the way everyone, including the bosses, dealt with him." Warily.

In all, Geneen stayed at American Can's New York headquarters less than six months. In Chicago he had become acquainted with J. H. McNabb, autocratic head of the Bell & Howell Company, and now he had a job offer: McNabb asked him to take over as controller at B&H.

Although American Can was prepared to bear up under the loss, Geneen got the standard exit interview, a restrained attempt to change his mind about leaving. After all, he was a bright young fellow—only thirty-six, at an age and position where he should be settling into routine service. By the time he was fifty or so, he could hope for a position of consequence, perhaps even chief bean-counter. Why was he dissatisfied? He told them why and left. This was one time when he evidenced no pangs at leaving a company.

Typically, he had called Lou Rappaport at Lybrand first. He often would when some nice point of accounting theory or practice arose. In this case, he wanted to discuss the differences in SEC strictures on an officer of a publicly held company, which he was about to become, compared with those on an officer in a subsidiary. Rappaport was impressed that Geneen so foresightedly recognized that there were questions to ask.

In Chicago, the night before Geneen was to report for work, he stayed with Andy Johnson, the man he had tapped as head of the general ledger at Forest Park. Johnson was amazed: "Here was Harold going to that big job next day, and he slept soundly all night. No trepidation about the job, no nervousness. I'd have been tossing all night long. But not Harold."

3

Hitting His Stride

Joseph Hector McNabb was no fool. General manager of Bell & Howell for thirty-two years, president and chairman for twenty-six years, he had harnessed the inventions of Albert S. Howell to make Bell & Howell the greatest name in movie and slide projectors. McNabb *was* the company. "My predecessor," says Charles H. Percy, "ran everything out of his office. No one went to the washroom without an okay from him." Employees spoke of the B&H "spider web" organization chart: all lines led to McNabb.

Still, JH, as they called him, knew his company and himself. As World War II ended he realized that B&H had outgrown one-man rule. Volume in 1941 had just topped $5.5 million. War contracts for gun sights, aerial cameras, lenses, and projectors to run those soporific training films had pushed revenue to nearly $22 million by 1945. Even with the expected postwar drop, 1946's sales were almost double those of 1941. Moreover, McNabb had taken the company public, making further growth mandatory.

Modern financial controls were essential, and McNabb knew he was not the one to institute them. His notion of control, while rigorous, had always been rudimentary. "The joke around here," says one longtime employee, "used to be that if you wanted a box of pencils you better get approval from Mr. McNabb." No one else at B&H knew any more about budgeting and forecasting. The outgoing controller, John Hahn, had been there over thirty years and remained unbudgeably in the bean-counter tradition. McNabb was his own treasurer, and none of the trainees in an otherwise excellent training program was advanced in finance, not even McNabb's fledgling assistant treasurers. As one observer says, "It needed someone with at least five years' senior experience to install a budget system." McNabb knew he would have to look outside. His first choice, Ira Lutz, lasted less than a year; he lacked

Joseph Hector McNabb

the decisive force to shatter old-line resistance to a new regimen. McNabb kept looking.

Like Amertorp, B&H had a resident navy inspector during the war. It was probably through him that McNabb heard about Geneen. When McNabb made his offer in early 1946, Geneen jumped at it. His job was to establish financial controls and to rationalize expenditures. These were massive tasks, because the corollary to McNabb's very personal rule was that decisions on spending and organization were often whimsical. R&D projects went forward because JH trusted Albert Howell or were squelched because the new man phasing in as chief engineer did not yet command the same confidence. The separate B&H electronics division was typical. Headed by McNabb's half-brother, it kept nosing into areas of doubtful promise. One was the making of TV sets—when B&H lacked all essential engineering, manufacturing, and marketing knowhow. "Geneen must have been about the first to bring law and order to the whole control and systems end of the business," says an associate from those days. Not long after Geneen arrived, the electronics division merged into regular operations, and McNabb's half-brother faded away.

Geneen's workaday impact, if less flashy than the dismantling of a division, was more pervasive. "He was relentless in getting better cost control," says Everett Wagner, an engineer in charge of quality control who eventually became B&H's vice chairman. "It was a thread that stayed with the company. To this day, things he did are still with us." Geneen started with budgeting and forecasts. These are business staples today, but they had never existed at B&H—which is amazing, since for its size the company had an extraordinary degree of vertical integration. B&H made almost everything it used, from specialized machinery to plywood for camera cases.

Geneen devised a forecast and budgeting system and installed it on a practice level for 1946 and 1947, then for real in 1948. Marketing had to forecast sales; manufacturing had to forecast costs and capital investment requirements, with each item justified; engineering now had to estimate development costs for new products and to predict development schedules. All departments had to live with their budgets. For the first time profit plans were developed. And, another novelty at B&H, the break-even point for each product line was figured.

There was still a lot to do. In August 1946 Geneen hired a young assistant, John P. Buchan, and set him to work up a cash forecast for the company. Buchan was appalled to find that B&H had never generated even basic information for any such forecasts. Management did not know how much money would be in the till next Tuesday. They paid on piecework yet did not know their standard costs. "A large part of our early work," says Buchan, "was to develop records that would reflect expenses in departments and divisions, to develop budgets and make comparisons to see where the company was off schedule." Soon Geneen's office was a maze of stacked-up cartons holding commandeered paperwork from which he and Buchan would distill the relevant records.

Geneen did not invent financial controls; indeed, the first thing he told Buchan was to read *Budgeting for Management Control* by Rowland and Harr. But Geneen did have a singular vision of the potential financial controls promised business. "In those days," says Buchan, "at accounting seminars they would say, This is how we can help top management. Not that they *were* top management, or should be. That was not Geneen's concept." Geneen considered himself a key part of top management, and his discipline the way to better management. His favorite dictum was that you do not make money, you save it. But control was just the start. With the overview his figures gave him of the whole enterprise, he could help steer the functioning departments. "He'd get into tooling with the manufacturing people," says Buchan. "How to tool an item, how long a tool should last, whether you should use die casting or sand casting, how much money to put into new tooling." He also figured how much the competing choices would save. Geneen showed them how marketing projections could reveal which programs would pay out. "That sort of thing had never been done at the company before," says Buchan. "All this really started Bell and Howell on its growth path. And it set—in my mind and in the mind of a lot of people— a pattern for financial people in other companies to follow that made them top management. I think Geneen established in modern business what a controller should be and what he should do."

For instance, B&H's oldest product was the model 134, an 8mm camera whose declining sales suggested that its end was near. Geneen determined how much the company would save on each model at successively increased levels of manufacture. Then he asked marketing how many more 134s they would sell at a lower price. The projected surge in sales meant that savings from volume manufacturing would more than offset the lower price. Model 134 got new life.

Model 220 was born of such thought. With prices and sales elasticity the order of the day, marketing got excited about a truly low-price camera. Model 220 came out at $49.95. But then Geneen's analysis of marketing's projections showed that at $39.95 the camera's extra volume would yield an even bigger profit. The price plunged. "And with an eight-millimeter camera under forty dollars," says Charles G. Schreyer, marketing director at the time, "we had the market by the balls. Even *Kodak* was worried."

The trick was lowering costs at every point, a movement that Geneen led. "He helped us call in suppliers," says Charles Percy, "and he would say, We're buying twenty thousand parts a year from you now; what would your prices be if we bought fifty thousand? He established the principle with us to go for quantity." Geneen also pointed the way to efficiency. "We went out in the factory one time," says Percy, "and he said to me, One of our greatest cost elements is compartmentalization. We're broken into very small units. We ought to knock out all these walls and have longer assembly lines. And why use floor space for inventory? Let's move it up to the ceiling and keep it moving around. He always had breakthroughs of that kind, and I found his thinking invaluable." Geneen's mark was evident everywhere.

Reviewing government war contracts, Geneen discovered that B&H had

Charles Percy's first B&H "cabinet" in 1949. Counting three rows, first row: Townsley on the right, Percy third from right. Second row: Geneen second from right, Harrod third, Roberts fifth, Stechbart sixth. Back row: Buchan third from right, Schreyer fourth, Phillimore seventh.

not charged enough for overhead. He fought a claim through the renegotiation board to a nice settlement.

He shifted from FIFO to LIFO inventory, lowering taxable earnings to conserve cash—vital for a growing company. LIFO was so unusual then that the switch inspired an immediate IRS audit. The auditor, as it happened, was a photography buff, keen on developing his own color pictures. Geneen gathered a library on color photography and became an instant enthusiast. He and the IRS man got along famously, and the changeover was allowed.

The company was ready to pass up one large military contract because their bid seemed impossibly high. But Geneen showed that they could afford to bid low—and make up the difference on spare parts.

What he demonstrated was not just that Harold Geneen, an individual with special talents, should and could be top management. Rather, he showed that any controller who followed his example would be top management, ex officio. "The material he had available to him for analysis," says Charles Percy, "was infinitely more helpful than a lot of the material that, say, color managers and vice presidents of engineering had—because he could picture the company as a whole. He *put* accounting into top management."

This did not always happen peaceably. "It was traumatic for some of us," says Malcolm G. Townsley, then a product development engineer. "The technical people felt constrained because before there had been much more freedom to explore new products." That sort of freedom, bordering on license, was exactly why McNabb had brought Geneen in. Nevertheless, says Townsley, Geneen "inhibited engineering for at least three years"—just at the pivotal period of postwar boom when B&H should have been enforcing its engineering dominance. The real quarrel was with Geneen's manner more than his mission. "He felt he was there to put budgetary control in forcibly," says Townsley. The engineers saw Geneen as interested only in his own job, not in helping them to do theirs. Since Geneen would always see a company's financial goals as the soul of its existence, people strong in the spirit of craft would always see him as uncaring. Malcolm Townsley is still bitter. "I think Geneen," he says, "is an authentic, stem-winding, ring-tailed bastard."

That was not the universal view at B&H. Geneen could be abrupt: "a staccato kind of guy," says someone who, despite this, "got along with him beautifully." Many thought well of him. "He was a warm person," says Everett Wagner. "I enjoyed him as a human being." Sometimes, over lunch, Geneen would entertain colleagues with tales of his new car, a Mercury whose radical design still had bugs in it. His stories of the crises, with himself as bewildered figure of fun, made him seem a human, appealing person. John Buchan, Geneen's closest assistant, adds, "I thoroughly enjoyed working for the man."

Geneen had another engaging trait. He was always open to cogent and informed argument. At ITT dogmatism would sometimes taint his reasonableness; but not at B&H. "If I had a case," says Everett Wagner, "I knew I'd get a good hearing." That was true even when accounting orthodoxy was questioned. Once Wagner wanted to modify the standard-cost definition of direct labor. Certain repetitive inspections were so integral to camera manufacture, he argued, that they should be reckoned as directly adding to the product's value. No doctrinaire controller would have brooked such heresy; but on reflection, Geneen agreed.

He also agreed with D. T. Davis—even more remarkable, since the issue here was cash owed the company. B&H pioneered the school audio-visual field, allowing schools to rent projectors when they could not afford to buy. The company was so lenient with credit that many schools and dealers owed impressive balances. B&H saw this as building an important market; Geneen saw it as shocking. "Why aren't those guys paying their bills?" he asked, unmoved by talk of cash positions, developing customers, good will, and the full faith and credit of school districts. "Bullshit!" he said, pointing to the books. "This dealer, D. T. Davis in Lexington, Kentucky. He's owed us money for two years. *I'm* going down there and collect." He came back with a smoked ham and a sheepish grin. Davis had shown him the books, taken him around, and explained the nature of the business. "The guy's right," Geneen said, "I understand it now."

Naturally, Geneen's forcefulness earned him a reputation at B&H. When Richard D. Higgins joined the company in June 1949, he says "it was with trepidation that I first went into Geneen's office. I had been told this is a sharp, heavy character in there and you better know your stuff. I laid out the issue and he started to address it. Well, in no time I was way over my head. He was talking, rapid-fire, very knowledgeably about the issue, and he just lost me. After a while he said, Are you with me? And I had a decision to make." Higgins made the right one. "I said, I'm sorry Mr. Geneen, I'm not sure I got all that. He must have been used to that because he graciously went all over it again." It was mostly the bluffers who got in trouble with him— then and later.

But there were two other kinds of people who would always have difficulties with Geneen. An example of the first is Scott Harrod. He was one of McNabb's two assistant treasurers when Geneen joined the company; he later became president of Harper Manufacturing, which he left shortly after Harper was acquired by ITT under Geneen. Harrod was, says an admirer, "a slow, careful, scholarly thinker, a very bright man who never wanted to be hurried or pushed." A less admiring observer says he always wanted to go at 30 miles per hour. Today, Harrod denies there was any friction with Geneen. But the consensus among B&H alumni is that the men clashed—as they would be likely to do, as antipathetic types. Harrod's languor, his complaisant approach to people and business naturally excited Geneen's impatience, and Geneen's headlong drive inevitably galled Harrod's more relaxed nature.

The second type of antagonist was more routine: the head-to-head career competitor. William E. Roberts was McNabb's other assistant treasurer in 1946, and he succeeded Percy as corporate secretary in 1949. "He and Geneen were very much alike, a couple of tigers," says Dick Higgins, who started off as Roberts's assistant, "and I think the cage got pretty small for the two of them." Perhaps Roberts had something of Geneen's style, but not his substance. "Both of them were very hardheaded men, stubborn," says Percy, "but Harold Geneen thought so fast! And Bill was—well, a plodder." Geneen would have no more patience with the pedestrian than with the invincibly languid. But where Scott Harrod had no desire to challenge Geneen, Bill Roberts had to try. His one true ambition was to be president of B&H. There was no question of succeeding McNabb; everyone knew Percy was next. But everyone was equally sure that Percy's ability and ambition would soon vault him beyond the company (in time he became United States Senator from Illinois), and Roberts was willing to wait. Then Geneen came along.

Roberts had been in the original executive training group during the thirties. He had grown up in the company and felt he knew it better than any Harold-come lately, however brilliant. He resented Geneen's march into top management—without the slightest deference to the old hands. One night when Geneen was working late as usual, Roberts stopped by his office on the way home. During the day disagreement had erupted between them over some sales projections. "Hal," he said, "you tell JH tomorrow what figures you're using and why." Geneen looked up, then threw his pencil down on the desk. "Hell no, Bill!" he said. "You tell him why you think I *shouldn't* use my figures." Roberts stalked out. He was set against Geneen, and Geneen took up the challenge. The conflict only sharpened when Charles Percy took over, and it was plain that Geneen had Percy's ear.

Charles Harting Percy was Golden Boy. B&H legend has it that McNabb named Percy president in his will. In fact he did not. But he did leave written instructions for the board of directors that assumed Percy's election, which had never been in doubt.

McNabb had taught Percy in his Christian Science Sunday school class. His own adopted son, Teddy, was near Percy's age and a cruel disappointment. He had come into the company, yawned, and gone off to be a dance band drummer and ball club owner in Banning, California. Young Chuck, though, was all a man could want as son and successor. At the University of Chicago he was president of his fraternity, president of the interfraternity council, and of the senior honor society; he was also captain of the water polo team, and he graduated as university marshall, his class's highest honor. He had to work his way through school, so as a freshman he entered the B&H cooperative training program, signing on full time when he graduated in May 1941. "Meteoric" inadequately describes his rise at B&H. In 1942, at age twenty-three, he was elected to the board of directors. After navy service from 1943 to 1945 he became secretary to the corporation. That is not generally a plangent title, but for Percy, titles did not matter. "Chuck just overshadowed everybody," says Dick Higgins.

When McNabb died on January 5, 1949, Percy was immediately elected president. He was twenty-nine years old. Fifteen days later another director died. One of the board replacements was a banker, and the other was Geneen, who was additionally elevated to vice president. Bill Roberts was elected secretary and Scott Harrod treasurer.

Percy prized Geneen's talents even more than McNabb had. With his modern outlook, he could gauge them better; more important, he had no desire to run everything himself. The two men had grown quite close, professionally and personally, during the previous two and a half years. Both were bachelors (since Geneen's divorce and the death of Percy's first wife), and each had ample time for the other. Moreover, their strengths were complementary. Percy could contemplate Geneen's brilliance without jealousy, secure in his own abilities. And he knew that Geneen's brain could immensely help advance his own plans for the company. For his part, Geneen surely admired, and perhaps envied, Percy's easy command of people and situations. Percy's popularity was effortless and universal; *everyone* called him "Chuck." Even so, he evoked respect and ungrudging deference from those a good deal his senior in age and service. What most delighted Geneen, though, was that under Percy he truly could be top management. Under McNabb, no one except McNabb had really managed B&H.

A measure of Geneen's position can be seen in what happened with the Rochester, New York, film plant. In 1947 the company introduced a line of microfilm cameras and readers. Bill Roberts was responsible for the project, and Geneen was in favor of it despite their differences. Indeed, Geneen advocated a further step. McNabb had bought a plant that could make microfilm. This would be the company's first diversification. Geneen urged McNabb to move ahead; it is always smart, he argued, to sell the blades that go with your razors. Percy was impressed with Geneen's studies, and when he took over he pushed the project forward in the surest way there was: he put Geneen in charge of it.

This was real top management. Even today, functional divisions do not often report to the controller. And Kryptar—the company's name—was a tough assignment, a perfect example of good science badly managed. The plant was not even finished; only one coating alley was in operation. B&H had hired an executive from Ansco to run Kryptar, but he would have to sit out a one-year covenant not to compete. Meanwhile Geneen had to mix in the day-to-day running of the plant, oversee construction work, and still handle his regular corporate duties. Another problem was that the microfilm business had a scientific and technical base about which Geneen was ignorant. Before one trip to Rochester, on his way to Chicago's Midway Airport, he dashed into a bookstore and emerged with a college chemistry text. His companion asked about it, and Geneen said, "I'm going to read this thing before we get to Rochester. Those chemists aren't going to snow me anymore. I'm going to know as much as they do." He never did, of course, but he picked up enough of the jargon to do what he did best: ask the right questions and accurately evaluate the answers, leading him to more questions.

Rochester did not go on-line until Geneen had left the company, and by then it was clear that B&H would have to flesh out the microfilm business with X-ray film and private labeling. But Geneen had gotten the project off the ground.

Percy counted on Geneen for even more than top management services; he used Geneen as his principal advisor and sounding board. When Percy became president, he found the flood of Boy Wonder publicity oppressive; he needed time out of the spotlight, a chance to plot the company's direction. One day he called Geneen on the intercom.

"Hal," he said, "let's get out of here, take a week off, and go where we can be alone and think about the future of the company." Geneen was understandably willing. Where would they go?

"Let's go out to Sun Valley and ski," said Percy.

"I don't ski."

"Neither do I. But we can learn."

Soon they were on a train for Sun Valley. "We did talk a lot about the future of the company," says Percy, "and he had a tremendous impact on my thinking because he could see, through financial control, what you could do with a company." Everything was splendid about the week—except, from Geneen's viewpoint, the skiing. "I still ski," says Percy, "but I don't think Hal's been on skis since then. It was unbelievable. In the morning he had to get in a hot tub to get his bones going again."

Despite their closeness, the relationship was bound to deteriorate given the disparity in their characters and views. "We left under the best of circumstances," Percy says today, "and we've been friends ever since." That is more nearly true for Percy than Geneen; on both sides strains developed during the fifteen months or so that Geneen served under Percy's presidency.

Geneen was always a single-minded businessman. To his way of thinking, no top executive should swerve from total concentration on his company. Percy had other interests. "Geneen got to feeling that Chuck was not working as hard as he should, that his priorities weren't right," says an associate who admires both men. Percy knew Geneen's mind. "I spent more time in civic things than he felt, probably, I should have," Percy says today. But Percy was, and is, unrepentant. His interests ran deep in the city and state; so did his feeling, as a corporate citizen, for community service. He thought McNabb's hand had been too heavy, and he considered it positive policy to let his executives know that his activity ranged beyond the walls of B&H.

The two also differed when it came to human relations. Geneen was not unpleasant or standoffish to subordinates, or insensitive to their welfare. He was often downright jolly. "And if you did a good job," says one admirer, "he'd praise you to the skies, unlike some of the other bosses." But his geniality had no context other than the business. His own lack of home life was not the point; neither before his divorce nor after his next marriage did home ever seduce him from work. He expected the same application from everyone. His assistant, John Buchan, says his own hours were "from eight-thirty until I dropped," and it took the threat of resignation, urged by Buchan's lonely wife, for those hours to taper off just enough to keep him on the job. "I'm very glad it worked out," Buchan says, "because I thoroughly enjoyed my association with the man." The way Geneen drove people dismayed Percy. Forbiding was not Percy's style; but he did remonstrate. "I kept telling Hal, You're just getting going around six o'clock; these people all have families, and that's when children want to see Daddy. Why do you require them to stay here? And he'd say, But I *need* them! Then he'd ease up a bit, but really he was oblivious of time."

One of Geneen's last acts at B&H was to brief Percy on Rochester. The operation was at a critical stage, with further investment needed. It was, to Geneen, the company's most important single issue. Geneen started rehearsing for Percy the small infinity of details that wanted watching, exhaustively outlining problems and likely solutions. After a while Percy was fidgeting, then suddenly he told Geneen he was sorry, but he had to leave. He was due at the Skull Club, the executive dining room. A veteran manufacturing man was retiring, and Percy was to present the sound projector that was the local version of a gold watch.

As Percy left, Geneen muttered, "Okay, that's it." He bundled up his briefing documents and started back down the stairway to his first-floor office. But he stopped on a landing, gripping the hand rail, knuckles white; he was quivering with rage. That . . . *butterfly!* Traipsing off to say bye-bye to someone when he should be sponging up every proffered fact about the company's greatest challenge. It was incredible!

The episode easily could have been avoided by two less irrevocably committed people. One could have pleaded a prior engagement and asked for a postponement. The other would have granted it. But nothing was more important to Percy than people: it would never occur to him that anyone would question the need for a fitting farewell to a faithful employee. On the other side, Geneen considered the briefest recess in concern for business unthinkable. Given this chasm of outlook, the wonder is not that the two drifted apart but that they had ever been so close.

No obvious breach developed between them. When Geneen moved on, they corresponded, and a curious thing happened. Geneen knew community involvement impressed Percy. When he relocated to Pittsburgh, smog control and urban refurbishment were major issues and civics became a motif in their letters. Geneen let on that now he was involved, too. "I like to think that I maybe contributed an interest on his part in the broader aspects of a corporate executive," says Percy, "rather than just running the business." Actually, Geneen's career as community patron was strictly an imaginary one, created expressly for Percy. Yet with all that says about Geneen's thirst for Percy's approbation, he retained a suspicion that Percy was not quite serious. Whenever subordinates in Pittsburgh wanted to tease Geneen, they had only to read some news item about the Boy Wonder. Geneen would look up and glare, mutter "Oh really?" or "He's not so hot," and plunge back to work.

Geneen's output was always prodigious. He would arrive at B&H sometime between 9:30 and 10:00, late as usual. "I could never encourage Hal to come in sooner," says Percy. But once there, his work was unremitting. He ate fig bars at his desk, telling people, "this is my energy," and kept on far into the night. He even resented time spent in corporate meetings. Once he had his secretary keep track of meeting hours, saying "Isn't that awful" when shown the weekly total.

Of course, it was not *all* work and *no* play. For exercise he swam and played volleyball at a health club in the Continental Hotel on Michigan Boulevard. Lunch hours were often spent with Percy and other executives at the nearby Evanston YMCA, where they would work out and have a salad. There was an occasional game of golf with Percy. Perhaps Geneen's favorite relaxation was to sit cross-legged on the bed in his Oak Park apartment, instruction book open, plunking away at his banjo to the distress of anyone within earshot. "He was lousy," says one friend. "I had a good ear, and it was murder." Geneen knew it. Very few people have heard him play; he reserved it for his own amusement.

All told, Geneen did not allow himself much time for a social life. In Chicago he met a woman named Elvonne Piper, and although friends speculated that they would marry, the romance did not flower. They stayed just friends—which was easy, because she moved to Cape Cod, Geneen's favorite place. Chuck Percy thought that Geneen dated, and once asked him for some advice. As a widower, Percy was an outstanding catch. "It was right after the war," he says, "and every friend I had knew some widow who wanted to get married again, and they'd introduce us." He asked Geneen, "What do you do when you start going with a girl and you suddenly feel sort of obligated, but you don't want to be involved?" Geneen shrugged. "I just put on my hat and leave." Perhaps. But when a woman threatened to walk out on him, Geneen was hooked.

June Elizabeth Hjelm was the secretary assigned to Geneen at B&H. She was, a contemporary says, "very pretty, very blonde," a particularly bright and energetic person. But even a work ethic imbibed from Scandinavian parents, heightened by a Yankee upbringing in Berlin, New Hampshire, left her unprepared for Geneen's exactions. Early in the spring of 1949 she told a confidant that she was going to quit. "He's not going to talk to me that way anymore; and he's not going to be unhappy with my work anymore; and he's not going to give me those rapid-fire memos, and expect me to be done in five minutes. I'm through. And I'm telling him so today."

Geneen was stunned. He had been more than satisfied with her work, her cheerfulness, and her intelligence. Then too, she was so very pretty and blonde. He urged her to reconsider; at the very least, he told her, they should discuss it over lunch.

That was the beginning. Geneen was never uxorious, but in most social matters he was unquestioningly conventional: people his age (thirty-nine) were supposed to be married. It was only proper. Propriety marked the relationship on both sides. There was evidently some question about the finality of Geneen's divorce, because office gossip had it that June insisted on clarification before she would keep company with him. The result was a dramatic flight to the city where the records were kept. Once that was settled, Geneen told June that he wanted her to leave B&H after all. He felt it was not proper to court her while she worked for him. She left in May.

Geneen himself left B&H not long after. Most people assumed that he left because he was miffed, feeling Percy was in his way. But that was not true. He had always known Percy would succeed McNabb. What's more, while he could well have hoped to follow Percy as B&H's next president, at his next job, even six years later, he was not in plausible line of succession. Finally, he enjoyed his work at B&H; he agonized over the move, visibly distressed.

So why did he leave?

"He was an awfully bright guy," says Everett Wagner, "in a job that was no challenge for his mind." Not even as top management, with Rochester to run, did B&H challenge him, and Geneen knew it. The long, dry years were past; his self-image was newly robust. Early in 1947 he got a surprise phone call from his Amertorp protégé, John Devaney. After the war Devaney had returned to American Can's machine shop in Cincinnati and had resumed his accounting studies at night. The moment Geneen heard Devaney's voice, almost two years after their last contact, he said, "You've passed your CPA exam!"

"How did you know?" Devaney asked, as puzzled as he was pleased.

"Why else would you be calling?"

Toward the end of 1947 Devaney was transferred to Chicago and they renewed their friendship. In the news, they learned that the head of a large corporation had just been deposed by his directors. Geneen said, "John, I can handle that job right now." He was feeling his oats and knew what he could accomplish if he found the right arena.

B&H was not it. Once again Geneen was entertaining offers. One came from McDonnell Aircraft (later, McDonnell Douglas). When he pumped John and Madeline Devaney about St. Louis, Devaney said he saw no future in aircraft. "Aw, come on, John," Geneen said, rattling off his own well-researched projections for the industry and throwing in the observation that air conditioning was another field of promise. The McDonnell offer did not pan out. Geneen kept looking, and the search grew more intense when he and June married, on New Year's Eve, 1949. He and Charles E. Phillimore, another B&H executive, were on a trip to Boston late in 1949, when he called June to check on her apartment hunting. They wanted to live on the Gold Coast, Chicago's Lake Shore Drive, and at last June had found the perfect place. Trouble was, the rent was around $500. "I know he was making under twenty thousand," says Phillimore, "and he did some figuring. He said, I can't pay that rent on the money I'm making, so I'll have to make more money."

In Pittsburgh, the Jones & Laughlin Steel Corporation was expanding after a self-assessment much like McNabb's. During the postwar boom there had been a management shake-up at the fusty old steel company. New management wanted modern and imaginative financial control, and their controller was not the one to give it. He was eminently retireable, once J&L found a successor. Michael Hopkins, a bigwig at the Central Hanover Bank—friend and patron of the man who would soon be president of J&L—was close to B&H, knew Geneen's reputation, and highly touted him to J&L.

In the winter of 1950, the steel company made Geneen an offer. "He came over to see me on a Sunday morning," says Chuck Percy, "and he said that Jones and Laughlin had said, Whatever you're making at Bell and Howell, we'll double it—and give you a major stock option. Hal said to me, What'll I do? I said to him, Hal, you're a smart guy; you ought to know what to do without asking my advice on it."

Percy could not match the salary offer even if he wanted to; Geneen was already at the top salary level in the company, apart from Percy's own. And a stock option was out of the question: nobody had one at B&H. In McNabb's valedictory letter to the board, he urged them to give Percy a stock option for fear that they could not keep him otherwise. Percy declined unless options were offered to other top executives too. Here was an opportunity to shake the board. Percy asked Geneen to make it clear, in his resignation, that the J&L stock option was the clinching inducement to leave. The ploy worked, and soon B&H joined the stock option world.

Next day, Geneen called John Buchan into his office. "You're the first person, after Chuck, I'm telling this to," he said. He had decided to take the offer and would be leaving B&H around May 1. Tears that had formed in Geneen's eyes now coursed down his cheeks. "If he developed a hardness later on," says Buchan, "it was not manifest at that time in his life."

4

The Shiny-Ass Clerk

The 1930s were especially hard at Jones & Laughlin. Rocked by the depression, the company was already degenerating due to chronic poor management. The Joneses and the Laughlins had become absentee owners who would neither lead nor relinquish control. When one capable manager, Tom M. Girdler, contrived to rise to the presidency of J&L, he moved his family to Sewickley, domain of the Pittsburgh aristocracy. This was thought so uppity that Girdler was roundly snubbed. When he projected a merger with Republic Steel, he stood suspect of darker pretensions and was dismissed.

But by 1935 events had drifted beyond the families' grasp. J&L desperately needed a new strip mill. That meant a bond issue and traffic with bankers —synonymous in Pittsburgh with the Mellons. It meant, in short, letting the camel's nose into the tent. Soon, Mellon Bank's Frank Denton became a dominant director. And in 1942 Charles Lee Austin, vice president of Mellon Securities Corporation, joined J&L as treasurer and board member.

After World War II service, Denton and Austin moved to modernize the company, nominating as CEO Admiral Ben Moreell, a prodigy of personality and leadership. Head of the Seabees, Moreell was the navy's first non-Academy four-star admiral. Though not a steel man, he had been chairman of the Coal Resources Board, and that was close enough. He came on board as chairman, president, and chairman of the executive committee in March of 1947.

Moreell was a beginning. However, at J&L old standpatters assembled row on row, firmly entrenched, to thwart reform. For example, there was the controller, Walter Dupka. Lee Austin commissioned a study that documented an urgent need for "more controls." But Dupka and his people were bean-

Lee Austin, from the J&L annual report, 1953.

Admiral Ben Moreell

counters, not controllers. That was when Michael Hopkins told Austin about Geneen.

The musty proprieties were of course observed; Geneen could not simply sweep in. He became "assistant to the vice president, general services" in May 1950. His nominal boss, Al Lawson, was a rarity: a lifelong J&L employee, with scant education, yet not an old fogy. Lawson was supportive; he smoothed Geneen's way and on occasion reined in Geneen's runaway impatience. That took some doing, because at first Geneen's "job" was simply to roam about, learn the operation, and get ready to replace Dupka in a year or so.

What Geneen saw astonished him.

The steel business takes a dollar of investment for every dollar of sales. A single mill is by itself a very large business—millions of dollars in plant, a thousand employees, an insatiable, belching giant, consuming mountains of material and great gulps of energy. Yet the operating people at J&L had no notion of costs, no concept of return on investment. Even the manager of the mill did not know the value of his inventory or the cost of his materials. Far from feeling responsible for saving or cost-effectiveness in capital expenditures, each division schemed to slice itself the maximum wedge of the J&L appropriations pie. The system for justifying appropriations was farcical. Company policy mandated a four-year payback, so schedules were routinely cooked to show that, yes indeed, this new machine would pay out in four years. And when it did not? No one knew, because make-good reports were never filed. Accounting never pressed for them. Not that it mattered; production and sales ignored the bean-counters with impunity.

Ronald G. Nestor, an accountant and industrial engineer who became one of Geneen's key people, saw the process firsthand. His works manager wanted a "hot scarfer"—an expensive machine that enveloped each steel bar in an oxygen flame to scarf off surface defects. But scarfing forms an overall crust that sloughs off. For bars with relatively few defects, spot-scarfing with a hand torch was more cost-effective. When Nestor's figures showed that their type of mill did not need a hot scarfer, his boss handed him a new work sheet. "Use these figures," he said. "Our job is to get all the appropriation money we can for this mill."

All this was bad enough; much worse, no one knew whether any machine or product line or mill was making or losing money. One month's production was compared only with the preceding month's, even though the product mix might be totally different. And no one could say whether either month's performance was objectively good or bad. Geneen summed up J&L: "Fourth in size, ninth in profit."

The time was right for a new broom. A month after Geneen started at J&L, North Korea invaded the South. Added to the postwar boom, the Korean War made the 1950s a golden decade for steel. Big profits were possible—with decent controls in place. But Walter Dupka mulishly resisted all change. So, at Austin's urging, the board of directors shelved Dupka early and elected Geneen controller as of January 1951.

What Geneen had in mind for J&L did not yet exist; but he knew where to observe a rough working model. He had always admired the methods of Alfred P. Sloan of General Motors. In 1944 Geneen's sister, Eva, had married Wilbur H. Norton, a long-time executive at Montgomery Ward, who became president in 1946. Forced out by chairman Sewell Avery three years later, Norton landed at GM as a vice president. Now he arranged for Geneen to inspect GM's system of budgets and control.

Geneen spent three weeks in Detroit and traced production through each department—noting, he once told an interviewer, how even "The man in charge of cutting holes had a budget that showed the cost of cutting, plus time." He returned, says an assistant from those days, "brimming with ideas," and not just for controls. "He introduced concepts that our salespeople had never dreamed of." One idea was market penetration. Another was knowing the profit on each product line. Still another was shooting for a share of market at least equal to J&L's share of industrywide production capacity.

Naturally Geneen needed help. Much of his time, during the first six months spent roaming around the company, was devoted to talent scouting. He looked for people who perceived—even if they did not know what to do about it—that something was wrong at J&L.

Charles R. Miller was an early find. Chief clerk in the Pittsburgh strip mill at age thirty-four, Miller took the view, then eccentric, that a works accountant should know what was going on in the mill. One day he was in the pit watching sheet steel being coiled when a neatly dressed stranger approached. "He said it was a good mill," says Miller, "and I said, Yeah but productivity's terrible."

"What do you mean?" the stranger asked.

"Well, delays, setup time, roll changes—things like that."

The stranger probed for details. "Finally," says Miller, "I figured I better be careful. I said, I don't know who you are. And I walked off. But I remembered his face." Two weeks later Chuck Miller was made senior auditor at headquarters, and when Geneen took over, Miller joined his team.

Ron Nestor was chosen for his industrial engineering background. Geneen saw possibilities in an accountant who could immediately relate costs to production efficiency.

Rank never mattered. Both Miller and Nestor were junior for the responsibilities Geneen thrust on them; Charles J. Lause, even more so. A recent Harvard M.B.A. (any M.B.A. was rare at J&L), Lause started in 1947 at the

Miller (left, front) and Moore (right, rear) at the 1954 J&L accounting department Christmas party.

1955 Christmas party of the J&L accounting department. Front row: Stanhope third from right. Second row: Haughton fifth from right, Nichols sixth. Third row: Geneen on right, Nestor fifth from right, Resler (with cigar) left. Fourth row: Lause on right (head tilted back). Back row: Gorman third from right, Flick fifth.

Cleveland works and in 1949 moved to Pittsburgh headquarters accounting staff. Geneen discovered him there, giving his seniors remedial cost-accounting courses. Always taken with such initiative, Geneen soon dispatched Lause back to Cleveland, this time as chief accountant, to install Geneen's new system. "It was like going in one jump from midshipman to admiral," says Lause.

Running short of experienced malcontents at J&L, Geneen's next move was to recruit outside. Walter L. Moore, for example, had no experience at all. In June 1951, about to leave Harvard with an A.B. in economics, he knew nothing about accounting. Indeed, he harbored a prejudice against it. His father, a Virginia dairy farmer, preached that the only worthy functions were production and sales. Furthermore, Moore had already signed as a marketing trainee with Burlington Mills when he saw the J&L interview notice. "I don't know what made me go," he says, "but I got the last time spot of the day. Geneen was twenty-five notches above the usual campus interviewer. And afterward he asked me out to dinner." Over dinner, Geneen described his plans for budgetary controls. He was riveting, messianic; he was not offering Moore a job but part of a crusade. Caught up, yet still wary, Moore finally asked, "You *sure* you're not talking about accounting?" By eleven that night, Moore was on the team.

Early on, Geneen set out to upgrade the status of J&L's "clerks." In line divisions they were easily overawed by the works manager. And without monitoring, abuses were rife in the divisions. Some were merely scandalous, others downright criminal. Geneen went on the attack.

The company was producing a movie about steel with a $360,000 budget. "Geneen smelled a rat," says the assistant assigned to ferret out the book juggling. The project's chief was fired. At some company mines, rock was crushed so that metallic ore could be separated magnetically. The residue, called "tailings," could be sold as road ballast—and it was, by the plant manager, who pocketed a tidy sum. The same manager's division used one make of trucks exclusively—and he drove a new luxury sedan, given him by the truck dealer. The manager of one J&L division was building cabins for his cronies with company labor and materials. Superintendents at other divisions had J&L employees mowing their lawns and chauffeuring their families. As Geneen spotlighted each peculation, the operating people became resigned to the independence of their unit accountants—if only to get Geneen off the subject.

Geneen had bigger fish to fry anyway. First Boston Corporation was about to underwrite a six-million-share J&L stock issue, and they demanded a five-year earnings projection. "Five years!" shouted one operations VP. "God, I don't know what we'll be doing tomorrow!" The sales department had no clue about sales levels even for the rest of the current year and did not care to guess. But production planning necessarily worked, however hazily, with estimates. Geneen got answers for the first year, then extrapolated the impact of new money on efficiency. "For two solid weeks we worked like dogs," says Ron Nestor. "We all caught Harold's enthusiasm." Finally the report was done. "Next morning," says Nestor, "Harold came in beaming." The projection had been such a hit that Lee Austin wanted to continue the discipline; it would bring substance to the listless J&L monthly review letters and meetings. The controller of J&L, after nearly 100 years of bean-counting, had a mandate to *control*.

First came budgets. At J&L they had always been a mystery; only capital expenditures were even vaguely budgeted, so no one could measure cost performance. "With costs," says James N. Imel, then superintendent of the Pittsburgh strip mill, "they'd only compare February with January." And since January's product mix might have been harder or easier to produce than February's, comparisions meant nothing except chronic disgruntlement for the operators.

Geneen's people pried a complete description of J&L's product line out of sales and approximate costs for each item from operations. The operations people were not deliberately balky. They honestly did not know their exact costs for any product or production level. No one had ever suggested that such knowledge could affect the cost of steel. Costs are costs, aren't they? No, Geneen said, they are variable; and to know how they vary with production is the key to their control. Besides, knowing exact costs for every product allows a measurement of performance. It solves the problem of comparing last month's oranges with this month's apples.

This cut little ice with most operators. The old system may have been dumb and unfair, but it was the one they were used to. "We made the people very angry," says Walter Moore, assigned to establish flexible budgets at the Pittsburgh works. "For instance, we made flexible allocations of electricity in the blast furnace, and said so much is variable by the ton, so much by the operating hour, and so much fixed. Then the electrical foreman says, Look, kid, we haven't got meters to tell us anything like that; all we read is the one meter once a month for the total. Besides, the mill generates its own electricity —so who the hell cares? I told Hal, I'm making them mad. And he said, That's good! You get it started and they'll be so peeved at the inequities in your budgets that *they'll* refine them." Sure enough, the crews soon installed their own meters to get accurate figures. They discovered that costs were not all fixed even at full capacity. What's more, lowering costs lowered the break-even point. That was vital. When demand dropped below capacity (which was often, even in the golden 1950s), important strategies emerged tied to the flexible budgets. With excess capacity of 1,000 tons a day, what should shut down? Two furnaces in Cleveland or one in Pittsburgh? It all depended on relative costs.

In time the figures became exact and the flexible budgets remarkably sensitive. By 1953 this system was the talk of the steel industry, and observers from other companies flocked to see how it worked. The budgets varied for each product in 10% increments from 100% capacity down to 50%. Geneen established budgets for units as far down in the organization as possible;

sometimes a single machine had its own budget. That solved ahead of time the usually intractable problem of laying people off.

"Human nature being what it is," says Harvey Haughton, who became Geneen's deputy in 1953 and succeeded him as controller, "the last thing a foreman wants to do is lay off any of his men." But in steel he often had to. J&L's old style had been crude: a 10% cut across the board or some such figure, often with cuts in inappropriate areas. Flexible budgets brought rationality. Geneen insisted that each foreman sign off on a cutback plan for each 10% reduction in volume. This might mean going from three turns to two, cutting back a shift. A blast furnace must run around the clock, but maybe the bar mill should go to a single turn. "We did this for all units in a plant," says Haughton, "and all the plants in the company. After a couple of years of head slapping, we had an overall plan."

Now the monthly managers' meetings had purpose. Budgeted levels were compared with actuals, and woe to the foreman who had promised to operate with thirty men at 70% of capacity if he actually had thirty-five on his crew. And he had better be sticking to the budgeted level of materials and energy, too. "You said you could do it, now do it!" was Geneen's constant cry.

Budgeting could be dramatically practical—as in the blooming mill incident. In a blooming mill, ingots get their first rolling, and any blooming mill devours vast quantities of lubricating oil. Even so, when Charles Lause installed budgets at Cleveland, the oil consumption proved to be way out of line. The superintendent was direct: "You guys don't know what you're talking about. I been running this fucking mill for twenty-five years, and I know how much oil we need." Lause kept pressing, and finally a leak was discovered: the extra, unbudgeted oil was going right down the drain. "I made a convert," says Lause. "Not a happy one, but he began to believe."

Budgets were working. And while they were being refined, Geneen placed the capstone on his system at J&L. This was his mill operating cost control program, the MOCC.

The basic recipe for steel is simple. Put iron ore in a blast furnace with coke and limestone, start a bonfire, and tap off steel. At that point, though, complications abound. Steel for tin plate is not like steel for wire or concrete reinforcing bars or structural shapes. Each type must be uniquely processed for malleability, resilience, and toughness that allows it to be rolled, molded, and cut into the shapes and gauges needed. A tin-plate ingot will be hot- and cold-rolled, then annealed, treated, and pickled quite differently from an ingot to be cold-rolled for automobiles. It may go through fifty distinct and tricky operations, with each separate operation an invitation to waste time and money. This need for varied and skilled processing makes the steel industry, uniquely, both capital- and labor-intensive.

Steel foremen had always said, Give me big tonnage and I'll make good costs. In rare times of full capacity that was true—if the company focused on the kinds of steel easy to produce, the "good rollers." When volume slacked off, profits plummeted, and the explanation was always on the order of, Well . . . coal costs more this month. Since J&L operations people knew only roughly what it cost to make a ton of any given kind of steel, they could scarcely know what costs to cut or how to cut them.

Geneen's MOCC would change that. Although a monumental task, beyond anything then known, the MOCC was at core a typical standard-costs program established with typical industrial engineering techniques. Geneen enlisted two consultants who would massage the numbers Geneen's own team gathered. "The trick was," says Charles Lause, "to accumulate all the standard costs for efficiently processing every kind of steel through each unit." They started with the records—how many hours, on average, it had taken to produce each item at each processing point. Then they refined historical data by observation.

Geneen had hit upon an amazing fact: the unions had long negotiated pay standards sensitive to subtle changes in how much work it took to process a particular ton of steel. That was the principle of the MOCC. It had eluded management, but even in the shipping department they realized that it takes least time to pack a ton of steel when the sun shines, a little longer in the rain, and a lot longer in snow.

Geneen's people started in the Pittsburgh strip mill, then went to the tin-plate mill. They were impressed by his restraint. Having established a standard, they were eager to hold crews to it. Geneen insisted that they start with interim standards. As one colleague puts it, "years and years of immaturity" had shaped work habits, and Geneen feared that the sudden imposition of true standards would be fatally disheartening. "Don't pin them on a cross," he cautioned.

Lee Austin became president of J&L on January 30, 1952. Now the managers' monthly review letters bloomed from a couple of pages to half-inch books crammed with performance statistics. Managers appeared at the monthly meetings flanked by their accountants (instantly upgraded) and sales and operating people. They had to answer for each variance from budget, explain each deviation from standard. "You didn't whip them about it," says Ron Nestor, "but at least you had a talking point." It might not be the fault of the workers. Maybe it was an antiquated machine or a failure of planning; perhaps a laggard foreman. Whatever the cause, the MOCC alerted management to trouble and pointed to the probable villain.

As a bonus, the MOCC let Geneen calculate exact costs and possible profits for each J&L product. Salespeople had always assumed that their job was to sell all the steel they could—of any kind; and both they and management had ignored production costs and profit margins. One of Geneen's team, Harry Stanhope, did a comprehensive cost-price study. Then the team prepared booklets that showed the company's cost and profit for each item. Now Geneen could prove the folly of the sales force's sell-everything policy. Instead, they should seek sales of the good rollers, the profitable items, even turning down orders that were too costly to roll.

This notion scandalized sales, but it was based on Geneen's solid grasp of historical reality. Steel companies do not all have the same equipment. At some point in the past J&L might have decided that half-inch-to-two-inch bars would be the big seller; the finishing mill accordingly installed equipment designed for maximum efficiency in producing bars of that size. If another company, in a different decade, saw a market for three-inch bars, the two companies would now have slightly different equipment. Large purchasers of steel normally spread their business among four or five steel companies, allotting so much for each. Geneen wanted J&L salespeople to tell customers, Please make the bulk of our fixed percent your one-half-to-two-inch bar business—and keep the rest for our competitors. That way, J&L's margins would rise on the same tonnage.

Then came the matter of "extras." Industrywide practice was to deliver coiled steel bound by one Signode strap. For another strap, the standard charge was, say, $1. But Geneen discovered that each strap cost J&L $1.30 to put on. Raise the price, he said. But $1 is the going rate, sales protested; they dare not ask more. OK, Geneen countered; we calculate that with 40% more strap business, it will pay to set up a special line that can do it for a dollar. So hustle up more business or stop taking orders for that extra.

It was worse when Geneen happened on an extra that for some reason cost J&L significantly under the industry rate. Why can't you get more of that business? he would ask—usually with Austin glowering on, approving the inquisition. Don't you realize the profit effect of just one thousand more orders a day? *That's* where your effort should be: selling, not just taking orders.

Inventory occasioned another clash. Sales and production always favor complete inventories; their jobs are easier with stock on hand. For sales, especially, it was an issue, part of their hankering for large, undifferentiated sales: whatever the customer wanted was right on the shelf and could be delivered tomorrow. Geneen said no. Large inventories affected profits; customers could wait for delivery of unusual orders, and maybe sales should not even accept such orders.

It all made perfect sense. And they hated it. Sales and production had always run the company, barely tolerating accountants. And now look! "I don't need any shiny-ass clerk to tell me how to run my business," said one deflated mandarin.

He was not alone. Opposition to Geneen came from five distinct groups. The first included those whose ox Geneen had gored. Most merely resented the upset of their comfortable old ways. "We were putting their feet to the fire," says Charles Lause. By the time Geneen left, most operating people recognized his system as the only rational way to run a steel business. "But along the way," says Lause, "they'd have gladly dumped all those hotshot young accountants into the Allegheny River." A small number of this group had reason to deep-six accountants. "We nailed those operating people," says

Ron Nestor. Two years before, operations had spent $6.5 million to rehabilitate Bessemer converters at the Pittsburgh works. Now they proposed to phase them out. Bessemers were dirty, and operations was catching flak from Pittsburgh's anti-pollution forces. But instead of trying to solve the problem, executive VP John Mitchell and his deputy, Gene Miller, opted for the easy way out, though it meant that J&L would abandon the lucrative market for free-cutting screw steel. Once, any such decision by operations was fiat. Now, an *accountant* challenged their plan as economic nonsense, indeed as dereliction of company duty. At one point the argument degenerated into a shouting match. But the Bessemers stayed.

Mitchell soon retired, and Miller took over. One of his early acts was to import Brazilian ore. That seemed a smart move. Brazilian ore assayed 67% iron as against the 50–52% for ore from J&L's Minnesota mines. Miller was still talking bows when Geneen showed Lee Austin his own department's analysis. Factor in transportation cost plus abandonment of property, and the Brazilian ore's advantage evaporated. Miller made outlandish counter claims, which Geneen coolly shot down. When Austin asked for a practical test, Geneen proved right. He kept on being right, and Miller soon opted for early retirement.

The chief industrial engineer, E. Gard Slocum, was soon gone as well. "Geneen wouldn't just take figures on faith," says Allen Motter, who was in Slocum's department; "he wanted to know what lay behind the figures." The blow-up came over the price of scrap metal. Steel furnaces are fed with the most economical mix of company-mined ore and scrap bought outside, a calculation that balances market prices and operating costs. When scrap prices started to drop, Geneen ordered that a study be done to determine when it would pay to change the usual mix. Meanwhile, Gard Slocum assured Lee Austin that the break-even price was $28 a ton. A week's hard work convinced Geneen that the true price was $23; at $28, J&L would lose money. Geneen asked Slocum for his backup figures. Slocum did not respond even when Geneen asked Al Lawson, Slocum's boss, to intercede. When Austin appointed a committee to investigate, their figure was within 50¢ of Geneen's.

That did it. Geneen had run into Slocum's fast answers before. He demanded that Austin do something. The president called in Lawson, who tried, desultorily, to defend Slocum: Austin had asked for the scrap break-even point on a Saturday; with no chance to delve into the figures, Slocum probably thought Austin wanted only a ballpark guess, and—

"Al," said Austin, "the controller of this company questions the integrity of your subordinate. And I agree with him. You'd better suggest that Slocum seek other employment."

A second group had a more principled reason for their opposition to Geneen. Their exemplar was John Timberlake, VP for sales. He was known as "Big John," an "old bull of the woods." To his *admirers* he was gruff, tough, bibulous, and overbearing, someone "you couldn't help liking," though he continually provided opportunities not to. "He was arrogance with a capital

A," says one of those admirers; "he treated his fifty-thousand-dollar executives like office boys." On the other hand, he was fiercely loyal to his collection of office boys, dead straight, and fair.

To Geneen's partisans Big John was "a drummer type; just a big noise from Winnetka elevated beyond his capacity." Maybe so; but he sold a lot of steel. And whatever else he was, John Timberlake was a *steel* man. It was his livelihood for fifty years; and more, it was his life. Certainly his hostility to Geneen was partly chagrin at having to knuckle under to a despised accountant. (It was Timberlake who called Geneen a shiny-ass clerk.) As he saw it, making and selling steel were the proper activities of steel men; niggling about profit margins and cost-price studies were not. So, while Timberlake understood the imperative of Geneen's "interference" with sales policy, and even came to appreciate it, he never stopped resenting it.

His position was not mere wrongheaded obstructionism. For a steel man, markets meant more than just balance sheets. Steel had largely become a commodity in regard to price, quality, and delivery. Only service and personal rapport distinguished the big producers. The big customers—auto, can, and construction companies—carefully nurtured all their suppliers so as never to be dependent on a single source. Each supplier got a set amount of business. However, each big customer reserved a respectable portion of orders to be awarded at discretion, a "kick-their-butts" component to keep service keen and responsive. This was the business you were fighting for. And you would not win it by telling good customer to wait a while for delivery or, worse, that you did not want some of their business. Who knows? Such highhandedness might jeopardize even your fixed percent. "When an order came in from General Motors," says a mill superintendent, "bingo! You had to get it to

John Timberlake,
from the J&L annual report, 1958.

them right away. If you didn't—well, the guy that bought for Fisher Body, Hookstra? He bought two or three million tons a year; that's a hell of a wedge on a steel company. He got what he wanted."

There was also a personal factor. Timberlake the steel man and Hookstra the auto man were a fraternity. How could you tell the Hookstras of the world that a shiny-ass clerk now called the shots? In time, Timberlake came part way around. Geneen had the backing of Austin, another numbers, not steel, man; and so much of Geneen's program made sense it impelled compliance. Even so, the personal antipathy was indelible. When the J&L board elected Geneen a vice president in 1954, Timberlake's "congratulatory" note reminded him that "A controller's still a bookkeeper, and two and two still make four, no matter what you think."

The third opposition group hated Geneen for an elemental reason: he treated them like dirt. In this group, E. L. Resler was at least first among equals.

Ed Resler, an assistant controller when Geneen took over, had been an accountant of the bean-counter persuasion "for about a hundred years," as Charles Lause puts it. An ex-Marine, nicknamed "Old Sarge," Resler was set in his ways. And his were not the ways of Harold Geneen. To his own secretary, Virginia Nichols, Resler was "a nice old man." To another secretary, Dorothy Flick, he was an "old fuddy-duddy," but a dear old one; even Geneen's bright young men liked him. Geneen did not.

Resler was in charge of the general ledger kind of accounting, which bored Geneen and his people. Unhappily, Old Sarge never did it to Geneen's satisfaction. "Geneen was always trying to get Resler to do it *this* way instead of an old-fashioned way," says one observer. And Geneen's way with the obdurate was not gentle. "Almost always when he went in to see Mr. Geneen," says Ginny Nichols, "the door would be shut, then he'd come out with his eyes on the ground, chomping on his cigar." Once, after Geneen's shouted obscenities echoed through the office, Geneen emerged "red as a beet," says Nichols. He realized that she must have heard, and he apologized for his language. Then out came Resler, equally red, muttering, "Don't let the bastards get you down" as he trudged to his own office. "Mr. Geneen hurt him so," says Nichols.

This kind of hurt gave birth to a gnawing hatred shared by many in the company. Geneen referred to Resler and his assistants as the "green-eyeshade department." In return, Resler and like-minded friends did not think Geneen was a "real accountant," just a flashy idea man and disturber of the peace. "There was a clique at J and L that hoped he would go away and stop stirring things up," says Walter Moore. "Clique" does not do justice to the size of the group. "Geneen was not very popular in the corporation," says someone who, himself, liked the man. He was too curt. Two of his nicknames—among his *admirers!*—were "Whizbang" and "Little Tojo."

The resentment he aroused endured. Years after Geneen had left the company, Ed Resler took the occasion of his own retirement dinner to hurl abuse at his departed tormentor. Over ten years later, others at J&L wrote an anonymous letter when the Federal Communications Commission was considering the takeover of the American Broadcasting Company by ITT. "Take it from us who knew Harold Geneen when he was vice president and controller of the Steel Company," they wrote on November 21, 1966, "it would not be to the advantage of the American Broadcasting Company to be placed under the aegis of ITT. He is a hard rider of the old school. . . . " It was signed "Former Associates of Harold Geneen at Jones and Laughlin Steel Company."

This sort of antipathy was matched by the admiration and affection of Geneen's team. Many remember those years as the high point in their professional lives; nothing since then has been as exciting or rewarding. Those who had grown up in the company were suddenly consequential, respected, even feared. Newer recruits might not have suffered the ignominy of long years as "clerks," but they, too, were elevated and energized by Geneen. If days were long, they were absorbing. There was always a ferment around Whizbang. Things never just happened with him, they exploded. Charles Lause was in New York on some mission when Geneen called and said, without warning, "I'm making you chief accountant at Cleveland." "And that was that," says Lause. When Geneen decided, in 1954, to reward Chuck Miller with the same job, he told Miller on a Thursday. "When do you want me to go?" Miller asked. "Tomorrow," Geneen said, stating the obvious. "Can't I wait until Monday?" Geneen finally consented to the delay.

Geneen's team thought the world of him. "I never met a more sincerely honest, straight-shooting, straightforward man in my life," says Charles Lause. "I had a high regard for Harold, and I find it difficult to believe that with his success he got bent." Geneen's later image is a puzzlement to them all. "I read these trade magazines," says Chuck Miller, "*Business Week* and what have you, and Harold is always tagged as someone very hard to work for—cold, forbidding. But he wasn't. He was *fun!*"

First there was camaraderie of a high order. His team numbered themselves among Geneen's few intimates, an elite. They were "a hot item," one of them insists, still proud of it. Part of the pride was that of a Marine Corps boot, derived from rigors manfully borne. They never got away with a thing. Geneen brought sloppy thought or wordy explanations up short with, "Come on, get down to the nuts of it." Or, more simply, "Cut the bullshit, yes or no?" Try to excuse slack performance and he would growl, "Don't give me any of that goddamn guff." On the other hand, from such a perfectionist, a satisfied nod is mighty praise, "well done" the accolade.

Besides, as one of the team recollects, Geneen could be very patient. He would spend all the time needed, listening to problems, helping contrive a better way to do the job. Both his acerbity and his patience were marks of inclusion. Geneen did not shout at the hopeless, he fired them; while he shouted at you, you had a job. That applied even to such as Ed Resler. Geneen made his life hell. But since Resler performed passably, his job was not in jeopardy, only his peace of mind.

Profanity was something else Geneen reserved for intimates. One mill superintendent was impressed because Geneen was the only corporate officer he ever heard swear. It certainly registered and set Geneen apart when he said of a presentation, "I want it to stand out like a turd in a pan of milk" or advised subordinates, "Never get into a pissing contest with a skunk."

Not everyone reacted to Geneen's manner productively, of course. Some, especially secretaries, froze in his presence. He never swore at women or around them, but his abruptness petrified the less hardy. "I had a girl faint one day," says his long-time J&L secretary, Valerie M. Gorman. "I came back from the washroom and she was outside his office, crying. She said, My pencil wouldn't move. It dropped on the floor and I got very weak." When Gorman went in to finish the dictation, Geneen said, "No, I want *her* back; I don't want her to feel that way." She would not return, and Geneen asked Gorman why. "Well," said Gorman, "you do kind of intimidate."

He would not change. What if there was a high turnover of secretaries, or if some staff froze? His team understood. One of them counseled a secretary just to stop Geneen whenever she could not keep up. That was exactly the right tactic. "He couldn't stand mousey people." says Val Gorman. She had stood up to him at the first, won his respect, and they got along wonderfully well.

For those who did win his respect, rewards flowed—regular maximum raises and promotions. Geneen got Val Gorman the top allowable secretarial salary, then he chivied the office manager for more. "He didn't tell me that," Gorman says. "The office manager did. Mr. Geneen had argued for two hours, but I couldn't be paid more than the secretary to the president. So he called me in and said, I've worked out a deal: you charge extra overtime each week."

Of course they all earned their pay. After a full day they trooped into Geneen's office to review the day's events and plan tomorrow's. Jim Imel was one of the few mill superintendents who instantly cooperated; Geneen inaugurated his MOCC program in Imel's Pittsburgh strip mill. But Imel rebelled at the hours. "I got to the mill at seven," he says, "and I'd get a call from Geneen's office, there's a meeting at four-thirty. We'd sit there until eleven o'clock. Finally I had to say, Hey! This after-hours stuff don't go. He says, Well, I figured you wouldn't want to come during the day, you have things to do. I says, Yeah, but I can't come here every night to sit around and talk with you guys."

The others had no choice, and it naturally strained home life. Dinner at home was rare; indeed, dinner anywhere was problematical. "He'd call a four o'clock meeting," says Harvey Haughton, "and his wrist watch alarm would go off at six. But he'd shut it off and say, We just want to take up one more thing." That was always good for a couple more hours. They might break for dinner; more often they would go straight through to eleven or midnight. "One night he and I were very busy," says Chuck Miller. "It was eight or nine and suddenly he said, Hey, we passed dinner time. I said, Yeah!— thinking he was going to call it quits. Instead, he opens his desk drawer, takes out a Clark bar, breaks it, and gives me half." That was unusual: Geneen normally kept Hershey bars with almonds to hand around, having switched from the fig newtons of his Bell & Howell days. When Charles Lause complained that he did not like chocolate with nuts, Geneen (someone you could always reason with) laid in a special stock of plain Hershey bars.

After hours, a further reward for his team was the intimacy of informality. Geneen would pull on an old black cardigan, often taking off his shoes, padding about in stocking feet. His profusion of ideas on every subject made him an enthralling companion, even on a Hershey bar diet. He had a ready wit, and there was much good humor, even joking. In the informality of after-five, the talk was not exclusively about business. For instance, there was his Growing Old notion. You never seem old to contemporaries, he reasoned, only to those who never knew you as young. He urged everyone to have many pictures taken when they were young so that their children, especially, could have a sense of them as something other than the Old Folks. Merits aside, he gave his team so much to think about in so many fields that, while they might be exhausted, they never were bored. Working with Harold Geneen *was* fun—so much fun, so rewarding and fulfilling in so many ways, that those who agreed with his aims and helped him achieve them often loved him.

There was one notable exception. Lee Austin was, by himself, the fourth group opposing Geneen. With him the antipathy was strictly personal. One of Austin's proudest boasts is that he hired Geneen, backed him, and promoted him—in every sense. They disagreed about virtually nothing of substance. There was no time for it. They were too busy squabbling over nothing.

"I witnessed a lot of this," says someone who admires both men. "After one shouting match, Lee came to my office, very disturbed, and said, Why can't we get along? I told him, Because you're too much alike." But, as with Bill Roberts at Bell & Howell, the differences were more telling than the similarities.

Austin was very bright; he had one of the few minds in the company on Geneen's level. After he graduated from Princeton in 1924 he went into banking. Though he had no useful family connections, by 1942 he was a VP and director of Mellon Securities. That was when he joined J&L as treasurer —the Mellon man put in to watch the kitty. His disdain for the steel industry's creaky methods moved Austin to hire Geneen; but it worked against him, given his personality. Where Geneen was curious about everything, and eager to learn the business, Austin never thought instruction necessary. What could troglodytes in such a backward business tell him about running anything? "Haughty and staid," one observer calls him. He was also forbidding and unapproachable, and something of a snob, especially intellectually. He terrified most people at J&L—with predictable results. "People told him what he wanted to hear," says Haughton, Austin's assistant before joining Geneen. "He liked that; but of course he got a lot of wrong answers."

For example, there was the problem of the new tinning line at the Aliquippa, Pennsylvania, works. It could use either the older hot alkaline or newer halogen process. An ad hoc committee found that an expensive Du Pont chemical made the halogen process cost more in this particular application. Their report went in. Back came a letter from Austin: his friends at Weirton Steel gave halogen high marks; the committee should restudy the issue. The committee reconvened, read the letter, and changed its vote. Later, when costs on the new line ran high, Austin raised hell, having it both ways.

This episode was typical. Austin seized seemingly every occasion, even the essential managers' monthly meetings, to humiliate, intimidate, and demote. That was never Geneen's way. Any horrors he inflicted were byproducts of his purpose—to clarify and solve problems. His system demanded openness in reporting problems and setbacks. He could scarcely expect openness if, like Austin, he punished confessions of failure. Geneen and Austin were born to clash; they grated on each other at every contact point. "They fought like two little boys over the top of the hill," says Val Gorman. She and Austin's secretary, Mina Mosher, would compare nasty memos their bosses had sent each other, bemused that two such brilliant men could carry on so. And over *nothing!*

For instance, one bone of contention was union relations. Even with the MOCC, some gap remained between standard and actual costs. Over the years, concessions to the unions had distorted labor costs. Where one man had once performed all steps in a single operation (like loading, banding, sawing up, and blocking), each step now required a different man. Industrial engineers claimed there was, on average, only 30% utilization of labor. But this was not cause for real dispute. In those good times, the company wanted to make hay, not principled stands. Policy was to avoid work stoppages. So, despite grumblings from some operating men, as an issue it was moot. As a stick for Geneen to poke at Austin, though, it was marvelous.

Jim Imel, Geneen's favorite mill superintendent, was due to talk at the superintendents' monthly lunch, which was always attended by the J&L brass. "He asked me what I was going to talk about," says Imel. "I said, I don't know. Something about planning, and—"

"You've got union problems, haven't you?" Geneen said.

"Sure."

"Why not talk about them?"

It sounded good to Imel. "Now what I didn't know," he says, "is that Geneen and Austin are having one big fight about this. So we sit down and write out a speech. I thought I was writing it, but he was putting words in there, and bingo! I've got a speech. It's a pretty good speech—about why don't management do something, not back down every time the union coughs. Because they're walking all over us." He gave the speech, and Austin immediately walked all over *him*. "Geneen saw the predicament I'm in, and I'll give him credit, he backed me up. But it was dawning on me: You dumb *fuck!* You got suckered in here, and you're too stupid to know it. And I see the works manager over there snickering."

Compared with the usual level of issues and tactics between Geneen and Austin, this was a miracle of maturity. Consider the great Time Clock Ploy. Geneen, of course, was always late to work. Austin knew it was a trivial fault but of course continually complained about it. He would call Geneen's office at 8:31 just to establish that Geneen was late. He would schedule meetings for 9:00 A.M., do no business, and dismiss them when Geneen breezed in at 9:30 or so, tartly blaming Geneen for everyone's wasted time.

Finally, Geneen sent Chuck Miller to get a time clock and a stack of time cards. From then on he punched in and out religiously—always late in the morning, much, much more than late at night. He never sent the time cards to Austin, though. They were his own documentation. Why let Austin know that his needling rankled?

"I could have handled him better," Austin sums up, "and he could have handled me better."

Austin was ostensibly the reason that Geneen left J&L. But opposition of the fifth group was more significant. That group was the board of directors —and the spirit of the steel industry itself. One episode concerned depreciation. Recent rulings had encouraged the company to accelerate depreciation, cutting taxes. Geneen argued that doing so distorted the balance sheet: it made investors think that J&L was making less money than it really was. Geneen proposed to accelerate for tax purposes but to make the balance sheet reflect actual profits, noting the reserve set up against future tax liability. It was not a startling innovation. Geneen pointed out that even Alcoa, a company of no great fiscal daring, reported depreciation both ways. But the J&L directors turned him down flat.

"Jones and Laughlin," says John W. Reavis, a director at the time, "was then still a company of the nineties; there were a great many old men running it." That included the board. Although the outside directors were not steel men, they thought like steel men, were stodgy and resistant to change. That put them profoundly at odds with Geneen. And from steel's point of view, they were right about him, for what Geneen really wanted was to phase J&L out of the steel business.

One of his first big board presentations was a scheme to move J&L into chemicals. During the depression many steel companies kept going by converting coal gas into chemicals. By now, J&L's equipment for it was antiquated, and the price of coal-based chemicals was not normally competitive with petrochemicals. But Geneen proposed economies of scale. J&L, he said, should raise a new complex to capture and process coal gas from all of the Pittsburgh steel companies. In time they might also edge into petrochemicals. The chemical engineers and cost accountants he consulted pronounced his plan sound. Capital expenditures would be a base contribution of $50 million, plus $20 million a year for five years; it meant $150 million equity in a $500 million chemical complex.

Even counting 30 years of inflation, a $500 million project is today no trifle; then it was daunting. But those were the days of lush cash flow for steel, and Geneen saw darker days coming. Steel had been good to the company for 100 years (J&L's centennial was in 1953). But steel was the past, chemicals the future; they should be J&L's future for the second 100 years.

His proposal did not stand a chance. Indeed, none of Geneen's dreams sat well with the board. "He had the acquisition bug," says Harvey Haughton. Lee Austin backed Geneen in this, and Geneen regularly dispatched Charles Lause to scout possibilities. Unfortunately, it was mostly scouting and little acquiring. Except for vertical integration, the board said no. Their notion of a high-yield acquisition was another limestone quarry or Great Lakes ore boat. Geneen argued that the return on steel's ancillaries was equally dismal as on steel itself; far from acquiring more, J&L should spin some off and use the money to diversify. Certainly, today's strongest steel companies are those that did diversify. But at the time, Geneen's urgings to get out of steel did not win the hearts or minds of the board.

It was a curious situation. Steel was no more in Geneen's blood than any other industry had been or would be. He would never be a steel man or any sort of industry man. He was always a return-on-investment man, a pennies-per-share man. Yet he eagerly sponged up the ways of the steel business. Why? First, he was omnivorously inquisitive about how everything worked. But mostly he abhorred making ignorant decisions. It was for the same reason that he read the chemistry text at Bell & Howell: so they could not snow him; he would know what questions to ask and how good the answers were.

Immune to the "romance of steel," Geneen was at the same instant making himself a steel expert—and pushing to get out of the business. By all standards of economic reason, Geneen was right and the board and the steel men were wrong. But the heart, even of a steel man, has its reasons.

Not that Geneen went unappreciated. In April 1954 the board elected him a vice president and member of the management committee. They did him only simple justice; no one had a broader management outlook. Geneen was into everything—purchasing specifications, the ratios of different kinds of scrap fed to the steel-making furnaces, whatever affected J&L costs and profits.

Ore inventory was a natural concern. Geneen knew the "inventory" was just huge outdoor piles. To take inventory, a grizzled superintendent would hold his thumb at arm's length, sight a pile, add Kentucky windage, and announce the number of tons on hand. Geneen was appalled. What kind of inventory was that? He commissioned aerial photographs of the ore piles. Trigonometry would render precise volume—except that his results showed less than half of what the superintendents said was there, and notably less than was *known* to be stockpiled. It seemed geometric volume was meaningless because the ore compacted. Well then, after boring to check average density, multiply visible volume by. . . . This time the answer was impossibly high. Ore was added to and taken from the piles in varying weather, and it compacted at crazily varying rates; even different parts of each stratum might differ wildly. Undismayed, Geneen hit on the perfect way to check inventory: he learned the old supers' technique. Soon he, too, had a calibrated thumb.

Most of Geneen's projects, of course, were more conventionally managerial. And in all of them he was highly valued. He was star of the dog and pony show J&L regularly put on for stock analysts. Gerald Tsai, Jr., a young specialist in steel stocks for Boston's Fidelity Management Research, attended one. Admiral Moreell talked, then Austin. The controller, programmed next, was not there. The admiral joked about how busy the controller was and how, anyway, he was never on time. At that point Geneen literally ran into the room—and proceded to dazzle the jaded audience with a recital of how his MOCC program helped keep J&L profits up. Back in Boston, Tsai told his boss, "All the others are going to buy Bethlehem; I think *we* buy J and L." They made money.

Two other of Geneen's projects established patterns he followed at ITT. With McKinsey & Co. as consultant, Geneen and director John Reavis worked out an executive incentive plan. Seeing him in action, Reavis became an instant Geneen admirer. Incentive plans are commonplace today, but this one was a model of enlightened corporate self-interest. There was only one problem: "It wasn't industry practice," says Charles Lause, "so he had a hard time selling the plan."

Geneen also pushed through a program of intelligence and psychological testing. It was not popular. Lee Austin considered it demeaning and would not take the test, while others complained, "If it takes some psychologist to tell me who my good people are—after ten years working with them—I'm no boss." That missed the point. Geneen knew that many in J&L rose through cronyism or because they posed no threat. But now if someone whose test results were poor was promoted anyway, the boss had a lot to explain. The tests' utility with new hires was even greater. And consensus was that test results seemed pretty accurate, despite a few howlers.

Grading Geneen's test was a problem. Most questions were yes-no or multiple choice, but Geneen scrawled answers all over each page. His secretary examined the test file. "He was a genius," she says.

With all this activity, Geneen did not have time for much except business. "Even at J and L," says Charles Lause, "it was a bit of a joke, his relationship with his wife. He probably saw her only in the morning." Before the evening conference hit full stride, Geneen would call home. "What's for dinner?" he would ask. "Roast beef? That sounds nice. Sorry I can't make it."

"I don't know how the marriage lasted," says Val Gorman. But it has lasted over thirty years. How indeed? Its account reads like a case study of neglect. Geneen would call June from Boston or New York or Cleveland, having forgotten to mention a pending business trip. One Christmas Eve, when J&L closed early, Geneen left at noon to have a drink with J&L's expert in stockholder relations. Engrossed in their talk, Geneen remembered in the evening that he and June had planned to go to Detroit—on a four o'clock flight. Another time, he had a cold and quit work early, taking Charles Lause home with him to finish some business. "On a table by the door was a stack of letters from June," says Lause. "She was in Florida, and the letters hadn't been opened. He saw them and said, Oh my God! she's coming home tomorrow—I'd better read these." Not exactly love's young dream—but on the other hand, she could go anywhere and not worry about any human rival.

"I suspect that he had no interest in women," says Val Gorman. "I think his interest in life was his job and his work and power." He barely seemed to realize that secretaries were female—except for not swearing in front of them. One of them was, as Val Gorman puts it, "well endowed," and the office was stunned one day to hear Geneen comment on the fact. That secretary herself says, "I never would have dreamed he noticed." (At ITT his obliviousness to even the routine male lubricities became legend. In Brussels one night he was striding briskly between two young associates, talking. They quickly overtook a pair of prostitutes dressed in regulation uniform, short tight skirts showcasing exuberant rumps. While his two companions ogled, Geneen kept expostulating as usual, head swiveling from one disciple to the other. Not until they were practically on top of the women did Geneen notice he had lost his audience. "What's the matter," he said, "what's the matter?")

In another marriage, Geneen's special ties to his mother might have been troublesome. Aida patently took precedence in Geneen's thoughts and affection. People who never knew June existed would hear all about his mother. When Aida decided to take driving lessons in her mid-sixties, Geneen bragged to nearly everyone at J&L how cute and spunky it was. She came for frequent visits, and Geneen spent a lot of time with her on Cape Cod. But a mother is not the rival that breaks up this kind of marriage.

On the other hand, June patiently endured notably offhand treatment. One evening Geneen called to announce that tomorrow morning he was going crow shooting with two colleagues. June was to have breakfast ready for them at 6:00 A.M. "He didn't ask her if it was all right, or anything," says someone who overheard the call, "just . . . brriiip! rattled off orders." Later, at Raytheon, during a conference at home, he called June in to take sandwich orders all around—in shorthand. "You could tell that she'd had it up to *here*," says a Raytheon colleague. It apparently was not so; but the compensations were not evident.

Their life-style was simple, even Spartan, considering Geneen's income. They lived in a one-bedroom apartment on Elsworth Street in an undistinguished neighborhood. When June needed a car she had to borrow the creaky Mercury Geneen still had from Chicago. The home he bought for his mother on Cape Cod, which doubled as his vacation home, cost only $10,000; the boat he bought was inexpensive. Furthermore, June enjoyed no perks because of Geneen's position. Once, when he was away, she called Val Gorman (with whom she was friendly) to ask if Gorman and another secretary would help address invitations for some club affair. But first she swore Gorman to secrecy. "Harold would be livid," she said. "He's told me never to ask you to do anything personal like this."

The Geneens' social life was rudimentary, totally subordinate to business. Dinner out was usually a business dinner, with people Geneen wanted to talk to. Sometimes he would include Chuck Miller. June liked to chat with Miller, and that kept her amused so Geneen could talk business. They had a few friends; but, like Miller, their function was mostly to provide companionship for June while Geneen worked.

Of course, as Val Gorman points out, June knew from her days as Geneen's secretary what to expect. So what *did* she get from the marriage? She could go to Florida, or anywhere else she wanted, nearly any time. Later there would be the greater latitude of even more money, with a house in Key Biscayne, another on the Cape, and (above all) a farm in her beloved New Hampshire, the perfect retreat from city life. Friends never noticed any want of affection between the pair. June simply made her own life within the easy confines of a nonrestrictive relationship. "Besides," says Val Gorman, with probably the clincher, "it must be fun being married to a legend—even if you don't see him much."

Lee Austin continued to be unawed by the legend. Admiral Moreell was named to the Hoover Commission on government reorganization in October 1953 and promptly contracted Potomac fever, becoming an absentee chairman. That left Austin in charge. In the context of Austin's increased authority, without the admiral's genial mediation, Austin and Geneen went at it. Things seemed fated to go wrong between them at every opportunity, even on the golf course—where a top-flight golfer once pronounced Geneen's the "wildest set of wrists" he had ever seen. Geneen hit a long ball but never knew where it was going. And he was too impatient to wait for other players to drift out of range before teeing off himself. At one company outing Geneen socked the ball and his companions watched in horror as it sailed straight down the fairway, skimming the head of Austin, who was in the preceeding foursome. "Any other time Harold would have shanked it," says Ron Nestor.

In the summer of 1955 Admiral Moreell dropped in from Washington to find turmoil, the Austin-Geneen wars having escalated to new ferocity. The admiral concocted a cooling-off solution. J&L regularly sent promising executives to the Harvard Business School thirteen-week advanced management program (AMP). Geneen was certainly promising; he might soon become financial VP. And going to Harvard would separate him from Austin. That it was a late, emergency decision is clear from the fact that the twenty-eighth AMP began on September 14, 1955, and Geneen arrived a week late. Dispensation took massive pull.

The status of executives sent to the Harvard AMP is evident from the cost: a thirteen-week absence at full pay, plus (in 1955) $10,000 tuition. Each class had about 160 members, split in two seminar sections; minimum age was thirty-five, the average around forty-five (exactly Geneen's age then). Members lived in six- or eight-man "can groups," so called because they shared a large bathroom. Geneen was in can group 5. He was proud of having been, even peripherally, at Harvard. The broadening was valuable and so were the contacts. One of his can group, Air Force Colonel Richard F. Silver, became his personal assistant at ITT. He did some business with another, Ralph C. Graham, both personal and at ITT. Another AMP classmate, William W. Lyon, became Geneen's personal banker, while Lyon's bank, Irving Trust, worked closely with ITT; John J. Graham, then at RCA, became the first of Geneen's many heirs apparent at ITT; Frank Conant, a VP at Chase Manhattan, arranged loans that let Geneen exercise his J&L stock options.

It was, however, a lackluster class. The two surviving professors, Kenneth R. Andrews and James Healy, recollect the members as being "salt of the earth, rather than sparkling" and remember others in the class more vividly than they do Geneen. To them, Ben Biaggini, who became chairman of the Southern Pacific Railroad, was the outstanding figure—voluble, emphatic, and persistent in class.

Union representatives sat in on some sessions, and Geneen once debated with them, charging a trend of union encroachment on company prerogatives in policy, organization, and administration. "He responded to the union members in an almost steely way," says Healy, whose field was labor relations. That make a big hit with his classmates.

Kenneth Andrews had one Administrative Practices case he always con-

Can group 5 at the Harvard AMP banquet. All the wives are there except June. Dick Silver (with glasses) is standing, left. Ralph and Mary Gene Graham are seated, far right. Geneen is third from right and Walter Gahagan is seated fourth from left.

sidered a telltale of executive thought. Safety guards in a mine had an inviolable rule: before a blast they were never to allow anyone past a certain point. One veteran worker was acting as guard when the foreman strolled by. At the last second the guard cried a warning. The foreman hurled himself down just before detonation and was uninjured. What, besides obscenities, should the foreman say when he picked himself up?

Most AMP students were in Andrews's "FSOB Club"—"fire the sonofabitch" was their favorite disciplinary solution. This case, though, divided them. Many pat FSOBers counseled lenience. After all, no one was hurt, the guard was otherwise a good worker, and workers did not, then, lightly voice commands to foremen. Andrews also invested the guard with five children and a heavy mortgage.

Cases had no "answers." But Andrews felt that here leniency was misplaced. The life-and-death nature of the situation demanded dismissal on principle. Geneen, while no knee-jerk FSOBer, tended toward sternness. In this case, though, he was for leniency. That surprised Andrews, who had expected him to discern the real issue.

Of course, Geneen dominated Russell Hassler's accounting class. It was designed to expose executives to activist financial control. For all their high rank and promise, most AMP members did not understand balance sheets. Worse, when Hassler asked accountants in the class to explain their art, they often got ludicrously tangled. Hassler would then say, "Well, you probably have the same problem in your company." That was one reason accounting was misprized by most managements. Naturally the professor doted on Geneen's mastery and clear exposition of financial control, and on his pioneering ideas. He invited Geneen to address one of his regular B-school classes. That vindicated Geneen's team at J&L; they had been sure, all along, he would teach Harvard, not vice versa.

Although Geneen found the AMP stimulating, he would not simply rusticate for thirteen weeks. He called Val Gorman every few days, dictating his usual endless memos. He also cut a number of classes, flying back to Pittsburgh. Business tinctured even socializing. He organized a dinner for all class members in steel-related industries, presenting a slide-talk analysis of the latest union-industry contracts. At the dinner were two guests: the head of J&L's health services and Geneen's mother.

The twenty-eighth AMP was to end December 9, 1955. On December 6 a newspaper story announced the appointment of David T. Schultz as president of Du Mont Laboratories, an early maker of TV sets. Schultz was senior VP and treasurer of Raytheon, a tolerably large electronics company near Boston. Company president Charles Francis Adams, Jr., sure to be deluged with applicants, wanted résumés from callers before he would see them. When Geneen called, Adams's secretary started to explain. He interrupted. "I think it's unfair to expect anyone to send in a résumé without knowing if there's an opening," he said. "and if there is an opening, it's unfair to conceal it. That means it's not open to everyone qualified." The secretary was dumbfounded: he was right. She promised to get answers and call back. When she told Adams, he was impressed; he would have to look into this one.

Meanwhile, the custom of AMP classes was for wives to join their husbands during the last few days of seminars and at a climactic banquet. All the wives of can group 5 gathered around the banquet table—except June.

A different Harold Geneen returned to Pittsburgh. Nothing would be settled with Raytheon for months. Charlie Adams, never very decisive, wanted Geneen to meet a number of his advisors before he made an offer. Geneen had turned indecisive too. Val Gorman had been promoted to stenographic department head, and Ginny Nichols, once secretary for Harvey Haughton and Ed Resler, took over. "I was scared to death," she says, "but he had really changed. I'd go into his office and the curtains would be drawn, and he'd be sitting with his back to me, just staring, meditating. He seemed more mellow, almost starry-eyed. I knew it was a funny period for him, whatever it was." He had always faithfully told secretaries where he would be when he left the office; now he disappeared for days.

Mostly, he was making the rounds of Charlie Adams's advisors, who were uniformly enthusiastic about him. Still he vacillated. "Do you really think I ought to take this job?" he asked one interviewer. It was the old story. He might never be a steel man, but he was always a company man. Any company he was with became his life, and it is hard to leave your life behind, even for a better one.

Yet he knew he had to. Someone later claimed that "Geneen felt that his boss, Charles Austin, was destroying his self-confidence. . . . " That is nonsense. Still, the lacerating relationship was harming Geneen's health. Driving home from the office late one night, his vision fogged. He pulled over and had to sit for quite a while before he could see clearly. "It scared hell out of me," he told a subordinate. Another time, visiting his sister, he rose from the dinner table, walked into the hall, staggered, and barely made it to a chair before he blacked out. A doctor assured him it was just overwork and tension. For Geneen, "overwork" meant nothing. Tension was the thing, and he knew where that came from. Austin, as boss, could always have the last word, and that was insupportable.

In February 1956 Austin reviewed sales and administrative budgets that had already gone into effect. He called Geneen in and told him to have department heads reduce their budgets. Geneen replied, "I'm dealing with vice presidents on my own level; I can't just demand they reduce budgets that have already been thoroughly discussed and authorized by you—unless you give me specific authority."

"Well," said Austin, "you're not going to *get* that authority."

Geneen sat dead still, a vein in his forehead throbbing; an assistant thought he was going to explode. But in a very quiet voice he said, "If I can't have that authority, then I can't take the responsibility." Austin turned coldly to Harvey Haughton. "Harvey," he said to Geneen's deputy, "I want you and

Walter Lewis to review the budgets and take the responsibility."

Geneen did not have to take this. Earlier, he had written in desperation to Charles Percy. Was there anything suitable at Bell & Howell? A poll of B&H executives showed that most felt Geneen's return "would be too upsetting." By now, though, Geneen's ambition was soaring, like his self-confidence. J&L had thrown him into contact with a lot of high executives, and he was unimpressed. "I've met some real idiots," he told a subordinate. He told another that his ambition was to be "president of a corporation larger than General Motors."

And now, for all his qualms about breaking the J&L tie, he had a plausible out. To force the issue, he formally complained to the admiral and agreed to a last effort at patching things up with Austin. He chose a weekend on Cape Cod, where Austin had a vacation home. It was a raw, early spring day, and a chill drizzle was falling. Geneen found Austin in his apple orchard, broadcasting fertilizer by hand. "I suppose I should have stopped what I was doing and talked to him," says Austin, "but when you're working in the field. . . . " Instead, Geneen sat on a wet rock and fumed while Austin finished the row. Afterward he declined an invitation to go in the house for their talk. The admiral had asked him to talk things over, but the two men quickly agreed there nothing to discuss and Geneen left.

His mind was probably set right then. Still, as late as April 26, 1956, when he was appointed by the directors to a pension plan board, he had not announced his intentions. Not long after that date, though, he told them he would go to Raytheon as executive vice president. He was getting $50,000 a year, plus stock options.

With the admiral's permission, Geneen also told key directors why he was leaving. One was William Whiteford; in meetings, Geneen had sensed that the chairman of Gulf Oil was sympathetic to him. Frank Denton was another matter. "He had in his mind," says Denton, "that I was Austin's backer." A pardonable assumption, given their friendship and common Mellon tie. "I remember his surprise when I told him, In no way have I been responsible for Austin's success or actions. I didn't even know, until Geneen told me, that he and Austin had differed. I couldn't and shouldn't have done anything about it anyhow." He took the news of Geneen's departure with equanimity. To his mind, Geneen was no real factor in running the company, just the guy handling the books. He did a good job at that, and they felt bad when he left—but so what?

What Denton did not tell Geneen was that Austin was also on his way out. Geneen found that out when he talked to John Reavis. "For God's sake," Reavis said, "didn't you trust us to solve that problem?" He and Denton, reminding the admiral that his retirement was due in 1957, had asked if he thought Austin should succeed him, and the answer was no. "I was fond of Lee," says Reavis, "and I respected him. He is brilliant. But he has a heavy hand with people." Reavis explained the situation to Geneen. Not that it mattered. Only the Austin problem would be solved. And Reavis recognized that the real problem was the esential imcompatibility between Geneen's nature and the poky ways of steel. Besides, Geneen was already committed. His resignation was effective as of June 1, 1956, and he would start at Raytheon June 7.

On August 30 Admiral Moreell called a meeting of all J&L executives. On stage with him was a stranger. The admiral said, "Gentlemen, here's your new president." It was Avery C. Adams, former president of Pittsburgh Steel, twelfth largest in the country.

Lee Austin was "promoted" to vice chairman and made head of the previously nonexistent finance committee. Everyone agrees that these were Austin's finest hours. His behavior throughout the period was exemplary, with never a complaint and no public comment. No matter what else he was, Lee Austin was a man. He stayed on until the following spring, then quietly retired.

5

The Brahmin and the Bull

One employee recollects that it was "a small company with two large missile programs." Harold Geneen called it "a two-hundred-million-dollar operation with management enough to run only a twenty-million-dollar company." On June 1, 1956, Raytheon Manufacturing Company was plainly in distress. Revenue was $175,490,000, net $1,255,000, down from the previous year's $182,505,000 and $4,532,000. Earnings per share had dropped from $1.62 to 45¢. Receivables were up from $15.3 million to $24.5 million, inventories up over $8 million. Only the missile division prospered—and everyone knew that was a triumph of science, not management.

If technological genius had been Raytheon's founding principle, so had managerial ineptitude. Shortly after World War I, scientist Vannevar Bush was consultant to a company called American Research and Development Corporation—AMRAD. An AMRAD employee, J. L. Spencer, showed Bush an invention he said was his own, not the company's; he had developed it at home, on his own time. It was a thermostat that kept flatirons from overheating. With the help of entrepreneur Laurence K. Marshall, Bush and Spencer started a new company to exploit the invention. Their defection doomed the failing AMRAD, and all of AMRAD's patents reverted to the company's bankroller, the firm of J. P. Morgan.

Among those patents was one for a new radio tube developed by an AMRAD scientist, Charles G. Smith. Now at loose ends, Smith approached Marshall with his latest invention, a home refrigerator. Marshall, Bush, and their backers formed another firm, called American Appliance Company, to develop and sell Smith's invention. Unfortunately, they had no idea of what their market should be or how to develop it. The new company looked like a goner. Just in time, Marshall remembered Smith's radio tube. He secured the patent rights from the house of Morgan for $50,000, mostly in shares of American Appliance. The trade name of Smith's tube was "Raytheon"—a beam of light from the gods. When it turned out that a company called American Appliance already existed, the new company adopted the name of the tube.

That sort of stumbling became a motif at Raytheon: muddled management kept afloat by excellent science. During World War II, the company did heroic work on radar—and made bushels of money, which Marshall promptly plowed into ill-considered ventures. Microwave transmission was one. Raytheon had the technology but lacked the necessary organization and marketing. With microwaves, as with refrigerators, Marshall was not so much ahead of his time as out of his depth. The Raytheon directors grew disenchanted. So did Morgan.

In 1938 Henry S. Morgan had placed Charles Francis Adams, Jr., on the Raytheon board to keep watch over the Morgan interests. Everyone who discusses him says the same: for a man of integrity and honor, for a Harvard overseer or a symphony trustee, call for Charlie Adams. But you might want to find someone else to run your business. Splendid men who made indifferent presidents was a family tradition.

Adams was the same age as Geneen, 28, when he joined the Raytheon board. Although a partner in Paine, Webber, Jackson & Curtis—so in theory an "investment banker"—Adams was more a banker-in-law. Harry Morgan had married his sister. Mostly, he was an Adams. Since he did not much care

Charles Francis Adams, Jr.

for the brokerage business, he was pleased when, in 1947, the Raytheon board pushed Marshall to take him as executive VP. By 1948 Adams was president and CEO, with Marshall as chairman; in May 1950 Marshall was out.

If the board assumed that an Adams *must* be able to run a company, Charlie Adams never made the same mistake. He always leaned on others. Unhappily, he had little talent for distinguishing the sturdy from the frail. Later, he relied on the likes of Geneen and Thomas L. Phillips. But in 1950 Adams surrounded himself at Raytheon mostly with ciphers. At first it seemed all right. While the company never achieved decent returns, business did grow after the Marshall years. But it was illusion, more science-to-the-rescue. Raytheon was the only electronics firm to hold prime contracts on two missiles—Sparrow and Hawk; it also had a handsome contract for B-52 Hustler radar.

So the company approached the post-Sputnik boom in a strange position. "We showed signs of being able to grow a bit in the future," says Adams, "but needed financial controls." Actually, it was more critical than that. "The Hawk and the Sparrow were going into big numbers," says the man who became Geneen's controller, "and the company couldn't afford such expansion without control. We had ten different directions we could grow in but not enough money. Maybe not enough to take care of what he had."

Despite that need for strong guidance, Adams at first offered Geneen only the newly vacant post of financial VP. But unless Geneen could run the show he was not interested. Adams's good sense prevailed. "Geneen was obviously bright as hell," he says, "and you had to give him broad responsibility to get the most out of him." For Geneen, it was a familiar situation. He found primitive organization with rudimentary control, rigidly centralized. But now, as executive VP, he finally had untrammeled power to do something about it. He quickly concluded, he told the policy committee, that "the company is operating with extremely minimum executive staff." There were only three profit and loss (P&L) centers in the entire company. One man oversaw all defense work; another headed up receiving and cathode-ray tubes, plus semiconductors; a third ran microwave and power tubes. None could say how any given product line was doing. Geneen's standard solution for such problems was to push P&L responsibility down as far as possible. For instance, one tube division was suddenly three divisions—receiving, industrial, and semiconductors, each with its own manager. "This is in line," Geneen reported, "with the complete decentralization of accounting which is under way."

That was also vintage Geneen. Books and accountants belonged at the lowest division levels. Tight controls would assure that healthy divisions (like missiles) made some real money; in the sick divisions (like receiving tubes) controls were critical to stop the hemorrhage. It was a personal issue for Geneen. Within a few months of his arrival, it looked as thought the Hustler radar contract had such huge cost overruns as to be unsalvageable; Raytheon might be the graveyard of his career. He knew the necessary controls could be exerted best, maybe *only*, on the spot. Receiving tubes alone would need 20 to 30 new accountants. Bookkeepers were dispatched to the divisions from headquarters, but the job was beyond many of them, and new accountants flooded into Raytheon. By the time Geneen left, they would number about 2,000, nearly 5% of the company's work force.

The new people included a corporate controller. For the job, Geneen recruited George Ingram, Jr., from Riegel Paper. Ingram was thirty-five, bright, hard-working, and largely at one with Geneen's concept of how to control a major corporation. Given the chaos then at Raytheon, he even favored what would be, at ITT, one of the most controversial and abrasive aspects of Geneen's system: divisional and plant controllers' reporting direct to the corporate controller. At J&L Geneen had never completely won this struggle. Now he could go all the way. On Raytheon organization charts, divisional controllers were connected to line managers only by a dotted line. In theory they were supposed to work in some amiably way of cooperation. In fact most of them did review reports with their managers. At least at Raytheon, Ingram insists, Geneen did not conceive of it as an adversarial relationship. But intentionally or not, the setup bred suspicion. Was the controller a friend or a spy? The controller and manager might form a harmonious team all month; but when the controller prepared his monthly report, it was supposed to detail every blemish on the manager's performance. Those reports were not known as the "Yellow Peril" merely because of their jacket color. Geneen did not seem to understand that the spirit of community he hoped for between controller and manager would have trouble surviving such monthly disruption. "It was inherent in Geneen's system," says Ingram, "to set people against each other. Two people would force an issue into the open, and a third would decide it." Still, Ingram is sure the independence of controllers was necessary to overcome the primitive conditions of financial control that they faced at Raytheon in those early days.

The urgency Geneen felt about getting controllers in place was dictated by his developing certainty that a company is best managed strictly by numbers. It took a year and a half to entrench his controls; then he was ready. The basic objective of the company, he announced, was an average 3% profit after-tax net on sales. With a three-times turnover, this meant ". . . nine percent return on assets or, since we borrow about one-half our capital, about eighteen percent return on the stockholders' investment after taxes." That was for government business. "In contrast," Geneen said, for commercial business, ". . . ten percent on the assets would be a reasonable goal."

The figures would be an unarguable measure. "Return," he said, would be the "measure of performance. . . . It will mean that we must lean backward to be critical of our own end performance and not excuse it on the basis of unforseen conditions." This was bold talk, since companywide profit on sales was then only 1.8%, less than two-thirds of objective. But Geneen dared to make those goals a flat promise to his bankers because he knew exactly how to proceed.

First he set ratios. Isolated facts mean nothing. Have your sales increased 10%? Wonderful; unless you added another person to your sales force of five, hiking your sales expense 20%. The important fact is your ratio between sales and salespeople; more important, between sales and profit. The point seems unaccountably hard to grasp. Even today, Fortune 500 companies are ranked by raw sales volume; profitability is a virtual footnote. Back in the mid-1950s, while ratios were recognized, their practical possibilities were not well understood. Someone who attended Harvard Business School at just that time says, "We had around fifty-five ratios to consider, all presented as being of about equal significance"—and so of equal nonvalue for running a business.

Geneen was determined to ignore—*really* ignore—any fact except as it related to profit performance. And it was his positive stroke of genius to see that he *could* manage a business with ratios, because all were subsumed or reflected by three key ratios: sales divided by the accounts receivable balance; sales divided by the gross inventory balance; and sales divided by gross plant.

With receivables, for instance, that means that if your annual sales are $100,000 and the average amount your customers owe you is $20,000, your receivables ratio is 5 because $\frac{100,000}{20,000} = 5$. If you speed up collection so that you are, on average, owed only $5,000, your ratio will jump to 20 ($\frac{100,000}{5,000} = 20$). The lower receivables, inventory, and plant are in relation to sales (and so the higher your ratios), the better.

All other ratios fit neatly into one of the three key ratios. With labor, for example: the isolated fact of higher labor cost in your plant this month is meaningless; perhaps it rose because you paid overtime to produce more units at lower per-unit cost, or added 2% to your work force in support of 7% greater sales. But Geneen was not interested even in such isolated *ratios* as labor costs to production or sales. Those would show in the inventory ratio, since higher labor costs increase the cost of goods in inventory—unless (always Geneen's point) you take some timely action, like increasing productivity, to offset the higher rate. Geneen's revolutionary insight was that this or that rate does not matter except in its effect on the relevant key ratio.

On February 27, 1957, Geneen outlined at a staff lunch how the ailing receiving tube division could get well. (For a detailed discussion, see Appendix III.) The division's performance graphs were a sorry sight. The receivables ratio was 7; they were owed $14.30 on every $100 of sales. Among competitors, only RCA had a worse receivables ratio. No competitor was worse with inventory; receiving tube's ratio barely topped 3.15, almost $31 of goods on hand for each $100 of sales. Their plant ratio was passable, almost 4.25; but a dismal 3.25 was forecast.

Geneen set some objectives. At minimum, all three ratios must be on a par with the best competition. But that was only a start. You were in business to make money, not products, not even comparatively favorable ratios. Government business accounted for 85% of Raytheon's total. Geneen wanted to look ahead, not back, so he used *new* government business as an example. The numbers for new business were somewhat different. A return of 34% on investment, Geneen said, was a necessary minimum; if you cannot realize 34% forget that business. It was needed to cover the level of profit Geneen demanded, plus interest, depreciation, and general and administrative costs.

New government business classically required a $50 investment for each $100 of sales. With ratios at decent levels, $10 would finance receivables, $25 was for inventory, $15 for plant. But Geneen insisted that new government business did not *have* to take that much investment.

With receivables, to achieve a competitive ratio of 10, the receiving tube division could take recognized steps: get billing out faster; dun aged accounts; be chary of business from slow payers. Now speed up more, and a ratio of 12 was perfectly attainable. Right away, you need less investment for the same amount of business. It was $8 instead of $10 (much less their current $14.30).

Geneen did not think to collect receivables faster than would produce a 12 ratio. But inventory could be much reduced. First, get progress payments of 75% of the balance owed, twice a month. That was easy. Of all the major competitors, only Raytheon was not getting progress payments of at least 50% of inventory. That was the more damning, since the others' percentages included a lot of commercial sales. After cash discounts, civilian controllers were eager to pay as slowly as possible; with the government all you had to do was ask—the right way. Geneen showed his people how. Soon, clerks were hand-carrying vouchers to Boston and waiting until they could fetch back a check. "Sometimes," says one awed controller, "we collected from the government *before* we had to meet the regular Thursday payroll for that work."

The second inventory reducer was subcontracting. If you subcontract half your work, still getting a 75% progress payment, that doubles the ratio on the other 25% of your inventory. With 50% subcontracted, half your inventory is the other fellow's lookout. With it all, the necessary inventory investment suddenly drops from $25 to only $10.50 per $100 of sales. What's more, subcontracting 50%, you need that much less plant investment. (And, with government work at that time, it was possible to get half your equipment furnished by the customer.) In all, plant investment drops from $15 to $4. Before, it took $50 to support each $100 new business. Suddenly, Geneen's way, it took only $22.50. See what that means to return on investment figured as a percent of sales. Before, to get your mandatory 34%, you needed a 17% return on sales. Now you needed only 8%.

This was more than a plan to rescue one hapless Raytheon division. It was the articulation of a basic philosophy for running any sizable business. The details would change; government business offered options not always available with commercial enterprise, but it also imposed some unique restrictions. In any case, Geneen's message was universal for all business: you must see the relationships between return and expenses and always distinguish what counts (here, return on investment) from what does not (return on sales). Even if you cannot directly increase sales, there are always alternate ways to control receivables, inventory, and plant, because many reciprocal factors affect each key ratio. With proper controls you get a good return on investment with level sales. Furthermore, if all you need for an acceptable return on investment is an 8% return on sales, management enjoys enormous flexibility. Achieve a better-than-8% return and you can increase profits, lower price, or both. That means bigger sales on the same investment, further sweetening key ratios.

It all came down to the fundamentals of business. "Geneen mastered the fundamentals," says George Ingram, "and he made them work." With such things as receivables, inventory, plant, return on investment, assets, and turn-over, says Ingram, "He didn't mention them once a month but *every* time you met. He didn't ever lose sight of them and wouldn't let you lose sight of them, either." He developed a shorthand test for any action or policy. "If anything happened," says Charlie Adams, "he'd say, That's going to be three cents a share next month."

That was not just for Raytheon's business executives. One manager had a plaque on his desk. "There comes a time when you must shoot the engineers and start production," it read. "Geneen laughed like hell when he saw it," says the manager; "he said, That's sure true." A satisfying thought, but impractical in a company whose life's blood was technology. So Geneen held meetings for all the company's technical people to explicate the significance to *them* of Raytheon's commercial prosperity. He hired a Waltham high-school auditorium for one mass meeting. For another, he gathered about seventy-five heads of engineering after hours at the Wayland Labs. "He went through very simple business arithmetic," says one observer, "how you netted down to the bottom line. He didn't talk down to them; but he made them realize that unless they contributed to the profit-making activity, there wouldn't be enough to feed back into the kinds of things they liked to do. It was very worthwhile."

His regular, monthly business review meetings—called "F&O" for "financial and operating"—were equally inspiring, if less benevolent in mood. At the F&O meetings he found out how each unit was following his system. Raytheon had long held managers' monthly meetings, and they were just as perfunctory as those at J&L had been before Geneen. They were Big Picture meetings, Geneen noted in a written critique, "and only a short time is usually available for the review of current operating results or specific current items requiring prompt actions or assignment of responsibility. More time should be spent analyzing our results. . . . "

First he restructured managers' reports. Henceforth they must contain sections showing each operation's detailed monthly results, with "explanatory and analytical comments needed to interpret or call attention to significant items." In fact, "no accounting figure statements will be presented without interpretive comment." He knew figures do not speak for themselves. Besides, making managers articulate the meaning of their figures fixes that meaning in their minds; it also reveals any lack of understanding. Comment should cover, Geneen wrote, "comparison of actual to forecasts, capital return on new equipment, effects of prices, costs, mix of products, overhead, etc. on profits."

He also required reports from "each line and staff member of the Management Policy Group on the tenth working day of each month, detailing the activity of his operation or staff function for the preceeding month." It must be comprehensive, including "competitive data, need for *action items*, request for policy, etc."

Everyone would receive a copy of all reports before the meetings. The object was "a complete interchange of management activity." As Geneen put it on another occasion, "Above all it is important that there be no 'covering up' of our problems at any management level. . . . If I were to look for any single indication of management's strength or ability *in any company* . . . the degree of 'openness and objectivity' in appraising its own performance would be the most single important index of management's strength."

He extracted from the reports heroically more than anyone else did. "I was flabbergasted," says one of the managers. "He'd pick up implications and details from my reports that *I'd* miss." These Raytheon F&Os set the pattern for ITT. It was here that Geneen honed his inquisitorial technique and developed the group review that marked the ITT system. Anywhere from 50 to 200 people went over the managers' reports, supported or challenged by the controllers' Yellow Perils.

That last feature set the tone of the meetings. "There was a certain amount of adversary feeling between managers and controllers," says George Ingram. More to the point, Geneen's system "put pressure on managers before their peers," says Ingram. "Nobody wanted to say, Well, I missed it again by a million dollars for the tenth month in a row. That probably had even more effect than the adversary aspect of it."

Indolent critics later argued that Geneen was shortsighted, that he cared only about this quarter's earnings. In fact, while Geneen reformed the F&O meetings, he established a "Committee for Long Range Statistics" to determine the company's future needs for space, manpower, and financing. And he instituted five-year planning. For the first time Raytheon managers had to confront such questions as: What will you be selling five years from now? To whom? How will you develop those customers? How much will you sell? At what price? What cost? How can you innovate to cut those costs? What about operating expenses? Overhead? Labor? If you'll need new hires, what are you doing about it *now?* Geneen was implacable about developing new business, contemptuous of managers who wanted to scant development funds whenever earnings were soft. "You're cutting off your future," he would say, "because you're in trouble now."

Not that Geneen slighted immediate results. Short-range planning became more precise. Immediately after each month's results closed, managers had to forecast earnings for the next three months, knowing their actuals (especially *next* month's) would be measured against forecast. "Ultimately," says Arthur V. Schene, the man who followed Ingram as controller, "we became very accurate and could predict very accurate short-term earnings—and we still do it today." It was a riveting exercise. With short-range planning, Geneen knew his managers were paying attention.

Unfortunately there were not enough managers. Geneen's first move had been to break up the old divisional fiefdoms. The former head of all government programs was shunted aside to staff. His former assistants took over, one each for missile systems, government equipment, and commercial equipment. Norman B. Krim was still called general manager of receiving tubes, industrial tubes, and semiconductors; but they were now separate divisions, each with its own manager, and Krim was often bypassed. Since Krim did not have enough top-level assistants to go around, Geneen insisted that he hire outsiders for two divisions. The first wave of hiring was stopgap, including the rush of divisional controllers. The second wave continued throughout Geneen's tenure, reflecting his vision of the company. Many of these recruits went with him to ITT.

Geneen once told a group that he was always on the lookout for management material, both for corporate posts and leadership "of whole possible Divisions or companies as yet unknown that we may buy or build." Then came his signature thought: "I personally do not lean to the theory that 'once a tube man always a tube man' or any other similar philosophy that restricts the ability of any individual of this management to grow in responsibility." Managerial ability *"is a readily translatable commodity from one responsibility to another. . . . "* A manager can manage anything. But to say a company is willing to promote from within says nothing. The question is whether management orchestrates internal managerial development—as does, say, IBM. Geneen never did. Nor did he particularly prize long-term service. His former subordinates routinely say that working for him was the best business training they ever received. But it was strictly informal, a by-product of doing the job. While this may be the best kind of training, it is not a program.

One of Geneen's earliest hires, in 1956, was David I. Margolis. He was twenty-six, fresh from an M.B.A. program at City College of New York and graduate work at NYU. He became an assistant treasurer; but his specialty was hyping Raytheon stock. "He was always on the phone," says a colleague, "talking to the analysts, either praising what Geneen had done or explaining it." He was sharp, hard-working, limitlessly ambitious—all the things Geneen admired. In time, Geneen would take him along to ITT as a top aide. When Margolis left ITT to take over Colt Industries with George A. Strichman, another Raytheon/ITT alumnus, Geneen was crushed. Although they remained friendly, Margolis and Geneen had little further contact: Geneen had time only for his own executives.

Alfred di Scipio and Martin H. Dubilier were not technically hires, since they worked for McKinsey & Company. But that in itself was significant. Geneen's concept of staff as an in-house consulting firm was rapidly developing. It was reflected in 1957 by a new organizational distinction between "operating division management" and "functional management." Unhappily, the latter, his staff cadre, was thin. For now, he had to go outside for consultants, mostly to McKinsey.

This experience planted in Geneen a remarkable trust in consultants, especially the young, quick, and self-assured. It was not a taste widely shared on the Raytheon line. "It didn't go down too well," says William T. Welsh, then number two in power tubes, speaking of Al di Scipio: "The great outside consultant telling us how to run the division was this kid who two years ago was a student, a Northwestern work-study intern at Raytheon, calibrating volt meters. But Geneen had an overwhelming faith in their pronouncements." (In fairness, di Scipio's field was marketing, about which, Welsh admits, "we were scared to death.")

McKinsey's Martin Dubilier was also in his early twenties, very bright, assertive, and abrasive. "I couldn't stand the guy," says E. Nevin Kather, who eventually became manager of power tubes. "You could never finish a sentence with him. He'd interrupt, and after a while it gets irritating. I threw him out of my office. I went to Hal and said, This guy's crazy; what he's proposing for my division won't work; I'm going to throw him out. And Hal said, Go ahead." But any consultant's generation of friction in no way diminished his value to Geneen.

Most executives probably deplore friction between subordinates; some may encourage it as useful. For Geneen, the question did not exist; friction was meaningless. A later disciple at ITT made the same point about those outsiders who thought it an oppressive scandal that Geneen at, say, 9:00 P.M. in New York, should unhesitatingly call a subordinate in Brussels, where it was 3:00 A.M. "So the guy was in bed, asleep. How does that affect the fact that Geneen needed some information right *then* to get on with the company's business? It doesn't fit into the equation." Just so, his system was to have people check on each other's results so the truth of the matter would infallibly emerge. Whether or not that caused friction was not his concern.

Of all his hires, no one was more Geneen's man than William T. Marx. Educated at CCNY, Pace College, and Columbia, he had started at Celanese Corporation in 1934 and worked up to personnel director by 1945. In 1957 Geneen pushed aside Raytheon's old-line personnel head and brought in Marx, whom many in the company liked. Those who did not—and this group was also large—considered him Geneen's spy and hatchet man. Certainly, Marx was alert to political currents, and he placed that sensitivity entirely at Geneen's service. The trouble was that Geneen developed a weakness for intelligence, indistinguishable from gossip, about who was up to what, who was loyal and who was not. A later, once-close associate says that "the only way you could live with Geneen and not be very competent was to feed that weakness." Marx was entirely competent; but he did feed the weakness.

Even while Geneen was getting the people and organization he wanted, he had to fight financial fires. In April 1955 Charlie Adams had plunged into a joint venture with Minneapolis-Honeywell Regulator Company, setting up a computer company, Datamatic. Honeywell put up $1.4 million and Raytheon supplied the technology, ownership being 60%–40% in Honeywell's favor. Thereafter, both companies had to contribute funds in proportion as needed. If one declined to ante up, the other could buy the delinquent percent of equity at a price equal to any outside offer, minus 10%.

The mainframe industry would soon become known as "IBM and the Seven Dwarfs." This showed why. Datamatic's model 1000 hit the market in September 1956; IBM almost immediately presented a competing model. By the spring of 1957 Raytheon had met eight capital calls for a half-million dollars each. Now Honeywell concluded they would have to expand dramatically or go under. Raytheon's share would be another $8 million.

When he reached Boston, Geneen had renewed his acquaintance with stock analyst Gerry Tsai. "One day," says Tsai, "he said to me, We're going to get out of the computer business. I said, Gee, Harold, this is the business of the future; how can you give it up? He said, Gerry, this is a poker game, and we don't have enough chips to play. Honeywell's going to squeeze us, squeeze us, *squeeze* us, and I'm going to end up owning only eight or ten percent anyway. Meanwhile I'm losing my ass. Why shouldn't I get out?"

Geneen went to Minneapolis and came back with Honeywell's offer— $300,000 for Raytheon's full share. Even when they upped the offer another $100,000, it was practically an insult. Geneen was furious. So was Charlie Adams, and at this point his brokerage contacts were vital. His old Paine, Webber colleagues promised $2.5 million for half of Raytheon's share. Before his Memorial Day date to take Honeywell's chief financial officer for a sail— and a talk—on his boat, Adams's frantic phoning extracted a promise from the senior partner of Bear, Stearns for another $2.5 million. Now Adams could enforce the contract price: $5 million, less 10%. Datamatic continued to lose money after the sale and eventually expired.

The receiving tube and semiconductor divisions, even after reorganization, were tougher problems, never solved by Geneen or anyone else at Raytheon. Eventually both divisions were special write-offs. Today, everyone who was at Raytheon then can explain where and why Norman Krim went wrong in the semiconductor business. There is no recorded instance of anyone pointing out his errors at the time. Indeed, RCA, GE, and other electronics giants were making the same errors that surrendered the field to Texas Instruments and the wunderkinder of Silicon Valley. Krim was an old receiving tube man. He saw transistors in terms of radio and hearing aid use, largely ignoring computers. And, for Krim they were simple, one-for-one tube replacements. "Krim, among many people," says one observer, "saw transistors not as a sweep of new technology but as a way to take this tube out of that socket and put another thing into the socket that was smaller and cheaper but that had the same circuitry. But solid-state technology meant you had to redesign from the ground up."

Krim was also beglimmered by germanium just as silicon was taking over. At one semiconductor exposition, Raytheon engineers proudly displayed a germanium transistorized radio that kept playing after a dunking in water. Texas Instruments engineers dunked their silicon version, set the two radios side-by-side, and blew hot air on them. TI's worked; Raytheon's did not.

Geneen did not give up. He was determined to make Raytheon's electronics business succeed. It would balance the military business—an important virtue to investors, because commercial business was considered more stable. Beyond that was the question of image. There was, he told the division managers, a *"need to succeed* as a management in the main *commercial electronics* field that we are in and have been pioneers in. . . . [I]t is basically the fundamental initial unit of the entire Company." Besides, missiles and radar were proprietary, electronics competitive. One was a triumph of science; the other would mean business success. So the prosperity of Raytheon electronics, Geneen said, ". . . will weigh people's judgment of the Company out of all proportion to its relative size in the total   and people's judgment means our ability to raise capital."

Geneen was wrong. The division continued down, yet no one noticed. Even with this drag, Geneen was making Raytheon boom. Summing up 1957, his first full calendar year in charge, he told employees that unprofitable investments had been liquidated, receivables and inventory reduced despite about $100 million more in volume. Some $30 to $35 million more capital was available just through these reforms. It was virtuoso control.

By now matters were so firmly in hand that Geneen could project to his bankers a set of performance benchmarks and, a year later, report point-for-point fulfillment. Promised (1957): 2.5 times turnover on gross assets; reported (1958): 2.8—close to his goal of three times turnover. Promised: 3% profit margin; reported: only 2.5%, but it compared with 1.9% for 1957, and the trend was up. Promised: $3 per share earnings; reported: $3.08. Promised: $23 million generated internally; reported: $60 million! Promised: minimized investment in fixed assets; reported: an astonishing 25 times turnover on plant. Promised: 15–20% return on investment; reported: 17%.

Everything was rosy. By the end of 1958 Raytheon was the largest employer in Massachusetts (36,000, up from 25,000 in 1957, 22,000 when Geneen arrived). From June 1, 1956, to December 31, 1958—the end of Geneen's last full calendar year at Raytheon—sales leapt from $175,490,000 to $375,156,000, pretax earnings from $4.3 million to $19 million, net from $1,255,000 (45¢ a share) to $9,403,000 ($3.08). This was over seven times better net on over twice the sales—in two and a half years—with the trend still up when he left in May 1959.

Investors agreed that it was an incredible accomplishment. On June 1, 1956, Raytheon stock closed at 15⅜; a year later, it was at 21⅛. The day Geneen reviewed his record for the bankers (November 5, 1958), Raytheon closed at 52¾, its P/E (ratio of price to earnings per share), about 18. Before he left, Raytheon would hit a high of 73⅞.

The entire financial world was impressed. Bill Welsh, marketing manager of microwaves and power tubes, thought he would become the next division manager. As consolation, when he was not chosen, Geneen sent him to Harvard's spring AMP in 1958. Soon after the course started, Geneen phoned. "I've been going through the roster of your class," he said, "and there's a guy from New York Trust, one from Banker's Trust, Hanover, Chemical—some more major institutions. We're going on the street to do some financing, and we're going for some bank loans. Those guys are going to get pretty friendly when the word gets around. Don't pick favorites. If a guy asks you to go to dinner, go to dinner."

"It was exactly the way Geneen foretold," says Welsh. "I called him and said, They've all taken me to dinner and they're all anxious to get to know the people at Raytheon."

"All right," Geneen said, "get them to agree to a date when they can get their most senior person to come from New York, and we'll have them all to dinner."

The dinner was held at The Country Club. Geneen charmed everyone. Then, as all relaxed over coffee, he said, "Now, gentlemen, you're used to dealing with a little country bumpkin called Raytheon, and I want you to know it's no longer a country bumpkin. We're going to put together a seventy-five-million-dollar credit. I have one requirement: that the Harris Trust Company participate. I'd like a New York bank to be the lead bank. You gentlemen caucus, select a lead bank, call me, and we'll work out a deal. Thank you very much for coming." Then he turned and left.

In June 1958 Raytheon signed agreements for $75 million in revolving credit. The credit line involved twenty major institutions, led by First National City Bank of New York.

The elements of Geneen's success would be hugely elaborated and refined at ITT, but all were evident by this time: decentralization of P&L responsibility; budgets, planning, standard costs, with managers accountable for meeting forecasts; unit controllers reporting directly to the corporate controller on line forecasts and performance; exhaustive monthly managers' reports inquisitorially reviewed at open meetings.

Most of all, there was Geneen's unrelenting push of his people. His own hours were as usual; one executive called Geneen "the night superintendent." And naturally he kept others with him. "He wasn't a very easy guy to work for," says one of them. "He had people working late every night, then first thing in the morning he wanted to know where the hell all the stuff was that he asked for at ten the night before. And he'd have people standing on their heads over weekends, weekend after weekend. It was a complete lack of sensitivity to the pressures he was putting on people who tried to lead balanced lives, with families and all that." His discussion with Bill Welsh about the Harvard AMP lasted until 9:00 P.M.—Christmas Eve. One New Year's Day he kept Norman Krim talking on the phone about an acquisition for *six* hours.

There was a more disturbing insensitivity as well. Geneen was profoundly at odds with Raytheon's New England humanism. What rankled was his disregard of any calls on people beyond work. Once, a subordinate told Geneen that he would have to miss a meeting scheduled for Sunday afternoon; his first child was being christened. Geneen exploded, "Goddamnit! Can't you have them reschedule for Sunday morning?" His whole attitude clashed with the company's spirit—and specifically with that spirit's exemplar, Charlie Adams.

"Adams always wanted everyone to be happy, everyone to win," says one of Geneen's staunchest admirers. "Adams wouldn't backhand anyone for anything. Geneen could do that very well." The admirer describes Geneen deftly "committing Zorro" on a defaulter: zip, zip, *zip!* and the wretch was in shreds. Adams hated that. He attended few of the F&O meetings; but at one of them, when Geneen was lighting into someone, Adams suddenly barked, "*Stop that!*" Later, privately, he insisted that Geneen not humiliate Raytheon people in public. The warning had no long effect on Geneen's style.

Another basic difference between the two men was portentous. Late in 1958, Geneen learned that the government might license tubes made by foreign companies for use in military products. His instinctive reaction to that threat of competition was to ask a subordinate for "complete information so that we can determine if there is any political action we should take." That would always be his reflex: to talk to the "right man," someone at the top. In dealing with the U.S. government," says a subordinate, "he'd say, You mean there's some *civil servant* who can make those decisions? Don't tell me that!" "The flaw," says another observer, "was his tendency to think that the world is made up of decision makers like himself."

Adams also dealt exclusively with those on top, but only ceremonially. "He knew all the admirals," says a former advisor, "but they weren't the people doing the buying." Adams was strict about leaving that to lieutenants on both sides. He would countenance no politicking to circumvent underlings. "If Charlie caught you even talking to politicians," says one subordinate, "you could be gone at once."

None of these differences proved a terminal irritant, since Geneen was making Raytheon hum. Moreover, not everyone found Geneen's spirit uncongenial. "It broke down into two groups," says one man who had grown up in the company. "Some felt Hal was an outsider, changing everything they were comfortable with, requiring a lot more work. They were saying, I've been getting along great—don't bug me. Others were eager to learn new ways, and experiment, and change—and work hard at it."

But there were never enough of these around to suit Geneen, and none who could work to his example. It was not only that Geneen cared nothing for the "balanced life" his subordinate mentioned; as the same man says, "he had *no* distractions." An interview with *Business Week* was set for 5:30 in the Peacock Lounge of the Waldorf Astoria. Geneen had brought June to New York. They were staying at the hotel, and she was upstairs, waiting to go to dinner and the theater. Everyone ordered a drink, and Geneen began to extol Raytheon. At 8:00, dinner shot and the theater in doubt, he was still at it. "He was having a fascinating time," says Raytheon's PR man, Richard P. Axten. "He had not even touched his drink. And I kept worrying about June, up in the room."

She was never a distraction. Neither was his increasing affluence. He now owned a condominium in Florida, the place on the Cape, and a bigger boat. But his life remained uncluttered. His apartment, for instance, was at 100 Beacon Street. That part of Boston abounds with delightful homes, but 100 is a plain, charmless highrise, now a dormitory for Emerson College. A rear window of the apartment overlooked the Hatch Shell, on the Charles River, where the Boston Pops gave concerts. When a visitor remarked how pleasant that must be, Geneen looked blank. What shell? What concerts? Soon after settling in, Geneen called Gerry Tsai and invited him to dinner for 7:30. "About eight-fifteen," says Tsai, "June says, I think I'll put the roast in now." Geneen liked Tsai and valued his good opinion; but nothing could tear him away from the office on time. He actually seemed to resent weekends when no meetings were scheduled. His secretary noticed that he was often grumpy Monday mornings, cheering up as the day progressed.

Geneen's only outside activity was a directorship of Boston's Shawmut Bank. Although he was not CEO at Raytheon, "we had an idea he was the driving force over there," the bank's chairman explained. Immensely flattered, Geneen loyally stayed a Shawmut director until the avalanche of ITT's woes in 1973, when he told the new chairman, Thomas Trigg, "I'm just not doing justice by you." The fact was, for all his pleasure in the appointment, Geneen's participation in board meetings had always been episodic. He was too busy.

By mid-1958 Geneen had made Raytheon quite profitable. But it could never be a really big winner, or truly secure, while it did 85% of its business with the government. Despite agreeable features like liquidity, low investment, and good turnover, government business had severe drawbacks. Post-Sputnik support for high technology quickly declined to bleak times when President Eisenhower's secretary of defense, Charles Wilson, slashed military spending. With government business, you could never tell, and you had no other customer to turn to. Commercial earnings, though, promised long-term growth. So now Geneen set a goal of raising the company's commercial business from 15% to at least 40% very quickly—and to 60% by 1963. It meant $50 million had to become $250 million. How could this be done?

For his first wave of hirings, Geneen had used the executive search firm of Boyden Associates. In summer 1957 he put Boyden to recruiting a commercial products man. The prime candidate was John T. Thompson, who had been with GE since 1939 and was GE's manager of distributor sales for electronic components at the time. In May 1958 Thompson became manager of Raytheon's new distributor products division.

First came internal expansion. The idea was to scour Raytheon for government products with commercial possibilities. It could be as simple as "civilizing" black box knobs and switches for the computer market—or as complex as using the six-month slack period in depth-finder manufacturing to make civilian band radios. Raytheon's pool of expertise was an advantage. Take those CB radios (10% net, the first year of operation): a 5% warranty fund was never tapped, mostly because Raytheon knew to pay 50¢ more to install military-spec crystals.

Still, internal expansion was risky and would not yield enough anyway. The safest, quickest way to grow was to acquire successful businesses and make them even more successful. This was the start of the funny-money acquisition era, and with a P/E ratio of 18, Geneen was ready. On August 12, 1958, he outlined his strategy to a ten-man acquisition group. One hundred and seventy-five million of their growth should be in bread-and-butter, minimum-risk fields: lamps, transformers, instruments and controls, components. For the other $75 million they could chance higher-return fields like radar and computer work. But all candidates must meet three absolute tests: at least 60% commercial sales, over $3 million annual volume; and a "good probability of expanding sales." Less rigid requirements included 10% net on assets, 4% on sales; 10% share of market—with no more than 40% sales currently to Raytheon, for fear of antitrust; a P/E ratio of no more than 15; market-to-book no more than 2:1. If an American company was being considered, it would need a low labor content as protection from foreign competition. Finally, there should be a "sound economic reason for becoming part of Raytheon," meaning demonstrable economies because of the association. Any candidate, though, with over 12% return on assets or "unusual strength and continuity in management" would qualify; those reasons were sound enough.

The group brainstormed likely product areas to enter and suggested specific companies they might acquire in each. Sometimes enthusiasm carried them away: North Electric, GE, and Motorola were proposed; but this was early in the go-go years, and minnows still merged with whales only one way. Electronic speed controls was a $100-million-a-year business, someone pointed out, and Raytheon was not in it. And how about resistance welding? They might acquire Weltronics, Robitron, Sciaki. Wire and cable presented tempting targets: Okanite, Simplex, Rome; Belden was a pretty big mouthful, but worth investigating. For relays they might look at Allen Bradley, Square D., C. P. Clare, and others; Signal was crossed off the list when it transpired that they were having problems. Electric components? The group rated chances of acquiring Cannon a minus, and the same for Clorostat, but Amphenol got two plusses; P. R. Mallory, Sangamo, Ward Leonard, and others were also possible.

Fed up with Norm Krim's windy excuses for his divisions' continuing dishevelment, Geneen had taken him off the line entirely. Now, helped by R. V. Peirce, Krim was assigned to track acquisition candidates. The group distilled eleven points for examination beyond the absolute criteria. They included such ratios as sales per employee and per dollar of capital investment; also labor relations, foreign competition, and possibilities of foreign distribution. Eventually, Krim would look at some 500 companies.

Leads swarmed in from everywhere. "Geneen might decide to pursue an acquisition in conversation with anyone," says a colleague. Even at ITT, with its elaborate search mechanism, Geneen's acquisitions often started as a casual talk with someone he met one Sunday on the Cape. In fact, some of his earliest ITT acquisitions began with such informal leads at Raytheon. One Raytheon employee belonged to an oddball golf club owned by a company called Surprenant. He mentioned it to Krim, who passed the word on; Surprenant was Geneen's second ITT buy. General Controls, another ITT acquisition, became a prospect at Raytheon when touted by Gerry Tsai. Cannon and Consolidated Lamp were two more ITT acquisitions first vetted at Raytheon.

The acquisition group met about every two weeks—at night, of course. The October 28, 1958, meeting was typical. It started at 6:00 P.M. Geneen hammered on the need for action; he wanted to approach ten to fifteen companies by the end of the year. The group evaluated the do-it-yourself field. Two companies were added to the look-into list: General Railway Signal and Eastern Industries, although Eastern might be too deeply into hydraulic pumps, totally outside Raytheon's competence. Then the group surveyed the list of interesting industrial classifications. They weighed the merits of various candidates, and Geneen told specific members to dig deeper into some. When Machlett Laboratories was mentioned, Geneen said he would follow through. This was a hot one.

Voltage regulators: Geneen observed that Superior Electric's return on net worth was high, around 21%. Dave Margolis should investigate its ownership and financial status.

Magnetic tape: Al di Scipio said that a Japanese company sought an American marketer. Trouble was, tape was so simple to make, anyone could get into the business. They decided to ignore struggling little Sony.

Relays: a splendid business. But Geneen said $8 million was too much above book to pay for Allied Control. And C. P. Clare's parent, Universal Products, was in race track totalizators, a connection that could be troublesome, especially since there had been some antitrust problems.

Thermostats: about 80% commercial, therefore a prime target. Geneen assigned a group member to uncover the reason for Fenwal's low return. Meanwhile, Norm Krim would talk to Fenwal's principals.

Motor controls: scrutinize Allen Bradley, Geneen ordered; and see if poor management accounted for Ward Leonard's low profits. And check Clark Controller.

So it went. They would stay out of magnetic tape equipment because Ampex cost too much to buy, and its formidable market share made happy competition against it implausible. Aircraft radio: Geneen was intrigued. Before the next meeting, Krim and another member must list all prospects in the field by product category, with details on ownership and sales; they must also make up a priority list for discussion and further study.

The meeting adjourned at 11:30. Just another Raytheon workday under Harold Geneen.

Yet for all the exertion, Geneen's only acquisitions at Raytheon were Applied Electronics Company, Inc.—APELCO—a small maker of marine radios acquired January 1, 1959, and Machlett Labs, acquired in May, just before he left. In addition, Sorenson & Co., was acquired the following July.

Why this tiny dividend for so much exertion? For one thing, mergers take time and unremitting application. Both ran out when Geneen left, as did the favorable P/E multiple. But there is another answer. One person you might expect to be involved in acquisitions is the company's president and CEO. Charlie Adams was never there. No corporate step is so momentous as a merger. Without the energetic press of the chief executive, the suit will not seem entirely serious to the company being wooed, or to the suitor's own directors. Geneen had been on the board since December 1956, but it was still Adams's Brahmin board. A board's nature and duty is to urge caution. They need prodding from the president, and this president was no prodder.

But why was Adams still president and CEO? Why not Geneen? Because this was the only thing Adams would not surrender. No one doubted that Geneen ran the company. "He collected most everything under himself," says Adams, "but I was relaxed about that. I was not one of those people scared to death that somebody was going to steal my prerogatives." Adams could say *"Stop that!"* and make it stick—while he was in the room. Indeed the only presidential prerogative Adams appeared to treasure was being president, having (however seldom he used it) the final say. For Geneen, that was the ultimate provocation. He had turned the company around. He wanted to run it without anyone's leave or even threat of veto. He wanted to be president.

Many of Geneen's former Raytheon coterie are sure that he was promised the presidency, and that Adams reneged. They do not understand Adams. Bill Welsh does. Although a convinced Geneen fan, Welsh says, "I cannot believe that Charles Francis Adams would go back on his word." Even those who are certain they *heard* the promise made only thought they did. "If Charlie Adams promised to walk down State Street in one white shoe and one brown, he'd do it," says Welsh. "Immediately after, he might shoot himself; but if he promised, he'd do it."

Adams flatly denies the presidency was ever promised, or even discussed specifically. Certainly Geneen had expectations, if only the implicit "Someday all this will be yours" kind. But Adams liked being president of Raytheon too much to give it up—the more so since Geneen had made the company so formidable. Geneen could wait.

Geneen, of course, would not wait. His résumé had been floating around for some time, and the break came when Boyden Associates, the head-hunting firm that had done so much recruiting for Raytheon, recruited Geneen. He disappeared for a week in the spring of 1959. On his return he told Adams that ITT had offered him the presidency. It was the usual story. "I really haven't made up my mind about ITT," he said. "Really—I haven't. I'm intrigued—but I want to be sure." Adams knew ITT somewhat. Raytheon had been courted by ITT's fantastical founder, Sosthenes Behn. Adams warned Geneen to get a foolproof contract, with real authority to run the company. Next time the two men met, Geneen announced that he was taking the offer.

Whatever reservations Geneen had about leaving any company, the decision made, that company could go hang. His manner in leaving Raytheon left a bad taste all around.

A year or so earlier, he had put in train a pilot incentive program, getting division head Nevin Kather to devise a bonus formula for his division's top executives. On inspection, Geneen had felt that the terms of Kather's plan were too tough. "Nevin," he said, "you'll never make a dime on this. But try it, and I'll make sure you all get *some* bonus." When the year's results were in, the division's return on sales had gone from 8% to 18%; return on equity from 12% to 30%: the group of five or six was owed some $300,000. "Oh my God!" said Geneen. "I haven't cleared this with Charlie Adams or anyone. Would you mind taking it over a three-year period?" Of course not; and of course Geneen was pleased at this evidence of the efficacy of incentives. But within a week, his departure was announced. "Practically as he was going out the door," says Kather, "I asked him, Hal, what about the bonus? He says, Take it up with Charlie. Adams says, I didn't know a damn thing about it, but if the company made a commitment, we'll do something. They made a fractional settlement."

Official word of Geneen's departure came on Wednesday, May 20, 1959. That morning rumors flew that Geneen was leaving for some unspecified "very large company," later identified as ITT; but neither company would confirm. By midafternoon it was official. Raytheon was the most heavily traded stock on the New York exchange (137,000 shares), dropping 6½ points. Next day, Raytheon was first again, with 87,000 shares, off another 1¼ points; it closed the week off another ⅜ at 58¼. Volume was 30,100, putting Raytheon in twelfth place. Next week it was off the charts, back to being country bumpkin for quite a while.

Geneen took more than stock value with him. Soon he took some key people. Bill Marx, George Strichman, and Dave Margolis went almost at once; others followed. But it could have been worse. Geneen just missed taking the company's future with him. Thomas Phillips was the star of the missile division and would finally become CEO, bringing stable success to Raytheon. Floundering just after Geneen left, Adams put a newcomer at the head of missiles. The division's top people were outraged. They promised wholesale defection, crippling Raytheon. Adams backtracked. But when he called to tell his stars that all was well, he could not locate Phillips, who was in New York. Geneen was taking him up into an exceeding high mountain and showing him all the kingdoms of the world, and the glory of them. The miracle was that Phillips resisted the recruitment pitch; Geneen was a nonpareil tempter. Had Phillips left, it is questionable whether Raytheon would have prospered.

A year or so afterward, when reporters wanted to talk about Geneen with Raytheon, the company insisted that he was "a closed chapter." Over twenty years later, though, his reforms and controls were still in effect.

6

It Makes You Question

Between 1914, when he started the company, and his death in 1957, Sosthenes Behn built the International Telephone and Telegraph Corporation into a world complex of telephone manufacturing and operating companies with almost $800 million in assets. At times, his baroque style overshadowed all else in an image-minded world. His office was a Louis XIV showpiece that featured a portrait of Pope Pius XI. He had given the pope a solid gold telephone. But behind the flamboyance lay a shrewd man and tough negotiator. Just before the Germans took over, Behn convinced Rumania's rulers to buy ITT's Rumanian operation for $13.8 million. Reasoning that Argentina would never give him a generous rate structure, he cajoled Juan Perón into buying most of ITT's Argentine interests for $93 million. Perón, who had been threatening to nationalize ITT, was beguiled when Behn stressed that only a ruler of Perón's stature could sign so large a check and have it honored. Behn's heart was with Franco during the Spanish civil war. Even so, he saw to it that the Loyalists' Madrid phone system remained in operation throughout the fascist bombardment. As always, he was sustained by the meals of his French chef, a constant companion. When Franco won, Behn sold the whole Spanish phone system to the government for $88 million—and cannily retained a monopoly for supplying phone equipment to the system.

Behn was, in a word, colorful. But by November 1947 he was also vulnerable. ITT's health depended on what parts of its body you looked at. For instance, there had been no dividend to stockholders since 1932, and the stock that had once peaked at $149¼ now hovered around $12. A $10 million loss in 1946 was followed by $3.1 million lost in the first half of 1947. On the other hand, the company had $93 million in cash on hand, and the book value per share of stock had risen from $33.61 in 1940 to $42.23 in 1946. The funded debt, bank loans, and fixed expenses had meanwhile been slashed. There was even talk at ITT of acquisitions: maybe Farnsworth radio, maybe Raytheon.

A cash melon of $93,000,000 is irresistible. Besides, in 1947 Robert M. McKinney happened to be searching for a target of opportunity. McKinney was the cousin of Robert Young, financier, railroad magnate, and sometime partner of Allan P. Kirby, president of the Allegheny Corporation. McKinney and Clendenin J. Ryan, grandson of Thomas Fortune Ryan, tried to force their way onto the ITT board. When Behn repulsed them, they formed a potent group for a proxy fight. The principals were McKinney, Young, Kirby, Charles Edison, former New Jersey governor, Arthur M. Hill, of Greyhound, and George Brown, partner in Brown & Root. Their counsel was former U.S. Senator Burton K. Wheeler.

Ryan, as spokesman, claimed his group represented 600,000 of the company's 6.4 million shareholders. All had gotten short shrift from ITT management. It was infamous, Ryan said, that no dividends were paid and that there had been no distribution of cash from those wartime sales. But no wonder. How could stockholders expect a fair shake when fifteen of twenty-five directors were company officers? Obviously, such a board cared only about inflating their own salaries and fees—$3.7 million in nine years—while the

ITT annual meeting, 1956. Sosthenes Behn at microphone, General Leavey in foreground.

stockholders got nothing. And what about all that travel and high living for Behn?

Behn responded: forget dividends; it was a marvel the company had not gone under, what with war damage to its overseas operations, the cutoff of revenues from Europe during the war, and the postwar devaluation of most currencies against the dollar. As for salaries, Behn got only $59,600, with $40,000 for each executive VP; no one else in the company made over $30,-000.

But Behn's heart was not in it. Rather than risk a proxy fight, he surrendered. Seven of the inside directors were to resign, making room for new directors nominated by Ryan, plus two nominated by Behn—including J. Patrick Lannan, another financier. A half-year later, Behn further agreed to the installation of a president, William Henry Harrison, a career AT&T man. Behn would remain chairman and CEO.

The company also started paying a modest dividend. It rose to $1.80 by 1956, but that was no sign of prosperity. Behn's adventures into domestic consumer products (Capehart-Farnsworth TVs and radios, Coolerator refrigerators) were debacles. In 1954 Behn, who had only 17,000 shares of stock, was stripped of power. The insurgent group set up an executive committee to superintend the company. Actually, they *ran* it—although Harrison became CEO in name. Behn stayed on as courtesy chairman.

In April 1956 Harrison suffered a massive heart attack and died. A week later Edmond H. Leavey was named as the new president. And at the annual meeting in May, after introducing Leavey, Behn announced his retirement.

Leavey—later called a "caretaker president"—was sixty-two when elected. But at that the directors expected more than they got. Unlike "Colonel" Behn and "General" Harrison, whose ranks were wartime commissions, Leavey was a *real* general—West Point, '17. That was the trouble. He had had only two years' business experience, in 1952, when Harrison brought him into ITT's Federal Laboratories. After Leavey succeeded Harrison, directors McKinney and Kirby took him on a get-acquainted cruise. They were appalled to discover that General Leavey had the army notion that a commander should let his staff run things.

The lack of firm direction showed. Although ITT revenue rose each year under Leavey, (1956–59), net income declined in 1957. It rose again in 1958, though not quite up to 1956's still unimpressive $1.96 per share. It was enough, though, to excite impressionable minds on Wall Street. The stock had stayed flat throughout 1956 and 1957 (range, 25¾ to 37¾); in 1958 it jumped from 29¼ to 65⅜. On February 5, 1959, there was a 2-for-1 split.

Good, bad, or (the real case) indifferent, Leavey's record was due to end with his mandatory retirement, at age sixty-five, in July 1959. Who should replace him? In approved army fashion, Leavey had made an executive VP, Charles D. Hilles, Jr., his chief of staff. Hilles was a highly competent corporation lawyer, exceptionally popular and pleasant. But his experience was not in corporate management. Another executive VP, Frederick M. Farwell, was also an evident presidential candidate. In fact, he had been recruited from IBM in June 1957, specifically as a possible successor. His field was marketing, and he became group executive for United States operations, yet he had administrative shortcomings. He did not, for instance, study carefully the terms of a big contract to provide First National City Bank with check-reading equipment; he was too immersed in plans for the new ITT building rising at 320 Park Avenue. The number of flagpoles and the location of bathrooms on the executive twelfth floor seemed his special concern. Robert F. Bender, the third executive VP, finance, was not as effective as hoped either.

Throughout the spring of 1959, impending reorganization was noised around the company, different slates proposed at each water fountain. All assumed inside succession. But the executive committee, composed of outside directors (except for Leavey), had privately rejected all inside candidates. The executive committee's power, however, was not absolute. With an equal number of directors potentially opposed, they had to act quickly and quietly, locating a candidate who wanted the job without any elaborate courtship; they had to present the full board with an accomplished fact.

Hugh Knowlton, a partner at Kuhn Loeb, as well as ITT director, was made head of a search committee. The natural first step was to engage a head-hunting firm. It happened that Boyden Associates was one that several of the committee, including Knowlton, had used before. G. Lawton Johnson normally handled Boyden's senior executive searches, and Hugh Knowlton called Johnson from ITT headquarters at 67 Broad Street. Could he come right down and meet with the executive committee?

Johnson found Knowlton in session with Brown, Kirby, Lannan, McKinney and Richard S. Perkins, a more recent addition to the board from First National City Bank. They sketched the problem and underlined the need for secrecy: he was to mull over prospects but do nothing until he heard from them. A week later Knowlton called. Johnson could go ahead. The search must be confidential; even the people under consideration must have no idea what company was interested in them.

Quite often, in these top-level searches, the company already has a few specific candidates in mind. Had the executive committee identified any possibles? Knowlton said that they had looked at people in the same sort of business and asked Johnson whether there was any chance of getting Geneen. Johnson had reason to think Geneen might be available. About nine months earlier, he had helped Geneen with a senior search for Raytheon. Geneen had said, talking about *really* top jobs, "Someday, when you have one, talk to me about it." That was touchy; Johnson explained that Boyden seldom moved an executive out of a client organization. Well . . . Johnson should at least talk about it.

It was no wonder that Knowlton and the others knew of Geneen and were impressed. Geneen's acquisition program turned on a favorable P/E ratio, and Dave Margolis had been tireless in propagandizing exactly the sort of people on ITT's executive committee. Geneen had always made himself available, highly visible with stock analysts, big investors, and investment bankers. A senior partner at Kuhn Loeb would naturally be alive to news of someone who had boosted the fortunes of a major company. Furthermore, Raytheon had much in common with ITT. "Raytheon was not as big as ITT," says Sidney Boyden, head of the search firm, "but it was not small. Like ITT, it was a multi-plant operation, with overseas subsidiaries, making electronic equipment for the government. Geneen was a financial man with strong operating experience at the policy level. Just what ITT needed."

Johnson managed to arrange a veiled interview by telling Geneen that some friends at Kuhn Loeb were interested in Raytheon and wanted to discuss the company's prospects over lunch the next time Geneen was in New York. He knew an audience like that would be a magnet and that Geneen's "next time" would be immediate.

The lunch at Kuhn Loeb was a triumph. A number of Kuhn Loeb partners were present, plus Knowlton and most of the ITT executive committee, introduced simply as interested investors. "Geneen talked for two and a half hours," says Johnson. "He told them about Raytheon, what he had done, what he would do and wanted to do with the company. Then he fielded all their questions. He was great!" When Johnson got back to his office and called Knowlton to check on the executive committee's reaction, he got a fast answer. Geneen was it.

Geneen had been staying at the old Ambassador Hotel on Park Avenue. By the time Johnson called, he had left for Boston. Next day, Johnson made an appointment with Geneen for dinner at Boston's Ritz Carlton. "When I told him what had been going on," says Johnson, "he said, Why you son of a bitch! Then he thought a moment and said, Lawton, that was pretty smart. How was I?"

Even though the possibility of Geneen's assuming the ITT presidency was now in the open, the board had to look over the candidate's wife without being obvious. Johnson confected another charade: a dinner meeting with board members was laid on for the Ambassador. Concurrently, Johnson's wife issued an invitation to June for dinner and the theater. After the meeting started, Mrs. Johnson called to say that they were on their way to dinner— at which point Johnson "suggested" that she drop up to the suite to say hello to some old friends. Naturally June tagged along. She came, they saw, she conquered.

Director Dick Perkins met with Geneen and Johnson at the Racquet and Tennis Club for the climactic session, at which Geneen would be formally offered the job. "I told him what we expected of him in running the company, which was not in very good shape at that time," says Perkins. "The company didn't go anywhere under Leavey, just staggered along, going sideways. I told him, There's a tremendous opportunity here for you. If you perform, we will recognize you financially and other ways—stock options and so on. If you perform, we'll recognize you; if you don't, we won't. Afterward he told me,

I think you're one of the toughest fellows I ever met. Anyhow, he moved in and he never stopped. He just kept right on going."

They were generous even at first. Geneen's salary from June 10, 1959, the day he started, to the end of the year was $76,830, with a $21,016 cash bonus, plus $8,984 worth of stock. He also received a stock option on 50,000 shares. His first full year's salary would be $138,545, with a bonus, cash and stock, of $50,000.

Of course Geneen was delighted. Yet something rankled. He had done a superlative job at three companies, bringing order to the chaos of Bell & Howell, turning Jones & Laughlin into a rational operation, rescuing Raytheon and making it profitable. Yet it had taken some head hunter to get him in as president of a company to which he was a stranger. "You know," he once told a young colleague, "it makes you question the justice of the entire system, that you can't make it just on hard work and your track record."

7

A Real Dog

When Geneen took over ITT on June 10, 1959, Merrill Lynch's Arch Angelo Catapano commented on the company's prospects. Although ITT faced huge problems, he said, "It has a solid core of earnings to fall back on from its foreign operation. . . . You could do nothing at the top of ITT and still make some money." What's more, Geneen's results at ITT would never be so startling as at Raytheon because ITT was a much better company. "ITT would earn something even if I were running it."

Geneen knew better. "There's a question how long it would have gone on before it cracked wide open," he said in those early days. "If this had gone on for three or five more years, maybe no one could have brought it back." John C. Lobb, who scrutinized the company as executive VP and (briefly) heir apparent, is even blunter. ITT, he says, was "a real dog."

Outsiders were easily fooled. In June 1959 ITT had 116 plants in 23 countries and still operated telephone systems in four Latin American countries, plus Puerto Rico and the Virgin Islands. In Europe the company manufactured mostly telephone equipment, with some odd lots of commercial products thrown in. For instance, ITT's Belgian company had become a major force in refrigeration; the Norwegian subsidiary made home freezers; the German company was big in TV sets and radios; the British company pioneered computer time-sharing service bureaus. In the United States, besides some telephone equipment manufacturing, ITT was mostly in defense work, with several lucrative contracts, including one to build a worldwide communications system for the Strategic Air Command. At the end of 1959, before Geneen's influence was really felt, ITT's volume was $765,639,896, up from 1958's $687,451,445; net was $29,035,688, up from $26,600,168. The profit margin for 1959 was 3.8%, earnings per share 95¢.

None of this was planned or controlled. The company was not managed; it simply existed. "Behn's concept of management," says Robert E. Chasen, who started with ITT in 1952, "was simply to organize to take advantage of all the tax laws—particularly European laws on dividends—and to get the best legal structure to maximize dividend receipts." No one knew what was happening throughout the company. Inherited subordinates assured Geneen that ITT made money in the United States and lost it overseas. He quickly found that the opposite was true: of 1959's $29 million net, $24 million came from abroad, only $5 million from domestic operations. And all of the United States net was from defense; ITT's domestic commercial operations had lost $6 million.

Such confusion was an ITT staple. Geneen found not a company but a confederation of nearly autonomous units. Every year, as one long-timer puts it, "they delivered a bag of money to New York—*maybe*." New York never knew how much would be in the bag until they opened the drawstrings and they could do nothing about it. Europe ignored the parent company. Geneen discovered that a German subsidiary had engaged a New York consulting firm for marketing advice without even telling headquarters, let alone asking for help. In short, ITT was a holding company.

At any time the thing could come apart. About one-third of ITT's earnings came from Latin America, where its assets were at grave hazard. In Europe the investment was secure against expropriation but was huge compared with a relatively meager return. What's more, there seemed little hope of dramatically increased business in Europe. Makers of telecommunications equipment got a fixed share of government business in their respective countries. In the United States Geneen saw serious problems even with the money-making defense group.

Earnings were unpredictable. "I used to get gray hairs," says a former high ITT executive, "because if the government of Chile refused to give us a rate increase, our earnings were going down no matter what else we did."

Geneen had to have earnings, and he needed more of them in dollars to pay dividends. Well over 90% of his stockholders were American, but 80% of his earnings were in foreign currencies. That meant unfavorable exchange rates in those days of the mighty dollar. Objectively, then, prospects were dim. But in Geneen's first public speech, while still cutting through the thicket of losing operations he blithely predicted "over the next five years at least a doubling in our earnings." And "I.T.T. will, in my opinion, emerge as one of the most important companies of this next decade." He explained that the company had a "very strong earnings base" and "enormous potential over and above its secure earnings base." It was a line his audience of stock analysts would swallow, even though his earnings were anything but strong, anything but secure. The potential, however, was real—*if* such an amorphous agglutination could be pulled together and managed.

Geneen started, as usual, with personnel. "There was a lot of deadwood," said an early favorite. "He cleaned out a lot of people who just weren't up to the job." He fired eight of the seventeen top corporate officers within a year. "Some," says John C. Lobb, "were really screwing the company. I think there was embezzlement and every other goddamn thing going on. Geneen finally didn't trust anybody. He just cleaned house."

The competent Charles Hilles was kept, as were others who could be useful. For example, he replaced John G. Copelin as controller, but made use of his general abilities elsewhere for many years. Others he tried out for a while. M. Richard Mitchell was one. He had been general counsel, and Geneen soon made him a vice president. Mitchell exuded dignity, intelligence, and erudition. He seemed to understand what Geneen wanted from a lawyer, telling a reporter, "Be specific. Give him the substance. Tell him on balance what the merits are. Give him the conclusion without twenty-seven qualifications." But two years later he was gone.

Adaptation to the new regime was the key to survival. Ellery W. Stone was a board member when Geneen arrived, and he looked the part. Geneen valued him as a figurehead, first for the defense group, then in Europe. Henry H. Scudder, based in New York, nominally ran Europe—"with a telegraph pad and a plane schedule," as Geneen once explained. Scudder quickly adapted to Geneen's ways, surrendering any pretentions to proprietorship over Europe. Scudder's deputy, James Basset, operated out of Zurich. He thought that the holding company, International Standard Electric, which technically owned the European subsidiaries, meant something and should continue to mean something. Scudder stayed at ITT for years; Bassett was gone quickly, remarking that he had survived the first three ITT presidents but not the fourth.

Even had Geneen kept everyone, there were not enough executives at ITT for his system. He immediately imported his trustiest associates from Raytheon: Bill Marx and Dave Margolis, plus Andrew C. Hilton and (a little later) Frank J. McCabe, who had been his personnel experts. George Strichman had joined Geneen at Raytheon from GE only a few months earlier and now followed him to ITT. James F. Lillis came from Burroughs as controller. Louis T. Rader came from GE to head the floundering U.S. commercial (USC) group.

Geneen also raided his old standby, McKinsey & Co. His first recruit was Al di Scipio as VP for marketing; then Gerhard R. Andlinger came as director of planning. Soon, di Scipio brought in Martin Dubilier—first as a consultant, then to join the company. A little later, John B. Turbidy, who had been a sometime consultant at Raytheon, signed on.

Geneen's recruiting technique was masterly, if simple. He offered people more than they had dreamed of getting and then hurled the ultimate challenge at them. Lou Rader is a case in point. He was a Ph.D. in electrical engineering from Caltech, an ex-professor (at Illinois Tech) who had made a successful transition to line operator at GE. Geneen had approached Rader for Raytheon. Rader, unenthusiastic, said he would "study" the offer. "That's the way to kill anything with Geneen," says Rader, "because he won't wait while you study anything." A year later, in the fall of 1959, Geneen called and said, "Lou, I want you to *seriously* think about coming to ITT. We've got fantastic opportunities to do everything." When Rader failed to jump at the chance, Geneen started his litany. "Lou, how much money do you make at GE?"

"Forty thousand."

"I'll give you eighty. How much incentive compensation do you get?"

"Depends on profit. It averages maybe fifteen, twenty—"

"I'll guarantee you twenty, minimum. What's your stock option?"

"Three thousand shares."

"I'll give you ten. Do you think you'll ever be on the GE board?"

"Never."

"I'll get you on the ITT board. Now, I can't absolutely *promise* that, but I'm quite sure I can do it. Do you like to go to Europe?"

"Sure."

"How often do you get there with GE?"

"Once every five years."

"I'll see you get there every quarter. They tell me you run one plant quite well."

"Hal, I run one plant very damn well."

"Do you think you could run seventeen plants?"

"I don't know."

"When will GE let you try?"

"Well . . . "

"I'll let you try tomorrow."

That was it: Do you want to be a *manager* or not? Do you dare high deeds or not? Money was never an issue with Geneen. The important thing was getting top-quality people. Geneen knew what he would demand of their time and energies, and he wanted to be sure none of them felt underpaid.

Take the case of Henry E. Bowes. Charles M. Mooney (variously known as "Red". and "Mellonbelly") was a genial underachiever who had somehow sold himself to Geneen. Hired as head of defense sales in Washington, Mooney took over the defense group when Ellery Stone shifted to Europe. Henry Bowes, a marketing specialist at Philco, was needed for defense sales. Mooney escorted Bowes to Geneen's office for the showdown session. "Mooney wanted me," says Bowes, "and Hal was very anxious for me to come. I'd had a pretty big job at Philco. Mooney had come out of the government end of RCA, and I don't think he'd been that big." They asked how much money Bowes wanted, and he told them: a lot. "They oh-ed and ah-ed for a while, then Hal said, That's it." Geneen led Mooney off to a corner of the huge office and after a few moments of earnest conversation came back to clinch the deal. On the way out, Mooney was all grins. "What do you think he was talking to me about over there?" Bowes could not guess. "Well, you make more than I do, and he was raising my salary so he could hire you."

Geneen was equally generous at the other end. "After you let a man go," he once said, "you may pay him enough to lie on beaches in Florida for the rest of his life. That's a different problem." Red Mooney knew that, and when the time came, he played Geneen with virtuosity. Mooney was way over his head, trying to run defense. Often as not he would be on the golf course or in Las Vegas when he should have been working, and it finally caught up with him. Someone had seen him cavorting in Vegas when he had told Geneen he was going to Washington to confer with Henry Bowes. "About a week later," says Bowes, "Mooney came to see me and said, I got caught, but I know how to handle Hal better than anyone in this place. There's a review coming up tomorrow. Watch!" At the meeting, Mooney baited Geneen, arguing, contradicting, ridiculing. "Hal was just sputtering, he was so mad at Mooney," says Bowes. "But after he had blown his stack in public like that, he couldn't just fire him and cut him off. He had to make him a *tremendous* settlement."

Geneen spent much of his first years discovering what his company consisted of and what it needed. There had never been much organization, and what existed was wrong. The ITT Laboratories in Nutley, New Jersey, and ITT Federal in Clifton, New Jersey, for instance, were separate entities. Each maintained duplicate functions, Labs its own production lines, Federal its own labs. Each pursued its own little unprofitable contracts. Between them the two divisions counted seventeen purchasing departments and eighteen quality-control groups. Yet they were really in the same business: one was the R&D arm, the other the manufacturer, for ITT's defense group. The money they made was in joint ventures like TACAN, VORTAC, and radar for the F-105. And despite the different addresses, they were literally across the street from each other. The staffing of each so faithfully duplicated the other's that when Geneen combined the divisions, firing was wholesale.

Even mismanaged, the defense group made money. ITT Communications Systems (ICS), with 175 employees, provided "overall systems planning and engineering services" that led to recommendations to the air force for worldwide communications. The budget was only about $8 million a year; but Geneen made sure that ICS began—"consistent with security regulations"—to let other ITT units know about opportunities for sales. As head of ICS, Geneen appointed retired Air Force Lieutenant General Roy H. Lynn, in December 1959.

The Federal Electric Corporation (FEC) was ITT's field service, maintenance, and operating division for such projects as TACAN, missile test ranges instrumentation, the Washington-Moscow hot line, the DEW line, and the White Alice military communications project in Alaska. Sales were about $70 million. FEC's head was John W. Guilfoyle, the unit's executive VP when Geneen arrived, made president in October 1959.

The combined Labs and Federal division showed the vagaries of defense business; its sales drooped from $135 million in 1959 to less than $120 million in 1960. Its head was I. Nevin Palley, appointed in January 1960.

The final unit, International Electric Corporation (IEC), demonstrated the perils of even profitable defense contracts. In September 1958 IEC had won a contract as system manager of project 465L, SAC's command system. This was the second largest communications system in the world, to be built from scratch—in time a $400-million plum. But Geneen arrived to find SAC unhappy. He immediately appointed a three-man investigating committee: Bill Marx; a senior partner from the company's outside auditor, Arthur Andersen & Co.; and Martin Dubilier, then still at McKinsey. The head of IEC, General Lanahan, was, says Dubilier, "a super guy." He had been Eisenhower's chief signal officer in NATO. Nonetheless, IEC's problem was weak management. Dubilier was recruited as Lanahan's deputy and replaced him in March 1960. Lanahan continued as consultant. The division prospered and became the nucleus for all of ITT's data processing capability, finally spun off as the Data and Information Systems division.

Compared with ITT's U.S. commercial operations, even the bad parts of the defense business looked good. USC's $6 million loss was the more remarkable because what Lou Rader says about one of its units applied to the whole: he did not see how it could be losing so much money on so little business. Rader's successor, John Lobb, observes that USC at first consisted only of "Kellogg and some other junk."

Kellogg Switchboard and Supply Company, in Chicago, dispensed telephone equipment to the undiscriminating few. The rest of the junk included Components, which shared the Clifton plant, even tinier Industrial Products in San Fernando, California, Royal Electric Corporation, in Pawtucket, Rhode Island, maker of wire and cable, and Kellogg Credit Corporation, in New York, which arranged financing for ITT commercial products buyers. Finally, there was Intelex Systems Incorporated, importers of equipment from ITT's European companies for installation in the automated post office in Providence, Rhode Island, and for bank check-handling systems. Intelex had its own subsidiary, Airmatics Systems, devoted to pneumatic tubes.

Geneen's standard fix was to find good people and send them in. George Strichman went to Kellogg. Joseph J. Bokan came from GE: a tough-talking, tough-minded man, Bokan would straighten out components and thrust ITT into semiconductors, which they had helped pioneer in their labs but had never marketed, falling almost irremediably behind. From Chrysler, Geneen recruited Glenn W. Bailey, another hard-driver, to expand ITT's wire and cable business.

At the same time, Geneen cut his inherited losses. There was the scheme to bring German railroad equipment to the yards in Kansas City; the contract was phased out because German and American gauge and meter measurements turned out to be incompatible.

In Chicago, George Strichman uncovered an inventory problem so severe that Geneen immediately required all USC units to estimate reserves they would need for 1961. He set aside twelve million, nine of it earmarked for Kellogg.

The least costly problem was with Airmatics. Their books were a maze of misinformation. Instead of operating at break-even, as reported, they actually had lost some $30,000—impressive only because their volume was so low. George E. Safiol, a young engineer, had organized the move from Behn's old headquarters at 67 Broad Street to a modern tower at 320 Park Avenue in 1961. His efficiency impressed Geneen, who sent him to Airmatics as operations VP; his two-and-a-half-year turn-around was the start of his career as one of ITT's best-regarded plant managers.

Intelex's automated post office in Providence was a larger problem. It was started in Eisenhower's administration. In January 1960, when Postmaster General Arthur Summerfield was told about the $600,000 cost overrun, he exhibited the sort of shocked outrage that often precedes refusal to pay. Geneen agreed to a $100,000 "sum-up job," at ITT's expense, setting right all of Summerfield's complaints. But with John F. Kennedy's election in November, the Democrats were back in. Summerfield had heralded the automated post office, "Operation Turnkey," a paradigm of Republican efficiency. The Democrats called it "Operation Turkey." All its "efficiency" meant was firing some sixty postmasters. Besides, said Summerfield's replacement, J. Edward Day, the damned thing did not work right anyhow. The Democrats refused to pay bills running to $300,000 a month. Rader complained to Day and was told, We're not mad at you, we're mad at the Republicans. Rader gave the story to the *New York Times* and was promptly chewed out at the next ITT board meeting. That was not the way to get things done. Board member George Brown, a Texas Democrat and Vice President Lyndon B. Johnson's early patron, could phone the Kennedy brothers—and be connected. He told Rader to hire a Washington law firm, Steptoe and Johnson, known for its ties to the administration; that and a little talk with a friendly congressman and all would be settled. Geneen beamed. Now *that's* how to get things done.

Intelex's problem with the First National City Bank (FNCB) of New York was less tractable. Within ten days of taking over, Geneen was faced with cancellation of a large contract for an automatic check-sorting and handling system for FNCB. No warning, no phone call, just an abrupt notice of cancellation. Geneen was furious. He demanded a study to prove that ITT's system was at least as good as any competitor's.

It was not. Conveyor belts designed and built by ITT companies in Belgium, France, and Germany carried checks and documents in Mylar folders labeled with machine-readable magnetic tape. ITT's pilot installation at the Valley National Bank in Phoenix had worked well enough; but the system was cumbersome on FNCB's scale. They thought it made their place look like a shoe factory. Besides, Honeywell's new magnetic ink technology had rendered ITT's system obsolete before it started. In April, prior to

Geneen's arrival, FNCB had asked ITT to justify its approach. ITT was still massaging the figures when the bank canceled.

They sent around two VPs who made the tactical error of talking tough to Geneen and talking up the competition. Geneen said of one, "He sounded like he had a Minneapolis-Honeywell record stuck in his throat." There would be a cancellation fee, and Geneen was determined to make it hurt. He renegotiated terms to include all costs incurred since the first of the year. Then he told every unit in ITT that any work, however tangential to the project, should be charged. When ITT and FNCB compared costs, they were about $4 million apart. Instead of going to law, they agreed to appoint an outside accounting firm to adjudicate. Geneen proposed Lybrand, and the bank agreed. The job was supervised by Lou Rappaport, Geneen's old oracle on technical accounting questions. Lybrand people surveyed costs claimed both in Europe and the United States. Thanks to Geneen's renegotiation of the rules for determining those costs, Lybrand handed ITT a triumph. When controller Jim Lillis came in waving the settlement check from the bank, around Christmastime, it was considered Geneen's first big victory.

Two other cutbacks were less triumphant in retrospect. Geneen liquidated ITT's position in L. M. Ericsson, the Swedish telephone giant, and in Nippon Electric Corporation (NEC). Ericsson was first to go. Behn had acquired the stock in the early 1930s, and when Geneen took over, ITT owned 23% of Ericsson's shares, which would normally represent working control but did not in this case. Although Ericsson even then had a reputation for high quality and advanced design, it did ITT no good. "We had directors on Ericsson's board," said Dave Margolis, whom Geneen sent to negotiate with the Swedes, "but they were not allowed to supply any information, even on such things as interim earnings." The Wallenberg family, led by Marcus Wallenberg, chairman of Ericsson, maintained rigid control, and Geneen was continually incensed; he never knew what was going on. Also, he needed the cash. At the time (early spring 1960), Ericsson stock sold at about $10 a share. ITT held 1,083,000 shares, about $11 million worth. Ericsson earned around $1.10 a share, although Geneen felt true earning power was nearer $2. The stock was plainly undervalued. He offered to sell the stock—to the company or the Wallenberg family or whomever in Sweden wanted it. Ericsson said it would gladly buy the block at what Behn had paid for it.

What! Geneen could sell it piecemeal, at market. Maybe, replied Wallenberg, but by law Ericsson stock could be sold only to Swedish nationals, and Geneen might find the market thin in Sweden, where people did not lightly disregard Wallenberg wishes. Geneen replied that he would make a secondary offering, in the United States, to Swedes, and would see how thin the market was out from under the Wallenberg nose. Convinced that Geneen meant it (he was proceeding with the SEC registration statement), the Wallenbergs agreed to negotiate. Dave Margolis returned from Stockholm with more than $20 a share, a total of nearly $22 million.

The story was much the same with Nippon Electric. Behn had bought about 22% of NEC in the early days, plus some 13% of smaller Sumitomo Electric Industries. When the sale was announced (the day before Kennedy's inauguration, January 19, 1961), Geneen said the decision was part of the company's "continuing review of its investment holdings around the world in relation to the company's growing demand for capital in its operating areas," which meant he needed money. But that was only half of it. Geneen was convinced that, like the Swedes, the Japanese were keeping information from him. And, again, he could not hope to control his investment. After the Tokyo riots that forced cancellation of Eisenhower's visit to Japan in 1960, Geneen got mad, resigned from the NEC board, and had Kuhn Loeb sell as much stock as the market would bear. It left ITT with 15%, plus the ill will of the Japanese, who felt a loss of face in not being brought in on the sale. In the next few years Geneen disposed of the rest of his Japanese holdings.

Both investments (especially NEC) would today be fabulously valuable. Even then, both companies were superior to ITT in telephone technology. What's more, unlike Europe, Japan had never departed from U.S. standards. An NEC design can be plugged into any American system, anytime. Later, this fact would haunt.

An exercise of "If only" can still bemuse many former ITT executives. If only Geneen had not sold. If only he had come to some sort of cartel understanding with Ericsson and NEC. The three would now dominate world telecommunications outside the United States. And even here, with the AT&T monopoly pried open, what a position ITT would be in today! If only.

None of this was manifest then. Neither company was disposed to share its technology with ITT; and in those days it would have taken a mystic to foresee the world conditions that made both companies such bonanzas. Besides, Geneen really did need the money.

He carefully husbanded any cash he got his hands on. "He managed cash very well," says Martin Dubilier. "There was a lot of debt at ITT and he wanted to get rid of it. He needed working capital to grow, and he did an extra-super job of managing cash—which wasn't common in industry twenty years ago." Nor were low-level P&L accountability, budgets, and long-range planning—all Geneen's multiple polestars, all intimately tied to cash management. "All ITT's cash was controlled at the corporate level," says Dubilier. "He doled it out as we needed it, and the capital appropriation form was a difficult one: you had to go through a nice rigmarole to get any money to spend."

His concern with long-range planning had started at Raytheon; but that had been such a homogeneous operation, so much of it directly under his eye, planning was less critical. ITT was a mélange. Its geographic diffusion, alone, demanded planning. "He needed a structure," says one aide from that period, "that would let him get his arms around the whole organization and find out what was going on, to influence decisions early in the game, rather when crises arose." That suggested a planning system to embrace both the short and long range for each business unit.

To design and install the planning system, Geneen recruited Gerry Andlinger, still in his twenties, from McKinsey. Born in Austria, Andlinger had won a scholarship to Princeton. He worked his way through in three years, then worked his way to a Harvard M.B.A. Army service during the Korean War made him a United States citizen. He then spent three years at McKinsey. "I always thought he would have made a good replacement for Geneen," says Lou Rader, "if a good replacement is someone with many of the same characteristics." Rader was thinking first of Andlinger's mind—but also of "a heart of steel."

Starting with no format, Andlinger went to two ITT companies—Standard Elektrik Lorenz in Germany and Compagnie Générale de Constructions Téléphoniques in France—lived in the pocket of each managing director and his staff for two weeks each, and devised a planning structure that fit observed operation. He then returned to the companies and with them worked up a planning format, with detailed instructions on how each unit should complete it. First, the unit had to define its business. Was it really in, say, publishing? Or in a broader area of communications, which left room for branching into ownership of TV stations? What were the unit's true managerial dimensions? Next came a thorough explication of the unit's operation: its size and growth rate; key competitors, their strengths and weaknesses; where the company fit in the market picture in its area—not just the raw number ("we're number two, and trying harder") but factors such as the trend of sales growth compared with the competition. Then the unit had to look five years out, establish benchmark goals for each year, and specify concrete steps toward each goal: R&D, new products, cost reduction, new facilities.

It was a never-ending cycle. As the system matured, bells and whistles were added; but the basic format remained. A later addition was the process of "0–1 objectives," an early statement of the company's goals for the coming year. After intensive staff review and revision forced consensus about the 0–1 objectives, the unit would prepare its business plan (an entire volume, says Jules Berke, a later planning director). Next came a preliminary budget, subject to further review. Included were what Berke calls "linking devices" to keep the budget in step with events throughout the planning period. When a final budget was approved by Geneen, it was, says Berke, "locked in concrete, never changed." This was the basis of each month's comparison between forecasts and actual results. By then it was time to start on next year's 0–1s.

"These declarations," says one veteran, "came early enough so Geneen could say, No, I reject that game plan: come up with an alternate—and have it make a difference. The reason it worked is that Geneen paid fantastic attention to each plan—seriously, weeks of his life reading the plans, annotating them, questioning companies for hours to improve their goals." Did a unit project 10% growth? Well, what would they need to grow at 25%? "He was always for more growth," says the same man; "he never cut anyone back. He shot the adrenalin in."

The business plan meetings and the monthly reviews, called general management meetings (GMMs), were central. Eventually they became mob scenes that took place in a special room nearly a block long that featured a table seating ninety-two. At the start, though, GMMs were held in the board room, with sometimes as few as five or six attending Geneen. What never changed was the wealth of fact unstintingly exposed about each unit. "Other chief executives of billion-dollar companies always feel they are automatically right," says an early aide. "Geneen was never like that. He never felt that he had the secret of rightness. He always felt that facts had the secret of rightness, and if you put enough of them together, your odds of coming up with a reasonable decision were pretty good."

The more facts the better—especially in the early days when all was new and strange. Without facts, Geneen easily got carried away by enthusiasm. At the first business plan meeting, he learned that ITT had a components operation in Portugal. He was entranced. He had become enchanted with Portugal on an early swing around ITT's major European facilities. The labor rate was around 19¢ an hour, he discovered, and land was extraordinarily cheap. Even better, as Geneen had toured one fazenda, the peasants had all stopped what they were doing, faced the visitors, doffed their caps, and bowed. Geneen talked about it for months. Now, in the plans meeting, Geneen unbridled his imagination. A components operation in Portugal? Well, it should be easy to move it into parts for telecommunications and, with that low-labor price break, export to Australia and Argentina; they could also move quickly into Germany, letting the Portuguese operation be parts supplier for the high-technology . . .

One man at the meeting started to grin. Geneen was serious; what was so funny?

"Mr. Geneen," he said, "I've been there."

"So?"

"Mr. Geneen, literally—not figuratively, *lit-er-al-ly*—that particular 'operation' is one man and one boy. And you've just conquered the world!"

Facts were everything, guarding him even against gamesmanship of his own people. After one early plans meeting, a line executive was drinking in the bar of the old Marguery Hotel, an ITT watering place, when Geneen came in with some staff. They all got talking, and Geneen asked the line man what he thought of the planning system. It would be wonderful, came the response, if it was always a matter of plans that would really work, not "made just to please or out-guess three-twenty Park." Geneen turned triumphantly to his subordinates. "See!" he said, "That's what I've been telling you guys." With enough facts, there could be no fudging by anyone. Facts would let Geneen comprehend the entire enterprise.

While operations in the U.S.—especially commercial—were by no means satisfactory yet, they were at least headed toward rational organization. And Geneen's attention was urgently required by Europe. Europe provided almost half the company's volume. It was, Geneen said, "the winning horse," and he meant to give it a hard ride.

8

An Uncertain Golconda

"The gold mine was abroad," said Geneen some years later. That described the situation more accurately than "winning horse," because for ITT, Europe's treasure was well hidden. On the surface, the situation looked prosperous enough. There were ITT companies in fifteen European countries, including Turkey and the Common Market, minus Luxembourg. These companies mostly made equipment for the government-owned telephone monopolies called "PTTs" for post, telephone and telegraph.

The nucleus of ITT-Europe was the old Western Electric empire, which Sosthenes Behn had snapped up in the 1920s when AT&T was forced into divestiture. Most of the company names, originally local variants of "Standard Electric," still reflected their provenance: Germany's Standard Elektrik Lorenz (SEL); England's Standard Telephones and Cables (STC); Austria's Standard Telephon und Telegraphen; Finland's Oy Suomen Standard Electric; Turkey's Standard Elektrik ve Telekomunikayson; Spain's and Portugal's Standard Eléctricas.

In 1960 it was thought that increasing European prosperity would surely bring with it a growing demand for phone service. But on inspection there was a severe problem. The government PTTs parceled orders among their in-country suppliers, following an inflexible formula. The Bundespost made sure that SEL got its unchanging share; but Siemens, and AEG-Telefunken got their slices, too. And while the whole market was indeed expanding, it was not doing so at any great rate. Government telephone monopolies were comparatively unresponsive to consumer demand. Their ministerial masters preferred to hold service rates down, which precluded very generous investment in new systems. For ITT-Europe, growth of domestic markets would always disappoint.

As for exports, ITT had captive markets for telephone equipment in Brazil, Chile, Cuba, Peru, Puerto Rico, and the Virgin Islands, plus the inside track in Argentina. In Spain, only ITT could sell equipment to the phone system Franco had bought from Behn. But competition for the rest of the world's business was fierce, not least among ITT's own companies. Geneen was appalled to discover that two of them had just knocked each other out of contention for a juicy contract in Egypt. As far as he could tell, ITT companies only competed, never cooperated, almost never talked to each other, much less shared engineering advances or marketing data. Nor had they any rational pattern of manufacturing. "Places with the lowest labor rates did no work," says someone who surveyed the scene for Geneen. "They imported subassemblies from expensive areas."

There was total lack of coordination. Germany's SEL made the best TV tubes, but England's STC spent lavishly to develop its own, inferior design. The excellent French laboratories needed production help. No one helped them, and they helped no one. At one Latin American group meeting, Geneen heard of troubles with some ITT telephone switching equipment. Later, what sounded like the same problem popped up in Denmark. Sure enough, Geneen found that both problems derived from equipment bought from an ITT company in France. The French had long since worked out the glitch —without bothering to tell anybody.

Geneen decided to try for a quick fix, at least with TV and radio manufacturing, which was inefficiently split among many ITT companies. At Raytheon he had dealt with Wells-Gardner Electronics in Chicago and been impressed by the company and its president, Robert S. Alexander. In late 1959 ITT and Wells-Gardner signed a know-how agreement. Wells-Gardner would standardize TV and radio manufacturing in a pilot program, then allot functions to the appropriate ITT companies. The first step was an inspection tour by Bob Alexander. He found the English receptive and immediately showed them how to save money in TV manufacture. The Germans were another matter. "They were building their sets like the Brooklyn Bridge," says Alexander. For starters, he suggested as a cost reduction that they omit one of three intermediate frequency stages. All TV sets had once been built with three IFs, but newer technology had rendered one superfluous. "Their attitude," says Alexander, "was, That's alright for the British and Americans, but the German people *demand* three!" The pilot program, Alexander reported back, was not going to work. Geneen had contemplated buying Wells-Gardner. Instead, he settled for inducing Alexander to join him at ITT.

If European managers were not ready for quick fixes, neither were they ready for cooperative export efforts. "They never thought beyond the boundaries of their countries," says Martin Dubilier, who had to wrestle with the problem. And without their willingness, nothing was possible. General

managers of the principal ITT companies were figures of national consequence; they might work for Geneen, but he could not just order them about.
They were too powerful, too entrenched.

Hermann Abtmeyer, for instance, had started with ITT it 1928 and had
directed Hitler's telecommunications while still in his twenties. He chaired
the Central Association of Electrotechnical Industry and was holder of the
Grand Cross. His company, SEL, resulted from a complex merger of seven
companies, the last in 1958 with the joining of Standard Elektrik and C.
Lorenz. "Abtmeyer," says someone who dealt with him, "held that company
together." And if he did not choose to cooperate? "Geneen's only recourse
with a guy like that," says Martin Dubilier, "was to fire him. But he couldn't
fire him because he had no one else available who could run that company."

It was the same with Spain's Manuel Márquez Mira. A thirty-one-year
veteran of Standard Eléctrica (SESA), Márquez was president of Spain's
Association of Telecommunications Engineers. He had also served in Spain's
parliament. Most important, his best friend was José Maria Clará Orellana,
head of the Spanish phone company. Push this man and who knew what
could happen.

In a showdown, any of the European managers had his country on his
side. "At any time," says one of Geneen's key aides in Europe, "that government could say, You will not send another dime to New York. Call it expropriation, call it anything you want; that was Geneen's problem. The European countries were back on their feet, and they felt their strength."
Expropriation was probably only a bugaboo, but who knew? At the least a
PTT could withhold enough business to erase profits if Geneen trifled with
their friend, and countryman, the general manager.

Yet Geneen had to make changes. The old system was not working, not
even for the separate companies; each had too much competition in its own
country. Without cooperation, none could flourish, because the most promising lines of business were international in character. Semiconductors are not
Belgian or Spanish; English wire is not distinct from German wire; there is
nothing Norwegian about a freezer; and as the American electronics industry
would soon learn, even TV and radio set buyers are not chauvinists.

Geneen saw all this well before the rest of the world, and a McKinsey
study confirmed his vision. ITT should be organized by areas: Europe, Latin
America, the Far East, North America, with a headquarters to coordinate
activity in each area. Establishing that authority was at once most essential and
most difficult in Europe. At first the Europeans did not take Geneen seriously.
They had seen Sosthenes Behn as one of themselves; but Geneen was an
American professional manager, and they disdained the breed's interchange-
able mobility. Today's XYZ Company president would be tomorrow's ZYX
Company chairman. They looked at their own one-company careers and
concluded that no ITT chief was permanent. Geneen was just this year's
General Harrison, the new model of General Leavey. "When Harold Geneen
was appointed," says Al di Scipio, "I believe their attitude was, This too shall

pass." They had refined a minuet for these visiting New York interlopers: first a hearty welcome, then a factory tour, a lavish and alcoholic dinner—and pour them on the plane. Every American suggestion met with immediate European agreement. During next year's tour, if the same suggestion arose, Oh yes, to be sure, they would get to it presently. "The first and second time around for Hal and Bill Marx and me," says di Scipio, "we got exactly that kind of royal treatment. They totally underestimated Geneen."

They were quickly disabused. First, Marx and di Scipio scouted around for a headquarters site. "We picked Brussels," Geneen explained, "because it's a good workaday town, easy to get into and out of, and it's neutral—wouldn't be offensive to others as France or Germany might." The first office was nondescript, up one flight of stairs, a dozen or so staff. And ITT-Europe's first president was equally unobtrusive, another general, Kenneth Fields. He did not have to shine; Geneen intended to run things himself.

Geneen's instrument of control was the European Advisory Council, the EAC, which consisted of Geneen, key New York staff, and Brussels staff. Each month, except August and December, EAC meetings brought together top people from all the European companies. That had never happened before. "It was a big revolution for the Europeans," says someone who attended regularly. "Here they were in one room, ex-RAF pilots and ex-Luftwaffe, French infantry colonels with German tank commanders. It was a shock." Geneen insisted that all Brussels meetings be in English. And they ran on New York time because ITT had discovered jet lag before the jet set. After the first few sessions, which had started early, following sleepless nights for the New Yorkers, Geneen ordained that no meetings would start before noon. And just as he encouraged his top people to call him "Hal," he insisted that the Europeans use each other's first names. "During the meetings," says one observer, "it was, Oh Pierre, Oh Fritz, Oh Miguel. Then once out the door it was back to Monsieur this and Herr that and Señor the-other-thing."

All that enforced homogenization was the least of it. The real shock came when Geneen confronted the Europeans with American managerial attitudes. "Their accounting was terrible," says John Lobb, "their reporting was terrible; nobody knew what was going on." They would proudly trot out their records of profitability (which left Geneen unawed, anyhow). Then Geneen would dig for what they knew about their enterprises. "Once they got past their easy operations," says Paul Vornle, then on Brussels staff, "they fell apart; they didn't know their ass from Adam." "I'm not asking you for any information that you should not already be getting regularly," Geneen told one discomfited managing director. He showed what he meant by incessantly probing every subject. Jean Bourgeois headed the telephone switching equipment operation at ITT's Belgian subsidiary, Bell Telephone Manufacturing (BTM) in Antwerp. "At dinner," Bourgeois remembered, "he asked me why we had lost a contract in Australia. It got so detailed I was drawing schematic diagrams all over the tablecloth to explain it. I'd never seen an ITT president interested in the characteristics of a switching system. He just kept on asking questions."

Geneen also demanded in Brussels the same openness about results as was expected in New York. "At last," says an ex-New York staffer, "they had to talk with each other, discuss their business plans and what the other guys were doing, and look on the board and see how the other guys had done. It was all up there for everyone to see every month."

There were stresses and dislocation. Geneen's managerial outlook was far advanced for America; in Europe, management remained feudally paternalistic. Geneen slowly ignited every time he discovered another European manager in a slump period happily "building for inventory" goods he could not hope to sell. Geneen would hector him to lay people off, close plants, behave rationally. He never quite won that battle.

Still, it now dawned on the Europeans that Geneen was serious. He was spending about 25% of his time in Europe, and so was much of his staff. "Those first two years," says Al di Scipio, "I spent more days in Europe than I did in the United States, though I was never assigned to Europe." Another staff member, in his first five years with ITT, crossed the Atlantic 125 times. Plainly, Geneen was there to stay, and so was the authority of Brussels headquarters and the EAC.

But area organization was no cure-all. "Geneen would come from a Latin America meeting," says James A. Yunker, then based in Europe, "and he'd say, Ted Westfall tells me he can't sell your equipment because your prices are too high. The European managers would say, Ah! but did Brother Westfall tell you this and that and three other things. Then Geneen would go back to Westfall and say, Those fellows say so-and-so; and Westfall would say, Oh-ho! but they didn't tell you . . . Well, it didn't take Geneen long to figure out that he needed some integrating mechanism."

His solution was to create a corps of product-line managers, PLMs. Based in New York, their writ would run worldwide. The concept was brilliant in several ways. Department heads in any organization are quite properly advocates for their peculiar biases: a manufacturing man mistrusts new products; an engineer aches to pursue each design to perfection; marketing wants to get going; finance demands a balance between sales and development costs. The divergent agendas meet in the general manager. But from ITT's worldwide perspective, even country managers were parochial about their products and operations. SEL forges ahead with portable radios. But what will that do to FACE's sales in Italy? BTM understands refrigeration. Should ITT be in home refrigerators? If so, how big is the market? In what countries? No one country manager could tell, certainly not make impartial judgments. A PLM could.

The PLMs' existence yielded Geneen a bonus. PLMs had no P&L responsibility and could not issue orders to the line. Nevertheless, they were empowered to go anywhere, look at anything, speak to anyone, compel answers. And they relayed their unenforceable decisions to Geneen. The most mulish manager would hesitate to flout the PLM's opinion. If things went wrong, the PLM was sure to say, I told them what to do, but they wouldn't listen—or, They didn't do it the *way* I suggested. The only sensible course, in dispute, was to surface all issues and surrender control of the decision process to Geneen.

It goes without saying that line operators resented the PLMs' authority-without-responsibility. PLMs could contrive to appear blameless anytime a unit missed its budget—which, when it happened, saw line people chopped, not PLMs. In Europe, though, line operators had less to fear. "Right from the beginning," says an aide, "Geneen handled those European managers with incredible finesse and softness and guile and skill. I was agape that he could be such a different human being over there from what he was in New York." At first, he would back his European managers in any dispute. After he gained the Europeans' confidence and respect, he shifted. Still behind the managers on telecom issues, he gradually sided with PLMs when it came to commercial and consumer products, where national considerations did not intrude. Soon, a PLM with taste for such sport could bully even a lordly country manager over some dereliction or lack of candor.

Geneen's complaisance never extended to those he found plainly unsuitable, however highly placed. Business in Britain, for instance, was a mess: the tube operation took a $1.1 million bath; a huge switching project called STRAD was written off for $2.38 million. Geneen replaced the British managing directors wholesale yet never found one to his liking in the early years. Since 1950 the managing director of France's Le Matériel Télé-phonique (LMT) had been Guy Rabuteau. With ITT for thirty-one years, officer of the Legion of Honor, he wanted to do things his way. In late 1960, after a long meeting, Geneen clapped his hands and said, "Well, Guy, we had a *good* meeting today. We're making a lot of progress." "Yes, Hal," Rabuteau replied, "because you are prepared to hear things you were not a year ago." He did not last much longer. Neither did Corneille Van Rooy, in Belgium. But observers marveled at how gently Geneen disposed of unsuitable Europeans. And a greater wonder was how few he had to discard. As one admirer says, "His greatest achievement was retraining the European managers—*without* replacing most of them—to accept and follow American concepts of management, competition, and control."

However gently disposed toward the Europeans, Geneen remained iron wherever ITT's central interests were at risk. For instance, he would go to the mat over computers. Before Geneen arrived, SEL and LMT had jointly contracted to construct a computerized reservation system for Air France. It is ironic that this should be the one instance of interunit cooperation, because it was a project of breathtaking naïveté. SEL and LMT just did not know what they were doing. The mainframe would be built in Germany and software developed in France. The price tag was $2.5 million. Not much later, when IBM developed the first workable system of that sort for American Airlines, each company contributed about $30 million for development. "It shows," says someone who was close to the ITT project, "the state of ignorance about what was needed—and the state of vanity about capabilities in those companies." It also speaks volumes about the genesis of cost overruns.

In early 1960, ITT could still brag about this new venture. But it was soon an unmistakable disaster. SEL and LMT could not deliver, perhaps at any price, surely not for $2.5 million. By fall of 1961, Geneen glumly allowed that ITT must stay in the business "at least officially" because they had two contracts "and have told the world of our competence." Penalty clauses had already amounted to $1.8 million, down-time penalties to another million. And that was just for phase one. Geneen warned a management meeting in Brussels that phases two, three, and four could cost more millions, plus damages. "We overmatched our ability in terms of our capabilities," he said.

It took a court fight to liquidate the contracts, and by then Geneen was no longer worried about saving face. Far from staying in the business, even nominally, he extirpated the division, 1,000 strong. And still he was not through. "He set up a whole group in Paris," recalls Tim Dunleavy, "whose sole job was to keep us out of computers." If this seems an extreme move, it was also a necessary one. The Europeans, particularly the French and Germans, were persistent computer bootleggers, ever trying to edge into the business. They did not do so out of sheer contrariness. E. Maurice Deloraine, ITT's luminous director of research in Europe, insisted to Geneen that electronic telephone switching, patently the wave of the future, would willy-nilly immerse ITT in computers; an electronic switching system *was* a computer. Geneen knew that, and he had no objection to ITT's using computers they bought or even to ITT's developing computers strictly for use in ITT switching systems. But there would be *no* mainframe projects for the market. If Honeywell and Raytheon could not compete with IBM, he would not let ITT try. One licking was enough. His ukase was so strong that when BTM sold an early electronic switching system to a Norwegian phone company, the descriptive brochure nowhere used the word "computer," though that was the guts of it.

Another Geneen non-negotiable fiat was a standard ITT phone system in Europe. Until World War I, all countries shared a single design. Then, for security reasons, the Germans changed their system, and to retaliate, most of the other countries adopted their own. To compound this chaos, different generations of technology were in concurrent use. Oldest was the step by step, introduced in 1889. Then ITT introduced an improvement, the Rotary, widely used for many years, but plainly obsolescent even before World War II. Electronic switching was the undoubted future; but a more efficient interim system was needed. It was Maurice Deloraine's responsibility, and after the war he encouraged both Bell of Antwerp and Paris's CGCT to come up with something.

Meanwhile, in America, Western Electric had introduced a new technique, crossbar switching, and their #5 was a success. So was L. M. Ericsson's version of the crossbar. CGCT developed an appropriately scaled-down version of the #5 called the Pentaconta. At a 1957 meeting in Antwerp, chaired by Deloraine, the decision was to go with the Pentaconta rather than the Antwerp design. That took care of France and Belgium. But although General Leavey, the caretaker president, was at the meeting and assented, the rest of ITT-Europe continued to go their own way.

When Geneen came along he was predictably all for standardization. He could not see why the system pronounced best by the company's weightiest scientist should not be *it* for everyone. But he was faced with a virulent outbreak of the not-invented-here syndrome. The various country managers protested that their PTTs would not accept a "foreign" design; it meant ruinously extensive retooling; the timing was bad; and on and on. As one observer puts it, "all hell broke loose for about a year." Finally, Geneen gathered all the players at a lengthy roundtable in 1960 and thrashed the whole thing out. Then he laid down the law, making Deloraine's 1957 decision writ for all of ITT-Europe. Or nearly so. "We have a marriage contract with Siemens and the Deutsche Bundespost," said Hermann Abtmeyer. "We can't change our switching system." The same was true for England.

Those holdouts aside, the move was a famous success. Geneen convinced six countries to standardize with Pentaconta: France, Belgium, Switzerland, Norway, Spain, and Portugal. Equally impressive, he convinced them that investment in expanded phone service would generate greater revenue; it was not just another no-return appropriation. Getting politicians to pony up more money is a hard sell, and investment never matched demand, but Geneen was a compelling salesman, and his efforts materially increased business for the Europeans.

More business legitimately requires a bigger staff. This particular growth, though, was exponential. "Some of the managers decided, Geneen wants numbers? Boy! Are we going to give him numbers!" says former staffer Paul Vornle. "In the second year—'sixty-one, 'sixty-two—we would have plans from each country. Volumes! There were armies producing projections, numbers, et cetera, and that created armies in Brussels who had to review the numbers and interpret them. The tab in Brussels alone ran between ten and twenty million a year." Geneen soon concluded that General Fields was inadequate to head such a yeasty operation. The signs were as usual. Toward the end of 1960 Fields confided to another executive that everything he said to Geneen "seemed to infuriate him." Geneen had a replacement in mind.

Marc A. de Ferranti had been a light of General Electric's international group for years. Unfortunately he had also been implicated in the GE price-fixing scandal of 1960. While his admirers maintain it was a bum rap, the judge thought otherwise. Now de Ferranti was available. He seemed perfect for ITT-Europe. His family was English, making him more acceptable to Europeans than a bluff American. Early in 1961, de Ferranti replaced Fields and was an immediate hit with everyone whose opinion did not ultimately count. His Brussels staff, his colleagues in the United States, the European managers—all were crazy about him. "His greatest contribution," says one of his staff, "was getting the Europeans to accept the *idea* of Brussels."

Geneen was unenchanted. Lou Rader, a friend from GE days, tried to impress de Ferranti with the differences between GE and ITT, the absence of autonomy. He tried to tell him about Geneen, but de Ferranti either did not listen or did not believe.

"Marc," said Geneen, talking about Europe, "you've got a real bucket of worms here."

"Yes I do, Hal. And you know something, every time I reach down in it to do something about it, I find there's another hand in there."

"Oh? Whose?"

"Yours."

When de Ferranti retailed that conversation, Rader was aghast. "You just don't talk that way to a man like Geneen."

Company rumor had it that Geneen was miffed at de Ferranti's mad popularity with the Europeans, suspecting it might undercut his own authority. Whatever the case, de Ferranti was a good deal too independent. He had been on the job about six months and was just moving into a house in Brussels. The move unluckily coincided with a sudden Geneen trip to Europe. On the phone, Geneen had mentioned that he would be landing in London on the weekend and was anxious to talk with de Ferranti—who explained about the household move but offered to meet Geneen's plane anyway. "Oh, no," said Geneen, "don't bother."

"He should have met him," observes Lou Rader, if only as a sign of deference. But he did not, and when Geneen tried to phone de Ferranti after landing, there was no answer. The phone was removed from the old home, not yet installed in the new, and for some reason no one could locate the president of ITT-Europe. The weekend passed while Geneen fumed.

That was *it*! When he returned to New York, Geneen dispatched Bill Marx to Brussels for a showdown on how Europe was to be run and who, finally, was running it. Marx laid out the case: the boss wants things done *this* way. "Well, Bill," de Ferranti said, "we were more decentralized at GE; we did things our own way. But now that I clearly understand what you're saying, yes, I'll do it his way."

It was too late. When Marx phoned Geneen with news of the concordat, Geneen interrupted. He had been thinking things over and had decided that the relationship would never work out. De Ferranti would have to go. Marx should tell him so, there and then.

"But Hal, he *said* he'd run the business your way. He understands what you want, and —"

"Goddamnit Bill! Listen to me. I want you to *fire* him. See?"

Marx hated this part of his job, and when he went to de Ferranti he was all sympathy, telling him, "I don't agree with this. It doesn't make sense. I know you said you'd follow procedures." That was a mistake. Today, Marx says that de Ferranti tended to be overemotional. The man flared. "OK, I know what to do," he said. "I'm going to sue ITT based on what you just told me." It took considerable persuasion for Marx to convince de Ferranti that suing ITT would be futile, that Geneen was entitled to choose his lieutenants and to change his mind. "What a business," says Lou Rader, to whom both de Ferranti and Marx told the story. "What a business!" An upshot was the ITT personnel department's de Ferranti Rule: no one would be hired into a senior position without spending at least a year on New York staff to see if he got along with Geneen. Geneen, too, had learned a lesson. His next choice as president of ITT-Europe was Ellery Stone, who did not insist on running things. Indeed, he was content to let his deputy do much of the work.

Through it all, Europe was growing ever stronger. Volume and earnings increased with improved control and outreach. And Geneen kept pushing for greater cooperation. He was moving toward a true multi-national organization—with rational manufacturing and distribution. A decade before the auto industry conceived of brakes being made wherever they could be made best and cheapest, chassis in another place, and engines in a third, with assembly near the market, Geneen was heading ITT toward that structure. And he, unhesitatingly backed any European manager who would reach across borders.

Hermann Abtmeyer was the prime example. Many managers resented him for his power and his push, and maybe just for being German. But he was Geneen's early favorite: "Hermann could do no wrong," says Tim Dunleavy; and it was because he thought internationally. In 1961 he volunteered to open a factory in Spain to feed cheap-labor PABX components to his own high-technology operation in Stuttgart. Abtmeyer was thinking about 60,000 square feet; before Geneen was done, it was up to 150,000. No one except Geneen and Abtmeyer favored the scheme. Unlike most, which required exhaustive documentation, this one was approved on the strength of a letter from Abtmeyer naked of investment figures or projected return. That was all right; it had vision and daring.

The Spanish manager of SESA, Manuel Márquez, was vivid in his objections. This would destroy his prestige, cripple his posture with the government. He would have nothing to do with it. In fact, the deal was set up with a new creation, Compañía Internacional de Telecommunicación y Electrónica, SA (CITESA). So touchy was the situation that Geneen labeled the final approval session an "export meeting" so that Márquez would not bother to attend.

In the face of such hostility from the most powerful manager in the country, the project predictably foundered. Geneen then talked Márquez into taking over the facility, making telephone handsets for export, and CITESA boomed. The idea was very sound.

Later, Abtmeyer fell from grace and was discarded. But early in the game he said, "I am one hundred percent for Geneen because in him we have finally found a man who can make decisions. He will transform our operation into one entity rather than a group of companies fighting one another. We have finally become active."

9

Plans for Christmas

To a casual observer, the real goldmine would have seemed to be not Europe but Latin America. When Geneen took over, ITT's Latin American companies yielded one-third of the corporation's profits on only about 10% of its worldwide investment. Some of the units enjoyed near monopolies: 92% of Chile's telephones were run by ITT, 75% of Peru's, 56% of all cable operations throughout Latin America. In 1962 the Chilean phone company's earnings represented 12% of ITT's whole profit. And there was an encouraging backlog of orders. In 1959, with 594,405 ITT phones operating in Latin America, orders were on hand for another 301,074. Even some diversification was under way, with plants in Brazil, Chile, and Argentina branching into such consumer items as office furniture, radios, and phonographs.

But this rosy picture was only an illusion. On his first swing around Latin America in January and February of 1960, Geneen was appalled. Too many of the local managers were practically beachcombers, "Harvard types who couldn't get a job in the States," says Klaus G. Scheye, a PLM who came from W. R. Grace with strong Latin American experience. "They went to Latin America before the war and were indispensable—because they hadn't trained anybody." Not that they had much to teach. "Their organization, accounting, and reporting were totally Victorian."

The telephone rate structures were shaky, too. Despite galloping inflation, governments that resented Yankee ownership anyway were disinclined to grant increases—a serious matter, since Latin American earnings bulked so large in the ITT corporate total.

What was worse, this dismal picture assumed a continued *favorable* political climate, and Geneen soon learned that life for ITT in Latin America would not be beautiful. In March 1959, three months after chasing Fulgencio Batista out of Cuba, Fidel Castro had appointed an "interventor" for various American-owned companies. Targeted were an electric company, several oil companies, thirty-six sugar mills, and the Cuban Telephone Company, owned 65% by ITT, which valued its share at $100 million. Under the intervention, ITT retained ownership but had no say in management.

On August 7, 1960, after Geneen was on board, Castro finished the job. In response to Eisenhower's "economic aggression" (a 700,000-ton reduction in Cuba's sugar quota), Castro expropriated the American companies. He might pay, he said, with fifty-year 2% bonds financed by future sugar profits. He did not, for the time being, touch other American companies in Cuba— First National City Bank and Chase Manhattan, the U.S. Rubber, Goodyear, and Goodrich plants, Coca-Cola, and others, including ITT's two international communications operations.

Only the details and lack of compensation were new. Otherwise, it was the same lesson Sosthenes Behn had learned in Spain and Argentina. Countries do not want their utilities run and owned by foreigners. Geneen realized that. He started negotiations with the governments of Brazil, Chile, and Peru, talking eventual buy-out of ITT's phone companies.

Meanwhile, something had to be done about Latin American operations in general. The corollary of Geneen's "managers must *manage*" is that troublesome situations, above all, need good managers. For Latin America, Geneen found his first manager at W. R. Grace, where any executive had to know the area. Ted B. Westfall was forty-one years old when Geneen hired him. Born in Oklahoma, he graduated from the University of Oklahoma with a B.S. in business administration and joined Price, Waterhouse in Houston. After navy service from 1944 to 1946, he went with the government's General Accounting Office. While working up to director of audits he earned a law degree from George Washington University. In 1952 he joined Grace. A year later he was treasurer, in 1956 executive VP. A head hunter spotted him for Geneen at the right time. The appointment of a new chief at Grace Lines only a few years older than Westfall convinced him that his string there had run out. He started with ITT in October 1960. "According to associates," wrote a *New York Times* reporter, "he not only looks like a fullback but knows how to handle the ball. . . . Mr. Westfall's proclivity for tenaciousness is not belied by his appearance—he is a bull-necked, 5 foot 9 inch clear-eyed 170-pounder."

Westfall toured his new territory for the first time in March and April of 1961, accompanied by Geneen. He found more assets at risk than he thought justifiable, given inflation and the political instability. The problem was compounded by Geneen's runaway enthusiasm. For instance, Geneen saw an opportunity in Brazil to manufacture refrigerator motors—not a bad idea, itself, but a further exposure of assets in a volatile environment. Westfall was determined to consolidate and cut back, while Geneen was determined to forge ahead. Nevertheless, Westfall operated in ways that deeply pleased Geneen.

His handling of P&L statements was typical. The P&Ls that ITT's Latin American managers sent to New York were stereotyped and determinedly cheery. Bad news traveled slowly and always arrived too late for intervention. When Westfall visited Argentina in August 1961, his review showed that inventory and receivables for TV sets had rocketed. The fullback hit the line, and many evasions later, the managers admitted to a fatal quality problem. They had high inventory because no one wanted their sets, and those poor wretches already stuck with shipments were uneager to pay for the trash. Why hadn't they halted production until the quality problem was licked? They were waiting for Westfall's arrival so the new boss could make so weighty a decision.

The system changed on the spot. Every Friday, each Latin American manager was to send New York a telex, called a "red-flag report," detailing everything wrong with his operation. Momentous defects would not wait for the next Friday; they demanded immediate red-flagging. Good news could follow by boat mail.

New York staff boggled to hear that Westfall also commanded his managers to copy Geneen with each red-flag report. Surely it was madness to rub the big boss's nose in your every mess! That showed they understood neither man. It was exactly what Geneen wanted: intelligence current enough to allow for his own participation in countermeasures. And no surprises. Since both men traveled a lot, they met only once or twice a month. But now they had an agenda of value, the accumulated telexes that absorbed them far into the night.

Geneen doted on Westfall—and the more so after the events of 1962 in Brazil. When United States Ambassador Lincoln Gordon met with Brazil's foreign minister, Francisco San Tiago Dantas, in February 1962, they took up an unexpected subject. The day before, Leonel Brizola, governor of the Brazilian state of Rio Grande do Sul, had suddenly expropriated ITT's phone company. The ITT company in Pôrto Alegre served about 19,000 phones, and there was a waiting list of 15,000. Although ITT set the company's value at $6 to $8 million, Brizola had put a mere $470,937 worth of cruzeiros in escrow as compensation. In 1959 ITT had discussed making an investment of $40 million to modernize and expand the system, but talks had ended when Brizola refused a rise in rates to cover the proposed investment.

Brazil's President João Goulart, while well over on the left, was dismayed by the expropriation. However, he was not entirely surprised. He and Brizola were related by marriage, and he thought the governor erratic and opportunistic. "I wonder what my crazy brother-in-law had in mind," he told his foreign minister. "Is he trying to spoil my visit to Kennedy?" Much of the press in Brazil was equally unapproving. But Brazil was still a democracy, a federal republic with states' rights. Brizola was within those rights, and all Goulart could do was volunteer good offices for negotiation.

Geneen wanted something more compelling on his side. Ever since Cuba, he had pushed the United States government to idemnify American businessmen for the risks of foreign investment. "What is required," he said, "is a Government policy that will help the United States citizen feel safe in putting his dollars to work in United States enterprises abroad." After his swing though Latin America with Westfall in April 1961, he had called for firm guarantees. "If such guarantees are made available—and only Government can do this—IT and T would invest one quarter of a billion dollars in South America during the next five years"—equal to about "half the replacement value of our present investment."

After Brizola's action, chances for special legislation looked good, but Geneen needed a compliant senator to sponsor it. The head of Geneen's new-born Washington lobbying office, William R. Merriam, had met Iowa Senator Bourke B. Hickenlooper at a dinner party. The senator agreed to introduce an amendment to the pending foreign aid bill. It would be known as the Hickenlooper Amendment. But it was drafted by ITT, and at 320 Park Avenue, it was known as the Geneen Amendment. It specified that the United States Government "shall suspend assistance to the government of any country to which assistance is provided under this act" whenever that government nationalized any American-owned property or subjected that property to discriminatory taxes or operating conditions—without arranging, no later than six months after the fact, "to discharge its obligations under international law." That meant they had to pay "equitable and speedy compensation." The amendment was to be retroactive to January 1, 1962, which would cover Governor Brizola's expropriation. At stake was $1,029,576,000 in Alliance for Progress aid, $357,190,000 of it bound for Brazil. Geneen demanded an eye for an eyelash.

He lobbied hard. Stockholders, he said, should help "persuade our Government that its Alliance for Progress should not grant aid to counties that expropriate private United States investments without fair and prompt compensation." He added, "We have been fighting hard for months to protect our investments in Latin America." Nevertheless, the amendment was in trouble. Much of Congress saw it as too raw a special interest item, and against the United States's long-term interest. The administration was dead against it, and Senator Hickenlooper was little help. He could not quite follow the nice points of strategy that would win Senate support. Geneen would phone him, growing angrier and angrier at Hickenlooper's dimness, more and more preemptory as he dictated the proper moves. "You can't talk to him like that, Hal," one listener protested, "he's a United States Senator!" "I know," Geneen replied, "but I need this, and he just doesn't understand."

There was another lobbyist in ITT's Washington office, a marvelously effective one, Dita Davis Beard. "The amendment wasn't going anywhere," she says, so she went to see Louisiana Senator Russell B. Long. "By this time we had become quite close friends," she says. Long, much brighter and more artful than Hickenlooper, knew how to help. In fact, after passage, he was furious whenever he heard it called the Hickenlooper Amendment. "I did all the work," he said, "I led the floor fight on that thing, I got the House to agree in committee." As we shall see, Geneen was grateful.

Meanwhile, negotiations dragged on in Brazil. Brizola's first position had been that ITT could challenge his actions through the state courts of Rio Grande do Sul. ITT knew that that was useless. Next, Brizola's minister of justice said he would negotiate with Ambassador Gordon, but not with ITT. It was not fitting for a government minister to palaver with private citizens. Gordon doubted the use of the negotiations but undertook them. When they led nowhere, ITT accused Brizola of having unilaterally broken them off; he accused them of having sent to New York "illegal earnings disguised as payment for technical services."

The expropriation did not interfere with President Goulart's trip to the United States after all. When he saw Kennedy in April 1962, Goulart was resolved to settle, once and for all, this nettlesome issue of utilities ownership in Brazil. In Washington, he promised Congress to end the problem with equitable buy-outs of all foreign-owned utilities. On the plane to Chicago and Omaha, Goulart told Ambassador Gordon that he liked Kennedy and wanted to smooth relations. "What about the ITT negotiations?" Gordon asked. They would be resumed as soon as Goulart returned to Brazil. Even if the federal government could not stop Brizola, it could assume responsibility for compensation.

On his return trip to Brazil, something happened to change Goulart's mind. Maybe it was the mild heart attack he suffered during a stop in Mexico; maybe he saw it as a way to recoup powers lost the previous fall when the Brazilian army had forced a prime minister on him; maybe on reflection he just thought he was doing the right thing. In any case, he made a tough, extreme left-wing speech on May Day that his more moderate ministers protested by resignation. The ITT negotiations were now stymied. In June, Westfall had to report no progress; he was not even getting a reply to his proposals.

After the Hickenlooper Amendment, things would change, and Geneen would prove right about its effect. President Kennedy was against it. So was Ambassador Gordon. A poll of other ambassadors showed them overwhelmingly opposed. From the desperation of Russell Long's rescue mission, much of the Senate, unlobbied, was probably against it. Still, it passed. Senator Hickenlooper skipped the vote on the bill because he would have had either to vote for foreign aid, which he opposed, or to vote against his own amendment. Senator Long paired against the bill. The amendment was law, and the six months' deadline for Brazil loomed. Lincoln Gordon took a careful translation to one of Goulart's top ministers and showed him that the drafting was air-tight. Absent compensation, the United States president was commanded, after six months, to cut off aid. No exceptions, no extensions. Actually, Kennedy would simply ignore the amendment—and nobody would call him on it. But a worried Brazil could not foresee that.

Within days, Dantas, now Goulart's finance minister, called Gordon to say that there would be a settlement. Westfall picked up the negotiations again and, with the bludgeon of Hickenlooper in hand, won the day. On December 21, 1962, settlement was announced. "It was done in a semiclandestine way," says Gordon. The price was $7.3 million. The Banco do Brazil lent ITT dollars in exchange for cruzeiros at an exchange rate rigged to favor ITT. The "loan" was repaid in cruzeiros at a different exchange rate, now rigged the other way to favor ITT again. The amount lent and repaid was the same in cruzeiros, but ITT ended up with 7.3 million dollars. This so-called "swap loan" way of settling was calculated to ease Brazil's humiliation at being blackjacked. That was fine with Geneen; he would take the cash and let the credit go; he knew his point had been made.

About ten days before the military coup of March 31, 1964, which deposed Goulart and temporarily banished democracy from Brazil, Geneen was again in Rio. In addition to his annual Latin American tour, he was to meet with the head of Nippon Electric, which seemed to be moving into the area, a fearsome threat. Geneen paid a courtesy call on Ambassador Gordon, their first encounter "He congratulated me for having brought about the negotiations," says Gordon, "and I said I wasn't happy about it. It happened because of that legislation, the Hickenlooper Amendment. I thought that was bad policy, and I thought he should know that I had opposed it when it was before Congress. He said something like, Well, it got us paid off, didn't it? And I said, Yes that's right, it did; but it seemed to me that seven million was pretty trifling in the whole array of Brazilian-American relations, and it was a pretty high price to pay—to extract seven million by blunderbuss legislation. And he got quite angry." In fact, Geneen stormed out of the embassy and scribbled a telex to Edward J. Gerrity, Jr., PR director and overseer of ITT's political doings. Gerrity was instantly to see the State Department about getting Gordon fired.

All along, the issue was not the money so much as it was Geneen's firmest principle. Geneen knew he would eventually have to pull out of the phone-operating business; talks continued, however desultorily, with Chile and Peru. But no one was going to push him out without paying dearly, one way or another. He would not just give away any part of his business, however small. The principle was not free enterprise but the safety and growth of his own enterprise. Nothing was more important than preserving ITT's assets, nothing more important than ITT's good. Ten years later that principle would metastasize. Meanwhile, its benign effect was to achieve for ITT unparalleled success and growth, unchecked by adversities of the economy or unfavorable circumstances of the market.

Geneen had to increase his earnings in the United States. The natural place to expand was where ITT had its presumed expertise, with telephones. That is really two businesses, manufacturing and operation. But the two are intimately linked in the United States. At the time, about 82% of U.S. phones were operated by companies in the AT&T system. This was a closed market for equipment, because all AT&T companies bought exclusively from

AT&T's manufacturing arm, Western Electric. Of the remaining 18%, almost half (45%) were operated by General Telephone and Electronics (GTE), which also had its own manufacturer, Automatic Electric.

ITT was not in a good position to fight for the independent business that remained. Geneen had Kellogg, which made PABXs (switchboards for businesses) and subsets (what you think of as *your* telephone) at factories in Mississippi, Tennessee, North Carolina, and Virginia. These products did well enough, but the big money in telecom comes from supplying entire phone systems, particularly the central switching equipment. And for reasons we shall examine later, few independent American phone companies wanted ITT switching equipment.

Geneen concluded that the way to sell more phone equipment of all kinds was to do in a small way what AT&T and GTE did, but in mirror image: his manufacturing company would acquire captive operating arms in the United States. Even inside ITT, many did not understand this strategy. "We tried to buy up little phone companies," says one doubter. "Only about four or five percent were even possibly available. So we were out talking to Ma and Pa operations in Nebraska and Dakota. But if you put them all together, what would you have?" You would have a marvelous business. Even apart from their allure as a captive market, independent phone companies were marvelously profitable. That was the problem: sky-high selling prices. John Lobb's first assignment for ITT was to scout phone acquisitions. "We tried three times," says Lobb, "but the companies were selling at multiples of twenty to twenty-five times earnings. And they didn't really *want* to sell." Furthermore, the big independents like United Utilities and Continental already had options in case Ma and Pa changed their mind. Later, when ITT could have afforded such ludicrous multiples, everyone feared to let Geneen in as a competitor. They consciously blocked him. Even AT&T.

In April 1964 Southern Bell—an AT&T company—announced its intention to sell the 18% share it had of Carolina Telephone & Telegraph, a small independent serving eastern North Carolina. That 18% was working control. Geneen offered $52 a share, $1 over market, for all 399,009 shares. Southern Bell mulled it over while AT&T assured the world that the decision was entirely up to the subsidiary. AT&T chairman Frederick R. Kappel, though, told his stockholders he could see "no compelling reason" for the sale, and the public offering was soon withdrawn. Southern Bell announced further that, no matter what, they would never sell to Geneen.

By that time, Geneen had challenged an AT&T move into the foreign written cable business and had bucked AT&T's request to lay a fourth transatlantic cable. Although the FCC let AT&T lay the cable, the commission kept them out of written messages, while allowing ITT to edge into cable voice transmission, once an AT&T exclusive. It is no wonder that Kappel was leery.

Geneen was not only convinced he could go head-to-head with AT&T, he always wanted to sue them—as he would successfully sue GTE—for restraint of trade. And if he could not sue, he would harass. He once had some of his people buy one share apiece of AT&T stock and then disrupt the annual meeting with questions. The ploy ended when Kappel called Geneen to complain and to observe that two could play that game. AT&T appeared unassailable.

"I don't think that the concept of a conglomerate was present when Harold first took over the company," says John Jobb. "I think it evolved after it became obvious that it wasn't practical to build a system that could fight AT and T. ITT's domestic telecommunications never got off the ground, and it hasn't to this day."

In any case, the organizational steps for conglomeration had been taken. The commercial group of ITT, headed by Lou Rader, would be the vehicle for growth. Even if all Rader superintended at first was "Kellogg and some other junk," the fact that with Geneen and Ellery Stone he was the only other inside director measured Geneen's evaluation of USC's importance.

Al di Scipio, when not in Europe, identified nonmilitary fields that ITT could enter in the United States. And in 1962 Geneen brought John Thompson from Raytheon to dig out of ITT's worldwide telecom products some commercial applications. At first, Thompson's operation amounted to about $80 million (and a $4 million loss)—some semiconductors, a little wire and cable, an empty building in West Palm Beach.

USC had some endemic problems. "There never was any product-line loyalty," says one hostile ex-executive. "ITT was not ever a long-run pusher. Product lines would come and go." That made it hard to motivate people on the line. More important, the technology was not there. ITT may have seemed a high-technology company, developer of HF/DF (called "huff-duff," a high-frequency direction finder especially useful for detecting submarines), the LORAN and TACAN navigation systems, and all that fancy switching equipment. But many of ITT's technical people thought Geneen saw engineering as an expense rather than a commitment. Certainly, ITT had no reputation for innovation. Especially under Geneen, their acknowledged forte was taking someone else's technology, managing and manufacturing it better and cheaper (especially cheaper), and making money.

Problems aside, Geneen soon had fashioned an organization that could absorb new businesses and had recruited the management to handle them. He also had what he needed to buy them. Profits had risen from $29,035,688 in 1959 to $36,059,034 in 1961. The stock range had risen from 14–23 in 1959 to 22–30 in 1961, the multiple averaging about 12.

There were only two acquisitions in 1960, and they were insignificant. But in 1961 the program turned earnest. When Geneen arrived, ITT owned 56% of American Cable and Radio. In 1960 AC&R's profit slumped badly, and some outside directors proposed eliminating the dividend. Instead, Geneen decided to eliminate them. In 1961 ITT bought the outstanding stock of AC&R for $19 million. This company became the nucleus of ITT's international communications business. It was a good move. Income from the newly acquired portion of AC&R alone climbed from $1.6 million to $4.2 million in seven years.

Another 1961 acquisition was Jennings Radio Manufacturing Corporation in San Jose, California, bought for $17 million—"a hell of a price," says John Lobb, considering its meager return of $400,000 on $5.9 million sales the year before acquisition. Geneen's reasoning was that high-technology Jennings, along with Gilfillan Radar, acquired in 1963, would convince Wall Street that ITT was not a stodgy plodder. "I guess it worked," says Lobb. "People bought the stock and pushed the price up so Harold could keep buying."

In 1961 Geneen also bought Surprenant Manufacturing Company of Clinton, Massachusetts. He paid $10 million for it—more than the Jennings price, really, since 1960 earnings were only $600,000 on $14.3 million sales. It was an interesting company. In addition to making wire and cable, owner Albert H. Surprenant had taken his company into some unexpected byways. There was a limping tile company, always losing money; and Surprenant Manufacturing had its own golf club, Runaway Brook in nearby Bolton. Miffed when turned down for club membership elsewhere because he was Jewish, Bert Surprenant had his company start one, and it was a showplace. Like any self-respecting golf club, Runaway Brook was picky about its membership, but along even more capricious lines than racial and religious. The criterion was Bert Surprenant's whim. Membership charges were so low, and the course such a beauty—one of the longest in the world, at 8,325 yards—that members blinked the fact that they had no rights. Reasons for expulsion included not playing well enough to suit Bert, and littering.

ITT kept the club going, changing its name to the International. Members were allowed to stay on, still at the low fee, but with even fewer rights; at any time the whole place might be preempted for an ITT outing.

In Europe, for all of 1961, there were only two acquisitions, both minor. That balance reversed next year. Although some big ones were in the pipeline, the only 1962 domestic acquisition was tiny National Computer Products, Inc., in Lawrence, Massachusetts, bought for $5 million. In Europe that year there were six acquisitions: one each in Finland, France, Italy, and Switzerland, two in the United Kingdom. It was mostly more of the same: telephone equipment, radio and TV manufacturing (although the Swiss company rented sets). But the French company was a significant departure. It was the Société des Pompes Salmson, makers of centrifugal pumps. This was the birth of ITT as the world's leading pump maker. At $5 million, Salmson was a steal.

Even if John Lobb is right, and Geneen did not start as a conscious conglomerateur, the accumulation of disparate companies was surely the logical extension of Geneen's career: never a steel man or electronics man or telephone man, always a pennies-per-share man. The former executive who complained about lack of product-line loyalty also says, "Geneen treated money like a commodity; he turned ITT into a bank." That is true. But

Geneen's product *was* money, and to that product he brought abiding loyalty. Since the sole object of his enterprise was to grow and to increase earnings, it made no difference what direction that growth took, whence those earnings came. Geneen was increasingly certain his management methods were valid for any business anywhere. And he kept positioning himself in those first years to realize his vision for ITT.

Opening a legislative office in Washington was an important step. Geneen's first head of PR, Ward B. Stevenson, showed himself unworthy by opposing the idea. He was supplanted by Ned Gerrity, who had joined ITT about a year before Geneen and who was all for lobbying. General counsel Richard Mitchell also got himself crosswise with Geneen by arguing that ITT should instead hire a Washington law firm for ad hoc dealings with Congress. Geneen knew better. His start-at-the-top outlook demanded unceasing contact with the powerful.

The office started small. For a while it was just Bill Merriam, whose aunt owned the F Street Club, a politicians' hangout, and whose social secretary mother was a Washington fixture. In early June 1961, the House Ways and Means Committee was considering a new tax bill that contained sections affecting dividend repatriation from abroad. Geneen wanted to talk to the committee about it, and Merriam was not clear how to arrange that, so he enlisted Dita Beard, whom he had known since 1939. An experienced political operator, Beard was supporting her five children by working days for the National Association of Broadcasters and shuttling cars at night for $25 each. Beard set up Geneen's testimony before the committee and laid on a convivial lunch that Geneen hosted for committee members afterward. She was captivated by Geneen and instantly decided that she would work for him for the rest of her life.

Merriam and Beard were tucked in a corner of the defense group's sales office; it would be a few years before they moved to their own office at 1709 L Street. When Beard arrived, she says, "No one at ITT had even heard of political contributions." Since Merriam did not know his way around Congress, she set out knocking on doors, "to put ITT on the political map." It was tough. Most people who had heard of ITT thought it was a foreign subsidiary of AT&T. Moreover, many female executive secretaries assumed that making an appointment for Beard would be frittering away their boss's time. But she was tireless and tough, a jolly, bawdy woman in her early forties who retained much of her once considerable beauty and who could drink and swear and tell dirty jokes with the best of them. She quickly became very popular, and she had the best help Geneen could provide—himself. "Hal," she would tell him, "I need the big gun, goddamnit. If you want this done, I have to have you here"—and he would appear. He even seemed to enjoy making the rounds with her.

At first things were tight. "I had to beg and whine and wheedle," says Beard, "to go to the first governors' conference." But after a while, "it was just too damn delightful that I could call a governor and say, My guys are coming down and we've got to have some help from you. That happened a lot." When Geneen saw how effective Beard was, he made sure she had a generous expense account and operating freedom.

To smooth her way past executive secretaries she instituted what she called "Ma Beard's Stud Farm." She dragooned all the ITT men she could, "anything with an arm and a leg in each corner," for massive parties. To these she invited the lonely women who guarded the powerful.

Another of her strokes was to arrange yearly political seminars with congressional speakers—honorariums being an uptown way of dispensing money to legislators. The first seminar, held at the Carlton, attracted only a dozen guests; the second, at the Shoreham, was bigger, featuring as speakers Russell Long and Michigan Senator Philip A. Hart. In time, 700 guests would show up, and other lobbyists marveled at the turnout. "There was no secret," says Beard. "No money changed hands or anything like that. It was just Harold's charm and wit, and the fact that I had become accepted—and the parties were a lot of fun."

Geneen was always alive to the uses and power of political favors. In 1962, a company owned by ITT director George Brown had bought the Shoemaker Arsenal in Camden, Arkansas, where five-inch rockets had been made. The extensive grounds were crisscrossed by railroad tracks allowing dispersion of munitions. Right away, Brown's company had torn up the tracks for salvage. This convinced the citizens of Camden that there would be no more work for them there. They set up a howl, echoed by Arkansas Senators John L. McClellan and J. William Fulbright, whose position gave their howls particular weight. Brown asked Geneen to take the heat off. Geneen called in Bob Alexander and said, "I want you to go down to Camden and start manufacturing something right away; I don't give a damn what it is."

There was some difficulty with this assignment. Most of the buildings were made of concrete, with rooms purposely small so that no more than five people would be killed in an explosion. But Alexander did find the shell of a warehouse with 85,224 square feet. ITT leased it from the Brown Engineering Company, put in offices and toilets, and put half the space to work. Within sixty days Alexander was importing subassemblies from other ITT plants for final assembly. The ITT Arkansas division was born. ITT Shareholders who might have wondered what benefit their company derived from bailing out a director like this would have been gratified to learn that Geneen next sent Alexander on pointed visits to McClellan and Fulbright to stress how generously ITT was treating their state.

Geneen did not miss many tricks. "He's always trying to find a big angle for making money," Lou Rader told a reporter several years after leaving ITT. "He calls them 'ploys.'" Richard Mitchell likened Geneen to a man in a field, certain that under one rock lay a pot of gold. It kept him very busy turning over rocks. It kept everyone around him busy, too, though never busy enough for Geneen. Resident psychologist Andy Hilton maintained that

Geneen could not finally trust even favorites like Marx and di Scipio or stalwarts like Rader and Henri Busignies, Deloraine's successor, because he knew they did not care as much as he did. A McKinsey & Co. partner was sure no one could everlastingly satisfy Geneen. "Even if a man does eight things right," he said, "Geneen would criticize the ninth."

It was getting to some of them. Jim Lillis, the controller, told Lou Rader it was becoming impossible to work for Geneen: that constant probing, plainly never quite trusting the answers. Lillis's self-confidence was cracking. So was general counsel Mitchell's. He had once told a reporter, "I wouldn't want to be on the witness stand with Harold Geneen questioning me," and of course that is where he was, every day. "Uncomfortable meeting," Lou Rader wrote in his journal, "boss in a mean mood, but tried hard not to be outrightly abusive. Will not try to understand an explanation, but demands a specific answer to his question." Once, Geneen asked the head of manufacturing what his cost-saving bogey would be that year. The man started to explain that it depended on how you measured the— "Don't give me that goddamn bullshit," Geneen snapped. "Answer my question." After that meeting Rader told Bill Marx, "I thought you should know—maybe you want to tell Hal—if he ever talks to me the way he talked to Harry, he'll be minus one vice president that hour." In fact, Marx did speak to Geneen about it, late one night in Brussels. Next day Geneen seemed subdued. The day after it was business as usual.

That meant a brutal pace, most demanding at the top. On one trip, Lou Rader left New York at 10:00 A.M. on a Monday. He got to London at 9:25, local time, that night. After a jam-packed two days he flew to Paris at 5:00 A.M. Three more days of meetings, and on Saturday night he slept on the train to Milan for talks with executives of an ITT subsidiary. Monday night at 6:10 he flew to Frankfurt, where he changed planes for Nuremburg, getting in at 10:50. After a full day, Tuesday, he was driven to Stuttgart. At 10:18 next evening he caught a train for Brussels, arriving at 7:22 Thursday morning. He was driven to Antwerp for the day at BTM, then back to Brussels to catch the 7:00 P.M. plane for New York.

The Brussels EAC meeting dates in November 1960 happened to include Thanksgiving Day. Geneen arranged Thanksgiving dinner for his New York executives, flying over turkeys, cranberry sauce, the works. His after-dinner remarks were gracious: he knew they missed their families, was aware of their sacrifice; but they knew why the need to sustain momentum meant keeping the EAC meeting schedule inviolable, and he appreciated their dedication and zeal. Both were at ebb just then. In that strained atmosphere, Jim Lillis started his gravelly chuckle, and Al di Scipio, sitting next to him, asked what was so funny. Lillis dug from his pocket a cable from his wife. He handed it over, and di Scipio read, "Dear Jim: what's he got planned for Christmas?"

It was this period that established ITT's revolving-door image. Some executives left ITT because they could not reconcile the commitment Geneen required with any idea of a full life. Bob Alexander, reminiscing, once said that he had a house in California, a house in Illinois, and an apartment in New York—and never got to stay in any of them. He was on the road. Finally, in late 1963, he wrote Geneen to give notice. After the next Brussels meeting, Geneen invited Alexander for a walk. They wandered the Grand' Place from one gilded café to another, talking. Geneen could not understand how anyone could bear to leave ITT. "This is quite a company," he said, "and I can't run it myself. I need help." Bob Alexander's help. Alexander was touched, but adamant. "If you want to know exactly the kind of life I don't want to lead," he said, "it's yours." Today Alexander says, "With ITT I couldn't set up a golf game once a week—or once a month—or a bridge date, or any social calendar with any of our friends." And yet, "I never enjoyed working for a man more. I wouldn't have passed up the experience I had at ITT for anything."

When Bill Marx left, also in 1963, he said, "If you're a young man of thirty or forty, and an eager, ambitious guy, you'll find Geneen highly exciting. But after a while, you'll say, Hell, this is a one-man band. I want to run things my own way and do things in a more reasonable climate."

George Strichman left in late 1962 to take over Fairbanks Whitney (now Colt Industries). Dave Margolis and Andy Hilton soon joined him. "I wanted to use my own wings," Margolis said. "When you work for Geneen you live in his shadow."

Before Lou Rader left in 1962 to become president of Sperry Rand, Geneen had people from all over the country call Rader to say what a dubious situation he was getting into. But when Rader persisted, Geneen took it in good grace and even threw Rader a testimonial dinner at the Waldorf.

Al di Scipio, wanting line experience, briefly became president of Intelex, the ITT unit involved with the automated post office. Then early in 1962 he accepted an offer to head the Friden division of the Singer Corporation. A firm admirer of Geneen's, nevertheless he says today, "I'm not sure if I'd still want to work for him."

Of course, plenty did. One young man who started with the company in 1961, leaving ten years later, says, when looking at Geneen's top people in the late 1970s, "Hell, I know them all! I saw them come, and didn't see too many go, except for bigger positions." Anyway, the defections bulked much less important than the unarguable fact that even during the early, troubled days, volume and earnings kept rising. It was not widely noticed until years later, but right from the start each quarter's earnings topped the previous year's.

And Geneen was looking at earnings a new way. Every large company concentrates on its P&L statement, its earnings per share. So did ITT's constituent units. But at ITT, most of those units were the size of entrepreneurial companies, and Geneen knew that the successful entrepreneur had to manage total assets, not just earnings. To instill this awareness in his managers, he devised a plan he called "operations cash management," in effect setting up a balance sheet for each profit center unit and charging them "interest" on the assets they employed in getting their earnings. This had never been done in large-scale American industry. Geneen wanted dollars; but they must not be gained with huge outlays of working capital or fixed assets. With this imputed interest, a measurable premium was put on such things as reducing inventory and receivables and capital expenditures.

It helped promote vigorous growth. In late October 1962 Ned Gerrity made the rounds of the executive floors, inviting everyone across the street to the bar of the Waldorf. They were celebrating ITT's having just reached one billion dollars in volume. Geneen had some gold medals struck, and distributed them to those who had been with him from the start. The medals read:

First
Billion Dollar
Year
in Sales and Revenues
Awarded To
_____
1962

Geneen's plans for Christmas and for 1963 included explosive growth and the true beginning of ITT as a conglomerate.

10

Trying Something New

I t was the best first-quarter net in ITT history: $9,407,958—or 56¢ a
share, against 49¢ for first quarter, 1962. Of course every quarter under
Harold Geneen was up over the previous year, each a new record. But
in 1963 that was still news.

The only one who disputed that things looked good at ITT was Geneen
himself. True, revenue and income had grown at better than 10% a year.
However, the percentage of domestic revenue had actually declined from
1959 to 1962. So had domestic profitability. In Europe, ITT made about
3.3¢ on each dollar of sales; the United States figure was only about 1.5¢. So
while things might *look* good at ITT, they would not continue to be good
without new strategy.

In March 1963 Geneen made a momentous board presentation. Considering his promises, projections for 1963 were not cheery. Net for 1962 had
been $40,693,850, up $4.6 million; but all Geneen could see for 1963—without some new infusion—was a rise to $43 million or so, well under his 10%
goal. Domestic earnings would be only about $8 million, less than half the
dollars needed to cover ITT's $17.3 million dividend.

The lack of domestic earnings particularly troubled Geneen because of
trends he discerned worldwide. Lowered "tides of U.S. prestige," he predicted, would distinctly affect ITT's overseas business. Even relatively stable
Europe looked scary. He wrote in his presentation document:

> In France there is now a strong anti-U.S. sentiment setting in and
> U.S. ownership of companies in that country will be heavily scruti-
> nized. . . .
>   In England, the new labor movement has set for its goal a nationalis-

tic policy and to a degree an anti-U.S. policy. Last week a socialist document circulated called for the nationalization of certain companies *including our STC company.*

In Belgium, the general thought will be much like France.

In Italy, we have seen a continuous wave for some six months now of ill-founded strikes which if not aided by Government have been at least allowed to continue as the Government itself is committed to a semi-Leftist approach and to increasing nationalization of industry. . . .

Only in Germany did Geneen find a government friendly to United States—an emotion "largely founded perhaps on nearness to the Russian border." But even in Germany there was a threat to ITT's prosperity that was inherent in ITT's doing business in Europe. About two-thirds of ITT's European income was derived from telecommunications business. And throughout the continent ministers were comparing costs, a movement sure to squeeze ITT's prices. The Common Market was even talking about "compulsory international bidding for all PTT supplies without reference to source country of manufacture." That would mean no more automatic share of Germany's business for SEL, England's for STC, and so on.

The picture in Latin America was worse. The area now contributed about one-quarter of ITT's total profit, and the trend there was unmistakably "toward nationalism and a failure up to now on the part of the United States to control those trends as they affect United States' private business." In addition, an invasion of increasing competition came from Europe and Japan.

In the Far East, besides the specter of Japan, Geneen saw the growth of local manufacturing. "In retrospect then," he wrote, "over the next decade our earnings . . . will be subject to increasing pressures pricewise, sourcewise and ownershipwise. . . . " But he had the answer: ". . . [I]t is clear that we must organize a goal program for acquisition."

That did not mean just doing more of what he had been doing; it meant a flood of acquisitions, much bigger and in new directions. Domestic net had been about 17% of ITT's total earnings when Geneen took over. He proposed to boost it to 40%; that would cover dividends with dollar earnings. To do it he set as a five-year goal the acquisition of $400 million in sales. His real aim—to make U.S. earnings 55% of ITT's total net—would take another $500 million. Companies under $100 million he would integrate into ITT as new divisions. Here he would stick to ITT's present fields. However, he would welcome any bigger, stand-alone businesses that came along. These would let him expand into such fields as chemicals, pharmaceuticals, insurance, "food stocks, etc." and office equipment—a happy direction for ITT because "the large growth earnings trends are almost wholly in these areas."

Geneen summed up to his directors: " . . . I think we should seek and take all good opportunities as they present themselves up until such time, at least, as we feel that our competence as a management has been stretched too wide in scope and we must of necessity slow down such a program." The board's reaction, Geneen said later, was, "They listened and they said, 'Well, let's go along as we go, sort of a case-by-case approach.' "

The choice of acquirable companies was not extensive. "The only companies we could buy," says John Lobb, "were those with a P/E ratio comparable to ITT's"—which had grown but still had not soared. And purchases had to be for stock, because Geneen needed what cash was available to finance internal growth. Furthermore, Geneen could not even offer all common stock, the kind companies like to use for acquisitions. "We had to use convertible preferred," says Lobb, "convertible three years out, or something, figuring by then we could get the earnings up so it wouldn't cause dilution."

That barely kicked off the problem. "The companies had to be dogs or we couldn't have bought them," says Lobb. "You can almost say that if a company can be bought, it's got troubles." Some disagree. Herbert C. Knortz, who replaced Jim Lillis as controller, maintains that Geneen bought good companies. It is a matter of definition and focus. To a line operator like Lobb, a company with sizable inventory and receivable problems, loss units, and standpat management is a dog; a controller sees the healthy balance sheet, the cash surplus, placement in a good business.

Further jaundicing an operator's view is the level of earnings needed to avoid dilution. Geneen habitually paid large premiums to acquire companies, and some wondered why so much was paid if they were such dogs. That, also, requires definition. Companies in the first great wave of acquisition were still run by entrepreneurs. The problems these companies faced were real; that is why they entertained Geneen's offers. But the problems that inspired thoughts of selling were not the same ones that challenged Lobb. The entrepreneurs' worries were on the order of estate settlement, unclear lines of succession, thinness of management, and lack of expansion funds. Of Geneen's early acquistions, only General Controls was in visible trouble, having lost money in 1962; and even those owners were far from desperate. All the companies might be willing to sell; none was anxious.

It all depended on price, especially since Geneen would never deal in unfriendly takeovers or hostile tender offers. He paid entrepreneurs handsomely enough to assure their unstinting enthusiasm and cooperation. He needed them, at least at first. Certainly, there were problems when they did not stay even for the transition. (If they stayed too long, that was bad too, but for different reasons, as we shall see.) Besides, Geneen was much taken with these entrepreneurs. He admired them even when they later became a pain.

Geneen's first acquisition of 1963, Bell & Gossett of Morton Grove, a Chicago suburb, displays all the important themes of his new acquisition policy and technique. It was also one of his best buys ever. Pumps were a fine business. Geneen's experience with France's Pompes Salmson had been uniformly happy. Salmson, growing 30% a year, could barely keep up with demand. Geneen wanted more of that action, and he happened to know a likely prospect. In his Bell & Howell days he had made friends with Courtland G. Newton, and their friendship had continued over the years. From time to time, Newton pushed Geneen to meet with the second most dynamic person he knew, R. Edwin Moore.

Ed Moore was a character. A huge, corpulent bear of unbounded vigor, he was equally renowned as a mighty hunter (he routinely walked away with his gun club's squirrel-shooting calcutta) and for his affecting rendition of "Jesus Wants Me for a Sunbeam." He was also an excellent businessman. Nominally second to Mr. Gossett, Moore had long been the company's driving force.

Geneen's friend Court Newton worked for a company that licensed equipment to Bell & Gossett. He had often talked to Geneen about Ed Moore, and about B&G—the industry leader, with 13 to 14 million pumps in operation throughout the country. As Moore rightfully boasts, "Nobody made a better pump or stood behind it better." When Moore took over in November 1962, following Mr. Gossett's death, Newton—a sometime consultant to B&G—became Moore's executive assistant. And now Geneen was talking to Newton about Moore. He had the idea that B&G should get together with Salmson for a joint venture in Europe. Newton arranged a meeting, and Moore spent two weeks in Europe examining Salmson. Geneen went too but got a cold and returned to New York; for his part, Moore got cold feet. Back in Chicago, he told Newton, "They've got some operation, but the joint venture is not for us. We'd be swallowed up at first bite." When Geneen called Newton and learned Moore's reaction, his immediate response was, How about acquisition?

That was different. For all his vigor, Moore was sixty-six years old. His partners were dead, and no clear successors were coming on. Besides, Moore was expansion-minded. This was a chance, he says, "to enlarge the future of the entire operation. We needed to move into strong hands, with money to do more." Geneen promised the world. As for purchase price, he was talking very fancy figures. "I got a call from him one evening," says Moore. It was an invitation to come to Geneen's vacation home in Key Biscayne to talk turkey. Moore, a self-styled "farm boy," affected ignorance. Key Biscayne? What was that? He didn't know about such matters, had to work too hard. "Cut the foolishness." Geneen laughed, "I'll see you there."

"Harold and Ed finally got through fencing with one another," says Newton, "and Ed was a better bargainer; he sold the company for more money than Wall Street thought he'd ever get. They were talking about it for two years afterward."

In 1962, B&G had earned $2.4 million on $41 million revenue. The price to ITT was close to $48 million in common and convertible preferred, about 20 times earnings. Geneen might have shaved a point or two, but he could not have bought for much less. The situation was typical. None of the problems of tight capital or succession was pressing or even particularly manifest to the B&G board. Moore easily convinced Geneen that ITT had to fork over enough money "to discount the known future of his company and to offset the claims of one block of his shareholders (identified with the Gossett holdings) that Bell and Gossett can make more money per share . . . by going it alone."

Sure enough, approval turned on the princely price. "It was a hairy period," says Court Newton, "because Ed Moore works in mysterious ways." The B&G board met at Chicago's Union League Club on the last day that ITT's offer remained valid. Newton took a room upstairs and held vigil with Stanley Luke, who was ITT's official negotiator—that is, the man who presented Geneen's terms. Geneen called from New York every hour, but there was nothing to report as time wore on. Finally, Newton said, "Stanley, maybe you better go down to that room and see how it's getting along. Otherwise we're going to see the night come and go." Luke came back aghast. "My God!" he said, "They don't even know what they're there for. They're just talking over old times." When Geneen called again he said, "Does Ed realize that if midnight strikes, we'll have to start over from zero?" A disgruntled ITT board might not renew the offer. Newton sent a bellboy to Moore with a note of urgency about the deadline. Luke again checked on progress. "He came back up," says Newton, "grinning from ear to ear." Moore had gotten the note and had gotten down to cases. "Ed wrote some numbers," Luke told Newton. "He turned to the board, showed them what he'd written, and said, Well boys, we just sold ourselves to ITT."

Actually, it was not quite so simple. As Moore had anticipated, there were demurrers; but also as anticipated, the board could not resist $48 million. One director, a banker, silenced the argle-bargle: "Now wait a minute," he said. "If this is for real, I won't stand for you fellows turning it down. I'll take you to court." That did it. The merger was announced on April 10, 1963.

From the first, B&G was a splendid acquisition, the centerpiece of ITT's most profitable industrial group. But if the process of B&G's acquisition was typical of those in 1963, so were the personal stresses and disappointments of its aftermath.

Ed Moore was used to doing things his own way. In many respects those were effective ways. He set up a course in modern heating and air-conditioning techniques for contractors; once students paid their way to Ed Moore's "red country school house" in Morton Grove, everything else was free. Some 20,000 contractors took the course and became lifelong disciples of B&G, faithfully specifying the equipment they had learned to know best. One ITT marketing expert told Moore, "You never have to have another idea."

Still, Moore's ways were not Geneen's ways, and Geneen's would prevail. The king of his own realm suddenly reported to someone else. That would have galled even without conflict. But the man Moore reported to, John Lobb, had to double earnings to avoid ITT stock dilution, and the first step as always was to scrap B&G's losers and low profit lines. First to go were what Lobb calls "Ed Moore's toys." Those included the two research companies in Colorado that Moore was sure would some day revolutionize communications. There was also the Gladstone, Michigan, company that manu-

factured electric motors, its shop equipment powered by overhead belts—
downright Victorian. And Gladstone had a subsidiary, Moore's special joy,
that confected precision gun sights and gun-cleaning equipment. On staff was
a craftsman many felt to be the country's premier gun sighter. Moore remains
bitter to this day about those amputations.

Another sore point was Geneen's early promise to get Moore on the ITT
board. He soon told Court Newton that he had tried but that the board would
not go along. Moore would have to settle for a corporate vice presidency.
(Geneen also had some personal bad news for Newton; he had been promised
a $300,000 finder's fee for the merger, but the board voted only $100,000.)

Worst of all, Moore's personality and autocratic spirit were outsized for
the ITT mold. Before long he was succeeded as president of B&G by his top
assistant, William A. Booth, a highly competent pump man but one with less
assertive corporate views. In theory, Moore would henceforth work on acquisitions; actually he did little but sit in his office, sourly trying to hold some
sway over the business. It should have been anticipated. "You have to get rid
of the Ed Moores," says John Lobb. "It's a mistake to keep the founder on
too long in an active capacity." Other retained entrepreneurs caused intermit-
tent stirs, Lobb says, "but Ed's the only guy who never gave up."

In some measure "Moore's Complaint" infects many ambitious executives at all levels in acquired companies. At ITT it became epidemic. Increasingly, Geneen felt that his best source of executive talent for the corporation
was the middle management of acquired companies. That might seem ideal
for young tigers: a choice of continuing their known career paths or exploring
corporate opportunities. But on inspection both alternatives had worrisome
drawbacks. At Bell & Gossett, for example, before acquisition, a young comer
might have ten or twenty or thirty people between him and the top. But he
could still plausibly see himself, someday, head of a thriving $45 million
company. Acquisition exploded the dream. From then on the head of B&G
would be picked by strangers in the corporate structure. It could even be an
outsider brought in for corporate broadening. Anyway, the position itself was
diminished: little autonomy, no immersion in corporate finance, certainly no
scope for stock option maneuvering. Someone who once was chief executive
of a company preeminent in its field would now be merely viceroy of one unit
of a group in a division of a conglomerate. The person he reported to might
have some clout. But the corporate side was no more enticing. If he switched
to 320 Park, the hot young executive would have to prove himself all over
again—without the edge of his industry-specific expertise. And he would be
in competition with a host of other hot young tigers. All around, it was a
daunting prospect. Many of the best found both choices unpalatable and left.
ITT handled the problem better than most, but these defections added to the
difficulty of running acquired companies in the early years.

The next 1963 acquisition was General Controls, in Glendale, California,
one that Geneen had considered at Raytheon. Beforehand, John Lobb went
to look it over. "I came back," he says, "and said the goddamn thing was a

mess. It probably could be straightened out; they were in a lot of good businesses—electronic controls, avionics. But ITT no way had the management to do it; nobody in the telecom business would understand what to do. So my recommendation was don't buy it. Of course the first company I got to run was General Controls."

In 1962 General Controls had lost some $1.2 million on nearly $36 million revenue, and the principals, the Ray brothers, were willing, though not anxious, to sell. Talks dragged through a half dozen meetings before the Rays sold for close to $18 million in common and convertible preferred stock.

Again, the Rays—who had made the company worth buying—were part of the problem. Bill Ray was chief engineer. "All he thought about," says someone who had to wrestle with the problem, "was engineering some new fancy thing and putting it in the line." That was fine with brother Jack, the sales manager, who "thought he had to have a complete line to compete." The other two, Alvin and Dick, were treasurer and plant manager, which made them constitutionally more sympathetic to Geneen's methods. They adapted and stayed; Bill and Jack had to go.

Next came Cannon Electric in Los Angeles. "There's never just *a* reason why you sell your company," says Robert J. Cannon. His father started Cannon in 1915, and soon the name was practically generic. Whenever there was a short circuit, especially in airplanes, someone was sure to say, "check all the Cannon plugs." But like many founding geniuses, the elder Cannon was no long-haul businessman. When he died in February 1950, the company bordered on bankruptcy. Nevertheless, it was basically sound, and by April of the same year, Bob Cannon had it back in the black, a very nice business, closely held, mostly by Cannon, his younger brother, a sister, and a half-sister.

Bob Cannon says that there were many reasons for selling. The declining business had occasioned layoffs, which had triggered an exasperating strike. Jim Cannon, who owned about 25% of the company, liked New England (he was chief engineer in the company's Salem, Massachusetts, plant) and would not move to southern California. That muddled succession. One sister had sold some stock. But the overriding reason was that Bob Cannon was tired of pushing on and was ready to sell.

There were plenty of offers. In 1962 Cannon earned about $2.3 million on somewhat over $50 million revenue, making it an attractive acquisition. "We turned away about one conglomerate a week," says Cannon. Litton was especially diligent in its pursuit. But Cannon did not like doing business with Litton. He thought they had given some of his company's designs to competitors.

Geneen was different. Cannon had played golf with him a few years earlier and had been impressed. Now, when ITT acquisitions negotiator Stan Luke came with an offer, Cannon listened. Geneen came out and toured the plant, and on the way to the airport in a limo the basic deal was cut for $33 million in the customary mixture of common and convertible stock. The merger was announced July 10, 1963. Trouble began almost at once. "Bob

Cannon was bitter," says John Lobb. Cannon says he was not, though he allows that a number of people in similar positions were. "But Bob made seventeen million dollars from the deal, his brother and sister made seven or eight. I told him he can't have everything—sell the company and still tell me how to run it. But he was bitter anyway, writing to the directors how we hadn't kept our promises." It is standard acquisition procedure, says Lobb, to tell the owners everything will stay the same and then to tell staff to double earnings, which cannot be done by doing everything (or even most things) the same. Conflict is the very soul of the situation. Bob Cannon left in November of 1964.

Albert Nesbitt perhaps foresaw the inevitable and left even sooner. His Philadelphia company, John J. Nesbitt, led in heating and air conditioning for schools, a natural fit with B&G. Geneen envisioned the combination of both companies' products and know-how, plus General Controls, to exploit England's recent discovery of North Sea gas fields. A part of his acquisition sales pitch was always to put his arm around the prospect's shoulder and rhapsodize about how together they would conquer the world. Albert Nesbitt was not wowed. His company had made $1 million on over $24 million revenue; he sold for about $19 million in stock, left his brother in charge, and quit the day after the merger became official, August 1, 1963.

Next month came the final 1963 merger—with Gilfillan Corporation, maker of radar in Los Angeles. This was a prestige acquisition. Geneen was willing to pay just under $19 million for a company that had netted only $786,000 on some $33 million revenue the year before, 24 times earnings.

Further possibilities seemed endless. In the fall of 1963 Geneen told his board that he had been talking to Travelers Broadcasting in Hartford. Their TV and radio station could be had for either cash or convertible debentures. Soon there was talk of acquiring the legal maximum of five TV stations. Mercifully, the business press did not discover Geneen's plans for TV; the acquisitions he actually made perplexed them enough. They decided he was "trying a piecemeal approach to growth"—which leads to the unstartling conclusion that Geneen had keener business vision than his critics. He saw how his acquisitions fit. For instance, Bell & Gossett had subsidiary pump companies—Marlow in New Jersey and Stover in Illinois—plus Reznor in Pennsylvania, a maker of heating units. With Nesbitt, these became the core of ITT's HEAVAC division (for heating, ventilation, and air conditioning). Geneen planned further acquisitions so ITT could some day provide builders with nearly everything they would need in the way of "environmental products." The talk was, lovingly, of "system selling." The English North Sea gas scheme was so typical as to be run-of-the-mill, and what seemed piecemeal to outsiders made perfect sense to Geneen. By 1965 the HEAVAC net was $5.2 million, up from 1963's $3.2 million. However, a significant part of that 1963 net—and even some of the corporation's overall 14% increase for 1963—was spurious, desperation accounting. In time, the acquisitions were marvelous. Right at first, though, they were not working. Geneen was in trouble.

11

A Paltry Putsch

John Lobb was group executive in charge of General Controls. "At the general management meetings," he says, "Ted Westfall would always ask me, How's that fucking General Controls? After about six months of that I said to him, I hope I live long enough to hear it called General Controls."

That seemed unlikely. "General Controls was nothing but problems," says Jules Berke, who had to help solve them. "Once, the manager made an impassioned plea: Please understand, these problems just keep coming out of the woodwork. And Geneen said, I'm surprised there's any woodwork left."

Other acquisitions had similar problems. Though not losing money, none was performing anywhere near expectation. Cannon, for example, made $1 million less than it had the year before. The least serious and soonest mended problem was Geneen's tenderness toward entrepreneurs. "In the early days," says Lobb, "Bill Ray had a pretty good pipeline to Geneen. No matter what I told him to do, he'd go around my back, and Harold would say, Don't be too hard on him, John." That continued until Geneen got so disgusted with results that he gave Lobb a free hand.

Then there were weaknesses built into the companies. Cannon, for example, was budgeted at about $1.8 million profit for the first year of ITT operation. Despite continued assurances that they would make budget, Geneen mistrusted a Cannon accounting formula that had been established when the company went public. A huge overhead charge went on the balance sheet automatically whenever a convoluted set of variable conditions obtained. If it happened, it would seriously affect profits. Toward the end of the year Geneen asked his staff, "Is that thing going to jump up and bite me?" They promised that it wouldn't: they understood it and had it under control. About two days later a telex came from Cannon's controller: "Sorry. We promised $1.8 million for the year; there's only going to be $1.3 million. The reason is that thing on the balance sheet."

Geneen's instinct in these matters was uncanny. Surprenant had declined to a $100,000 loss in 1964, and no one could imagine why. Geneen saw the numbers and asked, "What's happening to prices?" The fast answer was, Nothing—same as always. But investigation disclosed a subtle change in the business. It was now small-run orders, and without a special setup charge, the company's profit eroded at the old price schedule. Similarly, when the Brazilian phone company suffered mysterious losses, Geneen spread the books on his desk and managed to divine the problem that had eluded everyone on the scene.

But even uncanny instinct could not quickly solve the basic problem: to avoid dilution of ITT stock, acquired earnings *had* to double in about three years. But the acquired companies already commanded generous shares of their markets. Present earnings reflected the best efforts of people with an intimate and encyclopedic knowledge of those markets. The entrepreneurs had presumably maximized earnings running things their way, leaving no obvious scope for instant growth. In fact, volume was *supposed* to shrink at first; Geneen's invariable first step with a new business was to do less business, chopping even marginal product lines. That should have at least yielded increased margins. But the natural morale slump in any takeover was so magnified by the cutbacks that earnings suffered too. There was no reason for alarm. Geneen was building for the future, had a patently rational plan, and his methods were proven. Unfortunately he had to contend with the ITT directors.

Board impatience is a weakness of American corporate life. Much has been written about the contrasting Japanese willingness to bear years of flat or even lowered income in order to build markets. American directors are pious about the future, but they are fierce about the present. Why isn't *this* quarter's net higher? When do we raise the dividend? The ITT board was particularly exacting, containing as it did a high complement of raider types left over from the Behn coup and others more attuned to investment banking than manufacture.

Of course, Geneen compounded his own problem. It was he who set the tests of 10% annual growth and an unbroken string of higher quarterly earnings, who doubled the net in five years and immediately pledged to do it again in the coming five. He had trapped himself by raising the board's expectation. Now he was desperate. "I remember back in 'sixty-three," says Donald G. Thomson, then on staff, "every trick you could play with the books was played to get the income up. I had to get out a special report to inventory all the stationery and supplies around the world so we could capitalize them and get a one-time kick on income." It worked; each quarter in 1963 and 1964 continued to set a record. That was all right for the analysts and business press, but the board knew that Geneen had not delivered on his promises. "I saw Geneen one day, and he looked like he had been hit by a truck," says Thomson. "I remembered it because he was being built up as such a hero. How could he do anything wrong? I found out a year later that when I saw him, he was just back from the board room, where he was almost fired. None of the acquisitions was working."

Geneen's relations with the board were a wonder. "Hal was always running scared—and still is—with respect to the directors," someone who had earlier been one of Geneen's closest aides told a reporter in 1967. "He's never quite certain what any particular guy on the board is thinking. So he tries to keep them off balance." Wariness was only prudent. "They were a tough group," says Lou Rader. "Nothing namby-pamby about them." They were rich, powerful men, not one of them (then, at least) Geneen's creature. Quite the contrary. These men, who could lay low a titan like Behn, had plucked Geneen from relative obscurity. "It was years," says a former aide, "before he had them where they couldn't just fire him *next day.*" Besides, Geneen had considerable admiration and respect for them as individuals. "Hal stood in awe of people with great wealth," says someone who was then very close to Geneen, "people like Pat Lannan"—ITT director and a financier. He also had a genuine reverence for their function. Corporate birdseed aside, he meant it when he explained to a reporter why keeping the board informed was so vital. "The most sensitive place is the board room. That's the first key area. The board. They're the people who can and will take risks and have the courage to back decisions."

Under Geneen, "keeping the board informed" acquired new depths of meaning. "It was like final exams in school," says someone who helped Geneen cram. "He was like some little guy going in front of an examining board." Board meetings were on Wednesday. "Monday and Tuesday," says an aide, "everyone went bananas." Staff would deliver a thick briefing book to Geneen late at night; next morning a deluge of questions flooded back. "And you didn't just answer his question," says someone who had to answer many of them, "there'd be six, seven questions come back *off* your answer." All answers had to be convincing. "He might send twenty questions to some guy," says a former aide, "and eighteen would pop back; he'd have scribbled, What's this shit? Give me an *answer!*"

The topics were universal. Finance, currency conversion, debt structure, earnings ratios, politics in ITT countries; always the P&L to date, with exhaustive comment on any variances from budget; warranty problems, quality control, personnel, security. If a big order was lost, Geneen had to know exactly why so he could tell the board how the faults would be cured. "He didn't *need* all those things," says Tim Dunleavy, an inside director. "He could have danced with the board for months without ever having to ask for anything." But in one practical sense that did not matter. If the board never asked him anything, his infamous "board notes" assured that once a month he was on top of all the company's central issues.

The board did not even have to ask about matters up for a vote. Geneen meticulously briefed the outside members beforehand, trying to achieve consensus and exclude debate. What if, despite all, some proposal did inspire controversy at a meeting? "He would get it off the table right away," says an observer. "He'd say, We'll study that and report back. He would not let it heat up as an issue."

For example, there was the airplane problem. Geneen disliked commercial flights; they meant bending his schedule to the airlines. Moreover, he was afraid of highjacking. ITT had a Beechcraft that Geneen used whenever possible, but once, coming into Brussels, a malfunction made the plane skid dangerously. Geneen wanted a jet, a Grumman Gulfstream. He agonized over presenting it to the board, expecting resistance. And yes, having rubber-stamped millions, the board niggled over thousands for the Gulfstream. Geneen instantly backtracked; he would study the issue. "Next month," says the same observer, "he comes back with fourteen inches of documentation proving the need for the plane. He hands these around, and it goes through without a peep."

Geneen handled the board masterfully, but he resented the time it took. Even more, he resented the need to justify his actions, even to people he admired. He had his director of organization, James N. Hills, study companies that functioned with only inside directors. "He'd call nearly every month to see how it was coming," says Hills. "He'd say, Let's find a way to get rid of those outsiders."

It would never happen. Meanwhile, Geneen viewed any subordinate who appeared to court favor with the outsiders with utmost suspicion. In early 1963 Geneen offered a ride to one high-level staff man. "Soon as I got into the limo," says the staffer, "he turned on me ferociously. He accused me of saying something to someone on the board behind his back. I looked at him in total disbelief and shock, because I had never even *met* anyone on the board!" So what was it all about? "Somebody must have said something, and he was fishing to find out who it was; or maybe he was just teaching me my first lesson: Don't you ever say anything to the board."

It was that much worse when loose lips belonged to someone who was himself an inside director. Insiders "didn't count for anything," as one of them admits. But they had easy access to the powerful outsiders, and Geneen wanted to make sure that they did not use it. When Lou Rader was an inside member, Geneen sent him a memo marked "PERSONAL":

In order to spare you any possible future embarrassment should the question arise, you are hereby directed to check with me personally before accepting any invitations from Directors which would involve a discussion of the company's affairs.

I believe this is entirely in accord with normal corporate management practice and I am sure will prove to be the best procedure for all concerned.

"I had probably exchanged a few words with some director in the halls" says Rader, "and the guy went to Hal and said, "Lou tells me . . . ""

When Geneen thought that two people were exchanging more than a few words, he took drastic action. Jack Graham and Geneen had been classmates at the Harvard AMP and had stayed in touch. Graham was a division VP at RCA with a fine record. He admired Geneen. When asked to come to ITT, in December 1961, "I didn't walk," he told a reporter, "I ran." He replaced Lou Rader at the head of U.S. commercial in March 1962. "I thought he was a pretty damn good executive," says John Lobb, "one of the best guys we had around there." So did Geneen. In 1963 he appointed Graham to the board. And in early 1964, when the board pestered Geneen to designate a successor, he said Jack Graham was the logical choice. This may have gone to Graham's head, because he promptly plunged into perilous waters.

There was some disquiet in the ITT board room. In April 1964 the board authorized Geneen to pay up to $1.3 million (15 times earnings) for Hayes Furnace, a company that made gas-fired heaters, complementing Nesbitt. Geneen wrote to John Lobb that the board questioned why "we did not develop such products ourselves since basically they are of simple design. I suggested that the time element and total cost in addition to sales distribution dictated this choice. I think this comment might be of interest, however." He later said that it "was a casual comment and not one of great concern" to the board.

Yet while the idea was perhaps not of concern to the whole board, its tenor consumed at least one member, ITT director Robert McKinney. Following John Kennedy's election as president, McKinney was appointed United States Ambassador to Switzerland in July 1961. He resigned before Kennedy's assassination and was welcomed back on the ITT board in September of 1963. By then the 1963 acquisitions were either consummated or already arranged. McKinney would have voted no. Looking back, he says that what Geneen and his people did was "go out and get a bunch of dogs, then they sent for the dogcatchers—the investment bankers—who came to them with all the dogs they could find. They rounded up nothing but dogs." And to McKinney's dismay, Geneen wanted to acquire more.

In January 1964 Geneen told a special stockholders' meeting, "The corporation ha[s] no further acquisitions in mind at present. . . . " He just needed authorization for an addition half-million shares of cumulative preferred stock in case any opportunities came along. Come they did—and strayed ever further from what McKinney considered ITT's proper business. By the end of August 1964 Geneen paid about $34.8 million for Aetna Finance and agreed to acquire Barton Instruments for over $12 million. McKinney was horror-struck, remembering what had happened with Behn's purchase of Farnsworth and Coolerator. He had to do something, but he needed information and a plausible replacement for Geneen. "He did not endear himself to Mr. Geneen," says Richard Perkins, himself an outside director, "because he established contact with some officer in the company for inside information."

That was almost certainly Jack Graham. "One night we were at the Hilton for some big function," says Henry Bowes, then ITT marketing director. "We were all in dinner jackets. Jack had his wife with him, and he asked her if she would stay in the bedroom for a minute, then he told me he was making a pitch to run the company. I've got to believe some directors came to him; otherwise I don't think he'd have ever thought of such a thing. I said, Well, friend, if they came to you, I'd go right to Hal and say this is what happened. Because if he finds out, you're dead."

He did indeed find out. "Jack must have been talking to guys about, I'm gonna be the successor," says Tim Dunleavy. "And he may even have gotten so bold, I think, as to tell Hal he didn't handle people properly, the way Jack did—or something." Whatever way Geneen found out, the chill set in with record speed. "Geneen called me into his office," says John Lobb, "and said, Jack is leaving and you're taking his job tomorrow. He fell out of favor very suddenly. Geneen told me that Jack was neither physically nor mentally able to stand the strain of a company that was growing too big for him, and couldn't handle it any more." Graham went into limbo for a few months, sitting in his office with nothing to do. His resignation took effect in June of 1964.

McKinney was not through. The board meeting in October 1964 was part of Geneen's cosseting, a tour of Europe for ITT directors and their wives: Berlin, Rome, Paris, London, Madrid, and Lisbon. Such junkets were frequent and were unlovely spectacles. "We on the staff used to hate these deals," says someone who saw many of them. "You get these people together —all wealthy prima donnas and their wives—and put them together in hotel rooms for two weeks or so and there was an explosion every couple of days. Someone had a bigger car than the other guy, and someone had a Cadillac and the other a Mercedes. And one lady would complain because she had white roses in her room and the other lady had red roses, and one lady had a better view than another lady—and so forth and so on. It doesn't make you very proud."

At times the war of the roses got on even the directors' nerves. Once, at a hotel in Portugal, John J. Navin, secretary to the corporation, heard another employee taking a call. "Certainly I understand," the man said. "Would you like me to arrange a car?" Hanging up, he told Navin that a director "just threw his wife out in the hall with her bags, pocketbook, and passport and asked if I would get her a ticket back to the States and get her the hell out of the hotel and out to the airport. Excuse me while I go help her."

In the 1964 dust-up, John Navin played a more active part. On the plane from Madrid to Lisbon Navin overheard McKinney talking to fellow director Allan Kirby about the parlous state of ITT. The solution, McKinney insisted, was an extraordinary board meeting, minus Geneen, to elect a chairman, someone to keep Geneen in check. McKinney offered himself as candidate. Navin reported the conversation to Raymond L. Brittenham, ITT general counsel; Brittenham told Geneen; and an anti-putsch council was hastily convened. "It was then that I saw this guy *really* in operation for the first time," says a participant about Geneen. "He had a mutiny on his hands. We just went down the list of directors. Which of these guys could he count on in a shoot-out? We can count on this guy; this one's a question mark; you can't count on *him*, but you can on *him*. We worked down the list." Then Geneen went to work on the directors themselves. McKinney says that Allan Kirby and George Brown were at first both convinced of a need for change. If so, Geneen quickly turned them around. There never was a shoot-out. Back in New York, Geneen confronted McKinney. He was, says McKinney, "at a boil." He did not appreciate McKinney's taking so great an interest in the company's affairs. The other directors were content to attend meetings and approve things, and McKinney should be, too. Geneen ran down the list and demonstrated to McKinney that he had the board on his side, at which point McKinney resigned.

John Hanway II had replaced Bill Marx. He now cemented his position by suggesting that Geneen move his own election as chairman. On December 9, 1964, the board went along, and so Geneen was chairman, president, and CEO. At the same time, Ted Westfall was anointed as official number two, sole executive VP. Francis Hart Perry, Geneen's treasurer and then a favorite, was made an inside director. The following March, as a reward for helping quash the putsch, Ray Brittenham also went on the board.

Ironically, as McKinney made his play, the laggard acquisitions had already started to nose out of their slump. Geneen's system was taking effect. John Lobb describes the process for doubling an acquisition's earnings in three years:

> First we made an exhaustive analysis of profitability on each product line. I never bought a company—then or since—where they had done that. Don't ask me why; you'd think everybody would do it. They don't.
>
> Then we would give them maybe thirty days to justify keeping anything that was making less than, say, five percent, pre-tax.
>
> For things making something like five to ten percent, we'd give them maybe sixty or ninety days to come up with a program for product redesign, or changing marketing or distribution or improving manufacturing—whatever would get those returns up.
>
> Our objective was twenty percent, pre-tax. We didn't always make it, but we tried.
>
> What you can't improve, you shut down. Sell the machinery, liquidate inventory, and get rid of the overhead people associated with it.

That's everyone from accounting clerks to direct labor to vice presidents. You end up taking a fifty-million-dollar business maybe down to forty million. But its got fewer people and lower costs—so you make more money with the forty million than you did with the fifty million.

And something else happens. You may offer fewer lines, but you do a better job with them, give better service and delivery. So before long you sprint beyond the original $50 million—still at the higher margin. When Lobb left ITT in 1967, it was to do the same thing for Norton Simon at Crucible Steel, where he raised earnings 24% in the first quarter on 2% less volume. After the Crucible turn-around, he went to Canada's $480 million Northern Telecom. In his first year there, Lobb cut volume by $64 million but raised the profit from $4.5 to $12 million. "Next year," he says, "we sold between seven and eight hundred million, and made about twenty-three million—doing what I learned to do at ITT."

The process takes time. ITT's U.S. sales dropped from $620 million in 1963 to $567 million in 1964, from 44% of ITT's total to 37%. But it was the necessary first move toward what would blossom, in 1965, into a new direction for the company—one that led the way for all conglomerates. It would no longer matter whether an acquisition candidate fit existing corporate business or competence; the only test was profit potential.

For instance, ITT had been in the finance business for years, but only for those who bought ITT equipment, and for capital investments of ITT subsidiaries. Aetna Finance was in consumer loans, an entirely different game: 177 offices in 25 states, plus some life insurance. When Geneen bought Aetna, to signal the new direction he lumped all cognate units into a new subsidiary, ITT Financial Services, headed by Hart Perry. Their "business" was making money—through credit, insurance, mutual funds, whatever paid, but especially consumer-oriented finance.

The analysts and business press were very confused. *Business Week* reported that "eyebrows were being raised on Wall Street" and speculated that Geneen was galvanized by Transamerica's creation of a "financial department store." If so, they concluded, then it was not such a daring departure after all; even Sears Roebuck was planning to sell mutual funds through Allstate. They did not see that Geneen was on his own new track.

The alert might have noticed that it was the same in 1963 when he formed the Information and Data Systems division out of International Electric Corporation and Information Systems. The new entity continued bread-and-butter government work. But its thrust was in civilian data processing and time-sharing. Indeed, the big push was to process orders for Wall Street. Helicopters plied between a Garden City, Long Island, office and computers in Paramus, New Jersey. The business expanded to a new service bureau in Paris, with confident talk about Los Angeles, London, Stuttgart, Madrid, and Lille. Actually, the confidence was misplaced; ITT would get out of data processing fairly soon. But Geneen continued to seize all opportunities to move the company deeper into consumer and service fields.

That thought animated Geneen's decision to make ITT the second largest shareholder, after AT&T, in the new Communications Satellite Corporation. Comsat had been an early enthusiasm for Geneen, its novelty and possibilities nicely suited to his taste. Characteristically, he made himself an instant expert. In 1960 a financial analyst researching Comsat asked for a few minutes with Geneen. Naturally Geneen got wound up and kept the analyst enthralled for hours with a world view of satellite communication, its history, promise, problems, and applications. "If I'd started with Geneen," the analyst says, "I could have saved months of traveling and talking."

In 1964 ITT paid $21 million cash for 1,050,000 shares, 10.5% of Comsat. This hunk entitled Geneen to name two Comsat directors: Ted Westfall and Eugene R. Black, ex-head of the World Bank. Black was the first national notable Geneen recruited for ITT's board.

Feuding over Comsat had begun before the new corporation, let alone its satellite, was fairly launched. In August 1962 RCA chairman David Sarnoff campaigned to make Comsat eventually responsible for all international telephone and telegraph service from America. He and Geneen quickly were in a tiff. Sarnoff saw "the current and future needs of our nation in the space age" being best served by combining under a quasi-public authority. Geneen would never subordinate his own company's growth. That continued as the theme of his dispute with Comsat. As soon as the corporation was formed, in 1964, Geneen fought its claim to a monopoly of ground stations—receivers and transmitters of the satellite signals. Geneen wanted his own. He would brook no restrictions on the expansion of his business, surrender control to no one.

Plainly, however, he could never control Comsat. When someone once observed that he did, after all, name two directors to their board, he said, "I can assure you . . . our two votes on Comsat have never swayed *anything.*" He soon tussled with Comsat on nearly every point, including who would control television equipment on the United States Navy carrier *Lake Champlain* during the Gemini 5 splashdown.

What could he do? One of his financial staff remembers commenting that "inasmuch as we were their competitors in many ways, it was foolish for us to retain ownership in their stock—especially since it wasn't paying dividends." Selling the stock also happened to be extremely profitable. In May 1967 ITT sold 235,000 of its shares; the price had orbited. The 815,000 shares ITT had left were now worth over $50 million. Two offerings later, by the end of 1968, ITT was down to 100,000 shares and relinquished board representation. A company spokesman was frank about why they dumped the stock: Comsat was obviously going to "continue to pursue a policy designed to extend its role in the international communications field beyond that which we believe was originally contemplated. . . . " Needless to say, ITT was "in basic disagreement with this policy."

The disagreement was not just public relations. Geneen genuinely burned over what he saw as Comsat's perfidy in violating the bounds of its Congressionally assigned role as "the carrier's carrier." His anger was a residue of an idealism and naïveté he brought to ITT. "In the early days," says a former aide, "Geneen was totally incorruptible. He would accept no one who got business by bribing someone." He was sure that the person willing to work harder and longer, with more thought and dedication, would win. When other companies got contracts that he thought ITT deserved, it was a shock and a personal affront.

The same held true with his own exposure to politics. When PR man Ned Gerrity arranged Geneen's first White House dinner, both Geneen and June moped about the hotel suite beforehand, complaining bitterly. Why did they have to do such things? Gerrity detected enough diffidence so that he thought it necessary to buck Geneen up, assuring him that he was every bit as good and important as the others who would be there.

Geneen soon got into the swing. He always demonstrated an advanced talent for learning everyone's game and beating them at it. His maneuvering with the Hickenlooper Amendment was classic, and so was the aftermath. When a politician is on your side, you make sure he stays there. By 1964 Geneen enjoyed trips to Washington, making the rounds of congressmen and senators with Dita Beard. They were about to call on Senator Russell Long, who had ramrodded Hickenlooper through. The visit was at the senator's invitation, and Beard was wary. "Now Russ is going to hit you up for something," she warned Geneen, "I know it. *Please* don't do anything; just be nice." It turned out to be a social visit until Beard stepped out to confirm their next appointment. "I walked back in the office," she says, "and Hal was nodding his head and grinning, and I thought, Oh my God! What's he promised? When we left, Hal said, He's a nice fellow; we want to do something for him."

Nothing easier. "I was called into Geneen's office one day in 1964," says Klaus Scheye, then PLM for teleprinters made in England and Germany, "and he said, You're going to be manager of our U.S. teleprinter facility." The facility did not in fact exist. Scheye was to license Western Electric's design (the domestic market spurned foreign models) and set up in business. The location of the plant was immaterial—as long as it was in Louisiana. And Scheye was to be guided entirely by the senator as to selection of legal and real estate people involved in the deal. ITT never did make teleprinters in Louisiana. But they did put up the plant, and Long continued to champion ITT's interests. As *Business Week* put it during the 1967 hearings into ITT's merger with the American Broadcasting Company, challenged by the Justice Department's antitrust lawyers, "Most powerful among ITT's supporters was Senate Majority Whip Russell Long of Louisiana, usually a strong antitrust supporter; ITT recently broke ground for a new plant in his state."

By the end of 1964, ITT net was up 13.7% over 1963 on 8% greater revenue. Pennies per share were up 14%. Even more significant, just as Geneen had promised, the five-year totals had doubled—and then some:

revenue was up 101%, net up 118%. Someone who joined the company during the year was told, "Mr. Geneen has decided that we are going to be in the Fortune top ten." There was thought to be a timetable for it. Indeed, Geneen was about to make one of the key moves.

12
Trying Harder

Harold Geneen knew what he wanted to buy. In an imposing March 1965 report headed "BASIC ACQUISITION POLICY" he told his board, ". . . our *primary* interest in any acquisition is its rate of growth for the future. Since ITT is growing at a rate of 10% or better yearly on a compounded basis, any company that we acquire has to either grow at a rate of 10% plus or through our management efforts we must be able to produce a growth of 10% ahead."

That was a minimum. But for the spurt of growth that would soon propel ITT into the Fortune top ten, Geneen could not stick to the sorts of businesses he was already in. On examination, no telecom, electronics, or hard-goods manufacturing company grew faster than ITT. "We worked out the principal factors that contributed to higher earnings," says one of Geneen's top aides in those days. "And what it showed—contrary to popular belief— was that high-technology, high-capital businesses didn't earn as well as the average. It was service businesses that gave you higher returns. I remember the surprise of the board when we presented this."

Surprise or no, service businesses made sense. The expected United States population explosion and an acceleration of income and savings would surely produce more dollars looking for more services. And there was another consideration. "You can stop fifteen people in the street," Geneen would say, "and not one will know what ITT is. That bothers me." His passion to be known was not merely a matter of pride. Since some 155,000 of ITT's 190,000 employees worked overseas, "the true size of ITT is not fully recognized by the general investing public. . . . " That translated into lower prices for ITT stock, the coin Geneen used to make acquisitions. The greater visibility of service companies should help.

Geneen was not the first to ponder the population explosion or remark on America's movement toward a service economy. But he was the first large-scale industrialist to act on the implications. What bemused the others—and the analysts—was a conviction that the shoemaker must stick to his last. If the maker of telecom equipment was presumed incapable of overseeing a pump company, how could he conceivably manage a service company? Geneen had no doubts. The last five years, he told his board, had shown that his system was "a demonstrated and proven approach THAT WORKS." It would work for any kind of company. And he now had so many executives practiced in his system that ITT faced the "pleasant problem of finding enough 'fast-growing' companies . . . to provide opportunities to our expanding, proven and aggressive management group." His tigers wanted meat. It was immediately clear that a lot of business brokers and investment bankers were eager to help Geneen acquire. Among the most eager was Lazard Frères & Co.

Charles Percy thinks he may be the one who got Geneen interested in Lazard. (At Jones & Laughlin, however, one of Geneen's warmest supporters was Albert J. Hettinger, J&L board member and Lazard partner.) Percy had wanted to buy the Ansco Film division of General Analine. He found himself bidding against Sidney J. Weinberg of Goldman, Sachs & Co. "So I went to David Rockefeller," he says, "and said, I've got to find somebody smarter than Sidney Weinberg." Rockefeller said, "There's only one I know, and that's André Meyer of Lazard Frères." Percy let Geneen know of the high regard he had developed for the firm, for Meyer, and for Meyer's protégé, Felix G. Rohatyn.

Meyer thought of Rohatyn as a son. He had known Rohatyn's stepfather in France, before both families fled the Nazis to New York—Meyer in 1940 from the Paris branch of Lazard, the Rohatyns by way of Casablanca and Rio de Janeiro. Throughout high school and Middlebury College, Felix Rohatyn had studied physics, but a summer job at Lazard became permanent.

In 1960 Lazard helped Geneen buy Jennings Radio, their first deal together. Rohatyn met Geneen then but later said, "[H]e may not have as clear a recollection as I do." Although Rohatyn would become famous as the man who saved New York financially in the late 1970s, he was not then well known: as late as January 13, 1965, ITT negotiator Stan Luke would refer to him in a memo as "Felex Rohotzen." The date is significant, because one day later the merger of ITT and Avis, self-proclaimed number two in rental cars, was announced. Everyone at ITT would soon know Rohatyn and his firm much better.

In the Avis acquisition, Lazard acted not as investment banker but as principal, owning as they did 39% of the Avis stock—working control—since 1962. Back then Avis had been a demoralized company, run on a shoestring. But for all its dispiriting losses, since its birth Avis had grown nicely each year. It enjoyed a good position in a great business. Although poor second to Hertz in market share, it *was* number two, with a national name and a national network of outlets. It was ready to profit from the surge of travel spawned by passenger jets—if it got enough working capital and vigorous top management. Lazard arranged for both.

The flashiest new manager was Robert C. Townsend, a senior VP at American Express, imported as Avis president. Donald A. Petrie, president of Hertz-American Express International, came as chairman of the executive committee. Winston V. Morrow, once the Avis executive VP and general counsel, returned as manager of the vital rent-a-car division.

The newcomers jumped right in. Their first year, they could have posted a modest gain. Instead they elected to take all their lumps at once, a $648,000 loss, putting the past behind. Then it was straight up. Their advertising theme —"We're only #2. We try harder"—became famous. But there was one further item of reorganization. The Avis chairman was a lawyer, John T. Cahill. "Townsend couldn't stand Cahill," says Bud Morrow, "and was determined to get him out. The only way to do it was to make a new president so he could move up to chairman, himself." In September 1964 Morrow found himself president and COO of Avis, with Townsend chairman and CEO. Things were going swimmingly.

In December came the news that Lazard was selling to ITT. "Townsend was not very happy with this merger," Geneen said some time later. It was an understatement. Although Geneen's claim that he never made an unfriendly takeover bid was technically correct in that he never made a hostile tender offer, Avis management was as one voice against the deal. "Townsend was the soul of the opposition," says Morrow, "but none of us wanted the sale. We all thought that with Lazard Frères we'd soon be on the New York Stock Exchange and get rich. And whoever heard of ITT anyway?" But nobody at Avis had anything to say about it; Lazard controlled the stock, and André Meyer was nervous about reports of Ford's entering the rental-car field, and wanted to sell. "So we came in there with a chip on our shoulder," says Morrow.

Townsend wrote to Geneen five days after the merger announcement. Why *should* Avis still try harder? Five of Townsend's seven points addressed the incentive plan. The system had been to pay Avis executives "excessively low" salaries, made up for with bonuses limited only by results. In addition, about 160 of Avis's 2,000 people had stock options. Townsend insisted that their bonus pool continue and that their stock continue to be shares in Avis, not ITT; they would retain the legal rights of shareholders in the otherwise wholly owned subsidiary. Their share amounted to 6.7%, and their stock would appreciate as Avis prospered, not tied to ITT.

Geneen agreed. The pool of bonus money would be 15% of the pretax net. The stock deal was OK too. Anything! Geneen sensed the mood at Avis, especially Townsend's. "At that time," he said later, "my particular desire was to calm down, because the fellow was getting very excited." It was more of the usual acquisition technique. "When the courtship is on," says Morrow, "all sorts of things get said. Yes! We'll preserve the independence of your management, and you can have all the money you need for growth. Well, of course you soon learn that, No, they're going to have their own bureaucracy, and the reason they're rich is, they don't give away their money. It's almost a standard of disappointed chief executives who've been acquired."

Geneen's calming did not take. He assigned Howard C. Miller as PLM for Avis. "When Miller first came out," says Morrow, "Townsend, Petrie, and I decapitated him. We didn't care for anything he had to say, we wouldn't change anything, we didn't agree to any of the forms—nothing! It was terrible, embarrassing. Townie and I threw a few hooks in there. But mostly it was Donald. He was an absolute terror; when Petrie is really ragging somebody, he's almost unbelieveable! Felix Rohatyn got a call from ITT bitching about the way we treated their man. He told us, When they send a staff person out, you guys shouldn't abuse him. You *ate* him. You don't *do* that."

Despite all, Geneen was patient with Townsend. As he later explained, "[I]t was my concern to keep this fellow intact and get through our initial problems and merger, and then see what the real problems were."

Even before the merger closed, Townsend announced that he would not stay. In his later best seller, *Up the Organization,* he cheerfully savaged conglomerates, hoping his epitaph might be that he had never worked for one a day in his life. It was an ungenerous comment, and technically misleading, because Townsend was kept on the payroll for about two years until his options matured. When they did, Avis threw him a parody of a retirement party, "with a gold watch," says Morrow, "and all the bullshit things corporations do." In farewell, Townsend said, "I'm only sorry that André didn't put Avis on the New York Stock Exchange—instead of selling us to one of the unjolly gray giants."

The merger closed on July 22, 1965. ITT paid $18.25 a share in common and convertible, a premium of 7.9% over the price of the stock when the deal was announced. The total price was over $51 million, of which Lazard got more than $20 million.

Soon afterward, Donald Petrie joined Lazard, leaving Bud Morrow to integrate his spritely company with the giant. Morrow's own fatalism about longevity in a conglomerate conspired with Geneen's courtship promises to make Morrow intransigent on the point of Avis's independence. First came the question of the name. When selling the deal to his board, Geneen had pointed out that "The [Avis] national advertising campaign will be an opportunity for us to get broad exposure for the ITT name at an extremely low cost." The issue came to a head at what Morrow calls a "sweater session" with Geneen. It was late at night, and Geneen was lounging in his black cardigan, ready to talk business forever. "Don't you think it would be a great idea to call it ITT-Avis?" said Geneen. "No, I don't," said Morrow. And he could make that stick, because it was in fact a singularly rotten idea. The soul of Avis marketing was its image as plucky, caring little "#2," having to try harder than hulking, presumably indifferent Hertz. But ITT positively dwarfed Hertz. Trumpet the ITT connection, and goodbye to Avis's image.

Other abrasions ranged from trivial to fundamental. At the light end, ITT's accounting and reporting forms were all labeled "MFG." Avis people resented having to use manufacturing forms, which they felt did not meet a service company's needs anyhow. Morrow complained until ITT controller Herb Knortz said, "All right, we'll change; it's now a Multinational Financial Giant form. Okay?" More nettlesome was ITT staff insistence that "return on assets" was a valid test of Avis performance. Morrow thought it an unfair distortion. The nature of any car-rental company is to have assets unusually high in proportion to return. Those cars cost a lot of money. But for the most part it is not the company's money; the cars are heavily financed. So while Avis's assets were indeed comparatively huge, they were much more leveraged, and Avis had much less equity in them, than anything an MFG staff (in either reading) ever saw.

But the real adjustment Avis had to make was to Geneen's confrontational methods at the GMMs and the exhaustive monthly managers' letter that preceded each one. The first full Avis letter ran to thirty-one typewritten pages, single spaced, except for charts of revenue figures. The other units' letters were equally long; each month's collection filled a massive notebook. "I thought, Who the hell's going to read all that crap?" says Morrow. "So to get our point across I tried to pep it up a little." At first, he wrote every word himself. "I spent some time," he says, "for a good turn of phrase so staff might read it and understand our position." To explain the difficulty of used-car sales in Italy, where Fiat controlled the market, he wrote, "The effect of being on the wrong side of a monopoly is seen first hand when one deals with Fiat." On the sunny side of monopoly, he reported that in Spain, "Despite appropriately bearish remarks" in his last letter, Avis had won an exclusive concession at all Spanish airports. Now all they needed was a telephone for their main office. Even with ITT help and appeals to the Minister of Information and Tourism, Avis was still on the waiting list in Spain. "If we don't get lucky soon in this area," Morrow wrote, "our next want ads may be for experienced semaphore signalmen, with perhaps carrier pigeons for long distance."

Of course, the monthly letters were only preparation for the GMMs. And everybody had to be prepared for those, because Geneen was sure to be. "When it came to your numbers," says Morrow, "he knew them as well as you did and was not exactly charitable if you weren't right with it. The first time, I was ready to talk about the large picture; but we got down to the numbers and I was stumbling all over the place. He probably decided I wasn't as bright as he had hoped. Next time I was ready." The only way to get ready was by total immersion in operations, total familiarity with results—which was exactly what Geneen wanted. "I never studied Avis as hard as I did just before a meeting at which Geneen would be present," says Morrow. It was the only way to live with Geneen. "Nobody ever took him lightly and survived."

Adjustments made, Avis prospered for the first couple of years. Revenues kept climbing, so did profits, and Avis was the showpiece of Geneen's grand strategy. "It was the first acquisition we made that *really* raised eyebrows," says the former head of Geneen's acquisition group. *Business Week* was flabbergasted. They could not "understand why ITT wants to get into the fiercely competitive auto rental business," thereby missing all available points about Geneen, ITT and the rent-a-car field. The furor was jam to Geneen. Barely a year and a half before, the business pages of the *New York Times* had referred to him as Harold S. Green. Now if you stopped fifteen people on the street, and it was Wall Street, virtually all would know ITT and Geneen.

The romance continued through 1966. Avis's pretax net was up some 31% over 1965 and would have been higher except for some accelerated write-offs and the ill-considered acquisition, by Avis, of National Auto Renting Company (NARCO), the largest independent truck leaser in New York City, a deal that did not work out. Current earnings were fine, wrote Morrow in his manager's letter for December 1966, but trouble loomed. "For the first time in some 18 reports, I note some cloudy factors on the horizon." By mid-1967, Chrysler—which supplied some 60% of Avis's cars in the United States—hit them with an astronomical increase in lease costs. The profit squeeze was on and earnings were flat. As month after month Avis failed to meet budget, the monthly letters ran to fifty pages and more; there was a lot to explain. And Morrow no longer needed clever turns of phrase to attract staff's close attention. If Geneen was unhappy, he says, "It was like throwing blood in the water to sharks."

His independence was compromised. He still did not budge on matters central to Avis's interest, but in areas he thought unessential he had to throw staff some sops. For instance, when ITT bought the Sheraton Hotel chain, there was a move to have Avis desks accept Sheraton reservations—the sort of cooperation Geneen loved. It was folly. Avis had always shunned identification with any one hotel or airline or travel agency for fear of alienating all the others. Morrow killed that scheme. But his return on assets remained a sore spot with ITT staff, and they found his ratio for finance leasing a special outrage. They seemed incapable of grasping the economics of leasing. A million dollars' worth of cars might yield only a $30,000 pretax net. On the other hand, those cars were leveraged over their hubcaps; the leasing company might need less than $100,000 equity to get financing. "That was our argument for finance leasing," says Morrow. "We don't put much in, and look what we get back: we had at least a thirty percent return on equity." But return on assets obsessed staff; and since Morrow had other wars to fight, he gave up on finance leasing for several years.

Nineteen sixty-eight saw an Avis comeback, with just over $9 million in pretax profit, $4.7 million after-tax. But even the comparative hard times were only that, comparative; flat earnings are better than none. And there were pluses. Avis kept growing. What's more, Avis supplied much of its own credit in the United States, preserving ITT's borrowing power. Some $5.5 million in Avis borrowing was once taken off the consolidated books and arranged through the unconsolidated financial services group; that increased the parent's credit. "They were really getting a free ride," says Morrow. "They put practically nothing in and they were taking fifty percent of our profits out annually. So whenever staff became belligerent, we had a lot of good things going for us. And we had occasion to remind them of it."

They also had peculiarly effective standing as minority stockholders. With that legal interest, the top Avis executives could stand fast when ITT treated Avis like a mere wholly owned subsidiary. "We became," says Morrow, "somewhat obstreperous about our rights. Financially, that was one of my sillier bits of activity." Had the shareholders kept quiet, they might have continued to share in the 50% dividend of a hugely expanding company. As it was, Geneen realized he had a monster in his midst. In 1967, when Avis bargaining power was low, says Morrow, "Howard Miller came to me privately and let it be known that either that stock came back in, one hundred percent, or we would be merged out and have to take a one-time payment." The valuation committee was dominated by ITT, so the pay-off would be laughable—and ITT would move in on management. "I thought about it," says Morrow. "Should I quit and make a fight? I finally decided it would be a lonely, losing contest, and the hell with *that*." Avis stock was traded for ITT shares.

Geneen did not mind. Avis was his special exhibit. It showed, he told security analysts in March 1969, how ITT companies resisted business cycles, growing "fast in so-called good times. But . . . while they grow less in poor times, they still nevertheless tend to keep growing at all times. . . . This has been the cornerstone of our growth and planning philosophies." About 70% of Avis's business came from airline travelers, but only 24% of the population then flew, and of those, only 6% rented cars. That meant room for steady increase, with a strong uptrend, good times or bad. Since the merger, Geneen said, Avis's "average growth has been 40.4% per year, and in 1966—the year of the last chill wind in Wall Street—its growth was still 57.6%."

What truly captured Geneen's heart was Avis's move in Europe. "We decided," says Bud Morrow, "to try to pass Hertz in Europe. To do it, we needed a national account program, which meant a full-blown sales force before we had anything like the underpinning to support it. Our concept had to be explained very carefully to ITT, because it violated most of the rules; typically you add salesmen as you get increments of income. So even when they agreed to our plan, we had to remind them of the agreement from time to time." Mostly, they had to remind the ITT treasury department. "A guy named Ohmes," says Morrow, "wanted to get rid of our whole European operation at the end of the first year because it didn't offer a proper return on investment. In fact, it was losing its ass: we were still getting started—all over, all at once."

Certainly Robert D. Ohmes thought Avis had no business being in Europe. "Their own numbers," he says "proved it was not economically justifiable." The market was very difficult. Repairs were harder, the resale market chancy, one-way fares across national borders a red-tape nightmare. But more fundamentally, Ohmes thought Avis had no business being part of

ITT. The debt-equity ratio of the rental-car business was simply wrong for a manufacturing company. "I always added," Ohmes says, "that if you could get Avis off the balance sheet, treated separately, everything I said, forget. But as long as it was consolidated, you had to justify this debt-equity ratio"—especially when invading a new market, because there would be additional debt. And that, says Ohmes, "would impinge on ITT's capabilities for getting funds for other areas."

The clash—and Morrow's feeling in general about ITT staff—was a pure example of Geneen's system. Staff was *supposed* to challenge the line. And line had to justify its plans, regardless of how weighty the project or how junior the challenger. Ohmes, not quite thirty years old, was a new hire in the acquisition group. But his analysis occasioned a formal investigation, chaired by Tim Dunleavy, to see if Avis's European operation should indeed be written off. Avis had only one edge. "Geneen liked the idea of an American company expanding in Europe," says Morrow. "Dunleavy was a little nonplussed; but he came back and said, Okay, Geneen says you can have another two million dollars—or something like that. What other company would have been as good as Geneen was? He had his eye on the long pull." Today Avis does about a half-billion dollars a year in Europe.

Geneen was equally farsighted about the Avis reservation system, ADVANCE—later called "The Wizard of Avis." This would be the first time a rental-car company had connected all offices with a Programmed Airline Reservation System (PARS)—the kind that had brought ITT to grief with Air France. The project started in earnest in late 1968. ITT Data Systems had bid for the job, but, says Morrow, "they just weren't up to it." Avis hired Greenwich Data Systems, recognized PARS experts, and Morrow beamed confidence and enthusiasm. Still, this was a huge undertaking. A lot of money was at risk in an area that made Geneen reflexively nervous. In 1970 Geneen posed five questions. Would the system really do all that was claimed for it? Would it really effect significant savings? Wouldn't a simpler, cheaper system do? After all, Avis clerks were scarcely computer specialists; could they make ADVANCE work? Finally, was interest figured into the appropriations request? The answer to this last question indicates the project's cost: interest alone would be $1,987,000 for five years. In fact, Morrow answered all the questions convincingly enough to still Geneen's doubts. But the clincher was probably his assurance that Greenwich Data would "accept considerable financial risks" to guarantee performance. Geneen knew painfully, from the other side, what that could mean. He was sold, and his patronage survived some horrendous difficulties. When his imagination was engaged, Geneen would always invest in the future.

Morrow had another ally beside's Geneen's vision. He became adept in the art of handling Geneen. He had learned during the hard times of 1967 to tell Geneen about sensitive matters well ahead of meetings. "If things were not coming through as we had expected," he says, "we would sit down and talk about it, so he understood what we were doing and where we were going. Then, when it came up in the meeting, Geneen would say, Oh, I know about that—and go right over it." That both defanged the staff and kept Geneen from having to take a publicly hostile posture. Most of all, Morrow learned to let Geneen have the last word, to talk himself out. Geneen might glare across a meeting table and say, "Well, we may have to write this off"—when the ADVANCE investment was already some $16 million. "He was sort of putting a chip on his shoulder," says Morrow. "I didn't say anything. I looked at him and he looked at me, and that was that. Earlier, I probably would have picked up the cudgels and lumbered in there; and that would have been very counterproductive." In private, Geneen would talk himself back around to his pro-ADVANCE position.

Geneen's intense pride in the new system figured largely in his fling as Avis's copywriter. He had always been intrigued by advertising; and although being anything other than number one was never to his taste, the Avis "# 2" campaign had been unanswerably successful. When Avis switched to the "Bugs" campaign—cartoons of the faults that can plague rental cars—Geneen was aghast. What was *this?* One night early in January 1972 he slipped on his black cardigan and scrawled thirteen pages of ad copy to Avis executive William C. McPike, with the message that he was passing on some random thoughts in hopes that they might provoke better ones. He commended the perkiness of the "# 2" campaign. Avis ads, he opined, must be bright, fresh, and positive—certainly not subtle.

His first idea was that Avis claim now to be # 1½ —and catching up! Maybe even # 1⅜. But that was just spitballing, as they say down at the agency. Idea number two was that Avis is fresher. Their cars turn over every six months, and The Wizard of Avis was tireless in remembering reservations. The Wizard was also brighter—able to add, to multiply, and most particularly to substract whenever a special rate was available. Yes indeed! Geneen wrote, The Wizard was bright as a penny, and most careful with each penny on the customer's account.

Idea number three was the prize: separate pieces of copy, each written in a form that looked like a particularly modern-design blank verse poem, celebrating the way Avis drives: much straighter, friendlier, and more beautifully than the competition. For instance, the customer should go *straight* to the Avis counter and see for himself: the only curved thing he would find would be the smile greeting him on the face of the Avis Girl.

To show how friendly Avis is, Geneen proposed telling Avis customers —Ernest, Percival, William, Harrison, and Lucille—that The Wizard wanted to know them better; after all, he was always looking out for their interests. So Ernie, Percy, Bill, Harry, and Lucy should just write their friendly names across their next statements, and The Wizard would reissue credit cards on a first-name basis. Hal then adjured Ernie and the rest of the gang to find out for themselves how much better things were at the Avis counter.

His final idea was:

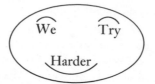

    Avis decided to wait that one out. Geneen was never insistent in such matters. And within six months came word of the antitrust settlement that mandated the divestiture of Avis.

What did ITT think of Morrow—and vice versa? He patently did a fine job of running Avis and was known as one of the brightest and wittiest people in the corporation. But he was never seen (nor, of course, did he want to be) as any sort of "team member." He visibly chafed under corporate discipline, never fit in, and was resented by some for this lack of community.

    Morrow's view of ITT—and especially of Geneen—is complex. The GMMs were not thrilling; the elaboration of reports comforted ITT but did not help in the field. Even so, the essence of the system was vitally useful. "You can't get to be big without what ITT demanded," says Morrow. And, like many others, he later adopted the system for his own, independent enterprises—minus whatever he considered its more oppressive and wasteful features.

    Morrow was never personally close to Geneen. After his refusal to be known as "ITT-Avis" came another meeting at which Morrow used a word that Geneen did not know. "He said, What's that mean?" says Morrow, "and I was surprised because it wasn't that involved a word. That was pretty nearly the last time I saw Geneen privately." A top ITT executive once tried for rapprochement, seating Morrow at Geneen's table at a company party. The talk turned to enlargement of ITT's publishing operations: what companies would complement ITT's subsidiary, Howard Sams. "Like a goddamn fool," says Morrow, "I cut in and said, "Why don't you hire some authors and editors and build publishing companies yourself? I could see it in his eyes: I was just dead. 'Develop' as opposed to 'acquire.' A funny look in his eyes, and I was gone, as if I had left the earth."

    Morrow's account of his own death in Geneen's eyes was premature. In 1983, when Morrow was president of a large title insurance company in Los Angeles, TICOR, Geneen and he formed a group of investors to take over the company. Morrow had always admired the man: "You could pick at various parts as I did—and other magpies like me did. We might comment and see the humor in something. But anybody would have to be terribly impressed with the immense balance that he put into ITT. He was head and shoulders over the other execs I've met. Maybe not as a person; lots of guys you'd like far better. But when it came down to who you want to run your company. . . . "

13

Harold in Europe— and Elsewhere

fter five years of Geneen's leadership, ITT's European revenue had more than doubled—up 108% on only 75% more plant; in 1964 European revenue was greater than ITT's worldwide revenue had been in 1959. This still was not enough for Geneen; he hankered after expansion in nontelecom and nongovernment business. ITT flacks unflaggingly bragged about the $150 million European TV and appliance operation, the two million logic circuits built for Burroughs, and such like. It was, though, mostly wind. ITT had to buy TV tube knowhow from RCA; and though European sales volume of components and consumer goods was respectable, profits were not. In fact, according to John Turbidy, then consumer products group manager in Europe, the whole operation was in disarray. In Britain, small companies with indifferent brands struggled along. In France, ITT had bought Oceanic for $4 million in 1965; an entrepreneur had run the hip-pocket enterprise at a tidy profit, but it did not prosper in the big time under ITT. Italy and Denmark were losers, Belgium was so-so. In Germany, strong Schaub-Lorenz made good radios and TVs but was about to enter a wrenching decline.

So despite Geneen's fond wishes, consumer products stayed a sideshow. In 1965, about two-thirds of Europe's sales of just over $900 million came from telecommunications. ITT supplied 30% of all European phone equipment in use by 1964, more than its two closest competitors combined. And Europe still provided over half of ITT's total revenue.

These facts dictated Geneen's organizational strategy for ITT-Europe. Since all turned on the good will of the host countries, the guiding principle was always to consult national sensitivities, and even crotchets. To start, ITT stressed the national identification of each unit. SEL was *German*,

LMT *French*, BTM *Belgian*, STC *British*, and so on. Their connection with ITT was a different matter. In Germany, where American methods were generally admired, the connection was transparent; for the French, who admire nothing un-French, it was opaque. In Belgium, where that issue did not matter but another did, ITT meticulously apportioned facilities between the Flemish and Walloon sectors. And, everywhere, the "Five-Man Rule" was ITT writ: no more than five executives in any European unit could be Americans, and they were almost invariably in finance. Managing directors reported to a country manager, who was, except in Spain, also a national of that country. As a final touch, Geneen recruited the most plangent names available for the boards of the European companies. The prides of his collection were Trygve Lie in Norway, Lord Caccia in Britain, and Paul-Henri Spaak in Belgium. The Belgian humor weekly, *Pan*, chortled over the fiery old socialist in bed with multinational conglomeration; they called him "Paul-HenrITT." Yet ITT had excellent relations throughout Europe; even the French considered it a model of corporate citizenship.

The Brussels headquarters group soon outgrew its second-floor walk-up. By 1964 it had a building at 11 Avenue de l'Empereur. On top, in big blue letters, was the name "ITT EUROPE" flanked by blue and white flags bearing the logo. The imposing structure curved around the corner between party HQ of the Belgian socialists and the national unemployment office. It was meeting place for ITT's European Advisory Council (EAC) and Strategy and Action Board (SAB).

The EAC was Geneen's European version of the GMM and was in session four days every month except August and December. Geneen and his senior New York staff flew over for virtually every meeting; the EAC was his principal instrument of control. "They are a hell of a lot of work," said one manager, "but the result is that no problem stays unsolved for more than one month." The SAB met about six times a year to discuss major product lines in excruciating detail. Each SAB was preceded by a week's confabulation among the operating people, the PLMs, and Brussels staff, with up to thirty product-line experts flying in from New York for the meeting itself. Then, each September, came the business plan review, a four- to six-week process. ITT executive opinion divided over whether the company initials stood for "International This and That" or "I Travel and Talk."

If the EAC was Geneen's instrument of control, the president of ITT-Europe was his remote finger on the button. Admiral Ellery Stone, who replaced Marc de Ferranti, was a perfect stopgap. He looked the elder statesman, had polish enough to satisfy Europeans, and, most important, harbored no pretensions about running things. Unfortunately, though not a "real" admiral, he had an authentic military inclination to leave the work for his adjutants. That created a power vacuum. Add the normal staff-line stresses, magnified by the natural U.S.-European mistrust, and the infighting around

Brussels was terrific. "The political aspects of the European organization are just not describable," says someone who saw them firsthand. "Geneen fostered them in a lot of ways because he put some people over there that really acted as his little spies, and there was a lot of intrigue going on all the time."

A good deal of the intrigue revolved around the question of succession. Stone was about to retire, and the most likely replacement was his executive VP, Charles Sherwood. But there were two drawbacks to Sherwood's candidacy: his wife, who hated Brussels, and his own inordinate pride.

The crunch came in the spring of 1963, at the first ITT Boca Raton gathering. ITT executives from around the world congregated in New York with their spouses, then went by private train to the Florida resort for a gala. Sherwood had been promised the trip with his wife, who yearned for a respite from Brussels. But the Belgian company, BTM, was then a shambles. The managing director would have to be replaced, and someone had to take charge meanwhile. The admiral sailed off to Boca Raton, leaving Charlie Sherwood to hold the fort.

Tim Dunleavy had followed Jack Graham from RCA to ITT in 1962. Now, as Geneen's executive assistant, he saw the cables back and forth between Sherwood and Stone. "They got into a pissing contest," says Dunleavy. "It was getting to the point of Charlie practically telling them, Stuff this job up your ass. So we realized we had a problem. And Geneen said to me, I think you better go over there and take Charlie's place."

Dunleavy took along two staffers, Jules Berke and Neil Firestone. At BTM they installed a new managing director—Frank Pepermans, who had run Ford's Belgian operation. That settled the crisis. Then Berke stayed on to solve a chronic BTM shipping problem. Meanwhile, Dunleavy became Stone's new deputy. And with that inside track, he succeeded as president of ITT-Europe in January 1965.

Nearly every ITT executive has an emphatic opinion about Tim Dunleavy. "Tim was . . . well . . . " says one former colleague, searching for the right word, "he was . . . an idiot." Hearing that, another says indignantly, "That's ridiculous. Tim was a very bright guy." Many maintain that Dunleavy was indeed quite bright—and smart enough to hide it. That was perhaps the essence of his role. To survive as president of ITT-Europe and a top Geneen aide, you had to be an extension of Geneen, making Geneen's moves, not your own. That could make anyone appear dumb. Unlike Charlie Sherwood, Dunleavy never pretended they were his own moves. "Charlie acted," says a former staff man in Europe, "like he was making his own decisions, like he was really running things. Now *that's* dumb!"

Being thought Geneen's boy excited neither shame nor resentment in Dunleavy. Actually, he says, it was inevitable. "Geneen was so objective, I had no conflicts. If it looked like I was doing things because he said it, it was because I recognized that they were the right things to do, and objectively I'd do it that way if it was my company."

The only consensus among ITT executives about Dunleavy concerns his personality. Short and corpulent ("I always say I'm the right weight, I'm just not the right height for it"), he was the company's Mr. Nice Guy. His chauffeur called him "a real sweet guy." His unfailing graciousness at ITT social functions bordered on ritual humility. He invariably played bartender on the company plane. On one flight he took orders from some poker players, mixing the drinks and bringing them over. One young man eyed his Scotch and water, held out the glass, and said, "More ice, Tim," and ever-jovial Tim scurried off to add ice. "And this kid was just some bag carrier!" says an amazed witness. Another colleague speaks of "that smiling Irish face." But Mr. Nice Guy was no softie.

Dunleavy's rise in Europe marked a watershed in the Geneening of the Europeans. Admiral Stone was the last president who boasted something of his own, non-ITT distinction; Tim Dunleavy was first of the ITT functionaries. Equally, Corneille Van Rooy, the deposed BTM manager, was last of those with an invincibly European business view; his replacement, Frank Pepermans, was first of the new, Americanized breed who revered "management principles" as ardently as any new-minted M.B.A. But the greatest necessary wrench was in attitude. Up to 1965, European managers could survive by adopting the vocabulary and form of Geneen's system. Now they had to embrace its substance.

Early on, the managers could get by with little more than a new style of thought about the proper relationship between managers and their enterprises. It had taken Geneen's marketing director to introduce one French managing director to his own sales manager. Geneen's EAC hammering soon ended that sort of disengagement. But most rising managers were of a new generation whose business careers encompassed only the postwar boom. Most had never known anything but upgraphs and sunshine. In the gloom of Europe's first postwar business downturn, in 1965, they discovered the less palatable logic of Geneen's methods.

The Europe-wide slump in consumer electronics was most pronounced in television, where ITT had its largest position. Color TV was plainly coming, though it was not yet marketable. What should have been equally plain was that black-and-white sales, already down, would continue to drop. But, as a top ITT-Europe executive explained, "The typical European businessman is simply not sensitive to the same danger signals as an American." Nor is he as ruthless. "Cutbacks" had once meant closing the marginal operations of prospering units; now they meant flat closings. It used to be that superfluous workers here could be reassigned there; at worst, a manager could flatter himself that, overall, he continued to employ more and more people. Now there were layoffs. "European managers," says the staff man Geneen assigned to ride herd on European layoffs, "equated power, prestige, and stature more with the number of people that worked for them than with how much the company earned. They were very reluctant to reduce work force, either direct or indirect, even when the business turned awful."

The TV operation in Britain, in trouble from 1963 on, was first to slump in 1965. By the third quarter, Germany followed. The consumer products VP of SEL was Hans Heinz Griesmeier. Throughout 1965 he either misread the signs or ignored their implications. "We told him it was going to happen," says Tim Dunleavy, "because we had seen it happen in the U.S. Geneen had climbed all over him for eight months, saying, You haven't been listening to our people."

"He had a huge inventory," says John Turbidy, the PLM, "and we just had to cut the hell out of the German operation. We had to cut back from about five thousand people to three thousand, and close several plants. And Griesmeier just didn't have the stomach for it."

By early 1966, even telecom business was off. ITT's German work force was cut from 37,000 to 30,000, and when the German managers protested, Richard E. Bennett, who had organized the North American staff, told them it was that kind of rigidity that had cost them the war. Another 3,000 people were laid off in the rest of ITT-Europe, and inventory was slashed almost $100 million. As a result, ITT was in good shape when the more general European recession deepened. In 1966, while the profits of Holland's Philips dropped 12%, Germany's Siemens and AEG-Telefunken 12% and 25% respectively, ITT was off only 3%; and ITT actually gained during the real recession of 1967.

Hans Griesmeier was among the casualties of the period. James A. Goodson was rushed in to oversee all European consumer products. Griesmeier left and eventually became a director of Grundig, then of Krauss Maffey, a company that makes the Leopard tanks. Another, more surprising casualty was Hermann Abtmeyer. Even though he was master of the largest, most profitable operation in ITT-Europe and was closest to Geneen in daring and vision, there were stresses—like the Air France fiasco and the failure of Abtmeyer's components adventure in Spain. Vision was vision, but failure was failure. His promotion of Griesmeier as successor was another black mark, once Griesemeier's frailty was exposed. So was his foot dragging over Dieter Moehring, a gifted young man in SEL who looked good to New York. Finally there was a personal angle. "Hermann got pretty loaded a couple of evenings in Brussels," says John Turbidy, "and in the hearing of a number of people began criticizing Geneen." Naturally it got back. By 1967 Moehring was at the EAC meetings in Abtmeyer's place. "Hermann became a sort of nonperson toward the end," says Turbidy. He died in 1971.

In Spain, the situation was even more complex. SESA looked like a rock in 1965, immune from downturns because it was by law Spain's sole source for telephone equipment. Managing director Manuel Márquez Mira was best of friends with the phone company's head, José Clará. Everything was so friendly, SESA sometimes started manufacture without waiting for a purchase order.

Márquez radiated courtly charm and wit. Not long after the Air France debacle, someone mentioned computers at a Brussels meeting, which naturally set Geneen off. There had been several late nights in a row, and although a small side meeting was to follow, this one was due to end around eight. A plate of sandwiches had been brought in for the stayers, but most had dinner reservations in a first-class restaurant. By nine Geneen had barely warmed to his theme, and people started chomping. At nine forty-five, with a lone sandwich left on the plate, Geneen asked for comments. Márquez said, "In the future, Mr. Geneen, let's have more sandwiches and less computers." Later, when the ITT directors came through Madrid, the fall of McKinney's attempted putsch, Márquez hosted a lunch. At the end he rose to say, "Mr. Geneen, some people call you a dictator." Unaware of the tension, and oblivious to the tableau of pregnant looks he had inspired, he went on, "But you're no dictator. We sit around Brussels and talk, and someone says something, and you say, Good idea! Dictators don't say other people have good ideas. So you're not a dictator. But you talk and talk. You say, Just ten more minutes! And an hour later, you're still talking. Again you say, Ten more minutes, and it goes on and on. Mr. Geneen, you're not a dictator; you just don't know how to tell time." With that he presented Geneen with an engraved watch—which Geneen added to the two he was already wearing, one on New York time, the other, Brussels.

But time, and Geneen's exactions, had taken their toll. "Márquez was showing his age," says Tim Dunleavy. At an audience with Spanish dictator Francisco Franco to mark the opening of some new plants, "Geneen promised we'd export five to ten percent of our production out of there, and old Márquez damn near died! Geneen and he began to drift apart."

Much of the drift was over succession. Márquez wanted his son, Manuel Márquez Balin. Geneen, unsure, accused Márquez of stacking the deck by not bringing along any other prospects. "It got to the point," says Dunleavy, "of them almost not talking." The issue sharpened when Franco suddenly replaced Márquez's old friend Clará, the head of the phone company, with the young minister of planning, Antonio Barrera de Irimo. Apparently Clará had been losing favor right along. Had Márquez missed the signs? Chosen not to warn New York of his friend's decline? Either way, says John Turbidy, "Geneen felt he had gotten a bad appreciation of the political situation for some time from Márquez." Now the situation was desperate. The usual five-year contract with ITT was up, and Barrera proposed to break ITT's monopoly. He wanted competitive bids.

Arthur G. Williams was installed as country manager to supervise negotiations. "Geneen came down on a number of occasions with Tim Dunleavy," says Williams. "And it's a funny thing: when Geneen was there, it was sweetness and light between him and Barrera; you'd have thought they were old friends. Same with Tim." But beneath the geniality, talk was tough. ITT was handicapped in the negotiations by Spanish law forbidding layoffs except in bankruptcy. So Geneen's strategy was to feign interest in other business. "We didn't let Barrera threaten us," says Williams. "He once said, You know, I don't have to buy anything from you people. And Tim Dunleavy said, Well, if we don't make telecom equipment, maybe we'll make shoes." Barrera finally agreed to a modified five-year contract: no more monopoly for ITT, just a substantial portion of Spain's telecom business. What won Barreva over? "Long, hard discussions," says Williams.

Meanwhile, the need to replace Márquez was urgent. Barrera was a prickly sort, "a very standoffish kind of guy," says Williams. And Williams, at thirty-seven, was near the new phone boss's age; plainly Márquez, incarnation of the old guard, would never get on with him, while Márquez's son, Manuel, had at least the virtue of relative youth. However, Manuel had a nervous tic, a rolling of his eyes. "You'd be sitting in a meeting," says Dunleavy, "and every so often you'd think the guy was having a fit or something. Geneen would out h that and say, Hey! Is that sonofabitch all right?" Geneen dispatched Jack Hanway to find out.

Hanway, who had married a Mexican, spoke some spanish, Geneen figured that might help. ("Geneen must have bought a hundred of those teach-yourself language books," says Tim Dunleavy. He had even taken lessons. Nothing helped. And he was touchy about his own incapacity for languages. Once during the succession talks, Dunleavy planned to spend the weekend near Márquez's summer home. On Friday, at the end of a phone call with Geneen, Dunleavy said, "If you want me the next couple of days, I'll be at the Felipe Segundo." Before he could give the phone number, Geneen snapped, "Who the fuck is he? Does he work for us?" Dunleavy explained that it was a hotel. "Well . . . don't use that goddamn Spanish on *me!*") Hanway, on return, reported that Manuel was all right after all; indeed, he was quite bright and capable, goggle eyes or no. He got the job.

But he could not warm to Barrera any better than his father could. "We used to talk about one-on-one," says Dunleavy, "knowing who Barrera eats with, sleeps with, does everything with, for chrissake! Who he plays golf with —you do the same things, and get to know the guy. That wasn't Manuel's cup of tea at that particular time. He didn't know how to do it. But eventually he learned." And in time, Geneen saw him as one of the most effective of the European managers.

In Britain, matters verged on hopeless throughout the 1960s. Creed and Company did indifferently well with teleprinters, but only under frequent staff prodding. The lead company, STC, was a perennial mess. Geneen had replaced the original managing director, but things did not improve under Rex B. Grey, a transplanted Texan. Alistair D. Mackay came next. Personable, gregarious, a hard drinker with impressive recuperative powers, Mackay was cherished by some at ITT for his song about a Scot who had forgotten to wear anything under his kilt; it was a treat to hear Mackay bawling out the line, "Doo-nald, where's yer troo-sers?" Geneen was not amused; STC was still a mess. Dunleavy argued that Mackay, who had many chums in the British PTT, should stay on at least until a new telecom contract was signed. But Geneen found Mackay's 1966 business plan dubious. Mackay was held over for a closer examination, and someone told Geneen of seeing Mackay come into the hotel at 7:00 A.M., off of a night's carouse, before the climactic Saturday face-off. He showed up looking as though he had just enjoyed twenty-two hours' sleep; but when Geneen bore in, neither Mackay nor his plan could hold up under the grilling.

There followed what one observer called "a charming but ineffectual group of managers" until 1971, when Kenneth Corfield was moved over from Brussels staff. Corfield earned Geneen's personal enmity, not long after his appointment, at a party in Brussels. A gallant Englishman, Corfield kissed June's hand when introduced to her. Geneen muttered to Dunleavy, "Hey, that sonofabitch was kissing all the way up her arm. We better look out for him." Geneen later felt that Corfield's acquisitions were not the right kind. Otherwise Corfield was Geneen's kind of manager, cutting costs, pruning unprofitable operations and unproductive people. Corfield told a reporter, "If there's one thing you learn at ITT it is that sales have no point unless they are profitable. Too many managers are still dazzled by volume, and talk proudly about how many people they employ. Nonsense, all nonsense. It is the bottom line that counts, not the top one." He stayed, made STC prosper, and indeed outlasted Geneen.

In Italy, ITT's business was either very, very good, or it was horrid. In 1964, it owned 51% of FACE (for Fabbrica Apparecchiature per Communicazioni Electtriche Standard S.p.A.), in Milan; the Pirelli company had the other 49%. "They wanted to sell," says Tim Dunleavy, "and all we wanted was to make sure we didn't look too obvious as we said, Well . . . we'll think about it." Geneen paid court to the firm's patriarch, Leopoldi Pirelli. The two hit it off, and Geneen invited the old man to visit ITT's Brussels operation. Pirelli regretfully explained that his health precluded travel; but they agreed to meet again, some three months later, in Milan. Geneen, enthusiastic, enjoined Dunleavy to make sure the meeting took place.

Dunleavy coordinated with FACE managing director Carlo Roda, a long-time ITT man. Both kept reminding their principals to keep open the scheduled date. The week before it, on a Thursday, Geneen telexed Dunleavy from New York to ask what day had been set. Suddenly nervous, Dunleavy telexed back the date and stressed the time their plane had to leave Brussels for Milan. Late Friday, Geneen telexed that he had thought the meeting was to be in Brussels; he had other meetings scheduled that day. Couldn't Pirelli come to Brussels? Dunleavy called Carlo Roda, who had been assuring Pirelli for three months that everything was set. Roda, downcast, agreed to tell Pirelli that something had come up and to ask if he could not travel this once. The answer came by wire:

TIM DUNLEAVY
BRUSSELS

IMPOSSIBLE LEOPOLDI PIRELLI COME BRUSSELS. REGRETS UNABLE SEE GE-
NEEN THIS MONTH.

NEW SUBJECT: DO NOT EVER ASK ME SET UP MEETING FOR GENEEN WITH
POPE. GENEEN SURE ASK LAST MINUTE, "CAN POPE COME TO BRUSSELS?"

REGARDS, CARLO

The missed meeting did not affect negotiations. ITT bought the Pirelli interest in FACE, a suberb investment.

Domel was different. Set up in 1963, ITT Domel Italiana was the sort
of project Geneen adored, an export outlet for German and Belgian consumer
products in Italy. They were sold mostly on credit, customers signing a book
of notes, called *"cessioni"* (assignments), and nicknamed "butterflies," perhaps
for their elusiveness when you went to collect. Dealers fobbed the *cessioni* off
on suppliers, and in default they might pay Domel (at best) in other goods.
On top of that inherent shakiness, the 1965 downturn killed the company.

Someone had to administer last rites, and the assignment was made in
classic ITT style. Dominick F. Sementa, an ITT staff close-out specialist, was
paged at New York's Kennedy Airport as he dragged back from a months-
long assignment in Brazil. He must go forthwith to Milan. When he protested
that he hadn't even seen his wife yet, he was told to take her along. In Milan,
Sementa found that three distributors were going to sue ITT because, suddenly without product, they would be forced out of business. He arranged
for enough TV sets to last them a year. They had twelve months to pay—
and to stock other lines. Everyone was happy, and Domel was unlitigiously
liquidated.

In Belgium, BTM prospered under Frank Pepermans, subject only to the
inevitable 1965 slowdown. In France, the two main companies, LMT and
CGCT, were sound telecom suppliers, not much troubled by recession. Indeed, most of ITT-Europe was toughing out the recession. Geneen once said
that the difference between good times and bad was that he had to work
harder to get the same results in bad.

From 1960 through 1966, ITT acquired as many companies in Europe
as in the United States, twenty-two, but of lesser size and consequence. The
preference was for non-PTT companies. That was bad news in the recession,
and eventually much of the direct consumer business languished. But Geneen's successful industrial diversifications far outnumbered the clinkers. For
instance, while looking at Sheraton Hotels, Geneen discovered that their $20
million subsidiary, Thompson Industries, which made auto parts, returned far
more than the hotels. That must be a good business! Soon Geneen bought
Alfred Teves in Germany, one of Europe's top producers of automotive
brakes. It was the start of what would become an ITT mini-empire in auto
parts.

Most ITT people say that Geneen himself ran Europe. How directly? Tim Dunleavy points out that, given the time difference, Brussels staff had put in six or seven hours before Geneen, in New York, woke up. But while the helmsman's hand is more often on the wheel than the captain's, there is no question as to who is setting the course. No one in ITT-Europe dreamed of making a major decision without Geneen's active participation and approval; and many minor decisions were his as well. Dunleavy might get fifteen to thirty phone calls a *day* from Geneen. Many were strategic; but even the seemingly insubstantial ones were Geneen's way of checking that his vicar was doing the job as he wanted it done. "He might ask me something like, How are things looking this month?" says Dunleavy. "Are we getting Germany to go along on tax incentives? Is Abtmeyer working on it? How's it coming? Now, he'd get that from his tax man in New York; but he wanted to see if I knew what the hell was going on, and to be sure I was talking to Hermann."

Geneen ran Europe—not least with his incessant pushing of subordinates for follow-up, or, as Dunleavy puts it, "keeping the heat on our people." Even STC, with all its problems, got business that its two British rivals—General Electric Company (no kin) and Pleissy—could easily have won. "We got dominant even though the government didn't want us to be dominant," says Dunleavy. How? By Geneen's pushing. "Geneen was always saying, When are you guys coming up with something new? I don't have to have all the answers, goddamnit! So you were trying to get things going or worked out before he got into the act."

Between 1959 and 1972, profits in Europe had increased some 530%. Everyone in the organization knew who was largely responsible.

LATIN AMERICA

The moment Geneen arrived, Latin America's importance to ITT diminished. Part was his determination to shift earnings toward the United States. The other part was his political wariness—even more pronounced in Latin America than in Europe (if you mistrust an Erhard or a de Gaulle, you positively dread a Castro or Allende). But Geneen could not just cut and run. First, the region continued to prove a bonanza. In 1965, 10% of ITT's worldwide sales were still there, 80% in telephone, radio, and cable operating companies—$143,796,000 worth—with their high profit margins on low investment. Even more important was Geneen's uncheckable enthusiasm for consumer business, anywhere. In 1965, Latin American consumer sales were $9,200,000, almost all in Brazil and Argentina and almost all in trouble.

Late on a Friday in December 1964, Geneen summoned marketing director Henry Bowes to his office. Brazil's consumer products were in an acute pickle. Bowes was booked on the night flight to Rio. He should meet Geneen in Brussels, a week from Monday, to report. Well . . . but . . . Bowes had been out of consumer goods for years and had never been near Brazil; how could he tell what—

"Well, hell," Geneen said, "you've *got* eight days." Bowes's new wife, Samantha, had been phoned, was packing, and would meet him at the airport. She was going along. A limo was waiting.

Geneen's signature was on more than the theatrics. "If you'd asked me could I do it," says Bowes, "I'd have said, No way!" But Geneen never asked. And Bowes discovered that at the GMMs he had absorbed more than he realized about Brazil and its consumer products. Finally, the fix was ad hoc and did not address the area's more profound consumer-product problems— another aspect of ITT marketing under Geneen.

Bowes was joined in Rio by Dominick Sementa, who stayed on. They found eighty-seven models of ITT TV sets, mostly losers. They cut back to the fifteen best sellers and changed styling, making their own cabinets from a beautiful local wood, jacaranda, in place of molded plywood whose rounded corners had tried to suggest the old RCA models. In three months the line turned a profit. However, another line—table-top stereos—would have to go; manufacturing space was needed to fill a new telecom contract. Sementa announced a mythical new line of stereo equipment. Full-page ads showed drawings of the nonexistent new sets. They were priced markedly higher than the current line—which would be sold at special close-out prices. "Then," says Sementa, "we notified dealers that each was allowed to buy only a certain amount of our current product. We cleaned it out, closed the door, and were out of the stereo business. Normally, on a liquidation, you're lucky if you get twenty to thirty percent; we got a profit."

It turned out to be only short term. Soon ITT was losing about 25¢ on each Brazilian TV and radio sales dollar. That operation was folded. And when Sementa returned to Latin America (after closing Domel) it was to liquidate ITT's consumer products in Chile and Argentina. Any future in Latin America would be in telecom, and that would have to change. The expropriations in Cuba and Brazil showed that operating companies were doomed. Geneen's only room for maneuver would be in negotiating favorable terms.

In Chile, President Eduardo Frei Montalva announced a February 1965 agreement to let the government and the public acquire 49% of the phone company by 1970. Meanwhile, ITT would add 185,000 new lines and expand telecom manufacturing in Chile. The accord did not survive wrangles over rate increases. But the agreement showed the trend.

In Peru, after a 1968 coup, the military government began negotiations for ITT's Compañía Peruana de Teléfonos Limitada. The talks dragged on. One sticky point was the Calvo Doctrine, which denied any authority higher than Peruvian law. It meant ITT would renounce all right of appeal. John G. Christy, an ITT negotiator, shuttled back and forth, briefing Geneen. He was enthralled by Geneen's solution: Christy should get the U.S. State Department to agree that if ITT surrendered its rights, *they* would undertake any necessary appeals to international tribunals. Christy was stunned by the simple daring—and by State's willingness to go along.

Another holdup was over caducity, the principle that provides for the lapse of treaties when the original causes of the agreement have disappeared. In this case the snag was not with the principle but with the word itself. Caducity sounded suggestive to the Americans, especially on the lips of one Peruvian negotiator, an attractive woman. When she also referred to telephone handsets as "instruments of connection," Christy and a friend amused themselves while the talks droned on by composing fake telexes. Their prize WAS: HAVE BEEN CADUCED STOP OUR INSTRUMENTS OF CONNECTION SEIZED. The Peruvian woman wanted to know what they were chuckling about; embarrassed, they could not explain, and the talks stalled for another week.

An agreement was finally signed in March 1970. Peru paid $17.9 million for ITT's 69.11% of the phone company. ITT would put $12 million of it into a new, luxury Sheraton hotel. Another $840,000 would go into an equipment plant, owned 60% by—and run by—ITT; for $560,000, Peru would own 40%, gradually increasing to 50%.

In Argentina, ITT lost all its operating companies. When seizing phone companies, Latin American countries generally excepted radio and cable operations, since they were international, and the countries feared retaliation or breakdown in service. But on September 19, 1970, Argentina nationalized all communications. "In some cases," commented the *New York Times*, "governments decided that the companies' profits over the years have more than compensated them for their investments." One official frankly explained that since communications were just another natural resource, countries wanted "the chance of exploiting them ourselves, rather than leaving them to the foreign pirates."

Geneen's eventual Chilean tragedy was not inevitable; he brought it on himself. But it followed from the situation he found in Latin America. Colonel Behn's freewheeling days were gone; Geneen's negotiations proved he knew that, and so (at least symbolically) did the 1966 replacement of Ted Westfall by Gerry Andlinger as Latin America group executive. Andlinger's was a more sinuous European manner than that of "Fullback" Westfall. Still, Geneen shared the general American business contempt for the region. The way you did business anywhere south of Texas was simple: you bribed people. "Geneen had a total feeling that you can buy anybody," says Klaus Scheye, a former PLM.

Geneen had at first found himself at a disadvantage because his competitors' governments were their complete business allies. "The Europeans," says Scheye, "and I'm speaking as an ex-European, were considerably more sophisticated in using their governments in Latin America. Ask the American ambassador to put in a word with the minister of telecommunications about a contract, he would see you as an ugly American and walk away." Without such help, ITT's notion of political ploy was puerile. Scheye was once sent to El Salvador to rescue a $10 million contract already awarded to L. M.

Ericsson. "I was the last hurrah," he says. He went armed with a list of "all the CIA contracts in El Salvador, all the FBI guys. I did not see the ambassador or anyone in the embassy. The CIA agents were supposed to introduce me to people who would maneuver the government to change from Ericsson to ITT. Obviously it did not work. But that was, to me, typical of the way they thought the system worked."

Scheye could only watch in envy as Holland's Prince Bernhard, for instance, toured Latin America. "He would leave beautiful gifts with all the right ministers," says Scheye, "and Philips would get the orders. We lost a contract to Philips for lighting the Lima airport after Prince Bernhard went through."

ITT learned its lesson. "The president of the Mexican telephone company was a Swede, as I recall," says Scheye, "and his son ran a sales agency in Panama, You paid five percent to that sales agency and you had to have a manufacturing facility in Mexico that the son owned, fifty percent. It was that simple. Everyone did the same—Ericsson, Siemens, ITT—and all got a share of business. We had made a handshake deal on the formula everybody used, and we were going to get x-million dollars of telephone equipment sales." Back in New York, Scheye called the legal department for someone to draw up the contract. "A young guy comes and I explain all this: five percent here, five percent there, the fifty percent company, and the equipment gets marked up so much to cover it—all that kind of stuff. The lawyer takes it all down. Then he phones me next morning and says, Look! I'm an officer of the court. This is plainly illegal, and I can't have anything to do with it. I called upstairs and asked what was going on, and I was told, It's very simple: we hired this young man from some federal regulatory agency, and he's a devout Catholic, goes to mass every morning. We'll send someone else."

Apparently bribery was acceptable anywhere in the world. Otherwise—in the United States and Europe—ITT observed a code of punctilio in most legal and business matters. In Latin America their philosophy was, on the other hand, anything goes. The Argentine government of Arturo Illia was increasingly at odds with ITT expressly because of that attitude. Service was miserable; some requests for phones dated back twenty-five years. But at each devaluation of the peso, ITT importuned the government for immediate rate increases, despite a law forbidding rate hikes for at least three months.

The U.S. Justice Department would later characterize Geneen's zeal in pressing ITT's cause as "excessive." In Latin America it was manic. Gerry Andlinger once told a reporter, "He taught me never to give up. . . . You come back from Brazil without a contract and he'll say, 'Did you see the President?' You think, 'What me? Me see the President and be thought a brash young man?' But you go back and see the President and you get the contract." And if the president does not feel duty-bound to hear special pleadings from private companies? And even if you see the president you still do not get what you want? Geneen would give his answer in Chile.

In business ethics as in all else, Geneen set the tone for his company. In

Argentina the four competing carriers agreed to stop plying customers with gifts. ITT broke the agreement—along with another that no carrier would advertise locally. In Peru, after ITT was prematurely bought out by the government, a competitor expressed relief, complaining that ITT habitually tried to pirate customers. In Chile ITT thought to convince Allende that if he paid them full compensation he could then seize the larger copper companies without payment, pointing to his dealings with ITT as sign of good faith; it was a tactic they had used with success in Peru.

A Latin American country's well-being or national pride was always subordinate to ITT's immediate interests. In Argentina, after a 1966 military coup deposed Illia, relations improved for a while. VP James R. McNitt, head of ITT World Communications, was a retired air force brigadier general. According to one reporter, he was "said to speak the language of the Argentine military." But when Argentina considered satellite communications, McNitt's accent was pure ITT. "The Latin American countries," he said publicly, "as well as the African countries—with the sole exception of South Africa—seem to prefer satellite communications. They are wrong." That was monumentally insensitive (especially coming from an American), resonating on several levels of racism—suggesting a Latin foolishness comparable to that of black, but not white, Africa. Moreover, it was transparently self-serving: ITT owned cable and radio companies whose business would be sharply cut by government-owned satellite communications.

Since the Argentines were determined to go ahead, the four conventional carriers tried at least to participate. Their study, under ITT direction, showed that in ten years profits would be only around $700,000. So why the fuss about government ownership? Why not let them in on it? Meanwhile, ITT's PR people turned the screws, including press propaganda against government monopoly. The campaign seemed about to succeed. Then Comsat conducted an impartial study at government request, and the game was over: it showed that the satellite ground stations would be amortized in three years and that profits would be around $50 million in ten years, not $700,000.

ITT did not even get to build the ground stations; its $11 million bid was undercut by an Italian firm's $6 million. The system went on-line in September 1969 and by 1971 had returned $16 million. The residual bitterness surely helped lead to expropriation. ITT's obstruction (with the other carriers) had held up the project about two years. That put Argentina fourth in Latin America to go on the satellite (after Panama, Chile, and Brazil).

In 1965 there had been virtually no Argentines practiced in satellite communications. They had needed help. When all they got was opposition, they developed their own experts. In 1972 an Argentine communications official told a reporter that if ITT had shown any concern for Argentina's needs, they might have saved their position. "They pressed too hard," he said. "They were not kicked out. They kicked themselves out."

It was the same throughout Latin America. ITT's operating companies were doomed by rising nationalism, not socialism. (The Peruvians and Argentines were military dictators. In Chile, although Pinochet paid Geneen's asking price for the company Allende had expropriated, he did not offer to return the company; neither did the military dictators in Brazil.) But the transition could have been lengthy and amicable. ITT might have stayed on as friend, consultant, maybe limited partner. As it is, in today's annual reports the region that once contributed a substantial portion of ITT's profits is not even listed separately. Latin America is subsumed in "Other."

FAR EAST

The other main portion of "Other" was never important to ITT and never would be. By 1965, Far East sales were $51.4 million, most of that in Australia ($26.6 million), India ($7.88 million), and the Philippines ($6.1 million). It was solid—plenty of cable and telecom—but nothing easily expandable, nothing to pique Geneen's imagination.

On his rare trips there he did not had much wipe for ITT. The manufacturing and control disciplines that gave him an edge on competitors elsewhere would either be meaningless, given the competing labor market, or impossible at such removes. Business coups in the Far East were on the order of the contract in India that ITT wrested from the Japanese. The Japanese government had agreed to a huge loan to India for the construction of harbor facilities. With a delicacy reminiscent of the Greater East Asia Co-Prosperity Sphere days, the Japanese ambassador wrote a letter saying, in effect, that if the Japanese company did not get the phone contract, the government might reconsider the loan. ITT got hold of the letter and sent copies to fifty Indian government luminaries.

That sort of thing makes for fine dining-out stories but not organized business expansion; and Far East organization appeared hopeless. Gerry Andlinger became Far East group executive after having installed ITT's planning system. In 1966, when he replaced Ted Westfall in Latin America, John Guilfoyle replaced him. Guilfoyle would proclaim that "Southeast Asia offers the largest potential growth area in the world and many new investment opportunities"—which, while doubtless true, did not interest ITT. Area headquarters was in Hong Kong, with an area director. However, the three largest subsidiaries—two in Australia, one in the Philippines—reported direct to New York. Guilfoyle himself was based in New York. And New York mistrusted, misunderstood, and misprized the area. For instance, Howard F. Van Zandt was country manager in Japan. He was a long-time ITT employee who had known Behn and had gone out to the Far East under Leavey. He had lived in Japan as a boy, been with the United States occupation forces, spoke Japanese, and knew many in government. As a manager, though, his effectiveness was limited by his company's hesitations. When he wanted to push those ITT product lines on which the Japanese were easing trade restrictions, the answer was no—the Japanese would only make cheaper, better copies. Van Zandt even presented New York with an opportunity that should have entranced Geneen: acquisition of a phone company. But it was on Guam, and headquarters pronounced it "too far away"—which it was from New York, though not from Japan. A chance to own half of Tokyo's New Otani hotel foundered on the ratio of public to private rooms: ITT's Sheraton people wanted to follow the American formula; the Japanese wanted more public rooms. The Sheraton people, says Van Zandt, "weren't acute enough to know that what was good in Boston might not be suitable in Tokyo." More likely, they did not care; they had their procedure, their concept of how things ought to be done, and they wanted to stick with what they knew. They were offered what turned out to be the last chance for foreigners to acquire hotel sites in Tokyo and Kyoto. But their formula called for cheap land to build on; it did not exist, so they passed. When New York was offered a joint venture to make telephone equipment in Taiwan, all they could think of was the danger of looming Red China, magnified in an area that seemed in all senses remote. (They went ahead with the venture in 1976, Richard Nixon meanwhile having made that part of the world safe for democratic capitalism.)

Guilfoyle was right, of course: it was a booming territory. Almost in spite of itself, ITT's sales in Japan alone increased from $1.38 million in 1965 to $2.76 million in 1972. But it was not enough to excite Geneen, so he did not involve himself, and without the pressure of his personal vision, the Far East was neglected.

The situation was much the same elsewhere in the world. Nineteen sixty-five sales in the Middle East were $15,978,000, just under 1% of the worldwide total—almost $5 million of it in Israel, just over $4 million in Turkey, and $3.2 million in Iran. In all of Africa, sales were about $1.5 million, over half in South Africa. All these figures would grow. Africa would become relatively more important as European sales flattened. But no one at 320 Park Avenue really cared. The focus was more and more on American companies, because that was where Geneen's methods were really paying off.

14
Unshakable Facts

s usual ITT's income for 1965 set a new record—$3.58 per share, up from $3.16. In 1966 revenue would top $2 billion, having doubled in four years. More important, the balance steadily shifted away from telecom and government business. Telecom was still the largest chunk: 34%, worldwide. But next highest was now Technical Industrial Products (TIP)—at 18%, ahead of defense and space's 16%. Components and consumer products were 14%; consumer and business services (nonexistent in 1959) were 10%. Phone operations in Latin America were down to 8%.

Curiously, the balance between domestic and foreign revenue was the same as in 1959, 42–58. The percentage of domestic revenue had at first dipped, hitting a low of 36% in 1961, which was understandable. Geneen's reforms in Europe started to take hold immediately, built on a solid base; U.S. nongovernment sales were created virtually from scratch. Profitability, though, was another matter. In 1966, with only 42% of the volume, U.S. companies contributed 50% of ITT's net. TIP was booming. 1966 sales of about $387 million were 43% of ITT's domestic volume, nearly one-fifth of its worldwide volume, and the constituent companies had all been acquired since 1959. While some had required heroic surgery, by now most were regular cash cows.

Arthur T. Woerthwein, the former Bell & Gossett executive who headed TIP, was under tremendous pressure to acquire. In one eighteen-month period the division picked up fourteen companies. And TIP was Geneen's joy. "Hard goods like that always appealed to Hal," says Herb Knortz, his long-time controller. "He liked pumps. He enjoyed selling brass. He used to say, You make money selling pipes, you don't make money selling electronics.

Now, that was an exaggeration for effect; but selling hard goods was more appealing to Hal than to sell soap or food products or things of that sort."

Of course, he was never a prisoner of his preferences. The facts and his growth strategy still demanded consumer and service businesses. Nor was there ever any question as to *how* Geneen would enter new fields. As Bud Morrow discovered, for Geneen the merits of development versus acquisition were not even arguable. Start-up time and money for a new business was ridiculous, the relative risk fearsome. Geneen eagerly developed businesses through internal growth. But nurture of a business you are already in, and growth of a new venture, are totally different.

Not that growth by acquisition is easy. "Acquisitions are a hard way to make money," says John Lobb. "There's more money lost than made on them. Geneen was one of the most successful." He had solved the four chief problems of acquisitions: what you can use to pay for them; how much to pay; which ones are worth buying; and how to make them pay off once you have them.

In the coin available to him, Geneen was at a disadvantage compared with go-go conglomerates of the time, such as Leasco, Gulf & Western, Ling-Temco-Vought (LTV), and Litton. ITT stock never performed as it should have. The P/E ranged from 14 to 19 in 1964; as late as mid-1966 it was around 17. Analysts grumbled about the "involuted capital structure," the "several issues of preferred stock," and the acquisitions they did not understand. Finally, though, the unbroken string of quarterly gains impressed enough investors so that by 1967 the P/E was well into the 20s—enough to give Geneen some buying leverage.

How much to pay is always a problem. Not even the most spendid company can return a truly outlandish premium. The vulgar opinion was that Geneen habitually paid too much. Controller Herb Knortz says no. "We never paid too much for a company," he says. "You could argue that Geneen should have skinned the cat a little more. But his basic philosophy was, If you make your mind up to go, pay the price and get on with it. What people haggle about is usually small in perspective of five years' earnings. Is there another five hundred thousand in inventory? It doesn't really matter. The question is, Is it a good company and do you want it and will it earn after you get it?"

·   The scope of that question had moved beyond Geneen's instincts. Just the volume of candidates was staggering. Almost every officer in ITT was under pressure to sponsor acquisitions. And once word got out that ITT was shopping, the brokers and investment bankers swarmed. In addition, acquisition decisions were soon of major complexity. What new fields should ITT *want* to enter? How do you identify and evaluate candidates in fields where you are a stranger? To get answers, Geneen established the best acquisition staff ever seen.

When Dave Margolis left, his replacement was to be Hart Perry, whose background was in the more rarefied strata of finance, not shirt-sleeve analysis. So Margolis recruited Robert H. Kenmore, an analyst who had been impressive when evaluating both Raytheon and ITT in the early days. Kenmore joined ITT in 1962, and in 1966—at age thirty-five—became ITT's youngest VP. His title was director of financial planning; his duty was orchestrating Geneen's acquisition studies. On ITT's widely disregarded organization charts Kenmore reported to Hart Perry; in reality he reported to Geneen, and it was byword that he would do anything for Geneen, nothing for anyone else. Indeed, Kenmore evoked remarkably high levels of hostility. A one-time colleague says, "Bob is the only person I ever *really* disliked in my life." The former head of an ITT division explains, "He was obnoxious but bright as hell."

Part of the unpopularity derived from what seemed self-importance. Many of Kenmore's fellows thought he was giving himself airs because they misapprehended his function. One otherwise astute observer says, "He ran a fucking *Xerox* machine. Geneen did the acquisition program, and Kenmore and those guys snipped Value Line reports to back up his ideas." True—but only the way it is also true that a law clerk snips decisions that help a Supreme Court justice decide cases. And for Kenmore's group, the case load was fearsome.

Their first step was a survey of business trends. All right, America was moving toward a service economy; what specific businesses did that suggest? The group evaluated ITT's present and potential fields for ten primary risk factors, including how much strain growth would put on management, level of capital investment (plus difficulty of financing), competitiveness of pricing, and labor content. Their study showed how chancy some of ITT's traditional fields really were—military work, electrical components, heating and air-conditioning manufacture. By contrast, such financial services as the small-loan business, life insurance, and mutual fund management were low-risk. So were other such service-economy fields as television broadcasting.

The group also evaluated the market size of various businesses, their historical growth rate of earnings, predicted earnings rate, return on equity, and average P/E ratio. TV manufacture was bigger than broadcasting ($2.5 billion versus $1.6 billion); but recently broadcasting had been growing at a rate of 13.5% versus 2.8% for TV manufacture, with a higher predicted rate, 8% versus 5%, and better return on equity, 19% versus 13%.

ITT already profited as a supplier to the building industry. But Kenmore's charts revealed negatives. Although the building market was huge—$25 billion—growth took a lot of management; financial risk was not low; and pricing competition was high, with no consumer franchise possible, which meant you were always at the mercy of the installer. Furthermore, recent growth had been dismal, with little improvement in sight, and there was very modest return on equity (ROE). Contrast that with the specialized field of building-trade protection systems and equipment. It was then only a $300 million business, but it had been growing at 11% a year, with 10% predicted; it offered 13% return on equity, and a 20 P/E ratio. Now *that* was a field to look at. So was life insurance, which practically grew by itself and offered a decent ROE and a terrific P/E. In time, Grinnell and Hartford would be the fruit of this thinking.

Having established such tests, any suggested business could quickly be examined. "When Avis came in," says Kenmore, "we could see right away it fit, even though we hadn't specifically identified the rent-a-car business."

That was some Xerox machine Kenmore ran. But it is easy to see how the casual observer would be misled. As Kenmore himself says, "Most of our work was an enormous collection of paper." Geneen insisted that they unearth every relevant fact about an industry, and about every company under consideration. With unremitting effort and murderous hours, the facts were "easy" to come by. "We didn't try to reinvent the wheel," says Kenmore. "We combed Wall Street for studies that already existed. If it wasn't Merrill Lynch that had done a twenty-page study of the industry, it was Kidder Peabody. Someone has already done a study on almost anything. We'd find those studies and very often talk with the people who had written them." To mask the acquisitions, the group ran some ITT pension funds. That helped secure Wall Street cooperation. "But," says Kenmore, "you have to go out and identify the places where high-priced people have done what you need. Most people stop looking too soon, and you can tell the difference in the output."

The acquisition review process soon settled into routine. One or two nights a week, Kenmore's group would load a mail cart with files and troop in at Geneen's call to review maybe fifty companies in four industries. They had developed a review matrix that covered a company on a single sheet of paper. "All the data was there, summarized," says Kenmore, "and if we wanted to go beyond, it was all in the files: annual reports, proxies, industry studies, company studies—everything on any company and industry we were remotely interested in." Formal sessions, with people like John Lobb and key group executives, were held every other Friday night.

The impulse for all this digging was Geneen's idiosyncratic view of facts and their role in decision making. It was the "secret" of his system; at ITT facts were a fetish. "I remember," said Felix Rohatyn, "he once stomped out of a meeting that had gotten too windy and wrote a memo titled 'Facts.' " It was dated November 16, 1965, and became compulsory reading for ITT executives.

> Yesterday we put in a long, hard, driving meeting, mostly seeking the "facts" on which easy management decisions could then be made. . . .
>
> There is no word in the English language that more strongly conveys the intent of incontrovertibility, i.e., "final and reliable reality", than the word "fact".
>
> However, no word is more honored by its breach in actual usage. For example, there are and we saw yesterday:

"Apparent facts"

"Assumed facts"

"Reported facts"

"Hoped-for facts"

"Facts" so labeled and accepted as facts—i.e., "accepted facts"—and many others of similar derivation!

In most cases these were not the *"facts"* at all.

The problem is not that people lie but that they do not bother to nail down the truth. They present as facts information for whose accuracy they cannot vouch. Almost as bad, they present as *the* facts less than all that is relevant; content with easy, surface truth, they stop digging. That was why Kenmore's group talked with the authors of brokerage house studies. Where did they get their facts? How much digging had they done? What confidence could Geneen have in the accuracy and completeness of the studies?

If you presented Geneen with what might seem an elementally simple fact—say, the value of physical assets in your unit—his first question might be, How do you know? If you told him, Our controller told me, his next questions would be, How does he know? Did you ask? Or have you uncritically accepted his statement and passed it along as fact without bothering to determine whether it was a fact, an opinion, or a guess? If you answered that the controller had surveyed all the title cards, Geneen might point to your fleet of trucks: Did anyone determine that they are really worth what the title cards say? And how about your heavy machinery? How do you know its real worth? Do you know what your sources of information did to find out? What *anyone* did?

Geneen wanted every manager an inquisitor, regardless of lacerated feelings. As he wrote in "Facts": "The highest art of professional management requires . . . the temerity, intellectual curiosity, guts and/or plain impoliteness, if necessary, to be sure that what you do have is indeed what we will call an 'unshakeable fact'."

It would take herculean work to develop unshakable facts, and for Geneen you had to go through the drill each time; it was, he wrote, "a never-ending discipline." You could *never* simply accept information on what you thought was "good authority." Too many people do. "Half-truths are the currency for most of the business decisions that are made in America," says Bob Kenmore. At ITT the digging was not voluntary. Geneen insisted, he wrote, that all his people learn to "tell a 'genuine snapping turtle' from the others" so as to "deal only with *unshakeable* facts in the future."

Facts, not people, "made" decisions at ITT. But Geneen interpreted what the facts said. If he did not *make* decisions, he reserved the right to announce them. And they could seem arbitrary. "Once he was looking at an annual report," says someone who attended most acquisition reviews, "starting at the back, with the financial statement, then working his way forward. He stopped at the president's letter, threw the report on the reject pile, and said, Well, we don't want that one. Why not? The rest of us thought the company was perfect for us. Well, he said, look at that guy's picture; I don't like the look in his eyes."

However decisions were made, Geneen's achievement in building his company from $765 million to $22 *billion* in twenty years is unparalleled, especially considering the businesses he was in. He never rode the wave of a basic industry as did Alfred Sloan at General Motors. He did not find oil in his back yard. He never benefited much from any of his era's hot industries: no skyrocketing with computers or solid state or space or television. His empire, while solidly based on European telecom, was built on the likes of Jabsco pumps and Twinkies. And although much was made of it, he did not just "buy earnings"—or even, really, volume. He had to expand whatever he bought, and rapidly, to avoid crippling dilution. And with the companies he already had, he had to keep them growing so that the perception of ITT as a sound investment would induce the public to buy his stock, and prospective acquisitions to accept it in payment.

How did he do it? The cement and spur of Geneen's system were his constant example and his leadership. Most successful executives work very hard; Geneen never stopped. In 1966 he spent a long day in Boston, addressing five separate meetings of security analysts. His enthusiasm and energy were so unflagging than an aide felt drained just listening. A letdown, afterward, would be human. But on the plane back that night he was hard at work on the next day's schedule. Another time, after a tumultuous but finally triumphant stockholders' meeting, Geneen was seen in a corner of the hotel lobby at 7:00 P.M., dictating to a secretary. Surely everyone else was out winding down, celebrating.

The number of hours Geneen put in at the office was staggering. Many wondered if he ever slept. Some insiders say he indeed slept very little, that he never got to the office before 10:00 only because he worked and exercised at home. On the other hand, when an underling in Spain arranged an 8:30 A.M. meeting with the minister of industry, Geneen emerged from his hotel bleary-eyed, threatening to fire the wretch if he ever again set such an early appointment.

In any case, the twelve- and sixteen-hour days were the norm. And since Geneen was visibly not sparing himself, how could *you* complain? John Lobb once ran into Henry Bowes in a San Francisco airport ticket line. As they talked, Bowes keeled over. Lobb, horrified, called an ambulance and was relieved to learn that it was only exhaustion, the ITT house disease. Bowes decided to resign on Labor Day, 1967, when he finally found time to compute his 1966 taxes and discovered that he had been in the United States only ninety-eight days during the year. About thirty of those were spent at home. Nevertheless, Bowes remembers his ITT days with fondness and Geneen with admiration. "He made us feel," says Bowes, "that we were really building something."

"You wanted to achieve for him," says Robert Ohmes, former staff man.

Everyone agrees that he evoked the best efforts from all his people. Partly it was the challenge of his seemingly impossible exactions. "This was my Mount Everest," says Ohmes, "my skydiving—being able to survive in that atmosphere, to work under that pressure, to be responsive to Geneen's demands and achieve for him. It's almost a macho kind of thing: see the stripes on my back? I could *take* it!" At the same time, when you did achieve for him, Geneen's praise was unstinting. Moreover, it was always for the right thing. He had perfect pitch for the notes of your self-esteem. Did you pride yourself on your intelligence? hard work? shrewdness? judgment? speed? That was what Geneen praised in you. The combination was irresistible. "He kept kicking you in the ass," says John Lobb, "and patting you on the back. He had this tremendous ability to get people to perform beyond what they thought was the limit of their mental or physical endurance."

Then there was Geneen's infectious enthusiasm. "I'd come back from Europe on a Friday night," says Lobb, "and I'd be exhausted. I'd say to my wife, Goddamnit, I'm not going anywhere for a week. Then, Sunday, Harold would call and invite us for a drink. We'd go and he'd say, John, we've found a company in California that sounds like it's made for us. If you get the early plane tomorrow you could go through that place in a couple of days and tell me whether we ought to buy it.

"And you know, he'd get me so charged up, I'd be off and running. He was very good that way."

Leadership at the top obviously spurs the entire organization. But Geneen's was particularly telling because he directly controlled an astounding number of executives. "He had the most of any chief executive I know," says a former staffer. "Most can do it for five or six; he did it with thirty or more." One result was the high-priced talent always piled up outside his office. Geneen wanted his own boot to do the kicking, his own hand the patting. It was bad enough that the president of ITT-Europe must be an ocean away; Geneen clutched his other key executives to him. Since much of U.S. commercial was centered around Chicago, John Lobb proposed moving his headquarters there. Geneen refused. "Of course I trust *you*, John; but I'd never know what someone else was doing out there."

One consequence of such intensely personal leadership was that ITT jobs were whatever Geneen said they were, minute to minute. He never let the people around him settle into niches. "Howard Aibel might be Geneen's lawyer," says Robert S. Savage, director of stockholder relations, "but Geneen'd have me check on some plainly legal point about proxies or nominations. It embarrassed me sometimes. The lawyers would say, What the hell are *you* doing here?" But they knew it was Geneen's way. "He didn't want people to say, Okay, *this* is my area of responsibility. The whole company was your responsibility." And anyone at hand was right for any job Geneen wanted done. Once, talking business on the beach at Key Biscayne, he suddenly remembered a letter he wanted to dictate. "You take it down, Mac," he said to Frank McCabe, his personnel director, and started rattling off, breakneck. "I'm sitting there in shorts, scribbling, the sand blowing all around," says McCabe, "and I'm getting about one word in three. I said, Wait a minute, Hal, I can't write this fast."

"You can do it," Geneen said.

"No I can't."

"Well, I can't *talk* any slower!"

Two other top-level executives pitched in, and the three got enough to reconstruct the letter.

"Everyone, always, was in boot camp," says another former executive. At the same time, everyone at every level was important, with company-ranging responsibility. When a subway strike threatened to cripple New York traffic, Mayor John V. Lindsay went on television to urge New Yorkers to consider whether their presence was vital in the office. Next morning, Geneen personally made the rounds, taking names of those who dared not consider themselves vital to ITT.

This enforced leveling (especially at the top) was an effective element of Geneen's leadership. However, it kept positions unclear, and that inspired some fierce jockeying. In late 1964, when Ted Westfall became ITT's only executive VP, he had already started into disfavor. While Tim Dunleavy thought Westfall genuinely wanted to ease Geneen's burden, with no thought of supplanting his authority, Geneen would reflexively see it as usurpation. Then, too, at his best, Westfall manufactured turmoil. The European managers could not stand Westfall's brusque manner and abrasive tactics. He was hated and feared by most ITT executives. "He was a bully," says one of them. Another confesses considerable satisfaction at having seen Westfall fall even faster than he had risen.

In Geneen's meritocracy creating turmoil, abrasiveness, rampant unpopularity—none was seen as a failing if you were effective. But, more and more, Westfall was only half-effective. He was all right mornings; after lunch he was drunk. Klaus Scheye followed Westfall from W. R. Grace and was one of the few ITT executives who liked him. "Ted," he says, "was a total victim of the alcoholism that was an occupational hazard at ITT because of the pressure and style." Westfall acknowledges what he says were two- or three-martini lunches, that he was in fact a heavy drinker. As for the effect, "I didn't suffer fools gladly at nine in the morning," he says, "and even less gladly after two." Actually, the effect was rather more vivid. Everyone at ITT knew that if you wanted to talk with Westfall, it had better be before noon. "He was totally vicious after two in the afternoon," says Scheye.

By February 1966, when three new executive VPs were named and Gerry Andlinger replaced him in Latin America, Westfall was in decline. Yet Geneen would never fire him. First he was in charge of North American telecom. That was taken from him, and by the end of 1968 his only responsibility was for ITT World Communications and ITT World Directories—overseas yellow pages—both of which he had built. Before the end, he lost World Directories. Still Geneen kept him.

It was Tim Dunleavy who was charged with the face-to-face task of relieving Westfall of his duties. "Ted said to me, What do you think I ought to do? I bit my tongue at first, and I should have kept biting it. But I said to him, You're still listed as executive vice president. They haven't taken that title away. I'd look on the outside if I was you. Because I don't think you're going anywhere here. You ask me as a friend, and I'm telling you as a friend. Jeez! I don't think it was two hours, Geneen's got me in his office saying, Who the hell are you to tell Westfall he's not going anywhere in this company? *You're* gonna fire him?—and all that sort of thing. And I said to myself, Oh, you bastard!"

(In the event, Westfall went on the wagon, retired at the end of 1974, then stayed as consultant on telecom to Geneen, as well as to Geneen's successors, Hamilton and Araskog—testimony to Westfall's abilities. He continued under contract as a consultant until 1982, when he was elected chairman and CEO of Comdial Corporation, a Charlottesville, Virginia, telecom equipment company.)

In 1966, with Westfall sinking, the question of succession became even murkier. The three new executive VPs were Tim Dunleavy, John Lobb, and Hart Perry. Boards of directors want an established line of succession. But— witness Jack Graham—having a single heir apparent leads the anointed to unwholesome thoughts. John Lobb was an inescapable choice. He was eminently "boardable," an independent operating man who had scored notable successes for ITT. The only evident drawback was age; he was just three years younger than Geneen. Still, he had to be the next executive VP. So how better confuse the issue than by also elevating Dunleavy and Perry? That was pure Geneen. Dunleavy was six years younger than Geneen, head of ITT's single most important entity, ITT-Europe. Perry, eight years younger, was, if anything, even more boardable than Lobb, and he starred in finance, a field of great moment in so highly leveraged a corporation.

In reality, none of them had a prayer. Dunleavy was unacceptable to the board. Perry had no real operating experience—and in any case would soon be in Geneen's "bad book," hectored out of the company. As for Lobb, business-circle rumors had it, in the words of *Forbes,* that Geneen "sent his staff in to put pressure on John Lobb because he became too strong and was being mentioned as a potential ITT president." Lobb denies there was any friction. But it is certain that, in the spring of 1967, when Norton Simon offered him the job of turning around Crucible Steel, Lobb took it. In 1966, though, all three seemed plausible enough as successors. It was resolution by mystification. And that, too, was an element of Geneen's leadership.

John Thompson was the components man who had followed Geneen from Raytheon. One Saturday morning he and his wife decided to take up paddle tennis. Thirty minutes after they started playing Thompson got a call from Geneen. "How did you know I was on the paddle tennis court?" he asked. "An hour ago I didn't know myself I was going to be there." Geneen laughed and said, "Mystique!" Another time, at a GMM, Geneen passed a folded note hand to hand around the huge conference table to Art Williams, over from Spain for the meeting. When Williams unfolded it, the note read, "Aunt Emily says hello." After the meeting, Williams rushed over: "Mr. Geneen, how do you know my Aunt Emily?" With a satisfied grin Geneen said, "I know more about you than you think," and strode away. It seems Aunt Emily was an executive secretary for the president of General Motors. She saw Geneen there one day and asked if he knew her nephew, Art Williams, who— "Oh, yes," Geneen joked, "that's the guy they put in jail for fixing horse races," and left. (Williams owned a couple of horses, and on trips to Spain, Geneen often gave him ten or twenty dollars to bet for him.) Geneen would keep them all guessing, all off balance: Thompson, Aunt Emily, successors, the press, his board, *everyone*.

Even so, some cracks showed in the mystique. An important weakness —one that saddened and alarmed his fervent supporters—became pronounced during this period. "In the first years," says one staunch admirer, "he was almost always open, understanding, patient, and easy to talk with. As the years went on, I think he became too—well, 'aristocratic.' Lots of guys in high places get to thinking they're the greatest—and he *was* the greatest—but I think he went a little too far. If there's one thing I could criticize him for, that would be it."

Increasingly, Geneen seemed oblivious to people's human needs. A review meeting for one unit brought executives from all over the country. The final session was held the day before Thanksgiving. When he kept the meeting going through the afternoon, Geneen was reminded that many had planes to catch. Sure, sure: there was just one more thing to cover. At 8:00 P.M. he was reminded again: Okay, just this final point. The meeting broke at 1:00 A.M. Another time, he had summoned the managers and controllers of all major U.S. units to a budget meeting called for 10:00 A.M. Wednesday. They waited for Geneen to show up all day Wednesday, then all day Thursday. At 4:00 Friday afternoon he breezed in, and the meeting started. "There were forty guys," says one of them, "just sitting for two and a half days."

It is one thing to serve a company's vital interests—even at 1:00 A.M., Thanksgiving, if need be; it is another thing to serve what seems nothing but one man's heedless convenience. And his demands had to be met immediately. When he called for information, says one staff man, "it was understood he wanted it within an hour or two." No matter that normally it would be a week's work. "If he said he wanted something by nine o'clock," says another staffer, "you didn't ask, morning or evening. It was always the *next* nine."

Most significant, he was developing an imperial refusal to be wrong. "At one review meeting," says someone who was there, "he didn't like something in some guy's plan and he suggested an alternative action. The guy said, Hal, if we do that, we'll have a disaster—and he ran down the reasons. Geneen said, Well, consider it anyway. He got off the subject but came back to it and said, You're going to do what I told you, right? The guy said, I think it's a mistake, but if you tell me to do it, I'll do it. Geneen said, I'm telling you to do it. The

guy wrote a memo saying, As you instructed, I have put in this plan. I still
think it's a mistake, but I'm going to do as you told me to do.

"About two months later, at another review, Geneen looked at this guy's
numbers, and there was a problem.

—What the hell happened here?

—Well, this was the program you told me to put in, and it didn't work
out.

—I told you to do that?

A few minutes later he came back to it:

—Now, why'd you do that?

—You know why, Hal. You told me to do it that way.

—No, I never told you to do that. No way! No way! I don't remember
that!

And Geneen remembers everything. About ten minutes later he exploded:

—Why you stupid sonofabitch, why the fuck did you do *that!* You know
better than to do dumb things like that!

He'd convinced himself. He wasn't out to get the guy; he didn't take any
reprisal. But he couldn't accept the fact that he had told the guy to do
something wrong."

In 1966 an office skyscraper rose at 437 Madison Avenue, around the corner
from ITT headquarters at 320 Park, and at last Geneen had a setting congenial
to his idea of the general management meetings. Part of the top floor of the
new "ITT Americas Building" was used for a second executive dining room;
but most of the top floor was one giant, windowless room, running the length
of the building, along Madison. The conference table that filled the room was
a hollow oval, the center reserved for projectors and amplifiers. Seats around
the perimeter were high-backed, blue-upholstered swivel chairs, ninety-two
of them, with smaller chairs for aides behind them. A microphone sat before
each place, and there were water carafes and glasses, but no ash trays; smoking
was forbidden. There were movie screens at either end and one in the middle
of the room, facing Geneen's seat, on which the units' recent performance
numbers were projected. The temperature was kept very low.

This room was the focus of Geneen's system. The facts would be discovered in this room; and from here assignments would issue to correct discovered flaws in performance. The system required extraordinary effort but was
unrivaled in its effectiveness.

Geneen did not think management decisions were hard to make. They
required no intuition or brilliance, just ventilation of the unshakable facts.
And he was certain that the chief enemy of candor was the pride of line
operators: the better they were, the harder for them to admit troubles. His
system was geared to surfacing those troubles. He once contrasted his theory
of management with that of a competitor. "There, they put a man in charge
of a division and leave him alone for two years. At the end of that, if he's
. . . achieved his goals, okay. If he hasn't, he's fired." It was not fair to the

manager or to corporate management. "I'm no laissez-faire, let-me-know-how-things-are-in-six-months guy. . . . I don't want some proud guy to get into his own Vietnam and then suddenly hand me his resignation." Geneen was not interested in punishment or "performance evaluation"; he wanted profit. "If a man loses eight million dollars for me," he would say, "I can't get it out of his final pay check."

The constant revelation of a unit's numbers was in the monthly letter, which imposed a rigorous and comprehensive format on reporting: there was little hiding room—especially since the unit's controller reported direct to Herb Knortz and would surely blow the whistle on any fudging. There is debate among ITT people as to whether Geneen read every page of every GMM report. But no question: it was suicide to assume that he had not read *your* stuff. A dozen or so "suitcases," crammed with reports, lined the window sills of his office, and he took along a couple every night, four or five each weekend, the whole caboodle on vacations. "You can't delegate anything you can't understand," he once told a reporter. "If you read it all, you have an idea of the situation, the people, the figures involved. There are a lot of things I don't need to know, but I don't know what they are till afterwards."

An added hazard, particularly for the duplicitous, was Geneen's memory. The manager of one Latin American company was jolted when Geneen noted that his current numbers did not jibe with those in a months-old report. The manager tried double talk, but it was clear that he had simply been lying, hoping no one would remember. Geneen cut him short: "I can't operate like this." he said, "See me after the meeting." And the fellow was gone.

The only acceptable tactic was total candor, because along with his memory Geneen had an uncanny ability to ask questions that would root out the nub of every issue. He was also implacable. "With most executives," says a former staffer, "after the second or third question, they've probed as far as they can. But he was able to ask the fourth and fifth question. And they were real questions, not rhetorical." Geneen once said, "I believe in pushing and pulling and kneading and whittling until you finally get those two purple drops." That they came out of someone's hide did not matter. Geneen frankly said that he had no patience with "the old theory of not criticizing a man in front of others." And there was now no Charlie Adams to say *stop that!* When he bore in, candor had better be not only total but timely: Why are your figures off? Why did we have to wait until now to find out? One manager answered, "I knew what results you were expecting, and I just didn't want to break your heart." Geneen glowered and said, "My heart's been broken ten thousand times. Once more won't hurt."

The purpose of his questioning, though, was seldom to humiliate; it was to get things done. And for that his depth of questioning was unequaled. "Someone wanted twenty-five million for a cable-laying ship," says Bob Savage. "Geneen said, What do you do now when you have to lay transatlantic cable? We borrow a ship from AT and T. Oh? And the questioning went on a long time. Does AT and T use its ship all the time? No. How much of the time do they use it? Maybe seventy-five percent. What do they do with it the other twenty-five percent? Nothing. Why don't we rent it from them for that twenty-five percent of the time?

"Even I could follow his reasoning, and I loved to hear his questioning," Savage says.

Once, Geneen made up for a reporter an example of how the questioning might go at a GMM, asking an executive about steps taken to close an unproductive plant:

> GENEEN: What has been done about it?
> EXECUTIVE: I told him to get rid of it.
> GENEEN: Never mind that you told him to get rid of it; what has been done to get rid of it?
> EXECUTIVE: Well, he says he doesn't want to sell it, because it will give him a black eye in the community.
> GENEEN: I don't care about his status in the community. I want that plant sold.
> EXECUTIVE: Well, I'll talk to him again when I get back.
> GENEEN: That's not enough. I want that plant sold, and I want to know what's being done about it.

Many people thought the GMMs a towering waste of time. Geneen might become intrigued by what seemed the five-cent problem of some nickel-and-dime unit and pursue it relentlessly, hour after hour, while everyone else sat stupefied with boredom. Of course, it was Geneen's constant dictum that the corporate bottom line was the sum of all the units' bottom lines, however small. And one staff man is sure that he "wasn't interested in all those five-cent problems for themselves—he just wanted to expose the guy's thinking process." Perhaps. But it did not matter. Anyone who thought the GMMs were a waste of time did not understand how ITT was run. They were not a waste of Geneen's time, and that was all that finally counted. They kept *him* informed. Besides, as Geneen once explained: "It sounds overly simple, but it's just a matter of more people doing more work, and doing it together and . . . better. I know if you have sixty people working together as a group for two days you're going to get better answers . . . than if you have one guy talking to one other guy.

"In other companies you have one fellow who may [talk] to twelve people. Then they [talk] to, say, forty. . . . But with us, we've got one hundred and twenty people all operating on the same line at any time, on one problem alone.

"If someone has a marketing problem, that could involve patent, technological, legal, and other aspects. And that problem comes out on the table and gets aired right there and then before people with expertise in every one of these areas. . . . I don't think there's any other way to get three hundred problems on the table at one time."

In the course of the GMM there would develop action assignments.

Richard Silver, Geneen's old can group mate from the Harvard AMP, had become his personal assistant. Colonel Silver wrote down the action assignments as Geneen pronounced them and published a list after each GMM. Each listing was short and pithy, even when the assignment demanded operatic effort in a desperately short time. For example, GMM action assignment #25, made at the March 1968 meeting, was: "Determine opportunities for increased manufacture and sales of new products by TIP Group. Report by May GMM." Action assignment #5, made at the GMM of February 13, 1967, was: "Assess the feasibility of establishing a lighting products group, combining the ITT facilities associated with the manufacture and distribution of lamp bulbs and lighting fixtures." The study was completed April 14.

The only way to get an action assignment off Silver's list was to report its accomplishment. Even if there was no due date, you were certain to be interrogated about your progress at every subsequent meeting. Managers and group executives got "big-picture" action assignments ("Prepare program to diversify TIP products and product lines"). Staff was assigned fire-fighting chores, requiring specific fixes (like, Find out why Cannon still cannot get product out the door, and do something about it; or, Cut General Controls's inventory).

Staff rode herd on everyone. The first item covered at each GMM was a review of staff and PLM activity. Geneen insisted that they all continually think how to save the corporation money. They filed weekly activity reports and had to specify the financial consequences of whatever they did. "Last week," one report ran, "I reorganized marketing at the Milan plant, shifting or eliminating three direct salesmen and a sales manager. Annualized saving, $100,000." Geneen did not mind the most arresting exaggeration. At one meeting he said, "I've added up all your reports and I'm really impressed. Last month you made an annualized savings greater than ITT's total after-tax profit."

Geneen had always valued staff as an in-house consulting firm; but ITT's monolithic North American staff (with later name and organizational changes) did not exist until it was proposed and put together by Rich Bennett, who became its first director in 1965. In 1966 Bennett was succeeded for nine months by James S. Rice. Then Maurice R. Valente became staff director until a basic reorganization in 1969.

Staff played two roles for Geneen. First, they were his eyes and ears on the line. He fostered the traditional adversarial wariness between staff and line with a policy that one former staff man calls "dynamic tension." Others called it spying. Geneen chose, the staffer says, "to build conflict into the organization, to make sure all the big problems would bubble up to him, so he could preserve for himself the option of being involved in the decisions." That was true at the highest levels. Henry Bowes, as director of marketing, reported both to John Lobb and directly to Geneen, and Lobb says he realized that part of Bowes's function was "to keep me honest." Staff had unquestioned access to every unit, were included in everything, had to review nearly every step of every plan, process, and new product. And that was with *no* problems in sight.

The second function of staff was to sniff out problems. The smart ones would pore over a unit's plans and monthly letters, marking them up as assiduously (if not so incisively) as Geneen himself, alert for spots that invited probing. Their objective, says George J. Haufler, who went from line to staff, then back to line, "was to raise tendentious questions at the GMM, hopefully to win an action assignment." Having lots of action assignments was a mark of success—that, says Haufler, and "being able to come to the next meeting with a boastful report about the success you have achieved" in fixing whatever had plagued the line. Haufler felt that he was shot down by staff, so his tone is bitter. But that, indeed, was what was supposed to happen. It was what Geneen counted on to keep ITT successful.

Staff might unearth a problem by poking around the units or by analysis of the numbers. A line manager might even own up to a problem as he was supposed to. "In any event," says John Turbidy, former Brussels staffer, "if he was not solving the problem, in came the outsider, the independent person who could give a more objective explanation of the problem *and* could help fix it. That was the ITT system at its best."

Some problems were easy. One staff inventory expert solved a problem by padlocking the supply-room door, making the workers use up materials already on the floor. Other problems were more involved. At Creed, in England, the teleprinter operation was disheveled in every department, from R&D through sales—and with such tension that the R&D director and the manufacturing manager were not speaking. One staff recommendation was to dissolve the company. That situation took upwards of two years to resolve. A staff man returned to England every couple of weeks, having set specific remedial actions to be taken between visits.

Staff was also used to take the heat off local management. "Geneen was a very firm believer," says Maurie Valente, "in moving management to the side and letting staff do some of the things that were less palatable for people who would have to live with the situation later: firing, reducing inventory, moving product out, pruning jobs or activities or markets, and so on." That would probably have been Geneen's eventual solution for the manager who did not want to close his home-town plant.

With so much help," says Don Thomson, who went from staff to line, "it was difficult to screw up." Furthermore, you were explicitly not diminished in Geneen's eyes for needing help and requesting it.

Even so, many thought that in time staff grew out of all useful proportion and out of control. John Lobb used to kid Geneen about it: "I'd tell him he could add a dollar per share just by eliminating staff." Maybe so; but most agree that until the 1970s, the system worked with stunning success. Certainly staff was the first line of Geneen's system, and as much as any other factor, it positioned him for the explosive growth of 1968.

Everything was working. Volume in 1967 was up nearly $1 billion over

1965; net was $122,760,000, up 60% from 1965. From 1965 through 1967, Geneen made forty acquisitions, seventeen of them foreign. Overseas, the only major ones were 66.9% of Oceanic for $4 million (1965) and Teves for $75 million (1967). At home, the important ones in 1965 were Avis ($51 million), Hamilton ($17 million), and Press Wireless ($4 million). Nineteen sixty-six was bigger: Wakefield (lighting, heating and controls, and abrasives) for $12 million, Jabsco Pump for $9.6 million, Consolidated (Champion light bulbs) for $7.7 million, Howard W. Sams (publishing, including Bobbs-Merrill; *Who's Who* was soon added) for $29.2 million, and Airport Parking Company of America (APCOA) for $26.3 million.

The growth value of acquisitions in 1965 was $115,024,000. In 1966 the acquisitions did not grow; they declined in volume (due to the recession) to $113,862,000—although there was still growth in acquired net, from $4.34 to $4.94 million. Then, in 1967, the growth of acquired companies shot up: volume to $506,172,000, net to $20,308,000. That was proof of how Geneen's system maximized growth, because new acquisitions in 1967 dropped off sharply. He bought Ampex/Lustra for $8 million to supplement Champion; Cleveland Motel Corporation (six Holiday Inns for $9.5 million) was an addition to APCOA's motel operations; Mears Motor Livery ($2.1 million) was for Avis; and Modern Life Insurance ($5.2 million) supplemented Hamilton Life. Everything else was under a million dollars.

Geneen's acquisition zeal was not slackening. Rather, his lawyers insisted on restraint. The antitrust people at the Department of Justice were already grumbling over the biggest acquisition of them all, the one Geneen wanted most: American Broadcasting Company.

15

ABC, Number Three in a Two-and-a-Half Universe

elevision broadcasting, said Geneen's acquisition group, was "one of the most attractive fields for ITT entry," a "tight oligarchy" protected by "limited access to new competitors, without the burden of regulated rates." The question was how to get in it. Should Geneen buy individual stations, or should he try to buy a network? There were arguments on both sides.

The Federal Communications Commission (FCC) rule is that no one may own more than five regular TV stations (VHF, channels 2 through 13). Networks each have their five "owned and operated" stations (o&o's), and no more. However, networks also profit by providing programs shown on stations owned by others, the "affiliates." Buying five stations would be easy. But while it is marvelously profitable to own stations, the magnitude of that profit is limited because of the five-station rule and because the best stations in the biggest markets are already network o&o's. Furthermore, if Geneen first bought stations, he would have to sell them if he got a later chance to buy a network—since the network's o&o's would be far better stations. It would be a forced sale, too; and the FCC, which must approve license transfers, might not like such wholesale trading. It was this logic that kept him from acquiring, in the early 1960s, the first station he considered, owned by Travelers Broadcasting in Hartford. Another inhibition was Robert McKinney's sniping. While not enough to rally the board, it did incite other directors to hard-eyed looks at all "unusual" acquisitions. In October 1964, before the showdown, Geneen got a memo from Hart Perry about two proposed TV acquisitions, suggesting that they "put them on the back burner until the current Board sentiment is clarified. . . . "

By late 1964, even with the McKinney situation resolved, and despite inspection of many individual stations and chains, Geneen was still not in TV broadcasting. He wanted a network, with its much bigger numbers and much greater éclat. But networks were hard to come by.

Of the three, the National Broadcasting Company was spoken for, and even Geneen did not hope to acquire its parent, RCA. The Columbia Broadcasting System was a better possibility, and Geneen tried to move in twice, in 1963 and 1964. "Geneen called me up," says Klaus Scheye, then a PLM, "and said, Klaus, I want to buy CBS, but they don't trust me. I'm going to show them we're people they can live with by creating a small joint venture." The problem was the suspicion of CBS chairman William S. Paley. "The idea," says Scheye, "was to convince Paley that Geneen was human." An approach would be through CBS president Frank N. Stanton. Peter C. Goldmark, chief engineer at CBS and father of the long-playing record, had developed a process whereby the entire Bible might be contained on two records, "a million bits, or something like that," says Scheye. ITT would produce and promote the CBS discovery to the blind as a charity. Scheye would be PLM, and he went along to an exploratory lunch with Geneen, Stanton, and Goldmark. "Goldmark was giving us a dissertation on how wonderful this would be," says Scheye, "when Geneen said, You know, the average attention span is twenty minutes, so why would anyone want a million bits on a record? Stanton looked intelligent and kind of agreed with Geneen, but Goldmark got furious and said, There must be *something* you can do with a million bits!" Offended, Goldmark refused to cooperate further, which ended the joint venture and the approach to Paley.

That left the American Broadcasting Company. The first direct merger suggestion to both sides came in late 1964 from Geneen's old stock analyst friend, Gerry Tsai. "One day," Tsai says, "I was taking a walk in Scarsdale with Larry and Mrs. Tisch" [Laurence A. Tisch, chairman of Loew's Corporation]. "We were talking about ABC, and I said, You know Larry, I think ITT should buy ABC. And he said, That's a damn good idea!"

Geneen thought so too. His own people had already pegged ABC as much better than it looked to the casual investor—or dial turner. It was a poor third in what ITT analysts termed a "two-and-a-half network universe." In 1964 there was not enough advertising to support three networks, and with the lowest ratings, ABC did not get its share. Between 1963 and 1965 ABC's network operations had lost at least $15 million, the deficit offset by its o&o's and by an ABC subsidiary, the Paramount Theater chain. But TV advertising was burgeoning. ABC's revenues had jumped from $364 million in 1962 to $476 million in 1965 and $540 million in 1966. Bob Kenmore predicted that by 1970 the network would earn a total of some $100 million. And most of that money would be available for investment in other areas.

Nothing immediate came of Gerry Tsai's contact. But a bit later, Larry Tisch was playing tennis with Leonard B. Goldenson, head of ABC, and Tisch said he believed Geneen wanted to make a serious offer; would Goldenson listen? "Sure," Goldenson said; "I'm glad to talk to anybody in respect

Leonard Goldenson

to anything about ABC." Today, Goldenson says that he was not personally interested in a merger. "I stated to the board that if it were my company, I would not agree to it—because I felt we had our own strength and our own ability to move ahead." On the other hand, he says, "I didn't control the company; I was only chief executive officer, representing the stockholders" —of which, to be sure, Goldenson was a major one, with just over 97,000 shares.

Geneen called him on January 12, 1965, and was invited to dinner at Goldenson's apartment along with Hart Perry; Goldenson was seconded by his executive VP, Simon B. Siegel. The talk was general, mostly Geneen's customary rhapsodic visions. No price was mentioned. In February Geneen made an offer of around $64 a share, ABC then selling in the mid-50s. "Without any hesitancy," Goldenson later testified, "I said I wouldn't be interested."

The talks stalled. Even so, Goldenson was increasingly disposed to listen. In 1964 Norton Simon had tried to force his way onto the ABC board, and by mid-1965 Simon had bought about 9% of ABC's stock. If Goldenson did not find some corporate shelter, a "white knight," there was no telling who might take over. In June he talked with General Electric, but Justice Department rumblings about antitrust cooled GE's interest.

Geneen had not lost hope. He called Goldenson in November 1965. "Mr. Geneen asked if I would be interested in resuming discussions on a merger,"

Goldenson testified. "I said yes, provided that the price would be around $100 a share, I would be interested. He said he would like to think about it, and could he get in touch with me about a further meeting." The ABC numbers looked irresistibly good, and on November 23 Geneen and Perry met Goldenson and Siegel at the Waldorf for breakfast. Geneen's new offer was only around $80 or $81, and Goldenson repeated that he wanted $100. But with ABC stock stalled back in the low 50s, that was just haggling. Geneen went to $83 a share, and then—Si Siegel reported to the ABC board—"raised this figure in very small amounts a number of times" until he reached $85.50, which Goldenson and Siegel were convinced was Geneen's top price. It was not $100, but how it was paid could make a difference.

"He called me about a day later, or maybe that day," testified Goldenson, "and said he had an idea on how he felt they could work out a deal on a convertible preferred and a common that would translate itself, in his opinion, to our stockholders getting the equivalent of $100 a share. I said fine."

For each share of ABC stock, Geneen would pay .5719 share of ITT common and the same amount of a new preferred paying twice the common dividend, with a $2.40 minimum. Total cost would be about $400 million, some 25 times ABC's 1965 earnings.

On December 1 an agreement was announced, and on December 7 both boards approved. Next day Geneen wrote to Goldenson, welcoming him, hailing the "historic event," and promising ABC continuing autonomy. The last would be a vital point.

A lot of ITT executives were instantly smitten by show biz. Bob Kenmore, who was slated as liaison with ABC, installed three TV sets in his office to monitor each network. A manager in the Far East urged on ABC the charms of Micronesia for a TV special. And after a party ABC threw for ITT, complete with dog-and-pony show about the glories of broadcasting, says Goldenson, "a number of ITT executives came up and said, My goodness, we'd like to come to work for ABC rather than ITT." Indeed, ABC soon complained about the deluge of phone calls, and a stern memo directed that all contact be through Hart Perry—who, with Geneen, would sit on the ABC board.

On April 17, 1966, both sets of stockholders approved the merger. Application had already been filed with the FCC for transfer of the broadcasting licenses. Technically, ITT did not need FCC approval to buy ABC's network operations—only to assume responsibility for ABC's seventeen TV and radio stations. Review was reckoned perfunctory and approval automatic. The Justice Department had voiced no objections on antitrust grounds. And the FCC was a pushover.

One FCC staff member, on resigning, decried the commission's "almost hypnotic lethargy" and complained about "the sad state of the regulatory art as practiced by the FCC." A reporter referred to it as "a political dumping ground," with four of the seven commissioners confirmed standpatters who (one of the other three huffed) served the interests of the companies they were supposed to regulate, not the public.

The Department of Justice antitrust division, under Assistant Attorney General Donald F. Turner, appeared no greater threat. Turner was considered soft on big-business mergers. Later, out of office, he was hired as consultant to ITT on an even bigger deal.

In early June 1966, FCC chairman Rosel H. Hyde wrote to Turner to ask for Justice's conclusions, if any, about the merger. An exchange of letters established that Justice was indeed looking at it but could offer no opinion for some time. Meanwhile, the commission asked ITT and ABC for more information. Was ITT really prepared to give ABC the money it needed to improve its program services? And would ITT really allow ABC operating autonomy? Absolutely, said Mr. Goldenson. Positively, said Mr. Geneen.

On August 17 the FCC majority concluded that it was not even necessary to hold a hearing. But minority member Robert T. Bartley wrote a strong dissent. "I believe that the information and evidence presently before us are insufficient." Approval was not supposed to turn on "whether ABC or ITT or both will benefit economically" from the merger; the FCC's duty was to determine "that the public interest will affirmatively be enhanced. . . . " And the applicants had fallen woefully short of showing that. Furthermore, Bartley could see dangers in ITT's proprietorship. After all, ITT had world-spanning interests, and the 13% broadcast tail "won't wag the 87% nonbroadcast dog." Not that Bartley was suggesting "premeditated falsification of news or distortion of fact"—only "selectivity" in scheduling and selection of news and program material "in the interest of corporate . . . harmony."

The majority gave in. A one-day hearing was set for September 19, 1966. But that was hardly the "full evidentiary hearing" the minority had demanded. Bartley's fellow dissenter, Nicholas Johnson, later charged:

> From the outset, the outcome of this case was a foregone conclusion. . . .
> . . . It was anticipated the Commission would merely meet informally *en banc* with the principals of ABC and ITT and hear their side of the case. Only the questioning of three commissioners extended the case to a scant two days. The questioning of three of the commissioners in the majority, combined, occupied scarcely a full page of the 607-page record. The fourth commissioner's questioning was directed principally toward discrediting an FCC staff member, and assisting ITT's counsel's efforts to demonstrate the absence of any possible antitrust implications of this merger. . . .

He complained that the public had been forgotten and that that was the guts of the matter.

The whole affair—two hearings, endless letter writing, and press statements—was marked by posturing and hypocrisy on both sides. The trouble was that section 310B of the FCC code stated that grants of TV and radio broadcast licenses must serve "the public interest, convenience and necessity." Perhaps a new license for a new channel might do that; but no mere transfer —unless to take a station away from a bankrupt or maniac—could meet that requirement. The public was neither served nor disserved; it would simply receive the same fare at the same trough, while someone new got rich on local advertising. Yet license transfers were routine, meaning the law was routinely ignored. In fact, when the Minnesota Mining and Manufacturing Corporation sold the Mutual Broadcasting Company, it was without review by the FCC, since only network operations were involved, no stations. But that was radio, and dull, and Mutual was an off-brand anyway. This was TV, and sexy. When a majority member observed the plain truth—that the commission had no authority over the network—even the ABC-ITT lawyer had to allow that it would be "highly unrealistic and artificial" to pretend the network was not the real issue.

The motives of ITT and ABC were simple. Geneen wanted ABC because it would be a marvelous investment and might get ITT better known. Goldenson and the other ABC stockholders wanted the premium price Geneen would pay. Public interest was not engaged either way. But once challenged, the principals had to make some showing of public interest, which could only mean demonstrating ABC's *need* for ITT's support in order to survive. But Goldenson had assured his board that ABC could carry on quite happily alone. So it follows that most of the ITT-ABC testimony at the two hearings was nonsense, some of it perjury.

The opposition's tactics and disingenuousness were just about as bad. What damage to public interest would flow from the merger? In programming, ABC was the joke network. When one of its programs, "Peyton Place," achieved good ratings, ABC's prime time soon boasted "Peyton Place II" and "Peyton Place III"—along with "Batman" and "Batman II," "Gidget" and "Patty Duke." What mattered who purveyed such a schedule? So the FCC minority, determinedly against the merger, was thrown back on two lines of attack.

The first was to show that ABC in fact did not need ITT (which would still not have had anything to do with the public interest). But color TV was taking over, and it would cost ABC up to $75 million to convert. Also, NBC and CBS were going to show movies two nights a week. Naturally ABC had to do the same, which meant some $120 million to reserve a three-year film inventory. ABC did need money.

Very well, said the FCC minority; how about ABC's usual channels of finance? Goldenson testified that the terms of their loan with Metropolitan Life forbade them to borrow more than $6 million beyond current indebtedness. That was not true. Perhaps Goldenson did not know the facts. Perhaps he was confused. But his executive VP, Si Siegel, knew better, was in the hearing room, and indeed told Goldenson about his misstatement immediately afterward. Yet they did not correct the testimony.

The minority's reaction was discreditable. Until the truth transpired, the honest reaction would have been, "Well, maybe you do need ITT's financial support after all." Instead there was low comedy. Ah! said Nicholas Johnson, but the ITT board had not specified now *much* support they would tender ABC; so maybe ABC's need would not be answered by the merger anyway. Geneen was testifying then, and Lee Loevinger, one of the majority, interrupted. Had Geneen promised to support his wife when he married her? Of course. Did the minister ask him to specify the amount of the support? No. Did the amount end up being more, probably, than if he *had* been forced to state a figure? That was too much for minority member Kenneth A. Cox.

Cox: Was the minister required to make a public interest finding?
Johnson: That would have been the more relevant issue.
Geneen: I'm sure I would never have gotten the merger through.

The minority's other line of attack was more reasonable, one that might have touched on public interest. Yet it was rendered hypothetical by the fact that no answer would have moved the FCC minority's opposition to the merger, any more than the majority could have been swayed. It was the question of independence for ABC News and for the network's public-affairs programming. There were some interesting aspects to the issue. Over half of ITT's business was still overseas, and much of it could survive only with the blessing of host governments. Nicholas Johnson asked ITT director John A. McCone if there would not very possibly be conflict between ITT's business interests and potential ABC documentaries or news stories critical of foreign governments. "No," said McCone, "I couldn't imagine that." This was a startling failure of imagination in someone who, as former head of the CIA (and a high-powered banker) presumably knew what evil lurks in the hearts of men. But all right, how about the United States? ITT still did a sizable chunk of business with the government, including a number of space contracts. Wouldn't that put pressure on ABC to support the space program, willy-nilly? McCone could not see why: "I would question very much whether an ABC producer would support the space program because of the benefits to ITT. I think if he was going to support the space program he would support it because it was in the national interest to do so. . . . " That was certainly, he said, "the only reason I would support the space program, that it was in the national interest, not in the special interest of the corporation."

It is not necessary to doubt McCone's sincerity to see that this was no answer. Where national interest resides is not always clear. Later, in Chile, McCone, Geneen, the CIA, Kissinger, and Nixon—all would discover national interest in directions that Congress and most of the nation found abhorrent. If there is a point to public-affairs TV it is surely the exposure of competing views as to the national interest, not an explication of national interest as undisputed gospel. In a couple of years Geneen would urge a particular view of the nation's interest in antitrust laws. Would an ABC producer with larger corporate ambitions, following the merger, have felt free to champion a special on the unwisdom of allowing conglomerate mergers?

Geneen's assurances were unequivocal—but necessarily unpersuasive. "I can assure you without reservations," he said, "that the broadcasting operation of ABC will be kept separate from other ITT operations, and the operations of ABC as a licensee will be performed unaffected by commercial communications or other similar interests of ITT." He even put it in writing as a corporate policy statement.

What of it? "Mere assertions of good faith," as Commissioner Johnson called them, were in no way enforceable. Logically, a hands-off policy is not possible to guarantee; ironically, it was not even consonant with the law. Geneen was caught in the delicious bureaucratic absurdity of having to swear he would never interfere with ABC's operations, and concurrently swear that as new licensee he would stand ultimately responsible for those operations. As final paradox, he would be duty-bound to step in and halt any documentary he suspected of being produced solely because it accommodated ITT's interests.

There was simply no way to guarantee independence. And if there were, it would still not affect the chill factor. Producers would know what was and was not politic. You do not have to abort programs that are not even conceived—or at least not proposed.

That far, the FCC minority had a point. But all this assumed a network that, unmerged, would pursue hard-hitting public-affairs stories, and everyone knew that that was piffle. If ABC was the joke network in entertainment, its news and public-affairs operation was a bad one-liner. They had only recently, and with feet dragging, expanded their evening news from fifteen minutes to a half-hour. As for the independence of ABC public affairs even before ITT, Nicholas Johnson asked Goldenson if he recalled when ABC had ever run anything contrary to the interests of a major stockholder or member of the ABC board. Goldenson could not bring any instances to mind.

As questioning went on, the preservation of ABC's independence emerged largely as a pretext for the minority's fixed opposition to big-business mergers. But reality is seldom an important determinant in such proceedings, and the hearing continued. Scheduled for one day, it went two. Geneen displayed his usual command of the facts, going on interminably and once prompting his questioner to say, "I'm getting hoarse from listening." Everyone was also getting a little dippy. After one particularly convoluted question, which Goldenson said he had not understood, Commissioner Bartley suggested that the reporter read it back: "I am kind of interested in knowing what I said, too." On the issue of ABC's financial strength, Johnson observed that from 1964 to 1965 the other networks' combined profit had declined from $68 million to $65 million, while ABC's loss had been cut from $8.4 million to $5.6 million—which obviously showed that ABC was "improving at a rate faster than that of the other two networks." Then a lawyer argued that to forbid ABC the support of ITT merely because the combined strength might have an anticompetitive effect would, by the same reasoning, void recent Office of Economic Opportunity legislation. "That would eliminate our poverty programs," he said. "That would eliminate all the great social trends which we have witnessed during the past quarter of a decade" (i.e., two and a half years). Commissioner Johnson said, "I don't think you meant seriously to suggest that the increase in Mr. Goldenson's stock . . . [as a result of the merger] was an essential part of the Administration's War on Poverty."

The hearing ended with all minds exactly where they were when it began. The first break came on September 22, two days after the hearing. Wisconsin Senator Gaylord Nelson sent Chairman Hyde a letter urging the FCC to suspend decision until the Justice Department had spoken. Another letter asked Donald Turner for Justice's views. Nelson was soon joined in his requests by Michigan's Philip Hart and Oregon's Wayne Morse, who said, "The public was forgotten."

Soon everyone was writing back and forth urging action. Finally, on December 20, 1966, Turner sent Justice's opinion to the FCC. In an earlier letter Turner had advanced the astounding conclusion that even though the merger did not seem to violate antitrust laws, perhaps the commission should turn it down anyway, just because. Now he wrote that the antitrust aspects "seem sufficiently speculative" so that Justice was "not presently contemplating action . . . to enjoin consummation of the merger." Nevertheless, he saw the "possibility of adverse effects significant enough" to call to the commission's attention. The only "adverse effect" he mentioned worth considering was the probability that ABC did not need ITT to compete.

Turner's letter arrived at the FCC at 6:00 P.M. At 10:00 A.M. next morning the commission announced its decision, 4–3 in favor of the merger, which would take effect in thirty days. The forty-three-page majority opinion cited ABC's need, relying on Goldenson's still uncorrected testimony. Besides, the majority concluded, finally talking turkey, the FCC should not stand in the way of a profit-making deal.

Nicholas Johnson hit the roof. In an eighty-eight-page dissent he professed equal bewilderment at the majority's reasoning and its haste. "I would think it appropriate to at least read Mr. Turner's letter slowly."

Why was there such a rush? One reporter mentioned "rumor laced with bits of truth." Another wrote that it all revolved around the congratulatory message that President Johnson had sent ITT and ABC when the merger was announced. Speculation had it that ITT executives had been pressured into making political contributions. "The way was greased for approval of the merger right from the start."

Bribery was not unknown at ITT, but a fair-minded observer would not conclude that it was at work here. The four-man majority was resolutely business oriented and simply could not see what the pother was about. They were, however, no more intractable than the minority. Yet no one suggested that those three dissenters had been bribed by, say, the American Civil Liberties Union, which later tried to intervene against the merger.

Whatever the case, there was too much voluble opposition to ignore, so on January 18, 1967, two days before the merger was to have gone through, Justice petitioned the FCC for "leave to intervene." A stay was granted, and on March 16 Chairman Hyde voted with the minority for a new evidentiary hearing on April 10, 1967.

ITT and ABC got busy convincing the commission that the merger was a good idea, employing tactics of varying success and wisdom. The first involved a campaign of letters and telegrams to the FCC, with some predictable friends logging in. Senator Russell Long let Chairman Hyde know that Senators Nelson and Morse had not acted with the advice or consent of the rest of his monopoly subcommittee. He was for the merger. So were Nebraska Senator Karl Mundt, California Senator George Murphy, and *TV Guide* publisher Walter A. Annenberg. A New York State assemblyman pointed out that ABC was too poor to keep a regular television crew in Albany—though he likely mistook lack of interest for lack of money. The most curious letter read: "Stop stalling and approve the AMERICAN BROADCASTING COMPANY-INTERNATIONAL TELEPHONE AND TELEGRAPH merger. Leonard Goldenson is a great leader and needs this money to teach the world our message." It came from the W.E.B. DuBois Club of Florida, not thought to be a handmaiden of big business, any more than Goldenson was widely considered a vocal champion of black communism.

Then there were the telegrams. "We asked our affiliates, which was proper, if they agreed to inform the FCC," says Goldenson. Actually, ABC may even have suggested some text, and not just to affiliates. Gene A. Triggs, director of the Mississippi agriculture and industry board, wired the FCC majority, "Stand fast on recent decision of FCC giving ABC its rightful place in the competitive broadcasting." His boss, Mississippi governor Paul B. Johnson, also urged the FCC majority to "stand fast." So did many others. But there was another school of thought. An associate justice of the Mississippi Supreme Court wanted the FCC to "stand firm." So did the executive VP of radio station WILK in Wilkes Barre, Pennsylvania, and a spokesperson for WKTY radio, La Crosse, Wisconsin. In fact, there were about as many stand fasters as there were stand firmers.

Other, more forceful activity did not have its intended effect. On February 1, 1967, before the new hearing was voted, the FCC ordered Justice to produce documents and list witnesses it would call if hearings were reopened. The language of the order, the text of which was not released until evening, was preemptory, even harsh—as ITT's press release gleefully underscored. Ned Gerrity, head of PR, called Eileen Shanahan, the *New York Times* reporter in Washington who was covering the story, and got to her office with the press release at around 8:00 that night. Shanahan had finished her story for the first edition but planned a rewrite. She thought the ITT handout might make a paragraph. Gerrity hinted that he would like to see what she had written. "It was not a direct request," Shanahan later testified, "certainly not a demand." But it annoyed her, and she replied that his people could buy a paper in New York in a couple of hours. Well then, would the *Times* print the full text of the FCC's order? No; they printed full text only of historically significant documents, presidential messages and the like. Yes, but this was so unusual, all that snarling between government agencies. True, said Shanahan, but the *Times* had not run the equally venomous text of Justice's petition. "He insisted that the two things were quite different," Shanahan testified. "I can no longer remember the argument, because it didn't make any sense to me." But she did remember that his "tone was certainly accusatory and certainly nasty." If Gerrity wanted to call her editors and recommend running the text, he was welcome to use her phone.

The subject changed. Did Shanahan realize what was happening to the price of ABC stock? No, she didn't watch individual stock prices. Well, it had plummeted. Didn't she feel a responsibility to those who could lose money because of what she wrote? No. Her responsibility was "to find out the truth and print it."

An ITT spokesman said that at that point Gerrity merely remarked that it was odd to find Nicholas Johnson and Gaylord Nelson on the same side. Shanahan remembered it differently. Gerrity, she said, asked if she was aware that Johnson and Nelson were collaborating on legislation that would forbid any newspaper to own any broadcasting property—an edict that the *Times*, owner of some radio stations, would view with distaste. "Then he said," said Shanahan, "I think this is some information that you ought to pass on to your publisher before you write anything further about Commissioner Johnson's opinions on anything."

The information was not true; indeed, Johnson and Nelson had never even met. Shanahan did not know that, but she had had enough, anyway. She said she had to get back to work, and the interview was over.

On February 16, the day after Justice released a specification of issues, the head of PR in ITT's Washington office, John V. Horner, phoned Shanahan to protest her play of the story. In the release was the first public mention of ITT's estimate that ABC would generate $100 million in profits by 1970. That was certainly of moment in a merger based on poor-mouthing, and it was in Shanahan's lead. Horner cried foul: it was "no story" because at the September hearing the companies had insisted that all ITT estimates were their own and not based on ABC's figures. Furthermore, Horner said, Shanahan's story was unfair in stating that if the commission refused to reopen the case, Justice was expected to sue: Justice had issued a statement that it would *not* go to court. Shanahan was dumbfounded; she had seen no such statement. In fact, there was none—only a telegram from Justice to Gerrity saying that no decision had been made about suing and that none would be made until (if it happened) the FCC refused to reopen. Not quite the same thing, Horner admitted, but how could Shanahan say it *was* decided, in light of that telegram? She said that she had her sources, and she believed them. They continued to argue. But when Horner charged that her coverage had been unfair from the start, Shanahan shouted at him and slammed down the phone.

Along with a few more minor incidents, all this added up to what Shanahan considered the most intense pressure she had ever faced from the subject of a news story. She asked the financial editor of the *Times* in New York if such pressure was usual from ITT and was told that, no, relations with ITT had always been quite normal. Some weeks later, Shanahan got a call from a former boss who told her that Jack Horner had been asking very intimate questions about her—professionally and personally: Enraged, she checked with two other former employers and found that Horner had also asked one of them for dirt on her. She called the most prominent of ITT's Washington lawyers, Marcus Cohn. He had thirty minutes to get that nonsense stopped permanently. He asked for twenty-four hours but called back before the deadline. Without admitting it had happened, he assured her it would not happen again.

According to an ITT spokesman, the incident was more casual and benign. Jack Horner ran into Shanahan's former boss in the bar of the Press Club, and they discussed her over drinks. (The spokesman did not explain questions to the second ex-boss.) In any case, both Horner and Gerrity, as ex-newsmen, should have known better—and especially with Eileen Shanahan. While a highly respected reporter, she was notorious for her hair-trigger temper and, according to a colleague, "boundless capacity for moral indignation." She was someone you could rely on to resent ITT's sort of pressure.

Two more journalists—these with the Associated Press—were also subjected to ITT-ABC pressure. Theirs was a tame story compared with Shanahan's. But if the two corporations did not scruple to squeeze reporters they did not even own, what chance would ABC's newspeople have?

The second FCC hearing began on April 10, 1967. The issues—unreal as ever—had at least been refined to four clear ones. First, competition: If Geneen had seriously considered buying o&o's, plus chains of profitable cable TV stations (CATV), might not ITT, if the merger were disallowed, use its vast resources to form a fourth network and *really* increase competition? Second, independence: Would ITT interfere in the gathering and reporting of ABC news and public-affairs programs? Third, financial necessity: With the cat out of the bag about ABC's borrowing power, did ABC need ITT's backing in order to compete? Fourth (and even Justice put little stock in it), technology: Would the merger stifle ITT's broadcast R&D?

As the hearing progressed, a fifth issue emerged: honesty. The testimony and behavior of many officials—mostly ITT's but also ABC's—lacked candor, responsiveness, and a sense of decorum. Perhaps Justice could not show perjury; but plainly there was equivocation and obstruction. In fact, on the first three issues, there was some out-and-out lying. Even more, there was what might be called "constructive perjury"—giving a consciously false impression of one's attitudes, interests, knowledge, and motives. The most blatant example of this was Leonard Goldenson's testimony about why ABC agreed to be bought. He says today that his *sole* reason was the high price

Geneen offered; yet he testified to ABC's financial need being the reason—which he today says he specifically discounted to his own board.

The problem Goldenson and the others faced is explained succinctly by Bob Kenmore: "When I went down for the hearings, and I was on the stand, I came away with the feeling that the frame of reference of a government lawyer and of a business executive are really so incompatible, it's like they were talking different languages. It's almost as if the questions and the answers didn't go together.

"They were saying, If you can't prove that ABC *needs* you, then we're not going to approve the merger. Well, once you establish that ground rule, you're almost trapped into playing by silly rules, rather than with the truth—which was that ABC would be a better competitor because of us, stronger, and so on.

"I think they were using phony arguments to buttress their case, and we probably used some arguments that weren't the most brilliant—taking extreme positions—to buttress our case."

Given those rules, specifically the language of 310B about public interest, if Goldenson had told the truth, the merger was cooked. The same was even more true about Geneen's interest in buying independent stations. It was transparent from subpoenaed memos and ITT actions. But given the construction Justice put on that interest, ITT witnesses felt they had to deny it was real. The result was the appearance of unceasing shiftiness.

For example, there was the spectacle of Stan Luke, who alternated with a bellboy running Court Newton's messages downstairs during the Bell & Gossett board meeting—*that* Stan Luke—testifying that he alone, regardless of lack of interest from Jack Graham and Harold Geneen, kept pursuing a possible TV station acquisition, Gross Telecasting, in Lansing, Michigan. A government lawyer observed that Luke was simply the fellow who carried out negotiations decided by Geneen and the board. So *they* must have told him to contact the station. "I contacted Gross on my own," swore Luke. He also had to pretend that he did not know what Chris J. Witting was doing at ITT—because Witting had been hired, after years at Du Mont and Westinghouse Broadcasting, and had been made an instant VP, specifically to head ITT's putative TV operations.

CATV was an even tenderer spot. ITT could point out that they had not, after all, *bought* any TV stations. But by the time of the ABC merger announcement, ITT had already invested $10 million in CATV and seemed committed for another $10 million in 1966. CATV operations were part of ITT's Federal Electric Corporation, then headed by Robert Chasen. Not long before Geneen's climactic meeting with Goldenson in November 1965, Chasen had written to Geneen that FEC was paying "maximum attention" to "the acquisition of CATV systems." He discussed plans for 1966 and 1967. Then, suddenly, ITT was no longer interested in CATV. Why? The timing was suggestive. So was ABC's vehement, public, and long-standing opposition to the spread of CATV. Chasen testified that there was no connection.

He had made the decision to abandon ITT's CATV investment on his own.

Earlier, to establish Geneen's interest in pay TV, Chasen had been asked if ITT had made any evaluation studies of a company called Sciatron. Chasen said no, whereupon the lawyer showed him exhibit J119, an ITT study of Sciatron. Chasen said he had meant that no *preliminary* evaluation study had been done. The lawyer said, "I can see I'm going to have to be very careful in framing my questions to you, Mr. Chasen." He was not careful enough. He asked if Chasen had discussed "what the ITT role in CATV should be" with anyone at ABC or with his direct superior at ITT, a group executive, or with the man Geneen had appointed to oversee CATV. Chasen said no. That was not entirely accurate; but the lawyer was on the wrong track, anyway. He never asked a direct question about discussions with the person who counted. "I was told direct by Geneen," Chasen says today, "that Goldenson had complained that our CATV operations conflicted with their theater business." Geneen ordered Chasen to freeze CATV operations. "I was a good soldier," says Chasen. "I just said, OK, I'll try something else." When Chasen left ITT in the late 1970s (he says it was because the fun had gone out with Geneen no longer in control), he became head of the United States Customs Service under President Jimmy Carter.

The second hearing stretched windily from April 10, 1967, to the twenty-seventh. Throughout, the behavior of ITT executives was downright stupid—given that the motif of their case was "You can trust us." Justice had asked that witnesses who were to testify later be excluded from the hearing room. During the first session ITT's general counsel, Ray Brittenham, shuttled notes to witnesses waiting in a nearby conference room. When called on it he stopped, but almost immediately the government complained that there were now two secretaries taking notes. They never did find out that Dita Beard, not yet famous, had carried a tape recorder in a capacious handbag. She gave the tapes to ITT's outside lawyers to pass on to Geneen—so, she says, "Geneen could see what the temperature was." But when she asked him, "Did you enjoy the tapes?" he replied, "What tapes?" At least the outside lawyers had better sense than to traffic in such matters; they had not passed the tapes on to Geneen.

In their final dissent, the minority professed indignant astonishment at all of ITT's shenanigans. "If ITT has behaved this way with the spotlight on it, how much credibility" could there be to assurances about the future when no one would be watching? To be sure, the deportment of angels would not have swayed the minority; but they had a point. ITT's PR department needed some good PR advice.

"It was all very heavy-handed, no question about it," Leonard Goldenson says. It all was part of what Justice termed the applicants' want of "completeness and candor."

On the morning of April 27, 1967, the FCC examiner pointed out that a record had just been achieved: a witness was on and off the stand in only ten minutes. The hearing was closed at 11:15 A.M.

In May both sides filed statements of facts and findings. On June 22 the commission announced its unsurprising verdict: 4–3 in favor of the merger, with a long, angry, denunciatory dissent. On September 7 the Justice Department filed suit with the Court of Appeals asking that the merger be disallowed. In October the case was heard, this time with no nonsense. In late December a reporter was sure the decision was expected "momentarily." It was never rendered, because the issue soon became moot.

Geneen's acquisition program had been in disarray for a year. "The lawyers," says a former staff member, "kept saying, Don't make waves, we're having enough trouble with ABC. Don't come in with too many other things." It meant giving up some plums. "We had a handshake deal to buy Holiday Inns," says Tim Dunleavy. But during the waiting period Holiday Inns' stock rose out of sight, and they backed out. The same thing almost happened with the home-building firm of Levitt & Sons, Inc. And other drawbacks to the merger soon presented themselves. It was clear that conversion to color was going to cost a lot more than anticipated, and revenues for ABC might be less. ABC did not look like such a marvelous deal anymore, and Geneen was growing leery. Most of all, says Tim Dunleavy, "Geneen just had a feeling that ABC was going to drag on for a long time."

According to the agreement, either party could cancel if the merger had not been fully approved by December 31, 1967. On New Year's Day, 1968, Geneen summoned his board—sending a limousine to fetch Tim Dunleavy from his home in Blue Bell, Pennsylvania.

For Leonard Goldenson, it ended as it started, playing tennis with Larry Tisch. It was the opening of Tisch's new Paradise Island resort in Nassau, and Tisch had invited many old friends. "I was sitting there by the tennis court," says Gerry Tsai, another guest, "watching Leonard and Larry play, and all of a sudden the loudspeaker said, Mr. Leonard Goldenson, an overseas call. So Leonard left, and when he came back, his face was white."

It was Si Siegel. "Si had received a call from Geneen," says Goldenson. "Geneen wanted to get to us before it was announced, but Si had already heard it on the radio. I didn't hear from Geneen until much later that day. He said the board had met and had decided to call off the merger. I said, Well good luck. What else was I to say? We were not consulted about it. No reason was given; no reason has ever been given to this day."

"It wasn't devastating," says ITT controller Herb Knortz. "We weren't broken up when we didn't get ABC." Geneen certainly was not. During the merger fight he and Goldenson had become very close, seeing each other both on business and socially, playing tennis, just visiting. "Buddies?" says Bob Savage, who saw them at work and play. "Great!" But as soon as someone was no longer important to ITT, he ceased to exist. "A little later," says Savage, "Geneen was at a meeting and was talking about broadcasting, and he said, What's that guy's name at ABC?" As for the others at ITT, "We just said," says Herb Knortz, "Well maybe it's all right; maybe they're not our kind of people, anyway. They're show people. And so we went merrily along."

16
The Glory Years

"And now," Geneen told a group of investors, "let me summarize the outlook for ITT in nineteen sixty-eight." To no one's amazement he predicted continued progress. Indeed, 1968 was an historic year for ITT, the advent of the most dazzling series of acquisitions ever accomplished by any company in so short a time, and prelude to the largest acquisition in corporate history to that date.

Having shed the restraint of ABC, Geneen was ready. During 1967 ITT's stock hit a high of 124, and on October 11 the directors proposed a 2-for-1 split, approved by stockholders on January 25, 1968. The reasonably good stock price was just what Geneen needed. With his system, his people, and a decent multiple, acquiring almost any company was now possible. All it took was the will. And in its audacious scope, Geneen's program was unparalleled. ITT's 1967 volume was $2.76 billion; yet in 1968 alone Geneen would pay over a billion dollars in stock to acquire companies.

This was bravery. "You have to be willing to use your stock and expose your company," says Herb Knortz. "A lot of people will 'gamble'—with five percent of their money. You can't do it with five percent. You have to play table stakes." That was Geneen's game. "Sure," says a detractor, "he was a high roller—with other people's money." But if it was their money, it was *his* company, and the company was his life. When the head of one substantial ITT unit seemed lighthearted about a potentially significant loss, Geneen said, "What are *you* risking? If it fails you'll get another job. I could lose the company." Bad acquisitions of this magnitude could sink the whole enterprise. Even so, Geneen knew he could not build what he wanted—the biggest profit maker in the world—without taking fearsome risks.

First of the 1968 acquisitions was Levitt & Sons, Inc. (LSI), the home builders immortalized by "Levittowns." LSI was easily America's biggest independent company of their type, with revenues in 1965 of about $74 million and a net well over $3 million. Geneen started looking at LSI in 1966. At the time, William J. Levitt controlled almost 80% of the LSI stock. He had gone public in 1960 and in early 1966 wanted to sell more stock. As an alternative, the LSI counsel, Joel A. Carr, explained the advantages of a merger. What's more, Carr knew who could find a buyer for LSI. He had been talking with Donald Petrie, by then a consultant to Lazard Frères. Carr and Felix Rohatyn had been in school together, and Levitt had known Rohatyn for years, belonging to the same country club as his parents.

"Mr. Levitt," Rohatyn wrote to André Meyer, "is apparently a rather mercurial individual, with a highly developed sense of his own importance and requiring a somewhat highly personalized approach." But Lazard could handle him. Although Rohatyn's first thoughts of a buyer turned to the large oil companies already active in real estate, he soon was extolling LSI to Geneen. Immersed in ABC, Geneen hesitated, and Lazard kept looking. One of their analysts observed that "Levitt and Lockheed talk the same language." There were other possible merger partners too. But by June 1966 Geneen was convinced that he wanted LSI, and he was considering a "ball-park price" of around $16 a share, a good premium since LSI stock stood between $11 and $12. It was 12 times earnings.

After the first ABC hearing in September 1966 a deal with LSI was set in principle, only "awaiting the ITT-ABC approval of the FCC." It was a long wait. With the Justice Department's intervention, Geneen's lawyers

Bill Levitt in 1975.

warned him off an immediate LSI merger. In January 1967 Bill Levitt promised to wait, and Geneen was suitably grateful. In truth, Levitt had little
choice; he was stuck. His stock was now around $19, though he had earned
a little less than expected in 1966. He was overpriced for a public offering and
no longer so attractive to corporate buyers who lacked Geneen's vision and
confidence. After the second ABC hearing and 4–3 vote, Levitt's patience was
rewarded. For appearance' sake they would hold off two weeks; but if Justice
appealed the ABC vote, they might as well go ahead. Justice did appeal, and
on July 22, 1967, the merger of ITT with LSI was announced.

The delay was costly for Geneen. Originally he had offered .25 share of
ITT common for reach LSI share—$17.50, with ITT stock at 70, LSI at 11⅛.
Now ITT was 102, while LSI had soared to 28¾. Geneen had to pay .285
share, $29.07, the total price over $93 million—by far his largest acquisition
up to then.

Even considering the price, Levitt looked to be a solid investment. "If
I had been on the ITT side," says an LSI executive from those days, "I would
have said, Jeez! It's an ideal company for us to gobble up and manipulate and
further expand. The numbers looked great, the management team, the sophis-
tication—nobody could touch us! The Kaufman and Broads, the Larwins,
they weren't anywhere near."

As usual, Geneen displayed no doubts about it being right for ITT. "He
said on many occasions," says another LSI officer from those days, "that the
building business was the same as any other manufacturing business." Bill
Levitt matched Geneen's optimism, especially given Geneen's promised support for expansion. "I said, Give us five years," Levitt says, "and we'll do a
billion a year." Forget "Levitt and Lockheed"; Bill and Hal, *they* talked the
same language. But not for long.

The acquisition was completed on February 1, 1968. In April, Levitt
called Geneen. "I said, Harold, this thing is not going to work. We can't
operate under the system you've got there." Geneen rushed out to Levitt's
Lake Success headquarters to calm him down, then wrote a seven-page memo:
LSI had to be treated differently from the other units, not held to the same
ratio standards or report writing. "It was directed to maybe a dozen different
people in ITT," says Levitt. "We got along all right for a week or two, then
everybody forgot about the memo." They also forgot about Bill Levitt. With
exquisite delicacy he was nudged up and out. His executive VP and groomed
successor, Richard A. Wasserman, became CEO.

Dick Wasserman was much more in the ITT mold than Levitt. He was
forty-two years old (Levitt was sixty-two), attractive, hard-working, and
bright, a product of the Wharton School, at home with Geneen's style of
reporting and number crunching. And he was every bit as eager for expansion
as Levitt had been. The result was, as a former ITT VP says, "an unmitigated
disaster." But that story belongs in the next chapter.

Geneen's second acquisition of 1968 was also affected by ABC. The
Holiday Inn franchises of his 1966 acquisition, APCOA, got Geneen in-

trigued with the hotel business. When the wait for ABC sank his deal for the whole chain, he started scouting other possibilities. One was Sheraton Hotels.

Ernest F. Henderson and Robert L. Moore were schoolmates, fellow World War I aviators and business partners. In 1937 they bought the Sheraton Hotel in Boston. Named for nineteenth-century cabinetmaker Thomas Sheraton, the hotel sported such a huge sign that the partners decided to make Sheraton their chain's name rather than spend money to change the sign. This spirit of Yankee thrift informed the whole operation. Henderson—president and dominant partner—would buy a dilapidated hotel in some city, refurbish it minimally, and keep trading up. Costs and salaries were depressed, depreciation maximized to avoid a taxable profit. "Sheraton never made a nickel," proudly says Richard Boonisar, Henderson's financial VP. The only blight on this enviable record was a subsidiary, Thompson Industries. Sheraton had bought Thompson Spa, a Boston restaurant whose single recommendation was a $4 million tax loss; they combined it with an Indianapolis company called Moldings, Inc., and watched with mixed emotions as the new auto parts company turned a profit each year.

In 1963 Moore retired as chairman. Henderson took that title, and his son, Ernest F. Henderson III, became president. Although forty-two years old, the son was universally called "young Ernie." Henderson and Moore wanted to get their estates in order, and Dick Boonisar had been told to talk to potential buyers. His talks included ITT, but there had been nothing like negotiations. In September 1967 Henderson suffered a fatal heart attack. The day after Henderson's death, Geneen called young Ernie at home. It was a futile call; "Ernie," says Boonisar, "had nothing to say about whether I sold or not." The Henderson interest was about 27% of the stock, but, says Boonisar, "his stock was all in the estate, and Bob Moore was the trustee. I had all the proxies."

Still, Ernie Henderson could not be ignored. Geneen gave him the usual trip to the mountaintop. With wide-body jets, he told him, travel was taking off. Backed by ITT, Sheraton could blossom from its mere 144 U.S. units and 10 overseas hotels to a world empire, a Sheraton in every terminal city. Then there were all those advanced management techniques that only Ernie, Sheraton's sole Harvard M.B.A., could appreciate. "He was feeding it to me," says Henderson, "and I was lapping it up."

The serious negotiation, however, was with Dick Boonisar—who was, says Henderson, "the father that my own father wasn't to me." Boonisar was lean, tough, a self-made man. When the executive of an ITT subsidiary first came to visit on business, Boonisar greeted him with, "Who the fuck are you?" and then wanted to know how many push-ups the visitor could do. Now Boonisar was chairman. One evening in October 1967 he got a call at home from Geneen. Could they meet? Sure; when? In a couple of hours; Geneen's secretary would call when he left for the airport.

The meeting place was Boston's Somerset Hotel. Geneen brought with him Tim Dunleavy, Hart Perry, and Howard Miller, who would be group executive. "Not one of those other guys uttered a word," says Boonisar. "They just sat there. Geneen says to me, Can you make a deal right now? I said, Sure, can you? And he smiled." Price was the only issue. Geneen said he would offer Sheraton's full market value, reflected in the annual report. Who could ask for fairer? "Look," said Boonisar, "I'm supposed to be a great trader. I can't come back with just what we say is our value, I've got to get a premium." Geneen raised his offer slightly, and Boonisar replied with notable unenthusiasm that he would discuss it with his board, making as if to leave. Geneen opened a door to the suite's bathroom and motioned Boonisar to join him, out of earshot of the others. "He asked me what I'd take," says Boonisar. "There were eight points' difference between us, and he said, I'll split the difference with you." The package of common and preferred came to just over $35 a share, a total of more than $193 million. APCOA's hotel people had looked Sheraton over and had set what they thought was a reasonable price: Geneen paid about $10 a share more. Now to make it pay off.

"The first thing Hal told me," says Henderson, "was to spread around a half-million dollars in raises." That scandalized him. The next thing Geneen did was raise profits. Even Boonisar recognized that Sheraton's no-profit, no-tax doctrine was impossible for a corporate owner catering to the market's demand for earnings growth. But this was appalling: with ITT's more profit-oriented accounting and depreciation, earnings rocketed in one year from $3 million (that pesky Thompson) to $18 million. Henderson saw, in anguish, $8 million forked over in taxes.

The third thing Geneen did was get rid of Henderson.

"Ernie was the wrong guy in the wrong place when his father was there," says the man who would eventually bring Sheraton to success for Geneen, "so he was certainly the wrong guy for ITT." Almost everything about ITT's style clashed with what Henderson calls "my philosophy of management"—which he epitomizes as, "We'll do it your way and you better be right." That was scarcely Geneen's idea of management. "Ernie had certain concepts," says Sheraton's long-time marketing director, and "ITT had certain concepts. They didn't jibe." Perhaps the most severe disjunction was in the sacred area of planning. "I can remember," says a former associate, "Ernie telling those people that the hotel industry is different, it's not like those other businesses you're in, you can't write a plan for it. That was clearly unacceptable to ITT, and I wondered how the hell long they would put up with it." It turned out to be not quite a year.

Philip L. Lowe had joined ITT in September 1967, just about the time negotiations for Sheraton started. He was PLM for financial services. Geneen liked him, and so did Howard Miller, Sheraton group executive. Just before Christmas 1968 he was offered a chance to return to his native Boston to replace Henderson. In his own way, Lowe was equally the wrong guy in the wrong place; to start with, he is a natural-born staff man. "I really think," he says, "I'm a better advisor than I am an 'orderer.' " Even more damaging, he knew nothing about the hotel business.

On January 9, 1969, Sheraton proxies in hand, Lowe voted himself in as president. Henderson, the news release said, had resigned "to pursue interests in the nursing home field."

Dick Boonisar had thought Geneen's expansion talk was just "snake oil" to enchant Henderson. Yet right after the merger, Geneen made his last annual spring tour around Latin America, picking sites for new Sheratons. "He was like a kid with a new toy," says a lawyer who accompanied him. He bought a hotel in Chile and told his people to buy land for another in Argentina. "Then," says the lawyer, "someone in Rio de Janeiro came to him with a package of land, and he personally negotiated that." The lawyer thought Geneen paid too much for the Rio land; others thought that anything was too much. "It was the crappiest site in Rio," says one of them, "and when I say crappy, I *mean* crappy. You stood on the cliff and you saw this brown line out into the bay"—a sewage effluent. It would take a special act of the Brazilian legislature to pipe the effluent out to sea. Meanwhile, hotel construction was stalled by a soccer club with squatter's rights on the beach. Their ramshackle clubhouse was perched smack on the planned hotel site. Eviction was complicated by the fact that the club's president was a local naval hero, a man known as The Captain. An ITT lawyer offered them $2,500 to move, but the club members liked their location. Finally, a Brazilian ITT employee told the lawyer to go back to New York; he would take care of things. Soon a bulldozer ran amok, by sad mischance smashing the shanty. The club accepted the $2,500, and building went apace. The sewage effluent outfall was finished a scant month before the hotel opening; as a stand-by, engineers planned to spray perfume throughout the building and grounds. In the end, Sheraton had one of the finest hotels on one of the finest sites in Rio. Geneen had seen something that eluded everyone else: they saw difficulties, he saw promise.

What Geneen did not see was the impossibility of Sheraton's land- and hotel-buying policy, and the inappropriateness of Phil Lowe, lacking all hotel experience, as manager. There were some bright spots. Ever the financial man, Lowe questioned Sheraton's bad debt loss of $4 to $5 million a year and learned that it was average for the industry: asking a hotel guest for identification was then thought infra dig. Lowe changed that. No credit cards or checks would be accepted without some positive identification bearing either signature or photograph. On one occasion David Rockefeller, leading a party of fifteen, had nothing to back up his Chase Manhattan credit card and was turned down by the desk clerk at Sheraton's Ritz in Minneapolis. Rockefeller called Geneen, who called Lowe, who called the manager. Geneen's staffers polled Sheraton managers countrywide; with few exceptions they were in favor of the loss-cutting program, and it continued.

An even greater triumph started at ITT's first marketing review meeting with Sheraton and their ad agency, Batten, Barton, Durstine & Osborn. Sheraton's ads featured a businessman with a large key stuck in his back, the copy urging him to unwind at Sheraton. Although BBDO's research proved the "keyed-up executive" campaign to be extremely memorable, Geneen had another opinion. At the end of the two-and-a-half-day review, ITT's Keith M. Perkins rose to say, "Mr. Geneen suggests that you get that goddamn key out of that guy's back and put him in the bar having a good time."

Sheraton needed a new campaign. In the spring of 1969, ITT's Howard Miller gave Sheraton's marketing director, William Morton, an assignment: come up with a one-number room reservation system to replace the more than 200 phone numbers Sheraton listed nationwide. Perhaps the greatest problem was picking one unforgettable number. It became a major project for ITT's marketing staff, and Morton did much research on his own. Surprisingly, it turned out that the phone numbers easiest to remember are not those ending in three zeros. Except for "Pennsylvania six-five, oh, oh, oh," which enjoyed an unfair advantage, people forget exactly which thousand to call. For instance, ITT's number was Plaza 2-6000; but for about three years, the man who eventually took over at Sheraton persisted in dialing PL 6-2000.

With the help of a psychologist, Morton settled on a number. Then came the real test: would Geneen like the whole promotion? "Everything was fine at the presentation," says Morton, "until we got to the one-call, magical, toll-free phone number." It was 800-825-3535. "Geneen stopped me and said, I don't think anybody will ever remember that number; I think you ought to do some research." Morton cited the volume already done. "But nobody will remember it," said Geneen. "Do some more research."

"Twice more in the course of the meeting," says Morton, "he stopped me and said, Bill, you do some more research."

The subject was researched-out. By winter 1970 the new system was on-line, and the new advertising campaign broke with saturation TV and full-page magazine ads, incessant repetition of "eight, oh, oh, three-two-five, three-five, three-five." The number was set to a catchy tune. The Boston Pops played it once; a singing dog performed it on Johnny Carson's show, it was a cocktail-lounge background music in a TV drama; it was played at skating rinks. Geneen bombarded Morton with ideas for further exploitation. Most gripping was a plan to install in every Sheraton lobby a grandfather clock that would chime the reservation theme. "But every time I saw Mr. Geneen," says Morton, "he'd say, I *told* you nobody's ever going to remember that number. You've got to *do* something about it. I never knew if he was kidding. I'd just smile and say, You're absolutely right!" Reservations, from the very first, increased handsomely.

Triumphs, though, were the exception under Phil Lowe's management. Sheraton did not need managing, it needed fixing, and it is hard to fix something you do not understand. "If you show me an insurance company's balance sheet," says Lowe, "I'll immediately know something about the company. I couldn't do that with the hotel business." Lacking a hotelier's experience, neither could he tell which of his subordinates were worth listening to and were worth keeping. "Any experienced hotel man," he says, "would have known who the bad apples were and would have had them the hell out of there a lot quicker. But you can't just fire twenty-two thousand people and start over."

ITT staff were worse than no help. Although they knew equally little about the hotel business, their knowledge of staff studies was encyclopedic. And, says one observer, "Phil Lowe said yes to everything they suggested. They'd send in people for studies, and he'd end up with two and a half doormen and three and three-quarters desk clerks." What else could Lowe do? "To operate under anything except the strictest ITT guidelines was unacceptable," he says. "I wouldn't have presumed, considering my limited experience, to insist that we had to run it *my* way! Who the hell am I?"

The problem was further complicated by Dick Boonisar's instant dislike for Lowe. Boonisar was—as Lowe puts it—"from the wrong side of the tracks." They both had gone to Harvard, but Boonisar was a scholarship day student. Boonisar was rough, Lowe smooth. And Boonisar was Lebanese, Lowe Jewish—although Lowe never knew "whether that was a problem for him or not." Boonisar is not sure either. "I don't think I'm anti-Semitic," he says, "honest I don't. Maybe—I don't know." In any case, Boonisar was soon telling everyone in Boston how badly Sheraton was being run, what a misfit Lowe was, and what fools ITT people were. Letters and emissaries descended to warn him to stop his public criticism of ITT and its appointees. Nothing helped. One morning, at the ITT club in Bolton, fed up with some latest bit of lèse majesté, Geneen ordered that Boonisar be fired by noon, employment contract or no. That seemed impolitic to Phil Lowe and Howard Miller: Boonisar was a close friend of then Vice President Spiro T. Agnew. They finally prevailed on Ned Gerrity to intercede, and the order was rescinded.

But Lowe could not save himself. Sheraton's expansion budget was $495 million, and it looked as though it would all be spent. The franchising department alone was at times making two new deals a day. Even the inattentive at GMMs knew that Sheraton debt was skewing the consolidated balance sheet. And the quality of Sheraton service, never high, was going downhill fast. Sheraton profits of just over $6 million were on budget for the first half of 1970, but it was mostly fancy accounting: revaluation of inventories, changing depreciation schedules, "all the standard things," says one expert, "that a hotel company in trouble does to show some earnings." Lowe recast his second-half projection to zero—which was optimistic. A new direction was essential, and Lowe was plainly not the one to chart it.

Geneen had long been urged to find a hotel man, and by spring 1970 he agreed. In May, Howard P. James, head of the Sahara hotels and casinos in Nevada, was offered the presidency of Sheraton. Bud James had worked in hotels since the age of eleven, had been to the hotel school at Cornell, had directed food and beverage operations for Hilton, worked for the Del Webb chain and, at age forty-seven, had been with Sahara for nine years. He took over in June. Lowe stayed as vice chairman to the end of the year. And, though he returned to 320 Park, he left soon afterward, having concluded that he did not want to join what he calls "the night shift" of executives waiting for Geneen's call.

There is dispute as to how much Bud James should be credited with Sheraton's recovery. "Bud claims to have invented 'get out of real estate,' " says controller Herb Knortz, "but Hilton was doing it before we were, and so were other chains; it's just the sensible way to operate a hotel business." However, that fact is a good deal plainer now than it was then. And Phil Lowe, who has no reason to praise his successor says, "James stopped the silliness of building big hotels we couldn't run." One of Geneen's aides who at the time warned him against all that real estate says, "Geneen's success with Sheraton solely depended on Bud James's persuading him that he was totally wrong."

The first thing James got rid of was the meddlesome attentions of New York staff. His first day on the job was spent in the monthly operations review meeting, which had to be held at a hotel in outlying Quincy because there was not enough room at headquarters for group executive Howard Miller and thirty-eight staffers from New York, plus forty-eight Sheraton division heads. "Once a month," says James, "they flew in here, even from Europe and Hawaii, to listen to this crap from eight in the morning to eight at night." New York staff surveys showed there was too much china and silver at the Palace in San Francisco; portion control of ketchup was out of hand at the Peabody in Memphis. "I called Geneen that night," says James, "and he said, Well, how did you like your meeting? I said, If there's ever again anything like that, you can keep your job." He did not mind GMMs with Geneen, or even operating reviews for himself, his immediate staff, an ITT treasurer, controller, and personnel director; but no more flying in hotel managers to huddle with a gaggle of staffers who could tell them nothing about running hotels. "And as a matter of fact," he added, "you can keep Howard Miller, too." Geneen said, "As of now, you report direct to Tim Dunleavy." At James's further request, Geneen also did away with the Sheraton PLM.

Then James started a major divestment of properties. Sheraton's assets ran between $700 and $800 million, with huge depreciation costs, making a decent return impossible. Accounting rules said that any hotel of which ITT owned less than 50% could come off the books, and James was determined to dispose of as many as possible. Geneen's only stipulation was that James not take any sizable capital write-offs. That was tolerable because the old run-down clunkers, those least salable, were already almost vanishingly depreciated. Indeed, the dilapidation of many hotels was one reason the chain was in trouble. From 1970 until 1980 Sheraton sold some 89 properties, and today they own fewer than 30 of the more than 400 units they operate. Naturally, they have a marvelous return on assets. It was no overnight turnaround; Sheraton lost money for the next three and a half years and did not become really profitable until 1978. But ITT no longer had to pump money in after 1973. And today, Sheraton is a money machine.

All through the transition, Geneen's vision died hard. He could not resist a good hotel. While he backed James totally, a few days at the Greenbriar—for his annual physical—and he wanted Sheraton to buy it. James would invoke The Strategy, and Geneen would yield. Then next month he would want James to buy the Gotham in New York; he had a scheme to tunnel under Fifth Avenue at Fifty-fifth Street, joining the Gotham with Sheraton's St. Regis—a plan James countered by demonstrating how much it would cost to divert the subway. But even if Geneen's visions were sometimes a trial, James says that Geneen's early strategy of taking Sheraton worldwide set the scene for today's triumph. "Whether it was a stroke of genius or he was just mad at not getting Holiday Inns, it was a smart thing and it's built a great company."

Geneen's next acquisition was even bigger, On April 26, 1968, he paid about $301.8 million in common and preferred stock for Rayonier, Inc, maker of chemical cellulose. One Rayonier project under ITT—building a pulp mill in Port Cartier, Quebec—"ranks high among corporate disasters," as one reporter put it. We shall see why in turn. But as the same article noted, the company was otherwise doing very well. Actually, Rayonier is a huge success in ITT—unaffected by Port Cartier, because that project was so massive it never was on Rayonier's books.

Next, on June 27, ITT announced acquisition of Pennsylvania Glass Sand Corporation for $113.8 million. With Rayonier, it formed ITT's new natural resources group and was a gem of a company, strongly positioned in the narrow and essential field of mining silicas for industry. It was so strong, Geneen had to pay about 22½ times earnings—some 18% after taxes, not easily increased even by Geneen.

The last big 1968 acquisition was Continental Baking Company, proprietor of (among much else) Wonder Bread and Twinkies. The merger was announced in May and consummated on September 13 for $275.7 million. Geneen was enthralled by the complexities of a high-volume, quasi-commodity business selling consumer goods. "And I was always amazed at his grasp of *our* business," says James Pomroy, a Continental marketing VP in the early days of the acquisition. Geneen would spend hours in the GMMs discussing the motivation of bread deliverymen and what a woman walking a supermarket aisle *really* wanted. But the company disappointed Geneen because, for all its volume (about $1 billion a year, even then), it never yielded a real profit.

Actually, volume *was* the problem. Continental needed huge sales to support its national investment in bakeries. That meant selling packaged, sliced white bread, a commodity item. Price had to be kept low to meet local competition, and it barely covered the overhead of national distribution and all those bakeries. So while the Hostess cake division made money, the much larger bread division was lucky to break even. In 1945, earnings had been as large as those in the early 1970s on much less volume.

Nineteen sixty-eight also saw lesser acquisitions, including some small but well-known companies, such as Speedwriting, Inc. ($7.9 million) and Transportation Displays, Inc. (TDI) for $3.9 million; the smallest was Bramwell Business College, bought for $40,000. In all, there were twenty acquisitions in 1968, costing over one billion dollars. "In those years," says Tim Dunleavy, meaning from 1967 until the events of 1973, "Geneen was the most objective person in the world, and we were building a company beyond anything ever conceived. We called them the glory years."

It was the only multinational conglomerate where central management truly functioned multinationally. The impulse was Geneen's. When détente with the Soviets was in the air, Geneen would say, "Let's do something about that," and suddenly ITT was signing contracts with Russia and was a presence at Eastern European trade shows. (One deal was to market Russian watches, and when one was taken apart for examination, Geneen's capitalist heart warmed to find the elegant cases Italian and the communist technology crude, one transistor connected directly to the power supply.) Geneen would read about night infiltrations in Vietnam and would say, "We're an electronics company; we ought to be able to develop a night viewer that catches those infiltrators." And a new, very profitable product line was born for ITT.

He cherished the concept of his units complementing each other. Could Drager in Germany use multiplex equipment made by England's STC and Belgium's BTM? And while wiring a building for telephone lines, could they add a few more and install sensing equipment for fire alarms? "I've never seen anyone, and never expect to," says one former PLM, "who could integrate these combinations the way he could." Even where they did not work, it was never for want of imagination. Rayonier needed lumber; Continental needed cocoa; ITT telecom needed copper. That suggested Africa. There were known copper deposits in Mozambique. A railroad in Angola to a seaport on the Atlantic was fueled by wood, which meant large plantations along the right of way. And ITT's Portuguese operations gave them entrée. Dieselize the railroad: that frees trees for shipping to Rayonier, making ITT such an economic force it could develop the copper and cocoa. Geneen dispatched his natural resources VP, J. Ronald Goode, to look things over. "Just one factor we hadn't put in the equation," says Goode, "the terrorists. I came back and said, Hey! We don't want to invest in Angola."

That was all right; Geneen had plenty more ideas. While discussing ITT's telecom manufacturing in Brazil, he had a flash: Brazil imported cement from as far away as Rumania—"and," says Ron Goode, "you can't move cement economically across the room." The problem was lack of identified limestone deposits; but Geneen now had the geologists of Pennsylvania Glass Sand. Limestone was located, and so was a joint-venture partner for know-how—first Kaiser Cement, which backed out, then Holderbank in Switzerland, world's second largest cement company—and a million-ton cement plant went up in Brazil.

This was true multinationalism, true conglomeration. It was not just the big deals and the glamour units that Geneen pushed overseas. Even Reznor, maker of entirely unsophisticated unit heaters, ended up doing an annual $1.4 million business in Europe during the glory years. Once, when some ITT telephone equipment was sitting uncovered on a dock in Africa, and Geneen could do nothing about it since it was a government-to-government deal, he said that maybe ITT should buy a small country and get a seat at the UN. "I was never sure," says someone at the meeting, "whether or not he was kidding."

During the glory years, what Geneen held became more than a chairmanship; it was an imperium. He bestrode a world industrial empire, and those he overawed were themselves people of considerable parts. "They were heavy, heavy hitters," says a former line executive. "I mean big guns, high-priced, bright, *bright* businessmen"—the people, in fact, now running ITT. And others: Charles T. Ireland, Jr., who came to ITT from the presidency of Allegheny Corporation and would leave to become president of CBS before his untimely death; Maurie Valente, who became, briefly, president of RCA; and Felix Rohatyn, widely credited with saving New York City from bankruptcy. They all deferred to Geneen. It was like class among race horses; on their own or in different company these men were front-runners, but not on Geneen's track.

There was a meeting in 1968 to discuss a $125 million convertible bond issue. Outside Geneen's office were Rich Bennett, Hart Perry, Herb Knortz, Lyman Hamilton, and Robert Ohmes, the staff man who had worked up the figures; also in the group were Felix Rohatyn, ITT director and partner of Lazard Frères, and Alvin E. Friedman, soon to be an ITT director, and then a partner in Kuhn Loeb. They were waiting until Geneen was ready to see them. "The doors open," says Ohmes, "and one of them says, We need a PR man to lead us in. Another says, Yeah, and a personnel man on the way out. They were all trying to be last in—these big, top, multi-six-figure executives —doing it in a joking way, but not *really* joking." They filed in and found seats. "We're all sitting absolutely straight," says Ohmes, "back rigid, feet on the floor, hands on the chair, no cigarettes. Mr. Geneen is on the couch with my material in front of him. He turns to Hart Perry and says, Jesus Christ! What the fuck is this shit?

"And it's *my* shit!

"Hart turns to me and says, Bob, will you please explain it to him? The issue is impact on earnings per share, and I'm showing five point three cents dilution while Geneen makes it eight cents. He says, Wait a minute, and rattles off his figures—boom, boom, ba-boom, the way he talks, like a submachine gun—and it all makes sense and everybody is nodding, figuring Ohmes is the sacrificial lamb and we're going to stone him. And Geneen says, What's the problem here, Ohmes?

"Mr. Geneen, I said, the bonds are going to be used to retire convertible preferred stock. So what we're trading is after-tax interest on one for the dividend on the other. If you do that adjustment, it's the difference between the eight cents and the five, three. Half the interest is covered by tax.

"Geneen said, Jesus Christ, that's right! And with that—ahhhh! Legs crossed, cigarettes lit, everybody relaxed, and for the next hour we just chit-chatted. The meeting broke, and I was almost carried out on their shoulders. They said, Boy! you answered the first question. The *first* question! If you hadn't gotten that, he would have been on a witch hunt."

Why such dominance? One answer was the moral force of his plainly superior dedication. Once, in Brussels, a meeting showed no sign of ending although it was already 2:00 A.M. The lights suddenly flickered. "You see, Hal," said Rich Bennett, "even the lights are getting tired."

"Only the lesser lights," said Geneen.

The other answers had to do with the rewards Geneen offered and the atmosphere he constructed. Of course, there was the money. "He's got them by their limousines," said one former executive. But that missed the point of ITT salaries; it was not just luxuries. "ITT pays people substantially more than *they* think they're worth," says the former head of one unit. It was surely more than they could get elsewhere. It meant the kids' private school, the summer trips, the wife's fur coat. A whole new style of family life was at stake. "We're overpaid by twenty percent on purpose," said one staffer, "to keep us so frightened we work like rats on a treadmill."

But Geneen wanted money to be carrot as well as stick; he felt his people deserved tremendous financial rewards. He established a stock option plan for them whose terms were so favorable that he declined to participate himself to avoid any appearance of self-interest. When ITT's stock plummeted during the scandals of 1973, never to recover, many ITT executives were strapped for interest on their options, and Geneen's disappointment for them was palpable.

As for himself, he liked money a lot. "He was very greedy," says a former close associate, now a detractor. In the glory years Geneen was by far the highest paid executive in the United States. By 1971 his salary and bonus totaled $812,494. "I remember," says a former staff man, "there was a lot of criticism when his salary went over seven hundred thousand. But once, at a GMM, some subsidiary asked for help in getting a large contract. Did Geneen have any contacts at the customer's? He left the room and came back ten minutes later to say, I just got you the contract. I remember thinking at the time, Jeez! That man made his whole seven hundred thousand right now, today, and I saw him do it!"

Geneen had no doubts as to his worth. Asked about rumors that he wanted to be paid a million dollars a year, he said, "Wrong. I've set my eye on a *much* higher figure." And why not? No one was exercised when ITT paid an entrepreneur $50 million for a company that had taken maybe fifteen years to build. In fact, something like that had happened to Geneen.

Leonard S. Schmitz, a lawyer in Chicago, knew Geneen from the Bell & Howell days. His firm represented K. K. Knickerbocker, principal owner of Acme Visible Records, Inc., sleepy but sound, which made filing systems for business and was located in Crozet, Virginia. In 1960 Knickerbocker was thinking of selling. Schmitz told Geneen, who dispatched Dave Margolis to check out the company. Acme had $6,748,487 in assets (including a 53.4-foot yacht, the Sunny-K III). Sales for four months, ending January 30, 1960, were about $2.74 million, with an after-tax net of $248,410. Geneen formed a private group to buy the company. The price was $5,375,000 in cash, plus $1,676,660.67 in 6% notes (originally $1.6 million; the buyers paid a penalty of $25,000 a month, prorated, because the closing took place June 2, 1960, instead of March 1, as planned). In addition, the owners got 71,750 shares of stock in the new Acme.

It was a tremendous deal for Geneen. He was backed by Bessemer Securities Corporation, led by John M. Kingsley and Thomas W. Keeser, Jr., who became Geneen's close friend, executor of his estate, and an ITT director. William Elfers, partner in the Boston investment house of Greylock, also participated, grew close to Geneen, and became an ITT director. The $5,-375,000 purchase cash came from various sources. Three insurance companies put up $3 million among them. They got 6½% senior notes plus warrants for 70,000 shares of Acme. Bessemer paid $2,100,000 for $1 million in 6½% senior subordinated notes and a warrant for 141,916 shares common, 11,000 preferred. Carphi Securities (Elfers and his wife) paid $100,000 for notes and a 14,192-share warrant. Geneen and Schmitz each put up $87,500, and each got that many shares of Acme common.

Schmitz gave up his law practice to become Acme's new CEO. Geneen became a director. He once said that he had made more money from Acme than he ever did from ITT, "with one-tenth of 1% of my time."

By the end of the first full year of new management, sales were up from just over $6 million to $8.6 million, with profits around $465,000. The familiar plan was to double both every five years through internal growth and acquisitions. The plan took off in 1963, with Acme going public, the stock issued at 16. "Everyone was supposed to be looking out for acquisitions," says John B. Hinch, then national sales manager and later (post-Geneen) president. "It was a way of continually growing," says George W. Horn, Acme's controller and later financial VP. It worked; the acquisitions came in, and the five-year plan was on schedule. Sales in 1966 were $19 million, with $1.73 million net. And Acme was growing. Furthermore, management was hyping the company, wooing stock analysts and financial writers.

There was one annual board meeting in Crozet; the others were held on Park Avenue at the Bessemer office. Anyone who had ever attended a GMM would have felt right at home at an Acme meeting. "Geneen would ask you what your plans were," says George Horn, "how to do this, how to overcome that, if there was any down-trend. You didn't have to agree with him, but you had to do your homework. If he caught you without all the detail, he'd kill you. A general statement never got by Mr. Geneen." Once, the subject was a price hike. Geneen asked the national sales manager what he thought, and John Hinch said he did not think they could raise prices.

"Why do you say that?"

"I think we're getting all the market will bear."

Geneen exploded. "Goddamnit! How do I know that? Prove to me you can't raise prices. How do I know you shouldn't *reduce* prices, for Christ's sake! Quit giving me that fucking *sales* bullshit!"

Hinch knew it was not personal. Another time, after Geneen had raked him about sales expense levels, Hinch was in the bathroom at a urinal. Geneen came in, stood shoulder to shoulder, and, slapping Hinch on the back, said, "Remember, we're looking for that seventeen percent sales increase again this year—we've got you labeled 'Seventeen Percent' Hinch!" Both Hinch and Horn liked Geneen and admired him enormously.

By 1969 the company was ripe for sale. Acme had reached its limit of growth, absent an important infusion of new capital. Moreover, accounting rules were about to change, and good will would soon have to be amortized, making acquisition more attractive now than later. It was time to cash in. The buyer was American Brands, Inc. Acme's stock had hit $60, split 3-for-2, and was bought at $47.50 a share, a little over market. The total sales price was $51.8 million.

By now Geneen had 88,662 shares, worth $4,211,445. Even so, his per-

Geneen and his mother, Aida, at her Cape Cod cottage in 1967.

sonal finances were tangled. He was thought to be paying some million dollars a year on stock option interest. In the late 1960s he reimbursed ITT for the services of an internal-audits accountant, Raymond H. Alleman, to audit his own positions. The assignment lasted on and off for a couple of years.

One knot in Geneen's finances was a farm. June hated the city and was not wild about Cape Cod or Key Biscayne, but she loved her native New Hampshire. Around 1967 Geneen bought a working farm near Littleton. The cows needed pasturage, and the land he bought for that included forest, so soon Geneen was in the dairy business and the lumber business, with his own saw mill. June's brother, Billy Hjelm, ran the place, and she spent as much time as possible there.

Geneen still preferred the Cape. In 1960 he had bought a grand house in Oyster Harbors, but he rented it out, staying in Centreville at the cottage he had bought in 1952 for his mother. Out back was a shack fixed up as an office. His mother called it "Harold's sulking house." (Aida Geneen continued as the great outside force in her son's life. "Whenever his mother was at one of the ITT social functions," says a former staff man, "she was number one; she obviously took precedence over June." Aida died on February 14, 1971. Six months after her death, Geneen still choked up when he mentioned her, and a doctor who had treated her well, thereafter found his pet research project the recipient of devoted ITT technical support.)

Geneen favored the Cape as a place of escape. However, he never went there just to rest; his suitcases of reports were always with him. Even away from them he had neither taste nor talent for pure relaxation. He had to keep busy. ITT's PR department spoke of hobbies—his music, woodworking, photography, collecting show tunes and jazz; and there was a succession of boats, all named *Genie*—for Aladdin's friend who could produce such delights, and because "it's a bit close to my own name." *Genie IV* was a forty-eight-foot sport fisherman and cost some $100,000. But Geneen did not have hobbies; he had intermittent obsessions. Once he stopped by Dick Boonisar's house, and Barbara Boonisar mentioned lobstering. Geneen whisked a lobstering license from his wallet and soon the two of them were deep in discussion of that and such other New England arcana as clamming. Boonisar was only faintly surprised to find that Geneen had made himself as much an adept of these mysteries as his own wife, a descendent of Maine's first settlers.

Geneen hurled himself into anything he did. He would become so intent on even desultory conversation that driving with him was a foot-pressed-to-the-floorboard trial. The son of an old friend noticed that when Geneen got wound up talking, he steered *Genie IV* the same way. Once, at a restaurant, a dinner guest of the Geneens', finding his swordfish tainted, stopped eating after a single bite. June noticed that Geneen, gabbing away, was half-through his own portion. She reached over, took a bite, and made him stop eating.

He might have kept on even without the conversation; food meant little. In Brussels, city of fine restaurants, he preferred to have dinner sent in so work could continue. One Sunday he told a group that since they would be working late, he had ordered dinner for all: minestrone, minute steaks, and ice cream. Frank McCabe said, "How about some wine?" "Wine?" Geneen said, "you want *wine?*" McCabe wanted wine. "Oh shit," Geneen said to a flunky, "get him some wine." His own taste ran to calf's liver and steak, both well-done. Hamburgers were the nearest thing to a dining passion with him, and where others might discuss some marvelous little French or Italian find in New York, Geneen would weigh White Castle against Phoebe's Whamburger on Lexington.

Notwithstanding the monomania, preoccupation, and imperial style, Geneen occasionally did display some human hankerings. "He wanted to be liked," says an admirer. "He wanted to be one of the boys." Every now and then he would tear loose. After a talk to security analysts in San Francisco, he corralled Hart Perry and Bob Savage for a drink at the Top of the Mark. "Then we went to the Red Garter," says Savage. "We were the only people there over thirty, and a kid wanted to buy us a beer. He was just back from Vietnam and was going to start a health farm in New England. Geneen said, I know all about health farms, and he talked to him for, like, forty-five minutes. Then we went to Earthquake Muldoon's—with Geneen's limousine following while we walked."

At Earthquake Muldoon's, Clancy Hayes was performing. He was an old banjo player renowned for his six-string instrument. Hayes had fallen on hard times, was partly crippled with a bad back. Geneen was delighted to meet him. (He later decided to make the old man a star, and he gave the assignment to Continental's marketing people. They were aghast. "I'm not a promoter," says Randall W. Hackett, then Continental's marketing director. "I know how to position advertised products. People are another matter. And by the way, who the hell is Clancy Hayes?" Nevertheless, Hackett had to act; otherwise he could expect an endless procession of queries: What have you done for Clancy Hayes? The only plan he had was for a self-liquidating record offer on Wonder Bread wrappers. "So," says Hackett, "we were trying to come up with a record. Then one day I was in a meeting, and someone came in and said, Well, I hate to put it this way, but I've got some good news: Clancy Hayes just died.")

The night was not yet over. "Next," says Bob Savage, "we went to a place with a girl in a trapeze, bare-assed, swinging back and forth, and we wound up at this chili parlor. Mr. Geneen was lecturing this waitress on the importance of love: Love is what it's all about, the only really important thing in life." Did he convince her? "I don't know," says Savage. "He convinced me."

Maybe love meant more to Geneen than it appeared to. Christmas was especially difficult for him. He had vowed never to repeat the lonely holidays of Suffield, but a sense of holiday isolation was implicit in his life. There was a regular ITT executive Christmas party at the Waldorf, and Tim Dunleavy remembers one in particular. Geneen kept urging everyone to stay—in vain, because it was Christmas Eve. "I had to run home," says Dunleavy. "We had kids, and I wanted to help my wife get everything ready. He kept saying, Aw come on, hang around. But I said no." When everyone had left, Geneen collected June in his limousine, and they were driven around New York in the dusk, looking at the Christmas lights.

On the job, the imperial style was absolute. An ad agency had prepared a corporate campaign for ITT. For Geneen's inspection, they were required to have everything done up, full size, type set and color photography. But maybe he would have time to see it only en route somewhere in the company plane; so they had to prepare another complete set, portfolio size. And a third complete set, notebook size, in case Geneen had time to look at the campaign only in his limo. In fact, he never looked at it at all, and the campaign never ran. The total cost was over $25,000.

Geneen still wanted ITT to be better known, and near the start of the glory years he had a movie made, a forty-eight-minute hymn to ITT. When producer Charles F. Skinner first met with Geneen, there was the normal outrageous wait. It was supposed to be a dinner meeting, and very close to midnight Skinner's director, a diabetic, was staving off hypoglycemia with candy bars. Finally it was time. Dinner would be in ITT's Waldorf suite. Outside, it was pouring rain. Geneen and his entourage went with the two movie men down to the ITT garage. Geneen indicated that only Skinner was to be in his, the lead, limousine. The others piled into the string of other limos standing at the ready. The caravan left ITT, crossed Park Avenue, and pulled up to the porte-cochere of the Waldorf Towers, right across the street. Not a raindrop fell on any head.

Geneen carefully extended elements of the imperial style to his people during the glory years. Everyone had a grade number at ITT, the "officer ranks" starting at 19, with those at 21 and above eligible for bonuses. A fleet of limousines and drivers was always standing by. From grade 25 on you were not *supposed* to take a taxi to any airport; you went by limousine. That applied to any one of any grade going to Wall Street. "Geneen didn't want his people going downtown on the subway," says Bob Savage. In this sense, Geneen did have them by their limousines. A former staff man still remembers the neighborhood hubbub whenever he came home in an ITT limo.

That sort of thing meant a lot to those at ITT. "They were not very *classy* people," the wife of one executive used to say. Most had distinctly lower-middle-class backgrounds; they had not gone to prestigious schools or worked previously in the loftier companies. They were fighters who had clawed their way up, and Geneen wowed them. "He gave me," says Ed Roth, "my first glimpse of the champagne style."

Boca Raton was distinctly champagne style. Officially called the World-wide Management Conference, the first was held in 1963, with later ones in 1966, 1969, 1973, 1976, and 1979. It was a two week, all-expenses-paid saturnalia, with just enough "business" to placate the IRS. ITT executives and staff and their spouses were brought to the Florida resort from around the world.

Boca Raton was perfect. It may be America's premier citadel of expensive bad taste, sure to dazzle ITT's "not classy" people. And Geneen did it in splendid style. Six seagoing fishing boats waited at the dock. Women discovered that the beauty shop was free. Make a date for golf and you received an envelope containing a five-dollar bill for the caddie's tip. There was lavish entertainment nearly every night.

Nineteen seventy-three was typical: 495 male and 33 female employees were invited, and 434 of the men brought their wives. First arrivals were on May 13, a Sunday, and departure was Saturday, May 26. If, by chance, you were not met at the airport, Avis gave you a car. Jitneys ran to the beach club, where all cabanas had been reserved for ITT and drinks (with tip) were charged to your room—for which, of course, ITT paid. Although some guests had been at a truncated GMM in New York, from the time they joined the others the business schedule was not exhausting. That morning, Wednesday, the fifteenth, and the next, meetings started at 9:30 A.M.; but for once they ended on time—at 12:30—when buffet lunches were served in the Cathedral Dining Room and at the beach club. Both afternoons were free, with a "reception and Steak Roast" on Wednesday night and just plain dinner on Thursday. Friday morning's meeting was a welcome from Geneen and Dunleavy, then a "comprehensive audio-visual presentation of ITT's activities and capabilities," which also ended at 12:30 for the dual buffet. Friday afternoon all rested up for "Las Vegas Night" in Camino Hall, following cocktails in the Cloister Gardens and Loggia and a buffet in the Great Hall. They played for scrip, tradable for prizes. Saturday night everyone dressed for dinner with "entertainment by Mel Torme." Monday the pace picked up. Mornings, the twenty-first through twenty-third, came "the Conference" proper: talks by fifteen heavyweights from academia and politics, including games theorist Herman Kahn, the State Department's Thomas C. Mann, Duke University president Terry Sanford (formerly North Carolina governor, and future ITT director), pollsters Richard Scammon and Daniel Yankelovich, and Roy Wilkins, executive director of the NAACP. Another speaker was Lee Loevinger, a friendly FCC member in the ABC hearings. Most spoke for fifteen or twenty minutes, although Princeton physicist Marvin L. Goldberger and Harvard economist Jesse W. Markham each got by with ten.

Afternoons were free, nights filled. There was "Big Band Night" (the Glenn Miller Orchestra, with Buddy de Franco and Helen O'Connell), "Concert Night" (Beverly Sills, plus Skitch Henderson and company), "Carnival Night" ("games of skill for prizes") and just plain dinner Thursday, to the music of Lionel Hampton). Thursday morning, May 24, mementos were available in the Cloister Loggia—exquisite enamel and gold baskets from Tiffany's. Although no further activities were scheduled, no one had to clear out until after the final buffet at the beach club on Saturday.

Boca Raton was one of Geneen's master strokes. "When some guy would get an offer from another company," says Ed Roth, who now stages a mini-Boca (a long weekend at Greenbriar) for his own executives, "his wife would say, Are you counting that free two-week vacation we get at ITT?" One ex-staffer says, "My wife wanted me to work only for ITT." Another says, "I better be careful what I say about Geneen. My wife thinks he's the greatest." Wives adored him. He was unfailingly charming to them—as he was on social occasions even to those husbands who, a few hours earlier, he had been flaying. "At a party he'd ask what you wanted to drink," says someone who often absorbed abuse, "then he'd run—and I mean *run*—to get it."

The glory years acquisitions continued strongly into 1969. Thorp Finance was bought for $46.5 million on January 3. Some had bigger names than price tags. Marquis's *Who's Who* ($7.5 million) was added to Sams on March 28, and Decca Systems ($7 million) was bought on March 31. On April 25 came announcement of another big one, Canteen Corporation, leader in vending machines, price $245 million. The next one of note happened October 30— Southern Wood Preserving for $12.7 million. But meanwhile there was a lot of activity. Much of 1969 was a prolonged tussle with the Justice Department over Canteen, as well as the projected mergers with Grinnell Corporation, world's largest maker of fire protection sprinkler systems, and Hartford Fire Insurance Company.

Geneen had been after Grinnell for a while. Although, as Grinnell's president later said, "the company wasn't for sale," Geneen's offer in November 1968 was too good to resist: $171.65 a share for stock selling at $118, total price $251.3 million. Before the deal could close, Justice intervened. In April 1969, three days after the Canteen merger, Justice filed to enjoin consolidation pending an antitrust hearing. On August 1 Justice filed for preliminary injunctions forbidding the Grinnell and Hartford mergers. Geneen wanted no more ABC-style cliffhangers, and in September he announced that if the injunctions were granted he would call off the deals.

That was not necessary. On October 21, 1969, Chief Federal Judge William H. Timbers refused the injunctions, subject only to a hold-separate order, which meant that all three companies would continue to be run as discrete entities, easily unmerged if the government's antitrust suits prevailed. Grinnell came into the ITT fold ten days later.

Hartford was still elusive, and that was the big one. Considering Geneen's unremitting efforts to get the company and his tenacity in keeping it, Hartford Fire Insurance looked to some like his "Rosebud," a palpable connection to childhood's view from the Travelers Tower. But there is a less tortured explanation. ITT's growth needed it. The 1969 0–1s showed that, without some new boost, company growth would tail off from its habitual 10% plus to something around 6%. When Felix Rohatyn suggested Hartford, it looked like just the thing. "What intrigued Geneen," says Bud Morrow, "was that it would be the ultimate money tree. He could take a seventy-five-million-dollar loss and not even think about it. I heard him say that—seventy-five was the number he used. This would give him the final flexibility, the linchpin to go for what he wanted—becoming the number-one-sized corporation in the world."

Hartford was the sixth largest property and casualty insurer in the country, with assets just over $1.8 billion. The unrealized capital gain of its stock portfolio had increased annually an average of $28.2 million for the past ten years, a $300 million increase. It was a company in trouble. Nineteen sixty-eight had been a bad year for all insurance companies, and Hartford's stock stood in the low 30s, ludicrously undervalued, begging for a takeover. Carl A. Gerstacker, president of Dow Chemical and a Hartford director, made an offer. "Dow," says David C. E. Carson, then Hartford's head of underwriting, "tried to steal the company." Negotiations began in September 1968 and ended on October 22. Harry V. Williams, chairman and president, soon announced that Hartford's stock would be listed on the New York Exchange instead of being sold over the counter, and that the authorized number of shares would be increased, better enabling Hartford to acquire other companies.

That was whistling in the graveyard, for the outside directors wanted to replace Williams. He had grown up with Hartford and was a strong operating man, but the company now needed a financier. Also, Williams was distracted by a son's illness; and one director, Barney Flaxman, of Shields, Rowe & Model, had long been sniping at Williams, wanting to be CEO himself. The board's choice was Robert Baldwin of Morgan, Stanley. But on November 1, 1968, before anything could happen, André Meyer told Hartford that his client, ITT, was going to buy 1,282,948 shares of Hartford stock from a San Francisco mutual fund. That was just under 6% of the total. Next day, Meyer, Felix Rohatyn, and Geneen met with some Hartford directors. "Geneen," says Dave Carson, "did a great job of selling himself and selling his company." If the Hartford board was not yet won, it was well wooed, panic allayed. On November 12 the two companies proclaimed "accord" over the stock purchase. Later, ITT would buy another 500,000 shares. In late December, Geneen sent his general counsel, Howard Aibel, with an acquisition offer that would work out to $1.5 billion. The board seemed receptive, but if they wavered Geneen was determined to exert, in his phrase, "inexorable pressure."

On February 28, 1969, terms for merger were announced, and they were approved by both boards on March 11. By April 10 the merger seemed all set. Still, there was delay. On January 20, 1969, the Nixon administration had come in and with it a new assistant attorney general for antitrust, Richard W. McLaren. And while Nixon was probusiness and McLaren a prominent Chicago lawyer whose career had been built on defending clients against antitrust actions, McClaren filed against the Canteen merger in April. Perhaps it was a case of the defense lawyer who, knowing his clients, turns hanging judge; perhaps it was just that McLaren, counsel to the old-line and blue-chip, felt that these upstart conglomerates should be stopped.

The Hartford board asked for a delay, and Geneen's inexorable pressure continued. A group of Texas stockholders, led by bank president George O. Nokes, Jr., threatened suit if the merger were further delayed. The group had been advised to buy Hartford stock by Frank C. Oltorf, close friend of ITT director George Brown. The *Hartford Courant* called them "the Waco 10" when Nokes pleaded guilty to making illegal loans in connection with the stock.

After McLaren filed against Grinnell and Hartford in August and Judge Timbers turned down the injunction requests in October, things were back on track. On November 10, 1969, Hartford stockholders approved the merger. The only step remaining was a hearing in early December by the Connecticut insurance commissioner, and ITT was sure that was pro forma. Instead, says one observer, they "ran into a buzz saw." On December 13 William C. Cotter, the commissioner, disapproved the merger, criticizing among other things the employment contracts and stock options for inside directors and officers that Geneen had used to sweeten the deal.

Hartford CEO Harry Williams immediately called Geneen and suggested that ITT make a tender offer, direct to stockholders, which could force the commissioner's hand. Geneen agreed, and so did the Hartford board. The merger would save Williams's position as chairman. Also, as Dave Carson says, "the Hartford board was bailed out. They sold the stock for double its price the year before. The merger took them off the hook."

Meanwhile, Geneen wanted to know what was going on. The other insurance companies in town hated the merger—who was next?—and Ned Gerrity still bemoans the dirty pool he feels they played. Someone must have gotten to Cotter. "ITT unleashed all these people," says Carson, "trying to find out whose pay he was in. Who's behind this? Of course, nobody uncovered anything. I really don't think there was anything to uncover." Cotter was a faithful product of John M. Bailey's political machine, Bailey having attained prominence as John Kennedy's Democratic National Chairman. Cotter's reward was the insurance commissionership, and he would soon successfully run for Congress. Brought up in Hartford, the city's loyal, provincial son, he saw ITT as a bunch of New York slickers. "Who knows what they'll do?" Carson imagines him thinking. "They may take all the jobs away and move the company to Oshkosh." Cotter would keep Hartford for the Hartfordites —his friends, John Bailey's voters.

To counter such fears, Geneen promised great things for the city—a new, $12 million, 400-room Sheraton, and maybe another for a proposed civic center. And there was direct pressure on Cotter. A later SEC investigation highlighted ITT's "promise him anything" attitude. An ITT VP, Howard T. Cohn, would be liaison with Hartford. Five days before ITT made a formal request for rehearing, Ted Cohn wrote Geneen a memo showing, as an SEC investigator put it, that ITT was "more concerned with" telling Cotter what he "would like to hear than it is in giving a truthful response to the inquiry." Did Cotter object to the employment contracts? the stock options? Poof! they were gone—to be "reconsidered" once the merger went through.

At the same time, Cotter was besieged by everyone ITT could enlist to change his mind. Howard Aibel hired Joseph E. Fazzano, graduate of Yale

Law, a noted Hartford trial lawyer. The firms already on the case were not told they had co-counsel, and when the local outfit found out, they resigned. That was Day, Berry & Howard; the other firm was Covington & Burling. As a Connecticut assistant attorney general remarked about ITT, "They had the big one in Hartford and the big one in the United States. Why the hell did they need Joe Fazzano?" Fazzano later told Watergate investigators that he acted more as a lobbyist than an attorney. He and Cotter had been friends for five or six years, "but not a close friend," Cotter maintained. "Not an intimate." There were, he said, maybe a hundred and fifty lawyers in Hartford who would have had more sway, and he always denied that Fazzano had influenced him. He claimed that they talked about the merger only four or five times. But in that case Fazzano was wildly overpaid. He got $30,000 and said he earned it, talking with Cotter incessantly; indeed, he claimed he sold Cotter on the merger. Certainly he became ITT's conduit to Cotter. The second hearing was March 10–12, 1970. Cotter approved the merger on May 23.

What changed Cotter's mind? At the second hearing Geneen guaranteed that Hartford would stay in town and stay at least the same size for a minimum of ten years, with no assets (except part of the yearly net) going to ITT. Then there were the beneficences Geneen would heap on the city, the new Sheratons, maybe even moving another subsidiary's headquarters there. There was all that pressure, Fazzano and other locals after him to approve.

Next November, Cotter was elected to Congress. The tender offer was accepted by over 99% of Hartford shareholders. But the merger's problems had barely begun. McLaren's antitrust suit was pending, and in November 1970 the SEC began an investigation of some irregularities, with a reprise of the "inexorable pressure" theme. William J. Casey, then SEC chairman, later testified that he had gotten calls from White House aide John Ehrlichman and from Senator Edward Kennedy, who explained that he was calling on behalf of an old family friend, André Meyer of Lazard Frères. When asked what he thought about the contacts, Casey said they were "not proper."

But Geneen had what he wanted. One morning, he unaccountably arrived at a GMM early. He was talking with Colonel Silver and did not realize that the microphones were on. "It came over the mike," says someone who was there. "There might have been two or three guys in the room. I looked up because I heard his voice, and he said, Well! The Hartford acquisition is going to give us the opportunity to have *programmed* earnings! And the man was actually rubbing his hands!" There would be serious problems in the future with Hartford. Nonetheless, as another former executive puts it, "The Hartford portfolio was played like a violin."

So was Hartford's CEO, Harry Williams. "When we were courting Hartford," says Tim Dunleavy, "Harold was spending all kinds of time with Harry, and Harry thought that Harold Geneen was the finest friend he ever had." Williams naturally wanted to reciprocate Geneen's hospitality. Knowing his new pal liked hunting, he invited Geneen on grouse-hunting expeditions to North Dakota. But having to spend time on anything except business was a strain for Geneen. "Geneen said to me," Dunleavy recalls, "Goddamn that Williams, I've got better things to do than going grouse shooting." Nevertheless, he went; throughout the courtship and honeymoon he was always available. "They were getting along real well together," says Dunleavy, "and Gladys Williams felt the same about June." Then Hartford was safely in the fold, and the letdown came. "Mrs. Williams told a number of people that Harry was terribly hurt," says Dunleavy. "She said, Suddenly they dropped us like a hot potato." And the amazing thing is that Geneen genuinely liked Williams and enjoyed his company. "But not," says Dunleavy, "to the point of being a friend. He's a complex guy."

The glory years continued. While the Hartford merger was first coming to a head, in late November and early December of 1969, Geneen, some of his people, and Felix Rohatyn appeared before a House antitrust subcommittee, chaired by New York's Emanuel Celler. For Geneen it was a triumph. "The press," says Bud Morrow, "never picked up what a tour de force that was. The breadth of that man's mind in that testimony! It was the single most impressive performance I've ever seen by a businessman marshaling the facts of his enterprise."

Congressman Manny Celler was impressed too. "I want to compliment you, Mr. Geneen," he said, "on a very splendid statement, and if I want an advocate I am going to call on you. . . . Your statement . . . almost makes me believe that I.T.T. has wings." Even the essentially hostile subcommittee staff was impressed. Their report dismissed the other companies investigated: the meteoric growth of Leasco and Gulf & Western was a matter of hyped-up stock acquisitions; Litton was a holding company that "revels in decentralized and informal supervisory controls . . . know[ing] very little about the quality and content of day-to-day operations through the system"; National General's acquisition program was "flamboyant and opportunistic"; and as for Ling-Temco-Vought, "LTV is a paradigm of conglomerate growth and disaster." ITT was different. The company's "efficient modern management" was an example to all. Geneen was "[a]n individual with exceptional talents" and "without question a superior individual. . . . " The sternest staff criticism was that "[h]is exceptional drive and ambition . . . have produced an overly enthusiastic program for ITT's growth."

Besides Hartford, the only major merger consummated in 1970 was with O. M. Scott & Sons Company, the lawn people, for some $77 million. The real feat was continuing to do so well when so many other companies were not. "In a year like 1970," wrote a *Dun's* analyst, ". . . controls are the key . . . to profitability. A lot of companies thought they had controls, but this year anyway, they will not be able to prove it by their income statements. ITT will." They would the next three years, even as the country sank deeper into recession. In 1968, net was $180.2 million on just over $4 billion revenue; in 1973, net was $521.3 on $10.2 billion ($2.6 billion of which was from insurance and finance).

Perhaps the most interesting thing about the later part of the glory years was that they included 1972—with its revelations and scandal over the Hartford antitrust settlement, Dita Beard's memo, allegations of bribery and of meddling in Chile, and what most people regarded as a punishing Senate hearing. None of it bothered Geneen. "He enjoyed it all," says Tim Dunleavy. "He liked jousting with all of them."

The glory years also encompassed some notable and instructive defeats.

17
Nobody's Perfect

When the first shipment of ITT telephone subsets arrived at Gulf Telephone in Perry, Florida, they were, says Gulf's president, Ernest L. Cox, Jr., "a grave disappointment." Something was wrong with the transmitters. "The carbon they used was not the proper carbon." But ITT quickly made good. "Could have happened to anybody," says Cox. "Nobody's perfect."

In fact, Geneen's system posited imperfection; its whole purpose was error's early detection and timely remedy. But how about the few irreversible debacles? What do they tell us about the limitations of his system? Some inevitable defeats were a product of either structural weakness in the company or a peculiarity of the market Geneen wanted to crack. Continental Baking, says Randy Hackett, Continental's marketing director, "was going to be the next General Foods. Mr. Geneen had that vision. But it took a lot more than just willing it." They lacked the right distribution, organization, and marketing. "We were basically a manufacturing-sales company," says Hackett, "and no one wanted to pay for the R and D and massive advertising it takes to introduce new products."

With the light bulb fiasco, the problem was an impenetrable market. Geneen wanted a single, worldwide ITT product, and the lamp business fit the bill. In the mid-1960s Geneen bought Claude Paz, a European company, and the United States company Consolidated Electric Lamp, which made Champion light bulbs. Consolidated was a family business, run by the Marsh brothers in New England. It seemed a thriving outfit with a good market base that Geneen could expand. What he could not know was that Consolidated existed on sufferance, nourished by GE, Westinghouse, and Sylvania as proof that the lamp business was not, after all, the oligopoly everyone thought. The oligarchs, though, feared Geneen. When he took over, complaisance ended. For instance, the equipment used to make bulbs was very complex and was made exclusively by GE, Westinghouse, and Sylvania. While the Marshes had only to ask anytime they needed equipment, it was not for sale to Geneen. He even tried to get the Japanese to copy the equipment, but nothing worked right. At the same time, what had been a most benign climate of sales competition for the Marshes turned wintry overnight. In the 1970s Geneen was finally persuaded to sell—though it took heroic effort to make him admit he was licked.

These were relatively minor stumbles. The pratfalls came when Geneen entered any business that depended not on system but on the specific know-how and industry experience of people or that by its nature or market could not—or should not—expand.

The proper management of some businesses might be called "intuition-intensive." This is particularly true of those where marketing and consumer demand are vital. They do not need "managers" so much as they need operators who know the lore of *that* business, who have—along with experience—a love, a flair, a feel for it. They need operators who will know what to do if not enough customers are staying at Sheratons, renting from Avis, buying Levitt homes or eating Twinkies. A professional manager cannot do it, and no one at corporate headquarters will be able to help. A professional manager may not even know enough about the business to pick the right operator.

Bobbs-Merrill is a case in point. Bobbs was the trade book division of Howard Sams, the publishing house Geneen acquired in 1966. It had never been especially distinguished, partly because its home base was Indianapolis. An editorial office in New York notwithstanding, Bobbs was considered somewhat "out of town" by authors and their agents. Its long-time successes were *The Joy of Cooking*, Ayn Rand's *The Fountainhead*, and the Raggedy Ann books; its great hope at the time of acquisition was *Mary Mead's Magic Recipes for the Electric Blender*.

Most of Sams was made for ITT; Geneen's system worked beautifully for divisions like Michie, a law book publisher, and Marquis, publisher of *Who's Who*. "When Michie does the state code of Alabama," says Eugene Rachlis, former publisher of Bobbs, "if they print fifteen thousand copies, they have orders for fourteen thousand. If the print order for *Who's Who* is fifty thousand, forty-eight have already been sold." Obviously that was not true for Bobbs. "You get advance orders," says Rachlis, "and you say, Okay that looks pretty good, let's print ten thousand—and you sell only four. Or you sell out the first printing, and you go for the second, and boom! the thing stops dead."

Geneen's kind of planning was meaningless; you cannot plan next year's best seller. No surprises? Trade publishing breeds surprises. And the return is meager. "Trade," says Rachlis, "works on about the same margin as supermarkets." Geneen seemed to understand. At one planning meeting he said that a trade house was something the corporation wanted. Perhaps he liked the prestige of a few best sellers. But no one in ITT understood trade publishing enough to choose the right person either to manage or run Bobbs.

The man selected to superintend Sams was a plausible choice for most of it—the routine, noncreative part: Stanley S. Sills had spent three years with the American Book Company. He was hired as ITT's publishing PLM in 1968 and in 1971 became president of the ITT publishing group. About the same time, Gene Rachlis joined Bobbs as editor-in-chief, soon to become publisher. Rachlis was, as a *New York Times* writer put it, "a well-regarded editorial executive." He was known as a fine editor, a bright, pleasant, thoroughly decent man. But he had difficulty attracting authors to an "out of town" house.

Rachlis's low profile might not have mattered had everyone indulged Bobbs as a corporate pet, justified by its occasional publishing triumph. But to attract tomorrow's money-and-glory manuscripts, it was clear that Bobbs needed to take some big risks. Laboring under Geneen's pressure for profit performance, Sills decided that those risks were unacceptable. Once, Bobbs offered a $50,000 advance for the biography of musician Ray Charles and could have had it. But that was a big number for Bobbs. Sills reviewed the deal and it did not go through. The house that did publish earned back $40,000 of the advance before the book was off press. Anyone can miss a deal; all publishers have horror stories of rejected best sellers. But Sills's decision reflected the style of his stewardship. That focus on numbers was what crippled Bobbs. Sills would learn that religious books were hot one year and urge God on Rachlis. Worse, he saw that the numbers on first novels were traditionally awful; that, indeed, the numbers are uninspiring on fiction altogether. The conclusion was inescapable, given ITT dogma of pruning losers and low-profit items. And economies were especially vital just then, because trying to make some *real* money, Sills had involved Bobbs in producing a Raggedy Ann movie. To make up for the $4 million loss Sills decreed in 1978 that by 1980 Bobbs-Merrill would no longer publish fiction.

It was a decision, wrote *New York Times* cultural correspondent Herbert Mitgang, that "brought nods of recognition and long faces in the industry." It was, he explained, "one of the rare public examples of what many authors and editors have been saying in private for years: The countinghouse that stands above the publishing house really does call the shots." Sills also followed the Geneen dictum of cutting expense by firing people—including two, Rachlis charges, whom Sills personally disliked (though, in fairness, both were now-dispensable fiction editors). Sills explained—in what Mitgang called "a coyly worded statement"—that "[t]his is not a cutback or a hatchet job. This is an alteration of strategy onward and upward." Bobbs would still publish cookbooks and other nonfiction, and "[t]hose are the kinds of books the public wants." If Bobbs-Merrill was never great, it was certainly respectable. Under ITT it faded rapidly. Gene Rachlis left in 1979. Stanley Sills left a year later, saying it was because Geneen was leaving.

Whereas with Bobbs the numbers were comparatively trifling, Levitt (LSI) showed how much money entry into the wrong business could cost. LSI was both kinds of wrong business rolled into one: it required intuition-intensive management and was nonexpandable. Hart Perry warned Geneen. He had started in the home-building industry and knew something about it. Just after Felix Rohatyn suggested the merger, Perry wrote to Geneen, "I basically do not believe that this is a business ITT should get into. . . . " At first Geneen agreed; but as a former ITT executive says, "Felix was extremely persuasive." Rohatyn explained that LSI had a formula of building only to contract in large developments; with that formula, backed by ITT, LSI's growth might be limitless. Trouble was, the formula was outdated, the seeds of debacle already flowering.

By the late 1950s, market conditions that had made Bill Levitt's on-site production-line methods in large Levittowns a phenomenal success had changed. With eased housing shortages and growing affluence, the trend was away from tract living. At the same time, LSI invaded new parts of the country. Local builders who could not have competed on a Levittown scale were at an advantage, with lower overhead, building on their own turf. As the court-appointed trustee later wrote, "Even at the peak of its success with its public offering in 1960, LSI was beginning to show the strains of expansion. The prospectus for this offering revealed that LSI's earnings in the first half of the 1950s were significantly higher than they were in the second half."

What's more, expansion attenuated control. It is a byword in the industry that the three important things in home building are "location, location, and location." It takes entrepreneurial intuition. You must hunker down in a potato field with some farmer and deal, somehow divining which farmer, which field, and what deal—and then what sort of houses people in those parts want, how to design and build them, how to get people to come, look, and buy, how to finance. "You've got to learn to spin on a dime," says Bill Levitt. The bigger LSI got, the more often someone besides Levitt himself was there to do the spinning. And that was before ITT.

By August 1969 Levitt was, practically speaking, out of LSI. "It fell apart," says a partisan observer, "because William J. Levitt wasn't there." If so, it was not the way this observer means. With his instincts, Levitt eventually might have faced the trend, scrapped dreams of being home builder to the nation, and resumed life as an entrepreneur. His personal prestige could have been proof against Geneen's pressure for expansion and the temptation of Geneen's open-handed financing. Such was rare at ITT, but it did happen. Hale E. Andrews of Pennsylvania Glass Sand flatly refused both pressings and blandishments. Although Geneen saw that company as his entry into the world of metallurgy, Andrews said, "We can't do anything well but mine sand. Leave us alone and we'll give you earnings." At LSI, with Bill Levitt eclipsed, there was no one to say no.

Dick Wasserman was a go-getter. He was very much taken with Geneen, who in return saw Wasserman as a likely successor. Wasserman's rise at LSI, wrote a reporter, occurred because of his "superlative talent for people man-agement—he was the sort of man needed to govern the far-flung empire Levitt was creating." Yet Wasserman's was exactly the wrong skill, because expansion was the wrong idea. Much the same was true of the other top LSI executives. One corporate higher-up called them "pound for pound the best management team in ITT." But their excellence was in directions it proved dangerous to pursue. Louis E. Fischer, for instance, was recruited from a consulting firm in June 1968 specifically to formulate plans for national expansion. In fact, among top management only Richard Bernhard, once project manager in Puerto Rico, and newly executive VP, was a hunker-down builder, though demonstrably no Bill Levitt. Far from saying no, such a management's signal skill was in saying, You bet! And in this situation Ge-neen's business plan was a blueprint for downfall. It was a competition among units for growth funds: the better your plan, the bigger your slice. "Wasser-man," says someone who saw him in action, "had them cheering."

With what plans? It was impossible to expand impressively through internal growth alone; the same group can make only so many building starts in a year. So LSI would have to swallow other full-blown builders. Worse, they would have to branch into other fields. Each move was catastrophic.

In March 1969 LSI acquired United Homes Corporation in Seattle, Washington—just in time for the collapse of Boeing and the attendant col-lapse of the Northwest housing market. United's sales dropped from $33 million in 1969 to $5 million in 1972; a 1969 net of over $1 million became a loss of well over $5 million in the next five years. The former owner cheerfully admitted that without the sale to LSI he would have been bankrupt. Next, LSI went into apartments and condominiums—just in time for a mar-ket glut and a change in accounting rules that made paper profits hard to realize in cash. Through 1974 the loss was almost $14.5 million. They opened a mobile home factory in Fountain Valley, California—just in time for that market to disintegrate. An expansion into commercial building lost almost $2 million in three years.

In everything, LSI enjoyed Geneen's unstinting support. The depart-ment of Housing and Urban Development was urging more modern con-struction techniques. Here was where ITT's manufacturing knowhow could shine. And so, says Dick Bernhard, "there was pressure put on us by Geneen and Rich Bennett to come into the twentieth century by taking building out of the field and putting it in the factory." The result was a 200,000-square-foot housing factory built from scratch in Battle Creek, Michigan. It got LSI one of twenty-two contracts awarded by HUD; it also got LSI a lot of trouble. The factory was a miracle of modern design: components were supposed to float down the production line on air bags. They did not. Nothing worked. The loss on modular housing from 1971 through 1974 was over $12 million.

The common thread of these defeats (except for United) was LSI's floundering in alien fields. By the early 1970s their supposed forte, single-family home building, was also in decline. While the market held firm the

Levitt name sold houses. But the recession killed the market. By 1972 the division was showing a loss—which reached over $9 million for 1974. When a trustee stepped in, the company averaged fewer than 200 sales in each of its 16 regional markets, and it was looking at a loss of nearly $11 million for just the first quarter of 1975.

Even that was not the worst. Any builder wants to do some land banking. The theory is sound: buy land now, cheaply, for tomorrow's projects. Relative poverty restrains most builders, limiting potential but also risk. LSI could dip into Geneen's purse. In just 1969 and 1970 they bought nearly $45 million worth of land, and eventually they had land worth between $80 and $100 million—"mostly," says Bill Levitt, "unusable." Wasserman points out that, had volume kept up, that amount of land banking would have been reasonable, even necessary. But it had to be the right land at the right time; the results suggest that they had been hunkering down in the wrong fields at the wrong time.

Geneen himself was responsible for another fiasco, Palm Coast. Rayonier already had timberland near Flagler Beach, Florida, a stretch some forty miles south of Jacksonville whose possibilities had failed to stir even Florida land promoters. "Geneen called me in," says Wasserman, "and said, We're going to do this retail land business. And I said, You won't like it, Hal, it's amoral, a suede-shoe business. He said, We have forty thousand acres, we're in the business now. Would you like to handle it or should we get someone else? I said, I love the business." Rayonier picked up another 60,000 acres at low, timber-company prices, then transferred title to LSI. The idea was to sell lots. But few wanted just lots, and ecologists challenged ITT's proposed improvements. When LSI was divested, Palm Coast reverted to ITT, and after a change of strategy and community development, and after a loss of over $100 million, Palm Coast is now at least inhabited.

The consequences of these dealings were not apparent under either Levitt or Wasserman. Wasserman resigned, to Geneen's distress, in June 1971. He left on the up-tick. In 1971 earnings had increased nicely from 1967's $6.6 million to $18.9 million (less United Homes's $2.3 million loss). Restated to reflect new accounting rules, that dropped precipitously; for instance, the single-family profit of $7.6, restated, was only $1.6 million. But any profit was a last hurrah, and Wasserman knew it. "The year I left," he says, "I said to myself, We did three hundred twenty million. Next year— they say go ahead ten percent, but you really want to make it fifteen to twenty percent—if I target twenty percent it means sixty-five million in a business where you can't just repeat. Everything's a new game. Where the hell are we going ahead sixty-five million? Maybe I'm a quitter, maybe I'm not as smart as the next guy, but it terrified me. I'm going to keep going up until they lop my head off. I knew when I left the thing would crash at some point, and I'm going to get the blame. But we had it working!"

At Geneen's urgent request Bill Levitt stepped in briefly, followed by

Lou Fischer (Dick Bernhard had turned the job down). But by the end of July ITT was under court order to divest Levitt. For that job Geneen brought back Gerry Andlinger, business plan installer, Ted Westfall's successor in Latin America, and then CEO of the Esterline Corporation. Geneen lured him back in January 1972 with a reported million-dollar contract.

All the principals say the same thing about Andlinger. As Dick Wasserman puts it, "they moved in a guy who I understand is very bright, very capable, very charming—who didn't know one single thing about housing." He was not supposed to run LSI, just take it public. The big losses were not yet quite evident, and Geneen told the ITT board they might realize $350 million on a stock sale. But it was soon clear that LSI was failing; a public offering was impossible. The loss for 1972 was $600,000. In 1973 that mounted to around $28 million, and through 1975 the total operating loss was close to $100 million. Andlinger angled for a corporate buyer. "They all looked at us," says an LSI executive from those days, "Gulf, Kaiser—and all they saw was a sieve." Only Bill Levitt was interested.

You could not give away LSI as it was. All told, the diversification units would lose about $60 million, and the hemorrhage was now obvious; another $56 million or so in inventory and receivables had to be written down, maybe written off. And there was all that land. Bill Levitt suggested splitting LSI into an "A" and a "B" company. "A" would contain the reasonable projects and land, "B" everything else. Levitt would buy "A" and ITT would dispose of "B" any way they could; that would at least get them out and satisfy the court order. In February 1974 Levitt asked Justice to approve his letter of intent. Justice wrongly sensed a sweetheart deal and took their time scrutinizing it. Meanwhile, Levitt audited the "A" assets and concluded it was not an attractive buy after all. In August 1974 the deal collapsed.

ITT took $113 million of debt off LSI's books, but that was still not enough to ensnare a suitor before time ran out. In January 1975 the court appointed as trustee the firm of Victor Palmieri & Co., specialists in such work; they had administered, for example, the nonrail assets of Penn Central. Edward P. Eichler, who had grown up in the industry, became chairman of LSI, with John Koskinen, a young lawyer, chairman of the executive committee. Andlinger went skiing in Austria, and when he came back, resigned and settled his contract with ITT amid mutual hard feelings.

The Palmieri people stayed with the "A" and "B" concept, though they made their own split. The "A" company posted a modest earning in 1976 ($2.4 million) and 1977 ($4 million), and on February 28, 1978, Palmieri sold its assets to Starrett Housing Corporation, another home builder, for $34.5 million. The total loss to ITT was never revealed, but one building industry estimate put it at over $260 million in 1975. Surely it was finally more.

Why did it happen? What does it tell us about Geneen and his system? "Dick Wasserman and Bill Levitt," says trustee John Koskinen, "have run a number on ITT, I think; a very skillful one. Their position is: ITT killed us because we had all these limitations—we couldn't pay salaries and we had to write reports and all these things. The irony was that ITT didn't have *enough* controls. There was too much money with no control on where it got spent."

Even if true, that explanation does not reach first causes. Start with the concept that a manager can manage anything—even when no one knows the business. It is questionable whether anyone can know national home building, whether it really is a business. Wasserman and Bernhard did not know it; they formed The Richards Group at Gulf & Western and that foundered too. No one at LSI knew any of the expansion businesses; nor did ITT. How can you control—or even intelligently discuss—what you do not know? The idiom even of LSI's basic business was so foreign to ITT that the dialogue of control was often babel from the start. A builder thinks of return on equity: for a million-dollar property he puts up, say, $100,000, leverages the rest, and hopes to sell for $1,100,000. He figures he doubles his money. "No you don't," Geneen would say, "you have only a ten percent return because you must measure by the assets at risk." Wasserman would explain that each contract had a so-called exculpatory clause, standard in the industry, specifying that the lender could look only to the property in case of default. The builder was no further liable. Geneen would say, "We would never walk away from our responsibility." Wasserman would insist it was an industry given; he would offer to have the exculpatory clause set in inch-high type. That still did not end it. Geneen would say, "Then what you're really doing is speculating. If anything goes wrong, your ten percent gets squeezed out." Exactly. *That* was the business. The degree of risk turned on the abilities, maybe instincts, of the speculator. How does a corporation control those?

Geneen's system was superb for dealing with the apposite part of any business. Avis, APCOA, Sheraton were less entrepreneurial or intuition-intensive than LSI only in degree. But that sort of business had to be running on the right formula already or Geneen needed enough time to find someone who knew enough to discover the right formula. With LSI he ran out of time. Yet neither could he have rescued the situation given time, for as we have seen there was another first cause to Geneen's few failures: his resolute pressure to grow would inevitably ruin a company that was in an inherently nonexpandable market (as Levitt was), because it impelled the company to expand in ruinous directions.

The most dismal example of this tendency was Nesbitt. Geneen had all the time he needed, and the longer it took, the worse it got. George Haufler came from Nesbitt, went to corporate, and returned as head of the environmental products division, embracing Nesbitt and Reznor. "Like many modest-sized companies," says Haufler, "Nesbitt succeeded because of its people and its proper orientation to its particular market. Nesbitt was a big fish in a small pond." The pond was heating and air conditioning for schools, and Nesbitt was indeed big. In a two-year period it got 96% of all the school jobs on Long Island. "That's the kind of dominance Nesbitt had in the Eastern educational market," says William D. McCloskey, then Nesbitt's Eastern regional sales manager.

How do you grow when you already own your market? Obviously you must enter new markets. After all, heating and air conditioning is the same all over, no? "Nesbitt," says George Haufler, "had skills which were not easily transferable into the broader industrial and commercial market." Their sales relationships were not transferable either. And since air conditioning was a late development in schools, Nesbitt's experience and technology was limited compared with that of the new competition.

Compounding the problem, while Geneen wanted growth five years out, he also wanted it this year, which meant a rush to market. "Our engineering department," says Bill McCloskey, "always put out a quality product—but we always blew our engineering PERT diagrams by about two years because we used to fuss with the product a lot." No longer. Geneen sent in an ITT staffer, Fred Weldon, as one of the first heads of environmental products. "Weldon kept saying he was going to have discipline in our engineering effort," says McCloskey. "Time goals would be met—and here's how to meet them. And we met them. And the product did not work."

Harry J. Smith left Nesbitt for Bell & Gossett within a year of the merger, but as a fond alumnus, he kept tabs. "Nobody will admit this," he says, "but they put out products that weren't completely tested. A rooftop unit went out and they had a million-dollar retrofit because it was always, Grow, grow! Get that product out there!"

Bill McCloskey was in charge of fixing the rooftop units—"the wrong way," he says. "After the customers had them." And all those modifications meant an inaccurate bill of materials, so suddenly there was a million-dollar inventory shortage, with New York insisting on physical inventories every six months—further impeding production and service. New York staff descended. Once, when Nesbitt was having production problems, Geneen got some letters complaining about quality. A staff team came to impose a brilliant quality-control system that further slowed down production.

Harry Smith overly simplifies when he says, "It was New York staff going in and trying to be heroes that drove that company down." But the constant intrusions did not help. An interesting contrast is with Reznor, which kept thriving without interference. Nesbitt alumni credit Reznor's location, tucked away in the northwest wilds of Pennsylvania, relatively inaccessible (Nesbitt was in Philadelphia, ninety minutes from Park Avenue). More likely, it was because Reznor never dominated its field and so had plenty of room to grow handsomely, still doing what its people knew how to do—maximized by ITT planning and control. Furthermore, Reznor's simple-minded technology was patently incapable of conquering other markets.

Each fresh downturn at Nesbitt brought new leadership. If a manager can manage anything, and a unit has trouble, try another until you find a real manager. Nesbitt and environmental products ate managers. The company had a new president almost yearly. Walter Moore, who had followed Geneen from Jones & Laughlin, succeeded Fred Weldon as head of environmental products. John K. Collins, Jr., from another subsidiary, soon replaced Moore. Collings was replaced by George Haufler after a year or so. Haufler also failed. Was none of them any good? John Lobb proposes a test for managers who fail at one place: what happens to them later? Collins became executive VP of Coca-Cola; Moore became head of a division of IU; McCloskey became general manager of Baltimore Aircoil. Haufler says his dismissal was triggered by his refusal to fire R. R. del Presto, then head of Nesbitt. Rocky del Presto became executive VP of Nytronics; Haufler started his own company.

Nesbitt, in contradistinction, sank. In the early 1970s someone decided that the real problem was labor costs. So a move was projected to Jackson, Tennessee. It did not help; the Jackson plant was closed in the late 1970s and Nesbitt was sold—by which time, says Haufler, "it had shrunk substantially in size, quality, and reputation." While Lyman Hamilton was still president of ITT, he said at a gathering of alumni, "If we ever do a book about how to screw up a good company, Nesbitt will be in it."

Managing a business is one thing, running it—still more, fixing it—another. What's more, you cannot find the right people to run a business that has a central flaw in its concept—the problem behind Geneen's chronic disappointment over ITT's failure to significantly penetrate the North American market for telephone switching equipment. Geneen had tried a succession of managers when James Rice became group executive in the late 1960s. "He was no better or worse than the others," says one observer. "We called him 'Jim Eleven.' " He had been hired to succeed Rich Bennett as staff director; but after about nine months Bennett, whose protégé Rice was, palmed him off on Ted Westfall, then in overall charge of telecom. People at the GMMs soon felt that Rice was over his head. Except for Hart Perry and Bob Benson, Jim Rice took more abuse at GMMs than anyone—until, ominously, Geneen simply would not talk to him. Soon he was gone. In his own defense, Rice points out that there had been ten people in his job in the previous ten years (he left in the spring of 1969), but that he so ordered telecom that his replacement, Howard Truss, lasted through the next ten years. But that does not mean much. Telecom was doing well enough through 1973, after which Geneen was distracted; and by then Geneen may have given up, realizing that his basic concept for switching equipment was wrong.

It was only switching equipment that disappointed, though that was the big item in the division. ITT's subsets did very well; the plant at Corinth, Mississippi, was magnificent. A good man was running it—George Safiol, who went on to become president of American Biltrite. In contrast, John Lobb, applying his test of managerial merit, says that Jims One-through-Eleven never made much of a mark anywhere else, either: Rice got out of business operation altogether and became an executive head hunter. But the difference was not people. For its subsets, ITT (like everyone else) licensed Western Electric's standard design, then maximized its potential with great controls. For a while Westfall flirted with the idea of licensing the Bell # 5 switching design, but in the end it was decided to adapt the French Pentaconta A-1, toast of ITT-Europe. The decision seemed sound. ITT already owned the technology, with hardware and experts, which made importation easier and cheaper than starting from scratch with the Bell design. But according to Jeffery McGee, head of Continental Telephone's Florida operations (which, itself, very happily used ITT equipment), the adapted French design "did not offer most independents the advantages they wanted." It required massive adaptation. Hearsay among independent phone companies was that hordes of ITT engineers labored months or years to get the few installations working right. One user, J. E. Corbett of Central Telephone in Tallahassee, Florida, says that problems are to be expected with any new installation, though the Pentaconta might have occasioned more confusion and delay than usual. But, he says, ITT kept competing against itself, introducing the Pentaconta right on the heels of its Kellogg crossbar, shortly followed by the electronic Metaconta, another import, exciting fears of phase-out, leaving buyers with staggering bills for replacement parts. A user in the Midwest found the equipment acceptable but maintenance costs exorbitant and financing difficult, with an oppressive amount of data required by ITT.

The differing views all come down to poor reception for ITT switching equipment. And in each case, the ITT decision was made on a basis of what ITT wanted, not what the market wanted.

Who should be blamed for all of the failures? The line people involved still blame the messengers. Gene Rachlis and one of his top editors, Barbara Norville, blamed Stanley Sills for what happened at Bobbs-Merrill; Rachlis felt that Gencen understood a trade publisher's problems. At Nesbitt, opinion was divided; the fault lay either with the pressure the head of TIP, Art Woerthwein, brought on successive heads of environmental products, or with the meddlesome New York staff. The Nesbitt people were sure Geneen supported long-term growth. Bill Levitt was sure Geneen understood; he blamed those who ignored Geneen's memo about treating LSI differently. For Dick Wasserman and Dick Bernhard it was staff that failed to grasp LSI's problems, that thrust inapplicable ratios upon them; staff, not Geneen. "Much as I had disdain for the ITT structure, for most of the nerds," says Bernhard, "I think on reflection that Harold Geneen was a hell of a guy, fair and brilliant." Wasserman says the same: the system was terrible, Geneen fabulous.

And so he was. Surely he understood their special problems; he took the time and trouble to understand every ITT unit. But who did they think animated the system—all of it, including the parts they loathed? Who put the pressure on Sills and Woerthwein? Who sent staff to Philadelphia; or more accurately, what spirit moved them to go? Would ITT top executives really ignore Geneen's Levitt memo unless they were certain he had no intention, really, of abrogating his system for LSI? Pressure to grow had to be kept on every unit, every moment. Staff did not do what they did because *they* wanted another quarter of increased earnings, or because *they* wanted ITT to become the largest money-maker in the world. Geneen's people were always about his business, doing what he wanted them to do. It was Geneen. To the great extent that it worked, it was his glory; where it failed, it was his fault.

Geneen's vision and dream were background to two other different kinds of failure: with people and with stock. People were bound to disappoint him. George Bernard Shaw had his Julius Caesar lament that in all the world he could find "no other Caesar . . . one who can do my day's deed, and think my night's thought." Geneen's cadre might have to keep up with his deeds, day and night; but he knew none shared his thoughts or dreams. They could never be his inheritors. As for the more independent, anyone good enough to succeed Geneen was disinclined to hang around until he was ready to be succeeded—which appeared to be never. One favorite after another let him down. When he told Dick Wasserman that the future might belong to him, Wasserman laughed and said it would ruin his backhand. Chick Ireland was quickly disillusioned and leapt at the chance to leave for CBS.

Michel C. Bergerac probably represented Geneen's most blighted hope. His brother, the French actor, Jacques Bergerac, had come to southern California; he urged Mike to join him. The latter took an M.B.A. at UCLA and before returning home to Biarritz did some translation work for Cannon Electric. Bob Cannon was impressed with him. When Bergerac wrote asking for a job so he could return to southern California, Cannon was delighted. Not long after the ITT merger, Bergerac joined the corporation. He went to Europe to take charge of some technical products companies. In the late 1960s, at an EAC meeting, Geneen concluded that an ITT pump maker, working under a licensing agreement, was not profitable because royalties were too high. He said Bergerac should either renegotiate the royalties or get out of that business. "Mike," says someone who was at the meeting, "said he'd already done it—and the sparks began to fly!" This was Geneen's kind of guy.

In 1971, at age thirty-nine, Bergerac became president of ITT-Europe. In three years he superintended the doubling of European sales, to $5 billion. He was clearly the leading candidate as Geneen's successor. But after how long a wait? The board extended Geneen's contract past the mandatory ITT retirement age, which he would reach in 1975. In 1974 Charles Revson, knowing he was dying of cancer, offered Bergerac the chairmanship of Revlon, with inducements that ran to $5 million.

Geneen felt betrayed. Here was another who, despite his favor, did not share his dream. In retaliation he hired one of Revlon's top marketing men, who was allowed a stunningly decorated office. Maybe Geneen would get himself a United States cosmetics company and show those guys something. It came to nothing. The marketing man was shipped off to Continental Baking, and Ned Gerrity got some flashy used furniture.

Other fallen favorites did not exactly leave. They either skipped a jump ahead of the posse, like Wasserman, or were ridden out, like Howard Miller. In the sunshine days, a favorite inevitably made to-the-knife enemies of Geneen's regulars. "The intimate staff," says Bud Morrow, "the Bennetts, the Dunleavys, the Hanways, and the others close to the throne, they would see this guy reporting directly to Geneen—although he might be miles away in line of organization—and he'd be getting everything he wanted, million-dollar appropriations, big budget variances. They might grouse to Geneen, but they'd be overruled. Then as soon as something went wrong, it was like being caught on the forward slope when your army's on the other side of the hill. It was murder."

Howard Miller had come to ITT in 1963 from the consulting firm of Robert Heller & Associates. He impressed Geneen, and by the late 1960s he was a VP and group executive for Avis, APCOA, Sams, Sheraton, and other consumer service units. "He got too far out front," says APCOA's Ed Roth. "I can remember at Boca Raton in 'sixty-nine, every time Geneen turned around he'd be calling for Howard—Howard, come to my room, I want to talk to you about this." Nor was Miller humble about his rise. "When Miller was riding high," says Morrow, "he offended a lot of people."

He was being publicly touted as a successor. "The *New York Times*," says Roth, "did an heir apparent story on him that was the beginning of the end." Ned Gerrity arranged an interview with *Times* writer Robert E. Bedingfield, who told a friend, "I don't know what the guy was talking about. He had nothing concrete to offer, but it sounded good as it rolled out." Geneen appreciated neither public heirs nor sonorities, but even that was all right while the favorite produced. Suddenly, though, Sheraton was failing, and it was Miller who had plumped for Phil Lowe. Then Miller took part in an ill-considered ITT venture involving cruise ships. Geneen would not fire him; but now his door was closed, his protection withdrawn. Miller was naked to his enemies. "They cut him to ribbons," says Ed Roth. "Bennett especially had the hooks out for him real big. He was lucky to survive." Canteen Corporation was to be divested, and Miller, cashing in his last chit with Geneen, arranged to go as Pat O'Malley's number two.

Easily the most feared and hated of Geneen's palace guard was Jack Hanway. "Blackjack," they called him, a tall, gaunt man who typed his own memos, answered his own phone, and would not unbend even to standard corporate lunchtime conviviality but instead took solitary walks, grabbing a hot dog from a sidewalk cart. He was a convinced loner. Once a jet pilot, his one diversion known to his fellows was playing a jazz trumpet.

He was Geneen's hatchet man, and naysayer, keeping Geneen's impulses from costing what they should not. Once, in Brussels, they joined some EAC staff people and their wives for dinner. Talk turned to the inadequacy of English-language schools. The wives planned an American school, had already made arrangements with some teaching nuns, and needed only $100,-000 seed money. Geneen immediately volunteered $50,000 from ITT. Early next morning the senior ITT man in the group got a call from Hanway. "Don't spend that money quite yet. . . . " The man, who knew Geneen and Hanway, assured Blackjack that he had not planned to.

That sort of thing was a surprisingly large part of Hanway's duty. Geneen might promise some importuner anything. Hanway, who was often in Geneen's office, would later summon the dazzled wretch to his own office. "No," he would say. "In spite of what you think you heard, *no*—you're not going to have unlimited use of a company plane, and *no*, you're not going to . . . " If the person protested that Geneen had promised, Hanway would say, "OK, and I'm telling you you're not getting it. Now you want to make something of it?" Some ran back to Geneen, who might then belabor Hanway for countermanding his "orders." But all knew Hanway acted only in Geneen's best interest as they both perceived them; there was never a question as to his loyalty. Furthermore, as a close observer says, "Hal always knew that Jack never told him anything but the truth." That was all he ever told anyone. "He's gruff and he's loud and he's crude and he's profane," says Maurie Valente, "but I've never known Hanway to give you anything but a straight answer, never evasive and never untruthful, just 'tell-it-like-it-is.' And no one was sacred except Geneen. Now, that doesn't create a lot of liking."

In turn, Hanway seemed not to like others much—perhaps for the reason that reportedly turns policemen misanthropic. Part of his job was to keep tabs on the derelictions of those who might cause problems for ITT—the drunks and thieves, the uncircumspectly lustful, the connivers and free-lance bag men. "I have seen," he once said, "some of the absolute worst moral and ethical conduct in individuals so that I almost wonder whether anybody you look at is what he seems to be."

His position with Geneen was so strong, he would often be the only one who dared say no. About once a month Geneen would meet with Hanway and Frank McCabe, director of executive personnel, plus Tim Dunleavy, Rich Bennett, and whoever else was currently helping in worldwide executive evaluation. The meetings, held in the ITT Waldorf suite, never started until eight or nine at night and typically ran until just about dawn. Once, at about 4:00 A.M., the group emerged from the Waldorf and crossed Park to their limousines waiting in front of ITT. Geneen said, "What's everyone going to do?" They stared at him. "Listen," he said, "is anybody hungry?" Silence. "I know a great place; we could have breakfast, and we could finish that part we never really got to—you know that guy in Brussels?" No one spoke; they wistfully eyed the chauffeurs standing by open limousine doors. Finally Hanway said, "Hal, we are not going anyplace with you. We are not having breakfast with you. We are going home. Good night."

Geneen needed a hatchet man; every corporate chief seems to. But he might have looked for a different person. Many of Geneen's problems with people derived from the atmosphere created by his choice of hatchet man; and whether it was by design or want of perception, this too was Geneen's fault.

The failure of ITT's stock—a relative failure even during the palmiest of the glory years—was different. It was a bum rap, born of misconceptions, ignorance, and wrongheadedness on the part of investors, the financial community, business press, and most especially analysts. Geneen deserved better.

He was victim of the Aristides Syndrome. In Athens, at the time of the Persian invasions, a political institution called "ostracism" let citizens send into temporary exile someone who had been charged with no offense. It was not a captious unpopularity contest but a means of breaking political deadlocks. Still, citizens needed no reason for their votes. For years Aristides had been acknowledged as the most righteous of men, a model of rectitude and fair dealing. Indeed, he was always referred to as Aristides the Just. However, when he clashed with another leader on a point of defense policy and it came to a vote of ostracism, he lost. One citizen, asked why he had voted against this great man, said he had never set eyes on him; "But, oh! I am so *bored* by hearing him called Aristides the Just."

The financial world got bored with Geneen the Brilliant. They got sick of reporting that ITT had posted yet another quarter with at least another 10% rise in earnings. It went on and on, thirty, forty, *fifty* straight quarters. And the financial world was not allowed to ignore it: Geneen was not reticent, his PR people not shy.

Nobody, the financial world said, can be that right that consistently. It must be done with mirrors or a sharp pencil. The analysts' complaint could not credibly be lack of disclosure. ITT consistently won awards from the accounting profession for the completeness of its statements and reports. In fact, those disclosures gave the analysts their clue. When ITT bought Sheraton, for instance, there was no chainwide practice of accounting for operating supplies like linen and china. They could be expensed or partly capitalized; individual units did as they pleased. A company like ITT that wants to show earnings naturally opts for capitalization and picks up a few million in one-time earnings, dutifully footnoted. Then the same thing would happen with Rayonier's woodlands. And Continental's trucks. In fact, not a quarter went by without some earnings boost through standardization of accounting procedures, all clearly noted. The analysts would pounce and say, Ah! *that's* how Geneen does it! It isn't real earnings after all. Then the talk was that pooling-of-interest acquisitions was how Geneen did it. But then the Accounting Practices Board ruled that good will had to be amortized, and while that chilled the go-go fever, Geneen somehow kept acquiring. When the Justice Department restricted his acquisitions, he somehow kept growing. Next the talk was about how *really* those earnings came from treating capital gains as income—especially with the Hartford portfolio. "Managed earnings" was how Geneen did it.

Of course ITT managed earnings. They smoothed them out, keeping the excess of a particularly lush quarter on the shelf against soft spots in next quarter's results. That way, both could show an 11% gain, not one 9.9% and the other 12.1%. But it always was close; you cannot "manage" even 3% or 4%. When a quarter lagged, Rich Bennett knew all the tricks, knew where unit managers would have a little tucked away against their own soft spots. When the corporation needed a boost *this* quarter, he was the one, says a former manager, who "ragged the units" for profits and "played the hard stick on them" at GMMs. "Geneen would ask me," says Bob Savage, "what's the Street looking for in quarterly earnings. And I'd say, The consensus is ninety-five cents. But Herb Knortz would say it looked under, and then they would start. First came the announcement that Geneen wants ninety-five, but it looks like only ninety-three. So all of you guys be thinking how you can sell another widget or something and get as much earnings as you can this quarter. And each guy would say, Yeah, I think I can come up with five hundred thousand over budget. They would write this down. And if the guy didn't make his forecast, he was in a little trouble. It was like the United Jewish Appeal."

The earnings were real and the growth was real. Everytime an analyst would discover some new *real* reason for the phenomenal record, the shout of "Eureka!" kept the stock unnaturally low. Everyone was sure the bubble would burst this quarter, surely the next. They never seemed to notice that *something* always kept the rise going. But in the market, expressed lack of confidence is a self-fulfilling prophecy, and at best the performance of ITT stock bitterly disappointed Geneen; even during the glory years it was nowhere near the multiple of less worthy companies.

By 1973, when the steam had gone out of the stock market anyway, the attacks on Geneen's credibility took on new substance. The stock would plunge. But that was for other reasons.

18
Starting at the Top

When Richard Nixon took office, his attorney general, John N. Mitchell, seemed to set antitrust policy in a speech before the Georgia bar association on June 6, 1969. It was strongly anti-conglomerate. In 1968, 91% of all mergers were between totally disparate companies, and Mitchell said he would "move aggressively to counteract this trend." In fact, "The Justice Department may very well oppose any merger among the top 200 manufacturing firms. . . . " That could refer only to conglomerates, since big horizontal mergers were already barred.

On the other hand, the tough talk might not mean anything. Another time Mitchell said that people should watch what the administration did, not what they said. A year later Geneen asked Mitchell about his policy. It seemed to attack ITT's and others' mergers because of bigness, not because of any proven anticompetitiveness. "I said," Geneen later testified, "that I thought his Savannah speech . . . could be taken or interpreted in that manner. He assured me that the policy of the Antitrust Division . . . was not against bigness per se, and he assured me that this was not the policy of the administration."

Of course it was *exactly* the policy—at first. John Mitchell, the Wall Street expert in municipal bonds, did not like conglomerate raids on his friends and clients any more than antitrust chief Richard McLaren did. But the pressures were different higher up. As a *Wall Street Journal* writer put it, ". . . a President who lets antitrust run free finds he's got a bear by the tail." Maybe established big business did not like conglomerates, but they liked unbridled antitrust actions even less. Policy at the antitrust division, though, had never changed. In April 1969 McLaren filed against the Canteen merger. The same month as Mitchell's Savannah speech, McLaren announced opposition to the Hartford merger, a month later against Grinnell, and on August 1, 1969, filed antitrust actions against both.

All that spring Geneen had been promising stockholders he would fight and urged them to rally round as they had with the Hickenlooper Amendment. He was incensed. One aide wrote to another, "Hal's posture is . . . that we have done nothing wrong, that we will do nothing wrong, and that (McLaren) is unfairly harassing us." In truth, McLaren's view of antitrust law was peculiar. None of his predecessors had thought that section 7 of the Clayton Act applied to conglomerate mergers; they had said with one voice that additional legislation was needed. McLaren disagreed and was pressing on. A mild attempt was made to show him the light: Ned Gerrity went to Washington to tell McLaren that ITT was a fine company and that he should not pick on them. McLaren ignored him. In any case, Geneen's instinct was not to deal at the McLaren level but to go right to the top, where real power dealt in orders, not pleas. In June 1969 he tried to see Nixon. His approach through Secretary of the Treasury Maurice Stans was unsuccessful. Under the circumstances a visit was deemed "inappropriate."

All right; there were other ways to get to Nixon. Geneen had prescribed "inexorable pressure" to achieve the Hartford merger; now it would preserve that merger. "It is probably a status symbol in official circles to have been lobbied by Harold Geneen personally," as it was put in the minority report of a Senate investigating committee, "and an embarrassment to have been visited only by Ned Gerrity or Bill Merriam." Geneen distributed the honor generously. Starting with Stans in early 1969, and through late 1971, after the settlement, Geneen talked antitrust with Arthur Burns, John Connally, Peter Peterson, John Ehrlichman, John Mitchell, Charles Colson, Paul McCracken, David Kennedy, James Lynn, and Peter Flanigan—and that was just in the administration. In Congress he talked with Senators John McClellan, Robert Byrd, his old friend Charles Percy, Vance Hartke, Philip Hart, Sam Ervin, and Daniel Inouye, and with representatives Gerald Ford, Hale Boggs, Clark MacGregor (later head of the Committee to Reelect the President), Jack Brooks, Peter Rodino, and Emanuel Celler. Meanwhile, ITT won every court battle with Canteen, Grinnell, and Hartford.

Grinnell went to trial on September 15, 1970. Whatever McLaren's feelings about conglomerates, to prevail under the Clayton Act, he had to demonstrate the anticompetitiveness of *this* merger. That was hard to do. Although Grinnell was largest in its field, it had strong competition; although ITT's backing would bolster Grinnell's finances, that itself was unlikely to let it dominate the market, unless there was reciprocity. If suppliers must buy from you in order to sell to you, the bigger you are (after a conglomerate merger) the greater the number of suppliers under the gun. In fact, reciprocity had been widespread at Grinnell before the merger. ITT policy, though, clearly forbade it. Geneen did not instinctively shrink from the practice: at Raytheon he had insisted that Hallicrafter and Wells-Gardner be given subcontracting work because—as a subordinate's memo put it—"Both of these

McLaren, left, and Kleindienst at hearing.

Kleindienst and Robatyn.

firms are important customers of our Receiving Tube division. Any work that can be placed with these firms would serve to further improve their relations with Receiving Tube by establishing a reciprocity basis." But ITT, in the spotlight and susceptible to antitrust actions, had to be careful. The instances of ITT reciprocity that Justice could adduce were spotty and equivocal.

Grinnell seemed to be going well for ITT. Nonetheless, Geneen was willing to settle the whole antitrust matter. On November 30, 1970, with *Grinnell* still in trial, and before *Canteen* started, he sent Washington lawyer Ephraim Jacobs to offer McLaren a deal. ITT would divest Canteen, Levitt, most of Grinnell, and others to be negotiated—all, if ITT were allowed to keep Hartford. "I called Mr. Jacobs," McLaren later said, " . . . and told him that I could see no reason for any such settlement as they had proposed." That may seem quixotic on both sides—especially when the *Grinnell* decision came down on December 31, 1970. It was strongly in ITT's favor; the judge expressed indignation that so weak a case had been brought. But both sides knew that the United States Supreme Court had historically backed the government on antitrust appeals. As another lawyer representing ITT wrote, "[I]f the government urges an expanded interpretation of the vague language of the Clayton Act, there is a high probability that it will succeed. Indeed, the court has at times adopted a position more extreme than that urged by the Department [of Justice]."

Geneen's immediate problem was to forestall McLaren's appeal of *Grinnell* to the Supreme Court. Notice of appeal was given on March 1, 1971. The government then had thirty days to "perfect" the appeal with a formal filing. Geneen and his troops got busy, and it was obvious that earlier efforts had paid off; they were preaching to the converted. On September 17, 1970, two days after *Grinnell* started, John Ehrlichman wrote to Mitchell:

> I was disappointed to learn that the ITT case had gone to trial with apparently no further effort on the part of Mr. McLaren to settle this case with ITT on the basis of our understanding that "largeness" was not really an issue in the case.
> ITT has passed word to us that the gravaman of the case remains "largeness" which is contrary to the understanding that I believe you and I had during the time that we each talked to Mr. Gineen.
> I think we are in a rather awkward position with ITT in view of the assurances that both you and I must have given Gineen on this subject.
> . . . Gineen is, of course, entitled to assume the Administration meant what it said to him.

That same day, McLaren gave a speech in which he quoted E. M. Forster's *Howard's End:* "It is the vice of a vulgar mind to be thrilled by bigness. . . . " Charles Colson sent Ehrlichman a copy of the speech, observing, "In sum, I think that we still have a problem here, which is a serious one and which is manifesting itself in Mr. McLaren's conduct of the ITT case."

On March 3, 1971, after the notice of appeal in *Grinnell*, Geneen and Bill Merriam, head of ITT's Washington office, saw Ehrlichman. In a thank-you note, Merriam wrote that they "came away . . . with the thought that you understand our position perfectly and are sympathetic." There was even a ray of hope. On February 15 Peter G. Peterson had become assistant to the president for international economic affairs and executive director of the council on international economic policy. He and his staff would study the question of antitrust in light of Geneen's assertion that domestic prosecution hurt his multinational's ability to contribute to America's balance of payments.

For the next few months, Peterson was never lonely. At one point Bill Merriam ended a letter with, "Please excuse me for bothering you every day, but I am sure things will get better sometime soon." Peterson wrote to Ehrlichman, "Here is the latest letter from IT&T on antitrust. Please keep in mind my reason for involvement is that the President asked Hal Geneen to talk with me about antitrust." And, wearily, "You probably have a very similar letter, but if you don't, here it is."

On March 20 (the usual ten-day deadline before a Supreme Court appeal is due) Solicitor General Erwin Griswold asked for and was granted a thirty-day extension on the *Grinnell* appeal. As the new (April 20) deadline approached, Geneen tried for another extension. For this he enlisted Lawrence E. Walsh, partner in the New York firm of Davis Polk & Wardwell, long ITT's outside lawyers. Judge Walsh (he had been one) had not done much with ITT before, and he was no antitrust specialist; he had other qualifications. Since John Mitchell had recused himself because his old firm had done work for ITT's Continental, Deputy Attorney General Richard G. Kleindienst was in charge of the ITT cases. Walsh was Kleindienst's friend. Moreover, as chairman of the bar association committee on the judiciary, he passed on all of Kleindienst's bench appointments. What Geneen really wanted was for Walsh to see Nixon, but the judge refused. Instead, on April 16 he called Kleindienst and sent him a letter and memo that urged Justice not to "advocate any position before the Supreme Court which would be tantamount to barring [conglomerate] mergers without a full study of the economic consequences of such a step." Kleindienst passed the letter and memo along to McLaren. At the same time, Geneen dropped off a copy to Peterson, and Merriam sent one to John Ehrlichman. April 16 was a Friday.

Sometime before 10:30 Monday morning (the nineteenth), Kleindienst called Walsh with the bad news that another extension was unlikely. McLaren had flatly rejected all of Walsh's arguments for delay. What's more, he had pointed out that this was the day before the deadline for filing, nine days after the deadline for a new appeal. Justice had already asked for one extension, "and it would be highly embarrassing to ask for another. . . . " But most of all, why ask for the opinions of other government agencies? It would be like abandoning Justice's antitrust policy "when the reasons for continuing it are just as strong as they ever were."

That sounded conclusive. Yet at about 4:30 that afternoon, Kleindienst called Walsh again. There would be another extension after all. A little before 3:00 P.M., Geneen had finally gotten action at the top.

According to Dick Kleindienst, he got a call from John Ehrlichman. "The president has directed you," said Ehrlichman, "to drop the ITT cases." Kleindienst says, "I told him, In the first place, I don't think the president said that, and in the second place, we can't do it because it's too late." Ehrlichman said, "We'll see about that!" And—click!—hung up.

Almost immediately afterward, Ehrlichman and George P. Shultz, then director of the Office of Management and Budget, had a meeting scheduled with Nixon. Ehrlichman and Nixon were to meet with John Mitchell next day, but Ehrlichman warned that by then it would be too late to turn off the ITT cases, "where God knows we have made your position as clear as we could to Mr. what's-his-name over there." Nixon supplied McLaren's name. Ehrlichman said McLaren was attacking conglomerates on a theory that had been contemplated by the Johnson Administration but "laid aside as too antibusiness." Nixon immediately put in a call to Kleindienst. While they waited, Ehrlichman pointed out that if the appeal were not perfected—by filing the next day—the case would end.

> PRESIDENT: They're not going to file.
> EHRLICHMAN: Well, I thought that was your position.

He had been, he said, "trying to give them signals on this," but "they've been horsing us pretty steadily."

> PRESIDENT: I don't want to know anything about the case. Don't tell me a
> EHRLICHMAN: Yeah, I won't.
> PRESIDENT: thing about it. I don't want to know about Geneen. I've met him and I don't know—I don't know whether ITT is bad, good, or indifferent. But there is not going to be any more antitrust actions as long as I am in this chair.

The call to Kleindienst came through. Nixon wanted something understood, and "if it is not understood, McLaren's ass is to be out within one hour. The IT & T thing—stay the hell out of it. Is that clear? That's an order." Clear enough, but not entirely palatable that late in the game. Kleindienst tried to stall.

> KLEINDIENST: Well, you mean the order is to—
> PRESIDENT: The order is to leave the God damned thing alone. Now, I've said this, Dick, a number of times, and you fellows apparently don't get the me—, the message over there. I do not want McLaren to run around prosecuting people, raising hell about conglomerates, stirring things up at this point. Now you keep him the hell out of that. Is that clear?

KLEINDIENST: Well, Mr. President—
PRESIDENT: Or either he resigns. I'd rather have him out anyway. I don't like the son-of-a-bitch.

Although Nixon said he did not need the legal ramifications spelled out for him, Kleindienst persisted in trying to explain how late it was to stifle the appeal.

KLEINDIENST: That brief has to be filed tomorrow.
PRESIDENT: That's right. Don't file the brief.
KLEINDIENST: Your order is not to file a brief?

And then the president of the United States of America said to the man who would soon be attorney general, "You son of a bitch, don't you understand the English language?" His order was "to drop the God damn thing. Is that clear?"

KLEINDIENST: [Laughs] Yeah, I understand that.

After they hung up, Shultz tried to discuss antitrust policy, but Nixon saw it all as personality. The trouble was that McLaren, "a nice little fellow who's a good little antitrust lawyer out in Chicago," was taken over by "all these bright little bastards" in antitrust, and with Mitchell and Kleindienst preoccupied with other matters, "they've gone off on a kick, that'll make them big God damn trust busters." Maybe that was all right fifty years ago, but not today. "That's my views about it," said Nixon, "and I am not—We've been through this crap. They've done several of them already about—They have raised holy hell with the people that we, uh, uh— . . . " Nixon did not finish the thought, but its direction was plain: "Well, Geneen, hell, he's no contributor. He's nothing to us. I don't care about him. So you can—I've only met him once, twice—uh, we've, I'm just, uh—I can't understand what the trouble is." It was McLaren, wasn't it? Then he would be out "In one hour. . . . And he's not going to be a judge, either. He is out of the God damn government."

Over at Justice, Kleindienst got to work. He ordered Erwin Griswold to request another extension. He did not give the solicitor general Walsh's memo; but then Kleindienst had not read it himself. That did not matter, though, because Walsh's argument for delay of appeal—that time was needed for an interagency review of antitrust policy—was never heard of again. Walsh's memo on April 16 bought time enough for pressure on an already sympathetic administration to do its work. When that pressure paid off on April 19, the Walsh thesis was no longer useful. Now the problem was to provide McLaren with a seemly out; Walsh's "policy review" was no good because McLaren had already specifically refused settlement on policy grounds. He could not be expected to do such an about-face on the issue. Chances are overwhelming that Nixon's intervention was reported to Geneen and that between ITT and the White House further moves were concocted to force McLaren's compliance without precipitating his resignation, which Nixon, for all the tough talk, feared, since it could precipitate a scandal.

Next day, April 20, Lazard's Felix Rohatyn asked Kleindienst's permission to present a new argument: the extreme hardship that divesting Hartford would wreak on ITT, the stock market, and America's balance of payments. The presentation on April 29 was in McLaren's office. Much of the antitrust staff was there, and so was Kleindienst, taking notes. They all had to wait almost an hour for Rohatyn to show up because he was meeting on another matter with Mitchell, everyone's boss. Geneen's representative was ostentatiously well connected.

Rohatyn made two kinds of argument: the irrelevant and the implausible. Certainly ITT's stock would drop with the forced divestiture; in fact it dropped with the settlement. So what? It was not the concern of Justice to protect stockholders from the consequences of their company's merger policies. As for allegedly crippling cash-flow problems divestiture of Hartford would create, again—even if true—so what? Most of the potential problem stemmed from the nearly $500 million premium paid for Hartford stock. Case law had established that such harm to stockholders or companies was no argument against an antitrust action, especially not in the face of so much warning.

Rohatyn's further predictions of horrendous "ripple effects" were at best dubious. Why should even a billion-dollar drop in the price of ITT stock have repercussions throughout the market? IBM regularly fluctuated in total value more than a billion a day with no ripples. And why should ITT, even shorn of Hartford, be unable to continue repatriating substantial foreign earnings? Long before acquiring Hartford, ITT had insistently trumpeted its performance along those lines as the miracle of American business. Actually, the merits of the argument were immaterial. Hardship injected a new element that could serve as a pretext for McLaren's change of mind, and that was all that counted. Now it was only necessary to effect the change.

On April 21 Mitchell had met with Nixon, obviously after talking with Kleindienst. It was politically impossible simply to turn off McLaren's appeal. He would surely resign if so humiliated. There was time to turn off the whole suit, said Mitchell, "[b]ut you just can't stop this thing up at the Supreme Court, because you will have Griswold quit, you will have a Senate investigation—Hart will just love this—and we don't need it. There are other ways of working this out."

On May 5 Ehrlichman wrote to Mitchell: "Following up our conversation at the Cabinet meeting the other day, I would like to arrange to talk with Dick McLaren about the present status of the ITT cases in order that we can achieve the agreed-upon ends discussed by the President with you." That talk must have been a classic application of stick and carrot. Above all else, McLaren wanted to be a federal judge. Everything might be possible if he cooperated, nothing if he did not.

Curiously, equity was on the administration's side. A president and his attorney general have the right to set their own antitrust policy, consonant with the law. In this case everyone—former attorneys general, antitrust chiefs, the trial courts—*everyone* except McLaren agreed that the law, as written, did not reach conglomerate mergers. ITT really was being persecuted. Putting an end to it could be, in Mitchell's phrase, "political dynamite" only in an administration obsessed with how everything would play in Peoria. Far from fearing McLaren's resignation, they could have dismissed him for unfairness and answered Democratic howls about probusiness bias with principled reason.

As it was, on May 12, 1971, McLaren took the first step toward caving in. By coincidence, the other theme of the scandal took shape that same day. It was at a party in San Diego following ITT's annual meeting. The previous winter, Ed Reinecke, lieutenant governor of California, asked ITT lobbyist Dita Beard for help. The Republican convention would take place in August of 1972, and President Nixon wanted it held in San Diego. That was his "lucky city," only twenty minutes by helicopter from his San Clemente home. Unfortunately, no one else wanted the convention there, especially the people of San Diego. There were not enough hotel rooms; and August was the one month when San Diego hotels were usually booked to capacity. And where would the city get the $800,000 cash (to defray expenses of the convention) required for such a bid? San Diego passed. Reinecke swore Beard to secrecy and said there was hope anyhow. She could help by checking on the availability of hotel rooms in the area, particularly to see if Sheraton's new 700-room Harbor Island hotel would be ready in time. Beard obliged. On April 20—although the April 1 deadline for bids had passed—the White House launched a major effort to change San Diego's mind.

San Diego was important to Geneen. There were already two Sheratons there, with a third soon to open. There was also a cable plant newly built to serve the Pacific area. A local congressman, Bob Wilson, had been instrumental in getting land on favorable terms for all four projects from the San Diego Port Authority. Geneen, grateful, and ever alert to the utility of a well-disposed congressman, was courting him, exchanging fishing trips, being accessible and attentive; like Hartford's Harry Williams, Wilson thought that he had found a true friend. Naturally he was invited to ITT's dinner party on May 12, held on the lawn of the Sheraton Half Moon, and naturally he was seated at Geneen's table. The day before, Wilson had learned that San Diego might still be in the running as convention host. When the subject came up that night, according to Wilson, Geneen was characteristically enthusiastic and generous:

[He] mentioned how important it would be for publicity for the opening of a large new hotel such as the Sheraton Harbor Island. I told him I was sure the community could come up with the sufficient financing [for the

$800,000 convention bid] if we were given a little time and if we got the proper underwriting. . . .

We kicked around the idea of my going to leading businessmen and getting commitments from them and putting together a bid package. He then suggested if I would take the lead he thought Sheraton would underwrite up to $300,000 and would, of course, be willing to actually commit for their fair share of the total amount of money needed. I told him I thought it would not be difficult to put a bid together quickly. He then told me he would see that they backed me personally for half the total amount needed, which would be $400,000. There was no written agreement, not even a handshake, but my personal knowledge of Mr. Geneen satisfied me as to the integrity of his guarantee.

As it happened, the size of the pledge became a bizarre issue. The whole $400,000 would not have been an unreasonable expenditure, since a condition was that the new Sheraton be the president's convention headquarters— "unbuyable publicity," as Dita Beard called it. However, it was never contemplated as a cash pledge, merely an undertaking to make up the difference if the balance could not be raised. With it, Wilson could announce that he "had" $400,000 to encourage pledges from others. When Sheraton head Bud James sent money it was a $100,000 check, with pledge of another $100,000 to match donations from other nongovernment sources. But when bribery was charged, Geneen decided that minimizing the size of ITT's commitment would make it seem less suspect (how much can you buy for only $100,000?). He resolutely refused to acknowledge anything beyond James's one check.

Back on the antitrust front, whatever had been promised or threatened, on May 12 Dick McLaren wanted an out. He called Peter M. Flanigan, a presidential assistant specializing in relations with business, and asked him to order a critique of Rohatyn's hardship plea, which was now in the form of a memo. He wanted Richard J. Ramsden, a New York stock analyst, to make the critique. The choice of analyst and of "conduit" (the word became an issue) were suggestive. As a White House fellow a couple of years before, Ramsden had critiqued a similar hardship plea. LTV had claimed that if their merger with Jones & Laughlin Steel was forbidden on antitrust grounds, LTV might go under. Ramsden allowed that LTV was probably right, and the merger stood. That result might have dictated the choice of Ramsden. But why get him though Flanigan? Although McLaren later said he did not know how to reach Ramsden, it was pointed out that a call from McLaren's secretary to Flanigan's would have solved the problem. It was McLaren who first called Flanigan a mere conduit, which term Flanigan embraced. But Flanigan was a high-powered operator, known as Nixon's "Mr. Fixit," no one's conduit; and he kept insinuating himself in the matter. For instance, McLaren never talked with Ramsden; Flanigan gave him his instructions, turning over Rohatyn's memo without identifying its self-serving source; and Flanigan received Ramsden's written report. That was another thing: Flanigan kept the report because McLaren was away when it was completed on May 17; when

McLaren returned, Flanigan carried it over and gave it to McLaren with Kleindienst looking on. Flanigan later called Kleindienst to relay Rohatyn's complaints over McLaren's settlement terms.

On June 17, 1971, McLaren told Kleindienst he was prepared to settle. ITT could keep Hartford. The two men immediately called Rohatyn, and negotiations started over terms.

On June 21 San Diego announced its bid for the Republican convention —and Bud James sent his check to Bob Wilson, although that was not announced until after the settlement, a circumstance many saw as suspicious. On June 23 the selection committee voted for San Diego over Miami, after a 3–3 tie was broken by a call from Nixon to the selection committee chairman, Senator Robert Dole.

On July 31 terms of the antitrust settlement were announced. To keep Hartford, ITT would divest Avis, Levitt, and Canteen, plus its two modest-sized insurance operations, and the fire protection part of Grinnell. In addition, for ten years ITT could not acquire any company whose assets were $100 million or over—$25 million if the company dominated its field—except subject to Justice review. This was not dissimilar to the settlement Ephraim Jacobs had proposed on ITT's behalf almost a year earlier.

On August 5, 1971, Sheraton's contribution of $100,000, with its challenge pledge of another $100,000, was made public.

The coincidence of events did not go unremarked. A member of Ralph Nader's group wrote to Kleindienst in September asking if they were connected. McLaren answered an emphatic no. In December, Lawrence F. O'-Brien, Democratic national chairman (whose Watergate office would be broken into next June) wrote with the same question and got the same reply, but from Kleindienst himself. Since both questioners had political axes to grind, no one paid attention.

John Mitchell was due to leave Justice on March 1, 1972, to become Nixon's second-term campaign manager. Kleindienst would replace him. On February 22 and 23 the Senate Committee on the Judiciary held nomination hearings. Although the more liberal Democrats were not thrilled, they concluded that a president should have the cabinet officers he wants, and the nomination was favorably reported to the full Senate by a unanimous 13–0. But before the Senate could act, everything changed.

Jack Anderson had been the assistant of Drew Pearson, proprietor of the syndicated newspaper column "The Washington Merry-Go-Round." On Pearson's death Anderson took over. His column for February 29, 1972, started off, "We now have evidence that the settlement of the Nixon administration's biggest antitrust case was privately arranged between Attorney General John Mitchell and the top lobbyist for the company involved." The company was ITT, the lobbyist Dita Beard. The evidence was her memo to Bill Merriam, dated June 25, 1971—just after McLaren's decision to settle, but before that decision was public and before the terms were thrashed out. The memo detailed Beard's understanding of ITT's San Diego pledge and reported on her discussion with Mitchell about an antitrust settlement when they met at a buffet in the governor's mansion after the Kentucky Derby on May 1, 1971. Anderson had obtained the original memo. His legman, Brit Hume, had interviewed Beard at her Washington office on February 23, then at her home the following night. She acknowledged both to Hume and later to Congressman Bob Wilson that the initial next to her typed name on the memo was her "own little 'd'."

The memo, headed "Subject: San Diego Convention," was devastating. Beard complained to Merriam about his phone conversation with a White House underling on the subject of ITT's commitment. They had "agreed very thoroughly," she thought, "that under no circumstances would anyone in this office discuss with anyone our participation in the Convention, including me." Only Mitchell, Haldeman, and Nixon (plus, of course, Lieutenant Governor Reinecke and Representative Wilson) were supposed to know "from whom that 400 thousand committment had come." She denied all knowledge, when asked, and so should everyone else in the Washington office. "John Mitchell has certainly kept it on the higher level only, we should be able to do the same." There was a question of whether the commitment was for "three hundred/four hundred thousand," but she advised that they all stay out of that, "other than the fact that I told you I had heard Hal up the original amount" (just as Wilson maintained). There was also confusion —which had occasioned the White House underling's call—as to how much of the commitment was to be in services and how much cash. Beard assured Merriam that, no matter what he and Ned Gerrity understood, it was not only services. "There would be very little cash, but certainly some."

Then came the crusher. "I am convinced, because of several conversations with Louie [Kentucky Governor Louis B. Nunn] re Mitchell that our noble committment has gone a long way toward our negotiations on the mergers eventually coming out as Hal wants them. Certainly the President has told Mitchell to see that things are worked out fairly. It is still only McLaren's mickey-mouse we are suffering."

She further complained: "We all know Hal and his big mouth! But this is one time he cannot tell you and Ned one thing and Wilson (and me) another!" Then she closed with another adjuration to keep quiet about ITT's commitment. "If it gets too much publicity, you can believe our negotiations with Justice will wind up shot down. Mitchell is definitely helping us, but cannot let it be known. Please destroy this, huh?"

On March 1 and 3 Anderson's column accused Kleindienst of telling "an outright lie about the Justice Department's sudden out of court settlement" of the case. He accused Mitchell of complicity and Justice and ITT of trying to lie their way out. Kleindienst immediately asked that his nomination hearing be reopened; he did not want to take office "under a cloud."

There were twenty-two days of hearings, beginning March 2, 1972, stretching to April 27, with 1,751 pages of testimony and exhibits. Of course, throughout, the senators did not know about *any* White House involvement except for Peter Flanigan's. And while it seemed improbable that so many high-placed people could be doing so much lying, if they were not lying, what happened simply made no sense.

The liberal Democrats on the committee plugged away. Birch Bayh of Indiana was the sharpest questioner when he was there, though during much of the hearing he was on a trip to Africa. John V. Tunney of California was a close second. Edward Kennedy of Massachusetts had fine staff work that give him penetrating initial questions to ask, but he often seemed inept, letting witnesses slip away. Philip Hart of Michigan sometimes joined in and was incisive. Sam J. Ervin, Jr., also joined in when testimony got implausible enough. The Republicans, except for Charles McC. Mathias, Jr., of Maryland, were obstructionist—Roman L. Hruska of Nebraska, Hiram L. Fong of Hawaii and Marlow W. Cook of Kentucky dimly so, Edward J. Gurney of Florida more cleverly. But the Republicans had a hard task, because the case they tried to defend did not hang together.

If there was no undue pressure, why had the Supreme Court appeal been postponed on April 19, 1971? Why was Flanigan so insistently *in* things? Why did Rohatyn keep talking to Kleindienst if—as Kleindienst swore—he had kept himself so severely out of McLaren's deliberations? Most of all, why McLaren's sudden decision to settle? As the minority report put it: "Basically, every reason given for the reversal of McLaren's previously steadfast refusal even to talk about a settlement allowing ITT to keep Hartford was either legally or equitably irrelevant, unsupported by any persuasive evidence, previously rejected, or contrary to fact."

McLaren drew a distinction between ITT's previous arguments for settlement and its final plea of hardship—with ripple effects. He said his decision relied on four things: Rohatyn's presentation; Ramsden's report ("which independently confirmed ITT's views"); the report of a Treasury official also at the presentation, which endorsed Rohatyn's claims; and on his own, twenty-five years of experience.

Rohatyn's presentation was self-serving. As Ramsden testified, "It was in no way based on any facts; it was in no way based on any analysis of data. It was basically unsubstantiated opinions. . . . " And Ramsden's own report? Without Hartford, ITT's stock would drop, its debt-equity ratio suffer, its borrowing power decline. There might be "some indirect negative effect" on ITT's balance-of-payments performance, and some cash flow problem, perhaps enough to cut the dividend. All unfortunate, none calamitous. As for the dreaded ripple effect on the market, Ramsden testified that his report "absolutely" did not even touch on it, and he did not believe there would be one; it was he who pointed out that IBM could harmlessly fluctuate a billion a day. The Treasury "report" was an even frailer reed—a hasty phone call from someone who had done no independent research and who said merely that Rohatyn's pitch *sounded* reasonable.

That left McLaren's experience. He must have known, right along, what divestiture would mean to a company and its stockholders. He had dismissed the hardship: "I thought that they made their bed," he testified, "they could lie in it." But that was before the picture Rohatyn had limned of divestiture's consequences. But all Rohatyn did, observed Senator Tunney, was raise "issues which would seem to have been obvious before the suit was ever filed." Anyway, this was Harold Geneen's ITT, not James Ling's LTV; it was not going belly-up, and McLaren's twenty-five years' experience surely told him that. On the other side of his experience, these cases were central to his theory of antitrust enforcement. He thought he was right and that his cause was just and vital. Would he really abandon it for such light reason—without pressure? It did not make sense.

Other themes, while fascinating, were peripheral. Surprisingly, since it occasioned the hearing and commanded so much time, attention, and theater, Dita Beard's memo was the most peripheral of all. But it was also the most entertaining. The story had everything. Beard disappeared for a time and was traced by the FBI to a hospital in Denver, where she languished at death's door (except for a remission long enough to allow a turn with Mike Wallace on TV's "60 Minutes") until the hearing was about over. She had been on a flight to a sudden vacation in West Yellowstone when she had collapsed on the plane and was brought to by a couple of pills and a restorative slug of whiskey. She had angina.

To check the memo's authenticity, White House aide Charles Colson dispatched E. Howard Hunt, who went to Denver, he wrote in his report, "wearing suitable physical disguise"—a red wig and heavy makeup. A small subcommittee also went to Denver to interview Beard on the same subject. Their session was cut short by her medical distress.

Dita Beard, flanked by doctors and a lawyer, testifying from her Denver hospital bed before a special subcommittee. Senator Cook is seated, facing camera; Kennedy is left, in profile; Tunney is right, back to camera.

The issue of authenticity was an afterthought, and nonsense. Beard told the subcommittee, and still insists, that she did not write the memo—at least as it appeared in Anderson's column. She could ascribe her earlier admissions of authorship only to confusion. The first paragraph of the memo seemed familiar: concern over the White House call, and keeping ITT's involvement quiet. She could have written that, she said, except for the last sentence about John Mitchell keeping it on a higher level. "I don't know," she told the subcommittee, "where in the world that mother came from." She could also have written the second paragraph, and the third, down to her assurance that some cash was involved in the ITT pledge. But from there on she could not *possibly* have written it. She would *never* put something like "Hal and his big mouth" in a memo. To be sure, she often said such things, but never in a *memo*. And she could not have written about Mitchell and the president and how the settlement was helped along by the pledge because she did not know any such thing.

That was true: she did not know. Her version of the post-Derby meeting with Mitchell varied greatly from his. She said he had harangued her about the intensity of ITT's pressure, but that she had pursued him and the subject of antitrust through the buffet line, and they eventually talked terms. Mitchell denied the harangue. He said it was the briefest of encounters; he simply told her to leave antitrust to the lawyers. With important qualifications, her version is more plausible. There certainly had been an exceptionable amount of pressure. However, when they met on May 1, Mitchell knew the case would be settled; why not pacify the woman by telling her that ITT would be treated fairly? And no reason not to mention terms. They were at issue, and although Mitchell and Beard had never met, she was well known, one of the top lobbyists in Washington. Mitchell might well conclude that she was capable of discussing terms.

All that being true, Mitchell would not have touched on Nixon's April 19 call to Kleindienst, or his own direct involvement. And he could not have discussed the influence of ITT's San Diego pledge when he and Beard met because the pledge had not yet been made. Furthermore, he would not have discussed it later with Governor Nunn—because Nixon's decisive intervention had already taken place, so the pledge could not have affected it.

Even so, that part of the memo was not spurious. It was written on June 25, after the pledge. Beard probably did not know that McLaren had agreed to settlement seven days before; it was not noised around the company; and of course he was no longer "mickey-mouse." Also, language of the memo suggests that a settlement was yet to come. But since Mitchell knew there would be one, and told her so, and she knew about the pledge, she would naturally assume there was some connection. The memo never said it was quid pro quo—just that Beard was "convinced" the pledge had helped. Of course we was. She was ITT's Washington dispenser of favors and speaking fees, arranger of rides in ITT planes and limousines for the powerful. One of ITT's other Washington lobbyists was a straight-arrow Mormon who took the legislative process seriously. Once, a Hartford executive asked him why a company would have both his kind of lobbyist and Beard's kind. Because, he said, there are two kinds of congressmen. The most sensible statement in the whole matter came from Senator Mathias, who wrote that he did not need Dita Beard to explain why "a corporate giant which must deal with some level of government every day" might make "a $400,000 commitment to a political party whose incumbent president is likely to be re-elected."

Why did Dita Beard write the memo? Her boss, Bill Merriam, could sit in the Metropolitan Club and talk about a sensitive ITT-White House contact loudly enough to be overheard at the next table. "Maybe," Merriam said, "I have a big mouth sometimes. . . . " His reaction to the memo crisis was to order wholesale shredding of papers in the Washington office. He explained that he got hundreds of memos across his desk each week. When asked if the shredded material included "such matters as are contained in the Anderson-Beard memorandum," Merriam answered, "Well, you would be surprised." Unable to leave bad enough alone, a few minutes later, asked if the shredding of embarrassing documents was company policy, he said it was when a memo like that was loose. But, observed Senator Ervin, he could not shred that one. "No," Merriam said, "That is right, but there might have been a lot of others in there like that."

Dita Beard despised Merriam and resented his being her boss. He, in turn, resented her: as Bob Wilson said to a reporter, "He's a busybody little guy and he resents Dita very much because she could get to Geneen and he couldn't, see?" She was Geneen's Egeria in Washington, and Merriam, who still did not know much about politics, resented it as he resented Beard's effectiveness. He got back by asserting his authority.

The day before the memo was written, Bill Merriam had been in the New York office. By coincidence, Bob Wilson had dropped by to see Geneen. Wilson and Merriam had talked about terms of the San Diego commitment, with Wilson finally saying, "Bill, look, you don't even know what you're talking about." Back in Washington, Merriam checked. When Merriam asked Beard about it, she tried to explain, but he kept insisting he did not understand; she should put it in a memo. That disgusted her. As she told the subcommittee, "I don't put anything in writing. . . . if it's important enough, you shouldn't, and if it is not important enough, why bother?" And here was Merriam, who could not understand the simplest matter, insistently telling her to put it in writing. Fine. Her memo would explain that she operated on a very high level indeed and that he was well advised to butt out, keep his mouth shut about things he did not understand, and *leave her be.* As for the authenticity question it was flapdoodle. As one ITT lawyer said, it had "nothing to do with whether or not what it says is true. . . . "

The true theme of the hearing—deceit—was not clear until afterward, when Watergate subpoenas evoked tapes and documents. There was much flat-out lying. John Mitchell, for example, said that the president "has never talked to me about any antitrust case that was in the Department." The tape of his April 21 conversation took care of that. Another Mitchell lie inspired lies from two minor figures, California's lieutenant governor, Ed Reinecke, and Edgar Gillenwaters, then California's director of commerce. The question was whether Mitchell knew about the ITT pledge before the settlement. We now know that it was a pointless issue; his intervention came before the pledge was made. But at the time it seemed of moment because Mitchell's line was to deny all knowledge of both the antitrust matter and convention arrangements. Unfortunately, Reinecke and Gillenwaters had truthfully told the press, right after Anderson's charges, that they had told Mitchell about the pledge in May. A call came to Reinecke's office from Mitchell's assistant, saying that Mitchell had consulted his calendar and showed no visit from Reinecke in May, but only in September. Reinecke immediately announced that he had confused spring with fall and indeed had not told Mitchell until September. Gillenwaters changed his story too. But both were stuck with their richly detailed press account of what they had told Mitchell. It was plainly a report on chances of the convention landing in San Diego, and the central role of ITT's pledge. Such a report was germane in May; it would be absurd in September, two months after San Diego had been selected. They did their best, but after pointing out the more glaring inconsistencies, Birch Bayh said, ". . . somebody is not telling the truth, or somebody is making a misstatement, and I have to say here just as one Senator, and I do not make this statement lightly, just listening to this conversation over the last couple of hours that your credibility has gone from 100 to damn near zero. . . . "

Gillenwaters smiled, and Bayh continued, " . . . if my impression is correct of what you have said both to the press and here under oath, you have committed perjury. . . . "

"Senator," Gillenwaters said, "if I smiled I am sorry. But if our credibility has gone to zero in your eyes then it must have shot up considerably elsewhere."

Dick Kleindienst's perjury, though, was the worst of the lot. He not only lied; he explained in exhaustive detail why he could not possibly be lying. There was the lie, direct:

SENATOR BAYH. No suggestions coming from the White House as to what action should be taken by the Justice Department?
MR. KLEINDIENST. No, sir.

There was the lie, serial—as when Kleindienst first swore he could not remember why the second appeal extension had been requested and, then, when his memory was "refreshed" about Judge Walsh's role, lied about that. There was the lie, knowing: " . . . there was no intervention by anybody, and I think that the record . . . that has been made before this committee, under oath, is abundantly clear on that point." There was also the lie, complete: " . . . as I have testified fully: In the discharge of my responsibilities as the

Acting Attorney General in these cases, I was not interfered with by anybody at the White House. I was not importuned; I was not pressured; I was not directed. I did not have conferences with respect to what I should or should not do. . . . " And there was the lie, circumstantial: "I would have had a vivid recollection if someone at the White House had called me up and said, 'Look, Kleindienst, this is the way we are going to handle that case.' People who know me, I don't think would talk to me that way, but if anybody did it would be a very sharp impact on my mind because I believe I know how I would have responded. . . . No such conversation occurred."

Kleindienst maintains that he understood the questions about White House interference to be "in the context of the White House staff." And, he says, "I never equated the President of the United States with the White House staff." Indeed, no one ever asked specifically whether Nixon had interfered; the questions were about interference from "anyone in the White House," or some such phrasing. "I was aware that I was walking a fine line," Kleindienst says. But he says he did not lie. "I'm a Christian, and I don't believe in taking my oath in God's name and violating it. I decided what I would do if I were asked a direct question, Did the president talk to you about ITT? I would refuse to answer, ask for a recess, then talk with him." And if Nixon refused permission to answer truthfully? "I would have withdrawn my nomination."

But Kleindienst also says that just before Nixon's call, Ehrlichman called with instructions "to drop the ITT cases." And Ehrlichman was White

Geneen after testifying at Kleindienst hearing.

House staff. Kleindienst might insist that Ehrlichman was merely speaking for Nixon—except that Kleindienst also is sure Ehrlichman was the one egging Nixon on in the matter. Ehrlichman says no, he was only following Nixon's orders—but that could go on forever. Richard Kleindienst lied under oath.

Geneen and most of his people were in a different position. They had broken no laws and had not obstructed justice; they had no need to protect present or proposed jobs or to curry favor by protecting their betters. Geneen could have set the tone and the line for his company and his people with a flat, honest exposition of his position: that ITT could make any contribution it wanted to a community trying to attract a convention; it was no bribe, and Beard did not know what she was talking about but was only trying to impress her boss and put him in his place; ITT had a right to petition government as often and as forcefully as they could for a redress of grievance; officials don't have to listen; and if any people objected to the intensity of Geneen's efforts for ITT, they should buy stock and vote against him as chairman. That would have been unanswerable in any way that could have hurt Geneen or ITT. The point was that they had done nothing wrong. They had applied all the pressure they could, but if there was wrongdoing, it was on the receiving end. If what they did was not illicit, they could not be blamed for trying; only the officials could be blamed if ITT succeeded.

Instead of being forthright, Geneen decided to pretend that nothing had happened. There had been no pressure, the memo was not real, the $400,000 did not exist, and the $100,000 was not ITT's but Sheraton's. He decided on a "PR" approach of bland denial, of maneuver and "cleverness." Again, Geneen's PR advisors needed good PR advice, though he did not see it that way; he was enjoying himself, "jousting," as Tim Dunleavy says. After Merriam testified, Geneen joked to aides, "Now I guess we'll have to acquire a company that makes paper-shredding machines." But then Geneen was more adept at obfuscation than his minions, so more relaxed. The others, in their testimony, weaseled and waffled, plainly uncomfortable. Information came from them not as assertions but as grudging admissions. They sounded shifty. It made ITT, which had done nothing wrong, seem guilty of something.

Those who were in fact guilty of specific violations did not come away too badly hurt. John Mitchell was never charged—perhaps because he already had his plate full with Watergate indictments. He was found guilty of one —obstructing justice and perjury—and went to jail. Dick Kleindienst was allowed to plead guilty to "refusing to testify" to a Senate committee. Even for a plea bargain, that was travesty. The hearing was called at his instance; he *insisted* on testifying, and his offense was specifically that he did testify, and lied. He was given a thirty-day sentence and a $100 fine, both suspended. The trial judge, George L. Hart, Jr., cited Kleindienst's hitherto blameless record and announced that his crime did not "reflect a mind bent on deception, but rather reflects a heart too loyal and considerate of the feelings of others."

Judge Hart must not have read the hearing transcript. Kleindienst was protecting his nomination as attorney general, which could not have been approved had the true story been known. As for his previous record, he simply had never before been brought to book. There was the Stewart case. Testimony showed that he had completely exonerated a United States attorney in San Diego when Kleindienst's own advisors accused the man of impropriety (others had accused him of worse); but the case was political, involving prominent Republican fund-raisers, including C. Arnholt Smith, one of Nixon's California patrons. Kleindienst also sat calmly, in another case, while someone offered him up to $100,000 as a donation to Nixon's campaign in exchange for intervention in a criminal case. Kleindienst did not call for the police; he did not even throw the fellow out of his office. He merely said that since the friend was already indicted, he could not help—and went on to discuss with the would-be briber possible appointments to a senator's staff. A week later, when Kleindienst discovered that the FBI was on the case, he decided it was a bribe, after all, and reported it.

Three of four Watergate prosecutors resigned in protest over the leniency shown Kleindienst. The Washington bar voted 4–3 to suspend him from practice for one month, although the three wanted to make it a year. The bar of his home state, Arizona, merely chided him.

They were less amiable next time. Arizona tried Kleindienst in 1981 for perjury in connection with a $23 million Teamsters' insurance deal. He claimed that he had been taken in by his client, "a convicted swindler and racketeer." The case involved Allen M. Dorfman, the convicted (later murdered) Teamster fixer. The jury acquitted Kleindienst. As one juror said, "The evidence didn't prove him guilty beyond a shadow of a doubt." Perhaps that was because the rules of evidence barred them from knowing that Kleindienst had charged his client $250,000 for five hours' work, half the fee split between a Washington PR man and a lobbyist. The Arizona Supreme Court set Kleindienst down for a whole year this time and made him pay $11,823 in costs. The United States Supreme Court barred him from further practice before it.

Ed Reinecke made a brilliant comeback. He was indicted for perjury, tried and found guilty, then sentenced to eighteen months, suspended. Some thought it very unfair that he was charged with a felony when his betters were let off with misdemeanors—especially since he had offered to testify against Mitchell in exchange for what he thought was immunity. But it all worked out with something like equity. Reinecke tried everything to beat the rap: claims that he had not been read his rights; offers of proof by a semanticist that the questions he was asked were unclear, and by an internist that his night flight from California to testify had disoriented him; a testimonial from Washington Redskins football coach George Allen to his "honesty and truthfulness."

Reinecke was sentenced on October 22, 1974. Early in 1975 he was a voting delegate at his party's state convention. His conviction was overturned later that year on the kind of grounds that doubtless make many of Reinecke's friends bombinate against pointy-headed judges. It seemed the Senate had not published a rule declaring one senator a quorum for the purpose of taking testimony—a procedural error. In 1983 Reinecke moved up from vice chairman to chairman of his state party. No one else was indicted, although Peter Flanigan's nomination as ambassador to Spain was blocked because of his involvement.

In December of 1972 Dick McLaren was elevated to the federal bench. He was cleared by Judge Walsh's committee in one day—not only the record, but an unheard-of celerity. Since he was from Illinois and would sit in that district court, Senator Charles Percy was his sponsor. The complaisance of the other Illinois senator was necessary, especially for so unusually fast a proceeding, and Adlai E. Stevenson, Jr., went along—later charging he had been lied to about the need for speed. Percy explained, and the explanation seemed to satisfy Stevenson. McLaren was already terminally ill, and he died not long afterward. That saved him from indictment.

Senator Hart was speaking about one particular episode in the hearing, but what he said is epigraph for the entire affair: "We are just one more chapter in this loaded story of why people lack faith in the system." For Geneen and ITT that remark would have ominous significance a year later.

19

Really a Painful Sight

Bill Merriam was not very thorough in feeding the shredding machine.

The Kleindienst hearing was in recess on March 21, 1972, when Jack Anderson struck again. On March 21 and 22 he published another series of memos from ITT's Washington files. These suggested that ITT had joined with the CIA during the 1970 elections in Chile to keep socialist Salvador Allende Gossens from the presidency. The main tactic was to be creation of economic chaos in Chile, leading to a military coup, and there was hint of cooperation by other American businesses. Whatever the truth of the memos, Allende was elected and at the time of Anderson's column was still president of Chile.

These memos, or ones like them, had been kicking around Washington since 1970. No one paid much attention. But now, with so much hullaballoo about ITT impropriety in *Kleindienst*, the Senate Foreign Relations Committee, chaired by J. William Fulbright of Arkansas, announced that a subcommittee would investigate the role of multinational corporations in United States foreign policy. With so many political overtones, though, a hearing would not be held until after the 1972 presidential election. In fact it started almost exactly a year after Anderson's column, running from March 20, 1973, in seven day-long sessions, to April 2—with Watergate raging.

Chile was much pithier than *Kleindienst* because the issues were clearer, and because of the subcommittee's makeup. Although Fulbright often sat in, there were only five regular members: Democrats were chairman Frank Church of Idaho, Stuart Symington of Missouri, and Edmund D. Muskie of Maine; the Republicans were Clifford P. Case of New Jersey and—coincidentally—Charles Percy. All were sharp; there was little posturing or meandering. Moreover, the Republicans were quite as interested as the Democrats in winkling out the truth rather than defending the administration. Percy sometimes lobbed soft questions, inviting witnesses to justify their activities, but he was never obstructionist or windy, and was often incisive.

As theater, one similarity with *Kleindienst* was striking: witnesses had the same interesting problem of having to deny or explain away what seemed manifest from subpoenaed documents. For instance, one memo was an unmistakable statement of collaboration between ITT and the CIA to implement a policy that was clearly spelled out. It was Bill Merriam's report to John McCone of Merriam's lunch with a CIA man. Merriam wrote that "[a]pproaches continue to be made to select members of the [Chilean] Armed Forces in an attempt to have them lead some sort of uprising—no success to date." At the hearing, Senator Muskie said to Merriam, "I think the burden of proof is on you and ITT to discount that implication, and you have not done it." Merriam replied, "Well, it is very difficult for me to do it." And Senator Church commented, "I should think it would be because it is right there on paper. [Laughter.] If words mean anything at all, it is right there on paper."

Such explicitness was a problem for minds more agile than Merriam's. Another ITT man wrote a memo proposing "a more active part during the preelection period to assure the defeat of Allende." He deplored the United States government's lack of zeal: "Why can't the fight be continued now that the battle is in the homestretch and the enemy is more clearly identifiable?" He recommended eighteen steps, including the cutting off of all aid and bank credit to Chile, not buying their copper or any other exports, and refusing to sell them strategic items. When asked if that was not a proposal to disrupt the economy of Chile, he said, "Not at all, Senator, I did not say that." But, said Church, "What other results could your recommendations have had . . . except to disrupt the economy?"

Those memos seemed clear. But the entire story of what happened in Chile and in Washington, as it emerged from documents and testimony, was so confused and contradictory that the denials and explanations left the central issue uncertain. Maybe it *was* all talk and no action; maybe neither the CIA nor ITT *did* interfere in Chile's election. There were too many bits of information missing, and unlike *Kleindienst*, where the one big fact of Nixon's phone call blew the case open, *Chile* remained a mystery until a series of small facts emerged, some as late as 1981.

The truly great difference between the cases made all the difference to Geneen and ITT. What had happened in Chile involved more than just corporate profit. At stake were people's lives and a country's liberty. So the atmosphere of this hearing was grim, the possible consequences for ITT devastating. Geneen did not enjoy himself this time; he was not jousting, he was struggling.

In Chile, presidential elections were held every six years, with a constitutional prohibition against anyone's serving consecutive terms. In 1964

Eduardo Frei had become president, leading his newly formed Christian Democratic Party (PDC). It was politically centrist, in favor of tax and land reform and the gradual nationalization of key industries like copper and communications by negotiated, compensated buy-outs; Frei called it "Chileanization." The 1970 PDC candidate was Radomiro Tomic Romero. The candidate of the left—a coalition of Socialist and Communist parties called Popular Unity (UP)—was Allende; he was for immediate nationalization of industry, utilities, and banks, with some undefined compensation, surely less generous than the PDC contemplated. The right-wing National Party candidate was Jorge Alessandri Rodriguez; he was for free enterprise. The election was scheduled for September 4, 1970. If no one won over 50% of the vote, Chile's congress would elect one of the two front-runners on October 24.

The story as it came out at the hearing made no sense. ITT's man in Washington had reported that the State Department thought the election too close to call. Yet ITT's man in Santiago, Chile, cabled that "most reliable indicators" showed Alessandri winning with 40% of the vote or more. Where was he getting his information? In any case, Geneen was concerned. When he and his people besieged the administration to get relief from McLaren's antitrust suits (all filed by August 1970), one theme was the danger ITT ran of expropriation abroad, especially in Chile, making the need for a strong domestic base the more acute. Geneen naturally told ITT director John McCone of his concern. Starting in May 1970 McCone talked with the then CIA director, Richard Helms, relaying to Geneen the disappointing news that the United States was not supporting any Chilean candidate. Helms did, though, arrange for Geneen to meet with a CIA official to discuss the situation. Both sides said the purpose of the meeting was a simple exchange of views; but in that case the choice of CIA representative was odd. On the night of July 16, in the ITT suite at the Sheraton-Carlton in Washington, Geneen met with William V. Broe, chief of clandestine services, Western Hemisphere. Geneen took the occasion to offer "a substantial fund" to the CIA to back Alessandri. One commentator observed that offering money to the CIA was bringing coals to Newcastle. Another wondered if Geneen really thought the CIA had a cash-flow problem. Broe turned down the offer, again on grounds that the United States was not backing a candidate. The meeting lasted less than an hour. On July 27 Broe made a quick phone call to Geneen. The chief of clandestine services testified that he was simply giving a news update.

On September 4, 1970, Allende won by 39,338 votes out of nearly 3 million cast, about 1% ahead of Alessandri. But since he had only 36.3% of the total, election was now up to congress, and ITT's man in Santiago reported that Tomic and Allende had made a secret deal that whichever finished ahead would get the other's support. Between them, their parties had about 155 congressional seats to about 40 for Alessandri's party, so it seemed inevitable that on October 24, 1970, an avowed Marxist, breathing expropriation, would become president. The prospect galvanized Geneen.

Salvador Allende at the United Nations accusing ITT
of fomenting civil war in Chile.

There seemed only one hope. ITT's man in Santiago reported talk of a plan to have congress vote for Alessandri, who would immediately resign, forcing a new election in which Frei would again be eligible to run since he would be succeeding Alessandri, not himself. Polls showed that Frei would easily beat Allende, head to head. This was called the Frei gambit by a later Senate staff, the Alessandri formula by most people, and the Rube Goldberg gambit by the United States ambassador to Chile, Edward M. Korry, who nevertheless favored it. The Alessandri formula ran against custom, but it was entirely constitutional.

Right after the September 9 ITT board meeting, Geneen told McCone that ITT would spend up to a million dollars to back any United States government plan for forming a stop-Allende coalition. McCone took the offer to Richard Helms and to Henry A. Kissinger, then Nixon's national security advisor. Oddly enough, having started at the top of the CIA and National Security Council (NSC), Geneen also had Jack Neal of ITT's Washington office tell Kissinger's assistant, Viron P. Vaky, of the million-dollar offer. Then, even more oddly, Neal called Charles A. Meyer, assistant secretary of state for Latin American affairs, never mentioning money, just offering State any assistance they might need from ITT. There was no response by anyone to these handsome offers. Yet on September 17 Geneen got the cheering news that the United States was going to do something after all. Or was it? A

September 17 cable from ITT's men in Santiago insisted that the "big push" had begun: "Late Tuesday night (September 15) Ambassador Edward Korry finally received a message from State Department giving him the green light to move in the name of President Nixon. The message gave him maximum authority to do all possible—short of a Dominican Republic-type action—to keep Allende from taking power." It then described an interview that an ITT agent had with Arturo Matte Larrain, Alessandri's brother-in-law and political mentor. It concluded with the happy assurance that "The leader we thought was missing is right there in the saddle (Frei), but he won't move unless he is provided with a constitutional threat." Of course, "That threat must be provided one way or another through provocation." That seemed clear enough. But at the hearing Ambassador Korry flatly denied getting any such message. There was no green light, no plot, no offers of help to the military, no provocation.

One of the ITT men who had sent the cable, Harold V. Hendrix, now crawfished. He had gotten the information, he testified, from a well-connected Chilean—not anyone in the embassy or having to do with the United States government. They were chatting in a coffee bar near the presidential palace, and the Chilean had not been quite so specific as the cable sounded. He had merely announced that a message had come to the ambassador from a source *"muy alto"* and it had been *"muy duro."* A very hard message from a very high source obviously could only be orders from Nixon to block Allende's accession to the presidency by any means short of calling in the marines.

On September 22 Geneen was in Brussels vetting European business plans (throughout all this, along with the antitrust fights, Geneen continued minding the store). Ned Gerrity, in addition to PR, was in charge of "intelligence" and lobbying, including the Washington office and ITT's men in Santiago. He now sent Geneen a memo saying that Bill Merriam had met with the CIA's Broe and had reviewed the actions suggested in the September "green light" cable. "It is clear," he wrote, "that the strategy outlined in the Hendrix memorandum is the best course to be followed." Broe had "suggested that all possible pressures be exerted." All this should have delighted Geneen's activist heart. At last, with Chile's run-off election barely a month away, someone was doing something. Events now moved from the odd to the bizarre.

Geneen had told Broe that in his absence Ned Gerrity was the man to see. On September 29, Geneen still in Brussels, Broe paid a call. Now the government did have a plan. Certain steps were already being taken, but he needed additional help to induce Chile's economic collapse. It was a five-part plan: banks should not renew credits, or at least should delay them; companies should be slow to deliver spare parts; Chilean savings and loan institutions, in trouble anyway, should be driven to the wall; all companies (ITT especially) should withdraw all technical help; where possible they should pull out. Broe gave Gerrity a list of companies whose assistance ITT might enlist. "I thought," says Gerrity, "the guy was wacko. Of course I didn't say that in the cable to Geneen." But Gerrity did seem to go pretty far out on a limb.

He wrote, "The idea [Broe presented,] and with which I do not necessarily agree, is to apply economic pressure. . . . " The stupefying thing was that Geneen agreed that the Broe plan was "not workable." ITT would pass.

How could that be? Geneen would spend a million dollars in aid of the Alessandri formula or any United States plan to stop Allende; his own agents assured him that only provocation was lacking; the CIA says, Here is a plan to provide what is needed. Will you help?—and Geneen says no. To make it the more unbelievable, immediately after Geneen's turn-down, Merriam reported to McCone that the word was still to keep the pressure on. One year later ITT would urge the eighteen-point economic-collapse scheme that was merely an elaboration on Broe's.

In Chile, action was clearer: there was murder. The chief of the army, General René Schneider Chereau, was a strict constitutionalist, determined to keep order and guarantee orderly succession. He announced that the army would back any decision by congress, and he threatened to shoot one general who was talking coup. Two days before the October 24 election he was assassinated by right-wing terrorists. Nevertheless, Allende was overwhelmingly elected and was installed as president on November 4, 1970.

From then on, ITT developed schizophrenia about the Allende government. And events seemed to justify the malady. In March 1971 ITT had a meeting with Allende. Tim Dunleavy was there with John Guilfoyle, ITT's group executive for Latin America, and Benjamin W. Holmes—a native Chilean, a friend of Allende's, and (at age seventy-one) long-time head of the phone company, Chiltelco. It was a very jolly meeting. They sparred a bit over some Chiltelco debt. Dunleavy said, "Mr. President, a telephone [company] is like a woman, no matter how much money you give her, she's always asking for more." He confided that no matter how much money he made, "[M]y wife manages to spend it." After guffaws all around, Allende said, "It's not like that here in Chile." Dunleavy said then maybe he should take out citizenship, and Allende, grinning, went to his desk and offered Dunleavy what he said were the necessary papers. "We all laughed," Dunleavy recalls. Best of all, Allende told his visitors he did not want to expropriate Chiltelco. He also told them about a telephone device he had invented, which Dunleavy promised ITT would look at, and when Allende spoke of his worry about phone taps and bugs, Dunleavy offered some scanning equipment, which the president accepted.

On May 26 Allende called Benny Holmes to his office and informed the Chiltelco manager that Chile would nationalize the company after all. Now the only issue was how much Chile would pay, and ITT's schizophrenia became pronounced. On one hand, they were considering the strategy that had worked for them in Peru. "Briefly," wrote Ned Gerrity to Geneen, "our thought is that we might suggest strongly to Allende that he make an agreement with us on the best possible terms" so that when taking over other companies, "he will be able to point to a satisfactory arrangement with us" —and pay less for the others, claiming ITT was the norm, the others exceptional. On the other hand, ITT memos regularly bemoaned the lack of other companies' cooperation in anti-Allende efforts. Senator Church remarked, thinking of the Peru strategy, "I can see why you did not get very much cooperation from other companies." Other ITT memos were downright bloodthirsty calls for the United States to cut off all aid to Chile.

Throughout the summer of 1971 Allende put the squeeze on Chiltelco. On September 29, 1971, he formally "intervened" in the company, appointing a government overseer. ITT's last Latin American phone company had been expropriated. The corporation claimed their share of Chiltelco was worth $153 million, $92.5 million of it covered by United States government insurance, for which ITT promptly made claim. Allende offered $24 million compensation and was indignantly turned down.

Geneen continued to look hopefully for signs that the Chilean economy was cracking and that Allende might be overthrown. In December 1971 Gerrity wrote to him, "A serious confrontation is predicted before mid-1972 by even the most cautious observers. Many Chile-watchers forecast a showdown by March 1972." It came—but in Jack Anderson's column, not Santiago. In April, Allende said, "[N]o one can dream we are going to pay even half a cent to this multinational company which was on the verge of plunging Chile into civil war."

That was the story as it publicly unfolded—with offers of money to the government, marching up the hill with the CIA, and then marching down again. It made no sense. ITT witnesses tried to explain it all away. On the subject of that talk with Alessandri's brother-in-law, Matte, for instance, ITT's Robert Berrellez wrote in his report, "At the end when it was mentioned we were, as always, ready to contribute with what was necessary, [Matte] said we would be advised." Surely, said the subcommittee lawyer, that meant "if money or anything else is needed you—presumably speaking on behalf of ITT—are ready to contribute whatever is needed." Oh no! In Spanish it was just a graceful assurance of being at his service. "It means," said Senator Church, "the same thing in Spanish as in English." And talk about how "everything should be done quietly but effectively to see that Allende does not get through the crucial next six months"? How ITT had been "trying unsuccessfully to get other American companies aroused . . . and join us in pre-election efforts"? It was just talk, not policy. "This must clearly be understood," said John McCone, "that this is differentiation between staff thinking and policy determinations." That is what staffs are for, "to think up alternatives, and then that is why you have bosses to make the decisions."

How about the bosses? Ned Gerrity, as senior VP, said that the million dollars offered to Helms and Kissinger was not calculated to block Allende. It would demonstrate to Allende ITT's "confidence in Chile." He quoted Geneen as saying, "I think we should go to the State Department and see if they have any kind of a plan to encourage private enterprise, do something in an extraordinary fashion at this point in time, to reassure Mr. Allende." (Of course, the offer was never made to State; it was made to the heads of the CIA and NSC.)

> MR. GERRITY. . . . and he talked about low-cost housing, he talked about some ideas he had on a farming program, he talked about—
> SENATOR CHURCH. Mr. Gerrity—
> MR. GERRITY. Senator.
> SENATOR CHURCH. [continuing]. How many houses would $1 million build?

One million for "constructive purposes" would not go far; 1.4 *billion* in aid during Frei's administration had not stopped Allende's election. But one million "is a very significant amount of money," said Church, "if it goes to finance covert political activity. . . ."

Gerrity could have saved his breath. Geneen had a better feel for what the subcommittee might swallow. When asked "for the record" if he claimed he had told Gerrity to pass on the word that the million was "for low-cost housing or technical assistance in agriculture," Geneen said, "No, I do not."

Predictably, Geneen did the best job of explaining away. Regarding the offer to Broe to "assemble a substantial fund" to back Alessandri—which Broe had already sworn to, making denial impolitic—Green said he could not remember that part of the conversation, and that since he had "no recollection to the contrary," he accepted it. Church tried to pin him down: did that mean Broe's version was accurate?

> MR. GENEEN. In think I previously testified to the committee that I did not have any independent recollection of this subject. I said that I felt that I may well have . . . from the shock of recognizing that, you might say, our Chilean investment was going down the drain, I might well have come back and said, "Can we?" in effect.
>
> I think it is clear that we are not talking about candidates, we are talking about what appears to be a reversal of the U.S. policy for many years down there . . . which is the basis on which we had been encouraged by five administrations to invest and go into Chile and my concern is one of help basically.
>
> Now, I have never talked to anybody before or afterward [about raising the fund] so I don't know what I would have been assembling, and I didn't mention any amount, so it is my reaction and conjecture that what I was really saying I was willing to work if it would help as against a policy problem as it appears to me.
>
> Mr. Broe . . . said it was not the Government policy and it died right there and I might add if I had given it more serious consideration I might have rejected it myself. But I thought of it, if I would place myself in the role probably of saying can I help, and it died right there as not being Government policy.

In effect he managed to admit making the offer while denying that the offer was real. He never let anyone bring up the subject without following his obligatory "acceptance" of Broe's story with insistence that it "rose and died right there as not being within any Government policy and that was the end of it." He never let the questioner define the area of his answer; he always brought the question around to his own view of matters. In the United States, for instance, political contributions by corporations are illegal. Senator Percy asked if they were also illegal in Chile. Geneen said he understood they were not—which was correct—"but we did not make a political contribution." All right, said Percy, even if legal, are they a "legitimate action" for a multinational in a foreign country?

> MR. GENEEN. We have not done it as a matter of policy and I raised the question only in terms of, as I said, in my reaction to Mr. Broe and it died there and I said I further thought I might have rejected it myself. If we had done that in theory it would have been within the U.S. policy. As it turned out it was not and it died then.

Did that mean he figured such a contribution would be all right if made as part of a government plan?

> MR. GENEEN. . . . I think our major concern was more one of what was happening and what appeared to be a reversal of a long term U.S. policy. And I think our main thought would have been, as I expressed it, and the only way I can construe it, can we help in any way in this matter.
> I don't think there was any question involved of candidates or anything else in the real primary sense of the problem.

Any time a question cut too close to the knuckle, Geneen's answer could be pure gibberish. He had been insisting that ITT always followed a policy of strict neutrality in the politics of host countries. Senator Church observed that he had "certainly violated your neutrality policy the first time you talked with Mr. Broe" and offered money to back Alessandri. Geneen said, "Two things: First, I think Mr. Broe was referring in the country, as I understood it, and second as I have said I think this was basically a question of, you might say, U.S. Government level at that time and that was my reaction." Enough answers like that and the most dogged questioner will give up. Geneen had testified most of the morning and all of the afternoon, and not long after that exchange, the hearings closed.

Church said that "it is obvious . . . somebody is lying. We must take a very serious view of perjury under oath." He also said, "It is a question of plausibility. You know we can only go so far in our capacity—" And Senator Fulbright interrupted, "For accepting fairy tales." But which were fairy tales? Who was telling them? Above all, why? The subcommittee did not know, and the last relevant pieces of information did not surface until 1981.

The first break, however, came on September 8, 1974, a month after

Richard Nixon resigned the presidency, fifteen months after the Chile hearings closed. In Chile, meanwhile, a declining economy, strikes, and food shortages had culminated in a bloody coup on September 11, 1973. It was led by the army chief, Augusto Pinochet Urgate, once Allende's supporter. Allende was murdered (or committed suicide) in the coup, and Pinochet instituted a savagely repressive dictatorship. So what had happened in Chile was of newly sensitive importance.

Richard Helms had left the CIA and was ambassador to Iran. The new director was William Colby. In April 1974 Colby testified before the House Armed Services Committee. Although the session was classified, any congressman may read any testimony before any congressional committee, and Michael Harrington of New York read Colby's testimony, then wrote a letter about it to the chairman of the House Foreign Relations Committee. The letter was leaked to Seymour M. Hersh of the *New York Times*. Hersh's September 8, 1974, story revealed that the CIA had spent at least $8 million between 1970 and 1973 trying to keep Allende from becoming president—and when that did not work, to keep him from being able to govern.

In the post-Watergate atmosphere of full disclosure, Nixon's successor, Gerald Ford, acknowledged the truth of Harrington's letter: $500,000 had gone to fund Allende's opponents before the election, another $500,000 during the election. When the Alessandri formula was projected, another $350,000 was set aside, though never used, to bribe Chilean congressmen. After enough further revelations in succeeding years, the reason for seeming contradictions in the hearings became clear. For instance, to see how Geneen's offer to Broe and his later turn-down of Broe's request for ITT help both made sense, you had to know what role the United States had played in the 1964 Chilean election when Eduardo Frei swept into office. The election was unusual on its face because Frei won 55.7% of the vote. In multiparty Chile, a plurality, not a majority, was expected. In 1958 Alessandri had won a four-way race, his margin over the runner-up less than 3%. That runner-up was Allende, who would probably have won if there had been only three candidates, since a left-wing priest had siphoned 3.3% of the votes away from Allende.

When John Kennedy became president in 1960 he was determined to help bring social justice to Latin America. Frei was Kennedy's kind of candidate, a moderate leftist, his Christian Democrats moderate reformers. Frei's Chile would inspire the rest of Latin America. In the 1962 congressional election the PDC became Chile's largest party, but Kennedy would risk no mischances. He ordered the CIA to funnel money into Frei's 1964 campaign (reportedly without Frei's involvement—although that seems unlikely, since over half the campaign was CIA-funded). The CIA also ran their own propaganda campaign to scare Chileans about a Marxist victory. With Ford's revelation, the CIA admitted to having spent some $3 million in 1964; Ed Korry, United States ambassador to Chile from 1967 to 1971, charged that it was $20 million. It was enough.

But it probably was not all that was spent. In 1963 Kennedy persuaded David Rockefeller to form a group of businesses that would invest in Latin America. Called the Business Group for Latin America (changed in 1970 to the Council of the Americas), its members included 210 companies representing 85% of all United States private investment in Latin America. In return, Kennedy had the Agency for International Development (AID) insure Council members against expropriation.

Frei was not a candidate Council members would instinctively cherish. While his Chileanization meant complete compensation, it also meant an end to lush profit opportunities. But he was the candidate Kennedy was pushing, and the Council supposedly offered $1.5 million to the CIA to spend for the 1964 election. John McCone, then CIA director, supposedly turned down the offer.

Reports of both the offer and the turn-down were probably red herrings. "Corporations never offer money to the government," says Ed Korry. "They offer to spend on their own." All they ask is direction as to plans and perhaps guidance or help in getting the money where it will do the most good. "In 'sixty-four," says Korry, "whatever they're saying, they *spent* the money."

Geneen knew all about it; he was on the Council's executive committee. He kept nibbling at the issue in his testimony, saying things like, "Now, I am sure, without knowing any details, that the Government seemed to take a very broad interest in the 1964 election. . . . " Perhaps he was hinting that they had better leave off or he would blow the whistle. But things had changed since 1964. The PDC had declined in favor in Chile, and so had Frei. His reforms were too pallid to satisfy many Chileans yet had gone too far to suit the Chilean oligarchs or the Council. Kennedy and his successor, Lyndon Johnson, had poured in about $1.4 billion of aid, but according to a United States congressional study, a shocking amount of it had ended up in the hands of Chilean bankers and their friends. Chile was in a mess.

When Richard Nixon became president in 1969, United States policy shifted. "Trade not aid" was the motto; and no more favoring the "democratic left." In fact, there were no early plans to back anyone. The group that coordinated such decisions was the 40 Committee, comprised of State, the Joint Chiefs, CIA, NSC, Justice, and Defense. It was dominated by Henry Kissinger.

The CIA station chief in Santiago, Henry D. Hecksher, wanted to support Alessandri. Korry would not hear of it; Allesandri, he said, was purely "the candidate of the rich." The United States should not back any candidate, he thought; the Chileans should elect their own president. On the other hand, it should not be Allende. Korry was a firm anti-Communist, having witnessed the take over of Eastern Europe as a newsman, and Hecksher easily persuaded him that the United States should at least work against the Marxist. Together, they proposed to the 40 Committee a "spoiling operation," akin to the scare campaign of 1964. Although State was leery of even that much interference, the spoiling operation was approved on March 25, 1970. A total of $425,000 would fund it.

That was not good enough for the Council of the Americas, who wanted Alessandri. On April 10, a group of them told Charles Meyer, a one-time Sears, Roebuck executive who had gotten his State job through the influence of David Rockefeller, that they would spend up to $500,000 for their man. Ed Korry learned of the offer and shot off an angry, denunciatory cable about allowing United States business to get involved, especially on behalf of the oligarchs' candidate. State said no to the Council.

Alessandri and his National Party needed money, and in July 1970 a CIA officer—probably station chief Hecksher—told ITT's Hal Hendrix about Alessandri's need. Hendrix relayed the information to New York, Geneen talked to McCone, McCone to Helms, and Helms dispatched Broe to meet with Geneen in Washington. There never was a direct offer of money to the CIA, no coals to Newcastle. Possibly Geneen asked if the CIA would deliver ITT's contribution and was turned down. But the purpose of the meeting, as a later congressional investigation showed, was to let Geneen know how to get the money to Alessandri (it was through Matte) and to the National Party (that may have been the subject of the short phone call on July 27). As Geneen later admitted, ITT followed the CIA's guidance and gave at least $250,000 to Alessandri and $100,000 to the party. This was matched by about the same amount from members of the Council.

Was the CIA acting on its own? Or—more likely, in light of the next development—was this Nixon's and Kissinger's way around a fight with State over backing Alessandri? This mystery remains.

After Allende's plurality in the September election, Geneen became really worked up. So much for the government's (relative) hands-off policy; now it was time for action. And now Geneen's million-dollar offer makes sense. It was not an offer so much as a proposal to spend that sum himself. It was made through McCone, who knew the CIA neither needed nor accepted contributions; and it was made to the head of the CIA and head of the NSC, not to State. Geneen assumed the CIA would guide him in placing the money to defeat Allende in the congressional run-off, as they had in the popular election, regardless of official United States policy. He was just upping the ante to match the parlousness of the situation. He did not have to spend the money, though, because government policy secretly changed.

Ed Korry was all for the Alessandri formula, however Rube Goldberg-ish. Korry was certain that Allende contemplated the end of further free elections: slowly, by constitutional means, Allende would wreck the constitution. On September 12 Korry was summoned to Valparaiso, where Frei had invited a State Department visitor. Korry wrote a cable that was the vehicle for Frei's plea to Nixon to "publicize" the fact that, as Frei said, the odds were fifty to one that Allende would turn Chile into another Cuba. Korry's cable reached Nixon on the twelfth. On September 8 and 14 the 40 Committee discussed Chile and authorized money to influence the coming run-off election. This support for the Alessandri formula was called "Track I." On the morning of September 15 a different sort of meeting convened. Augustin Edwards was Chile's premier oligarch. He owned the right-wing *El Mercurio* chain of newspapers; he also held the local Pepsi-Cola franchise. The head of PepsiCo, Donald M. Kendall, old friend of Nixon's, arranged a September 15 breakfast for Edwards with Kissinger and Attorney General John Mitchell so Edwards could warn them of approaching disaster in Chile. Kissinger was already convinced. The previous June he had told the 40 Committee, "I don't see why we have to let a country go Marxist just because its people are irresponsible"—the right and center unwilling to submerge differences that, to Kissinger, were nothing compared with a possible Allende victory.

Later on the fifteenth, Nixon called in Helms and, according to an investigation report, "instructed the CIA to play a direct role in organizing a military coup d'etat in Chile to prevent Allende's accession to the presidency." The word immediately went out to CIA station chief Hecksher. This was "Track II." Part of the strategy for fomenting a coup was summarized in Helms's notes of the meeting: "make the economy scream."

Korry would have screamed too if he had known about Track II. He was not told (another Helms note was "no involvement of embassy"); nor were State or the other 40 Committee members. But ITT's Hendrix and Berrellez did not know that. When someone in Augustin Edwards's organization told them about the plan, they assumed the United States ambassador must know. They could not find out directly, because they were then barred from the embassy. Immediately after the September 4 election Korry had gotten a call from Peter Jones, son of Korry's boss from his United Press days. Jones was an ITT regional VP based in Buenos Aires. His interest in politics was high, and part of his job was to prepare a quarterly assessment of political-economic developments throughout ITT's operations areas in Latin America. Now, on an open phone line, Jones asked Korry if it was all right to come to Santiago to assess the probable effect of the unfortunate election results. Korry was appalled at this kind of talk on a possibly tapped line—and at the idea of an ITT executive rushing into so volatile a situation. He told Jones to stay put, then sent for Berrellez and—first extracting a promise that Berrellez would not report the incident to New York—berated him for such foolishness. Soon, Korry got a letter from Jones: within an hour of their phone call, New York had called telling Jones not to meddle in Chile; Ned Gerrity's department was handling it. Korry now called in both Berrellez and Hendrix. It seemed the two had their knives out for Jones and must have had his phone tapped. What of Berrellez's promise? He had made it without reflection. Korry said to them, "As far as I'm concerned, you're a piece of shit, and I'm going to make certain that you never walk into this office again as long as I'm here." They could scarcely report that Geneen's men in Santiago were not allowed in the embassy, so they did not know, just then, what the ambassador did or did not know. Hence the "green light" memo.

With these facts revealed, the rest—for example, Geneen's turn-down of Broe's plea for help—is clear. The Chilean military, especially General Schneider, took a less lighthearted view of constitutional democracy than did Nixon or Kissinger. Besides, Allende was courting the military. They had starved under Frei, who at Kennedy's urging had put money into butter (after the oligarchs had skimmed the cream) rather than guns. Allende promised the military that their budget would soar. So a coup would be very hard to generate, especially before October 24. Helms needed all the help he could get. If he really could make the economy scream, though, it might propel the military along Track II; at worst, it might improve chances for Track I. And since ITT had been stridently for intervention, naturally Broe was sent to enlist Geneen on September 29. ITT could do much itself to ruin Chile's economy and could help line up other companies. But Gerrity was right: the plan was Wucku a desperation move. No wonder Geneen said no. A military coup would not bother him. But if the economy were wrecked, what would become of ITT's businesses there? How would that save them? Anyway, as he and Gerrity agreed, with under four weeks to go, the plan truly was not "workable." That did not mean Geneen was giving up. Merriam was right when he told McCone they were still keeping pressure on Washington. It was for a *real* Track II—wholesale bribery, or some sensible way to stage a coup.

ITT's seeming schizophrenia after Allende's installation now also makes sense. Bellicose talk in Washington could not hurt; maybe the government could still do something. Anyway, the danger of foreign expropriation was Geneen's main argument against antitrust; what better way to dramatize it? On the other hand, Geneen sincerely thought he could negotiate with Allende. The bloody coup, Pinochet's frightfulness, and Allende's death martyred Allende, a process that effaces flaws of character and policy. Actually, Allende was vain, frivolous, pretentious, and corrupt. The ideologues in his own party despised him; he was likely the only Marxist-Leninist ever to retain membership in a Masonic lodge. He had extremely expensive tastes, so he and much of his administration, as a State Department desk man put it, "were on the suck." Allende had established a five-man constitutional tribunal as a way around the Chilean Supreme Court in his nationalization moves. Two members were from the court, two were government appointees, and the swing vote was an old friend, Jacobo Schaulsohn. ITT put Schaulsohn on the payroll as a "consultant"—along with a member of Allende's copper board. These were the kinds of dealings and people Geneen was used to in Latin America. Especially after Dunleavy's affable March 1971 meeting, Geneen must have been flabbergasted when Allende announced expropriation and went ahead with it in September 1971.

After that, ITT's espousal of the eighteen steps—the very pattern for economic chaos Geneen had turned down in 1970—made perfect sense: ITT had little to lose, and in upheaval might get back Chiltelco. At very least they would get back at Allende. Naturally, though, ITT had to keep up negotiations about compensation (though Ed Korry says Allende never negotiated in good faith) to protect their claim for insurance. Indeed, one ITT lawyer, Richard Dillenbeck, had already complained that the more expansive exhortations for economic sanctions against Chile that were coming out of the Washington office might be considered provocative enough to jeopardize the claim.

There is no evidence that ITT was involved in the coup, or that the United States was directly involved, although the 40 Committee nurtured the opposition with massive infusions of funds. And United States economic pressure did help to destabilize the government. Furthermore, money given to legitimate political groups occasionally ended up with terrorists. The CIA, at least once, gave terrorists some guns. But technical military assistance came from Brazil, then only just peeping from the depths of its own right-wing military coup of nine years before.

On December 20, 1974, Pinochet's government and ITT announced a settlement: $125.2 million for Chiltelco. ITT's other properties had never been touched; in fact, members of Allende's government had been getting English lessons at one of the Sheratons—so perhaps Geneen's provident hiring policies paid off after all.

Concurrent with the settlement, Geneen announced that $25 million of the money, matched by Chile, would establish Foundation Chile, an agricultural research station to bring better food growing, processing, transportation, management, and overall planning to the country. It became a pet project, and he supported it in the face of red tape and cost overruns.

The elder Henry Cabot Lodge, no enemy of commerce, once said, "The businessman dealing with a large political question is really a painful sight." Chile was a case in point. People whose instinct and training have taken them into government are different from businessmen in basic outlook. Not just the "statesmen"; even the politicians, and even if they are venal or incompetent, are likely to have a broader vision of the world. They are accustomed to consulting and accommodating the varied agendas of differing interests. They cultivate a talent for compromise. Their objective in a fight is seldom to destroy; they can contemplate their adversaries' wider needs and are eager to build bridges for their retreat. Businessmen are educated to a more singular concern, and in this, as in so much else, Geneen led. He once told a reporter that making a profit was business's "most honorable motive," and we have seen how he never let anything stand in profit's way. He was surely right that the core logic of business is profit. His controller, Herb Knortz, says, "ITT is a *most* moral company." Morality is not the point of a company; profit is. The people of a company can try to operate on the highest moral plane; but insofar as they do so *and* it interferes with profit, they are unbusinesslike. In practice, ITT—especially under Geneen—was specifically amoral; there is little indication that ITT people much consulted their perceptions of what was right as against what was profitable. For Geneen, what was right was whatever contributed to his company's well-being. He was ethically punctilious, but according to his own quirky code. He would not let his people be blackmailed or shook down; but freely offered bribes were a regular part of ITT business practice. He would never "walk away from responsibility" for a Levitt mortgage; yet he embraced what Wasserman called the "suede-shoe business" of selling lots in Florida. In Chile the phone company had millions in bank loans outstanding, and although after expropriation, if Chile denounced the loans, the banks had no recourse to ITT, Geneen privately assured them that he would make good (though of course they were not to tell Allende that); at the same time he could entertain a plan to sell out the other expropriated companies as in Peru. He certainly had no scruple about the Chilean people or what Ed Korry called the "sweetness" of their society. A military coup in Chile would almost certainly mean that people would die; Geneen would have backed any plan to defeat Allende—including a coup— with a million dollars of ITT's money. In a moral company, anyone who sent to headquarters memos exhorting bloodshed, would have been fired on the spot.

To what end was all of Geneen's effort? The government insurance covered only $92.5 million of ITT's $153 million property because the rest represented assets acquired before the insurance was offered in 1963. Not a penny of either amount had come from New York. The original investment had long since depreciated; the insured assets and the residue had been gained entirely through reinvested earnings. For years Chile had been fabulously profitable to ITT and had cost the corporation nothing. To an accountant that might not mean much; to a moralist it would lighten the effect of the (admittedly unjust) expropriation. It might be argued that Nixon and Kissinger were worse; they acted, where ITT just passed some money and talked tough. But they acted at least with a vision, however stigmatic, of national interest. They were personally disinterested. Geneen's vision—his nightmare—centered on what ITT might lose on the bottom line.

How much did Geneen know about what his people were writing and saying and doing in and about Chile? He told one aide that he was unaware of much of it. Certainly he had a lot more than Chile on his mind. Equally certainly, his people did sometimes conceal things from him—like the fact that Hendrix was cooperating with the CIA, getting and giving information. It is also true that at ITT the imperative always was for activity. Often, in political situations, the only constructive thing to do is nothing, just watch developments. But ITT people could not fill their weekly activity reports with tales of watchful waiting. "He didn't mind if you made mistakes," says one staff man. "The thing you were eliminated for is if you lost by default, if you didn't have the guts to *do* something." He may not have known all details; certainly he knew about the key acts—giving money to Alessandri and the National Party. No one would have dared do that without his say-so. For the rest, he knew at least the broad outline of ITT's pressure on the government to do the morally repugnant things reflected in the bloody-minded memos from the field.

The question remains, why such wholesale lying at the time of the hearings? The one moderately honorable explanation is that ITT people lied at government instance, to conceal the CIA's involvement. But ITT had its own reason for lying. The atmosphere was different from *ABC* or *Kleindienst*, with much more opprobrium threatened. Still, Geneen was again ill-served by PR advice. Had he said, "Yes, we supported a particular candidate because we thought he was the only one who could beat the Marxist and preserve democracy; as a corporate citizen, we saw that as both our privilege and duty," it would have caused ITT much less damage. In fact, he said almost exactly that—but only after the revelations had already given the lie to much of his testimony. By then it was too late to dispel the bad impression: after all, if what ITT had done was not horrible, why lie about it? And what else, what further role—in the coup, perhaps—were they lying about?

Of course, concealment tempted, because the truth about ITT's CIA connection would trouble the governments of other countries where ITT did business. And temptation was compounded by the same arrogance the Watergaters displayed: we are too powerful to get caught. Then there was ITT's lulling experience with equivocation, stonewalling, and lying in *ABC* and *Kleindienst*. Nothing happened then; why should it now? So few are ever prosecuted for perjury before congressional committees, it is hard to blame the ITT people for being sanguine.

Actually, the results in Chile justified insouciance. Hal Hendrix got scared when Justice started presenting evidence to a grand jury in the late fall of 1976. The CIA's role was known, and they were reluctantly cooperating, declassifying documents. Since Hendrix's ties with the CIA were the guts of his perjury, he felt lost. On October 8, 1976, he started to plea bargain: in exchange for testimony against the others, Hendrix was allowed to plead guilty to the misdemeanor of withholding information from Congress. He was sentenced to one month in jail and a $100 fine, both suspended, with three months' unsupervised probation. It was essentially the same deal Richard Helms would receive for his perjury about Chile, except that Helms had to pay $2,000.

On March 20, 1978, one day before the statute of limitations would have run out, Justice filed perjury charges against Ned Gerrity and Bob Berrellez. (As we'll see, prosecution was finally dropped on hotly disputed grounds of national security.) Geneen was off the hook. So were McCone and all the others. The assistant attorney general handling the case, Benjamin R. Civiletti, "bristled slightly at a suggestion that the Justice Department had focused on 'low ranking people,' rather than senior executives, such as Mr. Geneen." It all depended, he told the *New York Times*, not on rank but "on the facts."

Justice would not discuss the matter further. Ed Korry contends it was a corrupt decision, made to protect the Kennedy and Johnson administrations from exposure of the extent of their use of multinationals to undermine other nations. That is unproven. But as we shall see, Justice is still covering the matter up.

Geneen and ITT beat the rap—but only the official one. By the summer of 1973 it looked as though there would be serious repercussions. First, they might not collect on their government insurance. On April 9, 1973, the government agency informed ITT that they would not pay the $92.5 million claim: ITT had withheld material information, and its actions had provoked Allende's expropriation and later refusal to pay compensation. The matter went to arbitration. In addition, the IRS was taking a fresh look at the ruling that had made the Hartford acquisition tax-free. That could cost $100 million. Worst of all, ITT was simply in bad odor; its stock had declined to half what it had been at the beginning of the year and would continue to drop. And soon things would get even worse for Geneen and his company. The glory years were over.

20

End of the Dream

None of the other hearings hurt. *ABC* ended a promising merger, only to clear the way for the glory years; *Celler* let Geneen shine; *Kleindienst* showed him as inexorable but not wicked. *Chile* ended the dream.

The effect on Geneen's position was not immediately apparent. ITT director George Brown said, "Hell, Harold Geneen told us it isn't true, so that's good enough for me, no matter what the damned papers print." Felix Rohatyn had earlier said, "He can run any company that I'm director of until he's ninety-two years old." In August 1974 the directors would in fact give Geneen a new, two-year contract, taking him beyond ITT's mandatory retirement age.

Public reaction was another matter. Although second-quarter earnings for 1973 (after *Chile*) were up 11.5%, ITT's stock took a nose dive. The 1973 high was 60⅜; on January 26, the day ITT announced agreement to acquire the publisher G. P. Putnam's Sons, the stock was 54¾. Then came *Chile*. On May 15, 1973, ITT closed at 35; that day, the *Wall Street Journal* noted that both Putnam's ($15.2 million) and a $22.6 million merger with Hydromatic Filter Company had been "suspended indefinitely." No one wanted ITT stock; its low for the year was 25. And it was not just *Chile*. Important money losses impended.

In April 1973 the IRS announced reconsideration of its 1969 ruling that had made the Hartford merger tax-free. Now it said that ITT might have fudged a sale that permitted the ruling; 17,000 former Hartford shareholders might have an immediate tax liability running to a possible $100 million.

The basis of the IRS's position was inane. For a merger involving an exchange of stock to be tax-free, the surviving company must give only its stock; it must not buy any shares for cash. There was no reason for that rule. The one-time head of enforcement of the SEC, Stanley Sporkin—scarcely business's lapdog—pronounces it inexplicable "tax theology." Perhaps the IRS hoped the rule might check the rush of conglomerate mergers. Inanity aside, it was the rule, and it appeared that ITT and Lazard Frères had broken it. Before ITT's tender offer, the company owned just over 1.7 million shares of Hartford stock, bought for cash. The rule meant that ITT had to sell those shares unconditionally, later exchanging ITT stock for them, just as for all other Hartford shares. Lazard arranged a sale to Mediobanca, a bank in Milan, Italy.

What does "sell" mean with stock? Surely, that if A sells to B, from then on if the stock goes up or down B, not A, takes the profit or loss. "If the buyer doesn't assume these stakes," the *Wall Street Journal* noted, "a deal isn't considered an unconditional sale by widely accepted legal standards"—or by common sense. And clearly that was not what happened with Mediobanca. As a stockholders' suit put it, ITT merely "parked" the Hartford stock with Lazard and Mediobanca. The idea was to avoid actual sale of the 1.7 million shares because they would be worth more once the merger was approved and consummated. ITT had two contracts with Mediobanca. The first was for payment of $1.8 million for the bank's "services." The second gave Mediobanca three sale options. Only the first set of terms constituted a real sale, and that was just for show; Mediobanca rejected it immediately. Options two and three involved no risk for the bank, with number three (the one selected) particularly unlike an arm's-length transaction. Mediobanca would remit to ITT whatever it realized when it, in turn, sold the shares—plus accumulated dividends. The bank would keep either 25¢ or 51¢ a share, depending on how long it waited to sell them. But Lazard would decide when to sell. In the event, the deal yielded ITT some $22 million more than if a real premerger sale had been made. Mediobanca earned $2.17 million—but had a secret contract with Lazard to split its fee. Further scandal turned on the fact that William Casey, then head of the SEC, convinced the commission to remove charges of fraud from an SEC complaint in the matter.

In March 1974 the IRS reversed its tax-free ruling. ITT appealed to the tax court. At the same time it promised to reimburse Hartford shareholders for any taxes due—at which point a shareholders' suit demanded that if ITT had to shell out, the amount be made good by the directors, past and present, who should have known about the fictitious sale and stopped it; there were some other defendants, too, including Lazard and Mediobanca. The suit was settled a year later with payment of $3.2 million to ITT by the directors and other defendants. In October 1977 Lazard settled a separate suit that revealed their $4 million-plus profit on the deal. The suit also showed that some 400,000 shares of the stock "sold" to Mediobanca were used by ITT in later acquisitions. ITT and Lazard said they knew nothing about that. In 1979 the tax court ruled in ITT's favor; "sell" did not mean what most people supposed. In 1981 ITT paid $18.5 million in final settlement, and the case was closed.

In 1973 and 1974, though, the effects of the IRS challenge were devastating, as was the government's refusal to pay ITT's insurance claim on Chiltelco. The successor insuring agency to AID was OPIC—Overseas Private Investment Corporation. In April 1973 OPIC's decision not to pay was a shock. The case went to arbitration, and ITT won in November 1974. A month later the Chilean dictatorship announced it would pay compensation. But that did not help ITT's stock. In December of 1974 it hit 12.

As troubles do, Geneen's multiplied. In September 1974, when he was sixty-four, just back from vacation, Geneen was stricken with Bell's palsy, a painful neuritis that paralyzes one side of the face. It affected his speech, and recovery was slow. "He really stayed out of the active part of the business for six months," says Tim Dunleavy. But even before that, Geneen's involvement had slackened. *Chile*, the IRS, OPIC, lawsuits—all devoured his time. "He backed away from day-to-day operations," says one former staff man. Others noted that he sometimes did not show up at the GMMs—hitherto unheard of—and that when he did he was often called out for long phone calls.

When Geneen formed the Office of the President in 1967, it had seemed a joke; surely he would not share his power. Suddenly, now, the OOP members really were running things, along with senior staff. ITT alumni are of two minds about the effect. One is that the OOP exercised "authority without responsibility," with predictably depressing results. The other, as a former staff man puts it, is that "even at the very high level, decisions were not being made and things were not being done." People did not want to jeopardize their positions. "They'd say, Let's put it off, let's see what happens next week—by then maybe Mr. Geneen will be back."

The views are not mutually exclusive. Watchful waiting is only prudent when so strong a leader is temporarily distracted and distanced; strong stands may come back to haunt you when he suddenly materializes. Still, someone had to run things, collect the managers' monthly letters and staff activity reports; someone had to preside over the GMMs. The man the system was designed for might not be there, but it still had to be used; it was the only one they had.

Pride and a tincture of spite also balanced the equation. These bright, competent men could at last, however warily, indulge power that in any other corporation would all along have been theirs by right. And they could settle scores. The case of Ed Roth, head of APCOA, was typical. "I had a close relationship with Geneen," says Roth, "and I would use it to run around all the corporate crap." At a GMM, Geneen would ask Roth how some project was coming. "I'd say, Hal, it's been sitting in so-and-so's office for three weeks, and I've been waiting for an answer. He'd turn to the guy down the table—a Hanway, a Dunleavy, a Lester—and say, Where the fuck is it? And the guy would say, Blah-blah-blah. Geneen would say to me, What do you think of it, Ed? And I'd say, Hal, I think it's a sensational deal. And he'd say, Go ahead." Now came the reckoning. "From around the middle of 'seventy-three," says Roth, "that wasn't going to work anymore. Geneen wasn't showing up at those meetings. He was involved in Washington. Things were changing, the corporation taking over, and now all the vultures were coming in on me because I didn't have that clout anymore."

The absence of Geneen's active, detailed leadership came just when it hurt most. By terms of the antitrust settlement, big acquisitions could no longer aid growth. In the late 1960s, depending on the year, they had added 20% to 35%. In 1972, acquisitions added only 5%. Internal growth on enough of a scale to make up the difference needed Geneen's kind of control and vision and drive, especially since the Mideast oil crisis was plaguing the world's economy. Perhaps nothing would have been different even with Geneen undistracted and in full charge. But in 1970, while so many other companies faltered, Geneen's had forged ahead.

In any case, in the first quarter of 1974 an era ended. Under Geneen, for fifty-eight straight quarters ITT had racked up a profit gain of at least 10%. Now ITT's profit declined. It was down about 1.6%. Geneen told stockholders that the reason was a change in accounting rules for figuring foreign currency translations: all loss had to be taken in the first quarter $14.4 million after taxes, equal to 12¢ a share. Without that, he said, the quarter would have set another record. The rest of the year, he assured them, should be "correspondingly benefited" by the first-quarter charge. Results for all of 1974 "will be substantially unchanged by this factor."

So they were; but it did not matter. When the record had hit 50 straight quarters, one analyst told ITT's director of stockholder relations, "The best thing for ITT would be to have a down quarter, and then you would be believable." That was fine, says Bob Savage, "except that when the down quarter happened, everybody sold the stock." A different analyst called the 1974 first-quarter results "an analytical nightmare": depending on how you figured it, the decline might be as much as 27%, or there might have been a 6.8% gain. But he went along with Geneen's projections, estimating that net for the year would be about $4.40 a share, up from $4.08. ITT's treasurer, Lyman Hamilton, said "That's in the right neighborhood."

It was not. At the 1975 annual meeting, Geneen had to tell stockholders that profits for the year had declined. At $3.63 a share, 1974 was off 13% from 1973's all-time high. That did not qualify ITT as one of the hundred neediest cases; profit for 1974 was $451.1 million. Still, it was a blow.

October and November 1974 saw mass staff and executive firings. Those fired called it "the bloodbath." One survivor calls it "a culling of the herd." Rich Bennett explained to one of the culls that since the company had done so well in 1968, the staff functions and people added since then could be dispensed with. Nothing personal. Executive bonuses were cut about 7.2%, although salaries were increased. It was not a happy time.

Adding to these woes were divestiture problems from the antitrust settlement. The early action was not bad. ITT sustained a $19.3 million loss on sale of its small insurance companies, but sold Canteen Corporation to TWA at a $7 million profit. The first two public offerings of Avis stock were a success. In mid-1972 a block went for $38 a share, and another, in early 1973, for $47 a share. They equaled 48% of ITT's ownership and represented a profit of some $55.4 million. Then ITT stopped selling. The lead underwriters, Kuhn Loeb and Lazard, suggested putting the stock out more slowly so as not to depress the market. But Bud Morrow, then still head of Avis, was sure it was ITT's decision. "They were waiting for higher prices," he told a reporter, "that's all." What they got was collapse of the stock market and, with recession, a collapse of Avis profits—down to $4 million in 1974 from $11.3 million the year before. By mid-1975 Avis stock sank to 8. When the divestiture deadline passed, the court appointed a trustee, and ITT was in a pickle. They had to keep Avis healthy, and that included, once, buying a new issue of Avis stock for $17.3 million, $11.62 a share. Yet they had no say over Avis's operations or divestiture (except veto) and no participation in profits. It was a mercy, in 1977, when the court allowed the trustee to accept an offer of $22 a share from Norton Simon.

Levitt continued down. It lost over $20 million in 1974, the last full year under ITT, and then the corporation had to absorb the pariah assets of the "B" company so that "A" might turn a profit—in which ITT would not share —so it could be sold at a loss. It was a relief when the shell of LSI was sold to Starrett for a mere $34.5 million in 1978.

Grinnell was another problem. After antitrust chief McLaren agreed in 1971 to settle, the two sides took from June 17 to July 30 to thrash out terms because ITT wanted to keep the part of Grinnell not involved in fire protection. McLaren finally agreed. But hacking the company in two left the part of Grinnell that had to be divested with no earnings record and with a disproportionately high overhead. A public sale of stock was impossible; there were no private buyers either. In November 1973 a trustee was appointed. The company made a little money in 1974—$1.4 million on $114 million sales —and was doing even better next year when in September 1975 it was sold to Tyco Laboratories, Inc., for a minimum of $28.5 million and a maximum of $40 million, depending on profits.

Matters in Europe during this period were no more agreeable than in the United States. Morale had been sagging in many units for quite a while. Geneen's domestic expansion in the late 1960s drained most of the corporation's resources. "Our capital expenditure in Europe," says Art Williams, "was being limited to our depreciation." That meant little was available in his division for new projects. Williams thought the fun was gone, and he soon left ITT.

Then came the recession. It hit Europe hard in 1974, just as Mike Bergerac was lured to Revlon. Maurie Valente was not Geneen's first choice as replacement. He was slated as number two; but when the first choice proved unacceptable to the Europeans, Valente got the job. Most ITT alumni think that was a mistake. Valente was remarkably easygoing for a top ITT executive, and perilously so for such tough times. In addition to recession, he faced a "new" and uncongenial Europe. With the end of Antonio de Oliveira Salazar's dictatorship in Portugal, a socialist government eventually came to power, and in 1975 ITT announced the end of support for its Portuguese subsidiaries. No one was bowing anymore. Following Francisco Franco's death in Spain, a strike forced the closing of five plants in 1976. And the same year, in England, STC announced the imminent closing of a plant and layoffs of some 1,000 workers, a trend that would continue.

In France there was also nationalism, though the results were more gratifying financially. The French government pressured ITT to give up its 67.96% interest in LMT, selling to a buyer designated by the government— the French firm Thomson-Houston. "Stan Luke did the negotiating," says someone close to the deal, "but Geneen masterminded it from New York with those interminable phone calls. He wanted complete detail from as many sources as he could get. We were all talking to different people in the government, trying to get a feel for what they wanted. We had done our homework and figured that Thomson-Houston didn't have the money. But someone high in the government said, Oh that won't be any problem. When I mentioned this to Hal, he said, Well there it is! The government's going to finance it for them. From then on his whole tactic changed. They paid a tremendous price." The price was $160 million in cash, a profit of $89.7 million, plus assurances that the French PTT would continue to buy equipment from ITT's remaining company, CGCT.

Geneen consoled Valente that ITT-Europe's loss of this profitable unit was the corporation's gain: he would use the LMT money to get ITT domestically further into natural resources and energy—a classic case of cold comfort. Nor was Valente cheered to realize that some of the acquisitions inherited from Bergerac's bonanza days (including ironically, Rimmel, Dr. Payot, and Ma Vale, cosmetics companies) were now hitting his balance sheets with sizable losses. It was surely not all Valente's fault, but Europe did not prosper under him. He returned to the United States in early 1979 and became president of RCA at the start of 1980—a post he held for about six months before being fired by RCA's irascible chairman, Edgar H. Griffiths.

Another sign of the troubled times for Geneen was the tone of ITT's annual meetings. Before *Chile*, he had relished their give-and-take, even the occasional hecklers. But as *Chile* was different in spirit and temper from the other hearings, the annual meetings were different after Jack Anderson's first Chile column in March 1972. In Memphis that May there were angry pickets outside and pointed questions inside. Only 30 to 50 marched at Memphis, but they shouted things like, "ITT makes a profit on murder" and "ITT pays no taxes." After the meeting, one ITT flack commented, "It could have been worse," and it soon was. By 1974, in Seattle, anywhere from 150 to 500 pickets chanted "ITT must go," and "We want Geneen" as they rushed the hall, going after him, turned back only by mounted police.

Inside, there was new acrimony. Before, Geneen had cheerfully dealt with the likes of Lewis D. Gilbert and Evelyn Y. Davis, who regularly turned up at every company's meetings, where they asked what they imagined were discomfiting questions and proposed measures that were regularly defeated. At first, Memphis seemed like old times. Only stockholders were allowed in, and Evelyn Davis's go-to-meeting costume was a red, white, and blue striped hot pants outfit with top hat. But the heckling was no longer Gilbert and Davis nattering about executive compensation, preemptive rights and cumulative voting; now it was the Women's Strike for Peace, Clergy and Laymen Concerned about Vietnam, and Ralph Nader's Project on Corporate Responsibility. At the 1973 meeting in Kansas City, held in May, after *Chile*, Raimundo Valenzuela, a Methodist minister and one-time bishop of Chile, said he spoke for "a stockholder who shares the outrage all Chileans feel at the damage I.T.T. was willing to inflict upon our nation." Then he said, "Do you realize what the proposed action in Chile has done to the image of I.T.T. all over the world? . . . The unethical policies pursued in Chile are in the long run self-defeating. They can blacken your name so completely that foreign governments will be wary of dealing with you." Geneen said the bishop's comments were sincere but ill-informed.

He was less gentle with Robert Sterling. Just out of Columbia Law School, Sterling had met Raymond L. Dirks, an offbeat young specialist in insurance stocks, who had long opposed the ITT-Hartford merger. Two days later, Sterling was Dirks's representative in Kansas City. Unfortunately, Dirks had no proxy to give him, and one was needed to attend, much less speak at, a stockholders' meeting. Before the meeting, though, Sterling met Ned Gerrity and they had a fine time talking about their respective army careers. When Sterling told Gerrity about his lack of proxy, Gerrity obligingly introduced him to Susan Gross, of Nader's group, who had proxies to spare.

"The whole front row," says Sterling, "was big, huge fellows, ITT employees who formed a solid line so no one could get to Geneen." Sterling took his turn during the question period: If ITT director Felix Rohatyn's firm, Lazard, had split fees with Mediobanca, wasn't that a conflict of interest? He kept at it for nearly an hour. "I was scared stiff," says Sterling, "and at one point the bishop of Chile came over, sat beside me, and held my hand." At another point, when the questions were getting even stickier, Geneen asked Sterling how he had gotten his proxy, and Sterling said, "Oh, Mr. Gerrity helped me before the meeting." Geneen glared at Gerrity, who quickly shook his head: no, no, not me!

Then came the last straw. Sterling asked about the validity of newspaper reports that ITT general counsel Howard Aibel had testified before the SEC that the IRS was not talking just about reconsideration of their Hartford tax-free ruling, but revocation. Geneen said he did not know.

"Well," said Sterling, "he's sitting right there, why don't you ask him?"

"Why do you want to know?" said Geneen.

"It's a stockholders' meeting for asking questions. I'm asking one."

"Why *that* one?"

"Is it true?"

"I'm not sure."

"Why not ask him?"

"Let's find out why you're asking."

"Well, if it's true, your proxy should have disclosed it; it's material. And since it isn't on the proxy, we should adjourn the meeting. If it's not true, and he so testified, we've got a perjurer, and we ought to call a U.S. marshal to take him away." (In fact, Ned Gerrity later explained, Aibel had so testified —but had simply been in error.)

Geneen motioned to Lawrence Walsh—Judge Walsh of *Kleindienst*— and they huddled with some other Davis Polk lawyers. Finally, Geneen announced that Sterling was not qualified to ask questions because his proxy was invalid. Why? Because he represented a party of interest in a lawsuit with ITT.

"Who do I represent?" said Sterling.

"Ralph Nader."

"Well, I don't. But even if I did, the other party is ITT, and you certainly represent ITT, so you better leave, too."

Geneen said, "That's it!" and motioned. "The guards came over," says Sterling, "and threw me out. Ten minutes later, the bishop got thrown out right beside me."

Back inside, the other stockholders rounded to Geneen's defense. For all his carping, Lewis Gilbert greatly admired Geneen, calling him "one of the most capable men in the United States." Now he said, "This board is not to be faulted for the Chilean situation—for trying to carry out its responsibilities to American investors." Geneen said, "You're damned right!" Another stockholder complained that she had taken "a terrible whipping" on the stock of other companies nationalized in Latin America but that "you acted magnificently."

In 1974 a new issue arose at meetings: ITT's role in South Africa. At next year's meeting, Geneen said in exasperation that it "comes up time and again: Somebody says don't interfere in Chile . . . but please interfere in South Africa." Geneen himself was without racial prejudice; so, officially, was ITT. In 1972 Charles Evers, the black mayor of Fayette, Mississippi, and brother of murdered civil rights leader Medgar Evers, had come to Memphis to praise ITT for opening a new plant in his town, taking "scores of citizens off welfare rolls" and making wage earners of them. Rumor had it that Evers had offered to testify to Geneen's character in Washington.

Geneen was not for apartheid. Nor, as the deals with the USSR showed, was he uncompromisingly against socialism. He was for ITT and against anything that would hurt its most immediate good. That meant he had no reason to interfere in South Africa and every reason to interfere in Chile. It had nothing to do with racism or politics, just pennies per share.

The changed atmosphere was not confined to acerbity in meetings. The first bomb scare came in July 1973 in Hartford. In September the first bomb went off, causing a lot of damage to an ITT building in Zurich. "Every time ITT's name was in the papers," says Sheraton head Bud James, "another bomb went off." That was another reason Sheraton (and other units) muted their ITT connection. Later in September there were demonstrations and explosions in Rome and on Madison Avenue, demolishing four rooms in ITT's Building of the Americas. It continued in France, Germany, Lebanon, and New York—until mid-1975, when a bomb shattered the ITT office in Beirut. That ended it.

That year, 1975, also ended Geneen's hope for quick ITT recovery. He had predicted at the 1975 annual meeting that there would be improvement in ITT's earnings "probably sufficient to make the year 1975 as good or even better than 1974." But the second quarter was sharply down, 31%, and so was the third quarter, 26.6%. Even a fourth quarter up 21% did not help; ITT's net in 1975 was lower than 1974's, down about 12% to $398.2 million. That made two years in a row.

Ironically, Hartford did not help either; it hurt. Nineteen seventy-four was a bad year for insurance companies in general, but Hartford had some special problems. An insurance company does not make its money directly from premiums but on the interest, dividends, and capital gains it receives from investing that premium money. Any insurance company is happy if its underwriting expenses and claims payments equal the premiums. The catch is that the company never knows how great the total of claims will be against the policies written in any one year. Some are not paid out for several years. So—by law—they must maintain an adequate reserve. If more claims come in than expected, or bigger claims, or both, the company must add to the reserve, cutting its current year's net.

In 1971, its first full year with ITT, Hartford's income was $105.5 million, 26% of ITT's total. At ITT's direction, Hartford started realizing much more in the way of capital gains than it had before, a measure that pumped up earnings. At the same time, the sales force was encouraged to hustle for more business. The added business might mean not breaking even on underwriting, but that was all right; even a 2% loss would be acceptable. In 1970 Hartford wrote $1.125 billion in premiums; in 1971 they wrote $1.335 billion, about 18.8% more, compared with a 10% industry average growth. In 1972 premiums were up 14.5%. In 1973 growth cooled to about 11.6%, with the total of earned premiums up to $1.733 billion (in 1969, they had stood at $954 million, an 81.7% increase in four years). Much of the new business was in such high-risk areas as product liability and medical malpractice; both have an especially "long tail," trade jargon for claims that do not develop for a few years.

There were two results. First, Hartford had more premium money to invest, mostly in stocks; second, the ratio of claims to premiums seemed very good. In 1970 underwriting loss was only $13.7 million, 1.2%. In 1971 and

1972 there was actually a profit on underwriting. In 1973 a few chickens came home to roost, and the underwriting loss climbed to $38.7 million, which was 2.29%. That was not acceptable, and in 1974 premium "growth" was held to .9%. But it was too late. Now claims rolled in, and the 1974 loss soared to $123 million, a punishing 7.6%. At the same time the stock market, with Hartford's extra premium money in it, collapsed. On paper Hartford's portfolio of $880 million showed a $240 million loss. That meant Hartford's surplus—the readily liquifiable assets that protected policy holders—looked anemic, and the state examiners wanted it beefed up. One way was to sell stocks and put the money into presumably safer bonds; but that would turn a paper loss into a real loss affecting the balance sheet. Instead, ITT turned over $93 million in assets to Hartford. Ironically, when the merger was under attack, Ralph Nader's group kept insisting that Geneen planned to loot Hartford.

Of course, with all of this, Hartford, like ITT, was not losing money; but profit was in a tailspin. Instead of 1971's $105.5 million contribution, in 1974 Hartford's net was down to $01 million; instead of contributing 25% of the corporate total (24% in 1972), Hartford's share was down to 18%. The one bright spot in 1975 was that Hartford's profit, unlike ITT's did not continue the slide. But its net was up only a little over $1 million to $82.3 million. Harold Geneen was surely glad to see the dawn of 1976.

Maybe it was his illness, maybe the troubles in Washington, but to some associates, Geneen seemed a changed man after 1973. "He was not the same Harold Geneen that I worked with in the first thirteen years," says Tim Dunleavy. Dunleavy thinks *Chile* was more to blame than palsy: "He got himself twisted in the testimony and had to do some real fast word shuffling to keep himself out of trouble. All that preyed on him; it gave him a hell of a problem." It was not so much his business practice but his personality; even "his personal ethics changed," says Dunleavy. One executive who had not known him in the earlier days describes a man who, brilliant as ever, is testy and intolerant of dissent—much more worrisome than that earlier tendency toward the "aristocratic." "He won't listen," says the executive, "He's so egocentric, that if someone disagrees with him, he closes his ears. He only wants to hear an echo of what he has said or thinks. And if someone persists in trying to give a reason for some contrary position, he not only doesn't hear you, but what comes out of his mouth—and I don't think it's conscious, he's just so wrapped up in his own thinking—what comes out are strong remarks that discourage you, and finally you give up." That was not the Geneen who would always listen to sound counterarguments, ever the servant of facts.

And it was not the same Geneen who had always been accessible to the press and who had shrugged off or laughed off public criticism. Now, some professor at Stanford wrote a lengthy appreciation of Geneen's methods, mostly an innocuous rehash, generally quite favorable. Geneen, seeing it in draft, did not like it. "He called Stanford," says Bob Savage, "and said, We give a lot of money, and I want that thing killed."

In at least one way, though, Geneen stayed the same. He never lost his courage or his talent for leadership. Embattled, his dream for ITT glimmering, sick with worry over a possible perjury indictment and literally sick with palsy, he was still splendid. "Everybody said the first time we have a downturn this guy will blow his head off," says Tim Dunleavy. "He's a genius, working on a fine line, and if he snaps, he'll blow up. Well, we took the downturn, and Christ! He rose to it just as beautifully as could be."

His leadership was striking in the case of Continental Baking. For them 1974 had been a horror, with skyrocketing commodity costs. "On something like a billion dollars of sales," says Randy Hackett, "we made something like twenty thousand dollars, juggling our accounts so we were in the black." Then came the business plan meeting, and they were sure Geneen was going to eat them. Not at all, says Hackett:

> It was the best business plan meeting we ever had. We went through everything, and Geneen held up his hand and said, I know you people may not understand this, but next year is going to be the best year you ever had. Because you're going to be forced to do the things that you probably should have done in the last three or four years, and never did. And when you come out of this year, you're going to go ahead at an accelerated pace, as if this had been a pretty good year for you. I don't look at this by any means as gloom and doom: this is a good year.
>
> And by God he was right! Next year we went through the roof. For me that was an amazing piece of wisdom.

And it was an amazing performance.

Geneen displayed the same gallantry fighting back from the paralysis of palsy. It was a terrible blow, made worse by his extreme health consciousness, which bordered on hypochondria. Geneen was sure his palsy was really a stroke. Before the face-disfiguring paralysis wore off, he would see only his closest associates, and then only in his darkened bedroom. He had seldom bothered with adding machines; now he would not use even pencil and paper, wanting to do all ciphering in his head to show he still could. At the same time, he would try to remember the details of past events. It was a huge relief to find his memory intact. His speech, though, was impaired, and he hired a therapist, John Monaghan, to help him, then was so taken with the man's coaching, he kept him for help in delivering speeches.

The results of Geneen's leadership began to show. By mid-1975 ITT stock was double its December 1974 low of 12. And although the year's net was down, at the 1976 annual meeting in Phoenix, Geneen could announce that the first quarter of 1976 was way up—in fact had set a new record for ITT first-quarter earnings. And the rest of the year looked promising. Coincidently, a reporter noted that "It also is the first year in recent memory that demonstrators didn't parade outside. . . . " (It was, however, at this meeting that Geneen acknowledged the $350,000 payment to Alessandri and his party.)

Recovery continued throughout 1976; the year was up 23% over 1975. The $488.7 million net was not equal to that of 1973, but Geneen could confidently predict that next year's net would top 1973's. What's more, with his stock hitting 33, he could make an important new acquisition: Carbon Industries, a coal producer in Charleston, West Virginia. Along with next year's acquisition of Eason Oil Company of Oklahoma City, this pushed ITT into energy, an especially brave move since Geneen had to overpay mightily for companies in such a hot field.

There were two more signal, but less creditable, events in 1976. The SEC had been looking at charges of ITT's overseas bribery since 1968. Now, in March 1976, ITT announced "reason to believe" that employees had made some $3.8 million in what they termed "unauthorized payments." The former head of one ITT subsidiary says that when he heard the figure of $3.8 million, he wondered "which week that was for." It supposedly covered 1971 through 1975, but it was indeed not the total. ITT did not call the payments illegal or unethical. The official statement stressed that "in all material respects, corporate policies concerning compliance with the laws of host nations have been observed." In other words, where ITT had bribed, bribes were practically hallowed tradition. In any case, the statement noted, neither the directors nor "senior officers" knew the first thing about it.

The truth was something else again. The final figure in the SEC's complaint was $8.7 million—to which ITT admitted. The former head of SEC enforcement is sure there was still more, but that was all the SEC could nail down for those years. The total included over $385,000 to Italian tax agents for a favorable settlement—not quite the same as a little baksheesh, squeeze, or mordida to a customs inspector. It also included $400,000 to Allende's opponents from 1970 through 1972, part of it channeled through a phony company called "Lonely Star Shipping Corporation" and charged off as PR expense. Although it is not clear, this was likely in addition to the $350,000 that went to Alessandri and his party before the popular election. The countries where the SEC had uncovered a pattern of bribery were Indonesia, Iran, the Philippines, Algeria, Nigeria, Mexico, Italy, Turkey, and Chile. In Belgium, where a sterner view of these things was taken, the head of ITT's company, BTM, popular and respected Frank Pepermans, received a sentence of six months, suspended, for giving the former managing director of the state-owned phone company gifts worth about $7,500 over a period of some years. The official got another nine months added to his previous sentence of four years for a separate conviction involving about $100,000 from other sources.

ITT did not fight the SEC's bribery charges; they were too well documented. But they bitterly fought public exposure of the details. When the judge refused to seal the SEC complaint, ITT settled by signing a consent decree. That was in September of 1979, and by then Geneen was almost out of the picture.

The other big event of 1976 was the announcement in June that two more people had been added to the Office of the President. One was Lyman Hamilton, at age forty-nine an executive VP and treasurer. The other was a surprise: Rand V. Araskog, at forty-four the youngest and the only one not already an executive VP and board member; he had been a group executive in charge mostly of ITT defense and aerospace work, an area of diminishing importance to ITT.

None of the business press was sure of the implications—beyond the fact that Geneen had evidently lost none of his taste for mystification. His contract as CEO would expire at the annual meeting in 1977, but there was nothing to keep the board from renewing it, and some observers expected them to do so, at least for another year, as they had the year before. "One knowledgeable source said yesterday, though," went a *Wall Street Journal* story, "that he expected Mr. Geneen to continue as chairman after the next annual meeting, but to relinquish the title of chief executive to Mr. Dunleavy."

21

Penultimate Chapter

To anyone watching the ITT board from the mid-1960s to early 1970s, it might have seemed that the directors danced to Geneen's whim. His astounding success had them buffaloed. But these were rich and powerful men, not weaklings and not dependent on Geneen. They could turn on him at any time, and he never forgot it. Of course he had always hankered after a board with no outside directors. And when he later had problems, he ruefully agreed with an associate who said that he should never have had bankers on the board, only operating people who would understand—friends who would support you through thick and thin.

But even at their most complaisant and lackadaisical, the board kept chivying Geneen about succession. When he formed the Office of the President in 1967, part of the reason had been to demonstrate his intention of grooming a successor; members of an OOP surely had to be reckoned plausible candidates. Then in 1972, three years before the official ITT retirement age, Geneen named Tim Dunleavy president, while he stayed chairman and CEO. The move fooled practically everyone. The press, most of ITT, Dunleavy's rivals, Dunleavy himself—all thought he was next in line. Geneen and the board knew better. "Dunleavy couldn't possibly have succeeded Geneen, not possibly," says Dick Perkins, board member since 1953 and chairman of the personnel and compensation committee. "It really was a gesture of cooperation with Geneen that we stuck him in there as president." Dunleavy was popular with subordinates, a fine operating man and consummate politician. But CEO? "At that level," says Perkins, "he was out of his field. He wasn't the kind of fellow you could take into the board room of any other company, really. He wasn't presentable in that situation." (Now retired, Dunleavy sits on ten boards.) Had he been the genius Geneen was, the rough edges, the mangled syntax, the incessant "he don'ts" might not have mattered; but Tim Dunleavy was not known within ITT as an independent thinker. Perkins knew that Geneen dictated and monitored Dunleavy's moves. In short, Dunleavy was the perfect successor—for a man who had no intention of leaving.

Geneen was soon talking in board meetings about the unwisdom of arbitrary retirement ages. Anyway, who could replace him? He had advanced Dunleavy's candidacy three times and had been routinely turned down by the board. The other two OOP members, Rich Bennett and Jim Lester, while very capable executives, were not the board's notion of viable candidates—although the concept of boardability says more about the board than about the men themselves. There were no other likely candidates around. Geneen had always been so adamant about not going outside that it was not contemplated. Instead, Geneen was extended twice until 1977. But it was for want of an alternative; the mood of the board was no longer accommodating. They greeted the revelations and scandals from 1972 on with what Perkins calls "great dismay."

And there were factors beyond the scandals. The company's performance was no longer unalloyed triumph. True, 1974 had been a tough year for everyone. Nonetheless, over two-thirds of the Fortune 500 list had increased profits that year. In 1975, ITT's second downyear, the worst of the recession was past. And there had been some disturbing lapses of judgment.

One former associate observes that Geneen was always susceptible to imaginative promoters; any grandiose scheme could capture him. For example, in Indonesia, someone named Vladimir Gold had obtained a huge concession to log Philippine mahogany on the Siak River. In over his head, he convinced Geneen that it would be a splendid investment for ITT. The Rayonier people advised against. The usual method of assessing a logging project—called a cruise—does not work in jungles because you cannot see the trees for the forest; there may be hundreds of useless species for every one of the kind you want. But Geneen was enthralled by the scope of the deal and went ahead, forbidding his own natural resources PLM to visit the project to check it out. After losing millions, ITT was lucky to emerge with half its investment.

In contrast, the venture at Port Cartier on Canada's North Shore might have been a winner. However, it did show the dangers in Geneen's irrepressible enthusiasm, and the board must have seen it as cautionary. At their 1969 business plan presentation, Rayonier asked for an $85 million expansion in plant capacity for their Jesup, Georgia, facility. After approving the project, according to *Fortune,* "Geneen leaned back and said—as several people remember the gist of his words—'Great!' Pregnant pause. *'What else have you got?'* "

"If you wanted more," says Russell F. Erickson, then Rayonier's CEO, "you had to go where the timber was, and that was Quebec." As it happened, a large concession was available on the north shore of the St. Lawrence. Blanton W. Haskell, Rayonier's director of planning, had lately cruised Quebec's North Shore. And when Buck Haskell described logging rights in an area of some 52,000 square miles—"about the shape and size of Tennessee" —Geneen's imagination took off.

Russ Erickson retired before the full dimensions of what *Fortune* called one of business's signal disasters were evident. In general, Erickson much admires Geneen and realizes that many factors contributed to what happened. But he is sure that Geneen's headlong rush for the biggest and best was at the core. "He was the boss," says Erickson, "he wanted to go his way and didn't want to take advice from me, so I said the hell with it and retired."

Port Cartier was not a goofy project. Research by both ITT marketing and Rayonier persuaded Geneen of a coming boom in demand for rayon. Arable lands, now planted to cotton, would be needed for growing food; oil prices would drive up the cost of polyesters. Timberland, source for rayon's chemical cellulose, would be unaffected. Demand must follow.

With that as a given, two kinds of plant are possible. A sulphite process-ing plant is best specifically for the raw material of rayon, but it produces a weaker pulp, unusable for kraft, which was about 95% of the pulp market. The other kind of plant—using sulphate processing—could turn out (though less efficiently) both kinds of pulp. The strength of Rayonier's Jesup opera-tion was its ability to make both. Of the two, the technology necessary for sulphite plants was much less well understood. "It was special design versus proven design," says Erickson. Despite all, Geneen insisted on going full out for sulphite. "He was on this rayon kick," says Erickson. Furthermore, he demanded a plant to match the grandeur of their timber concession. There were standard plans for plants with a 600-ton capacity. "But Geneen wanted to go all out," says Erickson, "an eight-hundred-ton sulphite plant. He had blinders on, racing full speed ahead on this biggest goddamn rayon mill in the world."

That is partly hindsight. Cotton was not plowed under, the price of oil turned out a negligible factor in polyester price; rayon never caught on. But at the time, Quebec was by no means nonsensical. "The projections looked pretty good to me," says Erickson, "the numbers didn't look that bad." After all, it was the largest timber reserve in North America. The initial investment to exploit such inaccessible wood might be high, but with proper mechaniza-tion of harvesting, with processing right on the spot, and most of all with obviously increasing inflation, it looked like a marvelous opportunity. Of course, the mill had to be built and run on the banks of the Gulf of the St. Lawrence, next to the vast woodland. That was the real problem.

"The lesson to be learned," says Ron Goode, then ITT's natural re-sources PLM and VP, "is never build anything in a country, especially one with relatively sparse population, where they're building an Olympics facil-ity." The 1976 Summer Games were to be held in Montreal. Until then, says Goode, taking labor productivity around Rayonier's Jesup plant as 100, it was probably 110 in Quebec; by the time Port Cartier was built, it was around 10. "The Olympics," says Goode, "sucked skilled labor out of the area, and they provided an opportunity for agitation." There were labor problems from the first, not at all helped by *Chile*. Of course, the costs of building a distant mill (in effect, carving it and a town out of rock), the possibility of a tight labor market—all that was considered. Simpletons were not making the analysis or decision. "What wasn't factored in," says Goode, "was the fact that the labor wouldn't work, and when they did, they did a lousy job." When the mill was finished, strikes kept it shut more than half the time.

"It wasn't that opportunity wasn't there," says Goode, "and it wasn't that they made gross errors in analysis; it was that events in Canada overwhelmed them." The mill was closed for two weeks in 1975, supposedly to correct an unmanagable inventory. But Port Cartier was losing money on each ton of pulp produced, and in September 1979 the board voted to close down, taking an immediate $320 million write-off, with a final loss possibly running as high as $600 million. Rayonier had been bought in 1968 for just over $300 million.

Even with all this, it was not that the ITT board suddenly decided the emperor was wearing no clothes. He just appeared much less resplendent than before. And there was a threat of jail. In 1973 the press reported that Watergate prosecutors wanted a perjury indictment against Geneen in *Kleindienst*, though nothing came of it. *Chile* looked worse. Since October 1975 Justice had been gathering evidence, and would call witnesses before a grand jury a year later. In December 1975 an investigation revealed ITT's $350,000 payment to Alessandri and his party. Geneen acknowledged the payments the following spring but told stockholders he had not known about them. Could

Tim Dunleavy in the late 1970s.

the board have swallowed that? Could they doubt that Justice would try to prove that Geneen had perjured himself? Certainly when the government turned Hal Hendrix in late 1976 things looked bleak to Geneen. "Oh Jesus!" Tim Dunleavy reports him saying, "What did we get into! Wouldn't it be terrible to wind up in jail after all this?" It looked likely. In January 1977 Justice told ex-CIA director Richard Helms that a grand jury was looking at charges that he had conspired with Geneen and John McCone to "fabricate and coordinate statements" during *Chile*.

Even the prospect of Geneen's indictment, let alone conviction, was too much for the board. They did not want someone under indictment to be CEO of the company. There would be no more extensions past May 1977. They insisted on real succession, and that did not mean Tim Dunleavy. That was why in June 1976 two more people were added to the OOP. Dunleavy says it was he who suggested bringing Lyman Hamilton in, and that "Geneen bitterly opposed it; he looked on Hamilton as Hart Perry's boy." Hamilton was an insider in the ITT anyway, but with a kicker. The day of the announcement, Geneen and Dunleavy were due to visit Rand Araskog's New Jersey headquarters. In the limousine, Geneen informed Dunleavy that Araskog would also join the OOP. Dunleavy exploded. "Goddamn it," he said, "you never told me a thing about it until now. You've been thinking about this all along. Araskog wouldn't have been my pick." Actually, Dunleavy was a little surprised that Araskog was Geneen's pick. "I don't think Geneen thought any more of Araskog than he did anyone else," Dunleavy says. Araskog was, though, certainly a plausible choice, long seen as a bright comer, a good operating man with modest diversity of experience. Most of all there was what Dunleavy calls "charisma" between the two: Geneen liked Araskog well enough, and Araskog plainly adored Geneen. If there must be a successor, this is the kind to have: one who needs grooming, who figures to need and heed the master's presence and counsel for the foreseeable future.

The board wanted Hamilton. Geneen argued Araskog's operating experience and Hamilton's lack of it, but two other considerations prevailed. Hamilton's constituency was the New York financial community, the bankers and brokers vital to ITT; and Hamilton was skilled at making presentations, an important art to the board. Twenty minutes before the February 1977 board meeting, Geneen told Tim Dunleavy about the decision. "He sat with me, teary-eyed, and told me he didn't want Hamilton," says Dunleavy, "he wanted Araskog." Dunleavy's compassion was minimal. Inside directors were ignored; even so, the president of ITT felt that he might have been told a little sooner that he was about to be replaced. "Hal," he said, "I want to tell the board what I think." Geneen was appalled. "Oh, don't," he said, "don't get after the board. Jesus! I did my best to get you into this job, but they wanted someone else." Dunleavy stared at him a moment. "I think you're full of shit," he said. "I think you damned me with faint praise to get yourself an extension." He was adamant about addressing the board, and did, berating them, then offering his cooperation. They were unmoved by both declarations. On March 1, 1977, Hamilton would become president and COO, succeeding Geneen as CEO on January 1, 1978. Geneen would remain as chairman of the board, with Dunleavy kicked upstairs to vice-chairman.

Hamilton's background was not what one expects of a financier or head of a great company. He came from Los Angeles, where his father laid sidewalks during the depression for $17 a week. His brother was a fireman. His college was Principia, in Illinois. After college, interrupted by a two-year wartime hitch in the navy, he got a master's degree at Harvard's School of Public Administration and in 1947 went to work for the government in the Bureau of the Budget. After fifteen years he had risen to senior investment officer for the World Bank, annual salary $15,000. During those years of unremarkable civil service, only two notable things happened. In the late 1950s he ran government-owned companies in Okinawa's Ryukyu Islands (his only operating experience); of more significance, he met Hart Perry.

The prosperity of Hamilton's career at ITT was largely a matter of timing. During the 1960s, while Geneen stood in unblinking control, his attention riveted on finance, no one could have flourished as ITT's chief financial officer. Hamilton was lucky to be overshadowed by Perry, who was in that position. He was Perry's protégé, sheltered from Geneen, Perry's very presence a lightning rod.

Hart Perry was nine years older than Hamilton, and of more conventionally distinguished background. After the University of Chicago and World War II service, he spent five years in the home-building industry, then six years in the Bureau of the Budget, where he was assistant chief of the international division. Next he helped start the Development Loan Fund, now part of AID, and served as deputy managing director. In May 1961 he was recruited to start and head the ITT Credit Corporation. He shot up fast. In 1962 —the year that he recruited his old friend Hamilton as a vice president of ITT Credit—Perry was made corporate treasurer. In 1964 he was elected a senior VP, named head of ITT Financial Services, and became a member of the board.

He was bright, quick, and attractive, tall and distinguished, bearing a remarkable resemblance to Franklin D. Roosevelt, Jr. He was also a man of more character and conviction than his later absorption of Geneen's abusiveness would suggest. Once, before the war, some fellows in the fraternity house were at the piano, singing the "Horst Wessel Lied." Perry told them to stop, that they did not know what they were doing or what Hitler stood for. That was not an environment or age group in which such moral strength is common.

Above all, Perry had a fine grasp of his subject, with an excellent, articulate board presence. He was particularly effective in explaining ITT's growing complexity to the financial community. Yet it was not enough. Perry committed the unpardonable error of not being Geneen. "No one could keep up with Geneen when he went through one of his exercises," says an observer. "He'd say, If we pay seven times earnings for this company and give them a four percent preferred convertible at twenty-six and a quarter, that means about a one percent dilution on our stock, which costs us two cents a share, which we make back when we get their earnings up four percent, which will take another hundred million in sales—right, Hart? And Hart would just sit there and Hart wouldn't have a clue."

That was bad enough, but it was not all. In the plebeian precincts of ITT, Hart Perry had a patrician air. His work habits were fashioned by the protocols of international banking. He worked hard, but of course not as hard as Geneen, and given Perry's gentleman-banker disposition, the discrepancy was glaring. Not only did Perry have outside interests, a life away from ITT, he often took a nap in the afternoon, a temerity unheard of at ITT. Some assumed he must be under doctor's orders. But no; he just liked a snooze after lunch, confirming Geneen's growing thought that Perry was essentially lazy.

By 1968 Perry was irretrievably in what many called Geneen's "bad book." No matter what he did, Geneen jumped on him. "Hart would do an underwriting," says another former favorite. "He'd beat the underwriters over the head for a quarter point better than anyone downtown thought possible. They'd all be saying, My God it's a miracle! and Geneen would say, You bum, another issue where we've given away the store; we should have done a *half* percent better, and here's why and you don't know your job and I always have to do your job for you."

Other ITT executives could not believe the amount of verbal plummeling Perry seemed willing to take. "Geneen had a tremendous hatred of Perry," says Dunleavy, "just an insane hatred. It was crazy!"

To the fury of his admirers, Geneen's press image became that of a cold, overbearing Tartar; one magazine called his company, and by extension him, "the ogre of growth." But he never wanted to be thought any kind of monster, and Perry was bringing out the worst in him. All the annoyances chafed the more because the CEO was naturally in nearly daily contact with his chief financial officer. The greatest provocation was that Perry took it. "The bleating of the kid excites the tiger," wrote Kipling; Perry's acceptance of Geneen's abuse inspired new heights of abuse, which meant that Geneen hated Perry the more for "making" him abusive. By the late 1960s the hatred was certainly unreasoning, but not without reason. Oddly enough, the nadir in the relationship was reached when Perry was not even there. The ITT atmosphere, plus personal problems, culminating in the tragedy of a son's suicide, had driven Perry to look for help. In the summer and fall of 1971 he had taken a leave of absence and was in Denver for therapy. Naturally Geneen knew about it; he had approved the leave. But a nettlesome financial question would drive everything from his mind except a demand for immediate answers. When one arose that he thought Perry might help with, he said, "Where's Hart Perry?" to the group in his office. "He's in Colorado," someone said. "What's he doing there?" Someone foolishly joked, "He's probably playing golf"—and Geneen launched into a tirade against Perry that made everyone in the room who knew the circumstances cringe.

Lyman Hamilton in 1977.

Geneen seldom fired top executives, but Perry might have quit. There is a clue to why he did not in his having taken early retirement practically the instant his pension rights were vested in 1973. Before that, along with hell, he was given a lot of money. In his last full year at ITT his salary was $107,800 with a $95,000 bonus.

With Perry to shelter him, then with Geneen distracted first by the glory years, then by the scandals, illness, and ITT's hard times, Hamilton eluded Geneen's displeasure long enough to get in solidly enough with the board so that it no longer mattered what Geneen thought of him. If anything, the board and the financiers liked Hamilton even better than Perry, and he was an even more effective pleader for ITT's interests. He was pleasant, plainly competent, agreeably modest. Treasurer in 1967 (it was a mark of Geneen's growing displeasure with Perry that he took that job away and gave it to Hamilton), chief financial officer in 1973, Hamilton was the board's choice in 1977, and Geneen could do nothing about it.

The annual meeting of 1977—Geneen's last as CEO—was an ovation. He had only good news for the stockholders gathered in Orlando, Florida: 1976 was an up year, the first quarter of 1977 was the best in company history, the rest of the year looked marvelous, and profits would finally exceed those of 1973. The stockholders stood to cheer him. Lewis Gilbert said, "I would like to quote from 'Invictus,' Mr. Chairman. As you leave, your head is bloody but unbowed. And I'm proud it's unbowed."

When Hamilton became president on March 1, 1977, it was understood that he would study with Geneen until he became CEO on January 1; the relationship after that was not spelled out. Officially, the transition period was a harmonious marvel; Hamilton declared it one of "uncommon normalcy." But that was for public consumption; the period never was normal from his viewpoint. He had been insulated from Geneen's work habits as well as from Geneen's overmastering presence in finance. Hamilton was used to getting to the office about 8:15 A.M. and heading back to Montclair, New Jersey, at about 7:30 P.M. He took work home, but at least he saw his family. No more. Of course, while Geneen remained CEO, Hamilton's deference was decorous and essential, and Geneen undoubtedly had volumes to teach. "Hamilton was just being so nice to him," says Dunleavy, "and Geneen was being a pain in the ass." Since Hamilton assumed the pain would end on January 1, it was bearable. But Geneen assumed the deference would go on forever. "Lyman got along very well with Geneen when he was chief operating officer," says a friend of Hamilton's, "and I don't think that Geneen thought things were going to change when he became CEO. When Lyman began to differ with him, why Geneen was astonished and hurt."

Yielding the trappings of power was no problem. After January 1 Hamilton moved into Geneen's huge twelfth-floor office and Geneen moved up to a fifteenth-floor suite, the Office of the Chairman, which consisted of himself, two secretaries, and Tim Dunleavy, though the chairman and vice chairman were barely speaking. At board meetings Geneen at first displayed restraint. Some member would ask a question. Geneen, having mastered each subject as usual, would start to respond, only to visibly check himself, letting Hamilton answer. He was equally circumspect in public. At the 1978 annual meeting Geneen never opened his mouth; Hamilton ran the show.

By then, ironically, the single most urgent reason for deposing Geneen had evaporated. On March 21, 1978, the statute of limitations ran out on any perjury charge against him. Ned Gerrity and Bob Berrellez were indicted, but not Geneen.

The Justice official in charge of the case may have "bristled" when selective prosecution was suggested, but bristling is not explaining. To this day Justice does not explain its decision not to indict Geneen or its later decision to drop prosecution of Gerrity and Berrellez—and that in the face of massive and voluble protest on both points. A Freedom of Information Act request evoked about 1,600 pages of memos, mostly junk, and talk of another 1,400 pages that still cannot be released, after all this time, because they are being scrutinized for possible national security problems by the CIA. Four documents that discuss the issues of Geneen's nonindictment and the dropped prosecutions of Gerrity and Berrellez are—the Justice Department says— exempt from the Freedom of Information Act. They cannot be released.

Gerrity was charged on six counts for, among other things, swearing that no money was given to Allende's opponents, and for denying that money spent by ITT in Chile was for the purpose of preventing Allende's election by the Chilean Congress. Geneen's sworn statement included the assurance that ITT did not "contribute money to any person . . . to block the election of Dr. Allende." Later he swore, "We did not make a political contribution."

What is the difference between Gerrity's testimony, which got him indicted, and Geneen's? If Geneen had not known about the payments, that of course would excuse his testimony. But assume someone in ITT had the guts to make such a payment without telling Geneen. Geneen's system was designed expressly to surface anomalous numbers. It is unlikely that he would have missed the formation of Lonely Star Shipping, and expenditure of maybe $750,000 for "public relations" in a critical place like Chile—where, incidentally, ITT's entire legitimate advertising and PR budget for the crucial year of 1970 was only $60,000. And if somehow it had happened, is it thinkable that Geneen, facing indictment, would not have thrown the offender to the wolves? Certainly the working prosecutors considered Geneen among the "potential defendents" as late as October 1977, after Richard Helms copped a plea.

So what happened? The cover-up continues.

Bob Berrellez started to plea bargain well before the indictment. He was particularly vulnerable, since he and Hendrix had testified to substantially the same things, and Hendrix was now willing to testify against him. Hendrix had been a CIA asset all along; and according to a government document, "The CIA had used Mr. Hendrix without informing his employer and even to obtain information about Mr. Hendrix employer from 1970 up until the time that Mr. Helms testified."

The government thought the defendants might count on the unavailability of enough declassified material to convict them. But Gerrity had another hope. He asked Tim Dunleavy, Jack Guilfoyle, and Geneen for letters that would show he had testified in good faith. Dunleavy and Guilfoyle obliged. "Geneen initially said he would give Ned a letter," says Dunleavy, "then he backed off and said no he wouldn't give him a letter. I think probably that was wise from a counsel's standpoint, but not as far as Ned was concerned. He figured Geneen was letting him sink. So I think that was the start of Ned's getting awfully upset." Another former ITT executive recollects a plane ride back from Europe with Gerrity and his wife, Mrs. Gerrity tearfully railing against Geneen's perfidy for an hour and a half. Gerrity kept repeating, "I'm going to get that sonofabitch one of these days, I'm going to get him!"

As it happened, exculpatory letters were not needed. In August 1978 Justice dropped three of the six counts against Gerrity; two of them involved perjury at the OPIC arbitration hearing and the third charged that Gerrity had suborned perjury from Hendrix. The government said they had to drop the counts because proving them would mean exposing information "vital to safeguarding national security U.S. foreign intelligence interests." As the *Wall Street Journal* commented, "It isn't clear why these three [remaining] counts would involve any less risk of disclosing sensitive information than the other three."

They would not. As Berrellez's trial got under way, Justice asked for a protective order letting the trial judge, in closed hearing, screen defense use of "sensitive material." That was unheard of. A federal appeals court refused it, saying the trial court had "shown a proper sensitivity to the requirements of national security." The information in question was on the order of CIA station chiefs' names and station locations, plus contacts and relationships in Latin America—some eight years old. As the *New York Times* commented, it seemed "that the information might merely be more embarrassing than vital to security." Certainly that applied to the names of current Chilean government figures who had worked for the agency. Later it came out that Pinochet's foreign minister had been a paid CIA agent. But having worked against Allende would not imperil any member of Pinochet's government.

In February 1979 the government dropped prosecution of Berrellez; in March they dropped prosecution of Gerrity. Senator Frank Church, committee chairman, called it "outrageous." He said it was based on "spurious" grounds. In all conscience, the working prosecutors at Justice did their best. They had a hard, frustrating time getting evidence declassified when they were building their case for the grand jury in 1976. An internal memo complained that "declassification is a lengthy procedure. For example, a declassification request sent to the White House on May 1, 1976, is still pending (in July) despite attempted follow up, and two declassification requests of May 5, 1976, directed to the CIA and the Senate Foreign Relations Committee are still pending." In October the CIA admitted to a Justice lawyer "that their Agency only recently decided to allocate . . . resources to deal with our requests, but asked us to forget the past." Instead, the CIA forgot to cooperate. In November a Justice prosecutor complained to the CIA's general counsel "that the delay to date had resulted in our inability to use these materials when questioning witnesses before the grand jury." And in December another prosecutor was still expressing "concern about the Agency's handling of our requests for declassification."

The State Department was worse. In September an internal Justice memo pointed out, "The material they now claim should remain classified . . . is clearly—with the exception of Item 7 which we agreed should remain classified—not now properly classifiable." Protests did no good. In December a State lawyer told a prosecutor, speaking of the secretary of state and one of his top assistants, Lawrence S. Eagleburger, that "Eagleburger/Kissinger views on declassification are strict." He left the impression ". . . that State will continue to move slowly and will adhere to a hard line."

When the prosecutors went to trial, the policy-making level at Justice knew that the CIA had regularly fed Hendrix information. It could not have been a surprise that Berrellez and perhaps Gerrity had the addresses of the players. How damaging to national security could it have been to reveal secrets at least five years old? Besides, *what* secrets? When the investigation was just getting started, on December 8, 1975, three of the prosecutors wrote a memo to the Justice official in charge of the case lambasting early CIA uncooperativeness on declassification. "The agency arguments," they wrote, "appear particularly devoid of merit in light of the fact that much, if not all, of the same information has been made available to Senate and House investigating committees, has been disseminated in the public press, and has been made available for the review . . . of ITT representatives and others."

Today, Benjamin Civiletti, the former Justice official who "bristled," says that Ed Korry is "dead wrong" in his charge that decisions were made, and a deal cut, simply to spare various administrations embarrassment. Civiletti declined an interview but in a letter reaffirmed that the decisions were based on the law and the merits of the case: there was not enough admissable evidence to indict Geneen; there was not enough admissable evidence left, minus what had to be suppressed for national security reasons, to sustain prosecution of Gerrity and Berrellez; the working prosecutors made the initial decisions. Civiletti was shown the preceeding pages. He did not address any of the points made in them. The Justice Department, also shown those pages, would not comment.

If Korry is wrong, no one has yet come up with a more persuasive explanation for what seem to be strange decisions.

Aside from generating immeasurable relief, though, the failure to indict Geneen in 1978 did not otherwise much matter. He knew he was not going to recapture his title as CEO. Having the company run his way was something else: that was essential, the validation of his life's work. Yet it was not possible. Who else could run Geneen's company Geneen's way? Certainly not Lyman Hamilton, who had no intention of trying. The board had told him that as CEO he should run the company as he saw fit. "We'll handle the Geneen matter," they said. He thought they meant it and would make it stick, and for a while it looked as though they did and would.

Public self-effacement notwithstanding, Geneen's private tolerance of Hamilton barely survived the turnover. Soon he was sniping at Hamilton in board meetings, hectoring him with memos, at times insulting him to his face. Soon Hamilton's wife was complaining to ITT officers, "I don't know why Mr. Geneen won't let Lyman operate properly, or why he's mad at Lyman, or why he makes Lyman's life so miserable." The answer was easy: Hamilton was making Geneen's life worse than miserable; he was making it pointless. Hamilton was busily changing the canon on which Geneen had built ITT.

The most profound change was in corporate direction. Geneen's dedication had always been to growth. Hamilton was stressing profitability and return on equity. It was not all or nothing on either side, more a matter of emphasis, or maybe the route to profitability. Geneen had always pruned the unprofitable, but within a context of growth; Hamilton foresaw continued growth but declared the days of growth-before-all over; quality of earnings should henceforth be paramount. Hamilton prescribed less emphasis on turning losing units around, more on getting rid of them. A particularly reflective former staff man says that when he heard of the dispute, "My first reaction was that obviously Hamilton was right—you go for returns. But the more I thought about it, Geneen wasn't all that wrong. He was saying, If you get well-positioned in a basic industry, your profit can always come from productivity and pruning—and that's the best kind of reserve you can have. If you have a choice to make, grow, and then go after profits." You have to have the clay from which to shape the vase.

Hamilton would discard the less promising lumps. Of the 250-odd businesses in the company, about 50 were judged inadequate performers. With some the problem was weak local management and could be solved. With others the problem was "structural"—that is, chronically low market share, the wrong products, service, or location, or some other such endemic defect incorrigible without massive capital outlays. "We found 17 units that clearly don't fit in," Hamilton said. "It's our strategy over the long term to divest these. Ultimately, we'd expect to have 180 to 200 stars and prune off the rest." The "long term" started at once. In March 1978 a cable manufacturing plant in San Diego (which had figured modestly in *Kleindienst*) was closed. In May, Hamilton phased out the United States operation of Rimmel and was looking for a buyer for the rest of Rimmel and Dr. Payot. In June he announced negotiations to sell off food companies in Europe. Around ITT they talked of "getting rid of the dogs."

Those dogs were Geneen's pets. He had acquired them and he adjudged them still valuable, no matter how they looked to less practiced eyes. Divesting such companies was the easy way out, favored by the incapable, one he had never allowed as CEO. "We don't sell our mistakes at ITT," he had often said. "We fix them." Now selling was the policy. Geneen was resigned to a diminished role for acquisitions under Hamilton, but not to a dismantling of the structure he had built. It made him boil.

Hamilton's thoughts on organization were equally infuriating. In the summer of 1978 Hamilton commissioned a two-part study from the firm of John Kehoe, experts in stockholder relations, to determine whether or not ITT's stock was undervalued, and what variables could influence the stock's appreciation. It would employ a superb and complex new method for divining such matters, with the density of statistics and formulas and the opacity of language beloved of the soft sciences. The first part of the study, in December 1978, announced that ITT's stock was "appropriately priced," and that only a "higher return on equity" because of a rise in profitability would send the stock higher. The second part of the study, next March, purported to show how Wall Street looked at ITT, and the short answer seemed to be, With confused wariness. "ITT is consciously moving in a new direction," the report stated. "However, a very few members of the financial community recognize the change being implemented. Even fewer can or have translated the implications of that change into the numerical relationships that impact investment values." Decrypted, that meant the boys on the Street who never understood Geneen's conglomerate even in the days when they were flogging conglomerate stocks to their customers, did not understand Hamilton's conglomerate any better. They needed help.

Both findings were congruent with Hamilton's program. For years he had been telling analysts that ITT was not really an incomprehensible agglutination of 250 disparate businesses—in short, not a conglomerate. It was five easy-to-understand, easy-to-chart business groupings: telecommunications, engineered products, consumer products and services, financial services, and natural resources. The financial community had not responded with enthusiasm. Trouble was, Geneen ran the thing like a conglomerate: one big company with 250 units, each of which somehow received *close* attention from top management. That was the heart of Geneen's system, his contribution to the idea of management, his enduring monument, as the General Motors system had been Alfred Sloan's.

Not long before Geneen turned over the CEO's job, he told a gathering, "I want to get this company in such tight order that even Mickey Mouse can run it." Mickey Mouse happened to be standing within earshot, but what could poor Mickey do? The company had gotten so big and diffuse that it was arguable whether even Geneen could continue running it Geneen's way. When an associate asked Hamilton whether he really could run a company like ITT, he replied that his goal was to put it in such shape that *his* successor would never be asked such a question. That meant changing the management structure.

When Hamilton was chief financial officer, telling everyone about ITT's five businesses, Geneen had not minded. Analysts could be told anything they wanted to hear. But when Hamilton took steps to manage the company as though it really were only five coherent entities, Geneen exploded. No more concentration by management on all units? No more GMMs? Hamilton was telling associates that he eventually saw an organization of only those five corporate entities, each with its own CEO and integrated functional staff. That was another sore point: staff. Geneen had built the staff as the glory of his system, his in-house McKinsey or Booz, Allen. Hamilton called for a much diminished staff and was rapidly eliminating bodies both in New York and Brussels.

The system that was to be Geneen's enduring monument seemed unlikely to endure even through his term as lame duck chairman. Of course, he attacked. Every board meeting became a skirmish, and to Geneen's astonished humiliation, the board backed Hamilton. To the end, the board never quarreled with Hamilton's policy changes. They did not understand ITT any better than the stock analysts did (perhaps no one but Geneen understood it), so they were scarcely exercised over attempts to make it more comprehensible and manageable by those who lacked Geneen's gifts.

As for pruning the dogs, the directors were all for it. They had read the Kehoe report without dissent and had always viewed with affectionate condescension Geneen's tenacity in holding onto everything he bought. "It was a natural reaction for anyone who's built up a company," says Dick Perkins. "They're your babies. And he did have a remarkable record for turning around losers. But we thought Hamilton's concept was right." Finally,

Hamilton was, after all, their choice as CEO. When Geneen went from board room attacks to meddling with the functions and prerogatives of the CEO, and Hamilton protested, the board had to sustain the CEO.

Two instances of interference brought on the blow-up. The first involved Nesbitt's move from Philadelphia to Jackson, Tennessee. Geneen wanted to find out why the move was not working out. He had never bothered with chains of command. When he wanted particulars he always went directly to the executive involved, in this case Rich Bennett. That was bad enough; but then Geneen positively shattered corporate protocol. Hamilton had concluded that M. Cabell Woodward, Jr., head of Continental Baking, should become ITT's chief financial officer. Geneen felt that Cab Woodward was more valuable staying at Continental—an honest board room difference of opinion, except that Geneen went to Woodward and argued against his acceptance of Hamilton's proposal. Hamilton told the board he just could not run the company with that sort of interference. The board agreed and in July 1978 decreed that Geneen would no longer have access to employees, and that his role in management meetings would be curtailed. Next winter they barred him from management meetings altogether, without Hamilton's express invitation.

Oddly enough, the triumph worried Hamilton's partisans. Two days before the July meeting, Hamilton met with two friends in ITT's Waldorf suite, and they urged him to go for the kill. He should insist that it was impossible to run ITT with Geneen on the scene at all, and that one of them would have to go. "Either you're going to get Geneen or he's going to get you," one friend said. "You've been chief executive seven months, you're still in the honeymoon period with the board: the time to move is right *now*— don't wait! Now you've got the power, the board will be too embarrassed to oppose the man they just picked. Use the power." Hamilton demurred; it would be enough to have the board box Geneen in. "When he told me that," says Hamilton's friend, "I told him, Lyman, that's the worst thing you could do. Because now he's going to be stewing. He's half-pushed outside, with one foot out and one foot in, and he's just going to wait to get back in with both feet."

For a while, though, it looked like Hamilton's strategy was effective. Geneen was devastated, and Hamilton thought he had a mandate from the board to run the company as he saw fit. They probably thought so too. But Geneen had been their generous friend and hero for years. Even if they backed none of his policy quarrels with Hamilton, when he kept sniping they concluded that such implacable opposition from one of his caliber had to be treated seriously. They started scrutinizing Hamilton and were increasingly uncomfortable with what they saw. He seemed a changed man. "He was morose and suspicious," says Dick Perkins. "I'd say to him, Lyman, what in the hell's the matter with you? I've spent the last five years trying to build you up to get you in this position. Now you don't want to talk with me, you don't want to do anything. And he'd say, Well, that's the way it is." Even extreme suspicion was not surprising coming from someone who had inspired Geneen's enmity, especially since Hamilton saw himself encircled by Geneen's loyalists, both on the board and in the top echelon of officers. No one was *his* man. He had transformed the OOP into a true collegial management group, holding weekly meetings at which he solicited and listened to the opinions of Jim Lester, Rich Bennett, and Maurie Valente, who became a member on his return from Europe. The three men were delighted at that, and they were disenchanted with Geneen. But they were, finally, people Geneen had made. How far could Hamilton trust them? Rand Araskog, the other OOP member, was Geneen's known favorite, and Hamilton treated him warily from the start. Araskog had little responsibility, even though he was nominally chief operating officer—a point that later rankled the board. As for the other top people—Dunleavy, Aibel, Gerrity, Hanway—Hamilton was sure they were indelibly marked by Geneen, and he wanted little to do with them. He wanted his own people. Hardly unreasonable; but his choice of cohorts contributed to his downfall.

The first ally he tried to bring in was his old patron, Hart Perry. He wanted Perry to go back on the board, but the board resisted, and Hamilton wisely gave up on that one, next proposing that Perry replace Jack Hanway. That might have gotten somewhere. Directors do not as a rule agonize over the personalities of corporate officers. However, Hanway's fearsome reputation was so great that its effect on ITT morale and image had penetrated even the board room. Felix Rohatyn had long wanted him out. That was whistling in the wind while Geneen was CEO; Hanway knew too much and was too useful. Now it was possible, and Hanway himself thought he was on the way out. Then an article appeared in the *Wall Street Journal* praising Hamilton. Most of the quotes were prudently anonymous, but not those by Hart Perry: " 'Geneen,' Mr. Hart Perry says, 'is overpowering and volatile, while Hamilton develops his leadership and elicits strong team efforts.' He adds: 'Geneen tends to get things done through fear, where Hamilton gets them done through loyalty.' " It was in every sense a mistake. Perry had earlier spoken to a *Journal* reporter on another subject, his remarks about Geneen made in passing. The reporter left the paper, and the writer of the piece about Hamilton's rule, Priscilla Meyer, used the earlier interview. Perry's remarks were not off the record, Meyer says, but Perry did not realize that they could be used, and the two of them had "a very emotional conversation" about it after the piece appeared.

To bring Perry into New York headquarters as a high officer now would be a direct insult to Geneen that the board would never countenance. But if not New York, how about Washington? That would accomplish two things: get Hamilton a trusted friend in a sensitive inside spot and undercut Gerrity and Aibel, both of whom had proprietary feelings toward ITT's lobbying office. Geneen's opposition to all of this was unremitting; he wrote the board a long denunciatory letter about Perry and buttonholed members with defamatory attacks on Perry's record and character. And now Geneen was seconded by Ned Gerrity, a nonpareil at plots and counterplots, who was further miffed because Hamilton was cultivating Keith Perkins, Gerrity's number two man in PR, with an obvious eye toward replacing Gerrity. With it all, Hamilton dispaired of bringing Perry back.

The very effort did him no good with the board. It brought his judgment into question. But even more damaging than his failure over Hart Perry was his success with Gerry Andlinger. When Andlinger left ITT the second time, in 1975, it was with a huge contract settlement—despite the Levitt debacle. That left bitterness. Now Hamilton wanted Andlinger to take over Europe. He had great confidence in Andlinger's operating record and ability; in addition, he thought Andlinger's European background would help him restore the confidence of managers who had felt little but drift in direction the past few years. Tim Dunleavy was appalled. He went to Hamilton and told him that in his view Andlinger was the wrong man for the job. In the first place, Andlinger, he felt, had done poorly with Levitt. More important, in light of the recently revealed bribery in Latin America, the man who had been in charge of ITT in the area might well be an embarrassment to the board. When Hamilton prevailed and put Andlinger forward, Geneen opposed him, saying much the same, but with no special heat. He was down on Valente, was indifferent to the only other plausible candidate, John Guilfoyle, and knew that Levitt had been beyond a simple fix. Andlinger's appointment went through in late 1978. But the contention itself weakened Hamilton with the board; his embroiling them in such unseemly disputes was of a piece with the other actions that were inspiring the board's growing disenchantment with him.

Those others hit board members in their most vulnerable spots, their pockets and their pride. The money was the lesser of it. Felix Rohatyn and Alvin Friedman, as directors of ITT, both had reason to dislike Hamilton's policy limiting new acquisitions. In 1978 Lazard's ITT fees dropped to $117,000, down from $957,820 the year before; Friedman's firm (now Lehman Brothers Kuhn Loeb) got a measly $130,687 compared with $1,200,027 in 1977. Also, ITT's stock had been in steady decline. 1977's high was 36⅜, the 1978 high two points lower, and by midsummer of 1979 the stock had not gone beyond 30⅞. Of the outside directors, only Pat Lannan had more than two or three thousand shares, so even that was more pride than pocket for most. But Hamilton's constituency was supposed to be exactly those like Morgan Guaranty Trust—which in June 1979 announced that it had sold off 1.2 million ITT shares, almost a third of its holding. Moreover it was a blow that the stock was selling below book value, an inferential rebuke to their choice of CEO.

Mostly, though, the board was miffed at Hamilton's assaults on their self-esteem. What was all that business with Perry and Andlinger about, anyhow? Why did Hamilton need an inner council, distinct from the board? Had they not installed him over the objections of their friend, Geneen? Yet Hamilton all but ignored them, relative to what was due from their creature.

During the most sizable acquisition he made on his own, the $147.5 million deal for Qume, maker of high-speed printers, Hamilton's consultation with the board had been barely perfunctory. "He antagonized everyone with his actions," says Dick Perkins. "He'd tell you about a situation, but he wouldn't tell you *all* about it. He wouldn't tell you anything untrue, but he'd leave out something that was significant to the decision." It was especially galling in contrast with the way Geneen had always made them feel integral to the action, totally ventilating his reasoning beforehand, then rewarding them handsomely in perks and flattering solicitude.

Hamilton seemed to understand nothing about the care of directors. One of the sorest points between him and Geneen—such a small thing that it escaped notice in the blow-up—was the issue of ITT's playgrounds: the fishing camp in Maine, the huge houseboat at Summerland Key, the hunting lodge at Riverview Plantation, a plush resort in Georgia. Hamilton had fired some 150 people in New York and Brussels, a measure that argued to him the need for a decent appearance of austerity, which those three luxuries did not much enhance. He wanted to eliminate at least one or two of them. After all, they were not used by customers so much as by ITT people, and—not incidentally—the board. Geneen exploded. These were central to ITT's champagne style for executives. Of course, he despised the whole idea of the staff cutback and the elimination of the faltering units the staff was supposed to help, so this was a handy focal point for his anger. Furthermore, he could be sure the issue would resonate with the board. They liked luxury too. More than that, they liked an evident concern for their good will, and here Hamilton had gone ahead on something that would directly affect them without consultation. Only Geneen's vigilance had saved the day. The board intervened in the matter, and Hamilton dropped it, but it made a very bad impression on the board. You do not treat such men like that.

You do not treat their friend, Geneen, the way he was being treated, either. Despite their willingness to make him step down, and to dock his power to interfere with the CEO's legitimate prerogatives, the directors were fond of him and resented denigration by the press and by Wall Street analysts. They assumed it was inspired by Hamilton or his friends. They were almost as indignant as Geneen himself at the *Journal* article quoting Perry and at a subsequent brokerage house report praising Hamilton's policies at Geneen's expense. "Geneen deserved better than this," said one director. "He built one of the finest organizations in history; he deserved to go out in a blaze of glory —not like this."

Hamilton completely misread the board's mood. He thought their backing of him on policy meant that they were on his side as opposed to Geneen's. He told associates that he was not concerned about the escalating pace and heat of Geneen's criticism in board meetings because "nobody on the board listened to Geneen anymore." As late as June 1979 he assured a friend that he "had control of the board."

On June 17 Hamilton left for a three-week trip to visit important customers and government officials in New Delhi, Singapore, Tokyo, Taiwan, Seoul, all over Asia. His friends thought he should stay home and stay alert. One of them says, "More than one guy said to him, Lyman, not smart! Watch your back. . . . " The trip meant that Hamilton would miss the annual picnic in Brussels, following the July EAC meeting. Geneen was going and had permission to attend the business sessions. ITT-Europe was in disrepair, both in operations and morale, earnings flat, the consumer business a shambles. To counteract the drift he had found, Andlinger had slashed costs, cut staff, and generally tightened the management reins. There had been divestitures, layoffs, and outright firings; old-time managers felt bypassed—what's more, projected changes in reporting and control would surely further erode their importance. When Geneen arrived amid this steamy upset, two news items greeted him. First, Hamilton proposed holding the next annual meeting in England, with closed-circuit TV transmission to the United States, a notion Geneen instantly pronounced one of the stupidest he had ever heard. Then Gerry Andlinger, only four months on the job as president of ITT-Europe, gave Geneen the *bad* news: they were going to sell off ITT's $1 billion consumer goods operation in Europe. Geneen was shocked and furious. This was the first he, as a director, had heard of the proposed major divestiture, yet things had gone so far that one local manager told him the prospective buyer had already been around to inspect his plant. Other managers complained that the sell-off would hit them hard. "Don't worry," Geneen assured them, "it won't happen."

At the Brussels picnic Geneen was called on for a speech. It was muted and amusing—some graceful words on ITT's momentum and how to keep it going—no stem-winder, but the response was galvanic. Geneen received a seven-minute ovation from the group, which numbered about ninety of the top European managers. They saw this as the great man's valedictory; their admiration and affection for him overflowed. He saw their enthusiasm as a mandate to save the company from the madmen bent on dismantling it. When he returned to New York he used the two weeks before Hamilton's return to advantage. He started with his closest allies on the board, Dick Perkins, Thomas Keesee, and William Elfers. "Whereupon," says one close observer, "they just dominoed the board. Felix Rohatyn says by the time it got to him it was, whatever, eight-to-one, nine-to-one. But a couple of others say they were last, too." Not that it matters. Geneen's determination to eliminate Hamilton was hot, while board support for Hamilton had grown tepid. And Geneen was calling on the loyalties of a lifetime. The personnel and compensation committee met: if Geneen was putting it that way, that strongly, Hamilton had to go.

Hamilton returned to New York on Tuesday, July 10, and breakfasted with the executive committee the next morning—as usual on board days. The other committees would meet through the morning, and after lunch the full board would meet at two o'clock until 5:30 or so.

This breakfast was different. It was at the Links Club, and included

Rand Araskog in 1979.

personnel and compensation members, because Dick Perkins had been deputed to tell Hamilton he was out. Breakfast, and Hamilton's ITT career, were over before 9:00 A.M. (With the time difference, it was afternoon in London when Gerry Andlinger was called out of a meeting to take an urgent call. He was nearly as stunned as Hamilton had been. It was anticlimax when the ITT 727 landed in Brussels two days later with Jim Lester and Jack Hanway, come to extract Andlinger's resignation.)

The inside directors did not know a thing about Hamilton's ouster until the full board met that Wednesday afternoon—without Hamilton but with his resignation on the table. Tim Dunleavy was vacationing in Poland, so only four insiders were present: Herb Knortz, the most independent of top ITT executives, Ray Brittenham, Jim Lester, and Rich Bennett. They were shaken. With Herb Knortz leading, the four protested—particularly the board's initial explanation that Hamilton was being dismissed for want of integrity. "If there was one man in ITT," says an observer, "who you would trust with your purse and your wife and go away for the weekend, it was Lyman Hamilton." The insiders would not let him be traduced this way. Well, then, it was not integrity so much as judgment: the outside directors no longer had confidence in Hamilton's judgment. That, of course, was unanswerable. Anyway, the outside directors, the *real* directors, wanted Hamilton gone; disagree too long, too loudly, and maybe it's time to reexamine *your* position.

When George Brown was a director, he used to explain the wonted consensus of boards by telling of the old days in Texas. If there were four men with guns at the waterhole and eight men with guns appeared on the ridge, the four skedaddled; conversely, if eight men held the waterhole and four came upon it, the four quietly moved on. In neither case was there a fight. The insiders knew they were outgunned. Rand Araskog was the new president and CEO. Geneen had the man he wanted, someone he had brought along and groomed as successor. Surely Araskog knew who had made him and would listen. Surely, now, the company would be run the way Geneen wanted it run.

It still could not be. When ITT stock started to slip further in reaction to Hamilton's firing, Araskog announced that there would be "no significant policy changes." That was reassuring: the financial community had welcomed Hamilton's attempts to make understandable the company only Geneen understood, and to run the company only Geneen could run. But Araskog meant it. He later called ITT "probably the most complex organization in American business." He said, "The company has grown so much that even Mr. Geneen might not have wanted to keep running it the old way. I know I can't." Geneen wanted him to try, and he immediately started hectoring Araskog as he had Hamilton.

"Finally," says Dick Perkins, "Rand came to me and said, I just can't live with this fellow. If you brought anybody from the outside to run the company and made him chief executive, he would not take the job with Geneen as chairman.

"And that was true. So we thought about it and talked about it in the personnel and compensation committee, and we took it up with the executive committee, and we decided what we had to do."

As with Hamilton, Perkins was the one who had to do it. "It was another distasteful job for me," he says, "a very difficult and sad job, for I always liked Geneen very much." It took eleven trips to Geneen's office. "He talked," says Perkins. "He didn't want to hear what I had to say. He didn't want to step down."

In November 1979 Geneen announced that he was resigning as chairman at the end of the year at his own request. The company bought out his contract. He continued on the board until March 1983, when he said he would not stand for reelection at the annual meeting in May. His life with ITT was through.

He had been chief executive from June 1959 through 1978, chairman until 1980. Revenues went from $765 million to over $22 billion, with profits (except for the mid-1970s) to match. He brought enormous strength and balance to a company that had been floundering. He changed the way business looks at itself, plans, then controls and adjusts the outcome of those plans. He was not so much an example to other businessmen as he was a reproach. You think you are dedicated? centered on your enterprise? a tough-minded, illusionless servant of reality? You call yourself daring? a workaholic? Look on Geneen and despair. Someone once commented about the brief inheritor of RCA that "Bobby Sarnoff thinks he's Geneen, but he ain't." Long after leaving ITT, Henry Bowes was hired as a consultant by J. Peter Grace, of W. R. Grace, specifically because Bowes had been close to Geneen. Grace used to ask, "Would Geneen do it like this?"

Because of his stunning success, Geneen convinced business that it should try to emulate him. He apotheosized the rational and analytic. It was not just that before, accountants were bean-counters, and after, they could be chairmen. Planning, analysis, and control had always been recognized as Good Things—like pure thoughts and chewing each mouthful twenty times —that are not necessary for real life. Geneen showed they were essential for his kind of assured results. He made those aspects of good business practice not just admired but *practiced.*

The other side of the coin was a ruinous tendency to overprize management-by-the-numbers. The analysts, the accountants, the dealmakers, the lawyers, the controllers—all the number crunchers—they took over and no one was left to do any honest work. Production and the product were no longer glamorous. It was reason run amok, effacing the purpose of the enterprise. Today, a production chief whose twenty-five years of experience superintends a thousand workers may be lucky to earn as much as some "conceptualizer" three years an M.B.A.

The overwhelming majority of ITT executives found their service instructive and rewarding. It really was, as *Forbes* called it, "Geneen U." But Geneen's repeated boast of the jobs created by ITT growth, the people who got their livings from his company's success—all that was hollow. First, employment is something of a zero-sum game, with a relatively fixed labor pool, relatively inelastic markets. One company's larger share of market is generally another's decline, the work force gravitating to the winner. More to the point, the spirit of Geneen's practice was contrary to his boast. The last thing he worried about was jobs. At the first sign of soft profits, people were fired, plants closed; it was an article of faith with Geneen before he got to ITT. One old associate recalled his saying, when a department felt a squeeze, "Get rid of two bodies, one male and one female." To save on salaries, he was eager to get rid of *all* the bodies in Nesbitt's Philadelphia plant, never mind their length of service, and substitute cheaper bodies; he undoubtedly spoke of creating jobs, though, when in Jackson, Tennessee (or Fayette, Mississippi). He was not unique in this; a tour of Rust Belts will show it a pervasive logic for much of business, and hard to fault rationally. The issue is too complex for simple conclusions but it has often been suggested that the fabled productivity, loyalty, and quality-consciousness of Japanese workers derive importantly from feelings of job security.

If jobs were not Geneen's legacy, what was? In the 1960s, Lyndon Johnson's war on poverty included the Jobs Corp, training camps for disadvantaged youth, mostly minorities, where they would learn work habits and job skills. ITT's Federal Electric Company was awarded a contract to run the program at Camp Kilmer, the old army post in New Jersey. One ITT executive heard Geneen say, "I think there is money in poverty." He knew Geneen did not mean it the way it sounded, but given the project's high visibility and volatile implications, it was a perilous mindset. Soon there was intense dissatisfaction. The faculty—many from nearby Rutgers University —complained that FEC was running the place like a business, not an instrument of national policy; cost efficiency, not education, was the thing. Robert Chasen, who was then head of FEC, still bridles at those charges and says they were not true, that it was an idealistic venture from the start. And the Camp Kilmer operation was later acknowledged as one of the best in the nationwide Jobs program. But Geneen's attitude toward profit was inescapably part of his legacy.

Geneen had a vision that was sustaining, indeed compelling—for himself. The sophisticated young editor of a newspaper syndication service, discussing Geneen, says, "God! It would be wonderful to have that kind of grand passion." But it was entirely personal. It drove him. Because of his mind and his personality, he drove others; *he* was their inspiration and their vision. One of his early executives speaks of the pride they all felt in the mid-1960s because they were building something together; but that was while the issue of ITT's solidity was still in question. Instead of taking clearer shape as time went on, the *reason* for ITT, the coherence and satisfying human purpose of it, became less clear. The direction of ITT showed increasingly that what Geneen had in mind to build was nothing more than the *record* of growth that should have been in aid of some further goal. What Geneen was building was the increasing number of pennies per share he could report each year. It was not a rallying cry that could enlist many for the long haul.

Some speculate that with ABC—or without antitrust divestitures and *Chile*—Geneen would have made ITT the greatest money-making organization in the world. But a thoughtful admirer says he thinks that what ultimately kept Geneen from his goal was a want of soul. That may seem overly metaphysical, but it feels right as an explanation. The sadness of Harold Geneen's story is not that he missed his goal but that such gifts served so narrow a purpose.

"The final chapter hasn't been written on ITT," says someone, once close, who is now no friend of Geneen's. It will, he says, be interesting to watch how they change a company that has to be changed—because they cannot change themselves into Geneens. As it happened, Rand Araskog's first quarter as CEO saw ITT's first reported loss (not just a dip in profits) since before Geneen took over. However it was not real: the $320 million Port Cartier write-off was taken then. But the $34.8 million loss in the third quarter of 1981 was real, and it was all Araskog's, with Geneen long gone. By 1983, income was $675 million on revenue of $20.249 billion. In the first quarter of 1984 profit dropped to $79 million, on $5 billion revenue, from first-quarter 1983's $137 million. Araskog explained that it was because of losses on foreign exchange, and he expressed confidence that the full year's earnings would be better than 1983's. (Coincidentally, Raytheon's first-quarter 1984 earnings were $79.2 million—on only $1.6 billion revenue.) ITT's 1984 second-quarter earnings were so far off that the dividend was cut more than 60%, and the stock nosedived 9⅞ points. It *is* interesting to watch—but without Geneen, only mildly.

Of course, it is not really without Geneen. As Bob Kenmore says with pride, Geneen and his acquisition program put ITT in some very sound, very good businesses. ITT is going along. Araskog prunes the losers and the hard cases. But it does not appear that the direction is toward either growth or profit.

Geneen went off on his own, forming ad hoc investor groups to take positions in companies and make leveraged buy-outs. In early 1984 he and Bud Morrow took over TICOR, the country's largest title insurance company. The price was $271 million.

Earlier, Geneen's old friend Gerry Tsai showed a visitor a feature story in *Barron's* about Pneumo Corporation. Geneen and his group had just bought 17.3% of the stock, with Geneen going on the board. "If you or I bought that much of Pneumo," says Tsai, "no one would notice or care. But when Hal does it . . . !"

Now, when Harold Geneen leaves his office in the Waldorf at 11:00 P.M. or midnight, he looks across Park avenue at ITT and glances up to the twelfth floor—the executive floor and his old office. All the lights are out.

APPENDIX I

*People interviewed for this book and
people whose names recur in the text*

Dates of interviews are given immediately after the name and age (if given) of the
people interviewed. Dates are by month/day/year. Where the interview was by
phone, it is so noted. Ages are at the time of interview.

For the reader's convenience, I also give the names of people who recur in the
text, on the second or subsequent times without identification. I do not include those
mentioned even several times if it is only in the context of one episode. Nor do I
include names easily identifiable, like those of United States presidents, senators, or
major Watergate figures.

A brief identification follows each name; positions are those held during the time
they had contact with HSG. For abbreviations, see Appendix II.

Abtmeyer, Hermann—head of SEL.
Ackerman, Solomon, 2/5/80 (phone)—NYU professor of insurance.
Adams, Charles F., Jr., 70, 2/12/80—head of Raytheon.
Aibel, Howard J.—ITT general counsel.
Alcorn, H. Meade, Jr., 6/20/80 (phone)—Suffield classmate, friend.
Alessandri, Jorge, Rodriguez—right-wing candidate, Chile.
Alexander, Robert S., 3/14/82—early ITT executive.
Alfieri, Frank T., 49, 7/1/80 and 7/21/80—ITT staff, finance.
Alleman, Raymond H., 45, 7/17/80—ITT staff; tax advisor.
Andlinger, Gerhard R.—installed planning system; came back to run LSI; then head
    of ITT-Europe for Hamilton.
Andrews, Kenneth R., 2/15/80—professor, Harvard AMP.
Araskog, Rand V.—HSG's choice as successor; current head of ITT.
Archibald, A. A. (Bill), 75, 5/20/80—engineer, J&L.
Austin, Charles Lee, 77, 2/9/80—president of J&L.
Axten, Richard P., 2/12/80—Raytheon PR director.

Bardes, Philip—Lybrand accountant; later, partner.
Barnes, Frank P., 8/8/80 (phone)—ITT scientist, phone expert.
Bartley, Robert T.—FCC minority in *ABC*.
Beard, Dita D., 3/6/82 (phone)—ITT Washington lobbyist.
Behn, Sosthenes—co-founder of ITT.
Bennett, Jerome E., 57, 1/24/80—ITT assistant controller, 1965–66.
Bennett, Richard E.—ITT executive VP, OOP member; manufacturing man.
Benson, Robert, 64, 6/12/80 and 7/2/80—ITT staff, finance.
Bergerac, Michel C.—head of ITT-Europe, early 1970s.
Berke, Jules, 54, 7/28/80—ITT executive.
Bernhard, Richard, 49, 1/30/80—executive VP, LSI.
Berrellez, Robert—ITT PR, in Chile.
Bishop, Warner, 7/18/80—classmate, Harvard AMP.
Boonisar, Richard, 6/30/80—Sheraton, finance VP, later chairman.
Bowes, Henry E., 64, 2/28/80—marketing director, ITT, 1960s.
Bowles, Edward L., 2/14/80—advisor to Adams, Raytheon.
Boyden, Sydney, 79, 2/29/80—principal, Boyden Associates, head hunters.
Boyle, M. Eleanor, 12/4/79 (phone)—secretary to Lawson, J&L.
Brandt, Coleman M., 44, 7/30/80—ITT staff, finance.
Brittenham, Raymond L., 7/2/80 and 7/16/80—ITT general counsel, then "law and counsel"; inside director.
Brizola, Leonel—governor, Rio Grande do Sul, Brazil; expropriated ITT phone company.
Broe, William V.—CIA, head of clandestine services, Western Hemisphere.
Brown, George—director, ITT.
Brown, George, MD, 8/5/80 (phone)—Suffield classmate.
Buchan, John P., 64, 5/6/80—assistant to HSG, B&H.
Buchanan, David L., 5/9/80—classmate, Harvard AMP.
Burowski, Irwin, 2/20/80—SEC lawyer.
Busignies, Henri—chief scientist, ITT.
Butler, Edmond, 70, 7/26/80—classmate, NYU; page, New York Stock Exchange.

Cameron, William—controller, Amertorp.
Cannon, Robert J., 3/12/80—principal, Cannon Electric.
Carbonaro, Victor L., 54, 7/10/80—ITT staff, 1960s.
Carson, David E. A., 2/7/80, 6/23/80, and 10/26/80—head of underwriting at Hartford until 1974.
Caruso, Joseph, 49, 2/14/80—account executive, BBDO, on Sheraton account.
Carter, Frank J., 79, 3/9/80—classmate, Harvard AMP.
Casey, William J.—head of SEC during *Hartford* and *Kleindienst*.
Catapano, Arch Angelo—Merrill Lynch analyst.
Chasen, Robert E., 8/22/80—head of ITT's FEC.
Christy, John G., 47, 5/22/80—ITT staff, Latin America.
Clará, José M., Orellana—head of Spanish phone company.
Correll, Arthur C., 3/16/80 (phone)—classmate, Harvard AMP.
Cortese, Edward, 50, 1/22/80—LSI executive.
Cotton, Robert H., 65, 3/2/80—scientist, Continental Baking; headed Foundation Chile.
Cox, Ernest L., Jr., 59, 9/12/80—head of Gulf Telephone, Florida.

Defliese, Philip, Sr., 6/17/80—Lybrand managing partner, dealt with HSG at ITT.
Denton, Frank, 80, 3/10/80—director, J&L.
Devaney, John, 1/19/80—accountant, Amertorp (St. Louis).

Devaney, Madeline, 1/19/80—Mrs. John Devaney.
Dillenbeck, Richard, 48, 6/16/80—lawyer, ITT, at time of Chile.
Dirks, Raymond L., 46, 7/19/80—analyst, insurance stocks, at time of Hartford acquisition.
Di Scipio, Alfred, 53, 8/6/80—Raytheon consultant, early ITT staff.
Dublilier, Martin H., 52, 12/26/79—Raytheon consultant, early ITT executive.
Dunleavy, Francis J. (Tim), 66, 8/16/80 and 8/17/80—head of ITT-Europe, executive VP, president and vice chairman; inside director.
Dupka, Walter—HSG's predecessor at J&L.

Edwards, Augustin—premier oligarch, Chile.
Ehrlichman, John D., 6/6/84 (phone)—Nixon aide.
Elfers, William—partner in Acme; ITT director.
Erickson, Russell F., 10/15/83—head of Rayonier.
Eshbach, Alton R., 5/20/80—executive, J&L.

Fausch, David A., 47, 2/13/80—head of Management Department, *Business Week*, in 1960s and early 1970s.
Fields, Kenneth L.—first head of ITT-Europe.
Federman, Hyman L., 2/5/80—classmate, NYU.
Flanigan, Peter M.—White House aide, "conduit" in *Kleindienst*.
Flick, Dorothy (Mrs. James Whitehill), 3/8/80—secretary to Lause, J&L.
Frei, Eduardo, Montalvo—president of Chile, 1964–70.
Friedman, Alvin E.—partner, Kuhn Loeb; ITT director.

Gadzinski, Chester, 6/3/80—ITT staff, engineering, 1960s.
Gahagan, Walter, 2/29/80—classmate, Harvard AMP.
Gendron, Edward C., 5/19/80—ITT staff, finance, 1960s.
Geneen, Aida Cruciani—HSG's mother; 1889–1971.
Geneen, Eva (Norton; Callison)—HSG's younger sister, 1912—(?)
Geneen, Lionel, 9/15/83—adopted son of Maurice, HSG's uncle.
Geneen, Robert, 9/13/83 (phone)—son of another brother.
Geneen, Samuel—HSG's father; 1888–(?)
Gerrity, Edward J. (Ned), informal interviews in winter and spring of 1980—PR director, ITT.
Gilbert, Lewis D., 7/16/80—stockholder "gadfly."
Goldenson, Leonard H., 74, 7/30/80—head of ABC.
Goode, J. Ronald, 53, 6/10/80 and 7/31/80—PLM, natural resources; VP; late 1960s, early 1970s.
Gordon, Lincoln, 8/5/80 (phone)—United States ambassador to Brazil; former professor, Harvard B-school.
Gordon, Michael S., M. D., 9/9/80 (phone)—treated Aida Geneen.
Gorman, Valerie M., 12/4/79—HSG's secretary, J&L.
Gormeley, James F., 57, 7/11/80 and 7/21/80—ITT staff, 1960s; specialist, inventory control.
Goss, James H., 1/16/80—trustee for Grinnell divestiture.
Goulart, João—president of Brazil, deposed in coup 3/31/64.
Graham, John J.—HSG's first ITT heir apparent; head of USC.
Graham, Mary Gene (Mrs. Ralph Graham), 10/17/84 (brief informal interview); views of June Geneen.
Graham, Ralph C., 70, 3/6/80—classmate, Harvard AMP; friend; later, briefly, ITT consultant for oil company acquisitions.
Graham, Richard F. ("D. Graham" in notes), 12/4/79—HSG's staff, J&L.

Grossman, Alfred, 2/5/80 (phone)—classmate, NYU.
Guilfoyle, John W.—ITT executive, later head of Far East, then Latin America at time of Chile.

Hackett, Randall W., 44, 8/7/80—marketing director, Continental Baking, from acquisition through most of 1970s.
Haidinger, Robert N., 46, 8/1/80—ITT wire and cable executive.
Hamilton, Lyman C.—ITT treasurer, chief financial officer, president.
Hanway, John II—succeeded Marx as ITT head of administration.
Hartman, William R., 51, 8/12/80—ITT staff; head of Grinnell during divestiture.
Haufler, George J., 48, 8/13/80—ITT staff; head of environmental products in late 1960s.
Healy, James, 2/15/80—professor, Harvard AMP.
Hecksher, Henry D.—CIA chief of station, Chile.
Haughton, Harvey, 66, 12/2/79—HSG's deputy and successor, J&L.
Henderson, Ernest F. III, 55, 2/10/80—son of co-founder, Sheraton; president.
Hendrix, Harold V., 58, 9/10/80—ITT PR, head of Latin America; connections with CIA.
Higgins, Richard D. 11/20/79—B&H executive.
Hilles, Charles D., Jr.—only pre-HSG executive VP kept at ITT.
Hills, James N., 53, 6/6/80 and 8/4/80—ITT pre-HSG; director of organization in early 1960s.
Hilton, Andrew C.—personnel and psychologist at Raytheon and ITT, early.
Hinch, John B., 60, 9/3/80—sales manager, Acme; later president.
Holmes, Benjamin W.—Chilean-born head of Chiltelco.
Horn, George W., 63, 9/3/80—controller, Acme.
Howe, Richard O., 64, 2/13/80—head of Boston office, BBDO, headed Sheraton acct.
Howes, Thomas, 46, 7/21/80—ITT staff, 1960s.
Hutchison, William, 48, 7/8/80—ITT staff, late 1960s, early 1970s.
Hyde, Rosel H.—Chairman, FCC; part of majority.

Imel, James N., 73, 2/26/80—superintendent, J&L.
Ingram, George, Jr., 59, 6/13/80—HSG's controller, Raytheon.
Ireland, Charles T., Jr.—top HSG aide, ITT, late 1960s.
Isreal, Lester W., 74, 5/17/80—engineer at Amertorp (Forest Park).

James, Howard P. (Bud), 57, 6/26/80—head of Sheraton.
Jennings, Alvin, 10/15/83—senior accountant, Lybrand; later managing partner.
Johnson, Andrew—head of general ledger, Amertorp (Forest Park).
Johnson, G. Lawton, 6/3/80—senior head hunter at Boydon Associates.
Johnson, Herbert, 69, 2/22/80—executive, J&L.
Johnson, Nicholas—FCC, minority member.
Jones, Peter, 4/20/84 (phone)—ITT regional VP, Latin America.
Jones, Sidney 6/25/80—classmate, Suffield.
Jones, Thatcher T., 2/5/80 (phone)—NYU professor, finance.

Kather, E. Nevin, 65, 2/11/80—power tube executive, Raytheon.
Keesee, Thomas W., Jr.—Acme partner, Bessemer partner; HSG's executor; ITT director.
Kehoe, John 8/12/80—specialist, stockholder relations.
Kenmore, Robert H., 49, 12/27/79 and 2/5/80—head of ITT acquisition group, 1960s.
Kilborn, Peter, 41, 6/9/80—business writer, *New York Times*.

Kirby, Allan P.—ITT director, with McKinney's group.
Kleindienst, Richard G., 10/16/83—United States attorney general.
Knortz, Herbert C., 59, 7/1/80—ITT controller.
Knox, Howard A., 12/4/79 (phone)—sales executive, J&L.
Korry, Edward M., 7/26/80—United States ambassador to Chile.
Koskinen, John, 41, 8/29/80—trustee group, LSI.
Krim, Norman B., 67, 6/25/80—receiving tube head, Raytheon.

Lannan, J. Patrick—director, ITT.
Lause, Charles J., 58, 1/8/80—HSG's staff, J&L.
Lawson, Albert T.—VP, general services, J&L; HSG's first nominal boss.
LeKashman, Raymond, 61, 8/14/80—marketing director, ITT, 1969.
Lester, James V.—executive VP, ITT; member OOP; insider director.
Levitt, William J., 73, 7/15/80—co-founder, head, LSI.
Lillis, James F.—HSG's first controller at ITT.
Lloyd, Grace, 82, 5/10/80—Percy's secretary, B&H.
Lobb, John C., 66, 2/28/80 and 5/21/80—head of USC, mid-1960s.
Loevinger, Lee FCC, majority member.
Lowe, Philip L., 63, 6/27/80—first replacement as head of Sheraton.
Lowis, David, 9/15/83—priest, Sacred Heart, Bournemonth.
Lucas, Darrell, 2/5/80 (phone)—NYU professor, marketing.
Luke, Stanley—ITT acquisitions negotiator.
Lyon, William W., 62, 9/8/80—classmate, Harvard AMP; at Irving Trust, especially,
    HSG's banker.

McCabe, Frank J., 56, 1/9/80—personnel director, Raytheon and ITT.
McCloskey, William D., 8/25/80—Nesbitt executive.
McCone, John J.—head of CIA; ITT director.
McCort, James, 3/16/80 (phone)—classmate, Harvard AMP.
McKinney, Robert M., 8/25/80—ITT director.
McLaren, Richard W.—assistant attorney general for antitrust, 1969–71; then a federal
    judge.
McNabb, Joseph Hector—head of B&H until death in early 1949.
Madge, George, 81, 1/18/80—accountant, American Can.
Margolis, David I.—HSG aide at Raytheon and ITT; specialist in stock analysis and
    promotion.
Markel, Felix G., 6/24/80—classmate, Suffield.
Márquez, Manuel, Balin—son of Marquez Mira; successor as head of SESA.
Márquez, Manuel, Mira—head of SESA until mid-1960s.
Matte, Arturo, Larrain—brother-in-law and political mentor for Alessandri.
Marx, William T., 6/14/84 (phone)—head of administration at Raytheon and early
    at ITT.
Marston, Randolph B., 57, 9/16/80—ITT staff, 1960s.
Merriam, William R.—head of ITT Washington lobbying office.
Meyer, Andrè—senior partner, Lazard Fréres.
Meyer, Charles A.—assistant secretary of state, Latin America.
Meyer, Priscilla S., 2/23/84 (phone)—WSJ reporter.
Miller, Charles R., 64, 12/5/79—HSG's staff, J&L.
Miller, Howard C.—PLM, consumer services, ITT.
Mitchell, M. Richard—holdover general counsel at ITT.
Moore, R. Edwin, 83, 5/9/80—head of B&G at acquisition.
Moore, Walter L., 53, 2/26/80—HSG's staff at J&L; later head of environmental
    products at ITT.
Moreell, Ben—chairman of J&L.

Moreell, Ben—chairman of J&L.
Morkish, Alfred O., 71, 2/27/80 (also Mrs. Morkish, part of the time)—plant manager, Amertorp (St. Louis).
Morrow, Winston V. (Bud), 4/16/80, and 9/23/80—head of Avis.
Morton, William, 6/4/80—marketing director, Sheraton.
Mosher, Mina F., 5/10/80 (phone)—secretary to Austin, J&L.
Mossberg, Lester, 2/5/80 (phone)—classmate, NYU.
Motter, Allen, 5/5/80—industrial engineer, J&L.
Moulton, Robert, 5/11/80 (phone)—executive, B&H.

Nestor, Ronald G., 69, 3/4/80—HSG's staff, J&L.
Newton, Courtland G., 9/9/80—friend of HSG's in Chicago; later, B&G executive, instrumental in acquisitions.
Newton, Grace, 9/9/80—Mrs. C. G. Newton.
Nichols, Virginia (Mrs. Warren Henshaw), 3/7/80—Haughton's and Resler's secretary; HSG's secretary after Gorman.
Norman, Virginia, 11/29/79—B&H secretary; briefly HSG's after June.
Norville, Barbara, 12/13/79 (phone)—fiction editor, Bobbs-Merrill.
Nuber, William F., 68, 1/25/80—accountant, American Can.

Ohmes, Robert D., 44, 7/11/80 and 7/21/80—acquisition and finance staff, ITT.

Parks, Newton, 12/26/79—partner, Booz, Allen.
Pepermans, Frank—head of BTM.
Percy, Charles H., 2/18/80—head of B&H, 1949; later United States Senator on *Chile* hearing subcommittee.
Perkins, Richard S., 7/29/80—director, ITT.
Perry, Francis Hart—ITT chief financial officer until 1973.
Petrie, Donald A.—Avis executive; then with Lazard.
Phillimore, Charles E., 5/27/81—B&H executive.
Piper, Elvonne, 11/15/80 (phone)—friend in Chicago and, later, on Cape.
Plum, Charles W., 65, 3/6/80—head of general ledger, Amertorp (St. Louis).
Pomerance, Norman, 53, 8/6/80—ITT staff, finance.
Pomroy, James, 46, 7/11/80—marketing director, bakery goods, Continental, 1969–70.

Rachlis, Eugene, 12/19/79—publisher, Bobbs-Merrill.
Rackmil, Bernard B., 2/5/80 (phone)—classmate, NYU.
Rader, Louis T., 2/22/80 and 9/4/80—head of USC, early 1960s.
Ramsden, Richard J.—author of report for McLaren in *Kleindienst*.
Rappaport, Louis H., 71, 3/3/80 and 6/30/80—accountant, Lybrand; later partner; HSG's guru on technical accounting questions.
Reavis, John W., 80, 5/16/80—J&L director.
Reinecke, Ed—appointed lieutenant governor of California; involved in *Kleindienst*.
Resler, Edward L.—accountant at J&L.
Rice, James S., 5/15/80—head of North American telecom, late 1960s.
Rohatyn, Felix G.—partner in Lazard; ITT director.
Roth, Edwin M., 5/17/80—head of APCOA.
Ryan, William A., 53, 5/12/80—ITT staff, 1960s.

Safiol, George E., 2/11/80—ITT staff; then plant manager, telecom.
Samek, Michael J., 60, 6/3/80—data-processing expert, ITT.
Savage, Robert S., 6/11/80 and 8/12/80—ITT stockholder relations.

Scharffenberger, George T., 11/18/82 (phone)—pre-HSG at ITT.
Schene, Arthur V., 63, 2/12/80—accountant, Raytheon; later controller.
Scheye, Klaus G., 57, 6/9/80—ITT staff, PLM teleprinters, 1960s.
Schmitz, Leonard S.—partner in Acme; chairman.
Schultz, Marilyn (Mrs. Harry Steen), 5/27/81—secretary, B&H.
Seelig, Gerald, 54, 8/7/80—ITT executive.
Sementa, Dominick F., 53, 8/4/80—ITT close-out specialist.
Sills, Stanley S., 1/17/80 (phone)—head of ITT publishing, 1970s.
Siegel, Simon B.—executive VP, ABC.
Schreyer, Carl G., 5/27/81—B&H assistant treasurer, VP.
Silver, Richard F., 70, 5/4/80—classmate, Harvard AMP; later personal aide to HSG.
Skinner, Charles E., 67, 9/9/80—producer of ITT movie.
Slawson, Paul S., 7/28/80—staff, ITT-Europe (especially Africa).
Smith, Eleanor E., 6/23/80—classmate, Suffield.
Smith, Dorothy, 6/23/80—Eleanor Smith's sister, several classes ahead.
Smith, J. Harry, 59, 8/14/80—at B&G after transfer from Nesbitt.
Sporkin, Stanley, 2/20/80—head of enforcement, SEC.
Stanhope, Harry—HSG's staff, J&L.
Staub, Walter, 73, 3/1/80 senior accountant, Lybrand; later managing partner.
Steen, Henry J., 5/27/81—B&H executive.
Sterling, Lionel N., 43, 7/8/80 and 7/22/80—ITT staff, finance, 1960s.
Stolle, John F., 5/10/80 (phone)—ITT staff, 1960s and early 1970s.
Stone, Ellery W.—ITT director; head of ITT-Europe, early 1960s.
Strichman, George A.—briefly at Raytheon; head of ITT's Kellogg, early 1960s.
Strobel, Norman G., 64, 1/16/80—accountant, American Can.
Stryker, George, 5/12/80 (phone)—B&H executive.

Thomas, O. Pendleton, 5/28/80—classmate, Harvard AMP.
Thompson, John T., 63, 6/9/80—components specialist at Raytheon, and ITT in 1960s.
Thompson, Margie, 90, 7/9/80—secretary to headmaster, Suffield.
Thomson, Donald G., 49, 9/15/80—ITT staff, then line in 1960s.
Timberlake, John—VP, sales, J&L.
Tisch, Laurence A.—chairman of Loews Corporation; intermediary in initial ABC contact.
Tomic, Radomiro, Romero—left-center candidate in Chile.
Townsley, Malcolm G., 67, 5/11/80—engineer, B&H.
Trigg, D. Thomas, 64, 2/11/80—chairman Shawmut Bank, Boston.
Tsai, Gerald, Jr. 7/27/80—stock analyst; friend of HSG's since J&L days.
Turbidy, John B., 46, 5/22/80 and 8/15/80—staff, ITT-Europe, 1960s.
Turner, Howard S., 68, 1/17/80—chemical engineer, J&L.

Vail, Irene, 3/9/80—secretary to HSG, Raytheon.
Valente, Maurice R., 8/5/80—ITT staff, 1960s; head of ITT-Europe, 1970s; member OOP, late 1970s.
Van Zandt, Howard F., 72, 9/15/80—country manger, Japan, to early 1970s.
Vornle, Paul, 6/18/80—staff, ITT-Europe, 1960s.

Wagner, Everett, 11/29/79—B&H executive.
Walker, Tirzah (Tee) (Mrs. Daryl Chapin), 10/8/80—Suffield, two grades ahead of HSG.
Wasserman, Richard A., 53, 2/4/80—succeeded Levitt at LSI.
Welsh, William T., 59, 2/12/80—Raytheon executive; HSG sent to AMP.

Westfall, Ted B., 60, 2/28/80—first executive VP, ITT.
Widmar, Joseph, 45, 8/22/80—Justice Department prosecutor in *Grinnell* et al.
Williams, Arthur G., 52, 8/13/80—ITT-Europe, staff and line; country manager in
    Spain; 1960s.
Williams, Harry V., 2/29/80—head of Hartford at acquisition.
Woerthwein, Arthur T.—head of TIP.

Yunker, James A., 5/13/80—president, ITT Standard, Europe.

APPENDIX II

Abbreviations used in the text and notes

This list does not include abbreviations of public agencies when they are commonly known by their initials—such as CIA, FBI, SEC, and IRS. Nor does it include companies that are also known primarily by their initials—such as IBM, AT&T, GE, and GTE.

Listing is by alphabetical order of the initials, not of the full name.

AMP—Advanced Management Program, a Harvard Business School thirteen-week course for business executives.

APCOA—Airport Parking Corporation of America.

B&H—Bell & Howell.

B&G—Bell & Gossett.

BTM—Bell Telephone Manufacturing Company, ITT company in Antwerp, Belgium.

CEO—Chief executive officer.

CGCT—Compagnie Générale de Constructions Téléphoniques, ITT company in Paris, France.

Chiltelco—Compañía de Teléfonos de Chile, ITT company in Santiago, Chile.

COO—chief operating officer.

EAC—European Advisory Council, HSG's main instrument of control in ITT-Europe; analogous to GMM, below.

FACE—Fabbrica Apparecchiature per Comunicazioni Elettriche Standard S.p.A., ITT company in Milan, Italy.

FCC—Federal Communications Commission.

FEC—Federal Electric Corporation, ITT company in Paramus, New Jersey.

FIFO—an inventory accounting method, acronym for "first in, first out." You arbitrarily decide that a given item that you sell is the oldest such item in your inventory. In periods of rising prices, that has the effect of raising your profits, and also, therefore, your taxes. It is compared with LIFO (below), which results in apparently lower profits, lower taxes, and more retained capital.

F&O—financial and operating review meetings at Raytheon; analogous to GMM.

G&A—general and administrative expenses; overhead.
GMM—general management meetings at ITT; monthly review in New York.

HEAVAC—heating, ventilation, air conditioning—a product group at ITT.

J&L—Jones & Laughlin

LIFO—"last in, first out"; see FIFO.
LMT—Le Matériel Téléphonique, ITT company in Paris, France.
LSI—Levitt and Sons, Incorporated.

M.B.A.—Master of Business Administration, graduate degree. It refers also to those who hold the degree.
MOCC—mill operating cost control, a program of standard costs that HSG instituted at J&L.

NEC—Nippon Electric Corporation, Japanese phone equipment company.

0–1—preliminary budgets, preceding business plan at ITT.
o&o—owned and operated, the stations belonging to a TV network.
OOP—Office of the President.
OPIC—Overseas Private Investment Corporation, government insurance agency for corporations doing business overseas, insuring them against expropriation.

PABX—private automatic branch exchange, a switchboard used by a business to route incoming calls.
PDC—Christian Democratic party in Chile, left-centrist.
P/E—the ratio of the price of a company's stock to its earnings per share; the price divided by the earnings.
PERT—a method of scheduling multiple parts of complex jobs so that there is a smooth flow of progress; it is technically called "critical path programming."
P&L—profit and loss; the statement of how a company or unit is doing.
PLM—product line manager at ITT.
PTT—post, telephone, telegraph, the government-run agencies in Europe.

R&D—research and development.

SAB—Strategy and Action Board; adjunct of the EAC.
SEL—Standard Elektrik Lorenz Aktiengesellschaft, ITT company in Stuttgart, Germany.
SESA—Standard Eléctrica, S.A., ITT company in Madrid, Spain.
STC—Standard Telephones and Cables Limited, ITT company in London, England.

TIP—technical industrial products, a division of ITT.

USC—U.S. commercial, the overall nongovernment operation, domestically, of ITT.
UP—Marxist-Socialist party in Chile.

APPENDIX III

"Business philosophy" talk at Raytheon

I want to thank Charles D. McIntosh for clarifying what were meant to be charts illustrating HSG's talk given February 27, 1957—but were reproduced in the form I received without the talk that explained them (see Notes, p 365).

HSG showed the receiving-tube executives the inadequacy of their division's performance in achieving suitable ratios with a series of charts showing the turnover ratios of receivables, inventory, plant, and investment, plus net as a percentage of sales and of investment, comparing each to the record of their major competitors. With inventory, for instance, Raytheon's ratio was about 3.15. Among competitors, Cornell-Dubilier had a 4, Sprague was nearly 5, Sylvania was about 5.5, and both RCA and Tung-Sol boasted ratios just about 7.

As a minimum, HSG set as objectives for this division: receivables at 10, inventory at 4, plant at 6.7. Given these ratios, assume a $100 investment needed for each $200 of sales. It would be allocated like this:

Investment allo-cation of $100		To finance	$200 of sales	
20%	$ 20	Receivables	10%	$ 20
50	50	Inventory	25	50
30	30	Plant	15	30
100%	$100		50%	$100

What about return? HSG had insisted that 9% on sales was a minimally acceptable profit; here, that would mean 18% on investment. He also had to recover 6% interest on his investment (these were the good old days), 20% depreciation on his plant, plus general and administrative (G&A) expenses. In chart form:

Necessary return on new investment at plant operation level

	On $100 investment		On $200 sales
Pretax profit	18%	$18	9%
Interest (6%)	6	6	3
Depreciation (20% for each of 5 years	6	6	3
on plant, which is 30% of investment)			
G&A (figured as ¼ of 8% on sales)	4	24	2
	34%	$34	17%*

*Actually, HSG pointed out, it would be only 12%. With government contracts, at the time, both G&A and depreciation were recoverable. Hereafter we shall ignore that caveat as irrelevant to the point.

This was minimum; any less return and you should not be in that business. But the amount you had to invest for $200 of sales was not fixed. With new government business there was much you could do about it. First, speed up collection of receivables so your ratio goes from 10 to 12. At 10, it took $20 per $200 of sales to finance receivables; at 12 it takes only a little over $16. Second, get progress payments of 75% of what is owed you, twice a month. The investment needed to finance inventory would then be: $150 (75% of $200 sales) divided by the new ratio of 12, or (rounded off) $12; plus the other $50 divided by the old ratio of 4, also (rounded) $12. Suddenly, inventory takes only a $24 investment. Third, get the government to furnish half your equipment. To make up for rounding off the other way, above, HSG now called half of the former plant investment of $30, $16. In chart form:

Old investment	To finance	New investment
$ 20	Receivables (speed up collection to raise ratio from 10 to 12)	$16
50	Inventory (75% progress payments, twice a month): $150 with inventory ratio 12 = $12 50 with inventory ratio 4 = 12	24
30	Plant (50% government-furnished equipment): ½ of $30	16
$100		$56

Before, it took $100 to support $200 of sales; now you invest only $56 for the same $200 of sales.

When you apply the same return-on-investment percents as before, you still must have 18% profit. But now that is only $10—that is, 5% of sales instead of 9%. The same is true of the other items. Interest is 1.5% of sales, depreciation about another 1.5%. Only G&A (figured on sales) stays the same. HSG's way, to get your 34% on investment you must make not 17% on sales but now only 10%.

You could do even more. If you subcontract half your work, still getting a 75% progress payment, that raises the ratio on the other 25% from 4 to 8, or $6 per $200 of sales. The inventory charge on the 75% progress-payment part stays the same, at $12. The total is $18. But since half is subcontracted, total inventory is $9 plus $12 (the half you do not subcontract, figured at the previous rate). So your new inventory investment is only $21 per $200 of sales. What's more, subcontracting 50%, you need that much less plant investment—which accordingly drops from $16 to $8. Suddenly your total investment to make $200 of sales is only $45. You still get your 34% on investment, but now with only 8% return on sales. HSG evolved the same exercise with existing government business, where the available options were fewer, and showed how a necessary initial investment of $56 dollars per $200 of sales could be reduced to $22.

The advantages of HSG's outlook went beyond this reduction of necessary investment. With subcontracting, for example, he showed what it could mean to return on investment, all by itself. To illustrate, he examined a government radar contract that required plastic covers. Say the contract was worth $100 million exclusive of the covers. Assume it would cost $800,000 to make the covers against $1,-200,000 to buy them. In those days, cost-plus-fixed-percent was a standard kind of government contract, so you can anticipate a profit of 8% on total costs. It would take a $20 million investment to build the radars; making the covers would take another $450,000 investment. In chart form:

	To make own covers	To buy covers (subcontracting)
Size of contract without covers	$100,000,000	$100,000,000
Cost of covers	800,000	1,200,000
Total costs	100,800,000	101,200,000
8% profit on total costs	8,064,000	8,096,000
Investment to build radars	20,000,000	20,000,000
Investment to make covers	450,000	
Total investment	10,450,000	20,000,000
Return on investment	39.4%	40.5%

The difference between making and subcontracting the covers is only $400,000—a trifle as a percentage of the whole contract: .4%. But the difference is 1.1% on investment. Clearly, subcontracting paid.

Behind all this was HSG's abiding principle of seeing relationships between return and expenses and always distinguishing what counts (in this case, return on investment) from what does not (return on sales). It might not always be possible to increase sales, he was saying (as, indeed, it was not in government business); but if you control what, with reasonable exertion, you certainly could control—receivables, inventory, and plant—you could get a good return on investment and equity with level sales. HSG showed that you get the same return one of two ways: with relatively modest reductions in receivables, inventory, and plant—or by more than doubling sales, while keeping the dollar level of investment flat. There was no question which way was easier—or even possible. Altogether, this talk was indeed, as Norman Krim says, a complete business philosophy.

NOTES

Where a source is given simply as a last name, the quote or the substance of the text is from an interview I conducted with that person, q.v. in Appendix I. In many cases, several sources might mention an incident, but I cite only those that the text relies on. However where two or more sources were equally useful I give both, separating the names with "and"—e.g., "Dunleavy and Savage." Where one was first, and the other on being asked expanded the account, I separate the names with a semi-colon—e.g., "NYT, March 3, 1969; Ryan."

Where the source is the last name of a person with "ex.," "dep.," or "test." after it, the reference is to exhibits, depositions, or testimony in the *Grinnell* antitrust suit. These documents are on file at the United States Federal Court House in New Haven, Connecticut.

Although it came too late for me to rely on in writing about Chile, Seymour M. Hersh's biography of Henry Kissinger contains an excellent account, though of course focused more on government than corporate activities. His book is *The Price of Power: Kissinger in the Nixon White House* (Summit Books, New York, 1983).

I give no page references for any book, paper, or magazine that contains its own index or (like the *New York Times*, the *Wall Street Journal*, or magazines) can be looked up in the newspaper's own indexes or the *Reader's Guide to Periodical Literature*. The *Grinnell* file is not serially paginated.

The following abbreviations or short titles are used:

ABC—The file is in the Maryland annex of the National Archives. Washington National Records Center, GSA, Reference Branch, Washington, DC 20409 is the address. The file number is 173-75-9. There are many volumes in about thirty cartons. They include the application for transfer of licenses, documents, and filings in the case, correspondence, testimony, minutes of ABC and ITT board meetings, opinions, etc. Where exhibits were given a number, I include it. Where page numbers are given for testimony, the page given is the start of the relevant testimony; it may go on for many pages.

AR—Annual Report. The year is given after each. Unless otherwise noted, they are ITT ARs. My thanks to Ned Gerrity for supplying me with these and with PROXIES, below.

BW—*Business Week* magazine.

Celler—Investigation of Conglomerate Corporations, Hearings before the Antitrust Subcommittee (subcommittee no. 5) of the Committee on the Judiciary, House of Representatives, Ninety-first Congress on International Telephone & Telegraph Corporation. Part 3. (United States Government Printing Office, Washington, 1970)

Celler Staff Report—Ibid., a report by the staff of the Antitrust Subcommittee, etc. (1971)

Chile—Multinational Corporations and United States Foreign Policy, Hearings before the Subcommittee on Multinational Corporations of the Committee on Foreign Relations, United States Senate, Ninety-third Congress, on The International Telephone and Telegraph Company and Chile, 1970–71. Part 1 and part 2. (United States Government Printing Office, Washington, 1973)

Courant—The Hartford Courant.

DUN MS—Unpublished manuscript by Tim Dunleavy, *Having Fun While Working, or Good Business and Humor Go Hand in Hand at ITT.* A collection of anecdotes. I am grateful to him for providing me with a copy.

FOI—Internal memos and letters received from the United States Department of Justice as the result of a Freedom of Information request. My thanks especially to L. Jeffrey Ross, Chief, FOI/PA unit, Criminal Division, and to William B. Jones, of the unit.

HSG—Harold S. Geneen.

H&H—*House & Home* magazine, April, 1975. A long, penetrating cover story, "The decline of Levitt and Sons: what went wrong under ITT."

ITT—Sobel, Robert. *ITT: The Management of Opportunity* (Times Books, New York, 1982). Written with the cooperation of the present ITT management, but not of HSG.

Klein.—Richard G. Kleindienst—Resumed, Hearings before the Committee on the Judiciary, United States Senate, Ninety-second Congress, second session, on Nomination of Richard G. Kleindienst, of Arizona, to be Attorney General. Part 2 and part 3. (United States Government Printing Office, Washington, 1972)

KRIM DOC—memos, press releases, transcripts of talks, etc., plus notes of meetings. My thanks to Norman Krim for this treasure trove.

MOR DOC—Letters and memos supplied by Winston Morrow, to whom thanks.

NYT—*The New York Times.*

Ordeal—Scott, Otto J. *The Creative Ordeal: The Story of Raytheon* (Atheneum, New York, 1974). Commissioned by Raytheon.

PROXY—Unless otherwise noted, ITT proxy statements, year given.

Rader meeting notes—Collection of notes that Louis Rader took at EAC meetings.

Rader notes—Rader kept a sort of journal. He allowed me to copy entries from it. He also supplied me with memos and documents as noted. My gratitude for these and above.

Reporters' notes—These are notes and stories filed by members of a number of news organizations. I am most grateful to the source; they were of immense value.

SAV DOC—a series of documents given to me by Bob Savage. They are charts, listings, memos, reports—back up material for speeches and reports by HSG. In addition, Savage furnished me with two speeches HSG made. I am very grateful.

Secrets—Powers, Thomas. *The Man Who Kept the Secrets: Richard Helms & the CIA* (Knopf, New York, 1979). Excellent source.

SEC DOC—Transcripts of the court proceedings, "Security & Exchange Commission vs. International Telephone & Telegraph Corporation, et al." Misc. No. 76-0060. (Also later docket numbers.) The bribery charges. My gratitude to Stanley Sporkin for the file.

Sovereign—Sampson, Anthony. *The Sovereign State of ITT* (Stein and Day, New York, 1973).

State.—*Statement of Information*, Hearings before the Committee on the Judiciary, House of Representatives, Ninety-third Congress, second session, Pursuant to H. Res. 803, a resolution authorizing and directing the Committee on the Judiciary to investigate whether sufficient grounds exist for the House of Representatives to exercise its constitutional power to impeach Richard M. Nixon, President of the United States of America. Book V—part 1 and part 2. Department of Justice/ITT litigation—Richard Kleindienst nomination hearings. (United States Government Printing Office, Washington, 1974)

Staff—*Covert Action in Chile, 1963   1973*, Staff Report of the Select Committee to Study Governmental Operations, with respect to intelligence activities. United States Senate (United States Government Printing Office, Washington, 1975). Although I do not quote from it, an excellent source is: *The International Telephone and Telegraph Company and Chile, 1970–71*, Report to the Committee on Foreign Relations by the Subcommittee on Multinational Corporations (United States Government Printing Office, Washington, 1973). The first is the public document of secret hearings into CIA activity. The second is the staff summary of the hearings here called *Chile*.

"Suffield"—"The Story of Suffield." A handsome, illustrated pamphlet put out by Suffield alumni, with reminiscences by representatives from each class. My gratitude to the Smith sisters.

SUP RPT—Contained in *Executive Report, No. 92-19, Senate, 92nd Congress, 2d session.* Part 1 (Report) and part 2 (Supplemental Report). These are the reports of the Senate Committee on the Judiciary to the full Senate, together with individual views of senators, on the two hearings into Kleindienst's nomination. The supplemental report is on the second hearing, and is of course much meatier. I do not have the information but assume the imprimatur is U.S. Government Printing office, 1972.

Trustee's report—John Koskinen kindly provided me with the entire series of reports by the Levitt trustee to the court. I quote only from the first and the last.

WSJ—*The Wall Street Journal.*

INTRODUCTION

Michel Bergerac—Significantly, the ingredients of his early success at Revlon mirrored the classic Geneen/ITT strengths: budgeting, planning, and optimization of manufacturing (author's interview with Bergerac, summer, 1976). Just as significant, when Revlon was in some distress, by mid-1984, it was because indifferent R&D had meant lack of winning new products, while inflexible marketing had rendered the company unresponsive to changing demand. The situation was saved from desperation only by Bergerac's program of diversification into health care (NYT, May 31, 1984). For better and worse Bergerac had learned Geneen's lessons well.

PROLOGUE: The Lion in Winter . . . Pounces

On February 9, 1977—Dunleavy for "teary-eyed." For announcement of Hamilton's succession: WSJ, February 10, 1977; *Fortune*, March 1977. Both are excellent accounts, with details on Hamilton.

announcement startled everyone—WSJ, June 11, 1976, for another year's extension. Also implicit in two articles in *Fortune*, May and June 1975, analyzing ITT's problems with Hartford and divestiture: Geneen would not step down unless he could "have a good year behind him." All press comment was that Tim Dunleavy was the expected successor. In the March 1977 *Fortune* story, after Hamilton's election by the board, Hamilton is quoted as having thought Dunleavy would be next.

"favorable development"—WSJ, February 10, 1977.

Geneen was pronounced—*Fortune*, September 1972.

"Harold be thy name"—Knortz.

"There can be only one CEO"—WSJ, May 9, 1978.

"hodgepodge . . . fix the machine"—WSJ, October 11, 1978.

On July 10, 1979—Many press accounts. A sampling: *Time*, July 23, 1979; NYT, July 12, 1979; *Forbes*, August 6, 1979; WSJ, July 13 & 18, 1979. Also Perkins and Kehoe (who related second hand information from Hamilton and others).

"Lyman's been going around town"—Gerrity.

"Geneen was not the one"—Perkins.

CHAPTER 1: Making the Most of It

"Well, I don't really remember"—Reporters' notes.

In the England of 1910—Details from HSG birth certificate, #BXA 532684. Also Christchurch Directory, Library, Bournemouth.

a year later, in New York—New York City Directory, 1911/1912.

turn of the nineteenth century—Details about the Geneen family in Russia and England from interviews with Lionel Geneen, adopted son of Maurice, and with Lionel's son, Derek, conducted in Bournemouth by Sandra Smith, a genealogical researcher; and interviews that I conducted with Robert Geneen, a nephew of Maurice, in London, and extensively with Lionel in Bournemouth.

his wife, Hana—The spelling is from Maurice's British naturalization certificate, # 16552, October 23, 1928, supplied by Lionel Geneen, to whom thanks.

Samuel . . . one of the brothers— In HSG's company c.v. and his *Who's Who* listing, the name appears as "S. Alexander Geneen." There is no indication that he was ever called anything other than "Samuel." That is the name his wife gave on HSG's birth certificate. It is the name on his marriage certificate and the name he gave for listing in the various New York City Directories—in all cases without even a middle initial. When he filled out a request for a duplicate naturalization certificate in 1942 he signed himself "Samuel" with no middle initial.

married Minnie Cohen—Marriage certificate # MX680298; also his profession as jeweler.

married Aida Cruciani—Marriage certificate # BXA684999.

birth certificate read Eda—Certificate # BXA532684. Her maiden name in all ITT releases, and in HSG's *Who's Who* entry, is given as either "di Cruciani" or "de Cruciani." The name is plain "Cruciani" on all the above documents.

Samuel's strategic conversion—This is speculation, but solidly based on the analysis of Father David Lowis, a priest at Sacred Heart in Bournemouth. HSG's baptismal entry records no impediment, and also no notation of Samuel's agreement that HSG be raised a Catholic. Both suggest that Samuel and Aida were married both figuratively and literally in the church, which would have been impossible without a notation of the impediment of heresy had Samuel not already converted.

Eleven months later—HSG's father actually came earlier, aboard the ship *Camania*, landing in New York on February 13, 1910: Samuel's "Declaration of Intention" (to become an American citizen) # 37908. Aida was still in Bournemouth with HSG; she did not register his birth until March 3, 1910. "Eleven months" is what HSG always told interviewers: Reporters' notes.

baptized a Catholic—Entry 136 in Volume IV, page 32 of *Liber Baptisorum* at Sacred Heart, Bournemouth.

"quite a guy"—Reporters' notes.

entrepreneur had become president—NY City Directory, 1915/1916.

when Harold was five his parents separated—Reporters' notes and all published accounts. They all derive from what HSG told reporters over the years. However, there is some evidence that Samuel and Aida were not in fact separated until 1923 or so. In conjunction with Samuel's application for a new naturalization certificate, the examiner wrote that Samuel stated he had been separated "over eighteen years." The application was made in 1942. Also, Aida's first (and only) New York City Directory listing is in the 1923/1924 edition. On another document, in 1942, Samuel wrote in longhand "by me, 1939" above the answer "Divorced" where the form asked for marital status.

Blessed with a good voice—Newton.

what to do with the children—Suffield did not take female boarding students. I do not know what Aida did with Eva.

The school was founded—"Suffield."

when the headmaster was a boy—M. Thompson.

"Any backtalk to Pop"—S. Jones.

He devoted himself to their well-being—M. Thompson.

school had answered the call—"Suffield" '18.

"a Canadian martinet"—Ibid.

"shell shocked"—E. Smith.

"You walk your guard"—Ibid.

"Commencing tomorrow"—"Suffield" cutline for picture of Johnson.

"So there I was"—*Time*, September 8, 1967.

Camp Wampanoag . . . Morgan's Camp—Reporters' notes.

Harold sat out organized athletics—S. Jones and Markel.

his small size—E. Smith.

A once-close associate speculates—Gerrity.

"Harold was a very happy boy"—Walker.

The headmaster's wife—"Suffield" '17.

The housemother, Agnes Massiglio—M. Thompson.

feeling "how full those years were"—Reporters' notes.

smell of burning leaves—Gerrity. Except name of the bakery comes from an advertisement in Suffield Class of '23 yearbook.

In winter he hopped rides—Reporters' notes.

the "Huckleberry"—"Suffield" '04.

The Huckleberry's history—Speech to the Investment Group of Hartford and the

Connecticut Investment Bankers Association. February 15, 1968.

supplier of ice—Markel.

From the Travelers Tower—Carson quoting CEO of Travelers.

sweaters out at elbow—Reporters' notes.

for a Halloween party—Markel.

Itch—classroom story, Walker; scratched his head, "Suffield" '32, crotch, Markel & S. Jones.

Compulsory chapel—"Suffield" '17.

Daniel Sweeney—M. Thompson.

"I had knots on my knees"—Devaney.

Johnny Myers—His name is given as John Miguel Meyers, as a freshman in the '23 yearbook, as John M. Myers in the '24 yearbook; classmates thought they remembered "Myers." *Stuck-up*—Markel.

"a real good kid"—Markel.

football factory—"Suffield" '32.

"Can you play ball?"—S. Jones.

class baby—Class of '23 yearbook, poll.

want of political guile—Dunleavy.

"I got an idea"—Class of '24 yearbook, poll.

phrase signaled disappearance—"Suffield" '24, written by Walker.

By 1924—NY City Directory, 1923/1924.

Bluebird Record Company—"Suffield" '24.

"Harold," wrote Tee—"Suffield" '24.

An Alcorn graduated—Alcorn.

Connecticut State's attorney—*Courant*, June 18, 1926.

He tirelessly manipulated—Markel.

Though considered the best student—Class of '23 yearbook, poll.

"had to be the best"—S. Jones.

Alcorns replaced Walkers—HSG told Gerrity, years later, how grateful he still felt, how much a part of the Alcorn family, and how much he admired Mr. Alcorn, Sr.

"Meade was book-smart"—Markel.

never let Meade know of banjo—Alcorn.

"Farmer" Blenkhorn—S. Jones.

June 15, 1926—*Courant*, June 18, 1926, for all details on graduation.

"well-to-do family"—Dr. Brown.

"I went to work instead"—Reporters' notes. If his parents did not separate until 1923 or so, that might explain the lack of money and change of plans.

ambition to earn $50,000—Devaney.

someday, to "run something"—Madge.

job as a page—It is possible that his job was as a runner, not a page. It is sometimes so given, viz., NYT, September 5, 1971, but much more often as page. HSG's comment about learning a great deal suggests page rather than runner.

the "Room"—All details of the Exchange, and later of student life at NYU night school, except where otherwise noted, are from Butler.

"give me something solid"—*Forbes*, May 15, 1971.

charged $9 a point—NYU catalogue, 1928.

elected to Arch & Square—*Commerce Bulletin*, NYU newspaper, March 1, 1934.

boardinghouse . . . soliciting ads— NY City Directory, 1933/1934. This is his first listing, his profession given as "solicitor," although he was presumably working for Mayflower.

"Same merchandise on sale"—*Commerce Bulletin*, November 27, 1933.

Thomas's restaurant—Butler.

used to watch people eat—Krim.

"one-cent sale on taffy"—*New York Herald Tribune*, August 15, 1965.

interview . . . Norman J. Lenhart—*Ordeal*. The anecdote comes from Scott's book. But he gives the name as "Mr. Lehnard." Jennings says that the partner's name was "Norman J. Lenhart," and Jennings gives the impression of being very seldom wrong about stated facts.

"14- to 16-hour days"—Nuber.

Audit groups formed—makeup and ranks, Staub and Rappaport.

regularly drew brokerage audits—Rappaport.

no new partners since 1929—Jennings. Staub says 1930, but Jennings is sure none made partner after the crash

"This guy will never get anywhere"—Madge quoting Jennings who does not remember saying it, but might have, strictly in the context of Lybrand.

"apple pie order"—Staub.

"Harold's contemporaries gone further"—Jennings emphasizes that HSG was not unique in his beyond-accounting interests. He was also not the focus of much attention at the time, still just another accountant. "He was just getting to where he might have been noticed," Jennings says.

said Philip Bardes—In Reporter's notes. Jennings is surprised that Bardes would ask for HSG because Bardes's specialty was not Geneen's.

Geneen was right—Strobel told me the story. When I realized that, like Cannold, I didn't understand it, Madge explained. I am indebted to both.

dictum of Col. Montgomery—Staub.

Deeda Tilghman—Bardes, in Reporters' notes.

at Jones Beach—Bardes, in Reporters' notes.

CHAPTER 2: For the Duration

a cottage industry—Madge.

Blueprints greasy papers—Morkish.

war-work profit limited—Devaney.

oversee Amertorp staffing—Madge.

possess trivial abilities—Plum.

"by osmosis"—Madge.

no physical inventories—Devaney.

Amertorp eat expense—Plum.

William Cameron controller—actually, the title was "general auditor," a specific American Can rank. Geneen was called "controller."

"army . . . commission"—Reporters' notes.

"unacceptable to the navy"—*Ordeal*.

plan for production—*Ordeal*.

winter of 1942—American Can PR department.

"Harold had an obsession"—Devaney.

"discomfort of associates"—Devaney wrote a long letter to me before our interview. This is from that manuscript.

shoot pheasants—Devaney.

discovered hands-on cost accounting—As a CPA, he obviously knew about it, but he had never been immersed in it. A fellow accountant at Lybrand, Plum, had assignments virtually identical to those HSG drew and had no exposure to cost accounting except on the Sperry Rand audit, which Geneen did not join. It was certainly Devaney's impression that "When Geneen went into our operation, I'm sure he had minimum exposure to the details of cost accounting."

torpedo most complex—Devaney.

25 assemblies—all further details from Morkish, including routine of manufacture, with cost-accounting aspects from Devaney.

deeply involved . . . "mastercard"—Devaney.

"explain Harold to people"—Wagner.

placid general ledger—Plum.

managers' week, seventy hours—Morkish.

One New Year's Eve—Devaney. He was not the man, only the story teller.

Amertorp wife remembers—Mrs. Morkish.

only when contracts discussed—Isreal.

new, unskilled help—Morkish.

Ten months after . . . Newport—Company newspaper, "Amertopics" June 20, 1945, given to me by Morkish, to whom thanks.

cost of each torpedo lower—Morkish and Madge.

Newport point about quality—Morkish detailed some of the faults. Charles McIntosh, an Annapolis graduate, confirms the problems. They derived from the firing mechanism design, though, not manufacture. Morrow points out that there were similar problems in the first days of the war, presumably with the Newport torpedoes.

evidently never exercised him—This in inferential. In all the hours of description of HSG's activities and concerns at Amertorp, no one mentioned the quality problem. Morkish discussed it only in response to my question and had no reason to believe HSG was concerned.

On August 31, 1945—"Amertopics," August 31, 1945.

a manpower survey—Nuber.

"jumping out the window"—Strobel quoting someone else.

Cameron friendship . . . widow—Madge.

Conway dragged in—Strobel.

"knew he was brilliant"—Strobel.

Johnson was amazed—Plum.

CHAPTER 3: Hitting his Stride

General manager . . . chairman—B&H AR '48.

"spider web"—Townsley.

Volume in 1941—B&H AR '46.

"joke around here"—Wagner.

controller, John Hahn—In fact, he was called "comptroller," a term that HSG always preferred. That officer was always called comptroller at ITT. In *A Dictionary of Modern English Usage*, H. W. Fowler wrote, *"comptroller, cont-.* The first spelling is not merely archaic, but erroneous, being due to false association with *count* (F *conter* f. L *computare*)." I've used "controller" throughout. Hahn's skills and those of the trainees in finance from Townsley and Phillimore.

"five years' senior experience"—Townsley.

Ira Lutz—Schreyer and Phillimore.

decisions whimsical—Wagner.

R&D projects went forward—Townsley.

electronics division—Wagner.

"law and order"—Higgins.

degree of vertical integration—Buchan. Machinery & plywood, B&H ARs.

practice level . . . 1948—Townsley.

departments live with budgets—Buchan.

maze of cartons—Schultz.

favorite dictum—Percy

competing choices would save—Steen.

marketing projections reveal—Schreyer.

model 134 . . . 220—Steen and Schreyer.

government war contracts—Percy and Buchan.

FIFO to LIFO—Buchan and Phillimore.

pass up large military contract—Percy.

"staccato kind of guy"—Moulton.

D. T. Davis—Schreyer.

go at 30 miles per hour—Schreyer.

Harrod denies friction—Everyone I spoke with who addressed the subject agrees there was friction. Harrod declined an interview but wrote me a letter in which he denied the friction; he urged me to be wary of the sources of such information.

true ambition to be president—Lloyd. After Geneen left, Peter G. Peterson arrived. Peterson, who would later figure in the ITT antitrust matter, was obviously going to succeed. Roberts left for Ampex Corporation, and Buchan went with him.

grown up in the company—Percy.

Roberts stopped by office—Buchan.

B&H legend . . . McNabb's will—Higgins.

written instructions for board—Percy.

McNabb had taught Percy—Lloyd and Phillimore.

At University of Chicago—c.v., supplied by Percy.

McNabb died—B & H AR '48.

Percy prized Geneen's talents—Buchan, Townsley, and Percy.

help advance his plans—Townsley.

introduced line of microfilm—B & H AR '47. Roberts's leadership acknowledged in B & H AR '48.

plant in Rochester—Phillimore.

Kryptar—Account of conditions from Phillimore, Buchan, and Percy.

on way to Midway Airport—Buchan.

Rochester not on-line—B & H AR '50.

flesh out microfilm business—Buchan and Phillimore.

Percy counted on Geneen—Percy.

"praise you to skies"—Schreyer.

"children want Daddy"—At the time, Mommy was almost certainly at home. I see no reason to distort history by misquotation, even to avoid bruising legitimate sensitivities. HSG seldom made women stay late at B & H. Schultz says she stayed late only one evening and was called in to work only one Saturday. Later in HSG's career the rule was no discrimination: everyone stayed.

small infinity—phrase borrowed from Rader, with thanks.

community patron imaginary—Nestor.

ate fig bars—Buchan.

"Isn't that awful"—Schultz.

For exercise—Devaney.

Noontimes at Evanston Y—Schreyer.

plunking at banjo—Devaney.

Elvonne Piper—Newton. I spoke with Piper on phone; she confirms they were friends but would not discuss the relationship further.

she told a confidant—Buchan.

finality of Geneen's divorce—Steen.

dramatic flight—Townsley was told that by Bruno E. Stechbart, B&H chief engineer. Steen also knew of it.

married New Year's Eve—Marriage certificate 2114800.

New management wanted modern control—Austin.

leave B&H around May 1—Directors' minutes, Jones & Laughlin.

CHAPTER 4: The Shiny-Ass Clerk

Tom M. Girdler—Nestor. Name is given so in *Who Was Who.*

new strip mill—Denton and Nestor.

Austin in 1942—Austin and NYT, January 30, 1952.

Denton and Austin moved—Denton.

Admiral Ben Moreell—NYT, February 14, 1947. Name so given, pronounced More-ELL.

Lee Austin commissioned—Austin.

"assistant to the VP"—Directors' minutes.

Al Lawson . . . reined in—D. Graham's phrase. Nestor, Miller, and Gorman agree.

dollar of investment—Haughton.

responsible for saving—Nestor.

ignored the bean-counters—Haughton.

making or losing money—All J&L sources agree.

"Fourth in size"—Nestor.

elected Geneen controller—Directors' minutes.

Eva married Norton—*Who Was Who* for Norton. Details on his career from Montgomery Ward press release/history.

Geneen to inspect GM—Nestor for details.

"The man in charge of cutting"—Ordeal.

"brimming with ideas"—Nestor.

neatly dressed stranger—A mill superintendent, Imel, was most impressed with HSG's dress. Nestor says that the only flaw, except for scuffed shoes, as at Suffield, was his habitually droopy socks, anklets that slipped down to display skin beneath the trouser cuff. Nestor has a group picture at a J&L Christmas party with HSG's sock at half-shank. Later, head hunter L. Johnson chided HSG, urging him to wear either garters or strong elastic knee socks. HSG showed no more ankle. But, says Johnson, "He thought that was pretty fresh of me."

overawed by the works manager—Nestor.

producing a movie—Eshbach.

"tailings"—Nestor.

building cabins for cronies—Eshbach.

employees mowing lawns—Nestor.

six-million-share issue—Nestor.

budgets a mystery at J&L—Miller. There had been rudimentary budgeting elsewhere in the industry. HSG imported Myron Ott from U.S. Steel because of his work on standard costs.

description of product line—Miller and Nestor.

honestly did not know exact costs—Nestor.

important strategies emerged—Haughton.

talk of the industry—Nestor.

managers' meetings had purpose—All sources, but especially Haughton.

basic recipe is simple—Turner.

Give me big tonnage—Miller.

coal costs more this month—W. Moore.

two consultants—Myron Ott from U.S. Steel and Tom House, a Price Waterhouse partner.

impressed by his restraint—D. Graham, W. Moore, and Miller.

"years of immaturity"—Nestor.

"Don't pin them"—D. Graham.

Lee Austin president—NYT, January 30, 1952.

managers' letters bloomed—Nestor.

"didn't whip them"—Standards were imposed only at first; all were negotiable. None was valid until the men held to it signed off on it.

historical reality—W. Moore.

"extras"—W. Moore.

"shiny-ass clerk"—Nestor.

price of scrap metal—Nestor.

"arrogance with a capital A"—Turner.

fiercely loyal—Turner and Motter.

"a drummer type"—Nestor.

a steel man—Timberlake declined an interview but wrote me a letter with some particulars about himself.

Timberlake understood—His denseness is a shibboleth for HSG's true believers, but more balanced opinions—Turner's and Lause's—assure us that he was quite bright. When I mentioned Timberlake in my conversation with HSG, he said, "Oh, he's a good fellow."

steel a commodity—Lause. All his analysis.

"order from General Motors"—Imel.

Timberlake's "congratulatory" note—Gorman.

nicknamed "Old Sarge"—By Harry Stanhope.

"trying to get Resler to do it"—Archibald.

"green-eyeshade department"—Nestor.

not a "real accountant"—Archibald.

"Whizbang . . . Little Tojo"—Motter . . . Imel.

anonymous letter to FCC—ABC, correspondence file.

"a hot item"—Lause.

"the nuts of it"—Miller.

"Cut the bullshit"—Eshbach.

"goddamn guff"—Gorman.

could be very patient—Miller.

did not shout at hopeless, fired them—Haughton. In fact, HSG didn't fire them; he had Haughton do it.

mill superintendent impressed—Imel.

"stand out like a turd"—Nestor. This was racy stuff then. A burning censorship issue was use of the word "virgin" in a movie of otherwise oatmeal blandness called *The Moon Is Blue*. When Nestor told me of another time when HSG used the word "fuck," he asked his wife, who was passing through the living room, to leave: "I don't want you to hear this, dear."

One counseled a secretary—Haughton.

trooped into Geneen's office—W. Moore.

normally kept Hershey bars—Nestor.

a ready wit—The Korean War occasioned civil defense measures. Someone pointed out that no shelter had been designated for a group tucked away, unsupervised, in an annex at 311 Ross Street. They had a reputation as goof-offs. "Oh," HSG said, "they're in no danger—unless there's a direct hit on the coffee shop": Nestor.

Growing Old notion—Reporters' notes.

Graduated from Princeton—Austin.

given his personality—The consensus of all, including those who much liked him—Turner and Reavis, for instance.

Austin seized occasion to humiliate—Miller and Nestor.

born to clash—"Austin expected you to be humble," says Nestor—which of course HSG was not; he was not even noticeably grateful for Austin's backing; which he took as his rational due. Someone who liked both men says that he was amazed to see them, one weekend at the Cape, relaxed and congenial together at Austin's place. He thought that chemically impossible. And the wonder was that their personal antagonism never intruded on the appreciation they had for each other's abilities. "I've been in Austin's office when they'd been at it tooth and toenail," says the same friend. "Then Harold would leave, the phone would ring, and Lee would praise him to the skies."

union relations—Nestor.

policy to avoid work stoppages—Imel.

"he backed me up"—Imel did not blame Geneen.

Time Clock Ploy—Austin says starting time was 8:00, Turner says 9:00; the consensus is 8:30. Austin says he knew HSG's punctuality was not important—except that it was the "J and L way" for executives to be in the office when the work day started. Gorman inferred the purpose of Austin's 8:31 calls because he never left any message to call back.

depreciation episode—Nestor.

first big board presentation—W. Moore.

dispatched Lause to scout—Motter.

return on steel's ancillaries—The board had some reason. Vertical integration meant independence. That was fine in good times, which they were then in. HSG, though, looked beyond.

Ore inventory—W. Moore.

Most of Geneen's projects—Directors' minutes.

program of intelligence testing—Conducted by the Psychological Service of Pittsburgh, supervised by Dora Capwell. HSG also used them at Raytheon but had his own department at I T T.

rose through cronyism—Miller.

despite a few howlers—Lause, for instance, scored high on intelligence, but after the psychological interview, the comment was, "We do not see how this man can survive in a modern industrial society." Lause became controller of the Mobil Corporation.

"He was a genius"—Gorman.

"What's for dinner?"—Lause.

call June from Boston or New York—Gorman.

One Christmas Eve—Haughton.

That secretary herself—Flick.

Aida's driving lessons—Gorman.

going crow shooting—Haughton.

Later, at Raytheon—Krim.

"she'd had it up to here"—Ingram.

considering Geneen's income—When he left for Raytheon, he told members of his team that he was going for less money. His starting salary at Raytheon was $50,000. Gorman comments that HSG didn't live "any better than I live right now." All details from Gorman, except inexpensive boat from Bardes, in Reporters' notes.

include Chuck Miller—Gorman, confirmed by Miller.

a few friends—Nestor.

no want of affection—Both R. Graham and H. Williams comment on the quite obvious easy affection.

named to Hoover Commission—Austin; NYT, October 19, 1953.

"wildest set of wrists"—Nestor quoting John Roberts, head of Raimond Associates, a consulting firm HSG used.

At one company outing—Haughton.

AMP began September 14, 1955—Details from the book published as a memento for each AMP class, given me by Healy, to whom thanks. Geneen's late arrival: W. Moore and R. Graham.

$10,000 tuition—Andrews.

average age around forty-five—Andrews. He points out that HSG was in fact no prodigy at that point: controller of a steel company at forty-five is not spectacular.

shared a large bathroom—etymology of "can group" from John W. Pratt, a B-School professor, relayed by Joy W. Pratt in one of her usual delightful and very funny letters.

proud of having been at Harvard—In HSG's ITT c.v. and *Who's Who* listing; he remains a member of the Boston Harvard Club.

Lyon Geneen's personal banker—Bishop, confirmed by Lyon. At Harvard, Lyon still worked for what is now Manufacturer's Hanover Trust. But most of the ITT people knew him as a representative of Irving Trust.

Frank Conant arranged loans—Gahagan.

Hassler's accounting class—Andrews.

cut a number of classes—Gahagan.

dinner for all class members—Buchanan.

head of J&L's health services—Dr. John Lauer, whom HSG brought to ITT.

December 6 newspaper story—*Boston Herald*, December 6, 1955. Also NYT, that date.

Charles Francis Adams, Jr., deluged—Ordeal.

wives join their husbands—R. Graham. Doubtless, today, it is also vice versa; not then.

"Do you think I ought to take this job?"—Bowles. The story also appears in *Ordeal*.

"Charles Austin destroying self-confidence"—Sovereign. Austin was always called "Lee," not "Charles."

Driving home from office—Nestor.

Austin reviewed budgets—Nestor.

written to Charles Percy—Phillimore.

"met some real idiots"—Nestor.

ambition was to be "president"—Eshbach.

weekend on Cape Cod—Nestor checked, and the high that day was 55 degrees. Austin remembers that he was pruning, but Nestor specifically remembers HSG's gesture, as he told the story, of scattering fertilizer. Story also in *Fortune*, February 1961, but in scant detail.

late as April 26, 1956—Directors' minutes.

$50,000 plus stock options—Ordeal; Scott's source, the Raytheon directors' minutes.

Geneen told key directors—Reporters' notes. Reavis's and Denton's versions came from them.

Reavis recognized the real problem—HSG assured him that, no, he was happy in steel. "He made a point of it," says Reavis, "but I couldn't imagine him happy in it. It would always be slow-paced for someone like Harold. I know it would have been for me."

Geneen was already committed—Director's minutes.

Moreell called a meeting—NYT, August 31, 1956; Morell's quote from someone who attended the meeting.

CHAPTER 5: The Brahmin and the Bull

One employee recollects—Schene.

Harold Geneen called it—Reporters' notes.

Sales were $175,490,000—Raytheon AR fiscal '56. Geneen changed Raytheon's fiscal-year reporting to calendar year because the analysts and market preferred it that way.

everyone knew a triumph of science—Bowles. Catapano quoted to the same effect in Reporters' notes.

Shortly after World War I—Ordeal. The characterization of managerial ineptitude, however, is mine, not Scott's.

*Microwave transmission—*Bowles.

*Morgan placed Adams—*Bowles and *Ordeal.* Morgan was head of the firm of Morgan Stanley, which controlled the Raytheon stock, having split off from J. P. Morgan in an antitrust action.

*an "investment banker"—*Bowles and *Ordeal.* Bowles insists that Adams did not care for brokerage business. Bowles was very close to Adams, once a principal advisor.

*man who became Geneen's controller—*Ingram.

*Adams at first offered Geneen—*Krim.

*rudimentary control, rigidly centralized—*Ingram and Schene.

*he told the policy committee—*KRIM DOC.

*three P&L centers—*Ingram. Details from Raytheon AR '56.

*suddenly three divisions—*Raytheon AR '57.

*personal issue for Geneen—*Krim.

*Receiving tubes need new accountants—*KRIM DOC.

*about 2000, nearly 5%—*Ingram says 10% of work force, but Raytheon AR '59 puts that at 41,000. Two thousand is Ingram's figure.

*new people included controller—*When Schultz left, Allen E. Reed was controller. Adams made him treasurer also. Geneen would be his own treasurer, in effect, so he kept Reed on in that job and replaced him with a working controller after his own heart.

*reporting relations to the line—*Ingram.

*most did review reports—*Schene.

*"Yellow Peril"—*Schene.

*basic objective of the Company—*KRIM DOC. The meeting was on December 5, 1957. It was a talk to the management club of the receiving-tube division.

*Someone who attended Harvard—*Charles McIntosh. I am indebted to him for an interpretation of the material that follows. Geneen's talk had been reduced to a series of charts that were, to me, unintelligible. When Krim first gave me a copy, he characterized it as "a hell of a talk" and "a complete course in business philosophy: it shows how to set your objectives and what the alternatives are for reaching them —really excellent!" He said, "I still use it in my career." Since Krim today harbors the strongest imaginable animus toward Geneen, this is indeed praise. I was anxious to understand the charts, but it seemed a forlorn hope; they were unaccompanied by explanation, meant merely as visual aids for HSG's talk.

A year before I got to the charts, a free-lance advertising client asked if I would address his Pepperdine Business School extension M.B.A. class about Geneen; they were then studying ITT's organization. I did. A year later, the instructor asked if I would address the new class. I said I'd be glad to if he would decipher the charts for me. He said that numbers were not his specialty but that if he could not, he had a friend who taught at the UCLA business school who surely could. It was a deal.

When I showed up for the class and showed him the charts he was at a loss but said his friend had already agreed to look at them and, indeed, had expressed interest in seeing them. Despite a note and two phone calls to the Pepperdine instructor's office, I never heard from him again.

Remembering that Mac had gone to the Harvard B-school, I asked him to look at the charts. He puzzled over them for weeks, taking them to lunch nearly every day.

Finally he cracked them, and after explaining the basic scheme of them to me, he helped me work out the details. The charts as they are discussed in the text, and as they appear in Appendix III, are changed from HSG's original to make them intelligible—all thanks to Mac's kind and perceptive help.

clerks were hand-carrying vouchers—Schene.

One manager had a plaque—Kather. He had himself been an engineer.

auditorium of Waltham—Sovereign.

at the Wayland Labs—Axten. HSG explained in reporters' notes that although engineering was Raytheon's boast, "we see the need of a considerable effort on more mundane 'business' aspects of the company."

Big Picture meetings—KRIM DOC.

"no 'covering up' "—KRIM DOC.

"details that I'd miss"—Kather.

50 to 200 people went over reports—Ingram.

Indolent critics later argued—They are still at it. In January 1982 *Fortune* ran a particularly silly piece about ITT without HSG. Morrow, who at that time had no connection with HSG, wrote a letter to the editors pointing out that while he had "never been slow to point out this or that deficiency in Geneen's methods or his control system, my strongest surviving impression remains that Harold Geneen is far and away the most outstanding business executive I have ever encountered." Perhaps he didn't "build a succession that immediately worked but just as clearly he built, as none of his successors ever could have, an immense, vital and, above all, well-balanced corporation. While making quarters counted mightily, he did not lose sight of the value of growth and development. . . . " Maybe it was fashionable to take shots at Geneen, Morrow closed; indeed he had done so himself "under certain circumstances. Still, comparing him with what is around today, I have to think he stands out as a giant. His remarkable record deserves a much more even review than it ever seems to get."

"Committee for Long Range Statistics"—KRIM DOC: October 26, 1956.

confront such questions as—All from Kather.

managers forecast earnings—Schene.

break up fiefdoms—Raytheon AR '57 & '58.

always on lookout for management material—KRIM DOC.

David I. Margolis—Who's Who.

"always on the phone to analysts"—Kather.

Colt Industries—At the time called Fairbanks Whitney.

Margolis and Geneen little contact—Reporters' notes, confirmed by Strichman's son, whom I met informally.

reflected in 1957—Raytheon AR '57.

disciple at ITT—Kenmore.

William T. Marx—KRIM DOC: Raytheon bio.

old-line personnel head—Les Woods, who thereafter dealt with union negotiations.

Geneen developed a weakness—Consensus. Among those who cited specific instances are Bowles, Schene, and Welsh, all HSG admirers.

joint venture with Honeywell—Account in *Ordeal*. Details from Adams, Axten, Bowles.

Adams enforce contract price—Adams says that HSG had nothing to do with the sale. But Vail and, later, Rader got the impression from what HSG said about it that he did. It was settled in June 1957: Raytheon AR '57.

same errors that surrendered the field to TI—Analysis mostly Welsh. Also Kather and Bowles.

"Krim among many people"—Welsh.

beglimmered by germanium—Kather.

a "need to succeed"—KRIM DOC.

Summing up 1957—KRIM DOC.

Geneen could project to bankers—KRIM DOC. Projection was in 1957.

Raytheon largest employer—Raytheon ARs.

Raytheon stock closed—NYT, day following dates.

"Harris Trust Company participate."—Chicago bank serving B&H.

June 1958 Raytheon $75 million—Raytheon AR '58.

"the night superintendent"—Kather and *Ordeal.*

"wasn't a very easy guy to work for"—Ingram.

first child being christened—Ingram.

"Adams wanted everyone happy"—Welsh.

Adams barked, "Stop that!"—*Ordeal,* elaborated by Adams.

license tubes by foreign companies—KRIM DOC. The answer was, among other suggestions, that since L. M. Ericsson was the putative supplier, and since the Bofors company had produced fire-control equipment for Germany in World War II, "This might be exploited in denying Ericsson qualification approval." Krim did not say how.

"You mean there's some civil servant"—Welsh.

"He knew all the admirals"—Bowles.

"If Charlie caught you"—Welsh.

"broke into two groups"—Kather.

condominium in Florida—Vail.

Hatch Shell—Bowles.

His secretary noticed—Vail.

the bank's chairman explained—Horace Schermerhorn in reporters' notes.

participation in board meetings episodic—"That worried him more than it did us," says Trigg. They considered it quality time.

85% business with the government—KRIM DOC.

raising the company's commercial business—Notes taken by Krim at an August 12, 1958, meeting; also KRIM DOC.

Boyden Associates—KRIM DOC. The main contact was William R. Geary. Boyden charged $1,500 a month just for looking, with a commission of 20% of a year's salary, minimum $4,000, for each placement.

John T. Thompson—KRIM DOC.

"civilizing" black box knobs—J. Thompson.

civilian band radios—After HSG left, but his concept.

safest, quickest way to grow—Krim kept the charts used at the meeting. Di Scipio and another from McKinsey were in the group. Marx was head of personnel and organization, which had little to do with acquisitions; but HSG trusted his judgment, so he was in the group too. Margolis was also included for his judgment and for his stock-hyping activity. Other members included John H. Beedle (government equipment) and J. Penn Rutherfoord (industrial aparatus), both of whom knew the competition, John Mitchell, who was director of planning, J. Thompson (commercial products) and Percy L. Spencer, resident inventive genius. Krim was coordinator.

three absolute tests—KRIM DOC. This was for a company proposed as a new Raytheon division; if it would just be a new product line, it needed only over half a million volume.

"pursue an acquisition in conversation"—Ingram.

casual talk on the Cape—Dubilier.

It started at 6:00 PM—KRIM DOC.

Yet for all the exertion—Raytheon AR '59.

the ultimate provocation—He told Vail that it was "not for the money" that he was leaving. He gave her the impression that the proximate cause was Adams's refusal to fire Bowles, whom HSG had grown to see as a malign influence. She quotes him as saying, "I was called in here to do a job, and I've run into a stone wall."

résumé floating around—Jennings.

"haven't made up my mind about ITT"—Ordeal.

"very large company"—NYT, May 21, 1959.

most heavily traded stock—NYT, next day.

Floundering just after Geneen left—HSG had made two controversial hires: Richard E. Krafve and Charles D. Manhart. Krafve had been at Ford, blameless head of the Edsel project. He was going to be Raytheon's head of consumer products. Adams made him executive VP, succeeding HSG, and he was not popular. Manhart had been a government relations man at Bendix, and was hired to be the same at Raytheon. Adams was going to put him in as head of missiles.

when reporters wanted to talk about Geneen—Reporters' notes.

reforms and controls still in effect—Ingram and Schene.

CHAPTER 6: It Makes you Question

when he started the company—With his brother, Hernand. See complete account in *I.T.T.* Also *Time*, June 17, 1957.

Louis XIV showpiece—*Time*, ibid. *Forbes*, February 1, 1964, called it Louis XV. So did *Fortune*, February 1961. But Behn seems more baroque than rococo. Sosthenes, wrote *Time*, means "life strength." Other details of his career are in *ITT*, plus versions told me by McKinney and stories in DUN MS.

no dividend to stockholders—BW, November 22, 1947. The stock high is from NYT, January 1, 1930.

The funded debt—slashed in half, to $70 million; fixed expenses ratio from 7.6 to 3.9. All from BW, April 7, 1951.

Robert M. McKinney searching—McKinney. Also, BW, November 22, 1947; *Time*, June 7, 1954; NYT, November 14, 1947.

Ryan, as spokesman—McKinney says he was the lead partner; the news stories all make it Ryan.

Behn responded—*Time*, June 7, 1954.

Seven inside directors resign—NYT, December 24, 1947.

installation of a president—BW, July 10, 1948; it happened on September 1. Harrison was no kin to the president. He was a Roman Catholic and thought that was why he had not become president of AT&T: Chasen.

started paying modest dividend—AR '59.

Behn stripped of power—*Time*, June 7, 1954. "We dethroned him," says Perkins.

Harrison heart attack—NYT, April 28, 1956.

Behn announced retirement—NYT, June 24, 1956. Behn died in June 1957.

"caretaker president"—Sovereign.

"Colonel" Behn . . . "General" Harrison—Fortune, August 1956. Leavey was a commensal of Dwight D. Eisenhower, Class of '15.

get-acquainted cruise—McKinney.

revenues rose each year—AR '59; stock prices from NYT, January 1, 1957–59.

In approved army fashion—Rundown on candidates from Chasen and Hills, confirmed by Scharffenberger.

Hugh Knowlton head of search—L. Johnson.

First National City Bank—Now called Citibank.

most of the ITT executive committee—Except Lannan.

salary to the end of the year—PROXY '60, '61.

something rankled—W. Moore.

CHAPTER 7: A Real Dog

Catapano commented—Reporters' notes.

Geneen knew better—Fortune, February 1961.

"a real dog"—Fortune called it "a sick giant." Ibid.

ITT had 116 plants— Ibid. AR '58 says 101 "principal" plants in 23 countries.

worldwide communications system for SAC—Dubilier.

ITT's volume was $765,639,896—Relevant ARs.

profit margin for 1959—SAV DOC.

ITT made money in United States—Reporters' notes.

German subsidiary engaged an NY firm—BW, May 4, 1963.

Europe investment huge . . . meager return—Lobb.

serious problems with defense group—Dubilier.

"used to get gray hairs"—Westfall.

over 90% stockholders American—Kenmore.

his first public speech—NYT, March 15, 1960.

"a lot of deadwood"—J. Graham, in reporters' notes.

seventeen top corporate officers—Margolis was quoted in reporters' notes: there was at ITT "a management vacuum when Hal arrived."

M. Richard Mitchell—Hills. The following Mitchell quote: Fortune, February, 1961.

Stone as figurehead—Dunleavy.

"with a telegraph pad and plane schedule"—Reporters' notes. Much the same in Celler.

Scudder stayed for years—He was last listed in AR '68.

He immediately imported—Marx came on July 27, 1959: AR '59.

"I'll give you eighty"—PROXY '61: $86,520, with a $20,000 bonus.

"After you let a man go"—Fortune, February, 1961.

two divisions counted seventeen purchasing departments—Ibid.

firing was wholesale—Haidinger. There were fifty people, he says, in the industrial relations department alone, entirely duplicated across the street.

ITT Communications Systems (ICS)—Report by Stone on a manager's conference in Gerona, Spain. Courtesy of Rader.

Geneen found SAC unhappy—Dubilier.

Kellogg Switchboard and Supply Company—Rader and AR '59.

find good people—Rader and *Fortune*, February 1961.

German rail equipment in Kansas City—Rader.

George Strichman uncovered inventory problem—Rader notes.

Safiol had organized—Hills, confirmed by Safiol.

Intelex's automated post office—Rader.

precedes refusal to pay—Rader had told the authorities about the overrun.

damned thing did not work right—Rader had warned the post office of inadequate training and insists it was that, not the equipment.

George Brown, a Texas Democrat—See Robert A. Caro's biography of Lyndon Johnson, *The Path to Power* (Knopf, New York, 1982).

cancellation of a large contract—Defliese and Rader. Also Madge.

designed and built in Belgium, France, and Germany—Rappaport and Rader.

about $4 million apart—Rappaport.

Rappaport, Geneen's old oracle—One has only to chat with Rappaport to realize that he would have been conscientious and fair.

Lillis came in waving the check—Knortz.

Behn had acquired the stock—NYT, May 5, 1960.

"directors on Ericsson's board"—*Fortune*, February 1961.

Geneen incensed; never knew what going on—Lobb.

same with Nippon Electric—NYT, January 20, 1961.

Japanese were keeping information from him—Lobb. Van Zandt says that is not so; but Lobb was closer to HSG, and it was HSG's perception that counted, not reality.

Japan never departed from United States standards—Lobb.

bells and whistles—Rader, Dubilier, and many others credit Andlinger with the planning system format.

"Other chief executives . . . automatically right"—Kenmore.

components operation in Portugal—Knortz.

Geneen toured one fazenda—R. Graham. For six months HSG urged Graham to join him in buying land there. "We'd both love to have a place where you walk along and have those people bowing."

executive drinking in the Marguery—Samek.

"the winning horse"—Reporters' notes.

CHAPTER 8: An Uncertain Golconda

"The gold mine was abroad"—Reporters' notes.

on inspection a severe problem—Yunker and Lobb.

juicy contract in Egypt—di Scipio.

"Places with the lowest labor"—Alexander.

troubles with ITT switching—Turbidy.

try for a quick fix—Alexander.

Hermann Abtmeyer—Hitler's communications: J. Thompson; rest of Abtmeyer's back ground, AR '60; SEL merger, reporters' notes.

José Maria Clará Orellana—Thanks to the information section of Spain's Ministerio de Transportes, Turismo y Communicaciones for providing the full name of Clará and of Barrera, in chapter 13.

McKinsey study confirmed vision—Yunker. Headquarters for everything except Europe, though, was in New York.

Europeans did not take Geneen seriously—Largely di Scipio's analysis. Rader points out that they were generally better educated and more cultured than their American counterparts, which bred contempt.

Marx and di Scipio scouted for headquarters—di Scipio.

"We picked Brussels"—Reporters' notes.

first office was nondescript—di Scipio and Vornle.

no meetings before noon—Rader. He says the first few times, the New Yorkers actually got sick.

"Oh Pierre, Oh Fritz"—W. Moore. Lobb says the informality did not carry over even to lunch.

"I'm not asking you for any information"—Reporters' notes.

The concept was brilliant—Yunker analysis.

"Geneen handled Europeans with finesse"—Kenmore.

back European managers in dispute—Vornle.

bully a country manager—Samek.

Guy Rabuteau—AR '60.

how gently Geneen disposed of unsuitable—Dubilier.

reservation system for Air France—There were three contracts, including a small one for British European Airways. "All three were losing their ass," says Lobb. Main source, Rader meeting notes.

ITT could still brag—AR '59.

stay in the business "at least officially"—Rader meeting notes.

"sole job to keep us out of computers"—Led by PLM and ITT-Europe VP Mortimer Rogoff. "He killed the data-service concept," says Samek, whose baby that was, and who was very bitter. "He had a lot of influence with Geneen."

French and Germans computer bootleggers—Yunker.

no objection to ITT's using computers—Dubilier went to Europe expressly to run ITT's data-processing operation.

standard ITT phone system in Europe—I am indebted to Maurice Deloraine for the accurate history of the development of Pentaconta and its introduction at the 1957 Antwerp meeting. His version was strongly confirmed by Yunker and Rader, with Lobb and Marx adding details—to all of whom, thanks. Details of the country managers' objections and "all hell broke loose" are from Yunker. "We have a marriage contract with Siemens": reporters' notes.

Fields: "seemed to infuriate him"—Rader notes.

Marc A. de Ferranti—Rader et al. Also in *Forbes*, May 1, 1968. He received a sentence of thirty days, suspended, and a $3,500 fine: NYT, February 8, 1961.

de Ferranti replaced Fields—AR '60.

"His greatest contribution"—A. Williams.

Geneen dispatched Marx—Rader. He also heard HSG's version; HSG had Rader paged on a golf course on a weekend to tell him firsthand when he fired de Ferranti. Marx confirms the story in main but corrected some details.

Geneen learned a lesson—Bergerac was to be an exception; he was much more independent.

factory in Spain—Dunleavy.

approved on strength of letter—Rader notes.

Labeled session "export meeting"—Rader notes.

"one hundred percent for Geneen"—Reporters' notes, on December 4, 1960.

CHAPTER 9: Plans for Christmas

Latin American companies—Scheye.

92% of Chile's telephones—None of these figures is exact. One *Fortune* article made it 90%; BW wrote 92%, and ITT alumni agreed. I am persuaded, though, that they are approximately accurate. There was no ITT telephone, radio, or cable in Paraguay.

backlog of orders—AR '59. That included Puerto Rico and the Virgin Islands.

Castro appointed "interventor"—NYT, August 8, 1960.

Ted B. Westfall—NYT, January 12, 1963. Name so given, and Westfall says it is his full name—actually more than full: he gave himself the "B." when he grew tired of being Ted (NMI) [no middle initial] in the service.

"According to associates"—Ibid.

Westfall toured territory—The delay was because his first assignment was to clear up one of the perennial messes with ITT's Puerto Rican Telephone Company, known at ITT by the unlovely name of Ricophone. Ricophone service was a horror. Once, at a reception, Samek thought to strike some common chord with the famous mayor of San Juan, Felicia de Rincón, by telling her he worked for ITT. She turned and stalked away. The annual tour with HSG became a regular thing until Westfall fell from favor.

expropriated ITT's phone company—NYT, February 17 & 18, 1962.

$470,937 worth of cruzeiros—Time, March 9, 1962, collected in a book of press comments put together by ITT PR, given to me by Rader.

"crazy brother-in-law"—Gordon quoting Dantas.

press in Brazil—NYT, February 21, 1962.

pushed government to indemnify—NYT, October 13, 1960.

"IT and T would invest"—NYT, April 8, 1961.

Merriam met Hickenlooper—Beard.

the Geneen Amendment—Bowes.

terms of Hickenlooper Amendment—NYT, July 21, 1962. Also amount of aid at stake.

a special interest item—Ibid. "Moreover it is agreed on all sides that the expropriation provision is intended to be of primary benefit to the International Telephone and Telegraph Company of New York. This, in the official view, makes it 'special-interest legislation' in a general authorization bill, contrary to accepted legislative procedure."

Geneen would phone Hickenlooper—R. Graham.

Brizola's first position—Gordon.

Brizola's minister of justice—He was Francisco Brochada da Rocha.

ITT accused Brizola—NYT, February 23, 1962.

nettlesome issue of utilities—Another governor, Carlos Lacerda, had moved against two other utilities. The politics of expropriation were confused, more nationalistic than ideological. Goulart was on the left, and Brizola even further left. But Lacerda was distinctly right-wing, a fierce anti-Communist. General Pery Constant Bevilacqua,

2nd Army commander in São Paulo, congratulated Brizola on his actions. The Brazilian press, meanwhile, annoyed at ITT-orchestrated talk of Brazilian bad faith, was changing sides.

Hickenlooper skipped vote—NYT July 21, 1962.

Gordon took translation to—Hermes Lima, later on the Supreme Court.

settlement was announced—NYT, December 24, 1962.

scribbled a telex to Gerrity—He gave it to Scheye to encode.

principle, not the money—In fact, the fuss HSG made cost something in depressed stock values. The always impressionable market took him at his word about what a blow the expropriation was and bid down ITT's stock enough so that HSG soon declared (BW, May 4, 1963) that the expropriation was "exaggerated out of all proportion to what was seized—a $7.3 million company that was running in the red."

82% of United States phones—Thomas Leweck, GTE PR department.

Southern Bell—BW, April 25, 1964; NYT, April 14, 1964.

challenged AT&T move—Fortune, July, 1966; NYT, October 30, 1963.

one share apiece of AT&T—Scheye.

"never product-line loyalty"—Samek.

Taking someone else's technology—Charles McIntosh J Thompson says, "ITT's technological capability was laughable. Henri Busignies admitted that when we sat down to talk about semiconductors." They had to settle for a knowhow agreement with Fairchild Camera and Instrument.

Profits had risen from . . .—Relevant ARs.

two acquisitions in 1960—AR '60.

American Cable and Radio—SAV DOC: all percentages are approximate, most rounded off.

Surprenant . . . unexpected byways—Hills.

Runaway Brook—name from Haidinger; details from Schene, who was a member, except course length from DUN MS, confirmed by pro shop at club.

Europe acquisitions—Relevant ARs.

National Computer Products—Henceforth called National Transistor. But HSG was thinking big. He considered the Burroughs Corporation and Western Union, conducted talks with P. R. Mallory. His disenchantment with Rader stemmed from Rader's insistence that Mallory was "a bunch of rubbish" not worth acquiring. Geneen said it showed Rader was interested only in technology and not making money. Rader notes and di Scipio.

Europe, six acquisitions—AR '62 and BW, May 4, 1963.

owned the F Street Club—Beard.

tucked in a corner of defense group—Reporters' notes.

yearly political seminars—in 1961, *Aviation Week and Space Technology* commented on ITT's exemplary program of exposing company executives to local and national politicians.

company owned by George Brown—Alexander.

85,224 square feet—PROXY '63. A ten-year lease at $57,952/year.

"big angle for making money"—Reporters' notes.

under rock, pot of gold—Attributed to others, but Rader is positive Mitchell said it first.

Andy Hilton maintained—Rader notes.

"man does eight things right"—Alex Smith, quoted in Rader notes.

"on witness stand with Geneen"—Fortune, February 1961.

Lou Rader left New York—on February 15, 1960. Typed itinerary is one of many memos Rader gave me.

revolving-door image—BW, May 4, 1963.

a house in California—Forbes, May 1, 1968.

"kind of life I don't want to lead"—Ibid.

"young man of thirty"—Reporters' notes.

"Hell, I know them all"—Sterling.

each quarter's earnings topped—Geneen was particularly insistent on a good first quarter, and especially in the United States, where defense and space were much of the total. The military was always looser with money toward the end of the year when a budget had to be spent or lost.

looking at earnings a new way—Sterling.

one billion dollars—Hills. He showed me his copy of the medal.

CHAPTER 10: Trying Something New

best first quarter net—NYT, May 9, 1963.

volume and income had grown—ARs and SAV DOC. The domestic decline was because so much of it was in low-profit defense work.

3.3¢ on each dollar—Forbes, February 1, 1964.

momentous board presentation—Celler, p. 258. ITT board meetings were regularly held on the second Wednesday of each month. In March 1963, that was the thirteenth. The document HSG prepared was dated 3/11/63.

and office equipment—Knortz points out that this was then considered a hot item and that HSG was lucky he did not come across a suitable acquisition in the field, because the market quickly soured.

"They listened and they said"—Celler, p. 70.

Geneen bought good companies—also Gendron.

unfriendly takeovers—In a speech to Boston stock analysts on March 17, 1969, HSG said, "We have never made a hostile tender": SAV DOC. Kenmore insists that was policy. Where management didn't want to sell, as with Grinnell or Avis, there were special circumstances that made it, still, not an unfriendly takeover, and never a hostile tender.

Pompes Salmson—Forbes, February 1, 1964 and Haufler ex. 9.

renowned as a mighty hunter—E. Moore.

Moore driving force—Haufler ex. 9.

Newton worked for a company—Newton.

Newton Moore's executive assistant—Newton dep.

Newton arranged meeting—Newton.

self-styled "farm boy"—His visiting card reads "Agriculturist."

B&G had earned $2.4 million—SAV DOC. 696,422 shares common, 145,487 shares convertible.

problems not manifest—Haufler ex. 9; three days before HSG's offer, Chrysler had made an offer: they wanted B&G as the central unit of their Air Temp division.

announced on April 10, 1963—NYT, April 11, 1963.

Moore doing things own way—Lobb's analysis. Details on "school house" from E. Moore.

"never have to have another idea"—Bowes, quoted by E. Moore.

bad news for Newton—Newton is sure HSG tried; his wife is bitter. This was just around the time of their marriage, Newton's first wife having died, and Mrs. Newton says there were so many phone calls from HSG it was like being courted by both men.

best source of executive talent—Lobb.

difficulty of running in early years—When the size of acquisitions grew, a whole other set of problems arose, such as integration of staff functions.

acquisition of General Controls—Lobb and Alexander.

General Controls had lost $1.2 million—SAV DOC.

sold for $18 million—*Fortune*, July 1, 1966. 112,000 shares common, 314,000 convertible. SAV DOC rounds off price to $17 million.

"All he thought about was engineering"—Alexander. Berke points out that another problem was a serious strike.

Cannon Electric—Cannon, Lobb, and NYT, July 11, 1963.

closely held business—NYT, ibid., put family share at 86%.

$33 million—998,000 shares common, 164,000 convertible.

"Bob made seventeen million"—Lobb missed a sister, but his figures add up.

Nesbitt made $1 million—SAV DOC.

sold for $19 million—596,000 shares common, 80,000 convertible.

quit day after the merger—Haufler et al.

final 1963 merger—Lobb, already cited, on September 16.

pay just under $19 million—NYT, September 20, 1963; *Fortune*, July 1, 1966. *Fortune* had it as 27 times earnings; I make it to be 24 if the NYT figures are right.

1963, Geneen told his board—Minutes in ABC.

"piecemeal approach"—*Forbes*, February 1, 1964.

saw how his acquisitions fit—Newton test.

core of ITT's HEAVAC—NYT, December 13, 1964.

Geneen planned further—Haufler ex. 8. HSG's presentation included a letter from Newton, written at HSG's instance, outlining a program of complementary acquisitions.

HEAVAC net was $5.2 million—*Fortune*, July 1, 1966: *New York Herald Tribune*, August 14, 1965: HSG quoted—"There isn't a company we've bought that hasn't done better since we acquired them"—which, at the time he said it, was true.

CHAPTER 11: A Paltry Putsch

"nothing but problems"—according to SAV DOC, the company made $100,000 in 1963 and 1964 on $34.8 million and $29.9 million sales, respectively, down from $35.9 million in 1962, when it showed a loss.

Cannon budgeted at $1.8 million—Down from its 1962 profit of $2.4 million (SAV DOC) because of a declining market and Geneen's standard strategy of trimming the line.

Geneen asked his staff—Berke.

Surprenant had declined—Berke. From about a $600,000 profit the year before acquisition in 1960. Profit was only $100,000 in 1963: SAV DOC.

Brazilian phone company books—Sterling.

natural morale slump in takeover—Newton is still bitter: "We all assumed that Ed Moore was going to be at the head of the overall group." To Newton, Lobb was an affront. "Presuming on our friendship," says Newton, "I said to Harold, 'You're pushing this guy Lobb down our throats." He was indeed presuming. As E. Moore puts it, Newton "broke his pick with Harold." But Newton's reaction was widespread, another drag on the early operation of acquisitions.

Donald G. Thomson—A firm HSG admirer. He was sent to the Harvard AMP, where Andrews remembers vividly his brilliant analysis of why HSG was so superior to all other conglomerateurs, including Singer's Kirscher, who was then in the news and under discussion.

"Hal was always running scared"—Reporters' notes.

"years before they couldn't fire him"—Hills.

"The most sensitive place"—Reporters' notes.

"you didn't just answer his question"—Dunleavy.

topics were universal—Dunleavy.

disliked commercial flights—Chasen.

Beechcraft skidded—Dunleavy.

Graham record—PROXY '62. In 1963 J. Graham was elected to the board. So was Westfall, but for 1962, Graham was one of the three highest-paid ITT officers ($70,523, with $50,000 bonus), and Westfall was not; in 1963, when both were on the list, Graham's salary was higher. In 1962 Marx was paid more than Graham: $77,200, with $45,000 bonus. In 1963 Graham made $105,910 ($30,000 bonus), Westfall made $91,850 (bonus, $65,000, largest of anyone except HSG). PROXIES '63 & '64.

"I didn't walk"—Reporters' notes.

Graham logical choice—Dunleavy.

pay up to $1.3 million—Celler, pp. 37, 74, 270. Letter was dated April 9, 1964. The point was the context of the hearings: an examination of anticompetitiveness by the antitrust subcommittee. The tendency of conglomerates was to buy rather than develop. Actual purchase price was $646,855.

United States Ambassador—PROXY '64; under Truman, in 1952, McKinney had been an assistant secretary of the treasury.

special stockholders' meeting—"Summary of Remarks," January 15, 1964, Baltimore; included with PROXIES.

$34.8 million for Aetna—Celler, p. 37. And NYT, August 22, 1964.

resignation took effect—PROXY '65; he went to General Dynamics and died soon thereafter.

Itinerary of tour—McKinney; date of the tour: ABC file.

at a hotel in Portugal—DUN MS.

plane from Madrid—McKinney is sure it was there. Another source says it was in a bar in Madrid. Navin declined to be interviewed.

reported to Ray Brittenham—Brittenham succeeded Mitchell as general counsel but fairly soon fell out of favor and was replaced as general counsel by Aibel. However, he stayed with the corporation, according to ARs, as a "senior vice president, law and counsel." He left after Araskog took over and went to Lazard.

Geneen move his own election—HSG's election: NYT, December 11, 1964.

Lobb at Crucible—Forbes, May 1, 1968. Also Lobb, and his account, with his figures, of Northern Telecom.

ITT's U.S. sales dropped—SAV DOC. The domestic contribution of profit, though, dropped only 1% to 29% of the total.

in finance business—with ITT Credit Corporation and Kellogg Credit.

177 offices in 25 states—NYT, January 20, 1965. Included in ITT Financial Services was Great International Life Insurance Company of Atlanta, a joint venture, which sold insurance in Europe. Also (BW, January 23, 1965) Hamilton Management of Denver, proprietor of the $394 million Hamilton Fund, a mutual, plus its own life insurance unit.

the same in 1963—NYT, July 4, 1973.

1964, ITT paid $21 million—NYT, May 4, 1967. The percentage comes from *Fortune,* July 1, 1966; but *Aviation Week and Space Technology,* August 24, 1964, made it "approximately 20%."

Feuding over Comsat—NYT, June 29, 1963.

Geneen fought Comsat claim—*Aviation Week,* August 14, 1964.

"I can assure you . . . "—ABC.

Gemini 5 splashdown—NYT, July 23, 1965.

staff remembers commenting—Brandt. When he would get home late at night, his wife would worry that he hadn't had dinner. He would assure her that he'd in fact had a three-courses: a sandwich, coffee, and a pickle.

815,000 shares left—NYT, May 4, 1967; plus 1,250 shares from Press Wireless.

a company spokesman was frank—NYT, December 6, 1968.

residue of idealism—Hills.

Gerrity arranged White House dinner—Beard.

Gerrity bucks Geneen up—Rader.

Business Week put it—March 19, 1967.

new plant in his state—In Monroe, Louisiana. It still operates, having served several different divisions.

net was up 13.7%—AR '64.

five-year totals doubled—*Fortune,* July 1, 1966.

"Mr. Geneen has decided"—Thomson.

Chapter 12: Trying Harder

imposing report—It was part of the exhibits in *ABC,* found in *Celler,* pp. 70, 266.

population explosion—"190 million to some 360 million in the next 35 years," HSG wrote.

"Stop fifteen people"—*Newsweek,* December 13, 1965. Appears many places. This is earliest I've found.

"true size of ITT"—In BASIC ACQUISITION POLICY.

"demonstrated and proven approach"—BASIC ACQUISITION POLICY.

Robatyn history—NYT *Magazine,* March 21, 1976; *New Yorker* magazine, January 24, 1983.

Lazard helped buy Jennings—*Celler,* p. 228.

"Felex Robotzen"—*Celler,* p. 410.

Avis demoralized company—Morrow. Also, *Celler,* pp. 370–403, and HSG ex 7. Market growth had been 17% in the past five years: *Celler,* p. 372.

Robert C. Townsend et al.—*Celler,* pp. 379, 386.

posted a modest gain—Morrow. He says over $600,000; *Sovereign* makes it $648,000. The "#2" campaign was created by Doyle Dane Bernbach.

"Townsend not very happy"—HSG dep.

Lazard controlled stock—39% of stock, control: NYT, January 15, 1965, and *Celler,* p. 429; Morrow dep. Meyer fear of Ford: Morrow.

"excessively low" salaries—The phrase appears elsewhere. Townsend's letter: *Celler,* p. 404; e.g., Morrow's salary, as president, was $36,000: *Celler,* p. 462. The objective was "$110 million in fiscal 1968 at a pretax margin of 12%."

Geneen agreed—*Celler,* p. 406. Townsend had also made a demand—and this was the point of interest for the antitrust subcommittee—that "we can call on IT&T, for example when we are ready to go after the car leasing business of their own divisions, suppliers, friends, etc., and we will get real help." HSG replied that, in fact, "all our employees, to the extent useful, could become salesmen for Avis." Morrow said (Morrow dep.) that when he and Petrie (both lawyers) saw that, they were "horrified." He said, "You just simply do not go about things or expect companies to go about things in this way." He added, "Townsend was very naïve . . . about business in general." HSG, of course, was telling Townsend anything Townsend wanted to hear. (See next two notes.) Emanuel Celler said (*Celler,* p. 101): "Mr. Geneen, there is an old adage, that is, 'The Bible says do right.' I say don't write. You have written here." HSG could reply only, "I accept that, Mr. Chairman. But I think if we proceed into the program, we will find out what happened." They found precious little. HSG loved those combinations, but they weren't practical.

"desire was to calm down"—*Celler,* p. 102.

"keep this fellow intact"—HSG dep.

Townsend would not stay—*Celler,* p. 464.

Townsend kept on payroll—Morrow.

merger closed—*Celler,* p. 398. Morrow speculates that the small premium over market was because Meyer was using Avis as a sort of loss leader to cement relations with HSG. Also, of course, all the stock can seldom be sold at much over market.

price over $51 million—The price appears several places in *Celler,* each time a little different: pp. 37, 413, 429, 453, 454; SAV DOC is also somewhat different. The number of ITT shares also varies; most authoritative seems: 369,621 shares, common; 268,816 convertible convertible (p.453).

"The [Avis] advertising campaign"—HSG ex. 7.

"call it ITT-Avis"—It was so called on forms, etc. Morrow's objection was to public identification.

"good turn of phrase"—"Fiat": *Celler,* p. 1001; Spanish telephone: p. 1053. One phrase, Morrow says, "came back to haunt me." He wrote, in discussing Avis sales to ITT suppliers, "Considerable work has been done on this but to date we have not tasted blood" (p. 963). The antitrust subcommittee pounced on it as evidence of routinized reciprocity.

"acquisition really raised eyebrows"—Kenmore.

Business Week *flabbergasted*—BW, January 23, 1965.

Harold S. Green—NYT, July 7, 1963.

Avis's pretax net—SAV DOC.

NARCO ill-considered—*Celler,* p. 445, for details on merger. Morrow for "ill-considered."

Chrysler . . . bit them—Morrow dep.

Avis desks accept Sheraton reservations—Morrow dep.

1968 Avis comeback—*Celler,* p. 1202. SAV DOC makes the after-tax net $4.1 million.

monster in his midst—Besides the indulgences already detailed in the text, the bonus pool was by agreement 15% "in perpetuity" (*Celler*, p. 102)—and unlimited, both of which HSG saw as nonsense.

Avis his special exhibit—Speech, Boston, March 17, 1969. In the original, "This has been the cornerstone . . . " is a new paragraph.

70% of Avis's business—Morrow dep. HSG in his speech said "most."

Ohmes thought Avis had no business in Europe—"The reason they went ahead," he says, "was somehow that they were convinced you had to be in Europe to be successful in the U.S." Ohmes misunderstood. As Morrow explained in his deposition, they did look for additional United States sales to Europeans familiar with Avis when they were visiting the U.S. But the European operation was always meant to stand alone, potential profit its own justification.

started in earnest in 1968—There had been talk since 1965. Letter, August 7, 1970. MOR DOC. In it, Morrow answered HSG's five questions.

affect significant savings?—Morrow figured $6,060,000 annually, including $1.6 million in fleet reduction and almost $2 million in personnel—plus the incalculable marketing advantage of being first with a systemwide reservation system.

Geneen scrawled thirteen pages of ad copy—MOR DOC.

fine job of running Avis—Lobb et al.

no "team member"—Chasen.

ITT exec tried for rapprochement—It was R. Bennett.

CHAPTER 13: Harold in Europe—and Elsewhere

European revenues more than doubled—AR '63 & '64. SAV DOC has a modest difference, probably due to restatement. HSG wanted Europe to be a market for ITT consumer goods, especially those from United States units, hastening a 50-50 balance of business. In 1963 he set up ITT Industries-Europe to exploit "particularly . . . the products of certain of our recent acquisitions in the U.S." (AR '63).

ITT flacks bragged—Forbes, February 1, 1964; AR '66.

knowhow from RCA—J. Thompson.

European profits—Vornle.

Oceanic for $4 million—SAV DOC.

two-thirds of Europe's sales—ABC. Except "next two largest": AR '63.

SEL was German—Some critics, especially Sampson, find sinister implications here. But any other policy would have been senseless and inaccurate.

"Five-Man Rule"—Ryan. In August 1967, for instance, there were only sixty-one Americans in ITT-Europe companies; only one small unit had an American at its head, and he was temporary. However, Brussels staff included thirty-seven more Americans: reporters' notes.

invariably in finance—Cf. today: Japanese nationals in overseas Japanese companies are usually in engineering: Charles McIntosh.

country manager—Generally head of the country's weightiest company—e.g., Abtmeyer in Germany.

Trygve Lie, etc.—Reporters' notes. That was not unusual; the competition in Germany, for instance, had Ludwig Erhard.

Brussels headquarters group—Reporters' notes.

EAC in session four days—At that time, in contrast, the GMMs lasted only two days.

"hell of a lot of work"—Jean Bourgeois in reporters' notes.

"International This and That"—Dunleavy.

Admiral Ellery Stone . . . leaves work—Dunleavy.

"political aspects not describable"—Dubilier.

Dunleavy took along two staffers—Berke.

succeeded as president of ITT-Europe—NYT, January 8, 1965.

"a real sweet guy"—Fortune, January 1973.

Geneen's marketing director introduces—Bowes.

"typical European businessman not sensitive"—Lester, in reporters' notes.

"European managers equated power"—Hartman.

TV operation in Britain—Britain and Scandinavia had concluded a trade agreement in answer to the Common Market. Until then ITT had shipped German TVs to Scandinavia; because of lower duties, in 1963 they started assembling and shipping from Britain. "It was a disaster," says Turbidy. "The quality demands of the Scandinavian market were not satisfied by our UK quality." Germany got back the market.

Hans Heinz Griesmeier—Thanks to Fritz Ross, of Grundig, for supplying Griesmeier's full name and details (below in the text) of his later career.

Griesmeier misread signs—Dunleavy; with BW, June 24, 1967.

German work force cut—Reporters' notes; BW, June 24, 1967 says layoffs were 10,000, Europe-wide.

Richard E. Bennett told them—Thompson. His words are "that kind of thinking." Since Bennett had fought them in World War II as an artillery forward observer, he presumably had in mind rigidity, not tender heartedness.

profits of Holland's Philips—BW, June 24, 1967. Extrapolations of SAV DOC make it off 5.7%; and the BW story says its figures are from New York Security analysts because ITT-Europe wouldn't "talk numbers."

James A. Goodson rushed in—Reporters' notes.

there were stresses—Dunleavy.

Dieter Moehring—Turbidy was put in charge of an outside search for Abtmeyer's replacement, but Moehring got the job.

SESA manufactured without purchase order—Turbidy.

computers at Brussels meeting—DUN MS.

Márquez hosted lunch—DUN MS.

wanted competitive bids—A. Williams, Dunleavy, Turbidy, et al.

"Long, hard discussions"—A. Williams says that there never was bribery in Spain.

Creed teleprinters—Carbonaro.

Alistair D. MacKay—Dunleavy.

"charming but ineffectual managers"—Reporters' notes.

Corfield told reporter—Ibid.

Geneen . . . Pirelli—DUN MS.

Roda cable—I have changed the diction from DUN MS to conform with cablese.

Domel . . . "cessioni"—Sementa and DUN MS, which mentions *cessioni*. In 1983 ITT was back in the TV business in Italy. Many billboards proclaimed that ITT color had zero defects.

difference between good times and bad—Forbes, May 15, 1971.

as many companies in Europe as in United States—Reporters' notes, quoting Dunleavy.

Alfred Teves—Time, September 8, 1967.

mini-empire in auto parts—By 1971 ITT had seven companies in the field, with annual sales around $350 million: *Fortune,* September, 1971.

incessant pushing of subordinates—A. Williams quotes HSG as almost always greeting any assertion with, "What makes you say that?" and "What if *this* happens?" Williams would try to anticipate all HSG's questions, but somehow HSG would come up with the unexpected, and Williams would leave asking himself, "How could I have missed *that* one?"

profits in Europe increased 530%—*Time,* December 20, 1971.

10% worldwide sales still there—ABC.

making their own cabinets—For a while. Yet, according to Howes, R. Bennett returned sometime later with a task force to settle later troubles and made a make-buy decision to phase out the cabinetmaking.

losing 25¢ on each Brazilian sales dollar—Howes.

In Chile, Frei announced—NYT, February 3, 1965; AR '64.

49% of the phone company—Campañía de Teléfonos de Chile, known as Chiltelco.

In Peru, after coup—NYT, October 30, 1969, & March 26, 1970.

Peru paid $17.9 million—NYT, March 26, 1970.

Argentina nationalized—NYT, September 20, 1970.

(at least symbolically)—the reason for the replacement was practical. Westfall's growing incapacity.

"Geneen feeling you can buy anyone—Scheye is very down on HSG. Others (e.g., Hills and Savage) stress HSG's near naïveté and shock in the early days.

"Ask the American ambassador"—ITT's European companies in fact tried going through their national embassies.

Holland's Prince Bernhard—He was later disgraced and forced to resign his government posts when it transpired that he had been on the receiving end, too—accepting $1.2 million in bribes from Lockheed to influence Dutch plane purchases: NYT, February & March 1976, especially February 8 & 9.

Ilia at odds with ITT—Reporters' notes.

Justice characterizes Geneen's zeal—ABC.

In Latin America—The "Five-Man Rule" did not apply. The top executives were generally Americans or Britons, who worked for less and were less disposed to job-hopping. Reporters' notes had it that two-thirds of ITT executives in Brazil were non-Brazilian and that "Factories were staffed at the top by Americans" throughout Latin America. ITT set up training schools for workers but showed little enthusiasm for locals as top management; a signal exception was with Chiltelco.

Andlinger told reporter—Forbes, May 1, 1968.

stop plying customers with gifts—Reporters' notes.

military deposed Illia . . . McNitt—Ibid.

Argentine official told reporter—Ibid.

friend, limited partner—There was no vendetta against ITT. Through it all, no properties other than utilities were touched.

Far East sales $51.4 million—ABC.

New York mistrusted the area—Cf. HSG's feeling that NEC was withholding information from him. Van Zandt says it was not so; but that is surely the way HSG viewed the area. Minutes of ITT board meetings read (ABC's August 14, 1963): "A review was made by the President [HSG] of the current status of the Japanese tax claim. It was indicated that the Corporation foresaw little hope of success if the matter were to be decided by the Japanese tax courts. A discussion was held of the possible means of getting political help in resolving the case."

Guam "too far away"—Van Zandt used to go there to make particularly sensitive calls to ITT, because he felt the lines were more secure than in Japan, where they could be monitored.

sales in the Middle East—ABC.

Africa became important—Slawson.

CHAPTER 14: Unshakable Facts

income for 1965—AR '65; NYT May 12, 1966. Revenue was up to $1,782,939,000 from $1,601,534,000 in 1964—and 1964's had been considerably restated to reflect acquisitions, including Avis: up from $1,415,627,000. Net was up to $76,110,000 from (restated) $66,831,000.

revenue would top $2 billion—AR '66. $2,121,272,000, 14.3% over the 1965 total, which had to be restated to reflect an additional $73,000,000 in acquired revenue.

balance between domestic and foreign—It would go to 50-50 overnight if ITT's planned merger with ABC went through. See chapter 15.

U.S. companies contributed 50%—AR '66.

regular cash cows—Lobb says "they were spitting out cash."

Woerthwein under pressure to acquire—Ryan.

Start-up time and money ridiculous—Ryan.

internal growth—The point was to avoid dilution, which mandated growth. In 1965 companies that he had acquired between 1960 and 1964 earned about $21 million, compared with $14 million the year before: *Fortune*, July 1, 1966.

P/E ranged in 1964—Fortune, July 1, 1966.

Geneen paid too much—Westfall says there was "some dilution." Knortz's "never paid too much" is an exaggeration: note Pennsylvania Glass Sand, Carbon, and Eason.

every officer under pressure sponsor acquisitions—Ryan.

"obnoxious but bright"—Chasen. I found Kenmore most pleasant, accommodating and companionable—in the course of two lengthy interviews. The brightness was manifest; the rest was not. He left ITT in 1968 to form, with another ITT analyst, Gardiner S. Dutton, the Kenton Corporation, a mini–conglomerate of such upscale units as Cartier, Mark Cross, Ltd., and the Ben Kahn Furs Corporation (NYT, August 1, 1971). It hit hard times in the 1970s. Kenmore left, took an advanced degree at Stanford, then taught for a while at INSEAD, the French version of the Harvard B-School. When I interviewed him first, in late December 1979, he was back in New York, starting his own investment business. He could not have been more helpful; I certainly had no more incisive analysis from anyone.

"a fucking Xerox machine"—Pomerance.

"remember," says Rohatyn—NYT, *Magazine*, March 21, 1976.

compulsory reading—Still read by some. It is prominent on the office credenza, for instance, of Marston, in Dallas, Texas.

elementally simple fact—Charles McIntosh furnished me with the example.

"looking at an annual report"—A former staff man, hearing that, says it must have been something HSG saw in the numbers.

to $22 billion—Relevant ARs. The latter figure from AR '79, HSG's last year as chairman, includes regular sales and revenues of $17,197,423,000 plus insurance and finance revenues of $4,798,600,000, or $21.996 billion.

a long day in Boston—Savage. In fact, a reason for the visit and multiple talks was that rumor had it that HSG had been overworking and that his health was failing.

after triumphant stockholders' meeting—Gilbert. It was in the 1970s, after the scandals.

to office before 10:00—H. Williams. However, according to Miller, from the J & L days, June said that HSG had a hard time getting up.

underling in Spain—A. Williams; the minister was named Lopez Bravo.

Bowes decided to resign—Sementa said the "problem" was that Bowes "fell in love with his wife, Samantha," and wanted some time with her. Bowes says that when he resigned, he stopped on impulse at a brokerage firm near the George Washington Bridge on his way home, asked for an account executive, and told the young man assigned to him that he wanted to sell some ITT, about 14,000 shares. The fellow's jaw dropped. ITT was then near its all-time high of 124. They sold a bit at a time so as not to affect the market. When the last 1,000 were traded, the broker said, "Mr. Bowes, I'd like to show you something." He led Bowes to the parking lot and pointed at a spanking new, glistening Lincoln Continental. "You bought me that," said the broker. Those who complain that Geneen did not "create value" simply sold at the wrong time.

Bowes remembers with fondness—but says he wouldn't want to spend "five minutes more" in that atmosphere.

evoked the best efforts—The most usual leadership comparison alumni make is to George Patton. Vince Lombardi is a close second.

"my Mount Everest"—But Ohmes, too, is glad it's over and has discovered that "it was really after ITT that I did things I considered fun: elder of the church, teaching Sunday School, coaching." He also likes himself better now that he is not so narrowly focused, more relaxed.

perfect pitch for your self-esteem—Benson.

"he did it for thirty or more"—Alfieri. Lobb says there is no other executive he ever knew who was "face-to-face with so many executives under him."

"always in boot camp"—Hills.

subway strike—Story comes from Milton Stone, who was once being considered for a high executive position and whose wife then worked at ITT.

European managers could not stand—Lobb; Ryan.

another confesses satisfaction—Marston.

three new executive VPs named—NYT, February 23, 1966.

only responsibility ITT World Communications—On a 1968 SAV DOC organization chart, only McNitt and his International Communications Operations reported to Westfall. By contrast, Lester, who was then just a VP, had Europe, Africa, and the Middle East reporting to him. Still, HSG stuck by Westfall. On the twelfth floor, a group of failed or obsolescent executives—known as the "zeppelin pilots"—waited for the axe or retirement. Westfall never joined them.

chairman of Comdial Corporation—L. A. Times, October 6, 1982, and December 8, 1982.

Lobb inescapable choice—He was quoted in BW, April 22, 1972, as saying that HSG had "told me I was being considered" as successor.

Perry no real operating experience—He was head of ITT Financial Services, but in ITT terms that did not count for much.

the words of Forbes—May 1, 1968.

review day before Thanksgiving—Pomroy.

called for information—Ryan.

"always the next nine"—Brandt.

"ITT Americas Building"—NYT, February 2, 1966.

executive dining room—It was thought to have slightly better food; but the overall ITT cuisine, perhaps reflecting HSG's uninterest, ran to the turkey roll as exotica. I wandered into 437 Madison, went to the fortieth floor, thinking to ask permission to look around. But no one was there, and everything was open, so I just looked.

ninety-two swivel chairs—Pomerance. I did not count them; but there did not seem so many to me.

"put a man in charge and leave him"—Reporters' notes. HSG specified the competitor but made that off the record.

"proud guy in his own Vietnam"—*Forbes*, May 1, 1968.

"man loses eight million dollars"—Yunker.

whether Geneen read every page—Sterling says that they once put dabs of rubber cement between some pages and later found them still glued. Thomson, though, says he once checked, and found every page marked up. In any case, for focusing the managers' attention, the next sentence is the operative one: you had to assume he read *your* stuff. On one hand that was inspiring. "Underlings spend all this time thinking and putting together strategies," says Hackett, "and they present the plan—and nobody ever reads it." HSG had read it, and showed that he had pondered the contents. "He always seemed to pick out exactly the right point to comment on," says Hutchinson. "Did he read every word? I don't know and I don't care. It would spoil the fun! But it had the effect of making me think, Okay, goddamnit! It *is* worth cranking these things out because somebody's paying attention—and isn't that wonderful!" On the other hand, HSG's attention could make you uncomfortable. When Pomroy was new to Continental, he was aware of a gap of logic in his section of the monthly letter but figured it would be passed over. HSG's first question went to the exact point. Pomroy, not knowing how sensitive the GMM microphones were, muttered, "Aw, shit!" HSG beamed as the amplifiers boomed it out, and said, "Caught you, didn't I?"

"You can't delegate anything"—*Fortune*, July 1, 1966.

Latin American manager jolted—Carbonaro.

had an uncanny ability—Dunleavy.

"after second or third question"—Alfieri.

"two purple drops"—*Time*, September 8, 1967.

"not criticizing a man"—*Fortune*, July 1, 1966.

Why are your figures off?—Carbonaro.

"didn't want to break your heart"—Yunker.

Geneen made up for a reporter—*Fortune*, July 1, 1966.

corporate bottom line the sum—Ryan.

"wasn't interested in five-cent problems"—Carbonaro.

Geneen once explained—Reporters' notes.

assignment #25—Haufler ex. 13.

assignment #5—Woerthwein ex. 6. The study concluded that a "single management" would help against the "formidable competitors," GE, Westinghouse, and Sylvania. It didn't: see chapter 17.

"program to diversify TIP"—Woerthwein ex. 9.

first item at GMM—Howes.

"Last week I reorganized"—Howes: a made-up example.

"Last month you made an annualized saving"—Howes.

"dynamic tension"—Gadzinski. Ryan says HSG just wanted to know what was going on, and he did not want it from one if he could get versions from two, not from ten if he could get it from twenty. Not that he thought that people lied; but the more

versions he could square, the closer he would come to the "unshakeable facts" of the matter.

padlocking the supply room—Gormeley.

Britain teleprinter operation—Carbonaro.

"difficult to screw up"—especially if, Thomson observes, like him you had been on staff and knew who the good ones were to ask for help.

not diminished in Geneen's eyes—Lester, for instance, was the manager most directly in charge of General Controls during its worst period. He never scrupled to ask for help. And he rose in the ITT hierarchy with laudable speed.

staff grew out of proportion—Yunker calls it "elephantitis."

Everything was working—Relevant ARs and SAV DOC.

growth value of acquisitions—SAV DOC.

lawyers told him to slack off—Brandt. Everyone agrees; but Brandt had it direct from HSG.

CHAPTER 15: ABC, Number Three in
a Two-and-a-half Universe

Television, said Geneen's acquisition group—ABC.

five regular TV stations—The economics are interesting. All three nets have o&o's in New York, Los Angeles, and Chicago, the biggest markets; for the other two, it's a matter of historic fortuity. ABC's are in San Francisco and Detroit, for instance, while CBS's are Philadelphia and St. Louis, NBC's Cleveland and Washington. They would all love to get Dallas, but nothing's available. The network produces shows and sells advertisers commercial time on those shows. The shows are provided to the affiliates, who run them locally, with the network commercials. Each show, however, has gaps, infrequently in the body of the show, always at each end, called "station breaks," and in these gaps the affiliates can sell time to local advertisers. (They also get some payment from the networks and share some expenses.) The greater the audience for a show, the higher the price of the time in the show and adjacent to it. And, eventually, the greater the number of affiliates willing to show the network's shows— hence the greater the number of people watching, hence the higher the price, etc. I am indebted to the operations departments of all three networks, and especially the affiliates relations department of NBC in Los Angeles, for this analysis.

logic kept him from acquiring—Kenmore.

memo from Hart Perry—The memo was dated October 13. Board meetings were on the second Wednesday of the month, which was then October 14.

Geneen tried to move in twice—Fortune, March 1969.

own people had already pegged—Also an outside firm of analysts, Roth, Gerard & Co.

ABC lost at least $15 million—BW, March 18, 1967; but Goldenson's reply to an FCC query made it: 4.6, 8.4 and 5.6 million dollars for the three years.

ABC revenues had jumped—Fortune, July 1, 1966.

Gerry Tsai's contact—There is some doubt about his role. ABC's directors' minutes (in ABC) mention contact by "Sai" [*sic*]. He himself says, "I arranged it," but Goldenson doesn't remember any call. He did testify, though (ABC test., p. 1483) about Tsai's contact.

Tisch playing tennis—ABC test., p. 1588.

dinner at Goldenson's apartment—ABC test., p. 1483: Goldenson.

"I wouldn't be interested"—There is some question as to whether the offer was as stated

or somewhere up to $75 (*Fortune,* March 1969). The market price of ABC on the first trading day, February 2, 1965, was 53¾ (NYT, next day). On the last trading day, February 27, it was up to 61½ (ibid.). Sources: ABC directors' minutes and test., p. 1486. Meanwhile, Kenmore sent HSG a memo pointing out that if the ABC talks stalled, there were many ready-made chains to approach: Storer, Cox, Capital Cities, Taft, Metromedia, etc. (ABC ex.).

talked with General Electric—ABC Directors' minutes; notes of special meeting of board: ABC ex.

"interested in resuming discussions"—ABC test., p. 1487.

ABC numbers irresistibly good—ABC test., p. 1119: Kenmore.

met at Waldorf for breakfast—ABC test., p. 1488: Goldenson.

Geneen went to $83—ABC directors' minutes.

"called me about a day later"—ABC test., p. 1488.

For each share of ABC stock—and the closing: NYT, December 2 & December 8, 1965.

"historic event"—ABC ex.

Kenmore three TV sets—Brandt.

manager in the Far East—ABC ex. It was Van Zandt.

deluge of phone calls—ABC test., p. 1280: Perry. There was talk, though, of cooperation: a proposal from an ITT Portuguese subsidiary to acquire a TV station in Mozambique was bucked to ABC for evaluation; there was discussion of ABC's using ITT transmission facilities to cover the 1968 Olympics in Mexico and using ITT's ground station in Vietnam to cover the war. ABC test., pp. 1274 and 1276: Perry.

Application had been filed—on March 1, 1966.

FCC staff member, resigning—Reporters' notes. It was D. E. Winslow.

Turner soft on mergers—*Time,* March 24, 1967.

Hyde wrote to Turner—ABC ex., dated June 6, 1966.

an exchange of letters—Reporters' notes. On June 6 Turner wrote Hyde to say, Yes, Justice was looking into the matter. Hyde wrote on June 30 to ask when they might expect a Justice opinion. On July 27 Turner answered, Not very soon.

not necessary to hold a hearing—The only formal opposition was from the owners of a station that wanted the ABC outlet in New York: ABC ex.

Johnson later charged—ABC. Dissent from FCC order of December 21, 1966.

serve "the public interest"—Quoted in the *New Republic,* October 15, 1966.

when Minnesota Mining sold Mutual—ABC test., p. 194: comment by Commissioner Loevinger.

"highly unrealistic and artificial"—ABC test., p. 400.

loan with Metropolitan Life—ABC test., p. 567. Details of how the truth transpired in ABC ex. J-279, Justice Department document headed "Completeness and Candor"; also test., p. 1330: Charbonnier; p. 1585: Goldenson; p. 2454: Siegel.

Johnson asked McCone—ABC test., p. 147.

"assure you without reservations"—ABC test., p. 168.

corporate policy statement—ABC ex.

"assertions of good faith"—ABC test., p. 328. And even granting the good faith, Johnson pointed out, ITT suppliers might very well feel impelled to advertise on ABC instead of the other two networks (except, of course, for those also doing business with RCA; a cruel dilemma).

the chill factor—As Johnson said to Goldenson, it "just runs counter to what we all know about human affairs" to expect that ABC personnel would operate as though ITT interests did not exist. ABC test., p. 240.

ABC ever run contrary to stockholders' interests—ABC test. p. 246.

"getting hoarse from listening"—ABC test., p. 518: Bartley.

other networks' combined profit declined—ABC test., p. 315.

lawyer argued that to forbid—ABC test., p. 380.

Turner's letter arrived—All documents in the paragraph are part of ABC, found, passim, in Volume 25; also Johnson's dissent.

"Rumor laced with truth"—Reporters' notes.

revolved around congratulatory message—*Newsweek*, January 2, 1967.

"leave to intervene"—ABC ex.

hearing on April 10—It was initially set for March 27 but Justice got it postponed.

letter and telegrams to the FCC—All found in ABC correspondence file, Volume 1. The New York assemblyman was Leonard P. Starisky.

Eileen Shanahan—Her version of events is from ABC test., pp. 2950–97. Her married name was Waite, and her beat was the U.S. Treasury, SEC, and Capitol Hill.

release might make a paragraph—ITT spokesman in reporters' notes. Shanahan said that he had phoned in the press release and just came by with a copy; the ITT spokesman said that she asked Gerrity to bring it by, saying, "If you can get it here in ten minutes, I'll read it over."

At that point, Gerrity remarked—Reporters' notes.

in Shanahan's lead—Also in the lead of the *Washington Post* story.

Shanahan got a call from former boss—Reporters' notes.

incident more casual and benign—Reporters' notes.

Horner and Gerrity ex-newsmen—Reporters' notes. Horner had some thirty years' newspaper experience, much with the *Washington Star*. Gerrity had been with the *Scranton Times*.

Two journalists with the Associated Press—Steven Aug and Jared Stout. ABC test., pp. 2997–3014. It was a question of requests for additions or modifications to stories.

not scruple to squeeze reporters—Did HSG know? There was no direct evidence that he ordered such shenanigans. But the FCC minority pointed out that Gerrity and Horner obviously "were not on a frolic of their own, and must have assumed they were serving ITT's interest." (ABC, p. 5370.)

sole reason was the high price—In fairness, Goldenson spoke to me without preparation and without much reflection. Although he specifically says that a *Fortune* story, March 1969, had it wrong that the Norton Simon episode influenced him, he did talk to a number of potential corporate buyers.

Stan Luke testifying—ABC test., p. 1012.

Chasen had written to Geneen—ABC ex. It was prepared for Guilfoyle's signature.

ABC's opposition to CATV—ABC test., p. 894: a petition to the FCC, dated October 16, 1964.

Chasen asked . . . Sciatron—ABC test., p. 867.

witnesses be excluded—ABC test., p. 900.

outside lawyers had better sense—Beard, who was no lawyer, knew the consequences. She says that she was aware that if discovered, "you know where my fanny would be."

"all very heavy-handed"—Goldenson finds that the more incredible because HSG "was

such a pro in every other way. But he felt he could bull his way through."

FCC examiner pointed out—ABC test., p. 3282.

September 7 Justice filed suit—NYT, September 8, 1967.

October, case heard—NYT, October 18, 1967.

decision expected "momentarily"—*America* magazine, December 23–30, 1967.

"Don't make waves"—Brandt.

same thing with Levitt—*Celler*, p. 858.

conversion to color cost more—Perkins and Goldenson.

not fully approved by December 31—It had originally been June 30, 1967, but was extended.

CHAPTER 16: The Glory Years

"And now," *Geneen told investors*—Speech to Investment Group of Hartford and the Connecticut Investment Bankers Association, February 15, 1968.

stock high of 124—NYT, January 3, 1968.

2-for-1 split—NYT, October 12, 1967; NYT, January 26, 1968.

Geneen's program unparalleled—There were flashier go-go mergers—by companies that were, in fact, flashes in the pan. But Geneen was offering stock in a *real* company; it was not funny-money stock.

head of unit lighthearted—Morrow.

Levitt revenues in 1965—*Celler*, p. 810.

Carr explained advantages—*Celler*, p. 774: memo from Rohatyn to Meyer.

Levitt had known Rohatyn—Levitt.

"a rather mercurial individual"—*Celler*, p. 774.

Lazard kept looking—Rohatyn wrote to Levitt, "Our friends uptown . . . are out of the running." *Celler*, p. 805. With ITT's lawyers urging restraint, the largest merger in 1966 was with Howard W. Sams, the publishing house, for under $30 million.

"Levitt and Lockeed talk"—*Celler*, p. 807: memo from Peter A. Lewis, later a partner, to Rohatyn.

"ball-park price"—*Celler*, p. 826: memo, Perry to HSG.

deal with LSI in principle—*Celler*, p. 839: Rohatyn to HSG with questions from Levitt; *"awaiting ITT-ABC approval"*—*Celler*, p. 843: Petrie and Raymond S. Troubh to Rohatyn and Meyer.

Levitt was stuck—*Celler*, p. 860: Rohatyn to Meyer.

hold off for two weeks—*Celler*, p. 870: notes by Fred Shinagel of Lazard, of meeting involving Luke, Carr (LSI attorney), and Levitt (part of the time).

Delay was costly—*Celler*, p. 828.

says an LSI executive from those days—"We'd been knocking out three to four thousand homes a year; those other guys were struggling to do four or five hundred."

"building business was the same"—Bernhard.

seven-page memo—Levitt says "seven or eight." He told me what was in it but wouldn't show it to me.

"unmitigated disaster"—Goode.

Holiday Inn franchises—Roth and Dunleavy.

Henderson and Moore—NYT, September 7, 1967.

Sheraton Hotel in Boston—Their first purchase was the Stonehaven in Springfield: ibid.

president and dominant partner—Howe. He says, "It was a typical one-man operation."

salaries depressed—Henderson and Boonisar. Henderson still proudly points out that Sheraton spelled backwards sounds like "not a raise."

Moore retired as chairman—He remained as chairman of the executive committee.

Henderson died—NYT, September 7, 1967. The call to Ernie Henderson was after midnight, and as Ernie's wife says, the father "was not yet buried."

mere 144 U.S. units—NYT, September 24, 1967. Sheraton owned 48, leased 19, and managed 11; 76 were franchises.

Boston's Somerset Hotel—HSG would later claim (speech to Boston stock analysts, March 17, 1969) that there were no rooms available in a Sheraton; Boonisar says it was for anonymity. Neither explanation makes much sense.

"half million in raises"—Henderson's own salary more than doubled, to $125,000; Boonisar's went to $105,000. Their bonuses were $42,000 and $35,000, respectively.

"wrong guy in wrong place"—James. All sources agree that Henderson was clearly over his head trying to run Sheraton, though as Lowe says, "nobody thought for a minute he was really running it."

"my philosophy of management"—Henderson says that he would get twenty assignments and have completed satisfactorily nineteen of them by time of the next review —and catch hell for the one undone, with no praise for the nineteen. He could not understand that.

Sheraton's marketing director—Morton.

"the hotel industry is different"—Howe. In fact, the Sheraton business plan was praised as the best first plan ever submitted by a new unit. Henderson is today proud of that; but it was not his doing. Sheraton's ad agency, BBDO, had always prepared elaborate, written marketing plans, not unlike ITT's; so Sheraton had a headstart. By coincidence, as a BBDO copywriter I worked on a branch of the Sheraton account just about this time. Although I never did any Sheraton work while in New York, when I was sent to the Los Angeles office of BBDO, one of my accounts was the local group of Sheraton hotels. I remember everyone's mild disgust when, to already small layouts, we had to add a tiny slug of type about the ITT connection: "A worldwide service of ITT." It was a good account.

Geneen's expansion talk—Lowe says $800 million was promised and $495 million actually set aside; Sobel in *ITT* says $865 million was budgeted.

"kid with a new toy"—Dillenbeck; NYT, May 20, 1968.

"crappiest site in Rio"—James.

Sheraton's bad debt loss—Lowe.

Sheraton ads . . . key—Caruso and Howe.

project for ITT's marketing staff—Hutchinson.

dialing PL6-2000—James.

"two and a half doormen"—Morrow.

Boonisar's dislike for Lowe—"I liked the guy," says Boonisar, "but I didn't like him running the company. This guy just didn't fit into the damn thing with me. The chemistry was absolutely wrong." Lowe says, "I took his sugarplum away."

franchising two deals a day—James.

"things a hotel company in trouble does"—James. Lowe says, "It was 'creative bookkeeping'—I'll put it that way." Of ninety-eight hotels in North America, only seven were showing a real profit.

head of the Sahara Hotels—Sahara Nevada Corporation. Earlier that spring James had been approached by a head hunter about the job of executive VP for Sheraton and had

turned it down. Ireland was the one who pushed Geneen hardest to find a hotel man.
"Geneen's success with Sheraton"—Benson. He had written HSG a memo warning of
the danger of Sheraton debt.

Staff showed too much china—On the other side, Hutchinson says that staff was not
trying to run the hotels, just point out operating anomalies and urge standard practices.

$301.8 million for Rayonier—Celler, p. 37. However, on another chart, p. 32 (both
furnished by ITT), the price is $293,133,000. *Fortune*, December 17, 1979, uses the
$293 million figure. First announcement had come in August 1967, three weeks after
the Levitt announcement. NYT, August 14, 1967.

"high among corporate disasters"—*Fortune*, December 17, 1979.

Rayonier huge success—Goode.

gem of a company—Lobb.

about 22 times earnings—NYT, January 30, 1968. The reason for selling, says Goode,
was for purposes of estate settlement; he is also source for "18% after taxes."

James Pomroy—At Continental only during 1969 and 1970.

motivation . . . supermarket aisle—Roth . . . Hackett.

for all its volume—Valente.

volume was the problem—Pomroy's analysis.

1968 lesser acquisitions—The disparity between pages 32 and 37 in *Celler* is sometimes
great. For instance, Bramwell Business College is shown as acquired August 19, 1967
(p. 37) and August 19, 1968 (p. 32). Jasper Blackburn Company was either the first
acquisition of 1968, on January 2 (p. 37), or nowhere near the first, on June 2 (p. 32)
—with the price varying between $15.7 million (p. 32) and $19 million (p. 37). Both
charts came from ITT.

détente with the Soviets—Slawson.

night infiltrations—Scheye. An often-run ITT add and TV commercial featured the
use of their device by sufferers of retinitis pigmentosa.

Could Drager use multiplex—Hoagland dep.

"I've never seen anyone"—Goode.

Brazil imported cement—Goode and Dillenbeck.

Reznor $1.4 million—Haufler dep.

telephone equipment in Africa—Bowes.

"heavy, heavy hitters"—Haidinger. But when HSG left a GMM for some reason,
everything came to a stop—although in theory some heavy hitter took over. "It was
then," says Haidinger, "that I was convinced that no matter how big ITT was, Geneen
ran it and no question."

"the lesser lights"—DUN MS—but told by many, an ITT legend.

"got them by their limousines"—NYT, September 5, 1971.

"more than they think they're worth"—Lowe.

"rats on a treadmill"—Milton Stone quoting Morton Rogoff, who was the man heading HSG's no-computers squad in Europe.

his people deserved tremendous rewards—Alfieri.

declined to participate himself—Alleman and PROXIES.

Geneen's disappointment palpable—Alfieri.

"salary over seven hundred thousand"—Sterling. He means total remuneration. HSG's
salary and bonus were, 1971: $382,494 salary, $430,000 bonus; 1972: $402,311 salary,
$411,000 bonus; 1973: $403,299 salary, the same $411,000 bonus; in 1974, a down year,
his salary was $407,610 and his bonus was cut to $381,000.

no doubts as to his worth—*Forbes*, May 15, 1971. HSG thought he was underpaid. "What do you pay someone who has contributed $11 billion to his company," he said. "Maybe if I study this hard enough I'll decide I'm worth $5 million a year and a lot of other guys around here are worth $2 million each."

Leonard S. Schmitz . . . Acme—Most of narrative: Hinch and Horn. Schmitz firm was McDermott Will & Emery. Knickerbocker is still very bitter about something but refuses to discuss it; the terms seem quite generous. There were many lawyers involved: Knickerbocker was represented by two firms, in fact. They were all gathered at the closing, carefully processing enough documents to fill two large bound volumes, intent on protecting their respective clients' interests in a deal that was massively complicated because so many principals were involved. They were at the People's National Bank of Charlottesville, around what bank officials assured them was the largest table in Virginia carved from a single piece of wood. It was buried in documents. Knickerbocker said to HSG, loudly enough for all to hear, "Hal, why don't you and I go down and take a look at the plant while these fellows are shuffling their silly papers." HSG looked embarrassed but went. The lawyers on all sides exchanged grimaces and shrugs and went back to work.

Acme had $6,748,487 in assets—All figures are from the bound volumes of the closing. I am most grateful to the source of these, and of the story, above.

Three insurance companies—Connecticut Life, Massachusetts Mutual Life, and Mutual Life of New York.

"one-tenth of 1%"—*Forbes*, May 15, 1971. Kingsley, Keesee, and Elfers were also directors: Acme proxy, December 1969.

bought at $47.50 a share—American Brands press release, June 22, 1970. According to the December '69 Acme PROXY, Keesee had 3,200 shares, Kinsley 1,500, Elfers 4,204, Schmitz 83,662. Bessemer had 349,454 shares, 32% of the outstanding stock.

bought a farm—Reporters' notes.

cottage bought in 1952—*Time*, September 8, 1967.

"mother took precedence"—Pomerance.

Aida died—NYT February 15, 1971

Geneen still choked up—Alleman.

a doctor who had treated her—Michael S. Gordon, M.D. My thanks for literature on his research project at the University of Miami School of Medicine.

succession of boats—Reporters' notes.

Barbara Boonisar—Anecdote: Boonisar; her descent, NYT, September 24, 1967.

driving a trial—R. Graham: also boat and swordfish. He was very impressed with HSG's hospitality and repeatedly stresses that as HSG's guest you never paid for a thing.

Phoebe's Whamburger—McCabe.

"wanted to be liked"—Goode.

he would tear loose—once, served by a topless waitress, also in San Francisco, HSG remarked, "If I had time, I could be a hell of a playboy" *Life*, May 19, 1972.

six-string instrument—John Mayer, an actor in Los Angeles and banjo enthusiast.

delighted to meet him—He also arranged for some well-paid appearances at ITT events, including Boca Raton.

collected June in his limousine—Dunleavy. He got it from the chauffeur. Dunleavy cultivated the company chauffeurs, feeling they are one of the best, yet most overlooked, sources of corporate intelligence.

Charles E. Skinner—He had been a child actor, playing "Whitey" in the original "Our

Gang" comedies. He was the producer of, among other things, the "Sgt. Preston" series on TV.

"officer ranks" at 19—Haidinger.

"From grade 25 on"—Lowe.

neighborhood hubbub—Sementa.

"not classy people"—Lowe.

loftier companies—That was not true in the early days.

did it in splendid style—Most details from Carson and Boca Raton program, 1973, which he gave me.

caddy's tip—Alexander.

495 male and 33 female—An assumption. It may be that some of the "Mr. and Mrs." guests listed in the program were female employees who brought husbands.

"work only for ITT"—Sementa.

"wife thinks he's the greatest"—Yunker.

"he'd run to get it"—Benson.

acquisitions continued into 1969—Celler, p. 32.

Canteen Corporation—NYT, October 17, 1968.

largest maker of fire protection—Haufler ex. 3.

$171.65 a share—NYT, December 3, 1968.

Justice filed to enjoin—NYT, July 31, 1969, and October 22, 1969.

discrete entities, easily unmerged—Because earnings were rapidly declining, HSG insisted on going back to ask for a modification of the order allowing him to replace the Grinnell president, Clarence Rison, with Hartman, and four other top Grinnell executives with other ITT people. Over Justice objection, he got the modification.

growth would tail off—Pomerance.

Hartford assets $1.8 billion—AR '70.

"tried to steal the company"—"In my opinion," says Carson, "and certainly in the opinion of Bill Griffin and Pete Thomas" (the two in charge of negotiating with Dow; DeRoy Thomas is now CEO of Hartford). "They told Dow," says Carson, "there was no way they were going to stand still for that kind of price." Thomas and Griffin declined comment.

Williams soon announced—NYT, November 13, 1968.

directors wanted to replace Williams—Carson.

board's choice was Robert Baldwin—Sovereign and ITT.

buy 1,282,948 shares—NYT, November 13, 1968. The firm was Insurance Securities, Inc.

"inexorable pressure"—Klein., p. 1218. Memo from Ireland to HSG: "Therefore, I think that during the ensuing delicate period our posture should be one of extreme alertness and in your own apt phrase from an earlier conversation, one of 'inexorable pressure'—right up to and through the movement [*sic*] the deed is officially consummated."

Hartford board asked for a delay—NYT, September 6, 1969.

Texas stockholders—Courant, April 1, April 4, April 13, and especially April 6, 1970.

McLaren filed—NYT, June 24, August 2, October 22, 1969.

Cotter disapproved—NYT, December 15, 1969.

Williams called Geneen—H. Williams.

"move to Oshkosh"—There was some reason to fear it, since the Connecticut tax on

Connecticut insurance companies was higher than that on companies based in other states doing business in Connecticut: Carson.

Geneen promised great things—Courant, June 3, 1970.

a later SEC investigation highlighted—Courant, May 27, 1973; also Cohn's memo.

Aibel hired Fazzano—Courant, June 24, 1979. They had known each other slightly in the army.

"big one in Hartford"—Courant, November 8, 1970.

Fazzano told Watergate investigators—Courant, June 24, 1979.

*talked merger only four or five times—*However, he did say that Fazzano had called his office often, speaking to others: ibid.

He got $30,000—Courant, ibid. It had earlier been reported as $25,000: *Courant*, June 7, 1973.

*conduit to Cotter—*When Nader's group attacked the merger, Cotter at first welcomed their help, then later found it an embarrassment when he was about to change his decision. ITT supplied him with arguments. "ITT," wrote an SEC investigator, "puts words in Cotter's mouth via Joe Fazzano": *Courant*, May 27, 1973.

*tender offer accepted—*AR '70.

*"played like a violin"—*Ryan.

Celler was impressed—Celler, p. 21.

*report dismissed other companies—*Celler Staff Report, pp. 85, 85, 281, 316, 360, 362.

*O. M. Scott & Sons—*NYT, November 16, 1970.

"a year like 1970"—Dun's, December, 1970.

*1968 net—*Relevant ARs.

CHAPTER 17: Nobody's Perfect

*Gulf Telephone in Perry, Florida—*I wanted to check on the assertions of Lobb et al. about ITT's failure in switching equipment. I concluded that since it would be indeed a random sample, I would try independent phone companies along the route of one of my research trips. My first response was with Cox in Florida, and he referred me to other independents in the area who he knew had some familiarity with ITT equipment. The only other independent I tried was in a Western state along my route. He had been in the Midwest.

*light bulb fiasco—*J. Thompson.

*never especially distinguished—*Bobbs did, however, publish William Styron and Mark Harris and had been Elmer Davis's publishers.

*Mary Mead's Magic Recipes—*ABC ex.

Stanley S. Sills—Who's Who. We spoke on the phone, and he told me a bit about his admiration for HSG but declined a formal interview.

*"well-regarded editorial executive"—*NYT, August 4, 1978.

*biography of Ray Charles—*Norville.

*wrote Herbert Mitgang—*NYT, August 4, 1978.

started in the home-building industry—Who's Who.

Perry wrote to Geneen—Celler, p. 329. He went on, " . . . although the record certainly suggests that Levitt has done a better job than most in producing a record of steady growth in recent years."

*"Felix extremely persuasive"—*Evidently. Soon, Perry was heard in the lobby of a Chicago hotel by Westfall arguing for the LSI acquisition.

market conditions changed—H&H and Koskinen and Trustee's report, et al.

Local builders at an advantage—Koskinen. "They ran their business with their wife and brother-in-law out of their Cadillac"—and added to lower overhead, they were more attuned to local zoning problems.

trustee later wrote—Trustee's first report.

"location, location, location"—Koskinen.

Levitt out of LSI—but not literally. He maintained an office there and was a consultant.

Hale E. Andrews—Goode.

"superlative talent for people management"—H&H.

"pound for pound"—Berke quoting Ireland.

"Wasserman had them cheering"—Morrow.

United Homes Corporation—WSJ, January 8, 1974.

Levitt name sold houses—Bernhard.

When a trustee stepped in—Trustee's first report.

land banking—"What we thought was a three-year inventory turned out to be seven years," Bernhard told H&H. He blamed sewer moratoria and no-growth legislation, etc. The trustee's report referred to "large land holdings without homebuilding possibilities."

ecologists challenged improvements—*Time*, June 28, 1971; *Dun's*, June 1971; *The Nation*, May 1, 1972. Also Beard.

Levitt followed by Fischer—H&H; Bernhard. Also Levitt.

operating loss $100 million—Trustee's final report, August 2, 1978. The 1973 loss is from the report; H&H had it as being $14.3 million.

diversification units lose $60 million—Trustee's final report.

August 1974 the deal collapsed—Levitt says Justice turned it down, but that is apparently not the case. H&H is on the other side; so is Koskinen, who says, "Levitt walked away from it."

firm of Victor Palmieri—He was later appointed head of Jimmy Carter's commission for relief of the Vietnamese refuges, the "boat people."

over $260 million in 1975—H&H.

we couldn't pay salaries—Almost all LSI alumni mention this. It was a holdover of HSG's personnel testing obsession. Anyone over the $25,000 level had to undergo rigorous stress tests and interviews, plus—until quite late in the game—personal salary review by HSG. In the mercurial building world, people just wouldn't wait, and often wouldn't go through the testing. That made it hard for LSI to hire good people.

whether national home building is a business—Koskinen points out that only two firms, Ryan and U.S. Home, have approached success with national operations, and both with rather specialized methods. He calls Ryan, for instance, a sort of "McDonald's operation"—a basic product that you either take or reject, no modifications.

idiom foreign to ITT—Wasserman. He remembers inventory control. "Wonder Bread would have a million-dollar overrun, somebody else would have five hundred thousand—and Levitt would have a *twenty*-million overrun." Why? Because a tract of 400 houses at $50,000 each was delayed by snowstorms and frozen ground. The explanation cut no ice with staff: "Their bells went off," Wasserman says.

How does a corporation control those?—Even if it could, the routine leveraging meant a debt-equity ratio that put ITT's consolidated sheet out of whack, meaning a severe cutback on other units' borrowings.

Nesbitt got 96%—McCloskey.

Nesbitt having production problems—W. Moore.

Moore succeeded Weldon—Weldon moved on before the problems were manifest; he was not "replaced."

gathering of ITT alumni—Rice, at the head-hunting firm of Spencer Stuart, organized it; there is a yearly get-together. I got a copy of the mailing list and found it valuable.

"called him 'Jim Eleven' "—Ryan.

palmed off on Westfall—Howes. Westfall thinks Bennett was simply trying to promote Rice.

Howard Truss—I had a most curious phone conversation with him. I told him the people I had talked with, and my impressions about ITT telecom, and asked to speak with him. He declined an immediate interview but thought that maybe we could play tennis together to see "what would develop." I told him that if he decided he wanted to speak with me, no net between us, I was available. He never called back.

For its subsets—"Give credit where it's due," says Cox. "They were very good."

licensing the Dell #5—Gadzinski is positive that the design rights were bought; no one else seems to think so. Gadzinski also says that systems were sold before there was a working model.

ITT owned the technology—Cox.

Hearsay among independents—Cox.

basis of what ITT wanted—E.g., the Pentaconta, massive financing documentation; compare the situation with Sheraton, where the ITT decision to concentrate on accretion of property gave way to what the market wanted, attention to service and convenience, once HSG got a manager who knew the business.

Levitt was sure Geneen understood—"Geneen," he says, "is one of the greatest managers, greatest authorities of management principles, I think, in the world."

it would ruin his backhand—H&H; Wasserman.

Jacques Bergerac, come to California—Valente.

did some translation work—Cannon.

"Mike said he'd already done it"—Pomerance.

doubling of European sales—*Time*, December 11, 1978.

leading candidate as Geneen's successor—Silver says ITT consensus was that Bergerac should have been made president to keep him, "But Geneen didn't want an active president."

Geneen felt betrayed—Pomerance.

an interview with Times—Savage.

Miller plumped for Lowe—who liked Miller and says he is distressed to think his own fall "might have affected" Miller's.

Pat O'Malley's number two—Morrow.

Jack Hanway—Details from Pomerance, who reported to him.

joined EAC staff for dinner—Yunker.

large part of Hanway's duty—Hartman.

"Jack never told anything but truth"—Hartman.

policemen misanthropic—Valente.

About once a month Geneen would meet—Hartman.

Aristides—H. G. Wells, *The Outline of History*.

disclosures gave analysts their clue—Knortz.

Accounting Practices Board ruled—Defliese.
"ragged the units"—Morrow.

CHAPTER 18: Starting at the Top

91% of all mergers—SUP RPT, p. 32.

Geneen asked Mitchell—Klein., p. 650.

"A President who lets"—WSJ, December 16, 1969, in SUP RPT, p. 149.

McLaren filed against Canteen—NYT, May 1, 1972.

Geneen promising stockholders—SUP PRT, pp. 39, 43.

"Hal's posture is . . . "—State., p. 895.

None of his predecessors—SUP RPT, p. 31. McLaren admitted that. Donald Turner, who had blocked the ABC merger, was now a consultant to ITT, and he assured HSG than the mergers did not contravene the antitrust law as written.

go right to the top—When Avis was trying to work out a deal for Chevrolets, HSG and Morrow called on the GM chairman and president. Morrow also asked whether his allocation of Cadillacs could be increased. The chairman pondered and said, no, he couldn't help them; they'd have to take it up with the division general manager. HSG was dumbfounded. What had this company come to since the days of Sloan, if the chairman couldn't just order something done?

he tried to see Nixon—State., p. 137.

"probably a status symbol"—SPR RPT, p. 12

Starting with Stans—Klein., pp. 777; 779.

At Raytheon he had insisted—KRIM DOC.

instances of ITT reciprocity—HSG's beloved "system selling" got a lot of lip service but never came to much. Memos made it seem that Rayonier and Continental were combining to increase overall ITT sales in Argentina; but it was inconclusive and at least explainable.

sent Ephraim Jacobs to McLaren—Klein., p. 101.

"government urges expanded interpretation"—Klein., p. 265.

Ehrlichman wrote to Mitchell—State., p. 192. "Gineen," *sic;* "gravaman," *sic.*

"vice of a vulgar mind"—State., p. 211.

"we still have a problem here"—State., p. 193.

thank-you note, Merriam wrote—State., p. 257.

Merriam ended a letter—State., p. 389.

Peterson wrote to Ehrlichman—State., pp. 388, 391.

enlisted Lawrence E. Walsh—Klein., p. 1033. Davis Polk partner F.A.O. Schwartz, Sr. had been the main contact, had attended board meetings in the early HSG years, and was known as "the conscience of ITT."

urged Justice not to "advocate"—State., p. 287.

Geneen dropped off copy—State., p. 304.

10:30 Monday morning—Klein., p. 1039.

A little before 3:00 P.M.—The transcript of the Nixon/Ehrlichman/Shultz meeting starts at 3:03 P.M. Kleindienst told me that the call from Ehrlichman came "immediately" before the call from Nixon, but there were about 3 to 5 minutes of conversation before the call, and there is no indication that the meeting started exactly at 3:03. I assume the call from Ehrlichman to Kleindienst was a little before three.

"made your position clear"—State., pp 312–20; 332. Nixon-Kleindienst at pp. 346–48.

"There is not . . . antitrust actions"—Sic.

"You son of a bitch"—This line was edited out of the original transcripts but was supplied later: NYT, October 30, 1973, and *Time,* June 6, 1974. Also Kleindienst. This seems obviously *where* in the conversation Nixon said it: it makes Kleindienst's "[Laughs] Yeah, I understand that" more logical.

That's my views—Sic.

Geneen, hell, he's no contributor—HSG was very proud of that line: Dunleavy. Beard, however, told a White House aide, James Hughes, a different tale. Hughes reported to Ehrlichman, "Dita cites a heavy financial support given by IT&T to the President's election": *State.,* p. 142, September 19, 1969.

"he's not going to be a judge, either"—This is most suggestive. It seems unlikely that the president would offhandedly know the burning ambition of someone so far down in the hierarchy unless it had been previously raised as a point: the carrot to encourage McLaren's tractability.

ordered Erwin Griswold—Griswold's version is at *Klein.,* pp. 242, 380.

Nixon's intervention reported to Geneen—Kleindienst agrees, though of course not with my construction of the reason: "to force McLaren's compliance," which Kleindienst maintains was voluntary.

Robatyn asked Kleindienst's permission—*Klein.,* p. 97.

IBM regularly fluctuated—Ramsden at *Klein.,* p. 1384.

Mitchell met with Nixon—*State.,* p. 372.

Ehrlichman wrote to Mitchell—*State.,* p. 829.

Reinecke asked Beard—She said (*Klein.,* p. 748) that it was in January or February; he said the earliest was April, more likely May (*Klein.,* p. 1468). Hers is the more credible version.

White House launched major effort—*State.,* pp. 425–77.

Bob Wilson instrumental—*Klein.,* p. 865. Including his version of the offer, below in test., p. 866.

completed on May 17—On that same day Griswold perfected the *Grinnell* appeal. Of course it did not matter any more. It could not be heard that term, and indeed it would never be heard because the settlement was already in train.

negotiations started over terms—Starting almost immediately, high executives at ITT (but not HSG) sold ITT stock; so did Lazard. In response to SEC charges of insider trading they said it was coincidence, and besides, most of them had sold only relatively small portions of their holdings. In addition, Savage says that at the time he, not knowing of the settlement, was telling people that it was a good time to sell. The matter was settled by consent decree.

Nader's group . . . O'Brien wrote—*Klein.* pp. 120, 1247. The Nader man was Reuben B. Robertson III.

"We now have evidence"—*State.,* p. 634; *Klein.,* p. 392.

Brit Hume—Albert B. Hume. His testimony and Anderson's, *Klein.,* pp. 391–538. Beard's memo is at p. 447.

"400 thousand committment"—committment, sic.

"very little cash"—This was part of her wanting to appear knowledgeable. It is doubtful that she knew the terms; and of course there was then no way of knowing how much of the commitment would be needed.

nomination be reopened—*Washington Post,* March 1, 1971, in *State.,* p. 637.

every reason given for the reversal—SUP RPT, p. 105.

decision relied on four things—*Klein.,* p. 253.

"no way based on facts"—Klein., p. 1356.

Ramsden's own report—Klein., p. 103. He estimated that ITT would drop 10½ a share from 64½.

The Treasury "report"—Klein., p. 1576.

"made their bed"—Klein., p. 165.

raise "issues obvious"—Klein., p. 341.

Beard disappeared for a time—When I first wrote, then called Beard for an interview, she said she'd have to think about it. One or two follow-up calls were inconclusive: she said neither yes or no. Many months later I found out why. She had written to HSG, whom she still adores. Geneen turned her letter over to Gerrity. Had HSG written her a brief line saying. "Don't talk with Schoenberg," I'm sure she would not have done so. When Gerrity said "Don't talk," her reaction was, "What do you want to know?" She was very helpful and open.

collapsed on the plane—State., p. 778.

Colson dispatched Hunt—State. p. 780.

"where that mother came from"—Klein., p. 724.

arranger of rides—she complained on "60 Minutes" that, for instance, Senator Vance Hartke "felt like this was sort of a personal taxicab company": *Klein.*, p. 1642.

straight-arrow Mormon—Carson. It was Bert Willis.

statement from Senator Mathias—SUP RPT, p. 15.

in the Metropolitan Club—Klein., p. 925.

Dialogues about memo shredding—Klein., pp. 935, 940.

"busybody little guy"—Klein, p. 878. Also description of talk with Merriam in New York.

"don't put anything in writing"—Klein., p. 753.

As one ITT lawyer said—Klein., p. 1152.

president "has never talked to me"—Klein., p. 552.

truthfully told the press—Washington Star, March 3, 1972, at *Klein.*, p. 1495.

". . . somebody is not telling the truth"—Klein., p. 1518.

Kleindienst's litany of lies—Klein., pp. 157, 249, 351, 353, 1682.

"acquire paper-shredding"—Time, March 27, 1972.

found guilty of one—NYT, January 1, 1974.

Kleindienst plead guilty—NYT, May 17, 1974; *Time*, June 17, 1974.

Hart cited Kleindienst—NYT, June 8, 1974; Time, ibid.

Steward case—Life magazine, March 24, 1972, at *Klein.*, p. 1739. Many references; this is the clearest.

in another case—Washington Star, by I. F. Stone, March 19, 1972 in *Klein.*, p. 1713. Again, best of many. The man who offered the money, Robert T. Carson, was an aide to Senator Fong, a member of the *Kleindienst* hearing committee.

leniency shown Kleindienst—NYT, May 29, 1974; August 13, 1975.

later perjury trial—Los Angeles Times, August 22, 1981; April 24, 1982; January 4, 1983. The Arizona bar petitioned to have him reinstated.

Ed Reinecke made brilliant comeback—NYT, July 28, 1972; June 3, 1974; June 30, 1974; July 21, 1974; July 25, 1974; October 3, 1974. The complaint of unfairness: *New Republic*, June 1, 1974. Conviction overturned: December 9, 1975. State politics: NYT, February 11, 1975; *Los Angeles Times*, January 31, 1983.

Flanigan's nomination—NYT, November 11, 1974.

McLaren elevated to bench—Chicago Sun Times, March 25, 1972; letter from Senator Percy to Senator Stevenson, April 7, 1972, at *Klein.,* p. 1576.

"one more chapter"—Klein., p. 121.

CHAPTER 19: Really a painful sight

kicking around Washington—Secrets. A newsman gave them to Senator Fulbright, who asked Helms whether there was anything to it and, on being told there was not, dropped the matter. *Time* had a set and so did a newspaper columnist.

subcommittee would investigate—NYT, March 23, 1972.

statement of collaboration — Chile, p. 644.

"it is very difficult for me"—Chile, p. 20.

"a more active part"—Chile, p. 629.

recommended eighteen steps—Chile, p. 939.

At stake were people's lives—A memo from the field warned that "the consequences" of a certain planned strategy would be "a bloodbath since the far left extremists wouldn't take this without reacting violently": *Chile,* p. 155.

ITT's man in Washington reported—Chile, p. 560.

man in Santiago cabled—Chile, p. 562.

danger of expropriation—Chile, pp. 8; 91; 34; 430; also NYT, July 3, 1972.

Geneen met with Broe—Chile, p. 244.

coals to Newcastle—Secrets; CIA cash-flow—Morrow: line was by a guest speaker at Boca Raton, 1973.

36.3% of the total—The figure is given differently in different places, and in fact, I make it to be 35.3%, with the vote totals given. Maybe there were some votes unaccounted for. See *Chile,* pp. 580, 581, 589.

vote for Alessandri—Chile, p. 582. Memo was dated September 7.

Geneen got the cheering news—Chile, p. 608.

from a well-connected Chilean—The truth. Korry says it was definitely one of Edwards's people.

"It is clear," he wrote—Chile, p. 617.

government did have a plan—Chile, p. 626.

Broe plan "not workable"—Chile, pp. 626; 636.

Merriam reported to McCone—Chile, pp. 641, 644.

meeting with Allende—Chile, p. 824 and DUN MS. Guilfoyle, who had followed Andlinger as group executive for the Far East, also followed him as group executive for Latin America.

strategy that worked in Peru—Chile, p. 799: Gerrity summarizing conversation with Dunleavy and Guilfoyle; also Guilfoyle memo on p. 200. Gerrity in the hearing justified this as "a very pragmatic approach": p. 201.

Allende put the squeeze on Chiltelco—He had refused rate increases, impounded records, and at one point arrested Holmes and some other Chiltelco executives (although he professed not to know about that). He charged the company with fraud in their management and with profits secretly and illegally exported to New York.

their share of Chiltelco—70%. As part of Frei's Chileanization, the government owned 24% and private investors, 6%.

"A serious confrontation is predicted"—Chile. p. 995. Gerrity's summary of a report from Berrellez.

Allende said, "No one can dream"—NYT, April 11, 1972, speech to Chilean union leaders.

offers of money—On some $450 million in profits, ITT had paid, because of tax credits, only about $2 million in U.S. income tax. That gave rise to:

> SENATOR CHURCH. And isn't it true you paid somewhere around $2 million to the Federal Government in taxes?
> MR. GENEEN. I think that is too low.
> SENATOR CHURCH. I think it is too low, too, but isn't that what you paid?
> MR. GENEEN. I think it is a low estimate. Let me get you the exact figure.

I do not find it in the *Chile* exhibits: pp. 467, 475.

talk with Matte—*Chile*, p. 163.

"everything done quietly but effectively"—*Chile*, p. 40: extract from memo.

"This must be clearly understood"—*Chile*, p. 103.

Ned Gerrity said the million dollars—*Chile*, p. 185.

$1.4 billion in aid—*Chile*, p. 116.

asked "for the record"—*Chile*, p. 496.

I think I have previously testified—*Chile*, p. 462. They very definitely were talking about candidates, specifically Alessandri and Allende.

Senator Percy asked—*Chile*, p. 476.

Geneen said, "Two things"—*Chile*, p. 506. The transcript reads, " . . . this was basically a question if, you might say . . . " but surely he said "question of."

"somebody is lying"—*Chile*, p. 427.

In Chile, meanwhile—NYT, September 12, 1973.

In April 1974 Colby testified—*Secrets*.

$500,000 to fund Allende's opponents—*Secrets*; *Staff*, p. 20.

Frei won 55.7%—*Staff*, p. 57. On p. 5 it is given as "57 percent."

Council supposedly offered—*Staff*, p. 16.

in hands of Chilean bankers—*Chile*, p. 704; a *Time* magazine file leaked to ITT.

the 40 Committee—*Secrets*; *Staff*, p. 20.

witnessed the takeover—*Secrets*; Korry.

spoiling operation approved—*Staff*, p. 58.

CIA officer told Hendrix—*Secrets*.

later congressional investigation showed—*Staff*, p. 12.

As Geneen later admitted—*Staff*, p. 13; NYT, December 5, 1975, May 13, 1976.

Allende contemplated the end—Seymour Hersh maintains that Kissinger's fear was exactly the opposite: that Allende would relinquish the presidency at term's end, which would make a democratically elected Marxist government respectable. Of course, whatever Allende's intentions, with his overthrow, elections were no more in Chile.

Chile's premier oligarch—*Secrets*.

"I don't see why"—*Secrets*: quoting *Uncertain Greatness*, by Roger Morris (New York, Harper & Row, 1977).

Later on the fifteenth—*Staff*, p. 23.

"Track II"—*Staff*, p. 11.

"make the economy scream"—*Staff*, p. 33 and *Secrets*.

Hendrix and Berrellez did not know that—Korry; P. Jones. Hendrix says Korry's version is overdramatic and that they were not really banished from the embassy at all. I believe Korry. Berrellez declined an interview. P. Jones's version of his call to Korry differs slightly; I have used his.

Allende courting the military—Korry.

"were on the suck"—Korry, who heard it on a tape recording.

Jacobo Schaulsohn—Korry; NYT May, 5, 1975: they spell his name Schlauson.

Dillenbeck complained—*Chile*, p. 723; Dillenbeck.

United States pressure destabilize—Korry says that was certainly not so while he was there; but he left well before the coup: *Staff*, passim, especially pp. 27, 28.

establish Foundation Chile—Cotton.

"really a painful sight"—*Saturday Review* magazine, June 26, 1976.

profit "most honorable motive"—Reporters' notes.

"most moral company"—The context was a discussion of accounting practices and disclosure.

specifically amoral—examples are passim in the text; two specifics will do: the later bribery, freely admitted; the instant firings and layoffs and plant closings to avoid even softening profits.

not let people be blackmailed—Roth and Wasserman.

freely offered bribes—Van Zandt once caught a visiting ITT executive, in Japan, soliciting kickbacks for his purchasing favors. Van Zandt sent him packing and complained to the fellow's unit. After a while the man was back, this time telling Van Zandt he had orders from headquarters—to steer clear of Van Zandt in his operations.

if Chile denounced the loans—Dunleavy.

He told one aide he was unaware—Savage.

"didn't mind if you made mistakes"—Sementa.

Civiletti "bristled slightly"—NYT, March 21, 1978.

withheld material information—FOI letter.

CHAPTER 20: End of the Dream

"Hell, Harold Geneen told us"—DUN MS.

"He can run any company"—*Fortune*, September 1972.

second quarter up 11.5%—NYT, August 8, 1973.

G. P. Putnam's Sons—WSJ, May 15, 1973.

low for the year—WSJ, January 2, 1974. Savage says they all sported buttons that read —referring to stock price goals—"73 in '73," then "74 in '74." After 1974 (low was 12) they discontinued the buttons. In many companies, "committees of corporate responsibility" were in vogue, and many, like the one at Phillips-Van Heusen, insisted that their pension fund get rid of ITT: NYT, June 17, 1974.

IRS announced reconsideration—NYT, April 19, 1973; June 19, 1973; December 20, 1973. WSJ, March 7, 1974; March 17, 1974.

"If a buyer doesn't assume"—WSJ, March 7, 1974.

ITT merely "parked"—NYT, June 19, 1974.

payment of $1.8 million—NYT, December 20, 1973.

Yielded ITT some $22 million—The total profit on the stock was $100 million.

secret contract with Lazard—Savage says that Rohatyn maintains he told HSG about the fee splitting at a party; HSG told Savage that was not so.

Casey convinced the commission—NYT, May, 21, 1973. In *Kleindienst,* Casey had precipitously shipped thirty-four boxes of subpoenaed ITT documents, plus an envelope containing particularly sensitive ones about contact with high administration officials, to Justice rather than turning them over to Congress as requested. At Justice they could be suppressed as part of a criminal investigation. The situation was saved because Sporkin made a bordereau of the documents, underlining their importance. These dealings held up Casey's appointment as president of the Export-Import Bank (NYT, December 4, 1973) but were no bar to his becoming head of the CIA in the Reagan Administration. And, despite all, Sporkin thought highly of Casey as a leader, later joined him at the CIA as general counsel: Sporkin.

IRS reversed its ruling—WSJ, March 7, 1974; March 17, 1974.

if ITT had to shell out—NYT, March 5, 1977. There were originally twenty-two ITT defendents, plus five others, although the figure was later given as twenty-one defendents.

Lazard settled—WSJ, October 14, 1977.

tax court ruled—WSJ, February 7, 1979.

final settlement—WSJ, May 11, 1981.

Chilean dictatorship announced—WSJ, November 5, 1974.

stricken with Bell's palsy—Fortune, May, 1975. In contrast with Dunleavy, *Fortune* had it that HSG was "back to work sooner than the doctors liked." My thanks to Dr. Robert S. Schoenberg, my nephew, for a description of the disease and its debilitations.

"backed away from day-to-day operations"—Carbonaro.

did not show up at GMMs—Howes.

Office of President a joke—At the time, someone in PR called Fausch, then head of the relevant *Business Week* department, offering an exclusive in exchange for a feature story on the momentous event. Fausch said, "You mean you want me to run a story about how Harold Geneen is going to share his power with some other guys?" "Well . . . " "Have you tried *Fortune?*"

"authority without responsibility"—Westfall.

"decisions were not being made"—Carbonaro.

"close relationship with Geneen"—Later, Roth bought APCOA back from ITT, a first for the corporation. He made the proposition to Dunleavy, who disappeared into HSG's office and emerged to say it was okay. Roth was hurt that HSG didn't come in person—though he did later send Roth a nice note.

added 20% to 35%—Fortune, September 1972.

ITT's profit declined—WSJ, May 3, 1974.

"best thing for ITT"—Catapano, quoted by Savage.

"an analystical nightmare"—WSJ, May 15, 1974; it was Harris S. Colt of Auerbach, Pollak & Richardson; "analystical" is *sic.*

1974 was off 13%—only the second quarter saw a gain, and that only 5%. The last quarter was a staggering drop of 40%. That was while HSG was out with palsy—probably a coincidence.

"a culling of the herd"—Berke.

one of the culls—Hutchinson.

bonuses cut about 7.2%—PROXIES '74 and '75.

$19.3 million loss—WSJ, January 18, 1974.

sold Canteen—WSJ, April 19, 1973.

public offerings of Avis—Fortune, June 1975.

court appointed a trustee—Richard Joyce Smith, a seventy-one-year-old lawyer, who had been trustee for the New Haven Railroad for fourteen years.

lost over $20 million in 1974—History of its disposal: WSJ, June 9, 1977; June 28, 1977; June 29, 1977; July 28, 1977; February 14, 1978.

1973, a trustee was appointed—James H. Goss, who spoke with me at length and was very helpful; he stresses that ITT behaved punctiliously in helping Grinnell get on its feet.

$1.4 million on $114 million sales—Fortune, June 1975.

Matters in Europe—Time, December 11, 1978.

slated as number two—Valente.

end of support for Portuguese—NYT, September 6, 1975. Salazar suffered a stroke in 1968 and died in 1970: *Columbia Encyclopedia.*

Franco's death—It occurred in 1975; plant closing: WSJ, January 12, 1976.

STC announced imminent closing—WSJ, September 27, 1976.

France also nationalism—NYT, June 4, 1976; June 16, 1976; July 23, 1976. The company is called "Thomson-Brandt" in the *New York Times* data base printout and "Thompson CSF" elsewhere.

price was $160 million—NYT, June 16, 1976.

ITT's annual meetings—Fullest accounts are in local papers. Sources are: *Memphis Press-Scimitar,* May 9 & 11, 1972; *Kansas City Times,* May 10, 1973; *Seattle Post-Intelligencer,* May 9, 1974; *Charlotte Observer,* May 8, 1975. I am grateful to the individual papers for providing me with copies of the relevant articles.

from 150 to 500 pickets—500 is the NYT estimate, May 9, 1974.

Raymond L. Dirks—Dirks had considerable trouble with the SEC on two occasions. In the first, he won an appeal to the United States Supreme Court; in the second, subject to appeal, he was "barred from association with any broker or dealer": *Los Angeles Times,* December 23, 1983; WSJ, ibid.

"huge fellows, ITT employees"—R. Sterling talked to them to find out.

"one of the most capable men"—Gilbert publishes, each year, a compendium of his visits around the country to corporate meetings. The quote is from the 1969 edition. Gilbert was kind enough to allow me access to his back copies.

"you acted magnificently"—Either she had not checked the value of her ITT shares recently, or she was the rare individual who can put principle above purse.

first bomb scare—et seq.: NYT, July 22, 1973; September 17, 1973; September 29, 1973; November 5, 1973; November 18 & 19, 1973; January 12, 1974; October 7, 1974; January 28, 1975; June 1, 1975.

predicted at the 1975 meeting—WSJ, May 2, 1975; November 13 & 14, 1975. For instance, the second quarter was 80¢ versus $1.16 in 1974.

insurance company does not make its money—Fortune, May, 1975 and Carson.

Hartford's income $105.5 million—WSJ, January 8, 1974, makes it $105.4, but AR '71 reads $105.49.

contributing 25% of the corporate total—AR '74; WSJ, ibid., makes it 26%.

sure palsy a stroke—Dunleavy.

speech was impaired—Savage.

ITT stock was double—WSJ, May 28, 1975.

new record for first quarter—WSJ, May 13, 1976.

Recovery continued throughout 1976—Ibid.

Carbon . . . Eason—Prices were: Carbon, $261 million (WSJ, December 31, 1976);

Eason, $133.4 million (WSJ, August 31, 1977). R. Graham says the Eason price was ludicrous. Others say Carbon was $100 million overpriced.

"reason to believe"—WSJ, May 13 & 15, 1976.

final figure $8.7 million—SEC DOC: Civil Action #78-0807, dated May 4, 1978.

"Lonely Star Shipping Corporation"—Ibid. and NYT, November 3 & 4, 1978. *ITT* gives it as "Lucky Star" but the cited sources are *sic.*

respected Frank Pepermans—WSJ, February 24, 1976. Many alumni, A. Williams most particularly, are very indignant, claiming these were nothing like bribes, only very casual gifts—much of it obsolete or reconditioned equipment used by ITT.

ITT did not fight—SEC DOC and NYT, August 9, 1979.

other big event of 1976—WSJ, June 11, 1976.

"one knowledgeable source said"—Ibid.

CHAPTER 21: Penultimate Chapter

ruefully agreed with an associate—Dunleavy.

chivying Geneen about succession—Fortune, September 1972.

named Dunleavy president—NYT, December 14, 1972.

"gesture of cooperation"—Dunleavy didn't think much of Perkins, either, and said so at our interview, not knowing what Perkins had told me.

Geneen was soon talking in board meetings—Fausch.

two-thirds of the Fortune 500 list—Fortune, May 1975.

Vladimir Gold—Goode. The story in the NYT (August 14, 1974) put the concession at 500,000 acres. Some sources mentioned the debacle as being in Surinam, but Goode says Indonesia.

according to Fortune—Fortune, December 17, 1979.

mill closed for two weeks—WSJ, March 5, 1975.

Rayonier bought for over $300 million—Fortune used the lesser figure of $293 million.

Watergate prosecutors wanted perjury indictment—NYT, November 1, 1973.

would call witnesses before a grand jury—FOI letter, July 12, 1976.

turned Hal Hendrix—FOI letter, October 8, 1976.

Justice told Helms—NYT, January 15, 1977.

Hamilton's constituency—Perkins.

Hamilton's background—Fortune, March 1977.

Hart Perry nine years older—Who's Who.

1964 elected senior VP—NYT, June 22, 1964.

resemblance to Franklin Roosevelt, Jr.—DUN MS.

"Horst Wessel Lied"—Ohmes.

nap in the afternoon—Hills.

"ogre of growth"—Les Info, October 22, 1973—given to me by Kenmore.

his last full year at ITT—PROXY '73.

Orlando, Florida, 1976—Miami Herald, May 5, 1977. This was part of group I sent for, and my thanks also to the *Herald.*

"uncommon normalcy"—WSJ, May 9, 1978.

getting to the office about 8:15—Fortune, March 1977.

moved into Geneen's twelfth-floor office—WSJ, May 9, 1978.

chairman and vice chairman barely speaking—Savage; Dunleavy (who admits relations were strained, though he did not say they were barely speaking).

statute of limitations ran out—NYT, March 26, 1978.

Gerrity charged on six counts—Department of Justice file: violations of 18 USC subsections 1001, 1505, 1621, 1622.

Geneen's sworn statement included—Klein., pp. 465, 476.

working prosecutors considered Geneen—FOI memo.

Berrellez plea bargain—FOI memo.

"CIA used Hendrix"—FOI memo.

count on unavailability of declassified—FOI memo.

Gerrity had suborned perjury—WSJ, August 21, 1978.

Justice asked for protective order—NYT, January 27, 1979.

Federal appeals court refused it—NYT, February 9, 1979.

current Chilean government figures—NYT, March 11, 1979. It might be argued that if such names were released, in future the CIA could not hope to enlist foreign nationals in such projects. To which the citizen of any democracy should answer: Good. It would be a positive policy restraint on government to announce that the subversion of democratically elected governments, of the right or left, is no legitimate part of America's business, and those who cooperate are liable to exposure. Those who cooperate in operations in dictatorships, and those in evident danger of more than embarrassment, would of course still be protected.

government dropped prosecution—NYT, February 9, 1979 (Berrellez); March 8, 1979 (Gerrity).

internal memo complained—FOI.

CIA admitted to a Justice lawyer—FOI memo.

a Justice prosecutor complained—FOI memo.

"concern about the Agency's handling"—FOI memo.

State Department worse—FOI.

State lawyer told a prosecutor—FOI memo. Lawrence S. Eagleburger: his name is misspelled in the memo.

CIA had regularly fed Hendrix—FOI memo.

1975, three prosecutors wrote memo—FOI.

sniping at Hamilton—Time, July 23, 1979.

Hamilton's wife was complaining—Dunleavy.

Hamilton stressing profitability—WSJ, May 9, 1978.

"My first reaction was"—Sterling.

"We found 17 units"—WSJ, May 9, 1978.

cable plant in San Diego—WSJ, March 29, 1978.

phased out Rimmel—WSJ, May 18, 1978.

sell off food companies—WSJ, June 12, 1978.

Geneen resigned to diminished role—WSJ, February 10, 1977.

two-part study from firm of John Kehoe—Now, Kehoe, White, Towey & Savage, Inc. Savage joined them after leaving ITT. My thanks to John Kehoe for supplying me with a copy of the report.

"Mickey Mouse can run it"—Time, July 23, 1979.

board never quarreled with Hamilton's—WSJ, October 11, 1978.

As for pruning the dogs—Perkins.

Nesbitt's move from Philadelphia—Dunleavy.

Hamilton concluded that Woodward—Perkins.

true collegial management group—Dunleavy.

point that later rankled—Perkins.

indelibly marked by Geneen—Dunleavy.

old patron, Hart Perry—Perkins.

Hanway himself thought he was on way out—Dunleavy.

quotes prudently anonymous—WSJ, October 11, 1978. For mix-up: Meyer.

Geneen opposed Andlinger—Dunleavy; Valente for "Down on Valente."

Lazard's ITT fees—PROXY '79, '78.

stock in steady decline—NYT, relevant dates.

only Pat Lannan had more—PROXY '79.

Morgan Guarantee Trust sold off—WSJ, July 18, 1979. Geneen also sold about one-third of his ITT shares.

selling below book value—Forbes, August 6, 1979.

Why need an inner council—Perkins. He says Hamilton also proposed to bring back Westfall and Marx.

$147.5 million deal for Qume—Perkins.

subsequent brokerage report—Newsweek, July 23, 1979.

"Geneen deserved better than this"—WSJ, July 18, 1979.

not concerned about escalating pace—Above two sources.

Geneen had permission to attend—WSJ, July 18, 1979. This account is particularly good and complete. Supplemented by all other sources that address the subject.

Geneen was shocked and furious—He was, after all, still chairman; no directors had been told of this major move.

personnel and compensation committee met—Perkins.

Hamilton returned to New York—Perkins and WSJ, July 18, 1979.

With Herb Knortz leading—Savage.

time to reexamine your position—Savage.

Araskog knew who had made him—NYT, April 6, 1980.

"no significant policy changes"—NYT, August 10, 1979.

Geneen announced he was resigning—NYT, November 15, 1979; December 12, 1979.

not stand for reelection—Los Angeles Times, March 9, 1983.

"Bobby Sarnoff thinks he's Geneen"—Reporters' notes.

no one left to do honest work—I'm indebted to Louis Marienthal for this insight and analysis.

production no longer glamorous—Like everyone else, I imbibe the spirit of the times. For my last book, *The Art of Being a Boss,* I interviewed Edgar B. Speer, then chairman of U. S. Steel, on the subject of rising through the ranks. I said something about how hard it must have been for him, a production man, since production wasn't very glamorous. He explosively disagreed.

zero-sum game—That is, with a stable economy.

"Get rid of two bodies"—NYT, September 5, 1971.

feelings of job security—Of course, cultural factors intrude. Mere job security is no guarantee of productivity, as a wait in any post office line will illustrate.

"money in poverty"—Berke.

"*that kind of grand passion*"—Carlos Sandoval.

pride they all felt—Bowes.

1983, income $675 million—Los Angeles Times, March 14, 1983; ITT investor relations department.

first quarter of 1984 profit—Los Angeles Times, April 20, 1984. Raytheon: *Los Angeles Times,* April 12, 1984. *Second quarter:* NYT, July 12, 1984.

take over TICOR—Los Angeles Times, February 2, 1984.

INDEX

The Best of the Business From Warner Books